Understanding Capital Punishment Law
Third Edition

Understanding Capital Punishment Law

Third Edition

Linda E. Carter
Professor of Law
University of the Pacific, McGeorge School of Law

Ellen S. Kreitzberg
Professor of Law and Director, Death Penalty College
Santa Clara University School of Law

Scott W. Howe
Frank L. Williams Professor of Criminal Law
Chapman University School of Law

ISBN: 978-0-7698-4902-7 (soft cover)
ISBN: 978-1-4224-8647-4 (eBook)

Library of Congress Cataloging-in-Publication Data

Carter, Linda E.
Understanding capital punishment law / Linda E. Carter, Ellen S. Kreitzberg Scott W. Howe. -- 3rd ed.
p. cm.
Includes index.
ISBN 978-0-7698-4902-7 (softbound)
1. Capital punishment--United States. I. Kreitzberg, Ellen. II. Howe, Scott W. III. Title.
KF9227.C2C36 2012
345.73'0773--dc23   2012016981

This publication is designed to provide accurate and authoritative information in regard to the subject matter covered. It is sold with the understanding that the publisher is not engaged in rendering legal, accounting, or other professional services. If legal advice or other expert assistance is required, the services of a competent professional should be sought.

NOTE TO USERS

To ensure that you are using the latest materials available in this area, please be sure to periodically check the LexisNexis Law School web site for downloadable updates and supplements at www.lexisnexis.com/lawschool.

Editorial Offices
121 Chanlon Rd., New Providence, NJ 07974 (908) 464-6800
201 Mission St., San Francisco, CA 94105-1831 (415) 908-3200
www.lexisnexis.com

MATTHEW◆BENDER

Dedication

For Michael, Michelle, and Laura-L.E.C.

For Tom, Erika, and Kristoffer-E.S.K.

For Jetty, Mario, and Jordan-S.W.H.

Preface

This book is written for students in capital punishment courses and for others, whether lawyers, experts, activists, or scholars, who are interested in an overview of this complex area of law. The primary emphasis of the book is an explanation of the constitutional law that governs death penalty proceedings in the United States. In the third edition, we have included new chapters on the military death penalty, the evolving attitudes on the death penalty reflected in moratoriums and reconsideration of the retention of capital punishment, and the death penalty worldwide.

In the few years since the second edition, significant changes have occurred in death penalty law, procedure and practice. We have tried to present the most up-to-date information and trends in death penalty law. New developments as of the time that we go to print are included, but additional cases are emerging even as we type. This is a dynamic area of law that will undoubtedly have further major developments in the next few years. Anyone studying or researching in this area should continue to look for the latest judicial, executive, and legislative actions.

We would never have been able to research and write this edition without outstanding work by our research assistants. We express great thanks to Anthony Corso, Marc Wiesner, and Alison Gilmore of Santa Clara Law; Eric Diamond and Regina Rivera of Chapman; and Jacquelin Hassell, Michael Youril, Jennifer McHugh, Jamie Garrett, Danielle Wheeler, Colin Roberts, Cassandra Shaft, and Tamana Zhublawar of Pacific McGeorge.

We also appreciate and thank our individual universities for their support of our research through research stipends and other resources.

Our families have supported our efforts through their patience and encouragement. We are truly grateful for their support.

As the law continues to evolve, so does this book. We consider this a work-in-progress, All comments, suggestions, corrections, or additions are greatly appreciated.

Linda Carter lcarter@pacific.edu

Ellen Kreitzberg ekreitzberg@scu.edu

Scott Howe swhowe@chapman.edu

TABLE OF CONTENTS

TABLE OF CONTENTS

TABLE OF CONTENTS

TABLE OF CONTENTS

TABLE OF CONTENTS

TABLE OF CONTENTS

TABLE OF CONTENTS

TABLE OF CONTENTS

TABLE OF CONTENTS

TABLE OF CONTENTS

TABLE OF CONTENTS

TABLE OF CONTENTS

TABLE OF CONTENTS

Chapter 1

INTRODUCTION TO CAPITAL PUNISHMENT LAW

§ 1.01   THE CAPITAL PUNISHMENT CONTROVERSY IN THE TWENTY-FIRST CENTURY

Capital punishment[1] is a controversial topic in the United States and in many parts of the world today. There are currently 140 countries that do not impose the death penalty by law or as a matter of practice. Fifty-eight countries continue to authorize the death penalty for a variety of crimes, including murder, adultery, corruption, rape and robbery, and, another 9, although abolitionist for murder and ordinary crimes, provide for the death penalty in exceptional circumstances.[2] The vast majority of countries in Europe have abolished the death penalty,[3] while the United States and countries in the Middle East and Asia retain it. Most of the executions in 2010 occurred in China, Iran, Saudi Arabia, and the United States.[4]

Even within the United States, there is division over the use of the death penalty.[5] Some states impose the death penalty, while others do not authorize it. There are also divisions over the applicability of the death penalty among those states that do authorize it. For example, some states substantially narrow the class of death-eligible murder defendants during the guilt-or-innocence trial, while

---

[1]   The terms "capital punishment" and "death penalty" are used interchangeably throughout the book.

[2]   *See* Death Penalty Information Center, *Abolitionist and Retentionist Countries, available at* http://www.deathpenaltyinfo.org/abolitionist-and-retentionist-countries (last updated Dec. 14, 2011).

[3]   As of December 2011, 47 countries belong to the Council of Europe. Since 1994, membership in the Council of Europe has been conditioned upon signing and ratifying Protocol 6, which requires abolition of the death penalty in peacetime. *See* Council of Europe, *The Council of Europe is a Death Penalty Free Area, available at* http://www.coe.int/lportal/web/coe-portal/what-we-do/human-rights/death-penalty. *See also Protocol 6 to the Convention for the Protection of Human Rights and Fundamental Freedoms Concerning the Abolition of the Death Penalty, as amended by Protocol No. 11* (April 28, 1983), *available at* http://conventions.coe.int/Treaty/en/Treaties/html/114.htm. More recently, the Council of Europe has promulgated Protocol 13, which prohibits the death penalty even in wartime. *See Protocol No. 13 to the Convention for the Protection of Human Rights and Fundamental Freedoms, Concerning the Abolition of the Death Penalty in All Circumstances* (May 3, 2002), *available at* http://conventions.coe.int/Treaty/en/Treaties/html/187.htm. As of November 22, 2011, 42 countries had ratified the Protocol, and 3 additional countries had signed, but not yet ratified it. *See* http://conventions.coe.int/Treaty/Commun/ChercheSig.asp?NT=187&CM=&DF=&CL=ENG. (websites last visited Dec. 29, 2011).

[4]   In 2010, there were 527 known executions in 23 countries, plus thousands that were believed to be carried out in China. Of the 527 carried out outside of China, 252 were in Iran; 53 in Yemen; 46 in the United States; and 27 in Saudi Arabia. *See* Amnesty International, *Death Sentences and Executions 2010*, 5 (2011), *available at* http://www.amnesty.org/en/library/asset/ACT50/001/2011/en/ea1b6b25-a62a-4074-927d-ba51e88df2e9/act500012011en.pdf.

[5]   *See* Franklin E. Zimring, The Contradictions of American Capital Punishment 123-33 (Oxford University Press 2003).

others allow defendants convicted of the broad category of murder to be subject to a capital sentencing hearing.[6]

The death penalty is authorized by statute today in 33 states plus the federal government and the military.[7] In most jurisdictions, the death penalty is a possible punishment only for certain homicides. There are, however, a few jurisdictions that authorize the death penalty for non-homicide crimes.[8] The overwhelming majority of states provide for execution by lethal injection. Other methods of execution include the gas chamber, electrocution, hanging, and the firing squad.[9]

Continuing controversy over the death penalty is also revealed by recent abolition in several states — New Jersey, New Mexico, Illinois, and Connecticut — and by a recently imposed restriction on the use of the penalty in Maryland.[10] The federal government, a few states, and independent researchers have conducted studies of the fairness of the imposition of the death penalty.[11] Issues include the possibility of executing innocent persons, the racially discriminatory imposition of the death penalty, and the uneven application of the death penalty geographically and socioeconomically. The debate continues in the legislatures, in academia, and in the media, making the death penalty one of the most controversial social issues today.

---

[6] *See* Section 9.03, *infra.*

[7] *See* Death Penalty Information Center, *Facts about the Death Penalty, available at* http://www. deathpenaltyinfo.org/documents/FactSheet.pdf (updated April 27, 2012) The 33 states are Alabama, Arizona, Arkansas, California, Colorado, Delaware, Florida, Georgia, Idaho, Indiana, Kansas, Kentucky, Louisiana, Maryland, Mississippi, Missouri, Montana, Nebraska, Nevada, New Hampshire, North Carolina, Ohio, Oklahoma, Oregon, Pennsylvania, South Carolina, South Dakota, Tennessee, Texas, Utah, Virginia, Washington, and Wyoming.

[8] *See* Section 8.05, *infra.*

[9] *See* Section 5.01, *infra.*

[10] *See* Steve Mills, *Illinois Bans Death Penalty*, CHI. TRIBUNE, March 10, 2011, at 1. *See also* John Wagner, *Md. Again looking at death penalty*, WASH. POST., Jan. 16, 2011, at C6 (noting that, in 2009, Maryland enacted a statute requiring that, "[t]o be eligible for the death penalty, there must be biological or DNA evidence, a videotaped confession or a videotape linking the defendant to the crime.").

[11] *See, e.g.*, California Commission on the Fair Administration of Justice, *Report and Recommendations on the Administration of the Death Penalty in California*, (June 30, 2008), *available at* http://www.ccfaj.org/documents/reports/dp/official/FINAL%20REPORT%20DEATH%20PENALTY. pdf; James S. Liebman, Jeffrey Fagan, & Valerie West, *A Broken System: Error Rates in Capital Cases, 1973-1995* (Columbia Law Sch. Pub. Law Research Paper No. 15, 2000), *available at* http://www2.law. columbia.edu/instructionalservices/liebman/liebman_final.pdf (calculating the rate of serious error between 1973 and 1995 to be 60% to 70% and finding that "the capital punishment system revealed by our 23-year study is not a success, and is not even minimally rational"); United States Department of Justice, *Survey of the Federal Death Penalty System, available at* http://www.justice.gov/dag/pubdoc/dpsurvey. html (websites last visited Dec. 29, 2011).

§ 1.02   CAPITAL TRIALS IN THE UNITED STATES: THE IMPORTANCE OF CONSTITUTIONAL LAW

[A]   Overview

Capital proceedings in current times are a product of complying with decisions of the United States Supreme Court. The "modern era" of the death penalty in the United States began in the mid-1970s. In a series of cases interpreting the Eighth Amendment's cruel and unusual punishment clause, the Court upheld the constitutionality of the death penalty as a punishment and defined parameters for constitutionally imposing it.[12] As a result of Eighth Amendment constraints, capital punishment law in the United States is largely a study of decisions of the Supreme Court interpreting the meaning of cruel and unusual punishment. A major body of jurisprudence has developed in this area.

The historical basis and evolution of contemporary society's views on the death penalty play a role in understanding and interpreting the Constitution. The history of capital punishment is a long one. The death penalty has been a form of punishment for centuries. For example, researchers have documented death-penalty provisions in the Code of Hammurabi, the Old Testament of the Bible, and Roman law.[13] Both the crimes punished by the death penalty and the methods of execution, however, have changed dramatically over time. At various points in history, capital crimes have included many offenses other than murder, such as witchcraft, petty treason (the killing of a husband by a wife), and blasphemy.[14] Early English common law included treason, murder, larceny, robbery, burglary, rape and arson as capital crimes.[15] Methods of execution in various time periods included boiling in oil, drawing and quartering, crucifixion, drowning, burning at the stake,[16] and beheading.[17]

---

[12] *See* Sections 4.01-4.04 and 6.01-6.06, *infra*.

[13] *See* Norman Krivosha et al., *A Historical and Philosophical Look at the Death Penalty-Does It Serve Society's Needs?* 16 Creighton L. Rev. 1, 3 (1982-83) (discussing the cyclic history and philosophy behind the death penalty and noting: "Ancient Chinese records document the use of the death penalty at a very early time. Likewise, the records of Ancient Egypt relate that criminals were sentenced to death as early as 1,000 B.C.E."); John Laurence, A History of Capital Punishment 2 (The Citadel Press 1960) ("For the oldest death sentence extant we have to search in the Amherst Papyri, which contains the accounts of the trials of State criminals in Egypt some fifteen hundred years before Christ.").

[14] *See, e.g.*, Laurence, *supra* note 13, at 4-5 (In Anglo-Saxon times, after the reign of Henry I, "high and petty treason were capital; so were all felonies, except mayhem, and petty larceny."); Krivosha, *supra* note 13, at 23 (listing idolatry, witchcraft, and blasphemy as capital crimes documented by the Massachusetts Bay Colony in 1636).

[15] *See* Krivosha, *supra* note 13, at 13 (At one point in English history, there were more than 200 capital crimes, including "shooting of a rabbit, the forgery of a birth certificate, the theft of a pocket handkerchief, . . . the damaging of a public building . . ."); Laurence, *supra* note 13, at 5.

[16] *See* Krivosha, *supra* note 13, at 16; Laurence, *supra* note 13, at 9. One of the early capital crimes was "petty treason," which was the killing of a husband by his wife. In an apparent effort to be kind in burning the woman at the stake, the woman was strangled before the flames consumed her. *Id.*

[17] *See* Laurence, *supra* note 13, at 6 (explaining how beheading was considered a more "honorable death").

In the United States, the death penalty came with the colonists and evolved as a reflection of early American society. Although each colony devised its own set of capital crimes, typical capital crimes included murder, rape, and the other English common law capital crimes.[18] Some colonies also had religion-based capital crimes, such as idolatry, witchcraft,[19] and blasphemy.[20] Both hanging and the firing squad were common means of authorized executions throughout the early history of the United States. The death penalty in early America was also linked to the discriminatory racial history of slavery. For example, nineteenth century capital crimes in North Carolina included concealment of slaves with the intent to free them, stealing slaves, and a second conviction for inciting insurrection among slaves.[21] The history of slavery was also reflected in the existence of capital crimes designed for African-Americans, such as the rape of a white woman.[22] Vigilante lynching, or hanging, as a means of execution was also inextricably associated with the racial history of the South.

Originally, the death penalty was mandatory for a capital crime.[23] The creation of degrees of murder was one way in which the harshness of a mandatory death penalty was limited. As states separated first-degree murder from second-degree murder, the death penalty was reserved for first-degree murders.[24] Ultimately, even with first-degree murders, most jurisdictions developed discretionary sentencing schemes.[25] These discretionary sentencing procedures were the ones challenged in the early constitutional cases.

In addition to being mandatory, the death penalty in early America was carried out in public. Public executions waned, however, as the nineteenth century ended, and the last public executions occurred in the 1930s.[26] The issue of public executions is once again topical as the media seeks to record or televise executions. As of the writing of this book, no executions in the United States are public. There is, however, increasing access for the victim's family members and the press to observe the executions.[27]

---

[18] *See* RAYMOND PATERNOSTER, CAPITAL PUNISHMENT IN AMERICA 5 (Lexington Books 1991).

[19] During the notorious Salem Witch Trials of 1692, twenty persons were executed and four others died while in jail. FRANCES HILL, THE SALEM WITCH TRIALS READER xv (Da Capo Press 2000). *See* discussion in Martha M. Young, Comment: *The Salem Witch Trials 300 Years Later: How Far Has the American Legal System Come? How Much Further does it need to Go?* 64 TUL. L. REV. 235, 242 (1989).

[20] *See* PATERNOSTER, *supra* note 18, at 5; Krivosha, *supra* note 13, at 23 (The "Capitall Lawes of New-England" in 1636 included crimes such as idolatry, witchcraft, and blasphemy).

[21] *See* PATERNOSTER, *supra* note 18, at 5; NINA RIVKIND & STEVEN F. SHTATZ, CASES AND MATERIALS ON THE DEATH PENALTY 23 (West 2d. ed. 2005).

[22] *See* STUART BANNER, THE DEATH PENALTY: AN AMERICAN HISTORY 140-41 (Harvard U. Press 2002); PATERNOSTER, *supra* note 18, at 117; RIVKIND, *supra* note 21 at 23.

[23] *See* PATERNOSTER, supra note 18, at 6.

[24] *Id.*

[25] *Id.* (By 1930 virtually all American jurisdictions had discretionary systems for imposing death or life.)

[26] *Id* at 7.

[27] *See* DENV. POST, April 12, 2001, at A8 ("Attorney General John Ashcroft [allowed] Oklahoma City bombing survivors and victims' families to watch the execution of Timothy McVeigh on a closed-circuit telecast."). *See also, e.g.,* Cal. Penal Code § 3605 (2011) (statutory provision on inviting the Attorney

Changing attitudes about the desirability and the effectiveness of capital punishment are reflected in statistics on executions in the United States. There was a dramatic decrease in executions between 1930 and 1970. In 1930, 155 persons were executed; in 1960, 56 persons were executed; and in 1970, no executions occurred. The last execution prior to the "modern era" of capital punishment occurred in 1967. Since 1977, however, with the advent of the Supreme Court's decisions reaffirming the constitutionality of the death penalty, there have been 1,277 executions as of December 22, 2011, with 43 persons executed in 2011.[28]

What are the characteristics of the modern era of capital punishment? Statutes today provide for protections against the arbitrary imposition of the death penalty. In its interpretation of the Eighth Amendment, the Supreme Court has created two major constructs. The first is the need to *guide the discretion* of the decision-maker to eliminate arbitrary and capricious reasons to impose the death penalty. The second is the need to provide the decision-maker with all relevant evidence to make an *individualized consideration* whether or not a particular defendant deserves the death penalty. These constructs, in turn, have led to the development of a bifurcated proceeding in capital cases. All capital cases in the United States have two phases: a *guilt phase* and a *penalty phase*. The chapters of this book explore the complicated body of case law that has developed in the course of interpreting the constitutional requirements for the phases of a capital trial.

[B] Organization of the Chapters on the Constitutional Constraints on Capital Punishment

Each chapter of this book covers an area of significance in modern capital punishment law. This chapter and chapter 2 are designed to lay out the context of capital punishment law. They briefly describe the history and the public debate for and against capital punishment. Chapters 3-6 provide an overview of the legal framework for challenges to the death penalty, methods of execution, and capital procedures. Chapter 3 is an overview of the legal sources that are pertinent in capital jurisprudence. Chapter 4 explains the challenges to the constitutionality of the death penalty as a punishment and describes the framework for analyzing issues under the Eighth Amendment. Chapter 5 focuses on the Eighth Amendment analysis as applied to methods of execution. The legal framework chapters culminate in chapter 6, which discusses the 1976 and 1977 United States Supreme Court cases that defined what was a constitutional death penalty statute and what was not. These cases from the mid-1970s are the foundation from which all of the later jurisprudence is generated.

General, immediate family members of victim, and 12 reputable citizens). *See also* Charlie Frago, *Suit Seeks to Open Execution Process in State to Public*, Ark. Democrat-Gazette, July 26, 2007 (reporting on federal lawsuit by coalition of journalists seeking to force Arkansas Department of Corrections to provide media access earlier in execution process rather than only after inmate strapped to gurney with lethal injection lines inserted); California First Amendment Coalition v. Woodford, 299 F.3d 868 (9th Cir. 2002) (permanent injunction to permit press to observe execution by lethal injection at earlier point in time, when inmate first brought into execution chamber).

[28] *See* Death Penalty Information Center, *Death Penalty Fact Sheet* (updated Dec. 22, 2011), *available at* http://www.deathpenaltyinfo.org/documents/FactSheet.pdf.

Chapters 7-12 cover the unique aspects of a capital penalty proceeding. Chapter 7 provides an overview of the process. Chapter 8 explores those areas in which the Court has found a categorical bar to imposing the death penalty, such as when the defendant is mentally retarded. Chapter 8 also discusses the status of the law on the execution of the retarded, children and felony-murder accomplices, as well as for crimes that do not involve murder. Chapters 9, 10, and 11 focus on aggravating circumstances, both as defining death eligibility and as an aspect of the death/life selection process. Chapters 12 and 13 explore mitigation and the decision-making process.

Chapters 14-19 look at the post-trial proceedings and issues. Chapter 14 addresses the direct appeal from a capital conviction and sentence. Chapters 15, 16 and 17 cover habeas corpus proceedings, with particular attention to the issues of ineffective assistance of counsel (chapter 16) and innocence (chapter 17). Chapter 18 explores the non-judicial, executive function of clemency. Finally, chapter 19 focuses on issues that arise while the defendant is on death row pending his or her execution. Legal issues of the defendant's sanity at the time of execution and the lengthy delay between conviction and execution are covered.

Chapters 20-23 address three issues that are not easily placed within any one part of the death-penalty process. These issues pervade the process. Chapter 20 focuses on issues of racial discrimination, and chapter 21 covers gender discrimination. Chapter 22 takes up the special issue of "volunteers," defendants who wish to die. They create unique problems for death penalty systems, which are premised on an adversary model. Chapter 23 also addresses a pervasive issue, the rights of defendants under international treaties, the use of foreign law, and extradition issues. Although many of the treaties have been in existence for some time, legal arguments based on treaty rights are still relatively new.

Chapters 24 and 25 discuss the use of the death penalty in the United States other than by the states. Most death penalty prosecutions occur in state courts. However, some federal crimes are punished by the death penalty, and several persons convicted of federal crimes have been executed in recent years. Chapter 24 focuses on federal death penalty statutes and the use of the death penalty in response to federal crimes. Likewise, some United States military crimes are punished by the death penalty, and the penalty has been imposed by military courts. Chapter 25 focuses on the military death penalty.

Chapter 26 briefly discusses the use of the death penalty outside of the United States. Although most countries no longer employ capital punishment, a small group, including China and Iran, continue to impose death sentences regularly.

Chapter 27 focuses on abolition issues, including moratorium efforts and arguments for abolition based on the costs associated with the death penalty.

Chapter 28 is the final chapter of the book. In this chapter, we explore developing issues in capital-punishment law. The televising of executions and the imposition of death penalties by military commissions are addressed, and questions of future litigation and debate are raised.

Chapter 2

THE DEATH PENALTY DEBATE

§ 2.01   MAJOR ARGUMENTS FOR AND AGAINST THE DEATH PENALTY

Is the death penalty a deterrent to violent crimes? Is it inherently inhumane and, if not, is it a just penalty for murder? Can the death penalty be imposed fairly? Is it cost-effective? These kinds of questions about capital punishment continue to be debated in legislatures, in the press, and in the classes in our schools and universities. The debates also extend beyond our borders, because the use of the death penalty in the United States is an issue of international significance.[1] Debates about the function and acceptability of the death penalty also surface in the judicial opinions of our courts interpreting the meaning of the Eighth Amendment to the U.S. Constitution. The Eighth Amendment prohibits "cruel and unusual punishments."[2] In assessing the death penalty and the procedures for implementing it under the Eighth Amendment, the United States Supreme Court has often focused on these same basic issues.[3]

The American public generally continues to favor retention of the death penalty. A recent Gallup poll[4] posed the annual question to the American public on the death penalty. In the November, 2010, poll, 64% of Americans favored the death penalty for murder and 28% were opposed. When given the choice between the death penalty and life without parole, the support for the death penalty dropped to 49%, with 46% opting for life imprisonment.[5]

The major points of contention in the ongoing debates over the death penalty can be divided into three areas. The first is whether the death penalty serves a legitimate penological purpose, and the two purposes that dominate the discussion are deterrence and retribution. The second issue is whether the system for deciding who will receive the death penalty is sufficiently accurate and nondiscriminatory to satisfy us that the process is fair. The third issue raises a pragmatic concern over

---

[1] *See* discussion in Sections 23.01 et seq., *infra.*

[2] U.S. Const. amend. VIII, provides: "Excessive bail shall not be required, nor excessive fines imposed, nor cruel and unusual punishments inflicted."

[3] *See* discussion of proportionality in Section 4.04, *infra.*

[4] *See* Gallup Poll, *Death Penalty, at* http://www.gallup.com/poll/144284/support-death-penalty-cases-murder.aspx.

[5] *See id. See also* Theodore Eisenberg, Stephen P. Garvey, & Martin T. Wells, *The Deadly Paradox of Capital Jurors,* 74 S. Cal. L. Rev. 371 (2001) (testing the paradox of support for the death penalty and concerns about its fairness as a problem of adequate alternatives and understanding of life without parole).

the cost of pursuing a death sentence in comparison to incarcerating the defendant for life. Each of these points will be discussed in the following sections.

§ 2.02 PENOLOGICAL PURPOSES

[A] Deterrence

Deterrence is a utilitarian concept. A utilitarian approach looks at whether the death penalty offers a net benefit to society. Deterrence is one way that a punishment could provide a net gain to society. In the death penalty context, deterrence is usually discussed as *general deterrence*. A punishment can serve general deterrence in two ways: 1) by preventing others who are contemplating crime from going forward, and 2) by ingraining the wrongfulness of the punished conduct into the societal mores. For the most part, researchers, writers, and the courts have focused on general deterrence as a way of preventing others from committing the same conduct. Thus, if the death penalty is imposed on a defendant for murder, other potential murderers should not commit a crime out of fear of having the death penalty imposed on them.

Consideration of the deterrence question also suggests the need to consider the issue of *brutalization*. The opposite of deterrence, brutalization reflects the notion that the use of the death penalty could increase the level of homicides.[6] Professor Roger Hood explains two levels on which the theory of brutalization could operate. First, "in the short term executions would stimulate the would-be killer by releasing inhibitions because he or she would be able to identify with the state as an 'enforcer' and 'executioner' seeking lethal vengeance." Secondly, "it has also been suggested that the drama surrounding executions stimulates certain people to see this as an alternative to suicide."[7]

There are two interrelated questions raised by the general deterrence argument. First, does the death penalty deter other murders more than if there were no penalty for murder? Of course, virtually everyone believes the answer to this question is "yes." But, the second and more important question is: Does the death penalty deter the crimes more than a lesser but still very severe punishment would deter them? If a lesser punishment would serve the same purpose, the harsher punishment is not necessary for the deterrence objective.[8] Thus, if life imprisonment without parole deters murders as well as the death penalty, deterrence alone does not support using capital punishment.

While far from conclusive on the deterrence issue, it is noteworthy that states without the death penalty do not have homicide rates that are above the average

---

[6] *See* RANDALL COYNE & LYN ENTZEROTH, CAPITAL PUNISHMENT AND THE JUDICIAL PROCESS 26-28 (3rd ed. 2006).

[7] *See* ROGER HOOD, THE DEATH PENALTY, A WORLDWIDE PERSPECTIVE 211 (3rd ed. 2002), *citing* WILLIAM J. BOWERS, G.L. PIERCE, & J.F. MCDEVITT, LEGAL HOMICIDE: DEATH AS PUNISHMENT IN AMERICA, 1864-1982 (1984), 271-335 (discussing "the hypothesis that capital crimes may be stimulated, not suppressed, by the execution of offenders" by condoning killing as vengeance).

[8] *See* COYNE & ENTZEROTH, supra note 6, at 25 (noting that, "if a lesser penalty achieves the same or a greater level of deterrence, no deterrent justification supports the enhanced punishment").

homicide rates in death-penalty states. For example, one study, conducted in 2000, found that "10 of the 12 states without the death penalty have homicide rates below the national average."[9] The same study found that, between 1980 and 2000, the homicide rate in death-penalty states was 48 percent to 101 percent higher than in non-death-penalty states. The study also noted that the differences did not appear to be explained on the basis of any obvious differences in the demographic profiles of the competing groups of states. This evidence is not dispositive regarding deterrence, however, because so many factors affect homicide rates.

Whether the death penalty has a marginally deterrent effect lacks a definitive answer. Some of the empirical studies on this question reach opposite conclusions. Other studies find the empirical results inconclusive on the deterrent effect or lack of one.[10] A major aspect of the difficulty of resolving the issue is that researchers cannot easily identify and control for the many possible influences on murder rates and, thus, cannot be sure that they have identified the marginal deterrent effect of the death penalty. The consistently low execution rates during the last three decades further compound the effort to draw inferences about the influence of executions from among the plethora of other factors that may afffect murder rates.

The most famous early study on the deterrence question, conducted in the 1960s, was by Thorsten Sellen, and he found no evidence that capital punishment deterred homicide.[11] Sellen's basic methodology was to compare the annual murder rates of adjoining abolitionist and retentionist states and countries. In addition to the paired comparisons, he focused on how murder rates changed after states abolished or reintroduced capital punishment. A variety of other researchers during that era also conducted studies similar to those of Sellin. Although these early studies were not all uniform in their outcomes, they suggested, on the whole, that capital punishment lacked a marginal deterrent effect. The "general consensus of the scientific establishment until 1975" was "that the death penalty does not deter."[12]

In 1975, an economist, Isaac Ehrlich, published an important article in a prestigious economics journal asserting that the death penalty did deter,[13] and his study was the subject of much controversy for several years. Ehrlich's work was a

---

[9] Raymond Bonner and Ford Fessenden, *States With No Death Penalty Share Lower Homicide Rates*, New York Times, p. 1, Sept. 22, 2000.

[10] *See* Hood, supra note 7, at 208-232 (discussing various studies conducted on the general deterrent effect of the death penalty and finding that conclusions that deterrent effects exist are unjustified); Coyne, *supra* note 6, at 25 (concluding that studies have produced varying results on whether the death penalty has a marginal deterrent effect); Nina Rivkind & Steven F. Shatz, Cases and Materials on the Death Penalty 12-13 (West 2nd ed. 2005) (noting that studies finding a deterrent effect "have been criticized as based on faulty assumptions and methodological errors"), *citing* M. Costanzo, Just Revenge 103 (1997) ("No proof exists that general deterrence results from capital punishment as opposed to life imprisonment.").

[11] *See* Richard O. Lempert, *Desert and Deterrence: An Assessment of the Moral Bases of the Case for Capital Punishment*, 79 Mich. L. Rev. 1177, 1197-1202 (1981) (describing the studies by Sellin and others).

[12] *Id.* at 1199.

[13] Isaac Ehrlich, *The Deterent Effect of Capital Punishment: A Question of Life and Death*, 65 Am. Econ. Rev. 397 (1975).

complex statistical analysis of yearly homicide rates and the rates at which convicted murderers were executed between 1933 and 1969. He concluded that "[o]n the average the tradeoff between the execution of an offender and the lives of potential victims it might have saved was of the order of magnitude of 1 for 8."[14] This dramatic conclusion reopened the debate about deterrence and was used by supporters of the death penalty to back up their case. However, a substantial body of criticism and research developed that created doubt about Ehrlich's conclusions. For example, critics noted that Ehrlich failed to consider that the existence of the death penalty probably makes it harder to convict for murder and that the reduction in deterrence effects from a reduction in conviction rates could entirely dwarf any increased deterrence effects from increased executions. Likewise, he failed to consider and control for other important factors that might have helped explain changes in homicide rates, such as the availability of guns throughout the period of his study. Even more fundamental, Ehrlich failed to include any measure of the duration of prison sentences or the likelihood of life sentences and, thus, failed to actually measure the marginal deterrent effect of the death penalty over sentences of prison for life. Moreover, a number of sophisticated studies using complex statistical analysis followed Ehrlich, and most of them found no evidence that executions deter.[15] Thus, up to the beginning of the new millennium, the notion that the death penalty deterred more than life prison sentences remained unsubstantiated in the view of leading experts.[16]

In the last decade, several new studies, mostly by economists, have reexamined the deterrent effect of the death penalty, with mixed results. Some have found no robust evidence of deterrence.[17] Some claim to have found a brutalization effect from executions in death-penalty states with low rates of execution.[18] Others claim to have found a strong deterrent effect from executions.[19] However, the later

---

[14] *Id.* at 398.

[15] *See generally* Lempert, *supra* note 11, at 1206-24. *See also* Peter Passell & John B. Taylor, *The Deterrent Effect of Capital Punishment: Another View*, 67 AM. ECON. REV. 445 (1977) (finding that Ehrlich's inferences were largely reached by attributing a spike in murders from 1963 to 1969 to the drop and ultimate moratorium in executions after 1962, which was suspect because the change in the murder rate in the 1960s occurred in death-penalty and non-death-penalty states alike and because Ehrlich's own model showed no correlation between murders and executions if his data from 1962 to 1969 were excluded).

[16] *See, e.g.*, HOOD, *supra* note 7, at 230. In his book, Professor Hood examines the flaws in the assumptions and methodologies of the various studies finding a marginal deterrent effect. He points out that the various problems with the studies "should lead any dispassionate analyst to conclude from the findings of these studies that it is not prudent to accept the hypothesis that capital punishment deters murder to a marginally greater extent than does the threat and application of the supposedly lesser punishment of life imprisonment."

[17] *See* Lawrence Katz, Steven D. Levitt & Ellen Shustorovich, *Prison Conditions, Capital Punishment and Deterrence*, 5 AM. L. & ECON. REV. 318, 319 (2003) ("Even if a substantial deterrence effect does exist, the amount of crime rate variation induced by executions may simply be too small.").

[18] *See* Joanna M. Shepherd, *Deterrence versus Brutalization: Capital Punishment's Differing Impacts Among States*, 104 MICH. L. REV. 203, 206-07 (2005) (finding that in many states with low execution rates, executions induce a substantial number of additional murders).

[19] *See, e.g.*, Hashem Dezhbakhsh, Paul H. Rubin & Joanna M. Shephard, *Does Capital Punishment Have a Deterrent Effect? New Evidence from Postmoratorium Panel Data*, 5 AM. L. & ECON. REV. 344 (2003); H. Naci Mocan & R. Kaj. Gittings, *Getting Off Death Row: Commuted Sentences and the*

studies have been criticized on methodological and other grounds.[20] Critics have concluded that the death penalty "is applied so rarely that the number of homicides it can plausibly have caused or deterred cannot be reasonably disentangled from large year-to-year changes in the homicide rate caused by other factors."[21] As a result, whether the death penalty deters remains a contested issue.

The prevailing view among experts in criminology is that the death penalty does not have a marginally deterrent effect over extended incarceration. In 1996, a survey of leading criminologists found that "approximately 80% of the experts in criminology believe, on the basis of the literature in criminology, that the death penalty does not have significant deterrent effects."[22] This study was repeated in 2008, after the appearance of several new studies asserting a deterrent effect and the academic responses to those studies.[23] The researchers found that "only 2.6% of the 2008 respondents agreed that executing people deters others from committing murder, while 89.6% of the experts disagreed."[24] Thus, few of the leading criminologists believe that the death penalty can deter murders more than lengthy incarceration.

Proponents of the death penalty argue that it is intuitive that the death penalty, as the most severe punishment, will deter potential murderers. Moreover, proponents argue that the burden should be on those who oppose the death penalty to refute a presumed deterrent effect. For example, Professor Ernest van den Haag has written that "[s]paring the lives of even a few prospective victims by deterring their murderers is more important than preserving the lives of convicted murderers because of the possibility, or even the probability, that executing them would not deter others."[25] The United States Supreme Court has also relied on deterrence as a justification for the constitutionality of the death penalty. In *Gregg v. Georgia*,[26] the Court acknowledged the inadequacy of the empirical studies, but

---

Deterrent Effect of Capital Punishment, 46 J. L. & Econ. 453 (2003); Paul R. Zimmerman, *State Executions, Deterrence, and the Incidence of Murder*, 7 J. Applied Econ. 163 (2004).

[20] John J. Donohue & Justin Wolfers, *The Death Penalty: No Evidence for Deterrence*, Economists' Voice, Vol. 13, No. 5, Article 3 (2006) *available at* http://www.bepress.com/ev/vol3/iss5/art3. Jeffrey Fagan, *Death and Deterrence Redux: Science, Law and Casual Reasoning on Capital Punishment*, 4 Ohio St. J. of Crim. L. 255 (2006); Richard Berk, *New Claims About Executions and General Deterrence: Déjà vu All Over Again?*, 2 J. Empirical Legal. Stud. 303 (2005).

[21] John J. Donohue & Justin Wolfers, *The Ethics and Empirics of Capital Punishment: Uses and Abuses of Empirical Evidence in the Death Penalty Debate*, 58 Stan. L. Rev. 791, 794 (2005).

[22] *See* Michael L. Radelet & Ronald L. Akers, *Deterrence and the Death Penalty: The Views of the Experts*, 87 J. Crim. L. & Crim. 1, 8 (1996). *See also* Ring v. Arizona, 536 U.S. 584, 615 (2002) (Breyer J., concurring). (citing to numerous studies and commenting that they are inconclusive).

[23] *See* Michael L. Radelet & Traci L. Lacock, *Do Executions Lower Homicide Rates?: The Views of Leading Criminologists*, 99 J. Crim. L. & Criminology 489 (2009).

[24] *Id.* at 503.

[25] Ernest van den Haag, *The Ultimate Punishment: A Defense*, 99 Harv. L. Rev. 1662, 1665-66 (1986). *See also* Cass R. Sunstein & Adrian Vermeule, *Is Capital Punishment Morally Required? Acts, Omissions and Life-Life Tradeoffs*, 58 Stan. L. Rev. 703, 705 (2005) ("We suggest . . . that on certain empirical assumptions, capital punishment may be morally required . . . to prevent the taking of innocent lives.").

[26] 428 U.S. 153, 185-86 (1976). The Court stated: "But for many others the death penalty undoubtedly is a significant deterrent [giving examples of murder for hire, murder by a life imprisonment inmate]."

was willing to assume some deterrent effect. In the interests of federalism, the Court was willing to defer to a state's determination that the death penalty has a deterrent effect.

Opponents of the death penalty respond that deterrence fails as a justification for the death penalty for several reasons. They argue that the burden should be on the proponents to justify such a severe penalty, and that the empirical evidence is, at best, inconclusive on the marginal deterrent effect of the death penalty over lengthy incarceration and, especially, life imprisonment without parole. Opponents also argue that the death penalty is unlikely to be a deterrent when it is imposed in a small percentage of death-eligible cases and seldom carried out.[27] In addition, opponents contend that most defendants who kill do not conduct a "cost-benefit analysis" of their actions.[28] This population of death-eligible defendants already fails to incorporate appropriate social values into their behavior,[29] and so a penological theory based on reinforcing acceptable behavior, the second deterrent purpose, is unlikely to succeed.

Another aspect of deterrence is *specific deterrence*. Unlike general deterrence, which focuses on the actions of other potential defendants, specific deterrence focuses on deterring the particular defendant who is charged with the crime. Thus, the question is whether the punishment will deter a convicted defendant through incapacitation.[30] In the death penalty context, proponents argue that executing a defendant is a specific deterrent that guarantees that the defendant will never kill again. Opponents argue that the death penalty is not needed as a specific deterrent. A defendant can be incapacitated with a sentence of life imprisonment.[31] Although it is possible for a death row inmate to kill while incarcerated, opponents argue that there is no evidence that death row inmates kill in prison at a rate any

---

The Court further stated that "[t]he value of capital punishment as a deterrent of crime is a complex factual issue the resolution of which properly rests with the legislatures . . . " *Id.* The *Gregg* decision is discussed in Sections 4.03 and 6.03, *infra.*

[27] *See generally* Jack Greenberg, *Against the American System of Capital Punishment,* 99 Harv. L. Rev. 1670 (1986) (describing the state practice of executions as rare and erratic). *See also* Hood, *supra* note 7 at 212 (stating that the probability of being executed if charged with a culpable homicide is 1 in 1,000).

[28] *See* Greenberg, *supra* note 27, at 1676 ("[The defendants] are impulsive, and they kill impulsively."). *See also* Paul H. Robinson & John M. Darley, *Does Criminal Law Deter? A Behavioural Science Investigation,* 24 Oxford J. Legal Stud. 173 174 (2004) (contending that the prerequisite conditions for deterrence to operate are rarely present).

[29] *Id.* ("This conception of general deterrence [ingraining right and wrong] seems deeply flawed because it rests upon a quite implausible conception of how this killer population internalizes social norms.").

[30] *See* Joshua Dressler, Understanding Criminal Law 15-16 (Lexis 4th ed. 2006).

[31] *See, e.g.,* Greenberg, *supra* note 27, at 1676 (noting that: "Very little reason exists to believe that the present capital punishment system deters the conduct of others any more effectively than life imprisonment."); David McCord, *Imagining a Retributivist Alternative to Capital Punishment,* 50 Fla. L. Rev. 1, 35 (1998) (describing the specific deterrence value of the death penalty as irrelevant because the more heinous murderers are unlikely to ever be released); Lawrence C. Marshall, *The Innocence Revolution and the Death Penalty,* 1 Ohio St. Crim. L. Rev. 573, 581 (2004) ("The advent of SuperMax correctional facilities now enables states to house particularly dangerous inmates under conditions that completely neutralize the inmate.").

greater than other inmates.[32]

[B] Retribution

In contrast to general deterrence, retribution focuses on the defendant who has committed the crime, rather than on the effect on other potential criminals. Retribution is satisfied if the defendant receives the punishment that he deserves for the crime.[33] Death as a punishment for murder is often viewed as "an eye for an eye." This rationale is drawn from philosophers, such as Immanuel Kant,[34] and from the Biblical concept of *lex talionis*.[35] Some scholars have pointed out, however, that the "eye for an eye" concept was intended as a limitation on the severity of the punishment that could be imposed, rather than as a justification to increase the penalty.[36] Thus, Professor Joshua Dressler has asserted that "[w]hat *lex talionis* in our modern society really means is that punishment should be

---

[32] *See also* Ring v. Arrizona, 536 U.S. 584, 615 (2002) (Breyer J., concurring) ("As to incapacitation, few offenders sentenced to life without parole (as an alternative to death) commit further crimes.") (*citing* "Sorensen & Pilgrim, *An Actuarial Risk Assessment of Violence Posed by Capital Murder Defendants*, 90 J. CRIM. L. & C. 1251, 1256 (2000) (studies find average repeat murder rate of .002% among murderers whose death sentences were commuted)); Marquart & Sorensen, A NATIONAL STUDY OF THE *FURMAN*-COMMUTED INMATES: ASSESSING THE THREAT TO SOCIETY FROM CAPITAL OFFENDERS, 23 LOY. L.A. L. REV. 5, 26 (1989) (98% did not kill again either in prison or in free society).

[33] DRESSLER, *supra* note 30, at 16 ("Retributivists believe that punishment is justified when it is deserved. It is deserved when the wrongdoer freely chooses to violate society's rules").

[34] William E. Connolly, *The Will, Capital Punishment, and Cultural War, in* THE KILLING STATE; CAPITAL PUNISHMENT IN LAW, POLITICS, AND CULTURE 190 (Austin Sarat ed., *Oxford University Press* 1999), states: "To act morally, according to the moral purist Kant, is to obey 'autonomously' a moral law each recognizes in itself. A crime thus deserves punishment because it is willed against the moral law that anyone is able to recognize and obey; and the level of punishment must be proportioned to the degree the will's disobedience contradicts its own essence." Connolly quotes Kant: "Accordingly, whatever undeserved evil you inflict upon another within the people, that you inflicted upon yourself. If you insult him, you insult yourself; if you steal from him, you steal from yourself; if you kill him, you kill yourself. . . . If . . . he has committed murder he must die. Here there is no substitute that will satisfy justice." *See also* RIVKIND, *supra* note 10, at 9 ("It (the 'Principle of Equality') may be rendered by saying that the undeserved evil which anyone commits on another, is to be regarded as perpetuated on himself. Hence it may be said: 'If you slander another, you slander yourself; if you strike another, you strike yourself; if you kill another, you kill yourself.' ").

[35] *See* McCord, *supra* note 31, at n.139 (1998) (describing the "modern manifestation of the ancient eye for an eye principle," quoting Leviticus 24:17, 20 (King James): "And he that killeth any man shall surely be put to death . . . . Breach for breach, eye for eye, tooth for tooth: as he hath caused a blemish in a man, so shall it be done to him again"). *See also* RIVKIND, *supra* note 10, at 8-9 (discussing religious support for the death penalty in the concept of *lex talionis*); COYNE, *supra* note 6, at 48-51 (discussing the debate over the propriety of death penalty across religions).

A number of denominations, most notably the Roman Catholic Church, have taken stands against the death penalty. Others, including the Southern Baptists, have taken positions in favor of the death penalty.

[36] *See, e.g.*, Norman Krivosha et al., *A Historical and Philosophical Look at the Death Penalty — Does It Serve Society's Needs?*, 16 CREIGHTON L. REV. 1, 3-6 (1982-83) (discussing the historical references to the biblical requirement of "an eye for an eye, and a tooth for a tooth."). Krivosha notes that this concept has often been misinterpreted: ". . . the concept of an "eye for an eye" was not intended to mean that one eye be removed for the another but, rather, that one may not be compensated for an eye if, the injury was only to a tooth." *Id* at 4.

proportionate to the offense committed, not that it must be identical."[37]

There are several versions of retributive theory. One version is based on the idea that a defendant's relationship with society requires moral balance. When a defendant commits a crime, this moral balance is askew until the defendant is punished for his or her actions and, by punishing him, society actually vindicates him as a responsible moral agent.[38] A second version holds that criminal punishment satisfies a widely shared demand for vengeance for a defendant's wrong. On this view, the death penalty is society's justified way of striking back at the defendant, rather than leaving the defendant's punishment to vigilante justice. A third account views the punishment as vindicating the injuries suffered by the victim or the victim's family. In this account, the death penalty reaffirms the victim's value as a human and eradicates the defendant's implicit message in killing that the defendant is more valuable than the victim. The latter two forms of retribution have a utilitarian component of achieving a goal for others.[39] An even more explicitly hybrid form of victim vindication and utilitarianism has been called "denunciation" or "expressive" theory. On this view, the punishment is educative and serves various ends that are beneficial to society. At the same time, the punishment is retributive in that it is a moral condemnation of the conduct in question.[40]

Proponents of the death penalty argue that a defendant deserves death because he or she has taken a life.[41] Thus, the "eye for an eye" rationale is often raised in support of the death penalty. On a more philosophical level, proponents argue that

---

[37] Joshua Dressler, *The Wisdom and Morality of Present-Day Criminal Sentencing*, 38 AKRON L. REV. 853, 860 (2005).

[38] *See* DRESSLER, *supra* note 30, at 18. *See also* Joshua Dressler, *1990 Survey of Books Relating to the Law; II. Crime and Punishment: Hating Criminals: How Can Something That Feels So Good Be Wrong?*, 88 MICH. L. REV. 1448, 1452 (1990) (discussing the idea that a moral equilibrium is established when people obey laws and "accept the burden of exercising self restraint" and "[p]unishment of the wrongdoer is fair and just, protective retributivists assert, because it restores the moral equilibrium.").

[39] *See* Greenberg, *supra* note 27, at n. 39. Greenberg sets forth the societal reaction and victim satisfaction views, but disagrees with them:

"Retribution is also said to have another utilitarian by-product distinct from a Kantian eye-for-an-eye justification: it satisfies demands for vengeance, preventing retaliatory killing. Yet, during the period of no executions (1967-1977) and in the overwhelming number of states that have abolished the death penalty, have not sentenced anyone to death, or have not carried out executions, it is difficult to find an instance of vengeance killing, although during this time there have been perhaps 360,000 murders (about 20,000 per year for 18 years). It is also argued that, particularly for those who have been close to the victim, who are members of his or her family, or who are fellow police officers, or for those members of the public who somehow feel an identification with the deceased, the death penalty provides personal satisfaction, repaying in some measure the loss they felt in the death of the victim. This hardly justifies the present system."

Id.

[40] *See* McCord, *supra* note 31, at 33 ("Under this expressive view, the signification of punishment is moral condemnation. By imposing the proper form and degree of affliction on the wrongdoer, society says, in effect, that the offender's assessment of whose interests count is wrong.") (footnote omitted); DRESSLER, *supra* note 30, at 19 ("Denunciation" may be an alternative to retribution or it might be viewed as a combination of retributive and utilitarian purposes.).

[41] *See generally* van den Haag, *supra*, note 25, at 1669; *see also* McCord, *supra* note 31, at 29 (discussing arguments for and against the death penalty). Professor McCord notes that it is publicly

death as a punishment is necessary to bring the defendant back into moral balance with society.[42] In response to opponents' argument that everyone has a right to life, proponents posit that a defendant has forfeited his right to life by committing the crime.[43] Although retribution can be distinguished from revenge,[44] some proponents also argue that revenge is a legitimate rationale for the death penalty.[45] A key United States Supreme Court case, *Gregg v. Georgia*,[46] which is discussed in Sections 4.04 and 6.03, *infra*, acknowledged the retributive models of society's condemnation of the crime and the prevention of lawless, vigilante justice as justifications for the death penalty. The Court stated:

> In part, capital punishment is an expression of society's moral outrage at particularly offensive conduct. This function may be unappealing to many, but it is essential in an ordered society that asks its citizens to rely on legal processes rather than self-help to vindicate their wrongs.[47]

Opponents of the death penalty argue that death is never a just punishment for a crime. Their fundamental argument is that killing a defendant is morally wrong because there is an inherent or universal right to life.[48] No crime can justify imposing the death penalty. By killing a defendant, the opponents argue, the state is engaged in the same conduct it condemns. Opponents also contend that revenge is never a justifiable purpose for punishment.[49] Moreover, they dispute the claim that there is evidence that the harm to, and grief of, victims' families is alleviated

---

accepted that "what is deserved for a criminal act is punishment that is in proportion to the seriousness of the act."

[42] *See* note 38, *supra*, and accompanying text.

[43] *See* Hugo Adam Bedau, *Abolishing the Death Penalty Even for the Worst Murderers*, in Sᴀʀᴀᴛ, *supra* note 34, at 43 ("Defenders of the death penalty typically reply (as John Locke did three centuries ago) that even if the right to life is "natural" and "inalienable," the murderer forfeits his life").

[44] *Id.* at 49 (stating that "revenge" and " "retribution" are not synonyms").

[45] *See* Gregg v. Georgia, 428 U.S. 153, 183 (1976) *quoting from* Furman v. Georgia, 408 U.S. 238, 308 (1972). The Court stated: "The instinct for retribution is part of the nature of man, and channeling that instinct in the administration of criminal justice serves an important purpose in promoting the stability of society governed by law." *See also* Bedau, *supra* note 43, at 50 (disagreeing with the propriety of revenge as a justification, but quoting from Nietzsche that "the thirst for revenge (and desire to use punishment as a vehicle for revenge) is "all too human."").

[46] 428 U.S. 153 (1976).

[47] *Id.* at 183.

[48] *See* Bedau, supra note 43, at 43. Abolitionists have contended: "[T]he right to life cannot be forfeited-because it is an absolute right. That is, the right to life prevails over every other moral consideration that might be thought to compete with or override it." *Cf.* Carol Steiker, *No, Capital Punishment is Not Morally Required; Deterrence, Deontology, and the Death Penalty*, 58 Sᴛᴀɴ. L. Rᴇᴠ. 751, 773-74 (2005) (asserting a human dignity argument against the death penalty that posits a difference between expectations and private murders on grounds that executions "damage or destroy the human capacities [to feel empathy, compassion, pity or love] of those of us in whose name the punishment is publicly inflicted").

[49] *See* Bedau, *supra* note 43, at 50 ("Revenge is simply too untamed and volatile, too indifferent to the claims of justice to play a role in civilized society"). *See also* Furman v. Georgia, 408 U.S. 238, 343 (1972) (Marshall J., concurring) ("Retaliation, vengeance, and retribution have been roundly condemned as intolerable aspirations for a government in a free society. Punishment as retribution has been condemned by scholars for centuries, and the Eighth Amendment itself was adopted to prevent punishment from becoming synonymous with vengeance.").

more by the death penalty than by life imprisonment.[50] Opponents further argue that retribution can be effectively satisfied by life imprisonment.[51]

§ 2.03 SYSTEMIC FAIRNESS

In addition to the debate over whether death in and of itself can be justified as a punishment for a serious crime,[52] a second level of debate focuses on the fairness of the system for imposing the death penalty. As discussed in later chapters, there is a complex procedural system for capital cases that includes a bifurcated trial, the presentation of aggravating and mitigating evidence, and an automatic appeal of the conviction and sentence. Opponents of the death penalty argue that, despite all of the procedural safeguards, the system remains arbitrary and capricious. Proponents counter that the system satisfactorily provides a balance of all interests.

Opponents contend that the flaws in the criminal justice system cannot be tolerated when the penalty is irreversible. Opponents argue that the discretion in the system, such as prosecutorial discretion whether to charge a capital offense and jury discretion whether to impose the death penalty, leads to unfair results.[53] Among other inequalities, they cite race and geography. For example, opponents cite studies that show that defendants are more likely to receive the death penalty

---

[50] *See* FRANKLIN E. ZIMRING, THE CONTRADICTIONS OF AMERICAN CAPITAL PUNISHMENT 59 (Oxford University Press 2003) (questioning the redemptive value of execution for the victim's family: "What is not known is whether pending death sentences delay the mourning and psychological closure associated with the loss of the homicide victim or whether the death of the offender in some sense accelerates the positive closure of relatives in relation to the victim's loss."); RIVKIND, *supra* note 10, at 11, *citing* HELEN PREJEAN, DEAD MAN WALKING: AN EYEWITNESS ACCOUNT OF THE DEATH PENALTY IN THE UNITED STATES (1993) (questioning the redemptive value of execution for the victim's family).

[51] Bedau, *supra* note 43, at 28. *See also* McCord, *supra* note 31 (proposing an alternative to the death penalty). *See also* Dan Markel, *State Be Not Proud: A Retributivist Defense of the Commutation of Death Row and the Abolition of the Death Penalty,* 40 HARV. C. R.-C. L. L. REV. 407, 480 (2005) ("[A] commitment to retributive punishment impedes neither the realization of humane institutions of criminal justice nor a revolt against the benighted, misbegotten, and often brutal status quo we continue to tolerate to our shame.").

[52] Greenberg, *supra* note 27. The two areas of debate, focusing on the purposes of punishment and systemic fairness, are not necessarily mutually exclusive, nor are they the only ways of assessing capital punishment in the United States today. Professor Greenberg has argued that the morality of the death penalty cannot be assessed in a hypothetical system, but must be evaluated within the existing system. *See also* ZIMRING, *supra* note 50, at 129 (describing a "value conflict" among people in the United States between "vigilante values" and "due process values" that creates continuing problems in deciding whether or not capital punishment should continue).

[53] *See generally* Stephen B. Bright, *Counsel for the Poor: The Death Sentence Not for the Worst Crime but for the Worst Lawyer,* 103 YALE L.J. 1835, 1842, 1844-45, 1855-56 (1994). The author suggests various factors that result in the arbitrary administration of the death penalty, including inadequacy of appointed counsel, the status and resources of the prosecution, and the political concerns of elected judges. *See also* RIVKIND, *supra* note 10, at 16-17 (discussing three major factors that lead to arbitrary imposition of the death penalty — prosecutorial discretion; incompetent counsel; and the politics of elected judges); COYNE, *supra* note 6, at 33-36 (discussing risk of executing the innocent); CHARLES BLACK, CAPITAL PUNISHMENT: THE INEVITABILITY OF CAPRICE AND MISTAKE (2d. ed. 1981) (emphasizing that a system administered by humans exercising discretion will produce mistakes); Adam M. Gershowitz, *Pay Now, Execute Later: Why Counties Should Be Required to Post Bond to Seek the Death Penalty,* 41 RICH. L. REV. 861, 869-73 (2007) (pointing to problems of racial discrimination, inadequate representation of defendants and geographical disparities among and within states).

if the victim is white.[54] Defendants are also more likely to receive the death penalty in a southern state. Opponents acknowledge that the criminal justice system in general tolerates variation. They contend, however, that while these inequalities may be tolerated with a less severe sentence, the same inequalities cannot be accepted when the sentence is death.[55] Opponents further argue that the system fails to provide adequate defense counsel,[56] which leads to the imposition of the death penalty in cases where it would not have been imposed if competent counsel had been provided. An argument gaining increasing force from opponents is the risk of convicting and executing innocent persons. As of December, 2011, 139 people in 26 states have been freed from death row since 1973.[57] Another recent study by Professor James S. Liebman found errors, indicated by a reversal rate in the courts, in 68% of death penalty cases decided between 1973 and 1995.[58] Opponents contend that the risk of error is too great to continue imposing the death penalty. Justice Blackmun epitomized the arguments of the opponents in a dissent to denial of *certiorari* where he stated:

> Perhaps one day this Court will develop procedural rules or verbal formulas that actually will provide consistency, fairness, and reliability in a capital-sentencing scheme. I am not optimistic that such a day will come.[59]

Proponents respond that the criminal justice system is fair.[60] They contend that discretion is inherent and desirable within the criminal justice system. In capital cases, the discretion is guided by legal standards that reduce the possibility of unfair or erroneous decisions.

If anything, they argue, the death penalty should be imposed more often in order to treat those who deserve it more equally.[61] In response to many of the complaints of the opponents, the proponents argue that there are ways to correct the problems

---

[54] *See* DAVID C. BALDUS, GEORGE WOODWORTH, & CHARLES PULASKI, JR., EQUAL JUSTICE AND THE DEATH PENALTY, 400-4 (1990) (finding that defendants in Georgia with white victims faced odds that were 4.3 times higher of receiving a death sentence than those with black victims). For additional discussion of the implications of race in capital cases, *see* Section 20.01 et seq, *infra.*

[55] *See, e.g.,* Greenberg, *supra* note 27, at n 42.

[56] *See* Bright, *supra* note 53, at 1842 (noting that "[w]hether death is imposed frequently turns on the quality of counsel assigned to the accused"); Gershowitz, *supra* note 53, at 71 (noting the problem with the quality of defense representation in capital cases). *See* discussion of challenges to ineffective assistance of counsel in Section 16.01 et seq., *infra.*

[57] Death Penalty Information Center, *Innocence and the Death Penalty* (2011), at <http://www.deathpenaltyinfo.org/innocence-and-the-death-penalty.> *Cf.,* Ward Campbell, *Critique of List ("Innocence: Freed From Death Row"),* available at <http://www.prodeathpenalty.com/DPIC.htm> (criticizing the statistics provided by the DPIC on "innocence").

[58] James S. Liebman, et al., *A Broken System: Error Rates in Capital Cases, 1973-1995* (2002) *available electronically at:* http://www.law.columbia.edu.instructionalservices/liebman/; James S. Liebman, *The Overproduction of Death,* 100 COLUM. L. REV. 2030 (2000).

[59] *See Callins v. Collins,* 510 U.S. 1141, 1144 (1994) (cert. denied) (Blackmun J., dissenting).

[60] *See* van den Haag, *supra* note 25, at 1663. Professor van den Haag contended that an unequal distribution based on race or other reasons does not affect the "justness" of the death penalty. He argued for separating the issue of maldistribution from the issue of the justice in imposing the death penalty.

[61] *See id.* at 1663-4.

without abandoning the death penalty.[62] For instance, standards can be established for the competency of capital attorneys, arguably alleviating the problem of incompetent counsel. Although proponents do not want to execute innocent persons, they contend that there are adequate safeguards in the system. Some proponents contest whether the figures on innocent persons executed or released are in fact accurate.[63] In addition, they point to safeguards such as clemency and DNA testing. Professor van den Haag has also argued that, if the death penalty is worth having, the risk of executing an innocent person is an acceptable cost.[64]

§ 2.04   FINANCIAL COSTS OF THE DEATH PENALTY

Another issue that continues to arise in the debate over the death penalty is the cost of litigating and executing in capital cases compared with the cost of litigating and incarcerating defendants in cases where the penalty sought and obtained is life without parole. Many proponents of the death penalty contend that society should not have to pay the costs to incarcerate murderers for life.[65] However, opponents of the death penalty argue that the death penalty is far more expensive than life imprisonment when all of the costs involved are considered.[66] While the differences will vary from state to state, the existing studies suggest that a death penalty system may be more expensive from a total-cost perspective than a system with a maximum punishment of life imprisonment without parole.

Death-penalty cases are costly compared to non-death-penalty murder cases because the former usually involve more expensive pre-trial investigations and

---

[62] *See* RIVKIND, *supra* note 10, at 16-17 (describing arguments of proponents). *See also* Amanda S. Hitchcock, *Using the Adversarial Process to Limit Arbitrariness in Capital Charging Decisions*, 85 N. C. L. REV. 931 (2007) (offering a solution by way of a pretrial hearing regarding the prosecutor's charging decision); Gershowitz, *supra* note 53, at 861 (proposing that legislatures force counties to post a cash bond before seeking the death penalty and that the bond be forfeited if pursuit of the death penalty is unsuccessful at trial).

[63] Stephen J. Markman & Paul G. Cassell, *Protecting the Innocent: A Response to the Bedau-Radelet Study*, 41 STAN. L. REV. 12 (1988). Professors Markman and Cassell argue that the risk of execution of the innocent "is too small to be a significant factor in the debate over the death penalty." They contend: "No sound reason exists for believing that there is currently an intolerable risk of executing an innocent person. Over the past fifteen years, procedural protections have been adopted to reduce as much as possible the likelihood that error will be committed or, if committed, that it will go undetected." *See also* COYNE, *supra* note 6, at 33-34; RIVKIND, *supra* note 10, at 16 (both describing the death penalty supporters' argument that few innocent persons are on death row and that there are procedural protections).

[64] *See* van den Haag, *supra* note 25, at 1665 ("Despite precautions, nearly all human activities, such as trucking, lighting, or construction, cost the lives of some innocent bystanders . . . analogously, for those who think the death penalty just, miscarriages of justice are offset by the moral benefits and the usefulness of doing justice.").

[65] *See* COYNE, *supra* note 6, at 39 ("The notion of law abiding taxpayers having to financially support convicted murderers for the rest of their lives is likely to influence jury deliberations. A juror weighing alternative punishments for capital murder might ask colloquially, 'You mean we should provide free food, shelter and television to this killer?' ").

[66] *See* ZIMRING, supra note 50, at 47, *citing to* Amnesty USA 2000. "Taxpayers in Texas are spending an average of $2.3 million on each execution — while lifetime incarceration costs from $800,000 to $1 million." *See also* RIVKIND, *supra* note 10, at 14 ("Various studies have estimated the cost of executing a murderer at between $1.5 and $4 million more then incarcerating the murderer for life").

trials, much more extensive and expensive post-trial litigation and, although a shorter period of incarceration, a still lengthy period of imprisonment before execution. The annual expense of incarceration for death-row inmates is also generally greater than the annual expense of incarceration for those serving life sentences, due to factors such as the perceived need for increased security on death row. In the end, it appears that savings achieved from reduced incarceration costs due to executions are outweighed by the increased costs of litigation associated with the death penalty.

Murder cases where the prosecutor seeks the death penalty are more expensive because of the perceived need for "super" due process when the defendant faces possible execution.[67] Often, the investigative costs and pre-trial litigation are greater. The defendant is more likely to be incarcerated pre-trial. If the case goes to trial, the jury selection process is also generally more extensive. The defendant, who is usually indigent, is often entitled to two appointed lawyers rather than one. Costly expert witnesses are used in greater number. The sentencing phase is much more formal and extensive, requiring the continued participation of the jury and the use of even more experts. As a result, a variety of studies from various jurisdictions have shown that the pre-trial and trial costs are greatly amplified if a murder case is pursued at the outset as a capital one.[68]

Post-conviction litigation and clemency proceedings are much more extensive and expensive in capital cases because, where the death penalty is imposed, the litigation typically proceeds through many more stages of state and federal post-conviction review and clemency appeals.[69] Where a non-capital sentence has been imposed, the review with appointed defense counsel typically proceeds only to a single level of appeal within the state system. In a death-penalty case, by contrast, the review will typically proceed to the state's highest court, then on a certiorari petition to the U.S. Supreme Court, back to state post-conviction proceedings, followed by multiple stages of federal post-conviction review, and ultimately by a clemency petition. At all of these stages, the defendant will usually be represented by appointed counsel. The cost of this additional litigation in terms of attorneys, experts and state judicial personnel averages in the hundreds of thousands of dollars.[70]

---

[67] *See generally* Ronald J. Tabak and J. Mark Lane, *The Execution of Injustice*, 23 Loy. L. Rev. 59, 133-34 (1989).

[68] For example, a recent report found that merely the mean *defense costs* at the trial level for a federal death case (including those that result in trial or a guilty plea) is $491,905, which is more than six times the mean defense costs of $76,665 for a federal death-eligible murder case in which the death penalty is not sought. *See* Jon B. Gould & Lisa Greenman, *Report to the Committee on Defender Services, Judicial Conference of the United States: Update on the Cost and Quality of Defense Representation in Federal Death Penalty Cases* 25 (Sept. 2010), *available at* http://www.deathpenaltyinfo.org/documents/FederalDPCost2010.pdf.

[69] *See* Tabak & Lane, *supra* note 67, at 135.

[70] For example, Kansas estimated that the costs of appeals for a death case would be 21 times greater than the appeal costs in the same case if the sentence was life imprisonment. *See* Coyne, *supra* note 6, at 42, *citing Performance Audit Report: Costs Incurred for Death Penalty Cases*, State of Kansas, Dec. 2003.

Incarceration costs in capital cases are also very high. In 2009, the average time between a death sentence and execution was 14 years and 1 month, and the average time on death row for currently condemned inmates was 12 years and 8 months.[71] A defendant sentenced to life imprisonment can still be expected to live in prison longer than one sentenced to death. However, the annual cost of maintaining a person on death row in most states may be higher than the annual cost of maintaining the person under a sentence of life imprisonment without parole. A California Commission recently concluded that "confinement on death row adds $90,000 per year to the cost of confinement beyond the normal cost of $34,150."[72] Thus, even regarding incarceration costs, a sentence of death is probably more expensive than is commonly understood.

Studies comparing costs have generally found that a death-penalty system is much more expensive than a system with a maximum punishment of life imprisonment without parole. In California, a state Commission estimated in 2008 that the annual cost of the state's present death penalty system is $137 million per year and that the comparative cost of a system that imposed a maximum penalty of life imprisonment without parole for the same offenders would be only $11.5 million per year.[73] A 2008 study by the Urban Institute in Maryland concluded that the 162 capital cases that the state prosecuted from 1978 to 1999 cost $186 million more than those same cases would have cost had the state not had a death penalty.[74] A 2005 New Jersey study by New Jersey Policy Perspective concluded that the death penalty since 1983 cost the state $253 million more than it would have spent if the most severe sentence were life imprisonment without parole.[75] A variety of studies in other states have reached similar conclusions.[76] These various studies also do not take into account the expense to all U.S. taxpayers from federal court time devoted to post-conviction litigation in capital cases. When added to the calculus, the additional costs from the use of federal resources reinforce the conclusion that the death penalty is expensive.

Cost arguments are also beginning to play a significant role in debates over whether to maintain the death penalty or to substantially reform death penalty

---

[71] *See* Tracy L. Snell, *Bureau of Justice Statistics, Capital Punishment, 2009 — Statistical Tables*, 12 tab. 9 & 14 tab. 12 (Dec. 2010) *available at* http://bjs.ojp.usdoj.gov/content/pub/pdf/cp09st.pdf.

[72] California Commission on the Fair Administration of Justice, *Report and Recommendations on the Administration of the Death Penalty in California* 82 (June 30, 2008) *available at* http://www.ddfaj.org.

[73] *See id.* at 84. A more recent study found the cost difference, taking into account more, but not all, of the actual expenses, to be $184 million annually. *See* Arthur L. Alarcón & Paula M. Mitchell, *Executing the Will of the Voters? A Roadmap to Mend or End the California Legislature's Multi-Billion-Dollar Death Penalty Debacle*, 44 Loyola Of L. A. L. Rev. S41, S109 (2011).

[74] *See* John Roman, *et al. The Cost of the Death Penalty in Maryland* 3 (2008) *available at* www.urban.org/UploadedPDF/411625_md_death_penalty.pdf.

[75] *See* Mary E. Forsberg, *Money for Nothing? The Financial Cost of New Jersey's Death Penalty* 16 (2005) *available at* http://www.njpp.org/reports/money-for-nothing-the-financial-cost-of-new-jerseys-death-penalty.

[76] *See generally* Testimony of Richard C. Dieter, Executive Director, Death Penalty Information Center, before the Judiciary Committee of the Colorado House of Representatives, Concerning H.R. 1094 (Feb. 7, 2007) (discussing numerous studies indicating that the costs of the death penalty exceed the costs of life imprisonment by at least several hundred thousand dollars), *available at* http://deathpenaltyinfo.org/COcosttestimony.pdf.

procedures.[77] Costs played a significant role in the recent decisions to abolish the death penalty in New Jersey, New Mexico and Illinois.[78] In part because of large state deficits that arose after the recession that began in 2007, the large expense has also recently become "a prevalent issue in discussing the death penalty" in a variety of states that have considered legislation to end it or restrict it.[79]

Whether the apparently high financial costs of the death penalty will cause a large number of states to curtail or abolish it remains to be seen. Critics of the death penalty, even some who would otherwise support the sanction, have begun to focus heavily on the costs as a reason for abolition.[80] They assert that the money devoted to the death penalty could be better spent in other ways. Yet, proponents of the death penalty assert that the cost studies do not consider expenses saved through the existence of the death penalty, such as its possible influence in encouraging guilty pleas in murder cases or in deterring murders.[81] Further, proponents argue that, instead of curtailing the death penalty, post-conviction review in death penalty cases should be streamlined to reduce the costs of the death penalty.[82] Proponents also argue that the extent to which the death penalty is used in murder cases should not rest on costs alone. Achieving appropriate retribution, they urge, is a worthy goal.[83] Ultimately, as these arguments suggest, the financial question involves disputes over a variety of contested factual issues and over the ultimate moral value of capital punishment.

---

[77] *See* Deboarah Hastings, *Death Penalty's Costs Boosts Opponents: States See Savings In Life Sentences*, THE WASHINGTON POST A3 (March 15, 2009).

[78] *See, e.g.*, Steve Mills, *Illinois Bans Death Penalty: Quinn Commutes 15 Sentences to Life, Angering Some Victims' Families*, CHI. TRIBUNE 1 (March 10, 2011).

[79] *Id.*

[80] *See, e.g.*, Donald A. McCartin, *Second Thoughts of a 'Hanging Judge': A Death Sentence in California Rarely Leads to Execution. Let's Abandon the Charade*, L.A. TIMES 23 (March 25, 2011) (arguing that "[i]t's time to stop playing the killing game" and that we should "use the hundreds of millions of dollars we'll save" to avoid "cuts to kindergarten, cuts to universities, cuts to people with special needs").

[81] *See, e.g.*, Mills, *supra* note 83 (quoting James McKay, Chief of the Capital Litigation Task Force for the Cook County State's Attorney's Office after news that the Governor of Illinois signed a bill to abolish the death penalty: "With the death penalty off the table, there'll be even more trials. There'll be no incentive to plead guilty. I do not believe for one second that taking the death penalty off the table will save the state of Illinois any money whatsoever.").

[82] *See, e.g.*, Hastings, *supra* note 77 (quoting Kent Scheidegger, Legal Director of the Criminal Justice Legal Foundation, a pro-capital-punishment group: "We should be revamping the appeals process so that these cases move more quickly" and so that states don't "calculate the cost as if these people are going to spend their whole lives on death row.").

[83] *See* California District Attorneys Association, *Prosecutors' Perspective on California's Death Penalty* 48 (2003) ("Whatever the cost, or its underlying cause, a fundamental question must be posed: What price justice?").

Chapter 3

SOURCES OF LAW

§ 3.01 OVERVIEW

Capital punishment is authorized in laws passed by state legislatures and Congress. There are extensive statutory provisions providing for the procedure and implementation of an execution. In addition, states may have state constitutional provisions that apply to capital cases. Despite extensive state law, the United States Constitution is the paramount authority in the field of capital punishment law. Although several constitutional provisions govern aspects of capital procedures, the Eighth Amendment's cruel and unusual punishment clause is the keystone. As with any constitutional provision, case law, especially from the United States Supreme Court, is important in interpreting the constitutional mandates. Additional, less utilized sources of law are international treaties providing for various basic rights. Thus, the sources of law in capital litigation include state and federal statutes, the United States Constitution, case law, and treaties.

§ 3.02 STATE AND FEDERAL STATUTORY LAW AND STATE CONSTITUTIONAL LAW

In all states that have the death penalty, there are statutory provisions that govern the capital trial and sentencing process. Similarly, there are federal statutory provisions governing capital cases based on federal crimes.[1] A typical statute 1) defines aggravating circumstances that elevate a murder to a capital murder, 2) provides for the presentation of mitigating circumstances, and 3) requires a procedure that takes into account the aggravating and mitigating circumstances in deciding the penalty.[2] Some states may also rely on state constitutional law as authority for either substance or procedure.[3] Thus, state law, and congressional statutes for federal crimes, are the first places to search to determine whether the death penalty is an authorized punishment and what procedures exist for imposing it.

---

[1] *See, e.g.*, 18 U.S.C.A. §§ 3591-3599 (West 2011).

[2] *See, e.g.*, CAL. PENAL CODE § 190.2-190.3 (West 2011); TEX. CODE CRIM. PROC. ANN. art. 37.071 (Vernon 2009).

[3] *See, e.g.*, CAL. CONST. art., 1 § 27, which provides: "All statutes of this state . . . requiring, authorizing, imposing, or relating to the death penalty are in full force and effect . . . "

§ 3.03   UNITED STATES CONSTITUTIONAL PROVISIONS

The first ten amendments to the Constitution are called the *Bill of Rights*. These amendments apply directly only to the federal government. Virtually all provisions of the Bill of Rights, however, have been incorporated into the meaning of *due process of law* under the Fourteenth Amendment.[4] The Fourteenth Amendment specifically applies to the states. As a result, the Eighth Amendment's cruel and unusual punishment clause and other pertinent constitutional provisions apply to state as well as federal capital trials.[5]

The Eighth Amendment simply states:

> Excessive bail shall not be required, nor excessive fines imposed, nor cruel and unusual punishments inflicted.[6]

The United States Supreme Court has relied heavily on interpretations of the Eighth Amendment to define constitutional capital procedures. Almost every chapter in this treatise involves interpretations of the Eighth Amendment's provision on cruel and unusual punishment. For example, the structure of a capital trial, discussed in Sections 7.01-7.03, *infra*, evolved as a result of decisions of the Supreme Court.

Other constitutional provisions that arise in capital litigation include the Fourteenth Amendment's due process clause, the Fifth Amendment's self-incrimination clause,[7] and the Sixth Amendment's right to counsel and right to jury clauses.[8] Due process often refers to the right to notice and a hearing, but it can also involve substantive protections. For instance, the Fourteenth Amendment's concept of due process of law includes a substantive prohibition of cruel and unusual punishment. Similarly, the due process clause includes the concepts of the Fifth Amendment's self-incrimination clause and the Sixth Amendment's right to counsel and jury clauses. Thus, each federal constitutional provision applies in both federal cases (directly) and state cases (through the Fourteenth Amendment). Each provision also has significance in all criminal trials, but raises unique issues in a capital case.

---

[4] U.S. CONST. amend. XIV, § 1 provides: ". . . nor shall any State deprive any person of life, liberty, or property, without due process of law . . . "

[5] *See* Robinson v. California, 370 U.S. 660 (1962) (recognizing that the Eighth Amendment's ban on cruel and unusual punishment applies to the states).

[6] The excessive bail clause has never been the subject of a Supreme Court case incorporating it into the 14th Amendment's due process clause, but the Court treats the clause as incorporated. Wayne R. LaFave et al., CRIMINAL PROCEDURE § 2.6(b) (West 5th ed. 2009); Browning-Ferris Indus. of Vermont, Inc. v. Kelco Disposal, Inc., 492 U.S. 257, 284 (1989).

[7] U.S. CONST. amend. V provides: ". . . nor shall be compelled in any criminal case to be a witness against himself . . . " *See* discussion of Fifth Amendment issues in Section 11.02[C], *infra*.

[8] U.S. CONST. amend. VI provides: ". . . the accused shall enjoy the right to a speedy and public trial, by an impartial jury . . . , and to have the Assistance of Counsel for his defence" *See* discussion of the Sixth Amendment right to counsel in Sections 11.02[C] and 16.01 et seq., *infra*. For a discussion of the right to a jury, *see* Section 10.01, *infra*.

§ 3.04　THE IMPORTANCE OF FEDERAL CONSTITUTIONAL LAW

Although the states and Congress have the primary responsibility for defining crimes and establishing procedures, the federal Constitution imposes limits on what state legislatures and Congress may do.[9] For example, if a state passed a statute authorizing the death penalty for shoplifting, the law would be unconstitutional under the Eighth Amendment. Thus, the states and Congress are free to establish death penalty crimes and procedures unless the laws violate the Eighth Amendment or other federal constitutional provisions. As a result, state and federal death penalty laws are designed to satisfy the commands of the Constitution. This means that the decisions of the United States Supreme Court, interpreting the Eighth Amendment and other constitutional provisions, create obligatory restrictions on the states and the federal government's imposition of the death penalty.

§ 3.05　CONSTITUTIONAL PREMISES

[A]　Federalism

One of the major premises underlying interpretation of the Constitution is federalism. States are free to create their own criminal justice systems within certain constitutional constraints. This means that there may be variation among the states on crimes and procedures. In interpreting the Constitution, the Supreme Court must decide which requirements are mandated by the Constitution (and thus applicable to all states), and under what circumstances the states have the freedom to design their own requirements. For instance, the Court has found that the Constitution requires the consideration of mitigating evidence in a capital trial; states are not free to have a mandatory death penalty.[10] On the other hand, the Court has found that the Constitution does not prohibit victim impact evidence.[11] Thus, states are free to allow victim impact evidence, to not allow it, or to impose any restrictions on it that they choose. It is rare that the Supreme Court decisions interpreting the Constitution are unanimous. The justices' differing views on federalism are a source of the division in the Court in many of the capital cases.

[B]　"Death Is Different"

Another premise in many of the Supreme Court's cases is that "death is different" from other penalties less than death and that, as a result, different procedures are constitutionally required. The Court has stressed in many of its

---

[9] The Supremacy Clause in the U.S. Constitution provides: "This Constitution, and the Laws of the United States which shall be made in Pursuance thereof; and all Treaties made, or which shall be made, under the Authority of the United States, shall be the supreme Law of the Land; and the Judges in every State shall be bound thereby, and any Thing in the Constitution or Laws of any State to the Contrary notwithstanding." U.S. Const. art. VI, cl. 2.

[10] See Section 6.06, infra.

[11] See Section 11.03, infra.

cases that death, in its finality, is qualitatively different.[12] This irrevocable quality of the death penalty, in turn, requires a greater need for reliability when imposing it. Some procedures that are constitutionally required for capital cases are not required in non-capital cases. For example, capital sentencing schemes must allow for the consideration of mitigating evidence. Moreover, if there is a jury, each juror must be able to decide individually what is mitigating.[13] These requirements do not apply in non-capital, criminal cases. The "death is different" premise is not always invoked by the Court, however, nor is it accepted by all of the justices on the Court.[14] For instance, the appellate use of the harmless error doctrine is the same in capital and non-capital cases.[15]

§ 3.06 CASE LAW

As with any area of law governed by statutes or constitutional law, case law is important in interpreting the written law. The United States Supreme Court generates the most important body of case law in the capital punishment area. Other courts, however, also decide cases that govern in their federal circuit or state. Thus, federal case law interpreting the Constitution and federal statutes are sources for understanding the law. Similarly, state case law is a vital source for interpreting the state statutes or state constitutional law.

§ 3.07 TREATIES

Less familiar to most attorneys are treaties and other international agreements that provide guarantees. Treaties are an agreement between or among nations. Most treaties do not create individual rights. Nevertheless, the nation, and sometime its subsidiary states, are bound by the provisions of the treaty.[16] There are potential remedies in both domestic courts within the United States as well as international tribunals. Specific treaties raised in capital cases are discussed *infra* in Section 23.04.

---

[12] *See, e.g.*, Woodson v. North Carolina, 428 U.S. 280, 305 (1976); Ford v. Wainwright, 477 U.S. 399, 410 (1986).

[13] *See* Section 12.03[B][1][c], *infra.*

[14] *See* Atkins v. Virginia, 536 U.S. 304, 337-44 (2002) (Scalia, J., dissenting) (explaining that "death is different" jurisprudence has no support in history nor in current social attitudes).

[15] *See* Sections 14.02-14.04, *infra.*

[16] For a recent dispute involving the legal effects of a decision of the International Court of Justice regarding consular rights of foreign nationals in the United States, *see Medellin v. Texas*, 552 U.S. 491 (2008) (holding that decision of International Court of Justice that United States had violated Vienna Convention by failing to inform Mexican nationals, including petitioner, of their rights under the convention was not enforceable domestic federal law that overrode state limitations on successive habeas petitions and that Memorandum from President also did not require states to provide reconsideration and review of petitioner's claim).

Chapter 4

CHALLENGES TO THE CONSTITUTIONALITY OF THE DEATH PENALTY

§ 4.01   OVERVIEW OF CONSTITUTIONAL CHALLENGES TO THE DEATH PENALTY

Challenges to the constitutionality of the death penalty have fallen into three categories. The first cases challenged the unguided, standardless proceedings as an *arbitrary* imposition of the death penalty. These cases were argued under both the Fourteenth Amendment's due process clause and the Eighth Amendment's cruel and unusual punishment clause. The Court rejected the challenge under the due process clause in 1971, but, one year later, found the death penalty unconstitutional as applied under the cruel and unusual punishment clause.

Four years later, in 1976, after states had revamped their statutes to avoid arbitrariness challenges, the *death penalty per se* was challenged as a cruel and unusual punishment under the Eighth Amendment. The Supreme Court rejected this challenge and laid the groundwork for the structure of modern day death penalty statutes.

Since 1976, many challenges to the death penalty have raised issues of *proportionality*. These cases have contested the constitutionality of applying the death penalty to particular crimes or to particular classes of defendants. Specific challenges are discussed in later chapters (*see, e.g.*, Sections 8.01-8.05 on categorical bars to the death penalty).

This chapter describes the three types of challenges to the death penalty and particularly focuses on the analytical framework used by the Court to evaluate proportionality challenges.

§ 4.02   CHALLENGES TO THE ARBITRARINESS OF THE DEATH PENALTY

Two constitutional provisions have formed the basis of challenges to the arbitrariness of the death penalty: the due process clause and the cruel and unusual punishment clause.

The challenge under the due process clause was rejected by the Supreme Court in *McGautha v. California*.[1] In *McGautha*, the Court considered challenges from proceedings in California and Ohio. In each case, the statutory procedure allowed

---

[1] 402 U.S. 183 (1971).

for an unguided, open-ended decision by the sentencer. The defendants argued that the lack of standards for imposing the death penalty denied them due process of law. A divided Court rejected the challenge. Recognizing the value of jury discretion as an improvement over mandatory sentences, the Court viewed the task of constructing guidelines and yet maintaining discretion to be an impossible one and thus, not required by the Constitution.[2]

The challenge under the cruel and unusual punishment clause arose in *Furman v. Georgia*, considered the seminal case of the modern era of the death penalty.[3] In *Furman*, the Court invalidated the death penalty as applied in two states and effectively invalidated the death penalty nationwide as applied. Finding it unnecessary to decide whether or not the death penalty itself was constitutional, the dominant theme of the *Furman* Court was the arbitrary and capricious nature of decisions regarding who received and who did not receive the death penalty.[4]

[A] The Due Process Challenge

The Fourteenth Amendment provides that no state shall "deprive any person of life, liberty, or property, without due process of law."[5] Although certain substantive rights are embodied in due process, the clause is primarily the source of notice and procedural protections. The defendants in *McGautha* logically turned to the due process clause to argue for a procedure that would guide sentencers in deciding whether to impose death or life imprisonment. The case included a defendant from California (McGautha) and a defendant from Ohio (Crampton).

In each case, a jury had sentenced the defendant to death and, in each case, the jury had complete discretion on the sentence. In McGautha's case, for example, the jury was told:

> . . . Notwithstanding facts, if any, proved in mitigation or aggravation, in determining which punishment shall be inflicted, you are entirely free to act according to your own judgment, conscience, and absolute discretion . . .[6]

The instruction in Crampton's case was less descriptive, but conveyed the same unguided, standardless discretion: "If you find the defendant guilty of murder in the first degree, the punishment is death, unless you recommend mercy." The only major difference between the two cases was that McGautha's was a bifurcated penalty proceeding while Crampton's was a unitary trial in which the jury decided guilt and penalty in one verdict.[7]

---

[2] *Id.* at 207.

[3] 408 U.S. 238 (1972).

[4] *Furman*, 408 U.S. at 294-295.

[5] U.S. Const. amend. XIV, § 1.

[6] *McGautha*, 402 U.S. at 189-190 (emphasizing the complete discretion of the jury under instructions that stated, "beyond prescribing the two alternative penalties, the law itself provides no standard for the guidance of the jury in the selection of the penalty, but, rather, commits the whole matter of determining which of the two penalties shall be fixed to the judgment, conscience, and absolute discretion of the jury").

[7] *Id.* at 217 (rejecting Crampton's challenge that his fifth amendment rights had been violated,

Relying on the historical trend to incorporate more jury discretion in sentencing, the Court found no due process violation. Although acknowledging that the American Law Institute had developed guidelines for imposing the death penalty in the Model Penal Code, the Court noted that lower courts had uniformly rejected challenges based on the lack of standards and the fact that no state had adopted the Model Penal Code procedures. Moreover, the Court viewed the Model Penal Code standards as providing only minor guidance to the sentencer.[8] In the end, the Court concluded that it was virtually impossible to construct standards that had any meaning without limiting the range of circumstances to be considered. As a result, the Court found no constitutional violation in leaving the decision to the "untrammeled discretion" of the sentencer.[9]

Foreshadowing the arguments that would prevail in *Furman* under the Eighth Amendment, the dissenters protested the standardless, arbitrary sentencing procedures. In contrast to the majority, the dissenters suggested that flexible guidelines, not rigid rules, could be designed to limit some of the "unbridled" discretion existing in the Ohio and California death-penalty trials.[10]

[B] The Cruel and Unusual Punishment Challenge

The Eighth Amendment provides:

Excessive bail shall not be required, nor excessive fines imposed, nor *cruel and unusual punishments inflicted.*[11]

In 1972, three African-American defendants challenged their death sentences from Georgia and Texas as cruel and unusual punishments. Two of the three had been sentenced to death for rape; the third for murder. The death penalty was attacked as an unconstitutional punishment in and of itself and as applied to these defendants. In a decision with nine separate opinions, the Court held, in a 5-4 vote, that the death sentences were unconstitutional as applied.[12] The reasoning differed from justice to justice, but common themes existed.

The dominant theme among the five justices voting to strike down the death penalties was the arbitrary and capricious imposition of the death penalty.[13] As

holding "that the policies of the privilege against compelled self-incrimination are not offended when a defendant in a capital case yields to the pressure to testify on the issue of punishment at the risk of damaging his case on guilt").

[8] *Id.* at 207. Many states after *Furman* modeled their statutes after Model Penal Code provisions, in an attempt to provide guidelines. *See* Kyron Huigens, *Rethinking the Penalty Phase*, 32 Ariz. St. L.J. 1195, 1209-1210 & 1282 n.56 (2000). The Model Penal Code, created by the American Law Institute in 1963, provided for a bifurcated proceeding, proof of an aggravating circumstance, and consideration of mitigating circumstances. Model Penal Code § 210.6(2)-(4). In 2009, the American Law Institute retracted its approval for the standards that it had created. *See* Franklin E. Zimring, *Pulling the Plug on Capital Punishment*, Nat'l L. J., Dec. 7, 2009, at 1.

[9] *Id.*

[10] *Furman*, 408 U.S. at 400-402.

[11] U.S. Const. amend. VIII (emphasis added).

[12] *Furman*, 408 U.S. at 239-240.

[13] The five justices forming the majority were Justices Douglas, Brennan, Stewart, White and

Justice Stewart stated in his concurrence:

> These death sentences are cruel and unusual in the same way that being struck by lightning is cruel and unusual. . . . [P]etitioners are among a capriciously selected random handful upon whom the sentence of death has in fact been imposed.[14]

Moreover, part of the arbitrariness was a concern about a discriminatory effect based on poverty or race.[15]

A second theme was the failure of the death penalty to further a goal of punishment. Without an anchor in an acceptable theory of punishment, the death penalty was excessive. As Justice Brennan stated: "If there is a significantly less severe punishment adequate to achieve the purposes for which the punishment is inflicted, . . . the punishment inflicted is unnecessary and therefore excessive."[16] Deterrence especially came under attack. Four of the justices were unconvinced that the death penalty served any deterrent purpose.[17] Although alone in his position, Justice Marshall also argued that retribution was not an acceptable goal of punishment.[18]

There was no agreement that the death penalty was per se unconstitutional. Only Justices Brennan and Marshall expressed that view. In addition to finding the death penalty excessive and arbitrary, they further concluded that the death penalty was unacceptable to contemporary society. Their opinions, along with the individual opinions of Justices Douglas, Stewart, and White rejecting standardless capital sentencing, formed a five-justice majority invalidating the death sentences in the three cases before the Court.

The dominant theme of the dissenters was federalism. They asserted that the Court should defer to the state legislatures on whether and when the death penalty was sometimes an appropriate punishment. Moreover, they found that the death penalty served the penological goals of retribution and deterrence. They further parried the arbitrariness charge by noting that inequalities inevitably exist in the criminal justice system.[19]

Because the death-penalty states responded to *Furman* by enacting new death-penalty statutes, the stage was set for the Court to decide what kinds of systems, if any, might satisfy the Eighth Amendment. In three cases in 1976, the Court upheld the validity of revised death penalty statutes, although, in two other

---

Marshall. Although Justice White focused on penal goals, he also stated that "there is no meaningful basis for distinguishing the few cases in which [death penalty] is imposed from the many cases in which it is not." *Id.* at 313.

[14] *Id.* at 309-310.

[15] *Id.* at 242, 249-252 (Douglas, J., concurring); *id.* at 310 (Stewart, J., concurring).

[16] *Id.* at 279 (Brennan, J., concurring).

[17] *Id.* at 300-302 (Brennan, J., concurring); *id.* at 308 n.7 (Stewart, J., concurring); *id.* at 311-312 (White, J., concurring); *id.* at 347, 354 (Marshall, J., concurring).

[18] *Compare id.* at 343 (Marshall, J., concurring), *with id.* at 308 (Stewart, J., concurring) (saying that retribution is a valid goal).

[19] Justice Burger also indicated that McGautha had settled the issue of the discretion in the system under the due process clause and that discretion was not an Eighth Amendment issue. *Id.* at 401-404.

cases, it struck down statutes that imposed mandatory death penalties.[20]

§ 4.03　CHALLENGE TO THE DEATH PENALTY AS *PER SE* UNCONSTITUTIONAL

[A]　Overview

Just four years after *Furman*, five cases reached the Supreme Court that posed the question of the constitutionality of revised death penalty statutes. Each statutory scheme was an attempt to alleviate the arbitrariness of the statutes declared unconstitutional in *Furman*. Unlike in *Furman*, the Court confronted the issue of the constitutionality of death itself as a sentence. The key case was *Gregg v. Georgia*.[21] In *Gregg*, a majority of the Court agreed that the death penalty did not constitute a per se violation of the Constitution. A plurality of the Court laid out an analysis for assessing the constitutionality of the death penalty.[22]

The *Gregg* Court's analysis can be divided into two conceptually different parts. The first was an assessment of the *acceptability* of the death penalty both at the time of the Eighth Amendment's adoption and to contemporary society.[23] The second part was the Court's independent evaluation, regardless of the acceptability of the punishment to society, whether the punishment comports with an underlying value of *human dignity*.

[B]　Acceptability of the Punishment to Contemporary Society: Evolving Standards of Decency

In the first part of the analysis, the *Gregg* Court noted the common acceptance of the death penalty in 1791, when the Eighth Amendment was adopted. The Court further found that it was necessary to evaluate the death penalty under a concept of "evolving standards of decency."[24] Thus, the acceptability of the death penalty to contemporary society was an important element of the Eighth Amendment analysis. The Court considered the actions of state legislatures to be the most compelling evidence of the views of contemporary society. After *Furman*, 35 state legislatures had reenacted death penalty statutes. The Court found the actions of the legislatures convincing evidence of the acceptability of the death penalty in current times.

---

[20] The Court upheld statutes from Georgia, Florida, and Texas. *See* Gregg v. Georgia, 428 U.S. 153 (1976); Proffitt v. Florida, 428 U.S. 242 (1976); Jurek v. Texas, 428 U.S. 262 (1976). These cases are discussed in detail in Sections 6.03-6.05, *infra*. The Court rejected two statutes from North Carolina and Louisiana that imposed a mandatory death penalty upon conviction for a capital offense. *See* Woodson v. North Carolina, 428 U.S. 280 (1976); Roberts v. Louisiana, 428 U.S. 325 (1976). These cases are discussed in detail in Section 6.06, *infra*.

[21] *Gregg*, 428 U.S. at 153.

[22] *Id.* at 169-175.

[23] *Id.* at 176-179.

[24] *Id.* at 173. This concept came from the case of *Trop v. Dulles*, where the Court held that denationalizing the plaintiff as a punishment for deserting the United States Army during wartime was barred by the Eighth Amendment. 356 U.S. 86 (1958).

[C] Principle of Human Dignity: The Independent Evaluation of Excessive Punishments

In the second part of the analysis, the *Gregg* Court focused on whether the death penalty was consistent with the underlying concept of "human dignity" in the Eighth Amendment. This part of the analysis was not dependent on the views of legislatures or the general public. In fact, the Court emphasized that, regardless of the acceptability of a penalty to contemporary society, the punishment would be unconstitutional if it were inconsistent with "human dignity." Thus, the view of contemporary society was only a threshold question. This second part provided a check on the views of contemporary society. According to the Court, this human dignity concept "at least" included a guarantee against excessive punishments.

The *Gregg* Court proceeded to analyze the excessiveness issue by assessing whether the death penalty furthered an acceptable goal of punishment. If it did not, then the death penalty would be unconstitutionally *excessive*, as it would impose the "wanton and unnecessary infliction of pain."[25] The Court focused on retribution and deterrence as the critical purposes of punishment, mentioning incapacitation only in a footnote.[26] Finding retribution to be an acceptable reason to punish, the Court concluded that the death penalty could serve retribution as an expression of society's "moral outrage" at the crime.[27] Although acknowledging that the evidence of deterrence was inconclusive, the Court deferred to state legislative determinations that the death penalty served a deterrent purpose. The Court concluded that the death penalty was not inherently excessive punishment.

As an additional aspect of excessiveness, the Court raised the issue whether the death penalty was grossly disproportionate when imposed for fairly common forms of murder. The Court in *Gregg* quickly dismissed this concern, stating that the death penalty was not grossly disproportionate to the crime of murder.

§ 4.04 CHALLENGES TO THE PROPORTIONALITY OF THE DEATH PENALTY

[A] Overview

Broad challenges to the death penalty since 1976 have typically contested the proportionality of death as a sentence for a particular crime or to a particular class of defendants.[28] Proportionality is judged under "evolving standards of decency."[29]

---

[25] *Gregg*, 428 U.S. at 173.

[26] *Id.* at 183 n.28

[27] The Court emphasized the importance of retribution in providing the punishment the criminal offender deserves to prevent vigilante justice. *Id.* at 183-84. Justice Marshall responded in his dissenting opinion that this view is not purely retributive but rather utilitarian because of its emphasis on the beneficial results of imposing the death penalty. *Id.* at 238-39.

[28] An exception is the claim raised in *McCleskey v. Kemp*, 481 U.S. 279 (1987), challenging the application of the death penalty as racially discriminatory. *See* Sections 20.01 et seq., *infra*.

[29] Atkins v. Virginia, 536 U.S. 304, 311-312 (2002), *citing* Trop v. Dulles, 356 U.S. 86, 100-101 (1958). The Court stated: " 'The basic concept underlying the Eighth Amendment is nothing less than the

The Court has developed a two-prong test for evaluating proportionality challenges, containing the acceptability and human dignity analyses from *Gregg*. The first prong assesses the acceptability of the death penalty to contemporary society for particular crimes or classes of defendants. The primary sources for determining the contemporary standard of decency are legislation and jury verdicts. The Court looks for a "national consensus." The second prong is the Court's own, or independent, judgment. For this prong, the Court evaluates whether the death penalty for the particular crime or particular class of defendants furthers an acceptable goal of punishment. The Court has focused specifically on the goals of retribution and deterrence.

One of the recent challenges on proportionality grounds was to the execution of the class of defendants who are under age eighteen when they commit a capital offense. In *Roper v. Simmons*,[30] the Court found that the death penalty was unconstitutional under both of the proportionality prongs. The execution of juvenile offenders was contrary to the views of contemporary society, and their execution did not further either retributive or deterrent goals of punishment.

Simmons shows that a majority of the Court adheres to a two-prong approach to proportionality analysis. Each prong, however, has generated its own problems and controversies. Both the meaning of "contemporary society" and the acceptability of the "court's own judgment" analysis have triggered debate. The basis for including proportionality as an Eighth Amendment concept and each of the two prongs are discussed in the following sections.

[B] Proportionality as an Eighth Amendment Principle

Although there is agreement among scholars and jurists that the Eighth Amendment prohibits torture or barbaric punishments, there is some disagreement about whether it prohibits excessive or disproportionate punishments. Justice Scalia would limit or eliminate the proportionality analysis altogether. For example, in *Atkins v. Virginia*,[31] in which the Court struck down the death penalty as applied to mentally retarded offenders, Justice Scalia, joined by Justices Rehnquist and Thomas, stated that the Eighth Amendment is limited to barring modes of punishment that were either unacceptable in 1791 or are unacceptable under contemporary standards, as determined by legislation and jury verdicts.[32] Although conceding the existence of a proportionality concept in the Eighth Amendment for death penalty cases in an earlier non-capital case,[33] in *Atkins*, Justice Scalia appeared to reject proportionality as an aspect of the Eighth Amendment guarantee even in capital cases.[34] A majority of the Supreme Court,

---

dignity of man. . . . The Amendment must draw its meaning from the evolving standards of decency that mark the progress of a maturing society.' "

[30] 543 U.S. 551 (2005). *See* discussion of *Simmons* in Section 8.04[B], *infra*.

[31] 536 U.S. 304 (2002). *See* discussion of *Atkins* in Section 8.04, *infra*.

[32] *Id.* at 339-340.

[33] *See* Harmelin v. Michigan, 501 U.S. 957, 994 (1991) (proportionality is an aspect of death penalty jurisprudence, not Eighth Amendment jurisprudence in general).

[34] *Atkins*, 536 U.S. at 349 (Scalia, J., dissenting) ("The Eighth Amendment is addressed to

however, continues to find that proportionality is part of the Eighth Amendment guarantee.[35]

The Court has derived the proportionality concept from the language of the "cruel and unusual" punishment clause, which is generally traced back to the English Declaration of Rights of 1689. Although there is debate about the intent and meaning of the English law, it appears to have been designed at least to prohibit penalties that were not authorized by law.[36] In addition, some scholars believe that the English law was also designed to prohibit disproportionate punishments.[37] The framers of the Eighth Amendment, however, understood "cruel and unusual" additionally to bar torture or barbaric punishments.[38] As a result, there are three conceptual areas under the rubric of "cruel and unusual:" 1) punishments unauthorized by law, 2) disproportionate punishments, and 3) torture or barbaric punishments. The Supreme Court's cases have blurred the distinction between the latter two categories of disproportionate and barbaric punishments.[39]

Prior to the 1970s, the Eighth Amendment was interpreted in only a handful of Supreme Court cases. The earliest cases focused on the method of execution.[40]

---

always-and-everywhere "cruel" punishments, such as the rack and the thumbscrew. But where the punishment is in itself permissible, "[t]he Eighth Amendment is not a ratchet, whereby a temporary consensus on leniency for a particular crime fixes a permanent constitutional maximum, disabling the States from giving effect to altered beliefs and responding to changed social conditions"). Justice Scalia has indicated, however, that the analysis of the mode of punishment (which he accepts as appropriate) under a societal consensus analysis and the proportionality of a penalty (which he views as inappropriate) would be the same if the methodology for each, as he espouses, relied exclusively on legislation and jury verdicts. See Stanford v. Kentucky, 492 U.S. 361, 379-80 (1989).

[35] See Lockyer v. Andrade, 538 U.S. 63, 72 (U.S. 2003) ("Through this thicket of Eighth Amendment jurisprudence, one governing legal principle emerges as 'clearly established' . . . . : A gross disproportionality principle is applicable to sentences for terms of years"); Ewing v. California, 538 U.S. 11, 23 (2003 U.S.) ("The Eighth Amendment does not require strict proportionality between crime and sentence. Rather, it forbids only extreme sentences that are 'grossly disproportionate' to the crime"); Atkins v. Virginia, 536 U.S. 304, 344 (2002) ("We have repeatedly applied this proportionality precept in later cases interpreting the Eighth Amendment").

[36] Furman, 408 U.S. at 242 (citing Anthony F. Granucci, Nor Cruel and Unusual Punishments Inflicted: The Original Meaning, 57 CAL. L. REV. 839, 845-46 (1969)). See also Laurence Clausen, The Anti-discrimination Eighth Amendment, 28 HARV. J. L. & PUB. POL'Y 119, 136 (2004) (contending that the clause was intended to proscribe certain instances of invidious discrimination, in particular, efforts to single out an offender on a morally insufficient basis for more punishment than was customarily imposed).

[37] Id. at 318 (Marshall, J., concurring) (quoting Granucci, supra note 36, at 860). Some scholars have contended that a central concern of the framers of the Eighth Amendment was disproportional punishments. See Tom Stacy, Cleaning Up the Eighth Amendment Mess, 14 WM. & MARY BILL RTS. J. 475, 510 (2005) (concluding that an originalist inquiry, rather than affirming Justice Scalia's position, indicates "that the ban was meant to outlaw punishments that, while permissible in some circumstances, are disproportionate for the offense and the offender at hand").

[38] See Granucci, supra note 36, at 860.

[39] However, note that in the recent Atkins case, the Court stated: ". . . we have read the text of the amendment to prohibit all excessive punishments, as well as cruel and unusual punishment that may or may not be excessive." 536 U.S. 304, 311 n.7.

[40] In addition to a few early capital cases, one early noncapital case addressed the constitutionality of a fine and three months of hard labor for an illegal liquor offense and upheld the penalty. Pervear v. Commonwealth, 72 U.S. 475 (1867).

Electrocution survived constitutional challenge in *In re Kemmler.*[41] The Court also upheld the death penalty by firing squad, hanging or beheading in an early case from Utah.[42] As early as 1910, however, the Court interpreted the Eighth Amendment as including a proportionality concept. In *Weems v. United States,*[43] the Court viewed a punishment of a minimum of 12 years incarceration; mandatory ankle and wrist chains; hard labor; seclusion from family assistance or association; and the loss of civil rights, as cruel and unusual punishment in "both degree and kind." The Court stated that the punishment "is cruel in its excess of imprisonment and that which accompanies and follows imprisonment" and ". . . unusual in its character."[44] Thus, the Eighth Amendment, at least since *Weems,* has been viewed by a majority of the Court as encompassing both unconstitutionally barbaric punishment and disproportionate punishment. The Court has continuously reaffirmed the proportionality concept as a component of the Eighth Amendment in a series of capital and noncapital cases.[45]

[C] The First Prong: Contemporary Standards of Decency

If a challenge is mounted to the imposition of the death penalty for a particular crime or a particular class of defendants, all of the justices will turn to the views of contemporary society to assess the constitutionality of imposing the penalty. A majority of the Court approaches the views of contemporary society as the first prong of a proportionality test. For two of the current justices, this test is exclusive.[46] Moreover, conceptually these justices are evaluating a mode or act of punishment rather than a proportionality test.[47] Nevertheless, the constitutionality under either analysis requires an evaluation of contemporary society's views under an evolving standards of decency approach.

The inclusion of the views of contemporary society in the evaluation of proportionality is a modification of the analysis laid out in *Gregg.* As previously noted,[48] the *Gregg* plurality analyzed the views of contemporary society before it reached its excessiveness analysis, and proportionality was one aspect of excessiveness. Today, the Court has incorporated the views of contemporary

---

[41] 136 U.S. 436 (1890). William Kemmler was convicted of first degree murder and sentenced to death by electrocution. *See also* State of Lousiana ex rel. Francis v. Resweber, 329 U.S. 459 (1947) (holding that a second effort to execute Francis in the electric chair, after first try failed due to chair malfunction, did not rise to the level of cruel and unusual punishment).

[42] *See* Wilkerson v. Utah, 99 U.S. 130 (1879) (defendant had his option of methods of execution under the statute).

[43] 217 U.S. 349 (1910).

[44] *Id.* at 377; *see id.* at 368 (explaining that the Philippine constitutional provision prohibiting cruel and unusual punishment "was taken from [the 8th Amendment of] the Constitution of the United States, and must have the same meaning").

[45] *See, e.g., Andrade,* 538 U.S. at 72; *Ewing,* 538 U.S. at 22; *Atkins,* 536 U.S. at 344.

[46] Justices Scalia and Thomas take this view.

[47] *See, e.g., Atkins,* 536 U.S. at 349 (Scalia, J., dissenting) (assumption that Eighth Amendment prohibits excessive punishments is wrong; Amendment prohibits modes of punishment that were cruel and unusual in 1791 or in light of evolving standards of decency).

[48] *See* discussion in Sections 4.03[B] and [C], *supra.*

society into its excessiveness analysis. Moreover, the Court has, for all practical purposes, equated excessiveness with proportionality.

For example, in *Atkins*, where the Court found that the execution of persons who are mentally retarded was unconstitutional, the Court referred to the imposition of the death penalty as an excessive or a disproportionate penalty. The Court treated the first prong of the proportionality assessment as one involving "objective" factors. The Court noted that sixteen states had passed legislation prohibiting the execution of the mentally retarded since the Court had last examined the issue. The Court found that this legislative trend, and the fact that very few mentally retarded defendants had been put to death in states that allowed it, reflected a "national consensus" against the execution of the mentally retarded.[49]

[1] Whose Views Count?

The primary analysis in *Atkins* and *Simmons* focused on legislation and the practices of sentencing juries. However, in *Atkins*, there is also a reference in a footnote to the views of professional organizations, international bodies, and public opinion polls. Likewise in *Simmons*, the majority pointed in the text of the opinion to international bodies and to the practices of other countries. In dissent, Chief Justice Rehnquist and Justices Scalia and Alito in both cases strongly disagreed with turning to those sources.

This division over the sources of views for contemporary society or evolving standards is, at least in part, a conceptual difference over the appropriate meaning of the Eighth Amendment. Is the Eighth Amendment's evolving standard of decency based on what is occurring throughout the world or only within the United States? Do the views of the international community have persuasive value? The role of positions taken by pertinent professional organizations and public opinion polls is also debated. Should the Court consider the position of a group such as the American Psychological Association? Should the Court consider the results of a Gallup poll?

The six-justice majority in *Atkins* commented that international views, organizational positions, and polling results were not "dispositive," but provided "[support] to our conclusion that there is a consensus among those who have addressed the issue," and the five-justice majority in *Simmons* offered a similar assertion.[50] The status of other sources thus appears to have some persuasive value to a majority of the Court. The *Atkins* and *Simmons* majorities, however, relied primarily on domestic legislation and jury verdicts. Three dissenting justices[51] in *Atkins* and *Simmons* rejected utilizing any information other than domestic legislation and jury verdicts to reach conclusions about a national consensus or contemporary

---

[49] For a complete discussion of *Atkins*, *see* Section 8.03, *infra*.

[50] *Atkins*, 536 U.S. at 316 n.21; *Simmons*, 543 U.S. at 575-76.

[51] *Atkins*, 536 U.S. at 322 (Rehnquist, J., dissenting) (Justice Rehnquist was joined by Justices Scalia and Thomas); *Simmons*, 543 U.S. at 607 (Scalia, J., dissenting) (Justice Scalia was joined by Chief Justice Rehnquist and Justice Thomas).

views.[52] Thus, the justices have been placing significantly greater emphasis on legislation and jury verdicts than any other sources.

Should the Court rely on sources other than legislation and jury verdicts in future cases? The argument against considering additional sources is twofold: 1) legislation and jury verdicts are the most reliable indicators of the views of contemporary American society and 2) only the views of the American public are relevant to interpreting provisions of the U.S. Constitution. The counter-argument responds that 1) the other sources round out the picture of the views of contemporary society and 2) the concept of "evolving standards of decency" transcends our national boundaries.[53] *Atkins* and *Simmons* indicate that the Supreme Court will use the additional sources of the views of the international community, professional organizations, and public opinion polls as supporting evidence, but not as primary sources of national consensus. Moreover, in the recent case of *Kennedy v. Louisiana*,[54] in which the Court rejected the death penalty for child rape, the Court did not rely on these additional sources to identify the evolving consensus.

[2] Statistical Interpretation

The use of statistics in identifying a national consensus is another area of controversy on the Court. However, this disagreement is one of interpretation only and not a conceptual difference. When looking at the responses of legislatures, sometimes the Court simply does "headcounting." For instance, in *Coker v. Georgia*,[55] the plurality found that only Georgia authorized the death penalty for the rape of an adult woman. Similarly, in *Thompson v. Oklahoma*,[56] the plurality totaled up the number of states that had specified a minimum age for execution and found that all had set the age at 16 or older. In other situations, the numbers may

---

[52] *See also Stanford*, 492 U.S. at 377 (declining to consider "public opinion polls, the views of interest groups, and the positions adopted by various professional associations"); Thompson v. Oklahoma, 487 U.S. 815, 865, 869 n.4 (1988) (Scalia, J., dissenting) (criticizing the plurality's reliance on Amnesty International's account of international standards of decency). *See generally* Scott W. Howe, Roper v. Simmons: *Abolishing the Death Penalty for Juvenile Offenders in the Wake of International Consensus*, in DEATH PENALTY STORIES 41, 440-44 (John H. Blume & Jordan M. Steiker eds., 2009) (discussing the Court's focus on legislation, jury verdicts, and the Court's independent judgment).

[53] *See Thompson*, 487 U.S. at 831 (recognizing relevance of views of international community); Enmund, 458 U.S. at 796-97 n. 22; Coker, 433 U.S. at 596 n. 10; Trop, 356 U.S. at 102 and n.35; Victor L. Streib, *Executing Juvenile Offenders: The Ultimate Denial of Juvenile Justice*, 14 STAN. L. & POL'Y REV. 121, 138-140 (2003) (discussing the consideration of international and comparative law in analyzing evolving standards of decency).

[54] 554 U.S. 407 (2008). *See* Howe, *supra* note 52, at 442-46. In *Atkins*, the Court relegated the additional sources to a footnote. Although the Court referred to views of professional organizations, the international community, and polls as "[a]dditional evidence," the Court also stated that this information was "by no means dispositive . . . " 536 U.S. at 316 n.21. *But see Simmons*, 543 U.S. at 575-76 (pointing in text of opinion to the actions of international bodies and the practices of other countries). *See also* Lawrence v. Texas, 539 U.S. 558 (2003) (noting in the text of the opinion the position of the European Court of Human Rights as direct support for the unconstitutionality of a statute criminalizing consensual homosexual sodomy).

[55] 433 U.S. 584, 586 (1977). For a discussion of *Coker, see* Section 8.05[B], *infra*.

[56] 487 U.S. 815 (1988).

be interpreted based on showing a "trend." For example, in both *Atkins* and *Simmons*, the Court referred to the "consistency of the direction of the change," in addition to the absolute number of states which had banned the execution of the mentally retarded or of those who were under eighteen at the time of their offenses.[57]

Even headcounting can become complicated, however. Should the states with no death penalty be included? For example, to determine the acceptability of executing juveniles, opposite conclusions can be justified based on the inclusion or exclusion of the non-death penalty states. In *Simmons*,[58] the majority counted states that have abolished the death penalty in its determination of the number of states that opposed the death penalty for defendants under age 18 at the time of their crimes. Using this method, the majority found that 30 states opposed the death penalty for juvenile offenders. In contrast, the dissenters contended that states without the death penalty should not be counted.[59] With this methodology, the dissenters concluded that a majority of death-penalty states did not oppose the execution of juvenile offenders.

[D] The Second Prong: Furthering Goals of Punishment

The second prong is the Court's "own judgment" or "independent judgment." For this prong, the Court assesses whether the application of the death penalty will further retributive and deterrent goals of punishment. This determination includes an assessment of the culpability of the relevant class of offenders.[60] Unlike the analysis from *Gregg*, where the Court separated the goals of punishment from proportionality, the Court today treats the analysis of the goals of punishment as part of its consolidated excessiveness or proportionality test. For example, in *Atkins*, the Court found the death penalty disproportionate because neither retribution nor deterrence would be furthered by executing the mentally retarded.

A majority of the Court applies the "independent judgment" prong in each proportionality case. There is a minority view, however, that this second prong is

---

[57] *Atkins*, 536 U.S. at 315-16 ("Given that anticrime legislation is far more popular than legislation protecting violent criminals, the large number of States prohibiting the execution of mentally retarded persons (and the complete absence of legislation reinstating such executions) provides powerful evidence that today society views mentally retarded offenders as categorically less culpable than the average criminal"); *Simmons*, 543 U.S. at 566 ("[W]e think the same consistency of direction of change has been demonstrated. . . . ").

[58] 543 U.S. at 564. For a discussion of *Simmons, see* Section 8.04[B], *infra*.

[59] *Id.* at 610-11. In the recent decision in *Kennedy v. Louisiana*, 128 S.Ct. 2641 (2008), the Justices also disagreed over how to count states regarding the use of the death penalty to punish child rape. The problem concerned whether some states could have thought that the *Coker* decision outlawed the death penalty for that offense and, if so, whether to count them in tallying the number of states that had manifested opposition to the use of the death penalty for child rape. *See id.* at 2667-68 (Alito, J., dissenting).

[60] In both *Thompson* and *Atkins*, the Court further subdivided the "independent judgment" prong into 1) the culpability of the class of offenders and 2) the purposes of punishment. Thus, in *Thompson* the plurality looked at whether juveniles below the age of 16 as a class could be as culpable as adults. 487 U.S. at 834-35. For a discussion of *Thompson, see* Section 8.03[B], *infra*. In *Atkins*, the Court looked at the culpability of the class of mentally retarded defendants. 536 U.S. at 318-21.

illegitimate because it represents a "subjective" judgment by the Court. In several opinions, Justice Scalia has criticized the majority for using its subjective judgment, rather than looking at what he considered to be "objective" factors. By objective factors, Justice Scalia meant evidence of legislative action and jury verdicts.[61] As soon as the analysis shifts into evaluating whether the goals of punishment are furthered, Justice Scalia views the analysis as "subjective." The majority of the Court, however, insists on the validity of both the "objective" evidence of legislation and jury verdicts as well as the Court's own analysis of whether the punishment furthers an appropriate goal of retribution or deterrence.

Commentators have contended that reliance only on legislation and jury verdicts would defeat the purpose of the Eighth Amendment as a restriction on the will of the majority. For example, Professor Susan Raeker-Jordan has commented: "The Eighth Amendment prohibits cruel and unusual punishments; it does not permit whatever punishments the majority, through legislatures and juries, deems to be appropriate, just as the Fourteenth Amendment does not sanction whatever public opinion deems to be due process or equal protection."[62] The argument is that the structure of the provisions of the Bill of Rights and the due process clause of the Fourteenth Amendment as restrictions on federal and state action requires an analysis based on the Court's interpretation of the Eighth Amendment above and beyond evidence of legislative enactments and jury verdicts.

---

[61] For criticism of the focus on legislation and jury verdicts, see Susan Raeker-Jordan, *A Pro-Death, Self-Fulfilling Constitutional Construct: The Supreme Court's Evolving Standard of Decency For The Death Penalty*, 23 HASTINGS CONST. L.Q. 455, 457 (1996), which describes the "objective" evidence as rife with non-objective, death-slanted factors. For instance, Professor Raeker-Jordan notes that looking to only death penalty states skews the statistics of what the "majority" believes. Likewise, she contends that procedural mechanisms, such as emphasis on aggravating factors and death-qualification of juries, slant verdicts in favor of death and thus, make them an unreliable indicator of a majority view.

[62] *Id.*, at 553 (1996). In *Furman*, 408 U.S. at 268, Justice Brennan stated in his concurring opinion that "If the judicial conclusion that a punishment is 'cruel and unusual' depended upon virtually unanimous condemnation of the penalty at issue, then, like no other constitutional provision, (the Clause's) only function would be to legitimize advances already made by the other departments and opinions already the conventional wisdom. We know that the Framers did not envision so narrow a role for this basic guaranty of human rights."

Chapter 5

METHODS OF EXECUTION

§ 5.01 OVERVIEW

Historically, many methods of execution were used that are brutal or barbaric by today's standards. Methods such as drawing and quartering, boiling in oil, burning at the stake, or disemboweling,[1] although common and accepted in their own times, are considered barbarous tortures today. In the modern era of capital punishment in the United States, each new method of execution was developed to make the execution more "humane."

There are five methods of execution that have been used in the United States since 1976: lethal injection;[2] electrocution;[3] lethal gas (gas chamber);[4] hanging;[5] and firing squad.[6] Lethal injection is the primary method of execution for every state

---

[1] *See* Deborah W. Denno, *Is Electrocution an Unconstitutional Method of Execution? The Engineering of Death Over the Century*, 35 Wm. & Mary L. Rev. 551, 563, 567 n.87 (1994); Furman v. Georgia, 408 U.S. 238, 297–98 (1972).

[2] Lethal injection is administered with intravenous chemicals. Most executions by lethal injection involve three chemicals: the first causes loss of consciousness; the second arrests the inmate's breathing; the third causes cardiac arrest. *See* Deborah W. Denno, *When Legislatures Delegate Death: The Troubling Paradox Behind State Uses of Electrocution and Lethal Injection and What it Says About Us*, 63 Ohio St. L.J. 63, 95-100 (2002); *Descriptions of Execution Methods*, Death Penalty Information Center, http://www.deathpenaltyinfo.org/descriptions-execution-methods [hereinafter *Descriptions of Methods*] (citing W. Ecenbarger, *Perfect Death: When The State Kills It Must Do So Humanely. Is That Possible?*, Phila. Inquirer Mag., Jan. 23, 1994; J. Weisberg, *This Is Your Death*, New Republic, July 1, 1991) (last visited Feb. 6, 2012).

[3] Electrocution involves strapping the inmate into a chair. Metal electrodes are placed on the scalp, forehead, and leg. The inmate is usually blindfolded in some fashion. A power supply of 500–2000 volts is then administered. *Execution Methods, supra* note 2 (citing J. Weisberg, *This Is Your Death*, New Republic, July 1, 1991; H. Hillman, *The Possible Pain Experienced During Executions by Different Methods*, 22 Perception 745, 1992). *See also* Justice Brennan's description of an execution by electric chair in *Glass v. Louisiana*. 471 U.S. 1080, 1087–88 (1985) (Brennan, J., dissenting) (noting "extensive research that '[in] every case of electrocution, . . . death inevitably supervenes but it may be very long, and above all, excruciatingly painful' ").

[4] For execution by lethal gas, an inmate is strapped into a chair in a sealed room. Sodium cyanide is released beneath the chair and death follows from inhaling the gas. *See* Fierro v. Gomez, 77 F.3d 301, 307–09 (9th Cir. 1996).

[5] Execution by hanging is done with a rope around the inmate's neck. Death is caused by the fracture of the neck. In Washington, where execution by hanging is used, there are procedures to weigh the inmate and then to calibrate the drop to ensure as quick a death as possible. *Descriptions of Methods, supra* note 2; *see also* Campbell v. Wood, 511 U.S. 1119, 1127 (1994) (Blackmun, J., dissenting) (describing the details of Field Instruction WSP 410.500, Washington's protocol on execution by hanging, and the observations of a "veteran prison warden").

[6] Execution by firing squad involves multiple shooters aiming at the inmate's heart, usually marked

with the death penalty, as well as the federal government and the military.[7] Other forms of execution are authorized in some states but only after specific criteria are met — if lethal injection is found to be unconstitutional, upon specific request of the inmate, or when the inmate was sentenced prior before lethal injection became an option. Of the sixteen states allowing some secondary method nine authorize electrocution;[8] four allow lethal gas;[9] two allow hanging;[10] and, in two states, a prisoner may be executed by firing squad.[11] Similarly, the four states that have lethal gas only use it as a secondary option to lethal injection. The firing squad is only a possibility in two states.[12]After the 1976 reinstatement of constitutional death penalty statutes, the vast majority of executions were carried out with lethal injection. From 1976 to 2012, there have been 1097 executions by lethal injection. Electrocution has been the second most popular method, with 157 executions. Lethal gas, hanging, and firing squad are much less common. Eleven executions by lethal gas have taken place, three executions by hanging, and three executions by firing squad.[13]

§ 5.02 LEGAL CHALLENGES TO METHODS OF EXECUTION: ANALYTICAL FRAMEWORK

Despite extensive jurisprudence concerning almost every aspect of the death penalty, the Supreme Court has rarely reviewed the constitutionality of a particular method of execution. As one scholar observed, there appears to be a "complete constitutional disregard for how inmates are executed."[14] For decades, the absence of Supreme Court analysis left lower courts without a clear standard or analytical framework to apply when reviewing method of execution challenges.

---

with a white cloth. A typical procedure is to give one shooter a blank round without telling any shooter which round is blank. *Description of Methods*, *supra* note 2.

[7] *See Methods of Execution*, DEATH PENALTY INFORMATION CENTER, http://www.deathpenaltyinfo.org/methods-execution (updating statistics from U.S. Department of Justice, Bureau of Justice Statistics, 2006 Capital Punishment Bulletin) (last visited Feb. 6, 2012).

[8] Alabama (on inmate request), Arkansas (on request if underlying offense was committed before July 4, 1983) Florida (on inmate request), Kentucky (on request if underlying offense committed before March 31, 1998), Oklahoma (if lethal injection held unconstitutional), South Carolina (on inmate request), Tennessee (on written waiver to those whose underlying offense was committed before December 31, 1998), Virginia (on inmate request). *Id.*

[9] Arizona (prisoners sentenced before November 15, 1992 may select lethal gas), California (on inmate request), Missouri, and Wyoming (if lethal injection is unconstitutional). *Id.*

[10] New Hampshire (if lethal injection not available), Washington (on inmate request). *Id.*

[11] Utah (on request if underlying offense sentenced before March 15, 2004), Oklahoma (if both lethal injection and electrocution are found unconstitutional). *Id.*

[12] Utah eliminated the firing squad as an option in 2004 but still allows prisoners to choose this option if they were sentenced before 3/15/2004. Oklahoma offers the firing squad only if both lethal injection and electrocution are found unconstitutional *Id.*

[13] *Id.*

[14] Denno, *supra* note 2, at 70.

In its earliest cases, the Supreme Court declared that punishment involving torture or unnecessary pain is cruel and unusual.[15] In 1890, William Kemmler challenged his impending execution by the electric chair as unconstitutional. The Court avoided an analysis under the Eighth Amendment by reasoning that, since the Eighth Amendment had not yet been incorporated to the states, challenges to a state execution would be evaluated under other sections of the Constitution.[16] The Supreme Court upheld electrocution as constitutional under the Privileges and Immunities clause of the Constitution. In sweeping language, the *Kemmler* Court observed that Eighth Amendment prohibition of "cruel and unusual" punishments refers to "something inhuman and barbarous — something more than the mere extinguishment of life."[17]

Almost 100 years later, there was still no direct Supreme Court response to a method-of-execution challenge. Justice Brennan, however, dissenting to the denial of certiorari in *Glass v. Louisiana*,[18] identified several factors to evaluate a method of execution's constitutionality. He suggests that a method of execution would be cruel and unusual if it is either (1) inconsistent with evolving standards of decency or (2) involves the unnecessary infliction of pain, physical violence, or mutilation of the person or body.[19]

In deciding more recent method of execution challenges, lower courts applied an "evolving standards of decency" test incorporating an "objective" prong, which looks at legislative actions and jury verdicts, and a "court's own judgment" prong, which assesses whether the punishment contributes to a legitimate penological goal.[20] The courts have held that if a punishment does not further a penological goal (normally retribution or deterrence), then the punishment is "nothing more than the purposeless and needless imposition of pain and suffering" and, therefore, unconstitutional.[21]

---

[15] *See* Ellen Kreitzberg & David Richter, *But Can it Be Fixed? A Look At Constitutional Challenges to Lethal Injection Executions*, 47 Santa Clara L. Rev. 445, 472–79 (2007); *see also* Wilkerson v. Utah, 99 U.S. 130, 136 (1879) ("it is safe to affirm that punishments of torture [such as drawing and quartering] and all others in the same line of unnecessary cruelty, are forbidden . . . ."), *and* Denno, *When Legislatures Delegate Death*, *supra* note 2, at 71 (explaining that the Framers created a prohibition of cruel and unusual punishment in the Bill of Rights "expressly to proscribe the kinds of 'torturous' and 'barbarous['] penalties associated with certain methods of execution").

[16] *In re* Kemmler, 136 U.S. 436 (1890) (examining the electric chair under the privileges and immunities clause) Louisiana *ex rel.* Francis v. Resweber, 329 U.S. 459 (1947) (addressing double jeopardy permits the state a second opportunity to electrocute an inmate after the first attempt failed).

[17] *See Kemmler*, 136 U.S. at 447 (1890).

[18] Glass v. Louisiana, 471 U.S. 1080 (1985).

[19] *Glass*, 471 U.S. at 1083–84 (Brennan, J., dissenting).

[20] Evolving standards of decency language is used to evaluate whether the death penalty is constitutional as applied to a particular class of defendants, as in *Roper v. Simmons*, 543 U.S. 551 (2005) (excluding juveniles) and *Atkins v. Virginia*, 536 U.S. 304 (2002) (excluding mentally retarded defendants); and whether particular crimes may be punished by death, as in *Coker v. Georgia*, 433 U.S. 584 (1977) (excluding rape of an adult woman) and *Kenndy v. Louisiana*, 554 U.S. 407 (2008) (excluding rape of a child). *See* Section 8.09[B], *infra*.

[21] *Atkins*, 536 U.S. at 319 (quoting Enmund v. Florida, 458 U.S. 782, 798 (1982)). *See also* Gregg v. Georgia, 428 U.S. 153, 183 (1976) remarking "the sanction imposed cannot be so totally without penological justification that it results in the gratuitous infliction of suffering."

It is this second prong, whether a punishment serves a penological goal, that has been the focus of several method of execution challenges. In determining whether a penological goal is furthered, lower courts look at the degree of pain inflicted in the punishment and whether or not there was "unnecessary risk of pain" in carrying out the execution.[22]

§ 5.03 CHALLENGES TO METHOD OF EXECUTION BEFORE LETHAL INJECTION

[A] Overview

The first time the Supreme Court reviewed a challenge to a method of execution was in 1878. In *Wilkerson v. Utah*, the Supreme Court examined the use of a firing squad as a method of execution and found that it did not violate the Eighth Amendment prohibition on cruel and unusual punishment.[23] The Court noted "it is safe to affirm that punishments of torture . . . , and all others in the same line of unnecessary cruelty, are forbidden by [the Eighth] Amendment to the Constitution."[24] In the 1890s, the Court was comparing a state's use of hanging as a method of capital punishment to cases, especially from England, where the offender was tortured, dissected or burned alive as punishment. The Court observed that these earlier punishments all shared the "deliberate infliction of pain for the sake of pain."[25] In 1890, New York's practice of performing execution by electric chair withstood constitutional challenge under the Privileges and Immunities Clause because the Eighth Amendment had not been applied to the States.[26]

More than a century passed before, in 2008, the Court reviewed Kentucky's lethal injection protocol and found the method did not violate the Eighth Amendment's ban on cruel and unusual punishment.[27] During the interim, states used various methods of execution: hanging; firing squad; lethal gas; electrocution; and, finally, lethal injection.[28] Inmates filed challenges to each form of execution, arguing, for the most part, that it constituted cruel and unusual punishment under the Eighth Amendment. The length of time to die and the pain associated with the

---

[22] Kreitzberg & Richter, *supra* note 15, at 476 (comparing Campbell v. Wood, 18 F.3d 662 (9th Cir. 1994) (hanging was constitutional because it recognized and took steps to prevent the foreseeable risk of pain), and Fierro v. Gomez, 77 F.3d 301 (9th Cir. 1996) (use of lethal gas unconstitutional because it inherently involved a substantial risk of pain), *vacated*, 519 U.S. 918 (1996)).

[23] Wilkerson v. Utah, 99 U.S. 130 (1878).

[24] *Id.* at 136.

[25] Baze v. Rees, 553 U.S. 35, 48 (2008).

[26] *In re* Kemmler, 136 U.S. 436 (1890).

[27] *Baze*, 553 U.S. 35, 61–62 (observing that "what [the Eighth] Amendment prohibits is wanton exposure to 'objectively intolerable risk,' not simply the possibility of pain") (quoting Farmer v. Brennan, 511 U.S. 825, 846 & n.9 (1994)).

[28] Challenges to the firing squad, lethal gas, hanging, and electrocution are less likely to arise as most states abandoned these methods in favor of lethal injection. Some states still cling to providing a choice of methods. To the extent that a defendant opts for one of the older methods, the defendant maintains standing to challenge that method of execution.

execution dominated the early analysis by lower courts. Often, cases failed to reach the Supreme Court because a new form of capital punishment replaced the older, more controversial form while challenges wound their way through the courts.[29]

[B]   Firing Squad

The firing squad remains an execution option only in Utah and Oklahoma.[30] There are no detailed procedures or protocols in place for the use of a firing squad[31] and its effectiveness depends upon the accuracy of the shooting team of officers. As with lethal injection procedures, a doctor must certify the individual as deceased before the execution is completed.[32]

The constitutionality of the firing squad has been challenged with little discussion from the courts. The most recent challenge in federal court was in *Andrews v. Schulsen* in 1984.[33] The Court upheld the firing squad as constitutional. While offering no real discussion, the Court, cited its decision *Wilkerson v. Utah*[34] 100 years earlier. *Wilkerson* upheld the use of a firing squad since it comported with prevailing norms of the times; firing squads were used in military desertion and disobedience cases.

In 2010, Utah executed Ronnie Lee Gardner after twenty-five years on death row.[35] It was the third firing squad execution in the United States since the reinstatement of the death penalty in 1976. Gardner elected to be executed by firing squad over lethal injection.[36] There are four more death row inmates who are eligible to be executed by firing squad.

---

[29] *See* Michael Janofsky, *Utah Officials Preparing for Another Firing Squad, to be Used as Soon as Next Month*, N.Y. TIMES, May 29, 2003, at A16 (indicating that Troy Michael Kell's challenge to Utah's death penalty statute authorizing death by firing squad may delay his execution for years).

[30] Utah permits the use of a firing squads either where a court holds that a firing squad would be permissible, where a prisoner elected to have the firing squad prior to 2004, or if the state's primary method of lethal injection is held to be unconstitutional. U.C.A. 1953 § 77-18-5.5 (2004). Oklahoma permits the use of a firing squad only if lethal injection and electrocution are found unconstitutional. 22 OKL. ST. ANN. § 1014 (2011).

[31] Utah law requires only that the state "select a five-person firing squad of peace officers," and that "the department . . . adopt and enforce rules governing procedures for the execution of death." U.C.A. 1953 § 77-19-10 (2004).

[32] The use of doctors in execution procedures has raised ethical issues for doctors under the Hippocratic Oath. *See* Dr. Atul Gawande, *When Law and Ethics Collide — Why Physicians Participate in Executions*, 1221 N. ENGL. J. MEDICINE 2006). With firing squads the additional ethical issue of harvesting their organs has been debated, *see* Daniel Fu-Chang Tsai, Meng-Kung Tsai, Wen-Je Ko, *Organs By Firing Squad: The Medical and Moral Implausibility of Death Penalty Organ Procurement*, AMERICAN JOURNAL OF BIOETHICS, Vol. 11, Iss. 10 (2011).

[33] Andrews v. Schulsen, 600 F. Supp. 408 (1984).

[34] Andrews also raised a challenge under the First Amendment, claiming that Utah's method of execution had been raised under the Mormon doctrine of blood atonement. The court found this argument unconvincing and failing under the prevailing First Amendment standards. *Id* at 431.

[35] Kirk Johnson, *Double Murderer Executed by Firing Squad In Utah*, THE NEW YORK TIMES (June 18, 2010), *available at* http://www.nytimes.com/2010/06/19/us/19death.html.

[36] James Nelson, *Utah Allows Firing Squad Request to Avoid Execution Delay*, REUTERS (Feb. 10, 2012), *available at* http://www.chicagotribune.com/news/sns-rt-us-firing-squad-utahtre81a02a-20120210,0,3598692.story.

The small number of states that permit the use of firing squads opens a possible challenge that it no longer satisfies the Eighth Amendment's evolving standard of decency test. With few inmates eligible for its use, the firing squad will soon likely become a relic of the past.

[C] Hanging

Although at one point forty-eight states imposed death by hanging, state legislatures abandoned this practice over the years. When the Supreme Court struck down the death penalty in 1972 in *Furman*, only eight states still used hanging as a means of execution. In 1994, with only Washington and Montana performing hangings as a possible means of execution, Rodman Campbell challenged the method's constitutionality in the state of Washington.[37] The Ninth Circuit, sitting *en banc*, rejected Campbell's claim and held, in a 6-5 opinion, that Washington's hanging procedure was constitutional.[38]

Campbell argued, in part, that hanging was unconstitutional given the number of states that rejected the practice over the years.[39] The Court of Appeals disagreed and did not consider the evidence of the legislative trends in deciding this issue.[40] The court held that such evidence is relevant only on the question of the proportionality of a death sentence and not to a challenge of a method of execution.[41] The Ninth Circuit reasoned "[w]here the method of execution is contested, the Eighth Amendment prohibits only the unnecessary and wanton infliction of pain."[42] Using the "unnecessary pain" touchstone, the Ninth Circuit found execution by hanging, when conducted according to Washington's detailed protocol, was constitutionally permissible.[43]

---

[37] Washington's death penalty statute, WASH. REV. CODE § 10.95.180(1), provides "[t]he punishment of death . . . shall be inflicted either by hanging by the neck or at the election of the defendant, by [lethal injection]." For defendants who are unwilling to select their mode of execution, Washington imposes death by hanging. Campbell v. Wood, 18 F.3d 662 (9th Cir. 1994), *cert. denied*, 511 U.S. 1119 (1994).

[38] Campbell, 18 F.3d 662.

[39] *Id.* at 682.

[40] *Id.* (distinguishing between proportionality review which considers "contemporary standards of decency," and "methodology review" which "focuses more heavily on objective evidence of the pain involved in the challenged method").

[41] *See* Chapter 8, *infra*, for a discussion of proportionality challenges.

[42] *Campbell*, 18 F.3d at 682–93. The court in *Campbell* held that it was not necessary to analyze legislative trends because unconsciousness and death by hanging, performed in accordance with Washington's protocol, was quick and thus did not inflict an unconstitutional amount of pain.

[43] *Id.* at 687. The court affirmed the district court's factual findings as the basis for its conclusion, summarizing them as follows: "[T]he mechanisms involved in bringing about unconsciousness and death in judicial hanging occur extremely rapidly, . . . unconsciousness was likely to be immediate or within a matter of seconds, and . . . death would follow rapidly thereafter. The . . . risk of death by decapitation was negligible, and . . . hanging according to the protocol does not involve lingering death, mutilation, or the unnecessary and wanton infliction of pain." *Id.* The court relied on the fact that Washington's detailed protocol provided specifications to avoid possible difficulties including the appropriate placement of the noose knot and the width and length of the rope to avoid decapitation, and a requirement that the rope be boiled, stretched, and waxed, to reduce asphyxiation. *Id.* at 683. The protocol also included a chart for determining, based on the weight of the defendant, the appropriate distance the body should be dropped. *Id.*

[D] Lethal Gas

Challenges to lethal gas also reached the federal courts during the 1990s with varied results. In *Fierro v. Gomez*,[44] the Ninth Circuit found lethal gas unconstitutional while in *Hunt v. Nuth*,[45] the Fourth Circuit upheld the practice. Both courts focused on the level of pain and the possibility of consciousness during the procedure.

The challenge to lethal gas in California came to the Ninth Circuit shortly after it upheld hanging as a constitutional method of execution. In striking down lethal gas as unconstitutional, the Ninth Circuit again focused on both the risk of pain and the amount of pain inmates would suffer. The court concluded that execution by lethal gas violated the Eighth Amendment because the evidence showed an inmate would be subjected to severe pain and that there was a significant risk that such pain would last for several minutes.[46]

[E] Electrocution

In 1890, the Supreme Court was asked to examine whether electrocution violated the Eighth Amendment's prohibition against cruel and unusual punishment.[47] While Kemmler was waiting to be the first person put to death in the United States by electrocution, the Supreme Court avoided reviewing this method of execution by holding that the Eighth Amendment did not apply to the states through the Fourteenth Amendment and therefore was not a legitimate basis to challenge the punishment.[48]

---

[44] 77 F.3d 301 (9th Cir. 1996), *vacated and remanded by*, 519 U.S. 918 (1996) (remanding "to the . . . Ninth Circuit for further consideration in light of Cal. Penal Code Section 3604"). In 1996, between the Ninth Circuit's 1996 decision and the Supreme Court's subsequent remand, the California legislature passed AB 2082. That bill amended a single word in California's Penal Code to provide that, in cases where an inmate does not chose among lethal gas or lethal injection within 10 days of receiving the execution warrant, "the penalty of death shall be imposed by lethal *injection*" instead of legal gas as was previously provided. 1996 Cal. Stat. 84 (emphasis added). On remand, the Ninth Circuit found that Petitioners did not have standing or present a ripe claim "[b]ecause neither plaintiff has chosen lethal gas as his method of execution within the [10 day window] of California's amended death penalty statute." Fierro v. Terhune, 147 F.3d 1158, 1160 (9th Cir. 1998). While neither petitioner in *Fierro* was subject to execution by lethal gas, the method remains possible under California law. Cal. Penal Code § 3604 (Deering 2008).

[45] 57 F.3d 1327 (4th Cir. 1995), *cert. denied*, 521 U.S. 1131 (1997). The court also rejected a challenge to the statutory choice of methods of execution. The defendant argued that having a choice between lethal gas and lethal injection was cruel and unusual. The court found that a challenge to the constitutionality of lethal injection was moot where the defendant had chosen lethal gas, but implied in a footnote that lethal injection was likely to be constitutional. *Id.* at 1338 n.16. The Fifth Circuit, in *Gray v. Lucas*, without holding a single hearing on the issue, also declined to determine the constitutionality of execution by lethal gas. 710 F.2d 1048 (5th Cir. 1983), *cert. denied*, 463 U.S. 1237 (1983).

[46] *Fierro*, 77 F.3d at 309 (upholding "[t]he district court's findings of extreme pain, the length of time this extreme pain lasts, and the substantial risk that inmates will suffer this extreme pain for several minutes" to conclude "that execution by lethal gas is cruel and unusual").

[47] *In re* Kemmler, 136 U.S. 436, 447–48 (1890). For a complete discussion of challenges to electrocution see Deborah W. Denno, *Is Electrocution an Unconstitutional Method of Execution? The Engineering of Death Over the Century*, 35 Wm. & Mary L. Rev. 551 (1994).

[48] The Eighth Amendment states: "Excessive bail shall not be required, nor excessive fines imposed,

Several state courts heard method-of-execution challenges to electrocution and reached different conclusions. In *Jones v. Butterworth*,[49] the absence of pain was paramount in the Florida Supreme Court's decision to uphold electrocution as a constitutional method of execution. A majority of a divided Florida court accepted evidence that electrocution rendered an inmate immediately unconsciousness, and therefore found no "unnecessary and wanton pain" in the procedure.[50]

The Georgia Supreme Court examined electrocution in *Dawson v. State*.[51] Interpreting its own state constitution, the Georgia court held that electrocution violated the state constitution's cruel and unusual punishment clause. The court applied a two-prong test and determined that electrocution (1) inflicted unnecessary pain on an inmate during the execution procedure and (2) violated the state's evolving standard of decency. In *Dawson*, the Georgia court applied an analysis similar to the Ninth and Fourth Circuits by considering the amount of pain electrocution involves and the amount of time necessary for an inmate to die. The Georgia court went further and, as Justice Brennan considered appropriate in *Glass v Louisiana*,[52] also evaluated levels of physical violence and mutilation.[53] In deciding whether electrocution involved "unnecessary" pain, the court looked at the available alternative, lethal injection, and found that electrocution resulted in "cooked brains and blistered bodies" where the alternative, through "the 'science of the present day' has provided a less painful, less barbarous means for taking the life."[54] Electrocution violated the Georgia state constitutional provision on cruel and unusual punishment because it "involves more than the 'mere extinguishment of life,' and inflicts purposeless physical violence and needless mutilation that makes no measurable contribution to accepted goals of punishment."[55] Under the second prong, the Georgia court concluded that societal consensus had evolved

---

nor cruel and unusual punishments inflicted." *In re Kemmler*, 136 U.S. at 445 (quoting U.S. Const. amend. VIII). For its part, "[t]he Fourteenth Amendment did not radically change the whole theory of the relations of the state and Federal governments to each other." *Id.* at 447.

[49]   Jones v. Butterworth, 701 So. 2d 76 (Fla. 1997).

[50]   *Id.* at 79 ("As the Court observed in *Resweber*: 'The cruelty against which the Constitution protects a convicted man is cruelty inherent in the method of punishment, not the necessary suffering involved in any method employed to extinguish life humanely.' There was substantial evidence presented in this case that executions in Florida are conducted without any pain whatsoever, and this record is entirely devoid of evidence suggesting deliberate indifference to a prisoner's wellbeing on the part of state officials." (quoting Francis v. Resweber, 329 U.S. 459, 464 (1947) (internal citations omitted))). The court based its reasoning, in part, on a finding by the lower judge that electrocution results in the "brain [being] instantly and massively depolarized within milliseconds of the initial surge of electricity." *Id.* at 77.

[51]   Dawson v. State, 554 S.E.2d 137 (Ga. 2001).

[52]   Glass v. Louisiana, 471 U.S. 1080 (1985).

[53]   *Id.* at 1085 (Brennan, J., dissenting) ("The Eighth Amendment's protection of 'the dignity of man,' extends beyond prohibiting the unnecessary infliction of pain when extinguishing life. Civilized standards, for example, require a minimization of physical violence during execution irrespective of the pain that such violence might inflict on the condemned. Similarly, basic notions of human dignity command that the State minimize 'mutilation' and 'distortion' of the condemned prisoner's body. These principles explain the Eighth Amendment's prohibition of such barbaric practices as drawing and quartering.") (citations omitted).

[54]   *Dawson*, 554 S.E.2d at 144.

[55]   *Id.* at 143.

away from electrocution, as evidenced by the Georgia legislature's decision to replace it with lethal injection.

The last challenge to electrocution as a form of punishment came in Nebraska in 2008. At that time, Nebraska was the only state still using electrocution as its primary form of execution. In *State v. Mata*, the Nebraska State Supreme Court found that electrocution violates the Nebraska state constitutional prohibition against cruel and unusual punishment.[56] Today, there is no state that uses electrocution as a form of punishment except as an alternative method and only at the request of the inmate.[57]

§ 5.04　CHALLENGES TO LETHAL INJECTION AS A METHOD OF EXECUTION

[A]　Overview

Lethal injection is the newest form of execution. It was first used in Texas in 1982.[58] As a result, challenges to lethal injection are relatively recent.[59] Between 2006–2007 nearly half of the 76 non-volunteers executed in this country raised Eighth Amendment challenges to the chemicals and procedures used in lethal injections.[60] During that same time, numerous other inmates, not facing immediate execution dates, also filed challenges to their states' lethal injection policies and procedures.[61] These challenges argue, in part, that inmates suffer unnecessary infliction of pain from (1) the drugs selected; (2) flawed state procedures; and (3) the absence of medically-trained personnel to administer drugs and verify their effectiveness.[62] In 2006, federal district courts in Missouri[63] and California[64] held

---

[56] 745 N.W. 2d 229 (Neb. 2008). For a complete discussion *Mata, see* Mark Mills, Note, *Cruel and Unusual:* State v. Mata, *the Electric Chair, and the Nebraska Supreme Court's Rejection of a Subjective Intent Requirement in Death Penalty Jurisprudence,* 88 NEB L. REVIEW 235 (2009).

[57] The state statutes authorizing electrocution include: ALA. CODE §§ 15-18-82 to -82.1 (Supp. 2007); FLA. STAT. § 922.105 (2006); S.C. CODE ANN. § 24-3-53 (2007); VA. CODE ANN. § 53.1-234 (Lexis Supp. 2007).

[58] Kreitzberg & Richter, *supra* note 15, at 459.

[59] *See generally* Taylor v. Crawford, 457 F.3d 902 (8th Cir. 2006); Morales v. Tilton, 465 F. Supp. 2d 972 (N.D. Cal. 2006); Cooey v. Taft, 430 F. Supp. 2d 702 (S.D. Ohio 2006); Nooner v. Norris, 594 F.3d 592 (8th Cir. 2010), *cert. denied,* 131 S. Ct. 569 (2010); Cooper v. Rimmer, No. C 04 436 JF, 2004 U.S. Dist. LEXIS 1624 (N.D. Cal. Feb. 6, 2004).

[60] Petition for Writ of Certiorari, Baze v. Rees, 553 U.S. 35 (2008) (No. 07-5439), 22, 2007 U.S. Briefs 5439, at *10.

[61] *Id.* at 23 n.3.

[62] *See generally Morales,* 465 F. Supp. 2d 972; Kreitzberg & Richter, *supra* note 15; *and* Denno, *When Legislatures Delegate Death, supra* note 2.

[63] In Missouri, Judge Fernando Gaitan held hearings in *Taylor v. Crawford,* No 05-41730CV-C-FJG, 2006 U.S. Dist. LEXIS 42949 (W.D. Mo. June 26, 2006). The most compelling evidence there may have come from John Doe I, a doctor who was the primary executioner in Missouri who mixed the drugs, monitored the anesthetic depth, and who, after admitting to be dyslexic testified, "[i]ts not unusual for me to make mistakes . . . . But I am dyslexic . . . . I can make these mistakes [in my testimony and in referring to drugs]." *Id.* at *5. The district court, "after discovery and hearing, determined that Missouri's then existing protocol violated the Eighth Amendment." *Taylor,* 457 F.3d 902. The Court of Appeal later vacated the stay of execution and held that lethal injection does not violate the Eighth

extensive hearings on constitutional challenges to each states' lethal injection procedures. For the first time, states were compelled to disclose to the public many of the details of their lethal injection procedures. These details included the state's selection and training of the execution team, the exact protocol used for injection of the drugs, and the reports and logs from previous lethal injection executions.[65]

In addition to Missouri and California, other state and federal courts reviewed challenges to lethal injection procedures.[66] Without guidance from the Supreme Court, each court had to first determine the appropriate legal standard to apply. Because courts use different terminology in reaching their decisions, it is difficult to determine whether they apply a uniform test. For example, the Eighth and Tenth Circuit Courts of Appeal applied a test that looks at whether the execution procedure involves "the unnecessary and wanton infliction of pain."[67] The federal district court for the Eastern District of Virginia looked to whether there was an "objectively substantial risk of harm."[68] The state Supreme Courts of both Connecticut and Kentucky held that a method of execution is viewed as cruel and unusual when the procedure creates a "substantial risk of wanton and unnecessary infliction of pain, torture, or lingering death."[69] Many challenges were unable to document more than minimal evidence of pain. Consequently, many courts found

---

Amendment and does not pose an unnecessary risk of pain. *See* Taylor v. Crawford, 487 F.3d 1072, 1085 (8th Cir. 2007).

[64] Hearings were held in September, 2006, in federal district court in California before Judge Jeremy Fogel in the case of *Morales v. Tilton*, 465 F. Supp. 2d 972. After five days of hearings and thousands of pages of stipulated testimony and evidence, Judge Fogel held that California's "implementation of lethal injection is broken, but it can be fixed." *Id.* at 974.

[65] Kreitzberg & Richter, *supra* note 15, at 479–80; *see also* DEATH PENALTY CLINIC, UNIV. OF CAL., BERKELEY SCH OF LAW, FORESEEABLE AND UNNECESSARY RISK: LETHAL INJECTION AND THE THREE-DRUG PROTOCOL, http://www.law.berkeley.edu/clinics/dpclinic/LethalInjection/LI/documents/kit/Kit.pdf (last visited Feb. 11, 2012).

[66] In New Jersey, a Court of Appeal ordered a halt to all lethal injection executions until the state could justify its procedures. *In re* Readoption with Amendments of Death Penalty Regulations N.J.A.C. 10A:23, 367 N.J. Super. 61(2004). New Jersey subsequently abolished the death penalty as a possible punishment. *See* Chapter 27, *infra*. In North Carolina, a federal judge ordered lethal injection executions must be monitored by medically trained personnel. Brown v. Beck, No. 5:06-CT-3018-H, 2006 U.S. Dist Lexis 60084 (E.D.N.C. Apr. 7 2006), *aff'd*, 445 F.3d 752 (4th Cir 2006). Although a new procedure was adopted, Governor Mike Easley recognized a *de facto* moratorium on executions until the new procedure's constitutionality was resolved. James Romoser, *A Death Sentence on Hold — State Officials Reject Judge's Ruling on N.C. Execution Policy*, WINSTON-SALEM JOURNAL, Oct. 3, 2007, at A1. More than five years after *Brown*, North Carolina is still reworking its practice. Paul Woolverton, *Legislature's Move to Repeal the Racial Justice Act Doesn't Mean Executions will Resume*, FAYETTEVILLE OBSERVER (Nov. 30, 2011), http://fayobserver.com/articles/2011/11/30/1140421. In Delaware, all executions are on hold pending the outcome of a challenge to the lethal injection process. *Descriptions of Methods, supra* note 2. In Maryland, the Court of Appeal ruled that the state had not complied with the Administrative Procedures Act, effectively halting executions until that issue is resolved. Evans v. State, 396 Md. 256 (2006), *cert. denied*, 552 U.S. 835 (2007). Maryland's judicial moratorium remains in effect. Peter Hermann, *Inmate Sues Over Incarceration; Victim's Family Faces a New Round of Anguish in his Claims of Mistreatment*, BALTIMORE SUN, Apr. 3, 2011, 6A; *State's Death Penalty Impasse Needs to End*, CAPITAL (Annapolis), Jan. 12, 2012, at A10.

[67] Hamilton v. Jones, 472 F3d 814, 816 (10th Cir. 2007); *accord* Taylor v. Crawford, 487 F.3d 1072, 1079 (8th Cir. 2007).

[68] Walker v. Johnson, 448 F. Supp. 2d 719, 722 (E.D. Va. 2006).

[69] State v. Webb, 252 Conn. 128, 146 (2000); Baze v. Rees, 217 S.W. 3d 207, 209 (Ky. 2006).

no constitutional violation in the state's procedures.[70] It was not surprising that the Supreme Court ultimately decided to hear this issue and to pronounce a standard for courts to apply when reviewing a method of execution claims. The case they chose was *Baze v. Rees*.[71]

[B]   *Baze v. Rees*

On September 25, 2007, the Court agreed to hear a challenge from two inmates on death row in Kentucky claiming that lethal injection, as practiced in Kentucky, constituted cruel and unusual punishment.[72] This was the first case in the modern era of capital punishment where the Supreme Court agreed to consider the constitutionality of a method of execution under the Eighth Amendment.[73]

Baze did not argue that lethal injection was *per se* unconstitutional. He argued the Kentucky procedure was unconstitutional as implemented by the State of Kentucky and asked the Court to clarify the appropriate Eighth Amendment analysis for such a challenge.[74] The record in the Kentucky case was thin — especially compared with the records developed in California and Missouri cases. Kentucky had only administered one execution by lethal injection. Not surprisingly, there was no evidence of systemic problems in the case. Kentucky had taken some precautionary measures not present in other states' protocols, including requiring the warden to remain in the execution chamber with the prisoner and requiring the execution team to practice at least ten sessions per year.[75]

In a plurality decision, the Court issued seven separate opinions, and upheld Kentucky's three-drug lethal injection protocol as constitutional. No single opinion was able to garner more than three votes. The plurality concluded that Baze failed to show there was a sufficient risk that Kentucky would improperly administer their protocol in a way that would risk serious harm to an inmate.[76] The Court held

---

[70] *See* Lambright v. Lewis, 932 F. Supp. 1547 (D. Ariz. 1996), *rev'd on other grounds*, 167 F.3d 477 (9th Cir. 1999); LaGrand v. Stewart, 173 F.3d 1144 (9th Cir. 1999); Provenzano v. Moore, 744 So. 2d 413 (Fla. 1999), *cert. denied*, 530 U.S. 1256 (2000); State v. Webb, 252 Conn. 128, 141, 147 (2000), *cert. denied*, 531 U.S. 835 (2000) (finding no unnecessary pain in the administration of lethal injection).

[71] 553 U.S. 35 (2008).

[72] Baze v. Rees, 551 U.S. 1192 (2007) (mem.).

[73] Up to this point, the Court's only direct ruling on a method of execution was in 1878 when it upheld the use of the firing squad. Wilkerson v. Utah, 99 U.S. 130 (1879).

[74] The first issue presented in the petition for certiorari asks: "Does the Eighth Amendment to the United States Constitution prohibit means for carrying out a method of execution that create an unnecessary risk of pain and suffering as opposed to only a substantial risk of the wanton infliction of pain?" Petition for a Writ of Certiorari at ii, Baze v. Rees, 551 U.S. 1192 (2007) (No. 07-5439). The petition also asks the Court to review the specific three drug combination used in Kentucky (and, at the time, by all other states except New Jersey) to determine whether the specific combination violates the Eighth Amendment. *Id.* at iii.

[75] *Baze*, 553 U.S. at 55.

[76] Baze and his co-petitioner, Bowling, conceded that if properly followed, the lethal injection protocol was humane and constitutional. *Id.* at 41. Their argument was that a significant risk existed that the procedures would not be properly followed. *Id.* They argued that if the sodium thiopental, the first drug, was not properly administered, an inmate would not be properly sedated and would experience

that to prevail in a challenge to the method of execution, it was necessary to show that the method presents "a 'substantial risk of serious harm,' an 'objectively intolerable risk of harm.'"[77] Chief Justice Roberts, writing for himself and Justices Kennedy and Alito, cited cases of botched executions that were held to be constitutional and stated that "an isolated mishap alone does not give rise to an Eighth Amendment violation, precisely because such an event, while regrettable, does not suggest cruelty, or that the procedure at issue gives rise to a 'substantial risk of serious harm.'"[78] A violation may occur when:

> the proffered alternatives . . . effectively address a "substantial risk of serious harm." . . . [T]he alternative procedure must be feasible, readily implemented, and in fact, significantly reduce a substantial risk of severe pain. If a state refuses to adopt such an alternative in the face of these documented advantages, without a legitimate penological justification for adhering to its current method of execution, then a State's refusal to change its method can be viewed as "cruel and unusual" under the Eighth Amendment.[79]

[C]   The California Litigation: *Morales v. Tilton*

Michael Morales argued that the lethal injection protocol in California was unconstitutional in that it created a "substantial risk that he will be fully conscious and in agonizing pain during the execution process."[80] Morales asked the court to examine whether this risk of pain was unnecessary and unconstitutional under the Eighth Amendment or the procedures conformed to underlying values consistent with human dignity.[81]

The California hearings took place over five days in September, 2006. Witnesses testified and evidence was presented describing the breathing patterns and movements of California inmates in the moments leading to their deaths. Expert testified about clinical trials studying the effect of the lethal injection drugs on humans and animals.[82] Judge Jeremy Fogel, hearing the case, visited the execution

---

excruciating pain that no one would be able to detect due to the second drug, pancuronium bromide, which acts as a paralytic and prevents involuntary muscle movement. *Id.* at 53; *cf.* Morales v. Hickman, 415 F. Supp. 2d 1037, 1047–48 (N.D. Cal. 2006) (describing specific measures California's Department of Corrections would need to take to perform lethal injection without violating the Eighth Amendment).

[77] 553 U.S. at 50 (citation omitted).

[78] *Id.* (citation omitted).

[79] *Id.* at 52.

[80] Plaintiff's Motion for Temporary Restraining Order; Memorandum of Points and Authorities in Support Thereof at 2, *Morales*, 415 F. Supp. 2d 1037 (No. C-06-926-JF). Morales's claims were heard in Federal District court before the U.S. Supreme Court heard arguments in *Baze v. Rees.*

[81] *See* Trop v. Dulles, 356 U.S. 86, 100 (1958) ("The basic concept underlying the Eighth Amendment is nothing less than the dignity of man").

[82] Morales argued that California's lethal injection procedure (Procedure 770) was rife with problems that contributed to a risk of unnecessary pain including (1) ineffective selection and inadequate training of the execution team, (2) inadequate facilities and oversight of the injection procedure, and (3) the selection and dosage of the drugs used. Morales v. Tilton, 465 F. Supp. 2d 972, 979–80 (N.D. Cal. 2006). In addition to live testimony, both sides stipulated to thousands of pages of deposition transcripts from

chamber at San Quentin and had the prison officials replicate the exact conditions of an execution.[83]

In December, 2006, Judge Fogel presented his findings that California's lethal injection procedure, as administered and practiced, was unconstitutional, "but . . . can be fixed."[84] This opinion was based, in part, on prison logs from the eleven lethal injection executions. Judge Fogel found evidence raising concerns that during at least six lethal injections in California "inmates may have been conscious when they were injected with pancuronium bromide and potassium chloride, drugs that the parties agree would cause an unconstitutional level of pain if injected into a conscious person."[85] In a strongly worded opinion, Judge Fogel took the Attorney General and the Governor's office to task for not being more proactive to fix a system with such glaring deficiencies.[86]

In response to the Judge's order, the state submitted proposed revisions to California's lethal injection procedures, including changes in the selection, training, and supervision of the execution team.[87] The proposal retained the use of the same three-drug cocktail previously used, modifying only the quantity of the drugs administered.[88] In light of the decision in *Baze*, Morales must return to federal court to review the new procedures and determine whether they satisfy *Baze*. This litigation should keep executions on hold in California through the end of 2012.[89]

---

participants in the lethal injection procedures allowing them to stay anonymous and out of the public scrutiny.

[83] In his opinion, Judge Fogel describes the room itself, the existing gas chamber, as "too dim . . . to permit effective observation," sealed during injection "as if lethal gas were being disseminated, rendering it virtually impossible to hear any sound," observed from a "small anteroom" which may be "so crowded with prison officials and other dignitaries that even simple movement has been difficult." *Id.* at 980.

[84] *Id.* at 974.

[85] *Id.* at 975.

[86] *Id.* at 983.

[87] Response by the Governor's Office to the Court's Memorandum of Intended Decision Dated December 15, 2006, *Morales*, 465 F. Supp. 2d 972 (Nos. C 06 219 JF RS, C 06 926 JF RS), *available at* http://www.clearinghouse.net/chDocs/public/CJ-CA-0004-0034.pdf (last accessed Feb. 11, 2012).

[88] Judge Fogel declined to uphold the revised protocol in California without a hearing. The federal litigation was prolonged due to a challenge that the revised lethal injection regulations adopted by the California Department of Corrections and Rehabilitation in 2010 violated the California Administrative Procedures Act. On December 16, 2011, Marin County Superior Court Judge Faye D'Opal agreed and held that California's lethal injection regulations invalid in their entirety. Sims v. Cal. Dep't of Corr. & Rehab., No. CV1004019 (Super. Ct. Marin Cnty. filed Dec. 16, 2011).

[89] The cases were reassigned to Judge Seeborg earlier in 2011 when Judge Fogel left the bench for an administrative position. Counsel have stipulated to a new discovery schedule cutoff date of August 15, 2012. By September 15, 2012, they will identify any material issues of fact that will require an evidentiary hearing. These dates are seven months later than the cutoff dates the parties agreed to in May, 2011. The 6-page stipulation indicates ongoing discovery followed by depositions of lay and expert witnesses. It also indicates that Acting San Quentin Warden Michael Martel recently selected a new execution team. The case is proceeding under docket Nos. 3:06-CV-219-RS & 3:06-CV-926-RS (as *Morales v. Cate*), and No. 3:06-CV-1793-RS (as *Pacific News Service v. Cate*). According to an October 5, 2010, order from Judge Fogel, "[i]t is the Court's understanding that [the state] will not seek to obtain any execution dates until at least thirty days after the conclusion of any further evidentiary hearing in the present action."

[D] Post-*Baze* Challenges

If the Supreme Court thought *Baze* would put an end to lethal injection challenges and litigation, they were wrong. Executions were slow to resume. After peaking in 1999, in 2008 there were 37 executions, in 2009 it went up to 52 but back down to 46 in 2010 and 43 the following year. The number of executions continue to decline while challenges to the method of execution continue.

While the Supreme Court rejected the constitutional challenge to Kentucky's use of lethal injection, it left open the possibility that lethal injection could be cruel and unusual under different circumstances.[90] Challenges were filed and remain pending in numerous states.[91] These challenges attempted to distinguish their state's protocol from the Kentucky protocol reviewed by the Court. Many tried to submit a more complete record showing the risk that some error, mishap, or other problem would occur.

Quite aside from ending challenges to executions by lethal injection, *Baze's* less-developed record and new test weighing alternative procedures (as opposed to alternative methods) invite new rounds of record-heavy, medically complex litigation into courts.[92] These issues are addressed, in part, by Supreme Court review of lower court decisions premised on certain evidentiary shortcomings.[93] Inmates challenging the failure of the state to provide more detailed record keeping have had some measure of success.[94]

Scheduling Order at 2, Morales v. Cate, Nos. 5-6-cv-219-JF-HRL & 5-6-cv-926-JF-HRL (N.D. Cal. Oct. 5, 2010).

[90] Roberts stated that a constitutional violation may occur when a substantial risk of serious harm is demonstrated and an "alternative procedure [is] feasible, readily implemented, and in fact significantly reduce a substantial risk of severe pain." Baze v. Rees, 553 U.S. 35, 52 (2008). "If a State refuses to adopt such an alternative in the face of these documented advantages, without a legitimate penological justification for adhering to its current method of execution, then a State's refusal to change its method can be viewed as 'cruel and unusual' under the Eighth Amendment." *Id. See* Eric Berger, *Lethal injection and the Problems of Constitutional Remedies*, 27 Yale L. & Pol'y Rev. 259 (2009) (questioning the Court's motives in selecting *Baze v Rees* instead of *Taylor v Crawford*, 553 U.S. 1004 (2008), which was pending certiorari at the same time and whose record included substantially more documentation). *Compare also* the record in *Morales v. Tilton. See* Kreitzberg & Richter, *supra* note 15.

[91] *See* Elisabeth Semel, *Reflections on Justice John Paul Stevens's Concurring Opinion in* Baze v. Rees: *A Fifth* Gregg *Justice Renounces Capital Punishment*, 43 U.C. Davis L. Rev 783, 586 n.350 (2010) (noting challenges pending in Arizona, Arkansas, California, Delaware, Louisiana, Maryland, Missouri, North Carolina, Ohio, Washington, and the federal government (citing *Court Orders*, Lethal Injection-.org, U.C. Berkeley Sch. of L., http://www.law.berkeley.edu/clinics/dpclinic/LethalInjection/LI/orders. html) (last updated Mar. 29, 2010).

[92] *Baze*, 553 U.S. at 105 (Thomas, J., concurring in the judgment).

[93] *See, e.g.*, Brewer v. Landrigan, 2010 U.S. LEXIS 8327, (2010), *rev'g* Brewer v. Landrigan, 2010 U.S. Dist. LEXIS 113485 (D. Ariz. 2010) (reversing a district court order which relied on a department of corrections failing to disclose the manufacturer of sodium thioental).

[94] Harvey Gee, *Eighth Amendment Challenges After* Baze v. Rees: *Lethal Injection, Civil Rights Lawsuits, and the Death Penalty*, 31 B.C. Third World L.J. 217, 240–42 (2011) (surveying challenges based on state administrative procedure act grounds).

[E]   Administrative Procedure Act Violations

Another line of challenges to lethal injection procedures, begun before the Supreme Court decided *Baze v. Rees*, has been cases arguing that state departments of corrections violate a state's Administrative Procedures Act by failing to publish lethal injection protocols. While varying by state, Administrative Procedure Acts typically require a period of notice-and-comment before rules go into effect.[95] A court placing execution protocols within the scope of such acts requires state governments to publically describe methods, receive commentary and justify the ultimate decision. State courts, however, have disagreed with whether execution protocols are subject to Administrative Procedure Act notice and comment requirements.

The Tennessee and Missouri supreme courts, for example, have held their lethal injection protocols are beyond the scope of their administrative procedures acts.[96] In contrast, courts in California, Kentucky and Maryland recognize an obligation to promulgate and receive comment on protocols for lethal injection.[97]

In *Abdur'Rahman v Bresden*,[98] the Tennessee Supreme Court held "procedures in the lethal injection protocol were not 'rules' adopted by the Department of Correction in violation of the [Uniform Administrative Procedures Act]"[99] While noting that a " 'rule' is an 'agency statement of general applicability that implements or prescribes a law or policy or describes the procedures or practice requirements of any agency' "[100] the court found two exceptions applied. First, according to the court, the lethal injection protocol was a "statement concerning only . . . internal management . . . and not affecting private rights, privileges or procedures available to the public".[101] Second, it considered the protocol was merely a "statement concerning inmates of a correctional facility."[102]

In California, this litigation has proven successful for death row inmates contributing to the halt to executions since January, 2006. This challenge alleged the California Department of Corrections and Rehabilitation failed to satisfy Administrative Procedure Act requirements by adopting its lethal injection protocol.[103]

---

[95] "[A]dministrative law serves as the rule of law's handmaid, laying the groundwork for meaningful public justification by cultivating governmental deliberation, transparency, fairness, reasonableness, and integrity. Traditional administrative procedures such as notice-and-comment rulemaking facilitate public justification by compelling agencies to articulate objectively reasonable, public-regarding justifications for their policy choices." Evan J. Criddle, *Mending Holes in the Rule of (Administrative) Law*, 104 Nw. U. L. Rev. Colloquy 309, 314 (2010).

[96] Gee, note 94 *supra*, at 241.

[97] *Id.* At 241-24.

[98] 181 S.W.3d 292 (Tenn 2005).

[99] Id. At 312.

[100] Id. At 311 (citing Tenn Code Ann § 4-5-109(10)).

[101] Id. (citing Tenn. Code Ann § 4-5-109(10)(A)) (internal quotations omitted).

[102] Id. At 311-12 (citing Tenn. Code Ann § 4-5-102(10(G) (internal quotations omitted).

[103] Morales v. Cal. Dep't of Corr. & Rehab., 168 Cal. App. 4th 729, 737 (2008), *aff'g* No. CV 061436 (Super. Ct. Marin Cnty. Oct. 31, 2007).

Judge Faye D'Opal, a superior court judge sitting in Marin County, ruled in December, 2011, that California's procedure for revising their lethal injection protocol was invalid.[104] Judge D'Opal criticized state officials who, she wrote, flouted its own administrative law to adopt a revised protocol. Judge D'Opal chastised the state for failing to respond to public comments and "the department's own expert" who "recommended switching to a single, fatal dose of the currently used sedative, which would minimize risks of pain."[105] With the cost of the death penalty a paramount concern in the state, the Judge also noted the state's failure to include a "a fiscal impact assessment" since there was "uncontradicted evidence" that it would increase the cost of already costly executions.[106]

§ 5.05 SOURCE OF DRUGS LITIGATION

Controversy and litigation over the source of sodium thiopental for executions is ongoing in a number of states. Thirty states use sodium thiopental as the first lethal drug in their three-drug protocol. In May, 2010, Hospira, the sole U.S. manufacturer of sodium thiopental, announced the drug would be unavailable "because of an unspecified 'manufacturing issue.' "[107] By September, 2010, state departments of corrections received notice from Hospira that "they do not want their drug (Sodium Thiopental) used for executions."[108] In January, 2011, Hospira, believing they "could not prevent the drug from being diverted to departments of corrections for use in capital punishment procedures," publicly announced sodium thiopental would no longer be available for lethal injection executions and that they would cease manufacturing the drug.[109] Existing drugs from Hospira that were still in circulation had expiration dates in 2010 or 2011. What followed was a national scramble by departments of corrections to obtain the sedative and perform executions according to existing regulations.[110]

The California Department of Corrections and Rehabilitation, for example, engaged in a self-described "secret mission" to secure this drug from the Arizona Department of Corrections. A flurry of e-mail correspondence reflects a sense of

---

[104] Bob Egelko, *Judge Rejects Officials' New Rules for Executions*, S.F. CHRONICLE, Dec. 17, 2011, at C6.

[105] *Id.*

[106] Sims v. Cal. Dep't of Corr. & Rehab., No. CV1004019, slip op. at 8 (Super. Ct. Marin Cnty. Dec. 16, 2011).

[107] Michael Kiefer, *Drug Shortage May Imperil Executions*, AZ. REP., May 17, 2010, at B1.

[108] E-mail from John McAuliffe, Corr. Cnslr. (Ret.), Cal. Dep't of Corr. & Rehab., to Scott Kernan, Under Secretary, of Operations, Cal. Dep't of Corr. & Rehab. (Sept. 28, 2010 8:02 PST), *available at* http://www.aclunc.org/docs/criminal_justice/death_penalty/aclu_v._cdcr/contact_with_hospira_and_other_states.pdf (last accessed Feb. 12, 2012).

[109] Press Release, Hospira, Hospira Statement Regarding Pentothal™ (sodium thiopental) Market Exit (Jan. 21, 2011), *available at* http://phx.corporate-ir.net/phoenix.zhtml?c=175550&p=irol-newsArticle&ID=1518610&highlight=thiopental.

[110] Jimmie E. Gates, *Lethal Drug Expires Soon*, CLARION-LEDGER (Jackson), Feb. 11, 2011, at B1; *DEA Seizes Ga.'s Lethal Injection Drug*, BOSTON GLOBE, Mar. 17, 2011, at 2; Greg Bluestein, *States scramble, go to unusual lengths to get execution drug*, BOSTON GLOBE, Mar. 26, 2011, at 12; Andrew Welsh-Huggins, *States: Death-penalty Drug Scramble, Higher Cost*, ASSOCIATED PRESS, July 9, 2011, *available at* http://www.businessweek.com/ap/financialnews/D9OC9L100.htm.

urgency to secure the drugs as quickly as possible.[111]

States began to look overseas for other sources for these drugs, generating new legal issues and ethical questions. Challenges by inmates questioned whether or not state agencies followed proper procedures securing the drugs. They also challenged the efficacy of imported drugs which the FDA had not tested, reviewed, or approved.

Nebraska recently experienced the complications involved in securing the required drug. In January, 2012, Michael Ryan challenged his execution by arguing documents with the imported sodium thiopental describing the drugs as "not for sale" indicated they were stolen.[112] The dispute worsened when the Swiss manufacturer of the drugs asked Nebraska to return them alleging they had been purchased from a broker and were never intended for executions.[113] The Attorney General announced Nebraska may more easily change its protocol to avoid the "circus sideshow" over the drugs.[114]

Each time a European source for the drug was disclosed, a public relations fiasco ensued, followed by a decision by the company not to export the drug for use in executions or a government ban on its export for that purpose.[115] In December, 2011, the European Commission imposed tough new restrictions on the export of anesthetics used for capital punishment including Sodium Thiopental and pentobarbital.[116] Catherine Ashton, high representative for foreign affairs and security policy and vice-president of the European Commission, said "[t]he European Union opposes the death penalty under all circumstances. . . . [T]he decision today contributes to the wider EU efforts to abolish the death penalty worldwide. This is a first step in response to the calls of civil society organizations and the European Parliament to strengthen the EU legislation."[117]

The source of the drugs, however, may be immaterial; challenges to a drug's effectiveness may require "evidence . . . to suggest that the drug obtained from a

---

[111] E-mails Between California and Arizona Departments of Corrections, ACLU of N. Cal., http://www.aclunc.org/docs/criminal_justice/death_penalty/aclu_v._cdcr/arizona_drug_swap.pdf   (last visited Feb. 12, 2012).

[112] Joe Duggan, *Sodium Thiopental; Death Drug Stolen, Says Ryan Lawyer*, OMAHA WORLD-HERALD, Jan. 5, 2012, at B1.

[113] Joe Duggan, *Bruning Suggests Change to One Drug in Executions*, OMAHA WORLD-HERALD, Jan. 10, 2012, at B2. "The Swiss manufacturer has maintained it gave the drug to the broker to develop a market for medical anesthetic in Africa. The Kolkata, India, broker, Chris Harris, sold the two samples of the drug to the Nebraska Department of Correctional Services for $5,411." *Id.*

[114] *Id.*

[115] David Jolly, *Danish Company Blocks Sale of Drug for U.S. Executions*, N.Y. TIMES, July 2, 2011, http://www.nytimes.com/2011/07/02/world/europe/02execute.html.

[116] Ford Vox, *Why America's Death Penalty Just Got Us Sanctioned by Europe*, ATLANTIC (Dec. 21, 2011, 3:10 PM), http://www.theatlantic.com/international/archive/2011/12/why-americas-death-penalty-just-got-us-sanctioned-by-europe/250324/; Kevin O'Hanlon, *EU to Ban Export of Lethal Injection Drug*, LINCOLN JOURNAL STAR, Dec. 13, 2011, at A1.

[117] Press Release, European Commission, Commission Extends Control Over Goods Which Could be Used for Capital Punishment or Torture, (Dec. 20, 2011), *available at* http://europa.eu/rapid/pressReleasesAction.do?reference=IP/11/1578 (last visited Feb. 12, 2012).

foreign source is unsafe."[118] On October 25, District Judge Roslyn O. Silver, of Arizona, unable to perform a *Baze* analysis on a "drug of unknown quality that was obtained from an unidentified, non-FDA approved source, "imposed a temporary restraining order.[119] On October 26, 2010, in a 5-4 decision, the Supreme Court lifted the restraining order. In a terse one page order issued after 7 P.M., the Court agreed with the Arizona prosecutors that there was no reason to force disclosure. "There was no showing that the drug was unlawfully obtained, nor was there an offer of proof to that effect," the court order said.[120] Justices Ruth Bader Ginsberg, Stephen Breyer, Sonia Sotomayor and Elena Kagen dissented voting to keep the stay in place.

Several state Department of Corrections sued the Food and Drug Administration arguing that when the Departments of Correction imported drugs from overseas, they did so in violation of the Federal Food Drug and Cosmetic Act (FDCA) by importing shipments of misbranded and unapproved drugs for use in lethal injection procedures. Judge Richard Leon in Washington D.C. agreed.[121] The court ordered the FDA to contact each State Department of Correction and demand return of all of the drugs imported for this use.

§ 5.06   BOTCHED EXECUTIONS

In addition to challenges directly confronting the method of execution, there have also been challenges to "botched" executions. Executions that fail in some way are possible for as long as capital punishment exists. The Supreme Court reviewed an early challenge in 1947 when Willie Francis of Louisiana was placed in the electric chair. The switch was thrown, but Francis did not die. Lawyers for Francis argued it was unconstitutional for the state to try to execute him a second time. The Supreme Court ultimately disagreed and held that "[t]he fact that an unforeseeable accident prevented the prompt consummation of the sentence cannot, it seems to us, add an element of cruelty to a subsequent execution. There is no purpose to inflict unnecessary pain, nor any unnecessary pain involved in the proposed execution."[122]

Botched executions continue to occur in every form of capital punishment. The electric chair was a frequent source of failure — some failures more egregious than others. In Alabama, 1983, John Evans's attorney, present at his execution, described the prison's three attempts to execute his client:

> At: 8:30 P.M. the first jolt of 1,900 volts of electricity shot through John's body. It lasts 30 seconds. Sparks and flames erupted from the electrode tied to his leg. John's body slammed against the straps holding him to the chair, and his fists clenched. The electrode burst from the strap holding it in place

---

[118] Brewer v. Landrigan, 2010 U.S. LEXIS 8327, *1 (2010) (vacating a temporary restraining order from the District of Arizona).

[119] Brewer v. Landrigan, 2010 U.S. Dist. LEXIS 113485, *31 (D. Ariz. 2010), *vacated*, 2010 U.S. LEXIS 8327.

[120] 2010 U.S. LEXIS at *1.

[121] Beaty v. Food and Drug Administration, No. 11–289 (D.C. Cir. March 27, 2012).

[122] Louisiana *ex rel.* Francis v. Resweber 329 U.S. 459, 464 (1947).

and caught on fire. A large puff of grayish smoke and sparks poured out from under the hood that covered his face. John's body tightened out and quivered. An overpowering stench of burnt flesh and clothing began pervading the witness room. . . .

. . . two doctors went into the chamber to pronounce him dead. One doctor put the stethoscope on his heart. He turned and nodded to us, the usual sign that a person is dead. But he meant the opposite, that he had found a heartbeat. . . .

. . . The guard reattached the electrode . . . .

. . . .

At 8:35 the second jolt of 1,900 volts of current was sent into John's body. The stench of burning flesh was nauseating. More smoke came from his head and leg. . . . Again, the doctors examined John. Again, they reported that he was still alive.

It was all out of control. . . .

I called out to [Commissioner] Smith: "Commissioner, I ask for clemency. . . ."

Smith ignored me. Again I made my plea.

"I'm his lawyer. I ask for clemency."

. . . .

Minutes later Smith announced: "The Governor will not interfere. Proceed." They were ready for the third jolt. . . . This jolt lasted 30 second.

At 8:44 the doctors pronounced him dead. His body was charred and smoldering. The execution of John Evans took 14 minutes.[123]

Also in 1983, Mississippi's gas chamber failed in the execution of Jimmy Lee Gray. Officials had to clear the witness room eight minutes after the gas was released when Gray's desperate gasps for air repulsed those watching. One defense attorney commented that "Jimmy Lee Gray died banging his head against a steel pole in the gas chamber while the reporters counted his moans." It was later revealed that the executioner was drunk.[124]

Lethal injection, hailed as the most humane form of execution, has numerous documented cases of difficulties. Ohio had two botched attempts in close succession. Christopher Newton, executed on May 24, 2007, was not pronounced dead until nearly two hours after the start of the lethal injection procedure. The prison staff "struggled to find veins in his arms to deliver the deadly chemicals, taking so long that at one point [Newton] was given a bathroom break . . . Prison officials said the difficulty resulted from the girth of the 265 pound, 6 foot inmate." According to a spokesperson for Governor Ted Strickland of Ohio, "[t]he Governor's understanding

---

[123] Denno, *supra* note 1, at 665–66.

[124] David Bruck, *Decisions of Death*, NEW REPUBLIC, Dec. 12, 1984, at 24–25.

is that the procedure worked exactly the way it is supposed to work."[125]

Two years later, Ohio failed in their attempt to execute Romell Broom. Efforts to execute Broom were terminated after more than two hours when executioners were unable to find a useable vein in his arms or legs. Finally, Governor Strickland ordered the execution to stop.[126] Strickland [granted clemency] at the urging of Ohio prisons chief Terry Collins after Broom was jabbed repeatedly with lethal-injection needles in both arms and both legs — a total of 18 attempts, Broom told his Columbus attorney, S. Adele Shank.

Media witnesses said Broom, 53, appeared to grimace in pain and clench and unclench his fists several times. At one point, he covered his face with both hands and appeared to be sobbing, his stomach heaving.

After numerous failures, Broom himself began pointing out new places on his arms to try. The prison team took a break after the first hour, but efforts to find suitable veins for the IV connections were unsuccessful in the second hour as well.[127]

As of January 2012, Mr. Broom remained on Ohio's death row awaiting the outcome of his appeal to prevent the state from attempting to execute him again.[128]

§ 5.07   ROLE OF PHYSICIANS IN LETHAL INJECTION EXECUTIONS

The Supreme Court has determined that the constitutional implementation of lethal injection executions requires that they be carried out in a manner that "significantly reduce[s] a substantial risk of severe pain."[129] To the extent that this standard requires the use of a physician or medical personnel to insert the

---

[125] Julie Carr Smyth, *Delayed Execution Intolerable*, CINCINNATI POST, May 25, 2007, at A1.

[126] Bob Driehaus, *Prisoner in Failed Execution in Ohio Wins a Stay Against a Second Attempt*, N.Y. TIMES, Sept. 19, 2009, at A10; Alan Johnson, *Effort to Kill Inmate Halted — 2 Hours of Needle Sticks Fail; Strickland Steps In*, COLUMBUS DISPATCH, Sept. 16, 2009, at A1. Bob Driehaus, *Ohio Plans to Try Again as Execution Goes Wrong*, NEW YORK TIMES, Sept. 17, 2009, at A16; *See also Some Examples of Post-Furman Botched Executions*, Death Penalty Information center, http://www.deathpenaltyinfo.org/some-examples-post-furman-botched-executions (last visited Oct 11, 2011) for more examples.

[127] Johnson, *supra* note 126.

[128] Andrew Welsh-Huggins, *Court Keeps Execution On Hold for Ohio Killer of 2*, Associated Press, Jan. 13, 2012, *available at* 1/13/12 APDATASTREAM 22:44:45. The United States Supreme Court has let stand an order by Ohio District Judge Gregory Frost who, on January 11, 2012, delayed the execution of Charles Lorraine set for January 18, 2012 saying the state had once again failed to follow its own rules for executions, failed to properly document the drugs used in its last execution in November and failed to review the medical chart of the inmate who was put to death. Reginald Fields, *Supreme Court Move Halts all Ohio Executions for now Justices Decline to Hear State's Appeal of Judge's Ruling*, PLAIN DEALER (Cleveland), Feb 9, 2012, at B1. In the November 15 execution of Reginald Brooks, evidence indicates that Ohio failed to review Brooks' medical chart prior to his execution as required by the state's policies. *In re* Ohio Execution Protocol Litigation, No. 2:11-cv-1016, 2012 U.S. Dist. LEXIS 3518, *26–27 (S.D. Ohio Jan. 11, 2012), *cert. denied*, 2012 U.S. LEXIS 1065 (Feb. 8, 2012).

[129] *Baze v. Rees*, 553 U.S. 35, 52 (2008) The Court's ruling required that states not reject alternate means of completing an execution if the alternative is "feasible, readily implemented, and in fact significantly reduce a substantial risk of severe pain." *Id.*

intravenous line to monitor the inmate, medical ethics and constitutional principles collide. Several state statutes require the presence of a physician to attend, to "pronounce" death or simply request their presence as witnesses.[130]

The American Medical Association ethical guidelines prohibit a doctor from participating in an execution and defines "participation" to include "prescribing or administering tranquilizers and other psychotropic agents and medications that are part of the execution procedure; monitoring vital signs on site or remotely (including electrocardiograms) attending or observing an execution as a physician; rendering of technical advice regarding the executions and performing acts specific to lethal injection executions."[131] Anesthesiologists are most directly called upon in lethal injection procedures. The President of the American Society of Anesthesiologists recently released a statement admonishing its members not to participate in executions stating, "Lethal injection was not anesthesiology's idea. American society decided to have capital punishment as part of our legal system and to carry it out with lethal injection. The fact that problems are surfacing is not our dilemma. The legal system has painted itself into this corner and it is not our obligation to get it out."[132]

Some doctors have faced challenges to their medical licenses for participating in executions. North Carolina's Medical Board has stated its belief that "physician participation in capital punishment is a departure from the ethics of the medical profession within the meaning of North Carolina's medical code of ethics.[133] In response to the Medical Board's statement that doctors involved in executions could face discipline, North Carolina's Department of Corrections filed suit to ensure the availability of doctors to aid in executions.[134] The North Carolina Supreme Court ruled that the state's capital punishment statutes required physician assistance in administering executions, and that the Medical Board had exceeded its authority by issuing a position contradicting the legislature's procedures.[135]

Inmates will continue to raise the legal and ethical issues surrounding the use of physicians in lethal injection executions. The complex questions asked surrounding the use of medical persons in this process is a reminder to recognize those who are called upon to carry out executions. There is a human toll on these willing and sometimes unwilling participants.

---

[130] Kreitzberg & Richter, *supra* note 15 at 300, fn 336.

[131] Code of Medical Ethics, Section E 206 (Am. Med. Assn. 2000), *available at* www.ama-assn.org/ama/pub/category/8419.html; Kreitzberg & Richter, *supra* note 15, at 499-505.

[132] Kreitzberg & Richter, *supra* note 15.

[133] *North Carolina Medical Board Position Statement — Capital Punishment* (January 2007), *available at* http://www.moratoriumcampaign.org/north_carolina_position_statement.pdf.

[134] Kevin B. O'Reilly, *North Carolina Medical Board Can't Discipline Doctors For Execution Work*, American Medical News (Oct. 29, 2007), *available at* http://www.ama-assn.org/amednews/2007/10/22/prsc1022.htm.

[135] *North Carolina Dept. of Corrections v. North Carolina Medical Bd.*, 363 N.C. 189, 203-204 (2009).

Chapter 6

MODERN DEATH PENALTY STATUTES

§ 6.01 OVERVIEW

The 1970s were truly a momentous time in the history of the death penalty. The Supreme Court first found no constitutional problem with the system for imposing the death penalty.[1] One year later, the Court held that the Georgia death penalty statute was unconstitutional as applied and implied that all other statutes might be unconstitutional as well.[2] In response, state legislatures around the country passed new death penalty statutes. Three of these statutes reached the Court for review in 1976.

In 1972, when the Court ruled in *Furman v. Georgia*[3] that the Georgia death penalty statute was unconstitutional, the impact was enormous. The result of the one decision was to effectively strike down 40 death penalty statutes nationwide and invalidate more than 600 sentences of death. Immediately following the decision in *Furman*, 35 state legislatures passed new death penalty statutes and states began prosecuting death penalty cases again. By 1976, more than 460 sentences of death were imposed. Five of the new statutes reached the Supreme Court to determine whether the new statutes adequately addressed the constitutional concerns raised in *Furman*.[4] Each of the state statutes that the Court chose to review took a slightly different approach in its death penalty scheme. They ranged from a mandatory sentence of death to virtually unguided discretion once a single aggravating circumstance was found. The Supreme Court struck down only the mandatory death penalty statutes, and upheld the other three.[5] Today, there are even more variations in death penalty statutes. In addition to examining the first three statutes to be upheld, three other variations will also be explored in this chapter.

What were the Court's concerns in 1972 when it struck down the existing death penalty statutes? How did the new death penalty statutes differ from those that were struck down in 1972? A look at the decision is *Furman* is helpful in order to understand what the Court required in a death penalty statute.

---

[1] McGautha v. California, 402 U.S. 183 (1971).

[2] Furman v. Georgia, 408 U.S. 238 (1972).

[3] Id.

[4] Gregg v. Georgia, 428 U.S. 153 (1976) (upheld); Proffitt v. Florida, 428 U.S. 242 (1976) (upheld), discussed at Section 6.04, *infra*; Jurek v. Texas, 428 U.S. 262 (1976) (upheld), discussed at Section 6.05, *infra*; Woodson v. North Carolina, 428 U.S. 280 (1976) (invalidated), discussed at Section 6.06, *infra*; Roberts v. Louisiana, 428 U.S. 325 (1976) (invalidated), discussed at Section 6.06, *infra*.

[5] *See supra* note 4.

§ 6.02   *FURMAN v. GEORGIA*

In 1972, the Supreme Court agreed to review three cases to decide whether the imposition of the death penalty constituted cruel and unusual punishment under the Eighth and Fourteenth Amendments to the Constitution. In a 5:4 decision, the Court reversed the three sentences of death, which had the practical effect of striking down all existing death penalty statutes. A majority of the Court, however, declined to declare the death penalty unconstitutional in all cases.[6]

The implications of the opinion were difficult to assess at the time because of the dramatic divisions within the Court. There was no majority opinion, and each justice wrote his own opinion, producing the longest single collection of opinions in any one case to date. Justices Brennan and Marshall held that the death penalty was unconstitutional in all cases. The critical opinions by Justices Douglas, Stewart, and White, in the "middle" of the Court, did not agree that the death penalty was per se unconstitutional. They found, however, that the procedures involved in the existing capital punishment statutes created a substantial risk that the death penalty would be imposed in an arbitrary and capricious manner.[7] It was clear that a standardless process that resulted in sentences of death was unconstitutional.[8]

Although not explicit in the various opinions of *Furman*, the Court's decision was viewed as requiring a constitutional capital punishment scheme to impose more structure in the manner in which death sentences were decided. It was the unbridled discretion given to juries that made the sentences of death unconstitutional. However, the Supreme Court was unwilling to state exactly what was necessary for a valid death penalty statute. It was up to the legislatures to respond, and they did. Death sentences imposed under the newly revised statutes of Georgia, Florida, Texas, Louisiana, and North Carolina were the first to reach the Supreme Court after *Furman*.

§ 6.03   THE GEORGIA STATUTE

The Georgia death penalty statute reached the Supreme Court in the case of *Gregg v. Georgia.*[9] In a 7:2 decision, the Court upheld the new death penalty statute and found that the statute addressed the constitutional defects that *Furman* found to be fatal.

What did the Court think was critical to the constitutionality of the Georgia statute? Although never clearly articulated in *Furman*, the Court now identified two distinct issues: 1) the discretion of the jury must be sufficiently directed and guided to ensure that the decision making is not done in an arbitrary and capricious manner and 2) there must be an individualized determination of the sentence that considers both the circumstances of the crime and the character and background of the offender.

---

[6]   408 U.S. at 257, 314.

[7]   *Id.* at 256-57.

[8]   *See* discussion of the opinions in *Furman* in Section 4.02[B], *supra*.

[9]   428 U.S. 153 (1976).

How was the discretion of the jury focused in the new statute? The Georgia statute created several procedures specifically designed to eliminate any arbitrariness in the imposition of a sentence of death. First, the statute provided that a capital trial should be a bifurcated proceeding — the guilt/innocence decision determined in the first phase and the sentencing decision determined in the second phase. Six crimes were designated in Georgia as eligible for death including murder, kidnapping for ransom where the victim is harmed, armed robbery, rape, treason, and aircraft hijacking.[10]

It was in the second (penalty) phase where new procedures were put into place. The statute made clear that the sentencing decision was a two step process. First, a jury had to find at least one statutory aggravating circumstance to be present (what the Court now calls the *eligibility* decision).[11] Only then could the jury consider additional evidence to decide whether or not to impose a sentence of death (what the Court now calls the *selection* decision).[12]

In an effort to eliminate arbitrary sentencing, the statute provided 10 statutory aggravating circumstances, at least one of which had to be found beyond a reasonable doubt by a unanimous jury for a case to be eligible for a sentence of death.[13] These aggravating circumstances included the following:

> 1) that the offense of murder . . . was committed by a person with a prior record of conviction for a prior felony,[14] that the offense of murder . . . was committed while the offender was engaged in the commission of another capital felony . . . , 3) the offender . . . knowingly created a great risk of death to more than one person in a public place . . . , 4) the offender committed the offense of murder . . . for the purpose of receiving money . . . , 5) the murder of a judicial officer, former judicial officer, district attorney, solicitor or former district attorney or solicitor during or because of his official duty, 6) the offender caused or directed another to commit murder or committed murder as an agent or employee of another, 7) the offense . . . was outrageously or wantonly vile, horrible or inhuman in that it involved torture, depravity of mind or an aggravated battery to the victim, 8) the offense of murder was committed against a peace officer, corrections employee or fireman while engaged in performance of his official duties, 9) the offense of murder was committed by a person who has escaped from lawful custody . . . , 10) the murder was committed for the purpose of avoiding, interfering with or preventing a lawful arrest . . .[15]

Once a case was eligible for a sentence of death, the jury then decided whether the appropriate sentence was life or death. To ensure that the sentencing decision

---

[10] GA. CODE ANN. §§ 26-1101, 26-1311, 26-1902, 26-2001, 26-2201, 26-3301 (1972).

[11] *See* Sections 9.01-9.03, *infra.*

[12] *See* Sections 9.03, 11.01-11.04; 12.01-12.04, and 13.01-13.06, *infra.*

[13] *Gregg,* 428 U.S. at 164-65 (1976).

[14] The Georgia Supreme Court in Arnold v. State, 236 Ga. 534 (1976) had already held a portion of the first aggravating circumstance to be unconstitutionally vague. It provided that a person was eligible for death if there was a "substantial history of serious assaultive criminal convictions."

[15] GA. CODE ANN. § 27-2534.1(b) (Supp. 1975).

was individualized, the Georgia statute authorized a jury to consider a broad range of evidence, including evidence not specifically listed in the statute itself.

The Georgia statute is a *nonweighing* statute. Once the eligibility decision has been made, the selection decision is very unstructured. The jury is not given any specific instructions on how to evaluate, weigh or consider the evidence presented in the penalty phase. Jurors are told they may consider all of the evidence presented in making its decision.[16]

As an added safeguard against random and capricious imposition of sentences, the Georgia statute provided for a highly specialized appellate process for capital cases. The trial judge filled out a detailed questionnaire at the end of the trial to evaluate how the trial proceeded. The judge was instructed to assess, among other factors, whether race was a factor in the trial or the sentence, whether the defendant was well represented by counsel, and whether death was appropriate in the case. The Georgia Supreme Court was directed to conduct a specific proportionality review to evaluate whether the death penalty was excessive or disproportionate in the case. The court had to compare the case to other similar cases in which death was imposed.

When the Supreme Court examined the Georgia statute, it concluded that the concerns in *Furman* that the death penalty not be imposed in an arbitrary and capricious manner were met by this statute. The statute both guided the discretion of the sentencer and allowed for an individualized determination of the facts and circumstances of the crime and the offender.

The Court upheld the statute, but decided that it was only facially neutral. In other words, it appeared that the procedures put in place in the statute would ensure a fair and reasonable capital punishment scheme, but the Supreme Court made it clear that the actual imposition of the sentences of death under the statute would be reviewed to ensure that it worked as promised.

§ 6.04   THE FLORIDA STATUTE

The Florida statute reached the Court at the same time as the Georgia statute. In *Proffitt v. Florida*,[17] the Court upheld the Florida statute with the same 7:2 vote. The Florida statute also tried to address the concerns raised by the Court in *Furman*. The statute had some features much like the Georgia statute, with some very important differences.

Both statutes created a bifurcated proceeding, with a guilt phase and a separate penalty phase. The same jury would hear both parts of the trial. The Florida statute also had a list of statutory aggravating circumstances, at least one of which had to be found by a jury before a case was eligible for death.[18] Florida also provided for

---

[16] Section 27- 2534.1(b) provided that: "In all cases of other offenses for which the death penalty may be authorized, the judge shall consider, or he shall include in his instructions to the jury for it to consider, any mitigating circumstances or aggravating circumstances otherwise authorized by law and any of the following statutory aggravating circumstances which may be supported by the evidence."

[17] 428 U.S. 242 (1976).

[18] The aggravating circumstances were: "(a) The capital felony was committed by a person under

an automatic appellate review if a sentence of death was imposed.

The differences in the statute were quite striking, however. Where the Georgia statute left the ultimate sentencing decision with the jury, the Florida statute provided that the jury made an advisory decision to the trial judge, who was the ultimate sentencer. A judge in Florida could impose a sentence of death even after a unanimous jury recommendation of a sentence of life.

Unlike the nonweighing formulation in Georgia, the Florida statute was a *weighing* statute. It provided a more structured process by which the sentencing decision was made. First the jury and then the judge had to balance all of the evidence presented in aggravation and mitigation. The statute further instructed the judge to impose a sentence of death when the aggravating circumstances outweighed the mitigating circumstances.[19]

Although the Florida statute provided for an automatic appeal, it was not defined with the kind of specificity found in the Georgia statute. It did, however, require the appellate court to reweigh the aggravating and mitigating evidence to make an independent determination of whether a sentence of death was warranted.

The Supreme Court found that the Florida procedures adequately channeled and guided the discretion of the jury, removing the arbitrary and capricious imposition of the sentences of death.

§ 6.05   THE TEXAS STATUTE

The Texas legislature created a very different structure than either Florida or Georgia had designed. It was reviewed by the Court in the case of *Jurek v. Texas*.[20] In Texas, capital trials were also bifurcated into two phases, a guilt phase and a penalty phase. However, the rest of the procedures differed significantly. The Georgia and Florida statutes each had a list of statutory aggravating circumstances that served to narrow the class of cases that were eligible for a sentence of death. This narrowing provided a rational basis for determining the few cases in which the death penalty was imposed from the many in which it was not.

---

sentence of imprisonment. (b) The defendant was previously convicted of another capital felony or of a felony involving the use or threat of violence to the person. (c) The defendant knowingly created a great risk of death to many persons. (d) The capital felony was committed while the defendant was engaged, or was an accomplice, in the commission of, or an attempt to commit, or flight after committing or attempting to commit, any robbery, rape, arson, burglary, kidnapping, or aircraft piracy or the unlawful throwing, placing, or discharging of a destructive device or bomb. (e) The capital felony was committed for the purpose of avoiding or preventing a lawful arrest or effecting an escape from custody. (f) The capital felony was committed for pecuniary gain. (g) The capital felony was committed to disrupt or hinder the lawful exercise of any governmental function or the enforcement of laws. (h) The capital felony was especially heinous, atrocious, or cruel." FLA. STAT. ANN. § 921.141(5) (Supp. 1976-1977).

[19] *Proffitt*, 428 U.S. at 248. Florida jurors were asked "(w)hether sufficient mitigating circumstances exist which outweigh the aggravating circumstances found to exist; and . . . (b)ased on these considerations, whether the defendant should be sentenced to life imprisonment or death." FLA. STAT. ANN. §§ 921.141(2)(b) and (c) (Supp. 1976-1977).

[20] 428 U.S. 262 (1976).

The Texas statute did not have any enumerated aggravating circumstances. The Supreme Court upheld the Texas statute and found that it performed the constitutionally required narrowing in the guilt phase of the trial. The Court held that the Texas legislature had limited the definition of "capital murder" to only five specific types of killings. These included:

> 1) murder of a peace officer or fireman; 2) murder committed in the course of kidnapping, burglary, robbery, forcible rape, or arson; 3) murder committed for remuneration; 4) murder committed while escaping or attempting to escape from a penal institution; and 5) murder committed by a prison inmate when the victim is a prison employee.[21]

The Court found that, once a jury found a defendant guilty of capital murder, it was the equivalent of a finding of a statutory aggravating circumstance — the finding was unanimous and had to be proved beyond a reasonable doubt.

Once the penalty phase of the trial began, the Texas statute was again significantly different. Instead of an open procedure allowing for the consideration of aggravating and mitigating evidence, the Texas statute provided for three specific questions that had to be answered by the sentencer:

> 1) Whether the conduct of the defendant that caused the death of the deceased was committed deliberately and with the reasonable expectation that the death of the deceased or another would result;

> 2) whether there is a probability that the defendant would commit criminal acts of violence that would constitute a continuing threat to society; and

> 3) if raised by the evidence, whether the conduct of the defendant in killing the deceased was unreasonable in response to the provocation, if any, by the deceased.[22]

The requirements for the questions were specific; if all of the jurors answered all of the questions yes, then death must be imposed. If at least 10 of the 12 jurors answered any one of the three questions in the negative, then the sentence was automatic life.[23]

The defendant argued that this rigid structure of three questions precluded a jury from considering any mitigating evidence about his background or character in making its decision of life or death. The Court disagreed. It held that Question #2 (the "future dangerousness" question) implicitly allowed for the introduction and consideration of mitigating evidence in order to fully consider and answer that

---

[21] Tx. Code Crim. Proc. Art. 37.071(b) (Supp. 1975-1976).

[22] *Id.*

[23] "The court shall charge the jury that: (1) in deliberating on the issues submitted under Subsection (b) of this article, it shall consider all evidence admitted at the guilt or innocence stage and the punishment stage, including evidence of the defendant's background or character or the circumstances of the offense that militates for or mitigates against the imposition of the death penalty; (2) it may not answer any issue submitted under Subsection (b) of this article "yes" unless it agrees unanimously and it may not answer any issue "no" unless 10 or more jurors agree; and (3) members of the jury need not agree on what particular evidence supports a negative answer to any issue submitted under Subsection (b) of this article." *Id.*

question. Interpreted in this way, the Court was satisfied that the Texas statute did not provide for a mandatory sentence of death. Through the answers to the questions, the statute allowed an individualized consideration of the defendant in the process of answering the questions. The Court even surmised that under the Texas system, the death penalty might be an available option in an even smaller class of cases than in the other states.[24]

In recent years, the Texas legislature has softened the rigidity of the original approach. Under the current system, the sentencer still responds to two questions in a yes or no format. One question poses the "continuing threat" query; the other raises the *Enmund/Tison*[25] question of the mens rea of an accomplice.[26] The same rules of unanimity for affirmative answers and 10/12 for negative answers apply. However, the Texas scheme now requires an additional inquiry by the sentencer as to the propriety of the death penalty even if the specific questions are answered affirmatively.[27] If the sentencer decides that death is not warranted, even if the two specific questions are affirmatively answered, the court must impose life imprisonment.[28]

---

[24] *Jurek*, 428 U.S. at 271.

[25] *See* Section 8.02, *infra*.

[26] Tex. Crim Proc. Code Ann. § 37.071(2)(b) provides:

"On conclusion of the presentation of the evidence, the court shall submit the following issues to the jury:

(1) whether there is a probability that the defendant would commit criminal acts of violence that would constitute a continuing threat to society; and

(2) in cases in which the jury charge at the guilt or innocence stage permitted the jury to find the defendant guilty as a party under Sections 7.01 and 7.02, Penal Code, whether the defendant actually caused the death of the deceased or did not actually cause the death of the deceased but intended to kill the deceased or another or anticipated that a human life would be taken. (c) The state must prove each issue submitted under Subsection (b) of this article beyond a reasonable doubt, and the jury shall return a special verdict of "yes" or "no" on each issue submitted under Subsection (b) of this Article."

[27] *Id.* at (d): "The court shall charge the jury that:

(1) in deliberating on the issues submitted under Subsection (b) of this article, it shall consider all evidence admitted at the guilt or innocence stage and the punishment stage, including evidence of the defendant's background or character or the circumstances of the offense that militates for or mitigates against the imposition of the death penalty;

(2) it may not answer any issue submitted under Subsection (b) of this article "yes" unless it agrees unanimously and it may not answer any issue "no" unless 10 or more jurors agree; and

(3) members of the jury need not agree on what particular evidence supports a negative answer to any issue submitted under Subsection (b) of this article.

(e)(1) The court shall instruct the jury that if the jury returns an affirmative finding to each issue submitted under Subsection (b) of this article, it shall answer the following issue: *Whether, taking into consideration all of the evidence, including the circumstances of the offense, the defendant's character and background, and the personal moral culpability of the defendant, there is a sufficient mitigating circumstance or circumstances to warrant that a sentence of life imprisonment rather than a death sentence be imposed."* (emphasis added).

[28] *Id.* at (g): "If the jury returns an affirmative finding on each issue submitted under Subsection (b) of this article and a negative finding on an issue submitted under Subsection (e) of this article, the court shall sentence the defendant to death. If the jury returns a negative finding on any issue submitted under Subsection (b) of this article or an affirmative finding on an issue submitted under Subsection (e) of this article or is unable to answer any issue submitted under Subsection (b) or (e) of this article, the court shall sentence the defendant to confinement in the institutional division of the Texas Department of

§ 6.06 THE MANDATORY STATUTES: LOUISIANA AND NORTH CAROLINA

In 1976-1977, the Court also reviewed and struck down two death penalty statutes that made the imposition of the death penalty mandatory upon a finding of first degree murder.[29] This time, Justices Stewart, Powell and Stevens joined Justices Brennan and Marshall to strike down both statutes as unconstitutional. However, both cases failed to produce a majority opinion.

Both North Carolina and Louisiana responded to *Furman* by making death sentences mandatory for everyone convicted of first degree murder. North Carolina's statute included a broad category of homicides within the definition of first degree murder; Louisiana limited its first degree murder statute to five categories of homicide.[30] The Court dismissed these differences as without constitutional significance.

Justice Stewart, in his plurality opinion, cited three principle reasons why the mandatory statutes were unconstitutional: 1) mandatory death sentences had long been viewed as unduly harsh and unworkably rigid, 2) mandatory sentences did not address *Furman's* concern with unbridled jury discretion — it merely shifted the discretion to the guilt decision in the trial,[31] and 3) mandatory sentences of death did not allow for particularized consideration of the character and background of each defendant.[32]

How is the Louisiana statute different from the former Texas statute? Although both statutes limited the definitions of capital murder, the Louisiana statute did not allow the introduction of any mitigating evidence. Once a defendant was found guilty; the punishment was death. In contrast, the Court viewed the Texas statute as accommodating the consideration of mitigating evidence, despite its structured questions.

Criminal Justice for life." The current version of the Texas statute now provides for "life imprisonment without parole" rather than "life" as the alternative to death. TEX. CRIM PROC. CODE ANN. § 37.071(2)(g) (2011).

[29] Woodson v. North Carolina, 428 U.S. 280 (1976) and Roberts v. Louisiana, 428 U.S. 325 (1976). The Court revisited mandatory statutes in Sumner v. Shuman, 483 U.S. 66 (1987). Shuman was convicted of murder of a fellow inmate while serving a sentence of life without the possibility of parole. Under the Nevada statute, a sentence of death was mandatory. The Court held that the sentence was unconstitutional because it failed to allow Shuman to present any evidence in mitigation.

[30] The Louisiana statute provided for first degree murder for 1) killing in connection with the commission of certain felonies, 2) killing of a fireman or a peace officer in the performance of his duties, 3) killing for remuneration, 4) killing with the intent to inflict harm on one or more persons, and 5) killing by a person with a prior murder conviction or under a life sentence, LA. REV. STAT. ANN. 14-30 (1974).

[31] This was the concern over jury nullification. The plurality worried that jurors, concerned about the harsh penalty that would automatically follow, might be reluctant to find a defendant guilty.

[32] *Woodson*, 428 U.S. at 293, 302, 303.

§ 6.07   VARIATIONS IN DEATH PENALTY STATUTES: GUILT-PHASE DETERMINATION OF AGGRAVATING CIRCUMSTANCES; THREE-JUDGE SENTENCING PANEL; AND BEYOND A REASONABLE DOUBT STANDARD TO IMPOSE DEATH

Although there are many variations in death penalty procedure, three stand out and are worthy of mention. These three variations are exemplified by the statutes from California, Nebraska, and Utah. First, in most states, the aggravating circumstance that is necessary to make a defendant death-eligible is determined in the penalty phase of the trial. In California, however, that determination is made in the guilt phase. Secondly, all states except Nebraska provide for a jury determination of death or life. Thirdly, most states do not specify the standard of proof for the sentencer's decision on death or life. In Utah, however, and in a few other states, the determination of death must be made beyond a reasonable doubt.

[A]   Guilt-Phase Determination of Aggravating Circumstances: California

The current California death penalty statute is different from most other death penalty statutes in two respects. First, California calls the death-eligibility factors "special circumstances" rather than aggravating circumstances.[33] The statute uses the term "aggravating circumstances" to refer to the additional evidence in aggravation that is permissible after the defendant is found to be death-eligible.[34] Secondly, and more significantly, California requires the finding of a special circumstance beyond a reasonable doubt in the *guilt* phase, rather than in the penalty phase of the capital trial. The jury in a typical case thus is tasked with deciding the defendant's guilt and death-eligibility in the guilt phase. In the penalty phase, the jury considers additional aggravating evidence, mitigating evidence, and the decision of life or death.[35] The California statute then uses a version of a weighing formula. The statute provides:

> [The trier of fact] . . . shall impose a sentence of death if the trier of fact concludes that the aggravating circumstances outweigh the mitigating circumstances. If the trier of fact determines that the mitigating circumstances outweigh the aggravating circumstances the trier of fact shall impose a sentence of confinement in state prison for a term of life without the possibility of parole.[36]

---

[33] Cal. Penal Code § 190.2 (West 2011).

[34] *Id.* at § 190.3.

[35] *Id. at* § 190.4.

[36] *Id. at* § 190.3. Interestingly, the current California jury instruction is not phrased in the mandatory language of the statute when aggravating circumstances outweigh mitigation circumstances. Instead the instruction provides: "To return a judgment of death, each of you must be persuaded that the aggravating circumstances are so substantial in comparison with the mitigating circumstances that it warrants death instead of life without parole." CALJIC 8.88.

[B]   Three-Judge Sentencing Panel: Nebraska

In all states, there is a right to a jury verdict on the aggravating circumstance(s) that makes the defendant death-eligible in light of *Ring v. Arizona.* [37] The decision in *Ring*, however, did not resolve the issue whether there is a similar right to a jury verdict on the sentencing decision. Although most states already provided for a jury verdict on the sentence, Colorado and Nebraska utilized a three-judge panel for the routine penalty phase decisions. [38] Post-*Ring*, Colorado revised its procedure to provide for a jury in the sentencing decision. [39] Nebraska, however, retained a three-judge panel for the sentencing decision. In conformity with the holding in *Ring*, Nebraska provides for a jury verdict on any aggravating circumstances. It is only after the aggravating circumstances are found that the case is turned over to a three-judge panel. [40]

The capital trial in Nebraska in fact occurs in three phases. First, there is a guilt/innocence determination. Secondly, there is a determination of aggravating circumstances. This second phase is either by the same jury as in the guilt/innocence phase or by a newly-impaneled jury if the defendant waived the jury in the guilt phase, but now wants a jury for the aggravating circumstances. [41] The third phase is the sentencing decision by a three-judge panel. The three-judge panel includes the judge who presided over the first two phases. [42] In order to impose a sentence of death, the three judges must unanimously reach that decision. In the absence of unanimity, a life sentence is imposed. [43] The judges are to consider:

(1) Whether the aggravating circumstances as determined to exist justify imposition of a sentence of death;

(2) Whether sufficient mitigating circumstances exist which approach or exceed the weight given to the aggravating circumstances; or

---

[37] Ring v. Arizona, 536 U.S. 584 (2002). *See also* Section 10.02, *supra.*

[38] Prior to *Ring*, Nevada had also provided for a 3-judge panel to sentence in several situations: 1) if a jury could not arrive at a decision; 2) if the defendant entered a plea of guilty or guilty but mentally ill; and 3) if the trial was conducted without a jury. These provisions were amended post-*Ring* to require a jury in all of those situations. For the legislative changes, *see* http://www.leg.state.nv.us/statutes/72nd/Stats200316.html#Stats200316page2082. For current statutes, see Nev. Rev. St. §§ 175.552 and 175.556 (West 2011). Ohio currently provides for a three-judge panel, but only in cases where the defendant pleads guilty. Ohio Rev. Code Ann. § 2945.06 (West 2011). Also prior to *Ring*, three states provided for single judges to sentence the defendant: Arizona, Montana, and Idaho. Arizona and Idaho now provide for jury sentencing. *See* http://www.deathpenaltyinfo.org/state-developments-post-ring. Montana provides for the trier of fact [jury unless waived] to find an aggravating circumstance, but then the court conducts the decision process. Mont. Code Ann. § 46-18-301 (West 2011).

[39] Colo. Rev. Stat. Ann. § 18-1.3-1201(2)(a) (West 2011).

[40] Neb. Rev. Stat. § 29-2521 (2011).

[41] Neb. Rev. Stat. § 29-2520(2)(b)(i) (2011).

[42] Neb. Rev. Stat. § 29-2521 (2011).

[43] Neb. Rev. Stat. § 29-2522 (2011).

(3) Whether the sentence of death is excessive or disproportionate to the penalty imposed in similar cases, considering both the crime and the defendant.[44]

[C] Beyond a Reasonable Doubt Standard to Impose Death: Utah

Most state statutes do not specify the standard of proof necessary to impose death. Utah and six other states require that the sentencer make a finding beyond a reasonable doubt in order to impose death.[45] The Utah statute, for example, states:

> The death penalty shall only be imposed if, after considering the totality of the aggravating and mitigating circumstances, the jury is persuaded beyond a reasonable doubt that total aggravation outweighs total mitigation, and is further persuaded, beyond a reasonable doubt, that the imposition of the death penalty is justified and appropriate in the circumstances.

The rationale for requiring that the sentence reach the conclusion of death beyond a reasonable doubt is grounded in the gravity of the decision. Just as a defendant is not found guilty without the factfinder's conviction of guilt beyond a reasonable doubt, the argument is that the decision of death is similarly one of great magnitude, warranting the highest standard of proof.[46]

---

[44] *Id.*

[45] *See* State v. Wood 648 P.2d 71 (Utah 1982); the other states requiring some sort of beyond a reasonable doubt finding are: Arkansas, Colorado, New Jersey, Ohio, Texas, and Washington.

[46] For a discussion of the beyond a reasonable doubt standard *see* Linda Carter, *A Beyond a Reasonable Doubt Standard in Death Penalty Proceedings: A Neglected Element of Fairness*, 52 Ohio St. L.J. 195 (1991).

Chapter 7

THE DEATH PENALTY TRIAL

§ 7.01 THE BIFURCATED TRIAL

Although capital sentencing procedures vary from state to state, every jurisdiction that authorizes capital punishment now requires two trials. The first trial decides the question of guilt or innocence and the second trial decides the question of the appropriate sentence. The second proceeding begins only after a judge or jury has found a defendant guilty of an offense that is punishable by a sentence of death.

The Supreme Court has never explicitly held that a bifurcated proceeding is constitutionally required. The only time the Court addressed the question directly was in 1971, in the case of *Crampton v. Ohio.*[1] *Crampton* challenged the constitutionality of the Ohio death penalty statute, in part, because it only allowed for a unitary procedure. A jury deliberated and delivered a single verdict on the question of both guilt or innocence as well as punishment. The Court, by a vote of 6:3, upheld the Ohio statute and declined to require a bifurcated proceeding.

The next year, when the Supreme Court invalidated death penalty statutes under the Eighth Amendment in the case of *Furman v. Georgia*[2], the keystone became guided discretion. State legislatures responded by enacting new death penalty statutes. Each newly enacted statute created a bifurcated system with a separate proceeding for the penalty determination.

When the Supreme Court reviewed several of these statutes in 1976, it acknowledged that the bifurcated procedure was one of the safeguards that helped ensure that the death penalty would not be imposed in a wholly arbitrary, capricious, or freakish manner.[3] The Court recognized that by conducting two separate trials, a jury will be better informed before making the life or death

---

[1] Crampton v. Ohio, 402 U.S. 183 (1971) (consolidated with McGautha v. California). Crampton challenged the Ohio statute under the due process clause and the Fifth Amendment. He argued that the unitary procedure violated his right against self incrimination — that his desire to speak during punishment compelled him to waive his right to remain silent on the question of guilt. The Supreme Court acknowledged that a bifurcated trial may be a superior means to conduct a capital case, but at that time declined to find that the Federal Constitution required it. *Id.* at 221. The Court held that a state might properly conclude that the compassionate purposes of jury sentencing are better served in a unitary trial. Crampton did not raise, and the Court did not address, any challenge under the Eighth Amendment.

[2] Furman v. Georgia, 408 U.S. 238 (1972). *See* Section 4.02[B], *supra.*

[3] Gregg v. Georgia, 428 U.S. 153, 188 (1976). Those who have studied the question of jury trials in capital cases suggest that a bifurcated procedure, one in which the question of sentence is not considered until the determination of guilt has been made, is the best answer. *See* Section 6.03, *supra.* In *Furman*

decision. In a unitary proceeding, a jury could hear evidence relevant to the question of penalty, but which may be highly prejudicial and therefore not properly admissible on the question of guilt. Even though acknowledging problems with unitary proceedings, the Court did not expressly hold that separate trials were constitutionally required.

Although there are two proceedings, only one jury is constitutionally required. In order to ensure that each juror could be fair if a penalty phase is held, jurors are questioned about their views toward the death penalty even before the trial on the question of guilt begins.[4] The *voir dire* of the jury panel in a capital case raises unique constitutional issues. This is discussed in Section 7.05, *infra*.

§ 7.02 THE PENALTY PHASE

The penalty, or sentencing, phase of the trial takes place only after a fact finder first determines that a defendant is guilty of an offense that is punishable by death. A penalty phase resembles the guilt phase in numerous respects. The lawyers give opening statements, call witnesses, introduce exhibits, and make closing arguments. Just like a trial on guilt or innocence, the court instructs the jurors at the conclusion of the penalty phase on how deliberations should proceed. The jury then deliberates and selects the appropriate sentence.

Since a penalty phase is like a trial on guilt or innocence, many of the same constitutional protections apply. For example, the Supreme Court held that the double jeopardy clause applies to a penalty phase and precludes a retrial of a penalty after an "acquittal" of the death sentence.[5]

Similarly, the Court held that a defendant's due process rights were violated when, during his penalty trial, the defendant was shackled with leg irons, handcuffs and a belly chain.[6] The Court expressed concern that shackles would adversely affect a jury's perception of the character of a defendant and may impair their ability to fairly decide whether life or death is the appropriate sentence in the case.[7]

---

v. Georgia, Justice Brennan noted "[s]ome legislatures have required particular procedures, two-stage trials . . . applicable only in death cases." *Furman* at 286. Chief Justice Burger, dissenting in *Furman*, noted specifically that "[t]he Eigth Amendment forbids the imposition of punishments that are so cruel and inhumane as to violate society's standards of civilized conduct . . . [but] is not concerned with the process by which a State determines that a particular punishment is to be imposed in a particular case." *See Furman*, at 397. The Court's analysis in *Gregg* more directly stated "When a human life is at stake and when the jury must have information prejudicial to the question of guilt but relevant to the question of penalty in order to impose a rational sentence, a bifurcated system is more likely to ensure elimination of the constitutional deficiencies identified in *Furman*. *Gregg*, at 192. Further, ". . . the concerns expressed in Furman that the penalty of death not be imposed in an arbitrary or capricious manner . . . are best met by a system that provides for a bifurcated proceeding . . . " *Gregg* at 195.

[4] A juror may not hold views either for or against the death penalty that prevents or substantially impairs them from considering both sentencing options. *See* Section 7.05[D], *infra*.

[5] Bullington v Missouri, 451 U.S. 430 (1981), Godfrey v Georgia, 836 F.2d 1557 (1988). Sattazhan v Pennsylvania, 537 U.S. 101 (2003), (a retrial of the penalty phase is not barred by the Double Jeopardy Clause where a life sentence was previously imposed by a court following a deadlocked jury).

[6] Deck v. Missouri, 544 U.S. 622 (2005). In a 7-2 decision the Court held that shackling a defendant during a penalty phase of his capital trial is a denial of due process.

[7] The majority of the Court acknowledged that the rationales that prohibited shackling during a guilt

[A]   Decision Making by Jury

Most death penalty statutes provide that the same jury sits as fact finder when deciding both guilt or innocence as well as the appropriate sentence of life or death.[8] Under these statutes the court must impose the ultimate sentence. Under some statutes, a judge may override a jury verdict of death to impose a sentence of life.[9] Another variation of a death penalty statute provides that in a penalty phase, a jury makes a recommendation to the judge of either life or death. The judge, under this statute, either accepts or rejects either sentence and is permitted to override even a unanimous recommendation of life sentence by a jury and impose a sentence of death.[10] This occurs with some frequency in Alabama whose statute provides that "[w]hile the jury's recommendation concerning sentence shall be given consideration, it is not binding upon the court."[11] Despite this limiting language, twenty-one percent of persons on death row in Alabama are there after a recommendation by a jury of life in prison.[12]

A handful of statutes initially provided that while a defendant had a right to a jury determination of guilt or innocence, a judge would be both the factfinder and impose sentence for the penalty phase of the trial.[13] In 2002, these statutes were held to be unconstitutional when the Supreme Court decided *Ring v Arizona*.[14] In *Ring*[15] the Supreme Court held that aggravating circumstances in a death penalty statute operate in the same way in which elements of a criminal offense operate. As a result, a defendant has a constitutional right under the Sixth Amendment to have a jury determine whether or not statutory aggravating circumstances have been

---

phase applied equally during a penalty phase. These included the need to 1) avoid prejudice, 2) permit a defendant to assist counsel and 3) to maintain the dignity of the judicial process. In his dissent, Justice Thomas (joined by Justice Scalia) argued that the underlying rationale against shackles was because of the pain they caused and the impairment to defendants who had no right to counsel. Since these rationales no longer applied, Thomas argued that the procedure no longer violated due process. *Id.* at 640.

[8]   Cal. Penal Code § 190.4(c).

[9]   "In every case in which the trier of fact has returned a verdict or finding imposing the death penalty . . . the judge shall review the evidence, consider, take into account, and be guided by the aggravating and mitigating circumstances referred to in Section 190.3, and shall make a determination as to whether the jury's findings and verdicts that the aggravating circumstances outweigh the mitigating circumstances are contrary to law or the evidence presented." Cal. Penal Code § 190.4(e). For a discussion of a case where a trial court overturned a jury's sentence of death, *see People v. Burgener*, 29 Cal. 4th 833, 129 Cal. Rptr. 2d 747 (2003).

[10]   These states included Alabama, Ala. Code § 13A-5-47(e) (1975), Delaware, Del. Code Ann. tit. 11, § 4209(d)(1) (2011) and Florida, Fla. Stat. Ann. § 921.141(3) (2010).

[11]   Ala. Code § 13A-5-47(e) (1975).

[12]   The Death Penalty in Alabama: Judge Override, Equal Justice Initiative (2011) (last accessed December 5, 2011).

[13]   *See* Ariz. Rev. Stat Ann. § 13-703 (2001); Colo. Rev. Stat. § 16–11–103 (2001) (three-judge panel); Idaho Code § 19–2515 (Supp. 2001); Mont. Code Ann. § 46–18–301 (1997); Neb. Rev. Stat. § 29–2520 (1995).

[14]   536 U.S. 584 (2002) The Supreme Court held that the defendant has a Sixth Amendment right to have a jury determine the existence or non-existence of the statutory aggravating circumstances that make a case eligible for a sentence of death.

[15]   Ring v. Arizona, 536 U.S. 584 (2002).

proved.[16] Under *Ring*, a death penalty statute, at a minimum, had to provide for a jury to find the aggravating circumstances that provide the basis for a possible sentence of death.

The question of whether or not a jury is required for all decisions in the penalty trial was left unanswered in *Ring*. The prosecution takes the position that *Ring* is limited to requiring a jury determination only for those aggravating circumstances that serve as "eligibility factors;" those factors that make a case eligible for a sentence of death.[17] Prosecutors argue that all other decisions during the penalty phase may be made by a judge. Defendants argue that the ultimate selection decision and the weighing process of aggravating circumstances against mitigating circumstances must be conducted by a jury. These arguments are discussed in Section 13.03, *infra*.

Defendants also argue that any factual decision that can be considered a prerequisite to the application of the death penalty to a case is governed by *Ring* and must be decided by a jury. For example, the Constitution requires that to be sentenced to death a defendant must be a major participant in the crime and that he act with reckless disregard for human life.[18] The Court has not yet addressed the question of whether or not a jury and not a judge must explicitly make this finding before sentencing a defendant to death.

In 2002, the Supreme Court held that it was unconstitutional to execute a defendant who is mentally retarded.[19] Statutory schemes are split on whether this determination should be made by a judge or a jury.[20] Most courts that have reviewed this issue have found that there is no constitutional right to a jury determination on whether or not a defendant is mentally retarded.[21]

---

[16] *See* Sections 9.01 and 10.01, *infra*. Ring v. Arizona, 536 U.S. 584, 606-610 (2002). This decision struck down death penalty statutes that provided for judge sentencing during penalty trials. The Court specifically did not decide whether the Sixth Amendment prohibited a judicial determination of the ultimate sentence as opposed to the statutory aggravating circumstances, nor did the Court decide whether the decision should be applied retroactively. In Schriro v. Summerlin 542 U.S. 348 (2004) (*Ring* should be applied retroactively.).

[17] *See* Section 10.02, *infra*.

[18] Tison v. Arizona, 481 U.S. 137 (1987). *See* Section 8.02[B][2], *infra*.

[19] Atkins v. Virginia, 536 U.S. 304 (2002). *See* section 8.03[6], *infra*. The Court examined the evolving standards of decency in the country, finding that the majority of states agree that mentally retarded offenders are categorically less culpable than the average criminal. Although the Court concluded that death was not a suitable punishment for the mentally retarded criminal, it left to the states the task of developing appropriate ways to enforce this prohibition.

[20] Carol S. Steiker, Jordan M. Steiker; *Atkins v. Virginia: Lessons From Substance And Procedure In the Constitutional Regulation of Capital Punishment*, 57 DePAUL L. REV. 721 (2008) ("Delaware and Virginia require a jury determination of mental retardation. DEL. CODE ANN. tit. 11, § 4209(d)(3) (2007); VA. CODE ANN. § 19.2-264.3:1.1 (2007). In contrast, Idaho and Nevada require the judge to determine mental retardation. IDAHO CODE ANN. § 19-2515A (2007); NEV. REV. STAT. ANN. § 174.098 (LexisNexis 2007). North Carolina and Oklahoma allow for determination by either a judge or a jury, but specify different burdens of proof for each. N.C. GEN. STAT. § 15A-2005; OKLA. STAT. ANN. tit. 21, § 701.10b (2007)."); John H. Blume, Sheri Lynn Johnson, Christopher Seeds; *Of Atkins And Men: Deviations From Clinical Definitions of Mental Retardation In Death Penalty Cases*, 18 CORNELL J.L. & PUB. POL'Y 689 (2009).

[21] Head v. Hill, 587 S.E.2d 613 (Ga. 2003) ("The absence of mental retardation is not the functional equivalent of an element of an offense." Rather, "mental retardation is a means by which a death penalty

§ 7.03   THE DECISION PROCESS

[A]   The Structure: Weighing v. Non- Weighing[22]

Although death penalty statutes take many forms, ultimately the sentencer must decide, on the basis of the aggravating and the mitigating evidence, whether the appropriate penalty is life or death. The exact manner in which this is done depends on whether the statute creates a *weighing*[23] or a *nonweighing*[24] procedure. The Supreme Court has found both approaches to be constitutional.[25] A weighing statute explicitly instructs a jury to balance the aggravating circumstances and evidence against all mitigating evidence presented.[26] Nonweighing statutes use the aggravating factors as a threshold requirement that makes a defendant eligible for a sentence of death. Once an aggravating factor is found to be present, it plays no further role other than to be considered, along with all the other evidence presented, to determine whether death or life is the appropriate sentence.[27]

§ 7.04   AUTOMATIC APPEAL

All the states and the federal government provide for an appeal from a capital conviction and sentence of death.[28] In most states the appeal is to the state supreme court.[29] Other states provide an appeal to the highest court that hears criminal

---

defendant may seek to have his possible sentence limited despite the fact that the statutory elements for the death penalty might be present."); U.S. v. Webster, 421 F.3d 308 (5th Cir. 2005) (nothing "in *Atkins* require, as a constitutional matter, the government to prove . . . by any standard, much less beyond a reasonable doubt-that a capital defendant is not mentally retarded."); State v. Johnson, 244 S.W.3d 144, 151 (Mo. 2010), ("Determining a defendant is mentally retarded is not a finding of fact that increases the potential range of punishment; it is a finding that removes the defendant from consideration of the death penalty.") *See* Section 8.03, *infra*.

[22] For more in depth discussion *see* Chapter 9, *infra*.

[23] Weighing states include: Alabama, Arkansas, California, Colorado, Connecticut, Delaware, Florida, Idaho, Indiana, Maryland, Mississippi, Missouri, Nebraska, Nevada, New Hampshire, New Jersey, North Carolina, Ohio, Oklahoma, Pennsylvania, South Dakota and Tennessee, Utah.

[24] Nonweighing states include Georgia and South Carolina.

[25] Gregg v. Georgia, 428 U.S. 153, 197-98 (1976) (nonweighing); Proffitt v. Florida, 428 U.S. 242, 250 (1976) (weighing).

[26] To return a judgment of death, each of you must be persuaded that the aggravating circumstances are so substantial in comparison with the mitigating circumstances that it warrants death instead of life without parole. CALIFORNIA JURY INSTRUCTION § 8.88 (2007).

[27] A Virginia statute provides: "If you find from the evidence that the Commonwealth has proved that circumstance beyond a reasonable doubt, then you may fix the punishment of the defendant at death. But if you nevertheless believe from all the evidence, including evidence in mitigation, that the death penalty is not justified, then you shall fix the punishment of the defendant at [a lesser sentence] . . . Any decision you make regarding punishment must be unanimous". VIRGINIA MODEL JURY INSTRUCTIONS — CRIMINAL, P33.125 (1998 Replacement Edition).

[28] *See, e.g.*, CAL. PENAL CODE § 1239(b) (West 2004) (Manner of taking appeal; Appeal after judgment of death: When upon any plea a judgment of death is rendered, an appeal is automatically taken by the defendant without any action by him or her or his or her counsel); People v. Stanworth, 80 Cal. Rptr. 49, 457 P.2d 889 (1969) (Defendant sentenced to death for murder could not dismiss the automatic appeal provided in such cases by section 1239(B); California Rules of Court (Rule 38), permitting an appellant

cases.[30] Although there is no constitutional right to appeal in a criminal case, presumably including capital cases, the Supreme Court has consistently recognized that appellate review is a crucial means of promoting reliability and consistency in capital sentencing. When the Court upheld death penalty statutes in 1976, each state statute provided for an automatic appellate review of every sentence of death. This was a significant factor to the Court in its determination that sentences of death would not be imposed in an arbitrary and capricious manner.[31]

Over the years, a high percentage of capital cases have been reversed on appeal. Studies of the civilian appellate system found the rate of serious error and reversal of capital sentences between 1973 and 1995 to be 68%.[32] Two years later, the same authors attributed high reversible error rates of capital sentences to a number of factors including juries that imposed the death penalty in cases lacking any "highly aggravated" facts, heavy use of a jurisdiction's capital system, and the impact of racial factors on the outcome of the case.[33] Studies of capital cases in the military court system revealed even higher reversal rates than in the civilian justice system.[34]

---

to dismiss his appeal, has no application to an automatic appeal and the right to dismiss is denied by the operation of section 1239(B), which not only invokes a right to review on behalf of the defendant but also imposes a duty upon the Supreme Court to make such review, which duty cannot be avoided or abdicated merely because a defendant desires to waive the right provided for him.).

[29] See VA. CODE ANN. § 17.1-313(A) (Michie 2003). In Virginia, the state supreme court, not the state intermediary court, reviews appeals of convictions where the defendant was sentenced to death.

[30] See TEX. CODE CRIM. PROC. ANN. art 37.071 § 2(h) (Vernon 2006). In the State of Texas, the judgment of conviction and sentence of death shall be subject to automatic review by the Court of Criminal Appeals.

[31] Gregg v. Georgia, 428 U.S. 153 (1976), Proffitt v. Florida 428 U.S. 242 (1976) (risk of arbitrary or capricious infliction of sentence of death is minimized by Florida's appellate review system, under which the evidence of the aggravating and mitigating circumstances is reviewed and reweighed by the Supreme Court of Florida to determine independently whether the imposition of the ultimately penalty is warranted), Jurek v. Texas, 428 U.S. 262 (1976) ("by providing prompt judicial review of the jury's decision in a court with statewide jurisdiction, Texas has provided a means to promote the evenhanded, rational and consistent imposition of death sentences under law.").

[32] See, e.g., James S. Liebman, Jeffrey Fagan, & Valerie West, A Broken System: Error Rates in Capital Cases, available at http://www2.law.columbia.edu/instructionalservices/liebman/ (last visited Dec. 25, 2011) (also finding that "the capital punishment system revealed by our 23-year study is not a success, and is not even minimally rational"); United States Department of Justice, Survey of the Federal Death Penalty System, available at http://www.usdoj.gov/dag/pubdoc/dpsurvey.html (last visited Dec. 25, 2011).

[33] James S. Liebman, Jeffrey Fagan, Andrew Gelman, Valerie West, Garth Davies, & Alexander Kiss; A Broken System, Part II: Why There Is So Much Error in Capital Cases, and What Can Be Done About It, available at http://www2.law.columbia.edu/brokensystem2/report.pdf (last visited Jan. 5, 2011). The study found numerous factors beside those listed above before suggesting reforms.

[34] See Chapter 25 infra. The Military Death Penalty, see also Col. Dwight K. Sullivan, USMCR; Killing Time: Two Decades Of Military Capital Litigation, 189 MIL. L. REV 1 (2006) (Finding the military courts' capital reversal rate to be 77.78% between January 1984 and December 2006.).

§ 7.05   JURY SELECTION

[A]   Overview

One jury is selected for both the guilt phase and the penalty phase of a capital case. The twelve persons selected as jurors first decide the guilt or innocence of a defendant. If the case proceeds to a penalty phase, these same jurors also make the penalty decision.[35] *Voir dire*, or the jury selection process, requires lawyers to assess a juror's attitudes and values and determine whether a juror can be fair and impartial. The specific procedures for the selection of a capital jury vary not only from state to state but also from judge to judge. There are few federal constitutional minimums that must be satisfied and parts of the process may be governed by state law. Much of the jury selection procedure, even in a capital case, is within the trial court's discretion and judges are afforded broad latitude as to the exact procedures permitted. The goal of jury selection, or *voir dire*, is to find twelve jurors who can listen to the evidence and fairly decide the case.

This chapter does not attempt to address the complex issues, approaches, tactics, or theories involved in the actual selection of a jury.[36] Nor will it address specific state laws regarding jury eligibility. This section will only address constitutional issues that arise in jury selection as they pertain to a capital trial.

Many of the procedures employed in capital jury selection are the same as in any other criminal trial. The first stage is the selection and summoning of prospective jurors.[37] The second stage includes the qualification of prospective jurors including a determination of whether any juror will suffer an undue hardship by serving on the jury.[38] The final stage involves challenges either to the entire panel or to individual jurors.[39] It is this final stage that raises the most questions and challenges.

---

[35] Ring v. Arizona, 536 U.S. 584 (2002). The Supreme Court held that the defendant has a Sixth Amendment right to have a juror determine the existence or nonexistence of the statutory aggravating circumstances that make a case eligible for a sentence of death. The Court did not decide whether a jury was required for the selection decision.

[36] National Jury Project Litigation Consulting, *Jurywork: Systematic Techniques*, Thomson Reuters Publishing (2011); James Gobert, Ellen Kreitzberg, Charles Rose III, *Jury Selection: The Law, Art and Science of Selecting a Jury*, Thomson Reuter's Publishing (2011); Robert B. Hirschorn, *Goals and Practical Tips for Voir Dire*, 26 AM. J. TRIAL ADVOC. 233 (2002); Jim Goodwin, *Articulating The Inarticulable: Relying On Nonverbal Behavioral Cues To Deception To Strike Jurors During Voir Dire*, 38 Ariz. L. Rev. 739 (1996); Barbara Allen Babcock, *Voir Dire: Preserving Its Wonderful Power*, 27 STAN. L. REV. 545 (1975).

[37] The United States Constitution permits each state to set its own requirements for jury eligibility or exemption. Potential jurors are often selected from voter registration lists, but also may be selected from other sources.

[38] A juror may be excused due to hardship. Typical hardships include: extreme financial burden; physical or mental disability that may create a risk of harm to the juror, obligation to provide necessary care to an elderly, sick, or infant relative.

[39] Duren v. Missouri, 439 U.S. 357 (1979); Castaneda v. Partida, 430 U.S. 482 (1977). Individual challenges are made when a juror indicates that he or she cannot be fair and impartial.

[B]   Challenges to the Panel

The Sixth Amendment guarantees a defendant that a jury is drawn from "the State and District wherein the crime shall have been committed.[40] The Supreme Court has interpreted this provision to require that jurors be drawn from a fair cross section of the community.[41] In *Holland v Illinois*,[42] the Court linked the fair cross section requirement to a defendant's right to an impartial jury.

A defendant in a criminal trial may challenge the composition of the jury venire by claiming that it fails to represent a fair cross section of the community. To raise such a challenge, he has to show 1) that the group alleged to be excluded is a "distinctive group in the community," 2) that the representation of this group in the venire from which the jury is selected is not fair and reasonable in relation to the number of such persons in the community and 3) that this underrepresentation is due to a systematic exclusion of the group in the jury selection process.[43]

Over the years courts have used different measures to assess whether or not underrepresentation exists.[44] In *Berghuis v. Smith* the Court declined to embrace any one particular test to measure disparities between the community and the panel from which the jury was selected. The Court, in a unanimous opinion, recognized that the dispositive issue is whether "underrepresentation existed," and, if so, was the underrepresentation "due to 'systematic exclusion'?"[45]

[C]   Challenges to Individual Jurors

Challenges to individual jurors include both challenges for cause and peremptory challenges. A challenge for cause is made against a juror if a lawyer believes that a juror cannot be fair and impartial because of a juror's attitudes, beliefs, relationship with the parties or the crime, or any past experiences of that juror. A judge decides whether or not to excuse the juror for cause after a challenge is made. Challenges for cause are unlimited in number so long as the

---

[40]   U.S. Const. Amend. VI — Jury Trials. The right to jury trial was incorporated into the due process clause of the 14th amendment and therefore binding on the states. Duncan v. State of Louisiana, 391 U.S. 145, 150, 88 S. Ct. 1444, 1448, (1968).

[41]   Taylor v Louisiana 419 U.S. 522, 530 (1975) ("we accept the fair cross section requirement as fundamental to the jury trial guarantee of the sixth amendment.")

[42]   493 U.S. 474 (1990).

[43]   Duren v. Missouri, 439 U.S. at 364.

[44]   The three measures commonly used include absolute disparity, comparative disparity and standard deviation. Absolute disparity is measured by subtracting a groups percentage in the jury pool from its percentage in the community from which it is drawn. A comparative disparity compares the mathematical ratio of a group's percentage in the jury pool with its percentage in the relevant population.

[45]   *Berghuis v. Smith*, 559 U.S. ___, 130 S. Ct. 1382, 1393 (2010). Smith is an African American who was tried before an all white jury. His venire panel included between 60-100 persons with, at most, three American members. Smith challenged the panel and claimed that African Americans were systematically excluded from the venire through the local system called "siphoning." Siphoning was a procedure where Kent county assigned prospective jurors first to local district courts and only after assigned any remaining jurors to county-wide circuit courts that heard the felony cases like Smith's, The Supreme Court held that the siphoning system did not systematically exclude minorities.

trial court finds that there has been a sufficient showing that a juror could not be fair and impartial in the particular case.

Unlike challenges for cause, a peremptory challenge allows an attorney to excuse a juror for any reason except on the basis of race, gender or national origin.[46] If challenged, a lawyer may have to state a race neutral reason for excusing that juror.[47]

Each state is free to determine the number of peremptory challenges allowed and to fix this number by statute. For example, in a federal capital trial, each side is allowed twenty peremptory challenges.[48] Under the military death penalty system, each side is given one peremptory challenge.[49] The exact procedures governing how and when peremptory challenges may be exercised varies from state to state. While aspects of the procedure may be set out in a statute, the trial court has broad discretion on how to implement the use of peremptory challenges. These procedures will only be reversed when a court finds an abuse of discretion by the trial court in its ruling.

Although the Supreme Court has repeatedly held there is no constitutional right to peremptory challenges,[50] it has suggested that the constitutional right to an impartial jury may impliedly require some peremptory challenges by counsel.[51] Justice Scalia writing for the majority in *Holland* agreed "[o]ne could plausibly argue (though we have said to the contrary) that the requirement of an 'impartial jury' impliedly *compels* peremptory challenges . . . ".[52] Scalia's suggestion invites the possibility that defense counsel's performance at trial may be evaluated, in part, on whether or not they exercise peremptory challenges to excuse jurors who may be unfair.[53]

---

[46] *See* Section 7.06, *infra*. Batson v. Kentucky, 476 U.S. 79 (1986).

[47] *See* Section 7.06, *infra*. Batson v. Kentucky, 476 U.S. 79 (1986). Swain v. Alabama, 380 U.S. 202 (1965). Swain argued that there had never been a Negro (sic) on a petit jury in either a civil or criminal case in Talledega County and that the prosecutors exercised their peremptory strikes in a way to eliminate all Negroes from serving on Petit juries. *Id*. at 223.

[48] Fed. R. Crim Pro 24(b), United States v. Johnson 495 F.3d 951 (8th Cir. 2007) (Court held no equal protection violation where defendant in a capital trial was not afforded more peremptory challenges than the government as would have been the case in a felony criminal trial).

[49] "Each accused and the trial counsel are entitled initially to one peremptory challenge of members of the court. . . . Whenever additional members are detailed to the [jury panel] . . . each accused and the trial counsel are entitled to one peremptory challenge against members not previously subject to peremptory challenge." 10 U.S.C.A. § 841 (2011). *See* Chapter 25, *infra*.

[50] Rivera v Illinois 556 U.S. 148,129 S. Ct 1446 (2009).

[51] Holland v Illinois 493 US 474 (1990).

[52] *Id* at 481-482, citations omitted. The Court's opinion, however, was based upon an early 20th century ruling declaring peremptory challenges statutory, not Constitutional, in nature. The Court held "[t]here is nothing in the Constitution of the United States which requires . . . [legislatures] to grant peremptory challenges to defendants in criminal cases . . . " Stilson v. United States, 250 U.S. 583, 586 (1919).

[53] Relying upon the Sixth Amendment right to a fair an impartial jury, some Circuit Courts of Appeal have found ineffective assistance of counsel for defense counsel's failure to exercise peremptory challenges. While courts generally allow broad deference to defense counsel's decisions during voir dire (Gardner v. Ozmint, 511 F.3d 420 (4th Cir. 2007)), under limited circumstances where the defendant can

[D] "Death Qualification" of a Capital Jury: Juror Attitudes Towards the Death Penalty

A capital trial is really two trials; one on the issue of guilt or innocence and a second on the question of punishment. This creates a more complicated dynamic during capital voir dire. Questions relating to a juror's attitudes about penalty must be explored even before the start of the guilt/innocence phase of the trial. In other words, jurors, in a capital voir dire, are asked about their willingness to impose a sentence of death on a specific defendant even before a decision is made about a defendant's guilt.

The process of determining a juror's views about the death penalty is known as *death qualification*.[54] The Supreme Court has held that because a defendant has a constitutional right to a fair and impartial jury, a judge may excuse "for cause" those jurors whose views about the death penalty make them unwilling or unable to consider both a sentence of life and a sentence of death. The test to apply in the death qualification process has shifted over the years from the test set out in *Witherspoon v. Illinois*,[55] to that set out in *Wainwright v Witt*[56] and *Uttecht v. Brown*.[57]

In *Witherspoon*, the United States Supreme Court held that the prosecutor in a capital case could challenge a juror for cause on the basis of that juror's opposition to the death penalty only where the juror makes it "unmistakably clear" that he or she "would automatically vote against the imposition of capital punishment without regard to any evidence that might be developed at the trial of the case."[58] During *voir dire* in Witherspoon's case, the prosecutor excluded nearly half of the potential jurors because they expressed some hesitation about being able to return a verdict of death. Only a handful expressed the view that they would not, under any circumstances impose a sentence of death. The Supreme Court rejected the state's approach to excluding jurors. The Court held that the mere fact a juror holds strong views in opposition to the death penalty is not, by itself, a disqualifying factor.[59] In *Lockhart v McMcCree* the Court observed: [T]hose who firmly believe that the death penalty is unjust may nevertheless serve as jurors in capital cases so long as they state clearly that they are willing to temporarily set aside their own beliefs in deference to the rule of law."[60]

---

show that a seated juror is "actually biased against him," ineffective assistance of counsel has been found. *Miller v. Webb*, 385 F.3d 666, 674 (6th Cir. 2004), Virgil v. Dretke, 446 F.3d 598 (5th Cir. 2006).

[54] *Examining Death Qualification, Further Data of the Processing Effect*, Craig Haney, LAW AND HUMAN BEHAVIOR, Vol. 8, No. 1-2 (1984) at 133; *"Modern" Death Qualification, New Data On Its Biasing Effects*, Craig Haney, Aida Hurtado, and Luis Vega, LAW AND HUMAN BEHAVIOR, Vol. 18, No. 6 (1994) at 619; *Life Under* Wainright v. Witt: *Juror Dispositions and Death Qualification*, Ronald C. Dillehay and Marla R. Sandys, LAW AND HUMAN BEHAVIOR, Vol. 20, No. 2 (1996) at 147.

[55] 391 U.S. 510 (1968).

[56] 469 U.S. 412 (1985).

[57] 551 U.S. 1 (2007).

[58] Witherspoon v. Illinois 391 U.S. 510, 522 n. 21 (1968).

[59] *Witherspoon*, Adams v. Texas 448 U.S. 38 (1980); Lockhart v. McCree 476 U.S. 162 (1986).

[60] *Lockhart, supra*, 476 U.S. at 176.

In the years following *Witherspoon*, trial courts took very different approaches when implementing the Witherspoon test. Nearly 20 years later, the Supreme Court revisited this issue in the case of *Wainwright v. Witt* where the Supreme Court rejected the test in *Witherspoon* and held that the law permits the removal for cause only those jurors whose views either for or against the death penalty are so strong that they would *prevent or substantially impair* a juror from considering both death and life as a possible sentence.[61]

If in response to a question about the jurors' views towards the death penalty, a juror states, "I would always vote for a life sentence" or "I would always vote for a sentence of death" then these jurors would be removed for cause; they are not able to follow the law. These jurors have indicated with unmistakable clarity that they will not consider both sentencing options. In each case, the juror would automatically impose a particular sentence regardless of the aggravating and mitigating evidence that might be offered.

If a juror, in response to the same question responds, "A decision to impose death would weigh heavily on my mind" or "Most defendants charged with murder should get death" then a trial court has significant discretion whether or not to remove these jurors. A court should explore further to see whether these jurors could follow the judge's instructions and consider both sentencing options.

"Death qualification" of jurors was to apply equally to those jurors whose views were automatic either for or against a sentence of death.[62] Trial and appellate courts around the country, however, often excluded only those jurors who indicated their opposition to the death penalty.

During the jury selection process, a trial court exercises significant discretion in deciding which jurors should be excluded for cause and which jurors should not. The Supreme Court in *Uttecht v. Brown* reaffirmed this deference and upheld the trial court's decision to excuse one juror for cause over a defense objection.[63] The juror had expressed reservations about the death penalty but also "indicated he would impose the death penalty where the defendant would re-violate if released."[64]

Justice Kennedy, writing for the Court, noted that a trial judge "is in a superior position to determine the demeanor and qualifications of a potential juror."[65] Kennedy cited four basic principles that govern the Court's review of the death

---

[61] Wainwright v. Witt, 469 U.S. 412 (1985). In *Witt*, the Court death-qualified jurors using the same standard to qualify jurors in any criminal case. A juror is essentially asked whether he or she is able to follow the Court's instructions and to obey their oath as jurors with respect to the consideration of a sentence of life or death. *Witt* rejected an earlier test set out in Witherspoon v. Illinois, 391 U.S. 510 (1968), where, to be excused for cause, a juror had to state that opposition to imposing death was *automatic*.

[62] Wainwright v. Witt, 469 U.S. 412 (1985).

[63] Uttecht v. Brown, 551 U.S. 1, 127 S. Ct. 2218 (2007) (held the Ninth Circuit exercised insufficient deference to the trial court's determination that a potential juror was unfit to carry out the duties of a juror in a capital case).

[64] State v. Brown, 132 Wash.2d 529 (1997).

[65] 551 U.S. at 17. Justice Stevens highlighted his disagreement with the Court's decision by reading a portion of his dissent from the bench. In another unusual step, Stevens identified Judge Kozinski by

qualification of jurors: "First, a criminal defendant has a right to an impartial jury drawn from a venire that has not been tilted in favor of a capital punishment by selective prosecutorial challenges for cause. Second, the state has a strong interest in having jurors who are able to apply capital punishment within the framework state law prescribes. Third, to balance these interests, a juror who is substantially impaired in his or her ability to impose the death penalty can be excused for cause; but if the juror is not substantially impaired, removal for cause is impermissible. Fourth, in determining whether the removal of a potential juror would vindicate the State's interest without violating the defendant's right, the trial court makes a judgment based, in part on the demeanor of the juror, a judgment owed deference by reviewing courts".[66]

Capital defendants have challenged the constitutionality of the death qualification process during *voir dire* arguing that it violates a defendant's Sixth and Fourteenth Amendment rights. Unlike jury selection in a non-death homicide, "death qualification" removes all jurors from the jury pool who have strong views against the death penalty. The defense argues that this exclusion produces a jury more likely to return a verdict of guilt during the initial trial and more inclined to return a verdict of death at the sentencing trial.[67]

[E] "Reverse" Witherspoon: Jurors who are "Mitigation Impaired"

In *Morgan v. Illinois*,[68] the Court held that jurors should be excused for cause if they would automatically impose a sentence of death once a defendant is found guilty of capital murder. A juror must indicate during *voir dire* that he or she is able and willing to consider the mitigating evidence that the defense intends to present during the penalty phase of the trial.[69] The Court reasoned that a defendant has a constitutional right to an individualized consideration of whether he should be sentenced to life or death. If a juror cannot follow the law when told

---

name as the Ninth circuit Court of Appeal judge who was reversed. Since Kozinski is recognized as one of the more conservative judges on the court, Stevens may have wanted to underscore the reasonableness of the Ninth Circuit reversal of the trial court. Writing for four dissenters, Justice Stevens stated that the majority erased the distinction set out in *Witt* between mere opposition to the death penalty (where a juror is entitled to sit) with an inability to perform the legally required duties of a juror (where a juror should be excused).

[66] *Id.* at 9 (citations omitted). The Court also observed that the requirements of the Antiterrorism and Effective Death Penalty Act of 1996 (AEDPA) provide additional limitations on the ability of a federal court to review a state court ruling.

[67] Craig Haney, *Violence and the Capital Jury: Mechanism and Moral Disengagement and the Impulse to Condemn to Death*, 49 STAN. L. REV. 1447, 1483 (1997) (concludes that when jurors are repeatedly asked whether they can follow the law and impose the death penalty they begin to believe that the law requires them to reach a death verdict) William S. Bowers, *The Capital Jury Project: Rational Design and Preview of Early Findings*, 70 IND. L.J. 1043, 1091 n.32 (1995).

[68] Morgan v. Illinois, 504 U.S. 719 (1992).

[69] Mitigating evidence is information that would tend to lessen the gravity of the criminal act in favor of a life sentence. It usually relates to the defendant's background, character, and the circumstances of the offense. For more information, *see* Section 12.01, *infra*.

to consider this evidence, that juror must be excused for cause.[70] The Court held that the inclusion of even one such juror denies a defendant the right to an impartial jury.

[F] Improper Inclusion or Exclusion of Jurors Challenged for Cause

When a trial judge decides during voir dire which jurors are qualified for a particular case, two possible errors can occur. A judge might improperly *exclude* a juror who is constitutionally qualified to sit on the case, or a judge might improperly *include* a juror who should have been excused for cause. The Supreme Court treats these two errors quite differently.

In *Gray v. Mississippi*,[71] the Court held that the erroneous *exclusion* of even a single juror requires an automatic reversal.[72] The constitutional violation occurred, the Court reasoned, the moment the trial judge impermissibly narrowed the pool of jurors eligible by excusing one qualified juror. The Court has held that a defendant's right to an impartial jury is a "basic fair trial right, [an error which] can never be treated as harmless . . . ."[73]

Despite this seeming unambiguous language in *Gray*, twenty years later in *Uttecht v. Brown* the Court severely limits the ruling in *Gray*.[74] In *Uttecht*, the Supreme Court granted the trial court broad discretion when excusing a juror for cause and then differed to that discretion. The result is that a trial court's exclusion of a juror for cause will only rarely be deemed improper on appeal.

The Supreme Court applied a different rule where the trial judge erroneously *included*, or failed to exclude for cause, a juror who indicated he would automatically vote for death. In *Ross v. Oklahoma*[75] the Court found no constitutional violation and upheld the defendant's sentence of death.[76] The Court reasoned that when a juror is improperly included, a defendant should use a peremptory challenge to correct this mistake. More importantly, the Court observed, none of the twelve jurors who ultimately decided Ross' case were alleged to have been unfair or partial.

---

[70] The Court referred to these jurors as *mitigation impaired*. "Any juror to whom mitigating factors are likewise irrelevant should be disqualified for cause, for that juror has formed an opinion concerning the merits of the case without basis in the evidence developed at trial." *Morgan*, 504 U.S. at 739. *See also* U.S. v. Fulks, 454 F.3d 410 (4th Cir. 2006); Mackall v. Angelone, 131 F.3d 442, 450 (4th Cir. 1997).

[71] Gray v. Mississippi, 481 U.S. 648 (1987).

[72] *Id.*

[73] *Gomez v. U.S.*, 490 U.S. 858, 876 (1989).

[74] Uttecht v. Brown 551 U.S. 1 (2007) The Court narrowed the applicability of *Gray* in *Uttecht* by stating "*Gray* represents a rare case, however, because in the typical situation there will be a state-court finding of substantial impairment; in *Gray*, the state courts had found the opposite, which makes that precedent of limited significance to the instant case." *Id.* at 9.

[75] Ross v. Oklahoma, 487 U.S. 81 (1988).

[76] The Court explicitly mentioned and refused to apply the rule in *Gray*. "We decline to extend the rule of *Gray* beyond its context: the erroneous '*Witherspoon* exclusion' of a qualified juror in a capital case. We think the broad language used by the *Gray* Court is too sweeping to be applied literally, and is best understood in the context of the facts there involved." *Ross*, 487 U.S. at 87-88.

The Court expanded on this reasoning in *U.S. v. Martinez-Salazar*.[77] When a defendant has a peremptory challenge and is able to remove a juror who should have been excused for cause, a defendant's Sixth Amendment interest is still protected since the objectionable juror does not sit as a juror in the case.

§ 7.06   PEREMPTORY CHALLENGES: DISCRIMINATORY USE

Unlike challenges for cause, there are a limited number of peremptory challenges for each side. The attorneys do not need to state their reasons for exercising a peremptory challenge. Peremptory challenges have long been the subject of controversy and debate.[78] In both noncapital and capital cases, the Supreme Court recognized the danger that peremptory challenges could be used as a pretext for racial discrimination. The Court began, in a series of cases, to regulate and limit their use. A discriminatory use of peremptory challenges has even greater significance in capital cases where jurors are asked to make decisions on both guilt and penalty.

To prove discriminatory use of a peremptory challenge, the Court initially required a defendant to prove systematic exclusion of certain groups from juries in all cases within that jurisdiction.[79] The Court essentially required a defendant prove that through the exercise of peremptory challenges, "the State in case after case, 'whatever the circumstances, whatever the crime and whoever the defendant or the victim may be, is responsible for the removal of Negroes . . . with the result that no Negroes ever serve on petit juries."[80] This task proved daunting at best and, as one court called it a "mission impossible" at worst.[81] There were rarely records documenting the racial composition of juries in court files or clerk offices that allowed a defendant to present the evidence required by the court.[82] This test survived over twenty years. The Court finally modified the test in *Batson v. Kentucky*.[83]

---

[77] 528 U.S. 304 (2000).

[78] For more in-depth discussion on the issue of race, ethnicity and peremptory challenges *see* Sheri Lynn Johnson, *Batson Ethics for Prosecutors and Trial Court Judges*, 73 CHI.-KENT. L. REV. 475 (1998). Charles J. Ogletree, *Just Say No! A Proposal to Eliminate Racially Discriminatory Uses of Peremptory Challenges*, 31 AM. CRIM. L. REV. 1099 (1993-1994). Judge Mark W. Bennet, *Unraveling the Gordian Knot of Implicit Bias in Jury Selection: The Problems of Judge-Dominated Voir Dire, the Failed Promise of Batson, and Proposed Solutions*, 4 HARV. L. & POL'Y REV. 149 (2010).

[79] Swain v. Alabama, 380 U.S. 202 (1965).

[80] Charles J. Ogletree, *Just Say No!: A Proposal To Eliminate Racially Discriminatory Uses of Peremptory Challenges*, 31 AM. CRIM. L. REV. 1099, 1101 (1994).

[81] Id., quoting McCray v. Abrams, 750 F.2d 1113, 1120 (2d Cir. 1984).

[82] Id., at 1102. As Professor Ogletree notes, between the rulings in *Swain* and *Batson*, only two appeals under *Swain* succeeded, both as a result of the same East Baton Rouge prosecutor admitting he always struck all blacks from juries. By comparison, seventy-five defendants failed to meet the *Swain* standard.

[83] Batson v. Kentucky, 476 U.S. 79 (1986). The Court in *Batson* found that the Equal Protection Clause of the Constitution protects two distinct rights: 1) a defendant's constitutional right to ensure that a prosecutor will not exclude jurors solely on the basis of race and 2) a jurors equal protection right not

In *Batson*, a defendant was permitted to challenge the use of a prosecutor's peremptory strikes by showing that they were being used against a particular race, ethnicity, or gender within that one trial. The Court constructed a three-part test to prove a constitutional violation. First, defense counsel must object to the use of a peremptory strike and make out a *prima facie* case of discrimination. This requires no more than an inference of discrimination and may be based on a prosecutor's pattern of strikes, his use of suspicious questions, his statements, or any other evidence that gives rise to an inference of discrimination on the basis of race, ethnicity or gender.

Second, if a court finds a *prima facie* case of discrimination, a prosecutor must offer a race neutral reason for the strike. Courts have set the bar low to meet this test with some courts accepting any prosecutor's stated reason as acceptable.[84]

Finally, in Step 3 the Court must determine whether or not the prosecutor acted with purposeful discrimination. In so doing, a Court may review all relevant circumstances and information including the other strikes made, the reasons stated for the strike, the demeanor of the prosecutor when he states his "race-neutral reason and any other information the court finds helpful. This determination by the trial court is upheld unless it is shown to be "clearly erroneous."[85]

In the years following the *Batson* decision, the Supreme Court added additional restrictions to the manner in which peremptory challenges could be exercised. The Court held that the defense was also prohibited from exercising peremptory challenges in a discriminatory manner,[86] that a defendant did not have to be the same race as the jurors who were excused in order to assert a challenge,[87] and finally that *Batson* included gender-based use of peremptory challenges as well as race-based use.[88]

Despite the Court's extension of *Batson* over the years, lower courts were inconsistent in their application of these standards. Hundreds of cases each year were litigated in lower courts challenging the use of peremptory challenges, by prosecutors and by defense counsel. While the Supreme Court adheres to the

---

to be excluded from jury service on the basis of race A violation under *Batson* could be based solely on a prosecutor's actions during a single trial rather than having to show a pattern of discrimination.

[84] 514 U.S. 765, 768 (1995) (accepting the prosecutors stated reason that a juror was excused because of the juror's hairstyle and facial hair. The Court stated the reason "need not be plausible let alone persuasive."

[85] Hernandez v. New York, 500 U.S. 352, 379 (1991). In Johnson v. California, 545 U.S. 162 (2005), the Supreme Court rejected California's test that required a defendant to show that the peremptory challenge was "more likely than not" a product of purposeful discrimination in order to satisfy the first prong of the Batson test. Justice Stevens, writing for eight members of the court, held that the California test was unduly onerous, and clarified that in order to establish a "prima facie case" of discriminatory use, Batson requires only that the facts provide an "inference" of discrimination. At this point the burden shifts to the side exercising the peremptory challenges to provide a race neutral reason for striking that juror. *Id.* at 168-169.

[86] Georgia v. McCollum, 505 U.S. 42 (1992).

[87] Powers v. Ohio, 499 U.S. 400 (1991). The Supreme Court held that a white criminal defendant could challenge the use of a prosecutor's peremptory challenges against a black juror.

[88] J.E.B. v. Alabama *ex rel.* T.B., 511 U.S. 127 (1994). (Violation in paternity and child support action because the state used nine of its ten peremptory challenges to remove male jurors).

principle that a discriminatory use of a peremptory challenge is unconstitutional, the ability of the courts to enforce the Batson principle in any consistent manner has proved more challenging.

The cases that have occupied much of the courts' time and energy over the years following *Batson* are those where peremptory challenges appear to have been based on race but where counsel offers a race-neutral explanation for the challenge.[89] Judges are reluctant to question the good faith and sincerity of the lawyer who offers a race-neutral explanation for a peremptory challenge of a minority juror, even though *Batson* seems to invite disingenuousness on the part of attorneys. It is the task of the trial court to determine whether the proffered explanation is a proxy for race or whether it in fact provides a race-neutral basis for excusing the jurors. At some level that will require evaluation of the challenging party's motives.

Lawyers have attempted to explain their peremptory challenges with a seemingly endless and often ingenious catalogue of reasons. Courts have found race-neutral reasons when counsel cited a juror's demeanor,[90] body language,[91] occupation,[92] the neighborhood in which the juror lives,[93] and the juror's religious practices.[94] Courts have upheld peremptory challenges as race-neutral based on the fact that the juror had defaulted on her federal student loan,[95] appeared unable to understand the legal principles involved or to understand the burden of proof.[96] In capital cases, prosecutors frequently cite a juror's views toward the death penalty as a race-neutral reason.

Whether a challenge is exercised on a discriminatory basis is determined in the first instance by the trial judge. Because the trial judge was present during *voir dire* and had the opportunity to observe the juror, considerable deference will be

---

[89] Michael J. Raphael & Edward J. Ungvarsky, *Excuses, Excuses: Neutral Explanations under Batson v. Kentucky*, 27 U. MICH. J. L. REF. 229 (1993) (examines problems with race-neutral explanations).

[90] U.S. v. Marrowbone, 211 F.3d 452, 456, 54 Fed. R. Evid. Serv. 541 (8th Cir. 2000) (inattentiveness); U.S. v. Cordoba-Mosquera, 212 F.3d 1194 (11th Cir. 2000); U.S. v. Chen, 131 F.3d 375, 379 (4th Cir. 1997) (upholding as race-neutral the peremptory challenge of black juror based on the juror's demeanor).

[91] U.S. v. James, 113 F.3d 721, 729 (7th Cir. 1997) (body language provided race-neutral explanation for peremptory challenge of black juror); U.S. v. Perkins, 105 F.3d 976, 978 (5th Cir. 1997) (prosecution's explanation that black juror shook his head and had disgusted look on his face was race-neutral); Washington v. Johnson, 90 F.3d 945 (5th Cir. 1996) (black juror's obstinate manner held race-neutral basis for peremptory challenge); Note, *Articulating the Inarticulable: Relying on Nonverbal Behavioral Cues to Strike Jurors during Voir Dire*, 38 Ariz. L. Rev. 739 (1996).

[92] U.S. v. Brown, 289 F.3d 989 (7th Cir. 2002) (teacher); U.S. v. Montgomery, 210 F.3d 446 (5th Cir. 2000) (social worker).

[93] U.S. v. Bishop, 959 F.2d 820 (9th Cir. 1992) (strike for living in low-income neighborhood was not race-neutral).

[94] U.S. v. Brown, 352 F.3d 654 (2d Cir. 2003) (race-neutral where based on religious activism although did not strike two white jurors who were churchgoers); U.S. v. DeJesus, 347 F.3d 500 (3d Cir. 2003).

[95] U.S. v. Roebke, 333 F.3d 911 (8th Cir. 2003).

[96] Splunge v. Clark, 960 F.2d 705 (7th Cir. 1992), superseded by statute on other grounds, as stated in Wheeler v. State, 749 N.E.2d 1111, 1114 n.1 (Ind. 2001) (questions were race-related and the justification was the juror's lack of understanding of the burden of proof).

given to a trial court's determination.[97]

Sometimes a prosecutor offers several reasons for a peremptory challenge, some of which may suggest (or admit) that the juror's race was a factor in the challenge but other factors which are ostensibly race-neutral were also involved. The question in these "dual motivation" cases is whether the non-racial reason is sufficient to allow the peremptory challenge to stand.

Over the years the Court's commitment to *Batson* seems to constantly shift. In the 1990's, the Supreme Court seemed to retreat from the strong pronouncements of *Batson* and accepted the prosecutor's "race-neutral" reasons at face value without seeming to question or analyze their reasons.[98] This was followed by the Court's strong affirmance of *Batson* in a Texas case that went up to the Supreme Court twice in as many years.[99] In *Miller-El v. Cockrell* the Court twice underscored the need for courts to exercise rigorous scrutiny of a prosecutor's explanations of their use of peremptory challenges and twice detailed the extensive evidence of discrimination.[100] The Court detailed the evidence of discrimination including the fact that all but one black venire person was struck,[101] the practice of "shuffling" the jury panel that shifts minority jurors who are coming to the top of the list back into the general pool,[102] as well as evidence that the Dallas County District Attorney's Office had a longstanding practice and policy of excluding black citizens from sitting as jurors in criminal cases.[103] The Court also conducted side-by-side comparisons and similarities between the black venire persons who were struck with the white jurors who were not and was unable to draw any rational distinctions between the two groups.[104]

---

[97] Purkett v. Elem, 514 U.S. 765 (1995) "the ultimate burden of persuasion . . . rests with, and never shifts from, the opponent of the strike."

[98] Herdandez v. New York, 500 U.S. 352 (1991) the Court upheld a prosecutor's strike of two Hispanic jurors and found race-neutral the prosecutor's concern that the jurors would accept the interpreters translation of the testimony. In Purkett v. Elem 514 U.S. 765 (1995) the Court allowed a prosecutor to strike two black jurors based upon their hair style and facial hair.

[99] Miller-El v. Cockrell, 537 U.S. 322 (2003). (The Court held that Miller-el was entitled to a hearing to present evidence of discrimination) Miller-El v. Dretke, 545 U.S. 231 (2005). In a 6-3 opinion, the Court ruled that Miller-El was entitled to a new trial in light of strong evidence of racial bias during jury selection at his first trial.

[100] The evidence of alleged racial discrimination included both a pattern and practice of discrimination in the Dallas County District Attorney's Office as well as the conduct of the individual prosecutor. The prosecutor removed all but one of the eleven African American jurors on Miller-El's panel.

[101] Justice Souter noted the "numbers describing the prosecutor's use of peremptories are remarkable. Out of 20 black members of the 108 person venire panel for Miller-El's trial, only 1 served . . . 'Happenstance is unlikely to produce this disparity.'" *Id.* at 240-241.

[102] *Id.* at 253. The Court describes a Texas practice during *voir dire* called the jury shuffle where "either side may literally reshuffle the cards bearing panel members names, thus rearranging the order in which members of a venire panel are seated and reached for questioning. . . . [T]he panel members seated at the back are likely to escape *voir dire* altogether."

[103] Justice Alito noted that despite the deference due a trial judge, "in Snyder's case, nothing in the record showed "that the trial judge actually made a determination concerning [the dismissed juror's] demeanor." Rather, "the trial judge simply allowed the challenge without explanation."

[104] *Id.* at 244-245. Justice Souter explained that the prosecutor mischaracterized one black jury member's answer to questions. The prosecutor exercised a peremptory challenge and struck the black

The intensive factual inquiry initiated by the Court in *Miller-El* reinvigorated *Batson*. Three years later the Court in *Snyder v. Louisiana*[105] reversed both Snyder's conviction and his sentence of death, holding that even a single race based violation was sufficient grounds for reversal. *Snyder* alleged a *Batson* violation after the prosecution dismissed all five of the remaining black jurors from a panel of thirty-six jurors.[106] The Court, as in *Miller-el*, conducted a side-by-side analysis of the struck juror with white jurors who were not struck, and found the prosecution's "race-neutral" arguments "implausible" and therefore pretextual. In *Snyder*, the prosecutor used a "backstrike" to remove the challenged juror, a procedure that allows an attorney to initially accept and seat a juror, only later to exercise a peremptory strike against that seated juror.[107]

Following *Snyder*, Courts of Appeal responded differently as to the degree of fact-finding required by a trial court. The Seventh Circuit took an expansive view and held that *Snyder* requires trial courts to provide more formal findings of the legitimacy of the peremptory challenge.[108] The Eighth Circuit expressed a more restrictive view of the need for findings.[109]

Scholars and advocates on both sides continue to criticize the use of peremptory challenges.[110] Some argue that *Snyder* failed to address the deep-seated racism that was clearly still present throughout the trial and continue to question whether or not peremptory strikes can be utilized without the risk of racial overtones.[111]

---

jury member alleging that the juror would only give death if he determined that the defendant could not be rehabilitated. Yet the prosecutor did not excuse a White and Latino juror who also answered they would consider rehabilitation as a factor in deciding whether to sentence a defendant to death.

[105] Snyder v. Louisiana, 552 U.S. 472 (2008).

[106] The Court did not rule as to the second juror after finding the first violation to be sufficient to support overturning the conviction.

[107] At least one Justice on the Louisiana Supreme Court found the backstrike of the juror suspicious State v. Snyder, 750 So. 2d 832 (1999) (Johnson J. dissent at 865).

[108] United States v. McMath, 559 F.3d 657, 666 (7th Cir. 2009). This reading of *Snyder* was echoed in the Second Circuit, which held that "[b]ecause the trial court failed to assess the credibility of the prosecution's explanation . . . it follows that there was no adjudication of [the defendant's] Batson claim on the merits. Dolphy v. Mantello, 552 F.3d 236 (2d Cir. 2009).

[109] Smulls v. Roper 535 F.3d 853 (2008). In *Smulls*, the court accepted, without formal findings, the prosecutor explanation that he struck an African-American woman because of the "glare on [the juror's] face, an aversion of her eyes and an irritated answer to one of his questions.

[110] A secondary issue not discussed here but worth note is the Circuit split over the appropriate remedy for a violation of *Batson*. As commentators have noted, the circuits are split between ordering a new trial, remanding for hearings to determine the credibility of prosecution arguments, and the narrow opinion of the Eighth Circuit — which effectively defeats any hope for post-conviction relief based upon a *Batson* violation absent explicit findings by the trial court. *See The Proper Remedy For a Lack of Batson Findings: The Fall-Out From Snyder v. Louisiana*, William H. Burgess and Douglass G. Smith, 101 J. Crim. L. & Criminology 1 (Winter 2011).

[111] *Batson, O.J., And Snyder: Lessons From An Intersecting Trilogy*, Camille A. Nelson 93 Iowa Law Rev. 1687 (July 2008), discussing the racial overtones resulting from the prosecutor in *Snyder*'s repeated references to the then recently decided O.J. Simpson trial, and the Supreme Court's Failure to address the issue in its opinion. *See also Batson Challenges in Criminal Cases: After Snyder v. Louisiana, Is Substantial Deference To the Trial Judge Still Required?*, Bobby Marzine Harges, 19 B.U. Pub. Int. L.J. 193, 215 (Spring 2010). *Report of the Council to the Membership of the American Law Institute On the*

While these — and other questions persist, the Supreme Court looked at this issue against just two years later in *Thaler v. Haynes*.[112]

The Supreme Court, in a *per curiam* opinion in *Thaler*, appeared to step back from *Snyder* and limit the need for factual findings by a trial court. Recognizing that *Snyder* directed courts hearing *Batson* claims to "take into account, among other things, any observations of the juror that the judge was able to make during the *voir dire*," the Court noted that neither *Batson* nor *Snyder* required "that a[n] . . . explanation [by a prosecutor] must be rejected if the judge did not observe or cannot recall the juror's demeanor."[113] In *Thaler*, one judge presided over the *voir dire* of the jurors while a second judge presided over the exercise of the peremptory strikes. When the defense objected to the strike of an African American juror, the prosecutor provided a reason based on the demeanor of the juror during *voir dire*. The judge presiding over the peremptory strikes found the reason to be race neutral but could make no independent findings about the juror since he had not observed the juror during *voir dire*. In reversing the Fifth Circuit grant of relief, the Supreme Court rejected a categorical rule and held that nothing requires "that a demeanor-based explanation must be rejected if the judge did not observe or cannot recall the juror's demeanor."[114]

Recent cases confirm that the controversy surrounding the use of peremptory challenges continues. Justice Marshall wrote separately in *Batson* to warn that the restrictions the Court proposed in that case would do little to end the racial discrimination that peremptory challenges inject into the jury selection process. Advocating the complete elimination of peremptory challenges, Justice Marshall wrote:

> Any prosecutor can easily assert facially neutral reasons for striking a juror, and trial courts are ill equipped to second guess those reasons. How is the court to treat a prosecutor's statement that he struck a juror because the juror had a son about the same age as the defendant, or seemed uncommunicative, or never cracked a smile and therefore did not possess the sensitivities necessary to realistically look at the issues and decide the facts in this case. If such easily generated explanations are sufficient to discharge the prosecutor's obligation to justify his strikes on nonracial grounds, then the protection erected by the Court today [in *Batson*] may be illusory.[115]

Many scholars argue that the years since *Batson* have proved Justice Marshall correct; that the purported protections provided in *Batson* were no more than illusory.[116] Lower courts frequently accept prosecutors' race neutral reasons

Matter of the Death Penalty, Carol S. Steiker and Jordan M. Steiker, AMERICAN LAW INSTITUTE, Annex B (April 2009).

[112] 559 U.S. ___, 130 S. Ct. 1171 (2010).

[113] *Id.* at 1175.

[114] *Kansas Law Review Criminal Procedure Survey*, 59 U. KAN. L. REV. 1187, 1275 (2011).

[115] *Batson*, 476 U.S. at 106 (citations omitted).

[116] *See* Sheri Lynn Johnson, *Batson Ethics for Prosecutors and Trial Court Judges*, 73 CHI.-KENT. L. REV. 475 (1998); Charles J Ogletree, *Just Say No! A Proposal to Eliminate Racially Discriminatory*

without challenge.

In 2005, Justice Breyer wrote a concurring opinion in the *Miller-El II* case, where he endorsed Justice Marshall's prediction of twenty years earlier that the only solution to race based use of peremptory challenges is to eliminate peremptory challenges completely. Breyer observed that despite extensive and compelling evidence of discrimination, the state's use of its peremptory challenges has been litigated for seventeen years and reviewed by twenty-three judges of whom only six found a *Batson* violation was present.[117]

Uses of Peremptory Challenges, 31 Am. Crim. L. Rev 1099 (1993-1994).

[117] Miller-El v. Dretke, 545 U.S. 231, 267 (2005) (Breyer, J., concurring).

Chapter 8

CATEGORICAL BARS TO THE DEATH PENALTY

§ 8.01 OVERVIEW OF CATEGORICAL BARS TO THE DEATH PENALTY

[A] Categories of Defendants or Crimes

In 1976, in *Gregg v. Georgia*[1] and its companion cases, the Supreme Court upheld the death penalty statutes of Georgia, Florida, and Texas, ruling that the Eighth Amendment does not impose a per se ban on capital punishment. Although *Gregg* held that the death penalty was not an inherently disproportionate penalty for murder, the Court did not address whether the death penalty was unconstitutional when applied to certain marginal categories of offenders or crimes. The Court subsequently addressed a variety of these kinds of claims. The most important decisions involved the imposition of the death penalty for 1) non-killer accomplices to a felony-murder,[2] 2) mentally retarded offenders,[3] 3) juvenile offenders,[4] and 4) crimes that do not involve the taking of a human life.[5] In the future, the Court may also take up the question whether the death penalty is disproportional for certain defendants who were severely mentally ill at the time of their crimes.[6]

Until recently,[7] the Court had been reluctant to exclude significant categories of crimes or defendants from consideration for the death penalty. The sections below

---

[1] 428 U.S. 153 (1976).

[2] *See, e.g.*, Enmund v. Florida, 458 U.S. 782 (1982); Tison v. Arizona, 481 U.S. 137 (1987). *See* Section 8.02, *infra*.

[3] *See, e.g.*, Penry v. Lynaugh, 492 U.S. 302 (1989); Atkins v. Virginia, 536 U.S. 304 (2002). *See* Section 8.03, *infra*.

[4] *See* Thompson v. Oklahoma, 487 U.S. 815 (1988); Stanford v. Kentucky, 492 U.S. 361 (1989); Roper v. Simmons, 543 U.S. 551 (2005). *See* Section 8.04, *infra*.

[5] *See* Coker v. Georgia, 433 U.S. 584 (1977); Kennedy v. Louisiana, *554 U.S. 407 (2008)*. *See generally* Section 8.05, *infra*.

[6] *See* Pamela A. Wilkins, *Rethinking Categorical Prohibitions on Capital Punishment: How the Current Test Fails Mentally Ill Offenders and What To Do About It*, 40 Mem. L. Rev. 423 (2009); Lyn Entzeroth, *The Challenge and Dilemma of Charting a Course to Constitutionally Protect the Severely Mentally Ill Capital Defendant From the Death Penalty*, 44 Akron L. Rev. 529 (2009).

[7] *See* Coker v. Georgia, 433 U.S. 584 (1977) (holding the death penalty inapplicable to the crime of rape involving an adult victim); Enmund v. Florida, 458 U.S. 782 (1982) (sparing from the death penalty certain accomplices to felony murder); Atkins v. Virginia, 536 U.S. 304 (2002) (excluding those who are mentally retarded from the death penalty); Roper v. Simmons, 543 U.S. 551 (2005) (excluding those who are juveniles at the time of the offenses from the death penalty); Kennedy v. Louisiana, 554 U.S. 407

detail the Supreme Court's response to these challenges.[8]

[B]   Challenges to the Proportionality of the Death Penalty for Categories of Defendants and Crimes

Most challenges to the death penalty have been based on arguments that a sentence of death is "excessive" or "disproportionate" (and therefore unconstitutional under the Eighth Amendment) when applied to a limited category of offenders.[9] In evaluating these claims, a majority of the Supreme Court applies a two prong test:[10] (1) whether capital punishment for the relevant group collides with the societal view of evolving standards of decency, and (2) whether capital punishment for the group would fail to fulfill "the two distinct social purposes served by the death penalty: retribution and deterrence of capital crimes."[11] Capital punishment is unconstitutional when applied to a particular group if it fails either test. In assessing proportionality, the Court also examines the culpability of the class of offenders in the relevant group as a whole rather than the particular offender before the Court.[12]

The Justices have disagreed about how to apply the first prong of the analysis focusing on evolving standards of decency. This inquiry asks whether a national consensus exists about the use of the death penalty against certain groups of offenders. Societal views may change over time, and the Justices are charged with determining whether a particular application of the death penalty comports with current views under the evolving standards of decency. The Justices have disagreed about the evidence they should consider in making this determination.

There is unanimity on the Court that objective evidence is the most reliable evidence of contemporary views and agreement, as well, on the need to examine recent jury verdicts and state legislative activity. The Court engages in a "counting" procedure to determine the number of death verdicts imposed under

---

(2008) (holding the death penalty unconstitutional for the rape of a child where the crime did not result, and was not intended to result, in the death of the victim).

Although not based on the same theory of excessiveness, the Court also has protected from execution those inmates who have been legitimately sentenced to death but who are insane when the state proposes to execute them. *See* Ford v. Wainwright, 477 U.S. 399 (1986); Panetti v. Quarterman, 551 U.S. 930 (2007). For more on the prohibition against executing the currently insane, *see* § 19.01, *infra*.

[8] For more discussion of these issues, *see* Corinna Barrett Lain, *Deciding Death*, 57 DUKE L. J. J. 1 (2007); Scott W. Howe, *The Failed Case for Eighth Amendment Regulation of the Capital Sentencing Trial*, 146 U. PA. L. REV. 795 (1998).

[9] The Court now uses the terms "excessive" and "disproportionate" interchangeably. Challenges under the Eighth Amendment can also argue that the punishment is inherently barbaric or unacceptable. *See* §§ 4.03-4.04, *supra*.

[10] Chief Justice Rehnquist, and Justices Scalia and Thomas would limit the proportionality examination to objective factors only. Justice Scalia appears to reject proportionality as an aspect of Eighth Amendment protection even in capital cases. *See* Atkins v. Virginia, 536 U.S. 304, 352-53 (2002).

[11] *See* Kennedy v. Louisiana, 554 U.S. 407, 441 (2008). The Court in *Gregg* had recognized incapacitation as a legitimate purpose served by the death penalty. *See* 428 U.S. 153, 183 n.28 (1976) (Stewart, J., concurring) (quoting *Furman v. Georgia*, 408 U.S. 238, 451 (1972)). However, more recent decisions concerning proportionality, such as *Kennedy v. Louisiana*, do not follow that view.

[12] *See, e.g.*, Roper v. Simmons, 543 U.S. 551 (2005); Atkins v. Virginia, 536 U.S. 304 (2002).

specific circumstances and the number of state and federal jurisdictions that authorize death under those same circumstances.

The counting of death verdicts has raised little controversy. For example, in 1988, when the Court addressed whether it was constitutional to execute a fifteen-year old offender, the Court noted that, for the previous five years, only five persons (including the defendant before it), who were under 16 years old at the time of their crime, were sentenced to death.[13] This was objective evidence of a national consensus against executing those who were 15 years old at the time they committed their crime.[14]

Other aspects of "counting" generate more disagreement and controversy. Specifically, disagreement exists over whether to count states that do not authorize the death penalty under any circumstances when determining whether a national consensus exists to impose the death penalty for a particular class of offenders or for a specific crime. For example, when analyzing the number of state legislatures that oppose executing those who are 15, should the Court have counted the twelve states that did not authorize the death penalty under any circumstances? How should the justices have evaluated death penalty statutes that were silent on the issue of youthful offenders?

In some of the early cases, the counting was easy. For example, in 1977, in *Coker v. Georgia*,[15] the Court found that Georgia was the only state that authorized the death penalty for the crime of rape of an adult woman and therefore held that the death penalty was unconstitutional for this crime. However, as the Court confronted greater division among the states on other issues, the disagreement within the Court became more pronounced.[16] Justice Scalia, along with several other Justices, has concluded that states that do not authorize the death penalty under any circumstances should not be counted when deciding whether a national consensus exists. Scalia asserts that these non-death penalty states are only relevant on the issue of whether there is a national consensus against applying the death penalty under any circumstances.[17] However, more recently, in *Roper v. Simmons*,[18] a five-Justice majority concluded, in an opinion written by Justice Kennedy, that the non-death penalty states should be counted in assessing whether there exists a national consensus against applying the death penalty under specific circumstances.[19]

---

[13] *See* Thompson v. Oklahoma, 487 U.S. 815 (1988).

[14] *Id.*

[15] 433 U.S. 584 (1977).

[16] *See, e.g.*, Atkins v. Virginia, 536 U.S. 304 (2002) (holding unconstitutional the execution of those who are mentally retarded); Roper v. Simmons, 543 U.S. 551 (2005) (rejecting as unconstitutional the execution of a defendant who was a juvenile at the time of the crime).

[17] States without the death penalty include: Alaska, Hawaii, Illinois, Iowa, Maine, Massachusetts, Michigan, Minnesota, New Jersey, New Mexico (although two inmates remain on death row under prior death-penalty statute) New York, North Dakota, Rhode Island, Vermont, West Virginia, Wisconsin, and the District of Columbia. Death Penalty Information Center, Fact Sheet, http://www.deathpenaltyinfo.org/documents/FactSheet.pdf (last visited Dec. 23, 2011).

[18] 543 U.S. 551 (2006).

[19] *Id.* at 564-67.

The Court has also divided over what evidence, other than legislative enactments, should be examined in identifying societal norms. Recent cases have raised questions of whether the Court should consider the views of the international community, professional organizations, or opinion polls in deciding whether there is an Eighth Amendment violation. Finally, there is also disagreement within the Court over whether the Justices should consider their personal views in conducting proportionality review.[20]

The sections below discuss some of the contexts in which the Supreme Court evaluated the constitutionality of the death penalty under the two prong analysis.

§ 8.02   FELONY MURDER AND THE "NONKILLER" ACCOMPLICE

[A]   Overview

The classic formulation of the felony murder doctrine states that "one is guilty of felony murder if a death results from conduct during the commission of or attempted commission of any felony."[21]

Most murder statutes allow a conviction for felony murder when a jury finds that a defendant participated in a serious felony and someone died during the course of the felony. Under these statutes, a jury does not have to find that a defendant intended to kill or attempted to kill.[22] All that a defendant must intend is to commit the underlying felony. Under the felony murder theory, a defendant may be equally guilty of felony murder whether he or she pulled the trigger of the gun or waited around the corner in the car. One scholar described the rule as follows:

> The felony murder rule disregards the normal rules of criminal culpability and provides homicide liability equally for both the deliberate rapist/killer and the robber whose victim dies of a heart attack, as well as for the robber's accomplice who is absent from the scene of the crime. . . . the felony murder rule can make a defendant guilty of murder when an officer or a victim mistakenly kills a third person . . . or even when the defendant is involved in a traffic accident while fleeing from the felony, resulting in a death.[23]

---

[20] *See* Atkins v. Virginia, 536 U.S. at 337. Justice Scalia (with whom The Chief Justice and Justice Thomas joined, dissenting) wrote: "Today's decision is the pinnacle of our Eighth Amendment death-is-different jurisprudence. Not only does it, like all of that jurisprudence, find no support in the text or history of the Eighth Amendment; it does not even have support in our current social attitudes regarding the conditions that render an otherwise just death penalty inappropriate. Seldom has an opinion of this Court rested so obviously upon nothing but the personal views of its members."

[21] MODEL PENAL CODE § 210.2 cmt. 6 (1980).

[22] "All murder . . . which is committed in the perpetration of, or attempt to perpetrate, arson, rape, car jacking, robbery, burglary, mayhem, kidnapping, train wrecking . . . is murder of the first degree." CAL. PENAL CODE § 189 (West Supp. 2010).

[23] Richard A. Rosen, *Felony Murder and the Eighth Amendment Jurisprudence of Death*, 31 B.C. L. Rev. 1103, 1115-16 (1990) (footnotes omitted).

Most death penalty statutes allow a defendant convicted of felony murder to be eligible for a sentence of death.[24] The intersection of the death penalty and the felony murder rule raises constitutional challenges and questions.[25] The Supreme Court has held that death penalty statutes must narrow the class of persons who are eligible for a sentence of death. These statutes, the Court has stated, should establish criteria to identify those individuals who are the worst offenders.[26] In contrast, the felony murder rule holds that all participants in a felony that results in death are equally eligible for the death penalty.[27] Applying the death penalty to a felony murder accomplice would allow a sentence of death for all participants in a crime, although their degrees of culpability may vary greatly. As one scholar described:

> The killing is murder by reason of the felony murder rule, the defendant is responsible for the killing under accomplice liability principles, and he faces the executioner because of the manner in which another person killed. Such a defendant may be at the outer reaches of personal culpability, yet still face death.[28]

Since a felony murder rule does not require any evidence that a defendant intended to kill, it allows the death penalty to be imposed on an individual who had no intent to kill.[29]

The Supreme Court addressed this issue in *Tison v. Arizona*.[30] The Court held that for a felony murder accomplice to be eligible for the death penalty, the government must show that the defendant either intended to kill or was a major participant in the crime and demonstrated a reckless indifference to human life.[31] The Court's analysis on this issue is discussed below.[32]

---

[24] Although many states permit the death penalty under a felony murder theory, several states severely restrict its use. For example, Virginia limits its application to the actual triggerman in all cases except murder-for-hire (VA. CODE ANN. § 18.2-31); the Maryland and New York rule is essentially the same as Virginia (MD. CRIM. LAW § 2-202; N.Y. PENAL § 125.27 (murder in the 1st degree); N.Y. CRIM. PRO. § 400.27 (procedure for determining sentence); Louisiana and Connecticut do not allow the death penalty under a felony murder theory (LA. C.CR.P. art. 905; CONN. GEN. STAT. § 53 a-46a).

[25] Steven F. Shatz, *The Eighth Amendment, The Death Penalty and Ordinary Robbery and Burglary Murders: A California Case Study* 59 Fla. L. Rev. 719 (2007).

[26] "That conclusion . . . is that the death penalty is exacted with great infrequency even for the most atrocious crime and that there is no meaningful basis for distinguishing the few cases in which it is imposed from the many cases in which it is not." *Furman v. Georgia*, 408 U.S. 238, 313 (1972).

[27] For a discussion of felony murder and the death penalty, *see* Rosen, *supra* note 23.

[28] Lynn Wittenbrink, *Overstepping Precedent? Tison v. Arizona Imposes the Death Penalty on Felony Murder Accomplices*, 66 N.C. L. Rev 817, 835-36 (1988).

[29] The case of Kenneth Foster in Texas brought that state's "Law of Parties" to national attention when Foster was facing execution on August 30, 2007, for a series of felony murders that occurred while he remained in a car, away from the scenes. The Fort Worth Star-Telegram joined others in asking the governor to spare his life. Editorial, *In the Law's Eyes*, FORT WORTH STAR TELEGRAM, August 19, 2007, *available at* http://www.star-telegram.com/225/story/206133.html. Governor Rick Perry commuted the death sentence to life imprisonment.

[30] 481 U.S. 137 (1987).

[31] *Id.*

[32] For more discussion of this issue, *see* Rosen, *supra* note 23.

[B] Categorical Bar for a Non-Killer Accomplice Without *Mens Rea*

In two cases, the Supreme Court established the standard for exempting non-killer accomplices from a sentence of death. In *Enmund v. Florida*,[33] the Court created a bright-line rule that excluded anyone from facing the death penalty who did not take a life, attempt to take a life, or intend to take a life.[34] Less than five years later, in *Tison v. Arizona*,[35] the Court modified this test. The Court held that a felony murder accomplice may receive a sentence of death if his participation in a felony is major and he evidences a reckless indifference to human life.[36]

[1] *Enmund v. Florida*[37]

Enmund was the getaway driver for a robbery that ultimately resulted in murder. He was waiting in a car about 200 yards from a farmhouse where the robbery-murder took place. Under Florida's felony murder statute, Enmund was guilty of first degree murder to the same extent as the actual killer and was sentenced to die.

The Supreme Court split 5:4 in *Enmund*, holding that the death penalty in Enmund's case violated the Eighth Amendment. In conducting its proportionality analysis, the Court began by evaluating the objective evidence to determine whether there was a national consensus against executing a defendant like Enmund. The Court identified Enmund as one who neither killed, attempted to kill, nor intended to kill.

In deciding to reverse Enmund's sentence of death, the Court considered the following objective evidence: (1) Out of 36 jurisdictions with death penalty statutes, only eight authorized a sentence of death for a defendant who participated in a felony where the other felon kills; (2) Of the eight states that had enacted new death penalty statutes since 1978, no state authorized capital punishment for a non-killer accomplice;[38] (3) Only six of the 362 persons executed between 1954 and 1982 were non-triggermen in a felony murder (and all six of these executions took place in 1955); (4) In October 1981, out of 739 inmates about whom information was available, only three (including Enmund) were sentenced to die absent a finding that they either participated in or hired someone else to kill the victim; and (5) Enmund was the only person on Florida's death row for whom there was no finding of a specific intent to kill.[39]

---

[33] 458 U.S. 782 (1982).

[34] *Id.* at 792-93.

[35] 481 U.S. 137 (1987).

[36] *Id.* at 152.

[37] 458 U.S. 782 (1982).

[38] These states were California (CAL. PENAL CODE § 109.2-17 (2003-04)), Florida (FLA. STAT. § 782.051), Georgia (GA. CODE ANN. § 17-10-16), Mississippi (MISS. CODE ANN. § 99-17-20), Nevada (NEV. REV. STAT. ANN. § 175.552), South Carolina (S.C. CODE ANN. § 16-3-20), Tennessee (TENN. CODE ANN. § 39-13-204), Wyoming (WYO. STAT. ANN. § 6-2-102).

[39] 458 U.S. at 789-95.

The Court then evaluated whether imposing the death penalty on a defendant like Enmund, who neither kills nor intends to kill, serves a legitimate purpose of punishment.[40] A majority of the Court concluded it did not. The Court did *not* believe that the threat of the death penalty would deter an assailant who had no intention of taking a human life in the first place. When the Court examined Enmund's own conduct and culpability, it did not believe that the death penalty was the appropriate level of retribution given his role in the crime. Deterrence and retribution are served, the Court concluded, when the death penalty is imposed on those who actually kill or intend to kill.[41]

Justice O'Connor, writing for the four Justices in dissent, concluded that no national consensus existed to exclude non-killer accomplices. Examining the objective evidence, she concluded that two-thirds of the states that permitted the death penalty (and nearly half of the states overall) permitted the death penalty for murder by a defendant who neither kills nor intends to kill.[42] This was not sufficient, she argued, to conclude that any consensus existed *against* imposing the death penalty on felony murder defendants.

Although the Court attempted to draw a bright-line rule in *Enmund*, a great deal of confusion followed. One scholar observed that the line drawn in *Enmund* seemed to move depending on who applied it.[43] At a minimum, it was clear that some minor accomplices who were not present at the scene of the killing were ineligible for the death penalty. However, courts around the country applied the test in different ways. Some jurisdictions applied a strict intent-to-kill requirement,[44] while others merely required a showing that the defendant anticipated that force would be used in the crime.

Five years later, the Supreme Court revisited the issue in the case of *Tison v. Arizona*.[45] Again, the Court was faced with a sentence of death imposed on a non-killer accomplice. Rather than clarify *Enmund's* "intent" rule, however, the Court extended the group of felony-murderers subject to the death penalty to those who either intended to kill or were a major participant acting with reckless disregard of life.

---

[40] *See* Section 2.02, *supra.*

[41] *See Enmund*, 458 U.S. at 801.

[42] *Id.* at 819-23. Of the 35 states that had the death penalty at that time, 31 authorized a sentencer to impose a death sentence for felony murder. Of those, 20 statutes permited death for a defendant who neither killed nor intended to kill.

[43] Rosen, *supra* note 23, at 1148-49.

[44] *See* State v. Branam, 855 S.W.2d 563 (Tenn. 1993) (reversing death sentence where accomplice was merely aware the triggerman was armed).

[45] 481 U.S. 137 (1987).

[2] *Tison v. Arizona*[46]

In *Tison*, the Court modified the *Enmund* standard to allow more non-killer accomplices to be eligible for the death penalty.[47] Two defendants in Tison were present at the time of the killing but did not pull the trigger or initiate the killing. A review of the facts of the case, the court's analysis and the statute provides additional insight.

The *Tison* defendants were brothers who helped their father and his cellmate escape from prison. The group's getaway car broke down. When a passing motorist and his family stopped to help, the group got in the motorist's car with the family and forced them to drive off the highway down a dirt road. The defendants' father told his two sons to walk back to their broken vehicle for some water. When the boys returned, they witnessed their father and his cellmate shoot the family to death. The Tison brothers were apprehended, convicted, and sentenced to death.[48] They challenged the constitutionality of their death sentences under *Enmund*, arguing that they neither killed nor intended to kill.

A five-justice majority upheld the Tison brothers' sentences of death, modifying the rule that had been set out in *Enmund*.[49] Justice O'Connor wrote for the majority and explained why *Enmund* did not cover the facts of *Tison*. She explained:

> *Enmund* explicitly dealt with two distinct subsets of felony murders. . . . At one pole was Enmund himself: the minor actor in an armed robbery, not on the scene who neither intended to kill nor was found to have any culpable mental state . . . The Court [in *Enmund*] held that capital punishment was disproportional in these cases. *Enmund* also clearly dealt with the other polar case: the felony murderer who actually killed, attempted to kill, or intended to kill. The Court [in *Enmund*] clearly held that . . . jurisdictions that limited the death penalty to these circumstances could continue to exact it in accordance with local law. The Tison brothers' cases fall into neither of these neat categories.[50]

The Court in *Tison* created a middle category of felony murder accomplices that fell between the two extremes explicitly addressed in *Enmund*. The Court then created a new test for this middle group. The Court held that a defendant may constitutionally receive the death penalty even if he does not actually kill, if his

---

[46] *Id.*

[47] Some commentators have questioned whether the Court was influenced by the heinous facts in *Tison*. "When the deaths of the Lyons family and Theresa Tyson were first reported, many in Arizona erupted 'in a towering yell' for retribution and justice." *Tison*, 481 U.S. at 159 (Brennan, J., dissenting) (quoting Paul Dean in the Arizona Republic, Aug. 16, 1978).

[48] The father of the Tison brothers died in the desert before he was apprehended.

[49] Justice White joined the majority in upholding the death sentence, ending his ten-year effort to exclude from death-eligibility those who did not specifically intend to kill. White first advocated this bright line rule in *Lockett v. Ohio*, 438 U.S. 586, 624 (1978) (White, J., concurring in part, dissenting in part, and concurring in the judgment of the Court).

[50] *Tison*, 481 U.S. at 149-50.

participation in a felony is major and if he acts with a reckless indifference to human life.[51]

Once again, the Supreme Court cited its proportionality review as the basis for its decision. As part of this analysis, the Court reviewed state death penalty statutes to determine their position on imposing the death penalty on felony murder accomplices. Justice O'Connor, writing for the Court, found "powerful" support that society does *not* reject the death penalty under the facts presented in *Tison*.[52] The Court concluded that a majority of jurisdictions authorize the death penalty when the defendant was a major actor in a felony in which he knew that death was highly likely to occur.[53] In addition, O'Connor noted that, even after the decision in *Enmund*, only 11 death-penalty states forbid capital punishment when a defendant's participation in the felony was major and the likelihood of killing so substantial that it raised an inference of extreme recklessness.

Tison expanded the number of defendants eligible for a sentence of death. However, as with the *Enmund* test, courts still engage in a case-by-case determination of whether a defendant possessed the requisite *mens rea* and level of participation to make him eligible for the death penalty. Not surprisingly, there is still variance among the lower courts in interpreting these decisions.

Let's suppose that five defendants are involved in a plan to rob a store. D1 initiates the plan, recruits the other members, but is not present in the store. D2 is present in the store and is the one who shoots and kills the victim. D3 is present in the store, shoots a gun, but misses and hits no one. D4 is the getaway driver who stays in the car that is parked around the corner. D5 is present in the store and takes money, but is not armed and engages in no violence. Under most felony murder statutes, all of the defendants could be convicted of felony murder.

The more difficult problem is to determine which defendants are constitutionally eligible for a sentence of death. D2, the actual killer, is clearly eligible for a sentence of death under either *Enmund* or *Tison*. D3 may be the next most culpable and eligible for death under both tests as well. He participated in the crime and used violence during its commission (albeit unsuccessfully). D3's presence and shooting is likely sufficient to qualify him as a major participant and, similarly, his shooting evidences his reckless indifference to human life. D1 may be the next most culpable as the "mastermind" of the plan. This should qualify him as a major participant. Although not present, he is responsible for the crime taking place. D5 is most like the Tison brothers. He actively participated in the crime, is present at the scene, but

---

[51] *See id.* at 152. Neither one of the Tison brothers was ultimately executed. In 1992, their death sentences were reversed on other grounds. For the re-trial, the court suppressed their statements to the police, leaving the government with no evidence to place the brothers at the scene of the shooting. Believing that, under those circumstances, a death penalty was no longer available, the government offered both brothers a plea with a sentence to life without the possibility of parole for 50 years. Randy Greenawalt, the father's cellmate, was executed by lethal injection on January 23, 1997. *See* David McCord, *State Death Sentencing for Felony Murder Accomplices Under the Enmund and Tison Standards*, 32 Ariz. St. L.J. 843 (2000); *Arizona Inmate Is Executed for 4 Killings*, N.Y. Times, Jan. 24, 1997, at A22.

[52] 481 U.S. at 153.

[53] *See id.*

does nothing to stop the violence. Under *Tison*, he is likely eligible for a sentence of death. D4 is like Enmund, a minor participant who is not present at the scene. As a minor participant, there would have to be evidence that he *intended* a killing to occur. He may be the only one who could successfully argue that he is not eligible for the death penalty. Yet, in many jurisdictions he would receive a sentence of death.

Many questions remain after *Tison* as to how courts should evaluate a defendant's participation in a felony. Uncertainty arises, for example, over whether a court should examine a defendant's role relative to others who participated in the crime and over whether the enormity of the crime itself affects the assessment.

[C]   How is the Categorical Bar Applied?

[1]   How Do the Courts Apply the Major Participant Reckless Indifference Test?

The two-part test from *Tison* requires 1) major participation in a felony and 2) evidence of a mental state of reckless indifference to human life.[54] The Court failed to define, with any specificity, the conduct or state of mind that would satisfy the constitutional minimum.[55] Since *Tison*, state and federal courts have attempted to reconcile the *Enmund* and *Tison* tests and apply them consistently.

Most commentators believed that the vagueness of the "reckless indifference" standard set out in *Tison* and the need for a case-by-case evaluation would open the door to many more sentences of death imposed under the felony murder scenario. According to one scholar, the number of death sentences in felony murder cases has decreased.[56] It is impossible to determine whether this is a result of more selective prosecution in felony murder cases, juror reluctance to impose death on non-killing accomplices, or the fact that some state statutes impose severe limitations on death eligibility when a defendant was not the person who killed.

State court decisions after *Tison* vary greatly in evaluating cases of non-killing accomplices. Some courts have specifically rejected the test in *Tison* in favor of the

---

[54] These terms are difficult to define. The Model Penal Code defines "murder" as a homicide that is committed recklessly under circumstances manifesting extreme indifference to the value of human life. Such recklessness and indifference are presumed if the actor is engaged or is an accomplice in the commission of, or attempt to commit, or flight after committing or attempting to commit robbery, rape or deviate sexual intercourse by force or threat of force, arson, burglary, kidnapping, or felonious escape. MODEL PENAL CODE § 210.2(1)(b) (1980).

[55] "We will not attempt to precisely delineate the particular types of conduct and states of mind warranting imposition of the death penalty here. Rather, we simply hold that major participation in the felony committed, combined with reckless indifference to human life, is sufficient to satisfy the *Enmund* culpability requirement." *Tison*, 481 U.S. at 158.

[56] *See* McCord, *supra* note 51, at 860-61. McCord created a case database by examining every case between *Enmund* and *Tison* that cited *Enmund*, and every case after *Tison* that cited *Tison* through 1999. After discarding cases without a real *Enmund/Tison* issue, he identified 189 cases. Of those cases, 101 were *Enmund* era cases (covering a span of five years) and 88 were *Tison*-era cases (but covered a span of 12 years). He observed that, although *Tison* is viewed as casting a wider net than *Enmund*, there have been fewer sentences of death since *Tison*.

more narrow "intent to kill" test in *Enmund*.[57] Others have applied the *Tison* test on a case-by-case basis, but are willing to find insufficient evidence to support a *Tison* finding.[58] Some courts also ask the jury to make a *Tison* finding as a recommendation to the judge.[59]

The cases of two recent death penalty defendants, Zacarias Moussaoui and Terry Nichols, presented the question of whether the enormity of the offense itself is enough to qualify a defendant for a death sentence — even where he was a minor participant in the crime. Zacarias Moussaoui is the so-called 20th hijacker in the World Trade bombing. He was charged with conspiracy to commit murder based on his alleged agreement with others to send planes into the World Trade Towers and the Pentagon. There is no question that Moussaoui was locked up in a Minneapolis jail from August 16 until after the attack on September 11. His incarceration, although not a bar to a conspiracy conviction, raises questions of whether he was a major participant in the crime and therefore eligible for the death penalty. Although his case went to a penalty trial, his jury sentenced him to life without the possibility of parole.[60]

Terry Nichols was charged with conspiracy with Timothy McVeigh for the Oklahoma City bombing. Nichols also was not present at the time of the actual bombing. Two different juries, one in federal court and a second in state court, rejected the death penalty and sentenced Nichols to life in prison without the possibility of parole.[61]

[2]   Who Decides the Major Participant Reckless Indifference Issue?

After *Tison*, the Supreme Court decided the cases of *Apprendi v. New Jersey*[62] and *Ring v. Arizona*.[63] These cases create an "elements rule," providing a Sixth Amendment right to a jury verdict on *any* factual finding that elevates the authorized punishment. In a death penalty trial, the rule applies to any facts necessary to elevate the authorized punishment from life to death.[64] In deciding which facts are considered "elements" for *Apprendi* purposes, the Court has stated that the inquiry is not one of form, but of function. The question is whether the

---

[57] The Montana Supreme Court chose to follow *Enmund* rather than *Tison*: "We now hold that pursuant to Article II, Section 22 of the Montana Constitution, the imposition of a death sentence by state courts in Montana must be reviewed for compliance with the proportionality and individualized treatment requirements set forth in *Enmund*." Kills on Top v. State, 928 P.2d 182, 200 (Mont. 1996).

[58] Jackson v. State, 575 So. 2d 181 (Fla. 1991) (evidence was insufficient to prove defendant's state of mind was one of reckless indifference to warrant the death penalty).

[59] State v. Rodriguez, 656 A.2d 262 (Del. Super. Ct. 1993).

[60] *See* Neil A. Lewis, *Moussaoui Given Life Term by Jury Over Link to 9/11*, N.Y. Times, May 4, 2006, at A1.

[61] *See* United States v. McVeigh, 153 F.3d 1166 (10th Cir. 1998); *Hung Jury Spares Nichols A 2nd Time From Death*, N.Y. Times, June 12, 2004, at A7.

[62] 530 U.S. 466 (2000).

[63] 536 U.S. 584 (2002).

[64] *See* Sections 9.02[A], 9.03, and 10.02, *infra*.

required finding exposes the defendant to a greater punishment than would be authorized without the finding.[65]

In *Ring*, the Supreme Court held that a defendant has a constitutional right to a jury finding of the statutory aggravating circumstances that make a case eligible for a sentence of death. One question still to be resolved is whether a *Tison* finding of "reckless indifference" and "major participation" must constitutionally be determined by a jury. The defense will argue that *Ring* applies to any factual finding that is a prerequisite to the imposition of an increased sentence. Therefore, a jury finding is required on those "elements" of eligibility that allow a "non-killer" to be sentenced to death in a felony murder context. The states will likely argue that no jury determination is required on the *Tison* finding. States will likely contend that a Tison finding should be viewed differently than statutory aggravating circumstances because it is not a punishment-enhancing factor articulated by the state but a limitation on the use of the death penalty articulated by the Supreme Court.

§ 8.03 PERSONS WHO ARE MENTALLY RETARDED

[A] Overview

Historically, the law has recognized that an individual's mental retardation may affect his or her capacity to face criminal charges or to be found criminally liable.[66] Modern statutes, for the most part, do not exempt a defendant from criminal liability on the basis of mental retardation, although his mental retardation may play a part in a court's decision on questions of competency.

While there are different definitions of mental retardation, three are used most frequently — those established by the American Association of Mental Retardation (AAMR),[67] the Diagnostic and Statistical Manual (DSM),[68] and the American Psychiatric Association (APA).[69] Although the definitions vary slightly, they are essentially identifying the same group of people.

Early classifications were based primarily on intelligence quotient (IQ) tests that helped establish categories more familiar to the public. Specifically, these four

---

[65] *See Apprendi*, 530 U.S. at 494.

[66] *See* Penry v. Lynaugh, 492 U.S. 302, 331-32 (1989). A person who is mentally retarded is distinguished from one who is insane. In *Ford v. Wainwright*, 477 U.S. 399 (1986), the Supreme Court held it was unconstitutional to execute someone who is insane. The Court defined insanity as lacking the "mental capacity to understand the nature of the death penalty and the reasons why it was imposed." Sue Ann Gerald Shannon, *Atkins v. Virginia: Commutation For The Mentally Retarded?*, 54 S.Car. L. Rev. 809 (2003). *See also* Luckasson et al, American Association on Mental Retardation, *Mental Retardation: Definition, Classification, and Systems of Supports* (10th ed. 2002).

[67] The American Association on Mental Retardation is the oldest and largest interdisciplinary organization concerned with mental retardation and related disabilities. *See generally* http://www.aamr.org.

[68] *See* American Psychiatric Association, *Diagnostic and Statistical Manual of Mental Disorders — Fourth Edition* (DSM-IV 1994), *available at* http://www.dsmivtr.org/.

[69] The American Psychological Association (APA) is a scientific and professional organization that represents psychology in the United States. *See generally* http://www.psych.org.

groups included: mild mental retardation within the IQ range of 50/55-70, moderate mental retardation within the IQ range of 35/40-50/55, severe mental retardation within the IQ range of 20/25-35/40, and profound mental retardation with an IQ score below 20-25.[70] Although IQ scores are still a large part of the measurement for mental retardation, they are only one component of a more complex set of criteria.

Mental retardation refers to a substantial limitation in an individual's ability to function effectively in everyday life.[71] There are generally three critical components to a finding of mental retardation: (1) substantial intellectual impairment (as indicated by IQ scores), (2) impact of that impairment on everyday life of the individual, and (3) appearance of the disability at birth or during the person's childhood.[72] An individual must meet all three diagnostic requirements to fall within the accepted definition of mental retardation.

The Supreme Court first addressed whether it is constitutional to execute a mentally retarded offender in *Penry v. Lynaugh*.[73] By a vote of 5–4, the Court rejected Penry's argument that the Eighth Amendment prohibited the execution of the mentally retarded. The Court concluded that, while the capital sentencer must be allowed to consider mental retardation as a mitigating factor, mental retardation did not exempt a defendant from the penalty of death.

In June 2002, Daryl Renard Atkins renewed the argument that it was unconstitutional to execute a person who was mentally retarded. This time the Supreme Court agreed. In a 6:3 decision, the Court in *Atkins v. Virginia*[74] held that it was a violation of the Eighth and Fourteenth Amendments to impose the death penalty on a mentally retarded defendant.

What happened between *Penry* in 1989 and *Atkins* in 2002 to cause the Court to change its mind? This section discusses how the Court approached the constitutionality of executing a person who is mentally retarded. It also examines the questions that remain following the *Atkins* decision.[75]

---

[70] *See* Luckasson, *supra* note 66.

[71] Mental retardation must be distinguished from mental illness, which is a medical and/or psychological disorder generally characterized by thought disturbances that may be temporary or episodic. Mental retardation is a permanent developmental or functional condition.

[72] James W. Ellis, *Mental Retardation And The Death Penalty: A Guide To State Legislative Issues*, *available at* http://www.deathpenaltyinfo.org/documents/MREllisLeg.pdf (last visited Dec. 23, 2011).

[73] 492 U.S. 302 (1989).

[74] 536 U.S. 304 (2002).

[75] For more in depth discussion of this issue, see James Ellis and Ruth Luckasson, *Mentally Retarded Criminal Defendants*, 53 Geo. Wash. L. Rev. 414 (1985); Lyn Entzeroth, *Constitutional Prohibition On the Execution of the Mentally Retarded Criminal Defendant*, 38 Tulsa L. Rev. 299 (2002).

[B] Between *Penry* and *Atkins*

In *Atkins*,[76] the Supreme Court agreed to revisit the issue of whether those who are mentally retarded could constitutionally be executed. The legal landscape looked very different in 2002 than it had looked thirteen years earlier when the Court first reviewed this issue. In 1989, when the Supreme Court decided *Penry v. Lynaugh*,[77] only Georgia, Maryland, and the federal government had death penalty statutes prohibiting the execution of the mentally retarded.[78]

After *Penry* upheld the death penalty for mentally retarded defendants, state legislatures around the country began passing bills excluding the mentally retarded from a possible sentence of death. In a period of five years, Tennessee, Kentucky, Arkansas, Colorado, New Mexico, and Washington all passed statutes prohibiting the execution of a mentally retarded defendant.[79] When Kansas and New York reinstated the death penalty in 1994 and 1995, respectively, their death penalty statutes also excluded those who are mentally retarded.[80] By the time the Supreme Court agreed to hear *Atkins* in September 2001, Arizona, Connecticut, Florida, Missouri, Nebraska, North Carolina, and South Dakota had also passed statutes that prohibited imposing the death penalty on those who are mentally retarded.[81] Even the Texas legislature adopted a bill to exclude those who are mentally retarded, but the governor vetoed the measure.[82]

[C] The Court's Proportionality Review

In deciding whether the death penalty is unconstitutional when applied to any class of defendants, the Court must conduct a proportionality review to determine whether a national consensus exists against executing persons in that group.[83] Over the years, Supreme Court decisions on proportionality review have often

---

[76] 536 U.S. 304 (2002).

[77] 492 U.S. 302 (1989).

[78] GA. CODE ANN. § 17-7-131(j) (1988); MD. CODE ANN. Art. 27, § 412(f)(1) (1989) (reorganized as MD. CODE ANN. CRIM. LAW § 2-202(b) (2002)); 21 U.S.C. § 848(l) (1988 ed.); *see also* 18 U.S.C. § 3596(c) (1994).

[79] *See* KY. REV. STAT. ANN. § 532.130 (1990); TENN. CODE ANN. § 39-13-203 (1990); N.M. STAT. ANN. § 31-20A-2.1 (1991); ARK. CODE ANN. § 5-4-618 (1993); COLO. REV. STAT. § 16-9-403 (1993) (renumbered § 18-1.3-1103 (2002)); WASH. REV. CODE ANN. § 10.95.030(2) (1993).

[80] *See* KAN. STAT. ANN. § 21-4623 (1994); N.Y. CRIM. PROC. § 400.27(12)(c) (1995).

[81] *See* ARIZ. REV. STAT § 13-703.02(g) (2001); CONN. GEN. STAT. § 53a-46a(h) (2001); FLA. STAT. ANN. § 921.137 (2001); MO. REV. STAT. § 565.030(4)(1) (2001); NEB. REV. STAT. § 28-105.01 (1998); N.C. GEN. STAT. § 15A-2005 (2001); S.D. CODIFIED LAWS § 23A-27A-26.1 (2000).

[82] House Bill No. 236 passed the Texas House on April 24, 2001, and the Senate version, S. 686, passed the Texas Senate on May 16, 2001. Governor Rick Perry vetoed the legislation on June 17, 2001. "In rejecting legislation that President Bush also opposed when he was Texas governor, [Rick Perry] bucked a nationwide trend toward protecting mentally retarded killers from execution." . . . " 'This legislation is not about whether to execute mentally retarded murderers,' " Perry told reporters in announcing his veto at the state Capitol. " 'It's about who determines whether a defendant is mentally retarded in the Texas justice system.' " Paul Duggan, *Texas Ban on Executing Retarded is Rejected*, WASH. POST, Jun 18, 2001, at A.

[83] *See* Section 8.01, *supra*. The Court used the term "excessive" punishment to denote the Eighth Amendment evaluation of whether the punishment is proportional. *Atkins*, 536 U.S. at 343-44. *See* Section 4.04, *supra*.

evoked stark divisions among the Justices. In *Atkins*, the divisions became even more acute, and the rhetoric, especially by Justice Scalia in dissent, more harsh.[84]

The Court in *Atkins* utilized a four step analysis. First, the Court examined the legislative action against or in favor of executing those who are mentally retarded. Second, the Court looked at how often the death penalty was actually imposed on those who are mentally retarded. Third, the Court considered national and international opinions on the subject. Finally, the Court brought its own views to bear on whether the death penalty, for those who are mentally retarded, violates evolving standards of decency and thus is barred by the Eighth and Fourteenth Amendments. Ultimately, the Court found that all of these considerations supported the finding of a national consensus against executing those who are mentally retarded and held it was unconstitutional.

When the Court evaluated the "objective" evidence, it counted nineteen death-penalty states that had statutes excluding defendants who are mentally retarded from execution.[85] The Court noted that all of the state legislatures passed this exclusion by overwhelming majorities. In addition, the Court identified several states, (like New Hampshire and New Jersey) that did not have the exclusion but had never executed a mentally retarded person. Finally, the Court observed that legislative change occurred in one direction only — excluding those who were mentally retarded.

The Court considered the views of religious and professional organizations[86] as well as those of the international community. All were strongly opposed to executing those who are mentally retarded. Based on this evidence, the Court concluded that public opinion, nationally and internationally, strongly disapproved of the execution of those who are mentally retarded.

The Court moved to the second prong of the proportionality evaluation and examined whether executing those who are mentally retarded serves any legitimate purpose of punishment and concluded it did not. The Court reasoned that those who are mentally retarded were not as culpable as other defendants; their deficiencies (including impairments of understanding, reasoning, processing information, or impulse control) distinguish them as a group from other persons who commit murder.

Perhaps the most controversial part of the Court's opinion was a discussion about the relationship between applying the death penalty to those who are mentally retarded and the possibility of convicting an innocent person. Several of the Justices were clearly troubled by recent death row exonerations, especially those defendants who were mentally retarded. These Justices noted that defendants who are mentally retarded are more vulnerable to the kinds of errors

---

[84] "Scalia's dissent was arrogant, caustic, and sarcastic in its disdain for the majority's reasoning. . . . dismissed the views of the leaders of his own religion, saying that Catholic bishops are so far from being representative. . . . [and] predicted that capital trials would become a game because defendants would feign mental retardation." Stephen Bright, *Capital Punishment: Accelerating the Dance with Death*, in THE REHNQUIST COURT 94 (Herman Schwartz ed. 2002).

[85] *See* Section 8.01[B], *supra*, for a discussion of the "counting" controversy.

[86] *See Atkins*, 536 U.S. at 316 n.21.

that have been cited as leading to wrongful convictions.[87]

[D] The Dissent's Proportionality Review

Chief Justice Rehnquist and Justice Scalia each wrote a dissent in *Atkins*, disagreeing not only with the judgment of the Court but with its approach to proportionality. Both argued that the majority went far beyond any appropriate proportionality review. This review, they argued, should be limited only to purely objective factors: state legislative enactments and actions by sentencing juries.[88]

Chief Justice Rehnquist took particular exception to the majority's "blind faith credence" in opinion polls that were submitted to the Court.[89] This information, he argued, was not only improperly considered but was completely antithetical to the considerations of federalism.

Justice Scalia wrote a blistering dissent that ridiculed the majority opinion. He claimed that the majority "miraculously extract[ed]" a national consensus from inadequate data and improperly counted the state legislative enactments. Scalia disputed the majority conclusion that eighteen death penalty states were opposed to executing those who are mentally retarded. He argued that only seven states should be counted, as they were the only ones that prohibited executions of those who are mentally retarded under *all* circumstances. Statutes in the other eleven states only provided various limitations and restrictions on these executions. Scalia also argued that prospective legislation, as passed by most states, did not support a finding of absolute moral repugnance required to exempt a class of defendants from the death penalty. Rather, it reflected the current preference between two "tolerable approaches."[90]

Scalia further argued that, even accepting the majority's numbers, they fell far short of the required number of states needed. Looking only at states with death penalty statutes, Scalia declared that the number of state statutes that excluded the mentally retarded from capital punishment ("a fudged 47%") more closely resembled the numbers in those cases in which the death penalty was upheld. Scalia compared his numbers in *Atkins* to those found in *Tison v. Arizona*,[91] (which upheld the death penalty for an accomplice who does not kill where 30% of the

---

[87] "The risk . . . is enhanced, not only by the possibility of false confessions, but also by the lesser ability of mentally retarded defendants to make a persuasive showing of mitigation. . . . mentally retarded defendants may be less able to give meaningful assistance to their counsel and are typically poor witnesses, and their demeanor may create an unwarranted impression of lack of remorse for their crimes." *Id.* at 320-21.

[88] Justice Scalia, with whom Chief Justice Rehnquist and Justice Thomas join, dissenting: "Seldom has an opinion of this Court rested so obviously upon nothing but the personal views of its Members." *Id.* at 338. "But the prize for the Court's Most Feeble Effort to fabricate 'national consensus' must go to its appeal (deservedly relegated to a footnote) to the views of assorted professional and religious organizations, members of the so-called "world community," and respondents to opinion polls." *Id.* at 347.

[89] "Everything from variations in the survey methodology, such as the choice of the target population, the sampling design used, the questions asked, and the statistical analyses used to interpret the data can skew the results." *Id.* at 326-27.

[90] *See Atkins*, 536 U.S. at 342-43 (2002) (Scalia, J., dissenting).

[91] 481 U.S. 137 (1987).

states prohibited executions under those circumstances), and *Stanford v. Kentucky*,[92] (which upheld executions of 16 and 17 year-olds where 42% of the states with death penalty statutes prohibited these executions). Scalia argued that eighteen states was not comparable to the numbers in cases where the Court struck down the death penalty. These cases include *Coker v. Georgia*,[93] (which struck down the death penalty for the rape of an adult woman when 97% of the states with the death penalty prohibited it), *Enmund v. Florida*,[94] (which struck down the death penalty for a non-killing accomplice when 78% prohibited it), and *Ford v. Wainwright*,[95] (which abandoned execution of the insane when no state allowed this practice).

[E] Post-*Atkins* Procedures

The decision in *Atkins* left two questions unresolved for each state to decide: (1) the definition of mental retardation, and (2) the procedure to determine whether a defendant is mentally retarded. Legislatures and courts have slowly set up procedures to implement *Atkins*.[96]

The definition of mental retardation has not posed a huge problem. The Court in *Atkins* relied upon the definition set out by the American Association of Mental Retardation,[97] but also recognized definitions from the Diagnostic and Statistical Manual (DSM),[98] and the American Psychiatric Association (APA).[99]

Each state was left to devise its own procedures to implement Atkins.[100] While all states place the burden of proof on the defendant, some require a showing by a "preponderance of the evidence"[101] while others require "clear and convincing"

---

[92] 492 U.S. 361 (1989). *Stanford v. Kentucky* was overturned in 2005 by *Roper v. Simmons*, 543 U.S. 551 (2005), which held that the death penalty was unconstitutional when applied to juveniles.

[93] 433 U.S. 584 (1977).

[94] 458 U.S. 782 (1982).

[95] 477 U.S. 399 (1986).

[96] After the Supreme Court's decision, *Atkins* was remanded to the Supreme Court of Virginia which further remanded the case for a hearing on the sole issue of whether Atkins was mentally retarded. In 2005, a jury found Atkins was not mentally retarded. On appeal, the Virginia Supreme Court unanimously reversed that finding. *See* Atkins v. Commonwealth, 272 Va. 144 (Va. 2006). The Virginia General Assembly had enacted emergency legislation to implement the *Atkins* decision. *See* VA. CODE ANN. §§ 8.01-654.2, 19.2-264.3:1(A). The legislation provided that a defendant has the burden of proving mental retardation by a preponderance of the evidence. *See* Atkins v. Commonwealth, 266 Va. 73 (Va. 2003).

[97] *See* 536 U.S. at 309 n.3. The American Association of Mental Retardation defines mental retardation as follows: "Mental retardation refers to substantial limitations in present functioning. It is characterized by significantly sub-average intellectual functioning, existing concurrently with related limitations in two or more of the following applicable adaptive skills areas: communication, self-care, home living, social skills, community use, self direction, health and safety."

[98] *See supra* note 68.

[99] *See supra* note 69.

[100] James W. Ellis, *Mental Retardation and the Death Penalty: A Guide to State Legislative Issues*, *available at* http://www.deathpenaltyinfo.org/MREllisLeg.pdf.

[101] In Missouri, a "fact finder" must determine whether a defendant is mentally retarded by a preponderance of the evidence. Ohio adopted the same standard but specified that the findings should be

evidence.[102] States differ on whether a judge or jury should make this determination. Some states provide a jury only if a defendant waits until the penalty phase to raise the issue, but provide a judge if the issue is litigated in advance of trial.[103] Following *Ring v. Arizona*,[104] many defendants argued that a jury finding of whether or not a defendant was mentally retarded was constitutionally required. However, few if any judges agreed.[105] Many states have not moved promptly to pass statutes to address the procedures that need to be in place in light of the Court's decision, and states have adopted varying definitions of mental retardation, some of which have been unduly restrictive, permitting the execution of some capital defendants who scholars contend have mental retardation.[106]

§ 8.04   JUVENILES

[A]   Overview

Suppose D1 and D2 commit a robbery, during which someone is killed. Both are arrested and charged with murder, and the government seeks the death penalty. D1 is 19 years old. D2 is fifteen years old. Should D2 be excluded from the death penalty simply because of his age? The question may be more complicated if we learn that D2 is the person who fired the shots or instigated the plan. The setting of a minimum age under which the death penalty is not available creates an arbitrary line that fails to distinguish for variations in maturity, experience,

---

made by a judge, not a jury. *See* Johnson v. State, 102 S.W.3d 535 (Mo. 2003); MO. REV. STAT. § 565.030.6; State v. Lott, 779 N.E.2d 1011 (2002); OHIO REV. CODE ANN. § 2929.03; ARK. CODE ANN. § 5-4-618; CAL. PENAL CODE § 1376; LA. REV. STAT. ANN. § 095.5.1.

[102] *See* ARIZ. REV. STAT. ANN. § 13-703.02; FLA. STAT. § 921.137.

[103] Most states that have legislated on this issue have chosen to have a pre-trial determination by a judge rather than a jury. *See, e.g.*, CAL. PENAL CODE § 1376; ARK. CODE ANN. § 5-4-618.

[104] 536 U.S. 584 (2002).

[105] Pursuant to the Sixth Amendment, *Ring* held that certain factual findings that expose a defendant to a greater punishment, must be decided by a jury. Defendants argued that mental retardation was similar to an element of the offense, as it was necessary for a defendant to be eligible for the death penalty. *See, e.g.* Head v. Hill, 587 S.E.2d 613 (Ga. 2003) ("the absence of mental retardation is not the functional equivalent of an element of an offense"; instead, "mental retardation is a means by which a death penalty defendant may seek to have his possible sentence limited despite the fact that the statutory elements for the death penalty might be present."); Webster v. US, 2003 WL23109787 (N.D. Tex., Sept. 30, 2003) ("[T]he status of not being mentally retarded does not raise the sentence for the capital crime for which [Petitioner] was convicted to one where the death penalty is available. Rather, the status of being mentally retarded prevents the death penalty from being carried out with regards to a federal defendant.").

[106] *See* John H. Blume, Sheri Lynn Johnson & Christopher Seeds, *Of* Atkins *and Men: Deviations From Clinical Definitions of Mental Retardation in Death Penalty Cases*, 18 CORN. J. L. & PUB. POL'Y 689 (2009). States without mental retardation statutes that began addressing *Atkins* through case law: Alabama, (Wood v. State, No. CC-94-7.60 (Ala. Cir. Ct. Pike County, Sept. 24, 2003)); Mississippi, (Foster v. State, 848 So.2d 172 (Miss. 2003)); New Jersey, (State v. Harris, 859 A.2d 364 (N.J. 2004)); Ohio, (State v. Lott, 779 N.E.2d 1011 (Ohio 2002)); Oklahoma, (Murphy v. State, 54 P.3d 556 (Okla. Crim. App. 2002)); Pennsylvania, (Commonwealth v. Graham, No.'s 3948, et seq. CD 1987 (Pa. Ct. Common Pleas, Dec. 18, 2003)); South Carolina, (Franklin, et al. v. Maynard, 588 S.E.2d 604 (S.C. 2003)); and Texas (Ex Parte Briseno, 135 S.W.3d 1 (Tex. Crim. App. 2004)).

intelligence and culpability among those involved. For years, the Court wrestled with the question of whether to set a minimum age and if so, what that minimum age should be.[107]

In 2002, the Supreme Court held that it was unconstitutional to execute a defendant who was mentally retarded.[108] Following this decision, the debate about whether it was constitutional to execute a defendant who was under eighteen at the time of the offense began to intensify.[109] One noted scholar and death penalty expert, Stephen Bright, of the Southern Center for Human Rights, stated that everything the Supreme Court identified about the unconstitutionality of executing those who are mentally retarded applied equally to children.[110] Even members of the Supreme Court were uncharacteristically public about the juvenile death penalty. In 2004, when the Court declined to hear the case of a seventeen-year-old sentenced to death in Texas, Justices Stevens, Ginsburg and Breyer wrote in dissent from the denial of *certiorari* that it would be appropriate for the Court to revisit the issue of executing juveniles at the earliest opportunity.[111] Less than two months later, the Supreme Court again declined to hear a case that raised this issue. This time, Justices Stevens, Souter, Ginsburg, and Breyer wrote in dissent that the rationale of exempting the mentally retarded from execution applied with "equal or greater force to the execution of juvenile offenders [and that] we should put an end to this shameful practice"[112]

---

[107] For an overview of juvenile death penalty statistics, see Death Sentences and Executions for Juvenile Crimes, January 1, 1973 – April 30, 2004, by Victor L. Streib Professor of Law Ohio Northern University, *available at* www.internationaljusticeproject.org/pdfs/juvDeathApril2004.pdf (last visited Dec. 23, 2011). For more in-depth discussion of this issue, see Victor L. Streib, *Emerging Issues in Juvenile Death Penalty Law*, 26 Ohio N.U.L. Rev. 725 (2000); C. Steiker and J. Steiker, *Defending Categorical Exemptions To the Death Penalty: Reflections On the ABA Resolutions Concerning the Execution of Juveniles And Persons With Mental Retardation*, 61 Law & Contemp. Probs. 89 (1998); J. Richard Broughton, *The Second Death of Capital Punishment*, 58 Fla L. Rev. 639 (2006); Dora W. Klein, *Categorical Exclusions from Capital Punishment: How Many Wrongs Make a Right?*, 72 Brook L. Rev. 1211 (2007); Victor L. Streib, *Moratorium on the Death Penalty for Juveniles*, 61 Law & Contemp. Probs. 55 (1998).

[108] *Atkins v. Virginia*, 536 U.S. 304 (2002). *See* Section 8.03, *supra*.

[109] Hughes, J., *For Mice or Men or Children? Will the Expansion of the Eighth Amendment in Atkins v. Virginia Force the Supreme Court to Re-Examine the Minimum Age for the Death Penalty?*, 93 J. Crim L. & Criminology 973 (2003); *see also* Jeffrey Fagan and Valerie West, *The Decline of the Juvenile Death Penalty: Scientific Evidence of Evolving Norms*. 95 J. Crim L. & Criminology 427 (2005).

[110] Adam Liptak, *3 Justices Call for Reviewing Death Sentences for Juveniles*, N. Y. Times, Aug. 30, 2002, at A1.

[111] Patterson v. Texas, 536 U.S. 984 (2002) (denying stay of execution); Patterson v. Texas, 528 U.S. 826 (1999) (cert denied). Patterson was later executed in Texas. *See also* Liptak, *supra* note 110.

[112] Although only four justices are needed to grant certiorari, five justices are needed to grant review when it is an original writ. *See* In re Stanford, 537 U.S. 968 (2002) (denying petition for original writ of habeas corpus).

[B]   The Road to *Roper v. Simmons*[113] and the Abolition of the Juvenile Death Penalty

[1]   The Fifteen-Year-Olds

The abolition of the juvenile death penalty began in 1988 in the case of *Thompson v. Oklahoma*.[114] In *Thompson*, the Court considered whether it was constitutional to execute a defendant who was under sixteen years old at the time the crime was committed. Although Thompson was only fifteen years old at the time of the offense, he was tried as an adult, convicted, and sentenced to death.[115]

Thompson appealed to the Supreme Court raising a single issue: he argued that because he was fifteen years old at the time of the offense, his capital sentence violated the Eighth Amendment. Ultimately, the Court agreed.

Thompson was a plurality decision. Although five Justices voted to reverse Thompson's sentence of death, only four were willing to draw a bright line and exclude from a sentence of death all defendants under sixteen years old.[116] The fifth vote, provided by Justice O'Connor, reversed Thompson's sentence of death, but on more limited grounds.[117]

The Court conducted a proportionality review and examined the objective evidence to see whether a national consensus existed against executing those who were under sixteen years old at the time of the offense. The plurality "counted" 37 states as unwilling to execute a fifteen year old — which represented near unanimity among death penalty states.[118]

Next, the Court examined death verdicts and learned that between 1982 and 1986, only five defendants under the age of sixteen, including Thompson, were sentenced to death.[119] The Justices reasoned that the infrequency of imposing a death sentence on a defendant who was younger than fifteen at the time of the crime

---

[113] 543 U.S. 551 (2005).

[114] 487 U.S. 815 (1988).

[115] Oklahoma, like most states, has a statute that allows for juvenile offenders to be tried as adults pursuant to a specific certification process. While the lower age for a direct file is fifteen years old, there is no limit as to how young an offender can be for a discretionary transfer.

[116] To underscore that juveniles have historically been treated differently from adults, the Court highlighted statutes in all areas of the law that created this dichotomy including eligibility to vote, to sit on a jury, to marry without parental consent, and to purchase alcohol. *See Thompson*, 487 U.S. at 823.

[117] EDWARD P. LAZARUS, CLOSED CHAMBERS: THE FIRST EYEWITNESS ACCOUNT OF THE EPIC STRUGGLES INSIDE THE SUPREME COURT 515-16 (1998); Victoria Ashley, *Death Penalty Redux: Justice Sandra Day O'Connor's Role on the Rehnquist Court and the Future of the Death Penalty in America*, 54 Baylor L. Rev. 407 (2002); KENNETH W. STARR, FIRST AMONG EQUALS: THE SUPREME COURT IN AMERICAN LIFE 32-34 (2002).

[118] The Court started with existing state death penalty statutes and determined that, of the 37 states that had death penalty statutes, 18 states set a minimum age of sixteen years or older. Nineteen states, including Oklahoma, did not specify any minimum age in their statutes. The plurality counted these "silent states" among those *unwilling* to execute a fifteen-years old, which created a total of 37 states. *See* 487 U.S. at 815 n.16. The opinion characterized the District of Columbia as a "state" for the sake of simplicity.

[119] *See Thompson*, 487 U.S. at 832.

made the practice "unusual" in the same way that the Court found sentences of death "unusual" and thus unconstitutional in 1972 in *Furman v. Georgia*.[120] The last execution of a defendant who had been younger than sixteen at the time of his crime occurred in 1948. This objective evidence satisfied the first prong of the proportionality review.

Turning to the second prong, the plurality found that the practice of executing a fifteen year-old did nothing to further any legitimate purposes of punishment.[121] The plurality concluded that the death penalty as retribution was inappropriate for youthful offenders for several reasons: society has a fiduciary responsibility toward its youth, youthful offenders have historically been viewed as having a lesser degree of culpability, and a young person still has a unique capacity to grow and change. The plurality also found that, especially given the infrequency with which the death penalty is actually imposed against this group, there was no deterrent effect served. With this evidence, the four justices in the plurality concluded that they should draw a bright line and exclude, as a group, all defendants who were under sixteen at the time of their offenses from a possible death sentence. Justice O'Connor provided the deciding vote. Her opinion straddled the line between the plurality and the dissent, adopting some reasoning from each while rejecting portions from each as well.[122] O'Connor voted to reverse the death sentence imposed on Thompson but rejected the plurality's bright-line rule that would exclude all fifteen-year-olds from the death penalty.[123]

O'Connor based her decision on the unusual facts presented in Thompson's case.[124] With an Oklahoma statute that was silent as to the minimum age for a sentence of death, and a "near consensus" nationally against executing fifteen year-olds,[125] O'Connor concluded that Oklahoma could not constitutionally execute

---

[120] 408 U.S. 238, 243 (1972). Although each justice in Furman wrote a separate opinion, several wrote on the subject of rarity: "the extreme rarity with which applicable death penalty provisions are put to use raises a strong inference of arbitrariness" (Douglas, J., concurring) and "the conclusion is virtually inescapable that it is being inflicted arbitrarily. . . . it smacks of little more than a lottery system" (Brennan, J., concurring).

[121] The four justices argued that juveniles, as a group, have the unique capacity to grow and change making retribution inappropriate and deterrence with little impact. *Thompson*, 487 U.S. 815, 835-38 (1988).

[122] O'Connor admitted that she *believed* a national consensus existed against executing fifteen-year-olds but was reluctant to adopt that conclusion as a matter of constitutional law. Instead, O'Connor wrote a narrow opinion and found that it was unconstitutional to execute Thompson under the particular circumstances of the Oklahoma statute. *See id.* at 858 (O'Connor, J., concurring). O'Connor found a middle ground on the second prong. She agreed that the blameworthiness of an individual or group should be considered as part of the Eighth Amendment analysis, and that certain qualities surrounding juveniles justify legislative decisions to treat them differently. However, O'Connor refused to substitute her own subjective judgment for that of a state legislature about the best age to draw the line for execution. *See id.* at 853-54.

[123] *See id.* at 858.

[124] O'Connor's opinion emphasized that her decision applied only to the facts presented in *Thompson*. She described the "peculiar circumstances" the Court faced and the "unique situation" presented and stated that the "conclusion I have reached in this unusual case is itself unusual." *See id.* at 857-58.

[125] O'Connor found that every state legislature that had expressly set a minimum age for capital punishment had set that age at sixteen. She also found that no legislature had affirmatively and

a fifteen-year old. Anticipating a future challenge, Justice O'Connor also noted that she would not feel compelled to strike down ambiguous legislation where the evidence of a national consensus was not as compelling as it was in Thompson's case.[126] In fact, that was exactly the issue when the Court examined the constitutionality of executing sixteen- or seventeen-year-old offenders.

Justice Scalia's dissenting opinion in *Thompson* raised arguments that would become the Court opinion in the next juvenile death penalty case.[127]

[2]   Sixteen and Seventeen-Year-Old Juveniles

Less than one year after it decided *Thompson*, the Court heard arguments in the consolidated cases of *Wilkins v. Missouri* and *Stanford v. Kentucky*.[128] These cases challenged the constitutionality of executing juveniles who were sixteen and seventeen years old, respectively, at the time of their offenses.[129]

Both defendants argued that imposing a sentence of death on a sixteen- or seventeen-year-old was contrary to the evolving standards of decency, and therefore unconstitutional. The Court rejected their arguments in both cases and upheld both sentences of death.[130]

Justice Scalia wrote the plurality opinion, using many of the same arguments from his dissent in the *Thompson* case. He found that there was no national consensus against imposing the death penalty against a defendant who was sixteen or seventeen years old. Once again, the Court disagreed over how to evaluate the objective evidence and how to "count" states. Scalia argued that, of the 37 states that had death penalty statutes, only fifteen did not impose the death penalty on a sixteen-year-old. Of those fifteen states, twelve required that the defendant be at least eighteen years old, and three required a minimum age of seventeen years

---

unequivocally endorsed execution of an offender younger than sixteen. *Id.* at 849.

[126] *See* 487 U.S. at 857.

[127] Although viewing the same objective evidence, Scalia counted the state statutes differently and reached the opposite conclusion. Scalia argued that the 19 "silent" states represented states that had determined that no minimum age for capital punishment need be set. Rather than count them as unwilling to execute fifteen-year-olds (as the plurality did), Scalia counted those states as willing to impose the death penalty whenever a juvenile was properly transferred from juvenile court and tried as an adult. *See* 487 U.S. at 859-78.

[128] 492 U.S. 361 (1989).

[129] Stanford was seventeen years old and sentenced to death in Kentucky under a statute that authorized the death penalty for defendants who committed crimes when they were sixteen years of age or older. Ky. Rev Stat. Ann. § 640.040(1) (1987). Wilkins was sixteen years old at the time of his offense, and was sentenced to death under a "silent" statute that specified no minimum age for the death penalty to apply. Mo. Rev. Stat. § 211.021(1) (1986).

[130] Neither Stanford nor Wilkins was ultimately executed. In June 2003, Gov. Paul Patton announced that he planned to spare Stanford's life to "correct an injustice" by the criminal justice system. Stanford, who was seventeen at the time of his crime, was thirty-nine. *See* Andrew Wolfson, *Patton Pardons 4 in Election Case and Will Commute Death Sentence*, The Courier-Journal, June 19, 2003, at 1A. Wilkins was also spared and ultimately pled guilty to three consecutive life offenses. His earlier plea and sentence of death were set aside by a federal judge who ruled that Wilkins suffered from psychiatric disorders. *See Youngest Ever Sent to Death Row Gets Three Life Sentences*, St. Louis Post Dispatch, May 22, 1999.

old.[131] These numbers, Scalia argued, fell far short of the numbers the Court required in earlier cases when it found that a national consensus existed.[132]

Justice O'Connor again provided the fifth vote. This time she joined the dissenters from *Thompson* and upheld both sentences of death. O'Connor found that unlike the evidence to execute a fifteen-year-old, there was no national consensus forbidding the death penalty on sixteen- and seventeen-year-old defendants.[133]

The Missouri statute in *Wilkins again* presented the "silent statute" issue as it failed to specify any minimum age. In *Thompson*, Justice O'Connor found that since nationally there was a "near consensus" against executing a fifteen-year-old, she was unwilling to impute any intent to do so in the face of a silent Oklahoma statute. O'Connor found no such consensus against the execution of a sixteen-year-old and was willing to find that Missouri implicitly authorized death for a sixteen-year-old.

Although joining in the holding, Justice O'Connor wrote separately in *Stanford* to make clear that she disagreed with Justice Scalia's Eighth Amendment analysis. O'Connor believed that the Court should evaluate any nexus between the punishment imposed and the blameworthiness of the defendant as part of the constitutional assessment[134]. Justice Scalia disagreed.

[C]   *Roper v. Simmons*:[135] The death penalty is unconstitutional for juveniles

By 2004, the stage was set for the court to finally reconsider the issue of the juvenile death penalty. The case was *Roper v. Simmons*[136] and it was argued in October 2004 and decided in March 2005.[137] In a 5-4 decision written by Justice Kennedy, the Court held that the Eighth and Fourteenth Amendments forbid the execution of offenders who were under the age of eighteen when their crimes were committed.[138]

---

[131] *See* 492 U.S. at 370-71.

[132] The Court found a national consensus against imposing a sentence of death when a person is insane at the time of execution (no states allowed). *See* Ford v. Wainwright, 477 U.S. 399 (1986). Only one state allowed the imposition of the death penalty for the crime of rape of an adult woman. *See* Coker v. Georgia, 433 U.S. 584 (1977). Only eight states allowed the death penalty to be imposed upon a defendant who neither killed nor intended to kill. *See* Enmund v. Florida, 458 U.S. 782 (1982).

[133] When Justice O'Connor counted the positions of the various state legislatures, she concluded that a majority of the states permitting capital punishment, including Kentucky, expressly authorized it for a defendant who was at least sixteen years old. Without a national consensus to forbid the death penalty, Kentucky's statute authorizing the death penalty to a defendant sixteen years old or older presented no constitutional issue.

[134] *See* 492 U.S. at 382. (O'Connor, J., concurring)

[135] 543 U.S. 551 (2005).

[136] *Id.* The opinion was joined by Justices Breyer, Souter, Stevens and Ginsberg.

[137] *See generally* Scott W. Howe, Roper v. Simmons: *Abolishing the Death Penalty for Juvenile Offenders in the Wake of International Consensus*, in DEATH PENALTY STORIES 415 (J. Blume & J. Steiker eds., 2009).

[138] *See* Charles Lane, *5-4 Supreme Court Abolishes Juvenile Executions*, WASH. POST, March 2, 2005, at A1; Charlie Savage, *Executions Barred for Juvenile Killers: In 5-4 Decision Justices Invoke Global*

Step by step, Justice Kennedy laid out the two prong analysis for the Court's Eighth Amendment jurisprudence. He reasoned that in light of the diminished culpability of juveniles, they are not among the "worst of the worst" offenders, and neither retribution nor deterrence provides adequate justification for the penalty.[139] He also compared and contrasted the objective evidence on the use of the death penalty against juveniles with that found regarding those who are mentally retarded. In finding that execution of juveniles was contrary to "the evolving standards of decency," Kennedy noted that a majority of states rejected the death penalty for juveniles and that the trend was consistently in favor of abolition.[140]

Justice Kennedy also asserted that the Court should bring its own independent judgment to bear on whether the death penalty for juvenile offenders was excessive. For the majority, he expressed the view that the application of capital punishment in this context was excessive. In support of this view, he identified three general differences between juveniles and adults that supported drawing a line to exclude them from executions. He argued:

> First, as any parent knows and as the scientific and sociological studies respondent and his amici cite tend to confirm, "[a] lack of maturity and an underdeveloped sense of responsibility are found in youth more often than in adults and are more understandable among the young. These qualities often result in impetuous and ill-considered actions and decisions. . . . The second area of difference is that juveniles are more vulnerable or susceptible to negative influences and outside pressures, including peer pressure. . . . The third broad difference is that the character of a juvenile is not as well formed as that of an adult. The personality traits of juveniles are more transitory, less fixed.[141]

Standard, THE BOSTON GLOBE, March 2, 2005, available at http://www.boston.com/news/nation/articles/ 2005/03/02/executions_barred_for_juvenile_killer; Vivian Berger, Stop Executing Minors, National Law Journal, April 26, 2004, available at http://www.deathpenaltyinfo.org/article.php?scid=38&did=926# bergernlj; Rosalynn Carter, No Death Penalty for Juveniles, THE MIAMI HERALD, April 7, 2004; William Sessions, Legislature Should Raise Execution Eligibility Age, THE LEXINGTON HERALD, Feb. 2004; Lee Bowman, New Research shows Stark Difference in Teen Brain, Scripps Howard News Service, May 11, 2004.

[139] See 543 U.S. at 569-70.

[140] Kennedy noted that in both Simmons and Atkins, the Court reconsidered an earlier position it had taken in 1989 in the cases of Penry v. Lynaugh (492 U.S. 302 (1989)) (holding it was constitutional to execute those who are mentally retarded) and Stanford v. Kentucky (492 U.S. 361 (1989)) (declining to draw a bright line for all juveniles and holding it was unconstitutional only for those who were fifteen). Kennedy noted that when Atkins was decided, the Court counted 30 states that prohibited the execution of a mentally retarded offender (including 12 states that reject the death penalty completely) and, in Simmons, the Court similarly counted 30 states that prohibited the execution of an offender under the age of eighteen. Kennedy noted that there were different rates of change: sixteen states abolished the death penalty for the mentally retarded between Penry and Atkins while only five abolished it for juveniles during that same time period. However, he noted that it was the "consistency of the direction of the change" that was significant. Finally, the Court also observed that at the time of Penry, only two death penalty states already prohibited execution for the mentally retarded, while twelve prohibited the punishment for those under eighteen and three more states prohibited it for those under seventeen. See id. at 562-67.

[141] Id. at 569-70.

Finally, Kennedy articulated an additional argument that raised significant controversy. He contended that international norms could provide "confirmation" of the Court's decision.[142] On this score, he presented a discussion of non-domestic sources followed by a conclusion emphasizing the "overwhelming weight of international opinion against the juvenile death penalty."[143] Although purportedly offered only as "confirmation" of a conclusion based on evidence of national consensus and the Court's own judgment, this latter discussion generated substantial dispute both within and outside of the Court.[144]

The *Simmons* decision was significant for several reasons. By abolishing the juvenile death penalty, it represented another major step in the Court's effort to prevent excesses in the use of capital punishment. In addition, the decision provided a foundation for a subsequent decision by the Court in *Graham v. Florida*[145] that life without parole for some juvenile offenders also violates the Eighth Amendment. The *Simmons* decision may also provide a grounding for future arguments that the death penalty more broadly is unconstitutional. The decision revealed that the Eighth Amendment can proscribe the death penalty in circumstances when forty percent of the states have not abolished it. Likewise, *Simmons* underscored that the failure of states to use the death penalty when authorized tends to support a finding that a national consensus exists against the penalty. The decision also confirmed the relevance of the Court's own views on excessiveness and arguably indicated the relevance of international norms on the use of the death penalty. In light of these points, one commentator has noted that, depending on future developments in the use of the death penalty by states, *Simmons* could provide "a blueprint for judicial abolition of the death penalty in the United States."[146]

§ 8.05 NON-MURDER CRIMES

[A] Overview

In 1976, the Supreme Court held that the Constitution did not create any *per se* bar to the imposition of the death penalty for the crime of murder. It left open the question of whether the death penalty is constitutional for crimes where there has been no taking of life.[147] The next year, the Supreme Court reviewed a case where the death penalty was imposed for the crime of rape.[148] Although the Court reversed the sentence of death, it did not explicitly limit the death penalty to crimes where there is a taking of life.

---

[142] *Id.* at 574-75. Kennedy also emphasized that, to the extent that the Court's earlier decision in *Stanford v. Kentucky* failed to consider the independent judgment of the court, it was inconsistent with historical Eighth Amendment jurisprudence.

[143] *Id.* at 575-78.

[144] *See* Howe, *supra* note 137, at 442-46.

[145] 130 S. Ct. 2011 (2010).

[146] Jordan Steiker, *United States:* Roper v. Simmons, 4 INT'L J. CON. L. 163, 171 (2006).

[147] *See* Gregg v. Georgia, 428 U.S. 153 n.35 (1976); Proffitt v. Florida, 428 U.S. 242, 248 (1976).

[148] *See* Coker v. Georgia, 433 U.S. 584 (1977).

In 2008, in *Kennedy v. Louisiana*,[149] the Supreme Court addressed whether the Eighth Amendment bars the imposition of the death penalty for the rape of a child where the crime did not result, and was not intended to result, in the death of the victim. The Court held that the Eighth Amendment prohibits the death penalty for this offense. As in *Coker*, the Court did not explicitly limit the death penalty to crimes where there is a taking of life, although it did strongly hint that the death penalty was unconstitutional for all "nonhomicide crimes against individual persons."[150]

In the modern era, state and federal legislatures have passed numerous statutes applying the death penalty to a variety of offenses, other than rape of an adult or of a child, that do not involve the taking of a human life. More than ten states and the federal government currently have laws that permit the death penalty for such non-homicide offenses, most frequently for the crimes of treason or kidnapping.[151] Montana allows the death penalty for certain non-homicidal offenses committed while the defendant is incarcerated.[152] Missouri imposes the death penalty for placing a bomb near a bus terminal,[153] and federal statutes allow a sentence of death for a drug kingpin and several other non-homicidal crimes.[154] Despite the passage of these statutes, the only person who has been sentenced to death for a non-homicide crime since 1977 is Patrick Kennedy, who was convicted of aggravated rape of a child and was sentenced to death in Louisiana on October 2, 2003. His sentence was the subject of the decision in *Kennedy v. Louisiana*, in which the Supreme Court rejected the death penalty for child rape. Because the Court in *Kennedy* did not clarify whether capital punishment is prohibited for all non-homicide crimes, questions remain about whether and, if so, when the death penalty can be applied to non-homicide offenses.[155]

---

[149] 554 U.S. 407 (2008).

[150] *Id.* at 438.

[151] ARK. CODE ANN. § 5-51-201 (treason); CAL. PENAL CODE § 37 (treason), § 219 (train wrecking), § 128 (perjury causing execution); COLO. REV. STAT. § 18-11-101 (treason) (penalty at § 18-1.3-401); FLA. STAT. ANN. § 921.142 (capital drug trafficking), § 921.141 (capital felonies) (West 2001); GA. CODE ANN. § 16-11-1 (treason), § 16-5-44 (aircraft hijacking), § 16-5-40 (kidnapping with bodily injury or ransom) IDAHO CODE § 18-4502 (first-degree kidnapping) (penalty at § 18-4504),; LA. REV. STAT. ANN. § 14:113 (treason); MISS. CODE ANN. § 97-7-67 (treason), § 97-25-55 (aircraft piracy); MO. ANN. STAT. § 565.110 (kidnapping), § 576.070 (treason), (penalty at § 557.021); MONT. CODE ANN. § 45-5-303 (aggravated kidnapping); WASH. REV. CODE ANN. § 9.82.010 (treason). For a discussion of the federal statutes, *see* Section 24.03, *infra*.

[152] MONT. CODE ANN. § 46-18-220 (attempted deliberate homicide, aggravated assault, or aggravated kidnapping while in official detention).

[153] MO. ANN. STAT. § 578.310 (bombs and explosives placed in or near bus or terminal) (penalty at § 557.021).

[154] 18 U.S.C. § 3591(b) (capital drug trafficking). A drug kingpin is defined as a leader of a continuing criminal enterprise or one who possesses specified quantities of drugs or drugs worth specified amounts of money. For other federal statutes making the death penalty applicable to non-homicidal crimes, *see* Section 24.03, *infra*.

[155] The United States Supreme Court held the death penalty unconstitutional for a kidnapping not involving the death of the victim in *Eberheart v. Georgia*, 433 U.S. 917 (1977). Eberheart had been sentenced to death in Georgia for both kidnapping and rape of a victim who was horribly brutalized but not killed. The Supreme Court vacated the death sentences imposed in Eberheart's case and in another unrelated case, *Hooks v. Georgia*, involving a rape. However, these cases were pending before the Court until *Coker* was decided and then the death sentences were reversed in an opinion citing *Coker* that

[B] Rape of an Adult Woman: *Coker v. Georgia*

[1] The Decision

In September 1974, defendant Coker was serving life sentences for murder, rape, and kidnapping when he escaped from a prison in Georgia. He broke into the Carver family home, threatened Mr. Carver with a four inch steak knife, and raped Mrs. Carver in the presence of her husband. He bound and gagged Mr. Carver in the bathroom and drove away, taking Mrs. Carver with him. Soon thereafter, Mr. Carver freed himself and notified police. Mrs. Carver was not killed. Coker was arrested, convicted and sentenced to death. He appealed to the Supreme Court and argued that his sentence of death was unconstitutional because there was no taking of a life.[156]

The Supreme Court reversed Coker's sentence of death in a decision that raised as many questions as it answered. The Court defined the issue before it as whether the death penalty violates the Eighth Amendment when applied to the rape of an *adult* woman.[157] Six of the justices agreed that a sentence of death was always disproportionate for the crime of rape of an adult woman.[158] Justice Powell concurred, but was unwilling to hold that the death penalty was always unconstitutional for the crime of rape.

The Court conducted a proportionality analysis and noted that at no time in the past fifty years had a majority of the States authorized death as a punishment for rape. The Court noted that, in 1925, eighteen states, the District of Columbia, and the Federal Government authorized the death penalty for the rape of an adult female. By 1977, when *Coker* was decided, Georgia was the only state with such a statute.[159] The Court noted that when the death penalty statutes were struck down in *Furman v. Georgia*,[160] *in* 1972, the legislative response was swift to re-enact death penalty statutes. However, none of the states, except Georgia, included rape of an adult woman as an eligible crime.

The Court was careful not to trivialize the harm inflicted during a rape, but did distinguish it from murder and the loss of life. The Court identified a fundamental difference between crimes that involve the loss of human life and those that do not, both in terms of the depravity exhibited by the offender as well as the injury

---

comprised only a few lines. The opinion did not mention the particular crimes on which Eberheart had been sentenced to death. As a result, *Eberheart* has not been uniformly understood as holding that capital punishment may not be inflicted for kidnapping, although that was the decision of the Court.

[156] *See* Coker v. Georgia, 433 U.S. 584 (1977).

[157] *See id.* at 593. Although the Court clearly referred to the victim as an adult woman, in fact she was 16 years old at the time of the assault and was considered an emancipated minor.

[158] Justices White, Stewart, Blackmun and Stevens joined the plurality opinion. Justices Brennan and Marshall joined in a concurring opinion. Justice Powell concurred, but was unwilling to hold that the death penalty was always unconstitutional for the crime of rape. Justices Burger and Rehnquist joined in a dissenting opinion.

[159] Florida, Mississippi, and Tennessee also authorized the death penalty in rape cases where the victim was a child and the rapist an adult. Fla. Stat. Ann. § 794.011(2) (1976); Miss. Code Ann. § 97-3-65 (1976).

[160] 408 U.S. 238 (1972).

suffered by the victim. Justice White wrote, "Life is over for the victim of the murder; for the rape victim, life may not be nearly so happy as it was, but it is not over and normally not beyond repair."[161]

Justice Powell argued that Coker's victim did not experience serious or lasting injury. He suggested that in another scenario, a rape victim might be so grievously injured, physically or psychologically, that life is beyond repair. In these cases, Powell argued, a sentence of death would be appropriate.[162]

Chief Justice Burger and Justice Rehnquist wrote in dissent and argued that the Supreme Court must show greater deference to state legislative decisions regarding appropriate punishment. They also argued that the decision in *Coker* would have serious repercussions as it would affect all existing and future statutes that impose a sentence of death in a non-homicide crime. The difficulty, they warned, would be that the government would now have to demonstrate that the harm caused by an offense punishable by death is significantly different, more permanent, and more depraved than the harm caused by rape.[163]

[2] Rape, Race and the Death Penalty

What is noticeably absent from the various opinions in *Coker* is any mention of the role of race in the application of the death penalty for the crime of rape.[164] Although Coker was white, commentators have often criticized the historical use of the death penalty as a punishment against black men for raping white women.[165] Early research showed that blacks were disproportionately sentenced to death for rape, particularly if the victim was white.[166] In the 50 years before *Coker*, over 95 percent of the executions for rape in the United States occurred in former Confederate states, and an overwhelming number of the executions involved African-American defendants convicted of raping white women.[167]

---

[161] *Coker*, 433 U.S. at 598.

[162] *See id.* at 603-604 (Powell, J., concurring in judgment).

[163] *See id.* at 616.

[164] For a discussion of this issue, *see* Sheri Lynn Johnson, Coker v. Georgia: *Of Rape, Race, and Burying the Past, in* Death Penalty Stories 171 (J. Blume & J. Steiker eds., 2009); Carol Steiker & Jordan Steiker, *Defending Categorical Exemptions to the Death Penalty: Reflections on the ABA's Resolutions Concerning the Execution of Juveniles and Persons with Mental Retardation*, 61 Law & Contemp. Probs 89 (1998).

[165] *See generally* Randall Kennedy, Race, Crime and the Law (Pantheon Books 1997); Carol S. Steiker, *Remembering Race, Rape, and Capital Punishment*, 83 Va. L Rev. 693 (1997) (reviewing Eric W. Rise, The Martinsville Seven: Race, Rape and Capital Punishment (1995)).

[166] *See* Marvin Wolfgang and Marc Reidel, Racial Discrimination, Rape and the Death Penalty in the Death penalty in America 194-205 (Hugo A. Bedeau, ed. 1982) (detailing Wolfgang's statistical findings). Wolfgang studied 12 jurisdictions in the South with substantial numbers of executions for the crime of rape. *See also* Steiker, *supra* note 165. The Martinsville Seven was a rape trial in Virginia in the 1950s where statistical evidence was presented to challenge the racial discrimination in the application of the death penalty.

[167] *See* Steiker & Steiker, *supra* note 164, at 96-97 (citing James Marquart et al, The Rope, the Chair, and the Needle: Capital Punishment in Texas 1923-1990 (1994)); Eric W. Rise, The Martinsville Seven: Race, Rape, and Capital Punishment (1995).

In selecting Coker's case for review, the Supreme Court chose to "hold" two other cases in which African-American men were sentenced to death for committing interracial rapes in Georgia.[168] These defendants had their death sentences overturned because of the broad ruling in *Coker*, but by choosing Coker's case, the Court did not have to address the race issue.[169]

[C]   Rape of a Child: *Kennedy v. Louisiana*

In *Coker*, the Court excluded the death penalty as a possible punishment for the rape of an *adult* woman. However, it left open the possibility that the death penalty could apply to crimes other than murder, and even to the rape of a *child*.[170] When *Coker* was decided, only two states, Florida, and Mississippi, had statutes imposing the death penalty for the rape of a child.[171] By 1990, the statutes in both Florida and Mississippi had been repealed, albeit for different reasons.[172] While these statutes were in effect, only one person was sentenced to death for the rape of a child, and his sentence was reversed in the state court.

In 2003, only Louisiana and Georgia had statutes authorizing the death penalty for the rape of a child. By 2007, six states had such statutes.[173] Louisiana was the first state after *Coker* in which the state's highest court upheld a verdict of death against a defendant for the rape of a child. The defendant was Patrick Kennedy. The Louisiana Supreme Court upheld his death sentence in 2007.[174]

---

[168] Eberheart v. Georgia, 206 S.E.2d 12 (1974) (companion case to *Coker*); Hooks v. Georgia, 210 S.E.2d 668 (1974) (held for Coker). The death sentences in these cases were vacated after *Coker*. *See* 433 U.S. 917 (1977).

[169] Some scholars posit that the Court may have been reluctant to reopen the controversial question of racial discrimination just one year after reinstating the death penalty. *See* Steiker & Steiker, *supra* note 164. *See also* Johnson, *supra* note 164, at 194-95.

[170] *See* Section 7.04, *supra*.

[171] Tennessee also had a statute providing the death penalty for child rape, but it was invalidated six months before *Coker* was handed down. Collins v. State, 550 S.W.2d 643 (Tenn. 1977).

[172] *See* Buford v. State, 403 So. 943 (Fla. 1981) (sentence of death for sexual assault was forbidden under the Eighth Amendment). Shortly after *Coker*, Mississippi upheld a sentence of death for rape of a child under twelve years old, holding that *Coker* was limited to rape of an adult female. Upshaw v. State, 350 So. 2d 1358, 1360 (Miss. 1977). Mississippi later amended its death penalty statute and subsequently, in *Leatherwood v. State*, 548 So.2d 389 (Miss 1989), the Mississippi Supreme Court held that the death penalty could not be applied in cases of rape.

[173] Louisiana, Montana, Georgia, South Carolina, Oklahoma and Texas had such laws. *See* Kennedy v. Louisiana, 554 U.S. 407, 423 (2008). The death penalty also was authorized for rape of a child in the military sphere in 2007. *See* Kennedy v. Louisiana, 554 U.S. 945 (2008) (denial of petition for rehearing).

[174] The Supreme Court of Louisiana, in upholding its death sentence to Patrick Kennedy, stated:

> [T]his Court upheld the constitutional validity of the death penalty for the crime of aggravated rape when the victim is under 12 years of age. In so doing, we distinguish the rape of a child from the United States Supreme Court's decision in *Coker*. For while *Coker* clearly bars the use of the death penalty as punishment for the rape of an adult woman, it left open the question of which, if any, non-homicide crimes can be constitutionally punished by death. Because, "children are a class that needs special protection," we concluded that "given the appalling nature of the crime, the severity of the harm inflicted upon the victim, and the harm imposed on society, the death penalty is not an excessive penalty for the crime of rape when the victim is a child under the age of twelve years old."

State v. Kennedy, 957 So. 2d 757, 781 (2007).

In *Kennedy v. Louisiana*,[175] the United States Supreme Court held by a vote of five-to-four that the death sentence violated the Eighth Amendment. Justice Kennedy delivered the opinion of the Court. Using the approach employed to overturn death sentences in prior proportionality decisions, the majority focused first on objective indicia of contemporary standards and second on the Court's own judgment about excessiveness, including an assessment of whether the death penalty for child rape legitimately furthers the social purposes of retribution and deterrence.

Regarding objective evidence of contemporary views, the Court noted that only five states other than Louisiana currently made child rape a capital crime. Louisiana, along with the dissenters, urged that the low numbers resulted from confusion over whether the *Coker* opinion allowed the death penalty for child rape, but the majority found that the *Coker* opinion rather clearly had not spoken to the issue. Louisiana and the dissenters also emphasized that the six states where the death penalty for child rape was a capital crime had enacted such legislation only recently and, therefore, given that five other states had proposed to do so, a consistent direction of change was afoot in support of the death penalty for child rape. However, the majority also was not moved by this argument, noting that only six states had actually enacted legislation and that this movement had occurred over a thirteen-year period. Further, the majority pointed out that Louisiana was the only state actually to have sentenced a defendant to death for child rape since 1964.[176]

In the Court's own judgment, the death penalty was also excessive punishment for child rape. The Court did not minimize the terrible harm caused the victim of a child rape. However, the Court emphasized the distinction between intentional murder and "nonhomicide crimes against individual persons, even including child rape."[177] The Court found that the harms caused by the latter category of crimes were not comparable to murder in their severity and irrevocability. Further, the Court concluded that applying the death penalty to child rape would not appropriately serve the ends of retribution and deterrence. The Court expressed a variety of concerns about excessive harshness to the defendant, infliction of undue stress on child victims, the reliability of some child testimony, and the possibility

---

Previously, Louisiana sought the death penalty against two defendants for the crime of child rape. After they were indicted but prior to trial, the defendants appealed the statute to the Louisiana Supreme Court. State v. Wilson and Bethley, 685 So. 2d 1063 (La. 1966). The Louisiana Supreme Court upheld the statute and sent the case back for trial. The U.S. Supreme Court denied certiorari, but three Justices wrote that the issue could be reviewed when and if the defendants were sentenced to death. Bethley v. Louisiana, 520 U.S. 1259 (1977). On remand to the trial courts, Bethley was given a life sentence, and Wilson was found incompetent to stand trial. Therefore, the case was not reviewed further.

[175] 554 U.S. 407 (2008).

[176] *See id.* at 422-34. After the Court rendered it's decision, Louisiana filed a petition for rehearing arguing that recent congressional and executive revisions of rape offenses under federal military law did not abrogate the death penalty for rape of a child, and, thus, the finding that the penalty was unconstitutional should be revisited. However, the Court denied the request, explaining that this fact did not draw into question the Court's conclusion that the penalty in the civilian context was unconstitutional. *See* Kennedy v. Louisiana, 554 U.S. 945 (2008) (rehearing denied).

[177] *Id.* at 438.

that application of the death penalty would add to the risk of non-reporting of child sexual assaults.[178]

While the *Kennedy* decision focused on child rape, the Court's opinion implied that the death penalty is also unconstitutional for almost all, but perhaps not all, non-homicide crimes. The Court articulated the prohibition as applying to "nonhomicide crimes against individual persons."[179] This language implies that the death penalty is unconstitutional for a crime such as kidnapping, which some jurisdictions continued to make a capital offense after *Coker*.[180] However, the *Kennedy* decision leaves open the question whether the death penalty is permissible for crimes against society more generally, including trafficking in large quantities of drugs, or crimes against the government, such as treason and espionage. These crimes are currently subject to capital punishment under federal law.[181]

[D] Crimes Against the Government

The most common crimes, other than murder, that are punishable by death, are crimes against the government. Typically, these include treason and espionage. Although there has not been a sentence of death pursuant to either charge in more than 50 years, these crimes are the subject of a great deal of current discussion and debate.[182]

Treason is the only crime defined in the Constitution of the United States.[183] Treason is the offense of attempting to overthrow one's government either by waging war against the government or by materially supporting its enemies. The requirement that an "enemy" be the beneficiary of the crime means it is less likely that there will be prosecutions for treason.

Prosecutions for the crime of espionage, especially crimes of "peacetime espionage" are much more likely and far more controversial. In the last two decades, there have been several prosecutions for espionage.[184] In 2003, the

---

[178] *See id.* at 434-46.

[179] *Id.* at 438.

[180] *See infra* note 151.

[181] *See* Section 24.03[B], *infra*.

[182] "But the death penalty? For what? In Ashcroft's case, his zeal is such that he demanded death for a hapless traitor who lacked both common sense and craft." Richard Cohen, *Ashcroft's Mission Unconscionable*, WASH. POST, Feb. 27, 2003 at A27.

[183] U.S. CONT. art. III, § 3 provides: "Treason against the United States, shall consist only in levying War against them, or in adhering to their Enemies, giving them Aid and Comfort. No person shall be convicted of Treason unless on the Testimony of two Witnesses to the same overt Act, or on Confession in open Court. The Congress shall have Power to declare the Punishment of Treason, but no Attainder of Treason shall work Corruption of Blood, or Forfeiture except during the life of the Person attainted."

[184] Some of the more high-profile prosecutions for espionage include Robert Hanssen (2001), a 25 year veteran of the FBI, Georgia Trofimoff (2000), the highest ranking U.S. military officer ever convicted of spying, and Wen Ho Lee (1999), a physicist at the Los Alamos, New Mexico nuclear laboratory who, after nine months in jail waiting for trial, was freed after all charges were dropped. The government did not seek the death penalty in any of these cases. *See* http://edition.cnn.com/2001/US/08/24/spy.timeline/.

government sought a sentence of death against Brian Regan, who was charged with attempted espionage under the Federal Death Penalty Act.[185] Regan, a former U.S. Air Force sergeant, went to trial and was convicted of two counts of attempted espionage for attempting to pass secrets to Iraq and China. The jury, however, declined to make the findings necessary to make Regan eligible for a sentence of death.[186]

The last Americans to be executed for spying were Ethel and Julius Rosenberg in 1953.[187] However, the Rosenberg case provides little guidance as to how the Supreme Court might view a sentence of death under the Federal Death Penalty Act of 1994. The Rosenbergs were sentenced to death under a different statute. Also, their sentences of death were not reviewed under today's Eighth Amendment proportionality analysis.[188]

It is unclear how the Supreme Court would apply its Eighth Amendment proportionality analysis to a crime of peacetime espionage. When the Court in *Coker* and *Kennedy* held that the death penalty did not apply in cases of rape or child rape, the Court looked primarily to the harm to the victim, and determined that it was qualitatively different than the harm caused by murder.[189] Espionage is very different from either murder or rape in terms of any evaluation of harm. Espionage, as defined in the Federal Act, does not require any death or any specific harm to the national security.[190] Even if some harm is believed to have occurred, espionage trials often take place before the extent of any damage can be clearly determined. There are added difficulties in connecting any perceived harm to the specific acts of a defendant. Finally, under the 1994 federal statute, the crime of *attempted* espionage is eligible for a sentence of death. Under this offense, any showing of harm is even more problematic.

The Court's Eighth Amendment proportionality review, as defined in *Coker v. Georgia* and more recently in *Atkins v. Virginia*,[191] and *Roper v. Simmons*,[192] and *Kennedy v. Louisiana*, sets the framework for the Court's evaluation of whether a

---

[185] 18 U.S.C. 3591(a)(1), 794(a) (1994) provides: "Whoever, with intent or reason to believe that it is to be used to the injury of the united States, . . . communicates, delivers, or transmits, or attempts to communicate, deliver or transmit, to any foreign government . . . any document, writing, . . . or information relating to the national defense shall be punished by death or by imprisonment. . . . [A] sentence of death shall not be imposed unless the jury . . . further finds that the offense . . . directly concerned nuclear weaponry, . . . or other means of defense or retaliation against large scale attack . . . ."

[186] The jury failed to find that the information intended to be delivered concerned nuclear weaponry. 18 U.S.C. 3591(a)(1) (1994).

[187] *Rosenberg v. United States*, 346 U.S. 273 (1953). The Rosenbergs were charged with conspiracy to commit espionage charging that they intended to deliver weapons to the Soviet Union that the Soviets could use to destroy the United States. They were executed in 1953. For more discussion on this issue see Ryan Norwood, *None Dare Call it Treason: The Constitutionality of the Death Penalty for Peacetime Espionage*, 87 Cornell L. Rev. 820 (2002).

[188] *See* Chapter 4, *supra*.

[189] Coker v. Georgia, 433 U.S. 584 (1977); Kennedy v. Louisiana, 554 U.S. 407 (2008).

[190] *Id.*

[191] 536 U.S. 304 (2002). *See* Section 8.03, *supra*.

[192] 543 U.S. 551 (2005). *See* Section 8.04, *supra*.

sentence of death is constitutional. The Court looks initially at legislative activity to see whether other jurisdictions impose the death penalty under similar circumstances. Then the Court examines the response of juries in similar cases. This type of comparison is not feasible for the crime of espionage. Peacetime espionage is only a crime under federal law, and is not amenable to a state-by-state comparison.[193] The paucity of death-penalty trials for espionage also makes it impossible to examine jury responses and verdicts as a guide to the acceptability of the punishment of death.

It is certainly possible that the government will attempt to seek the death penalty in an espionage case in the future. However, if a sentence of death results, the Court will have to define how it will evaluate the constitutionality of such a sentence.

[E] Drug Kingpins

In the Federal Death Penalty Act of 1994, Congress enacted new provisions extending the federal death penalty for the first time to leaders of a drug organization for crimes even where no death has occurred.[194] These "drug kingpin" provisions authorize the death penalty in two different circumstances.[195] One applies to leaders of a continuing criminal enterprise[196] or their triggerman who *attempt* to kill certain designated victims.[197] The second, and the more controversial, provision authorizes the death penalty for one who is in possession of large quantities of drugs or involved in a large quantity of receipts from the enterprise.[198]

If the issue were to come before it, the Supreme Court would face many of the same problems in evaluating the constitutionality of these provisions as it would in evaluating the constitutionality of the death penalty for espionage. However, these cases are not common. Many of the most powerful drug dealers are well insulated and will not be arrested with large quantities of drugs either by dollar amount or weight, taking them out of the reach of the statute.[199] Still others live abroad, in countries that refuse to extradite defendants to the United States if a defendant

---

[193] Norwood, *supra* note 187, at 833-34.

[194] *See* Section 24.03, *infra*, for a discussion of the modern federal death penalty. *See also* Neil Schur, *Assessing the Constitutionality and Policy Implications of the 1994 Drug Kingpin Death Penalty*, 2 Tex. F. on C.L. and C.R. 141 (1996) (arguing the drug kingpin provision is unconstitutional and ill advised); Eric Pinkard, *The Death Penalty for Drug Kingpins: Constitutional and International Implications* 24 Vt. L. Rev. 1 (1999) (arguing that the drug kingpin provisions are constitutional but the benefits of the act are weakened by international difficulties of securing foreign national drug lords).

[195] An earlier provision under 21 U.S.C. 848(e) (1988) authorized the death penalty for drug kingpin murders and drug related murders of law enforcement officials.

[196] A continuing criminal enterprise is defined in the Controlled Substances Act, 21 U.S.C. 848 (c) (1988), as violations "undertaken by such persons in concert with five or more persons with respect to whom such person occupies a position of organizer, a supervisory position, or any other position of management and from which such person obtains substantial income or resources".

[197] 18 U.S.C. § 3591(b)(2) (1994).

[198] 18 U.S.C. § 3591(b)(1) (1994).

[199] *See* Schur, *supra* note 194, at 160.

faces the possibility of a death sentence.[200]

---

[200] *See* Pinkard, *supra* note 194, at 15-23.

Chapter 9

OVERVIEW OF AGGRAVATING EVIDENCE: THE ELIGIBILITY FUNCTION AND THE SELECTION FUNCTION

§ 9.01 OVERVIEW

In addition to a finding that a defendant is guilty of murder or another permitted capital offense, there are two determinations that must precede a death sentence, which we will call the *eligibility* decision and the *selection* decision.[1] The *eligibility* determination poses the question: Is the defendant in the class of defendants on whom the death penalty could be imposed? The *selection* determination poses the question: Should a sentence of death in fact be imposed on this defendant? These two questions are separate and distinct.

The Supreme Court decisions in the decade that followed *Gregg*[2] called for capital cases to exhibit both "eligibility" and "selection" criteria. The criteria for the eligibility determination are aggravating circumstances. The criteria for the selection decision include aggravating evidence and mitigating evidence. Aggravating evidence includes statutory aggravating circumstances as well as other evidence offered in aggravation.

When discussing "aggravating evidence," it is important to identify the role it plays in a particular case. Whether particular aggravating evidence is used for the eligibility decision or the selection decision affects the terminology used to describe it, as well as the constitutional requirements that apply.[3] Thus, it is important to distinguish aggravating evidence on the basis of its function. Although the courts and statutes are not consistent in their terminology, we will use the term *aggravating circumstances* to describe aggravating evidence used to determine eligibility. We will use the term *aggravating evidence* to describe the composite of evidence, including aggravating circumstances, that is used to determine selection.

---

[1] When the Supreme Court first upheld the modern death penalty statutes in 1976, it did not articulate two distinct determinations as part of the sentencing process. In current case law, however, the Court uses this dichotomy. *See, e.g.*, Tuilaepa v. California, 512 U.S. 967, 971 (1994) ("Our capital punishment cases under the Eighth Amendment address two different aspects of the capital decision-making process: the eligibility decision and the selection decision.").

[2] *See, e.g.*, Zant v. Stephens, 462 U.S. 862 (1983).

[3] The terminology used to describe aggravating evidence is not uniform among state statutes, jury instructions, or in the decisions of the courts. In this book, we will use aggravating circumstances to refer to evidence offered as a basis for the eligibility decision. We will use aggravating evidence or factors to refer to evidence used as a basis for the selection decision.

Statutorily defined aggravating circumstances in the eligibility decision act as a filter to determine those cases for which the death penalty is a permissible sentencing option. There are thousands of murder cases committed each year around the country. Even though each one of these cases involves a loss of life, not every killing can be punished by a sentence of death.[4] The Supreme Court has held that a death penalty statute must, in some meaningful way, narrow the class of cases eligible for death. In doing so, each statute identifies those characteristics that legislators believe make certain murders worse than others. This is the function of aggravating circumstances.[5] Aggravating circumstances are the means to distinguish one killing as worse, and therefore, eligible for a sentence of death, from the many others that are not eligible.[6] Typical aggravating circumstances that appear in death-penalty statutes include multiple murders, the killing of a police officer, and a killing for pecuniary gain.[7] The California death-penalty statute lists 22 special circumstances, the finding of any one of which makes the case eligible for death.

The selection decision, on the other hand, uses a broader range of aggravating evidence. This aggravating evidence includes the aggravating circumstances as part of the evidence. Once a case is eligible for the death penalty, however, the function of the aggravating circumstances changes. They cease to act as a filter determining which cases are eligible for a sentence of death. They now become a possible reason to impose the death penalty on a particular defendant.[8]

There is a broad range of "aggravating evidence" in addition to evidence to support a specific aggravating circumstance. Typical evidence includes evidence that a defendant constitutes a future danger to society or evidence of a defendant's prior criminal record. Aggravating evidence also encompasses what is broadly defined as the *circumstances of the crime*.[9] Many statutes specifically state that evidence relating to circumstances of the crime may be considered. Even when not

---

[4] *See* Section 6.06, *supra*.

[5] Gregg v. Georgia, 428 U.S. 153 (1976). The Supreme Court recognized that this process helps to identify those crimes that are the "worst of the worst" and therefore appropriate for a sentence of death. In California, the death penalty statute provides a list of "special circumstances" that serve as a basis to determine which first degree murders are eligible for death. CAL. PENAL CODE § 190.1 (West 2011).

[6] In *Furman v. Georgia*, 408 U.S. 238, 293-94 (1972), the Court mentioned that proponents of the death penalty argue that the death penalty is imposed only in the most extreme cases, but the Supreme Court found that this was not true given state legislation and practices at the time.

[7] *See, e.g.*, CAL. PENAL CODE § 190.2(3) (West 2011) ("The defendant, in this proceeding, has been convicted of more than one offense of murder in the first or second degree."); GA. CODE ANN. § 17-10-30(b)(8) (2011) ("The offense of murder was committed against any peace officer, corrections employee, or firefighter while engaged in the performance of his official duties"); FLA. STAT. § 921.141(5)(f), (j) (2011) ("The capital felony was committed for pecuniary gain . . . The victim of the capital felony was a law enforcement officer engaged in the performance of his or her official duties.").

[8] This is in contrast to the role of mitigating evidence which serves as persuasive reasons to keep the defendant alive or in prison rather than sentenced to death. In making the selection decision, each juror must be free to give effect to all relevant evidence that has been presented in mitigation. *See* Chapter 12, *infra*.

[9] *See, e.g.*, TENN. CODE ANN. § 39-13-204(c) (2011) ("In the sentencing proceeding, evidence may be presented as to any matter that the court deems relevant to the punishment and may include . . . the nature and circumstances of the crime. . . . "); CAL. PENAL CODE § 190.3 (West 2011) ("In determining

listed, courts generally allow a sentencer to consider such evidence, including evidence about the victim and the victim's family.[10]

Some states choose to list admissible aggravating evidence in their statutory scheme. Other states have no statutory provision for additional evidence in the selection decision, but permit its admission by practice. If the aggravating evidence is listed in the statute, it is usually called *statutory aggravating evidence*. If there is no statutory definition, or if the evidence is different from what is listed in the statute, the evidence is generally referred to as *non-statutory aggravating evidence*.

Whether or not particular evidence is *statutory aggravating evidence* or *non-statutory aggravating evidence* can only be determined in the context of the specific statute under which the case is being tried. For example, evidence of a defendant's prior record may be specifically listed as aggravating evidence in one state statute and not listed as aggravating evidence in another statute.[11]

There are constitutional limits under the Eighth Amendment to the introduction of aggravating evidence. The evidence in the eligibility decision must narrow the class of cases that are eligible for a sentence of death.[12] The evidence introduced for the selection decision must provide a basis for an individualized decision that death is appropriate for this defendant.[13]

Chapter 10 discusses the use of aggravating circumstances to determine eligibility of a crime for the death penalty and the constitutional challenges that have been raised against the use of certain broadly defined aggravating circumstances. Chapter 11 discusses how statutory aggravating circumstances and other aggravating evidence are used in the *selection* decision process.

---

what sentence to impose for a crime, the court shall consider . . . [the] nature and circumstances of the crime committed. . . . ").

[10] *See* Section 11.03, *infra*. The Florida statute provides, "Any such evidence which the court deems to have probative value may be received, regardless of its admissibility under the exclusionary rules of evidence, provided the defendant is accorded a fair opportunity to rebut any hearsay statements." FLA. STAT. § 921.141 (2011). The Louisiana statute provides: "The sentencing hearing shall focus on the circumstances of the offense, the character and propensities of the offender, and the victim, and the impact that the crime has had on the victim, family members, friends, and associates." LA. CODE CRIM. PROC. ANN. art. 905.2 (2011).

[11] Most death-penalty states list prior record as statutory aggravating evidence. A few states list future dangerousness as statutory aggravating evidence. *See* Section 11.02, *infra*.

[12] In *Gregg v. Georgia*, 428 U.S. 153 (1976), the Court noted:

"Georgia did act, however, to narrow the class of murderers subject to capital punishment by specifying 10 statutory aggravating circumstances, one of which must be found by the jury to exist beyond a reasonable doubt before a death sentence can ever be imposed. In addition, the jury is authorized to consider any other appropriate aggravating or mitigating circumstances. GA. CODE ANN. § 27-2534.1(b) (1975). The jury is not required to find any mitigating circumstance in order to make a recommendation of mercy that is binding on the trial court. See GA. CODE ANN. § 27-2302 (1975), but it must find a statutory aggravating circumstance before recommending a sentence of death.

Id. at 196.

[13] *See id.* at 205 (noting that, for this purpose, "the jury is permitted to consider any aggravating or mitigating circumstances").

§ 9.02   AGGRAVATING EVIDENCE AND NARROWING

Every death penalty statute must narrow the class of cases that are eligible for a sentence of death.[14] This narrowing occurs when a statute establishes specific criteria that determine which cases are eligible for a sentence of death. The Supreme Court has never specified any single structure by which this narrowing or eligibility must occur, and has given states broad latitude in designing death penalty statutes. States have responded by creating different types of statutes with different approaches to accomplish the narrowing process.

In most states, the eligibility decision takes place during the penalty phase of the trial. A jury finds at least one statutory aggravating circumstance. A few states have chosen to have the narrowing process take place during the guilt phase of the trial. In these states, the legislature has defined capital murder to include some factor that is identical to statutory aggravating circumstances in another jurisdiction.[15] These statutes have merged the decision of murder plus an aggravating circumstance into one decision of "capital murder." Texas and Louisiana follow this model. California presents a hybrid model. Although a narrowing takes place in the guilt phase of the trial, it is performed by a jury making two separate decisions, rather than one as in Texas.

[A]   Eligibility/Narrowing in the Penalty Phase

Most states use the penalty phase of a trial to conduct the constitutionally required narrowing.[16] When this is the case, the capital murder trial begins in the same manner as a non-capital-murder case. A jury is selected and decides whether or not the defendant is guilty.[17] If a defendant is found guilty of capital murder, the case proceeds to a penalty trial. The same jury that decided the guilt of the defendant now decides whether the defendant is eligible for a sentence of death. The defendant has a constitutional right to a jury determination on the eligibility decision.[18]

During the penalty phase, a prosecutor presents evidence to support one or more of the statutory aggravating circumstances. For a case to be eligible for

---

[14] *See Gregg,* 428 U.S. at 153. *See also* Kansas v. Marsh, 548 U.S. 163, 174 (2006) ("[A] state capital sentencing system must: 1) rationally narrow the class of death eligible defendants; and 2) permit a jury to render a reasoned, individualized sentencing determination. . . . (citations omitted) So long as a state system satisfies these requirements, our precedents establish that a State enjoys a range of discretion in imposing the death penalty . . . ").

[15] *See, e.g.,* TEX. PENAL CODE ANN. § 19.03 (Vernon 2011), which defines felony murder in the same way that GA. CODE ANN. § 16-5-1 (2011) defines the aggravating circumstance of felony murder.

[16] Georgia and Florida are among the states that follow this approach.

[17] In a capital murder case, a jury is "death qualified" at the time it is selected. Under this process, prospective jurors are asked questions to determine whether their views about the death penalty would substantially impair their ability to consider a punishment of both death and life. Usually, the death qualification *voir dire* takes place prior to the guilt/innocence phase of the trial. *See* Sections 7.02 and 7.05, *supra.*

[18] "Moreover, *the jury's role in finding facts that would determine a homicide defendant's eligibility for capital punishment was particularly well established.*" Ring v. Arizona, 536 U.S. 584 (2002) (emphasis in original).

death, a jury must unanimously find at least one statutory aggravating circumstance beyond a reasonable doubt. Although most state statutes provide for a number of aggravating circumstances,[19] a finding of just one aggravating circumstance is sufficient to make a case eligible for a capital sentence. Once a case is eligible for death, the jury proceeds to the selection decision.[20]

[B] Narrowing During the Guilt Phase

Only a few states have chosen to narrow the class of death-eligible defendants during the first phase of a capital trial, when a jury determines guilt or innocence. Texas and Louisiana have taken this approach. In each of these states, the legislature drafted restrictive definitions of capital murder, and included within these definitions elements that mirror statutory aggravating circumstances found in other jurisdictions.

The Court has upheld this approach on the basis that the Constitution requires only that some narrowing takes place. The fact that it takes place during the guilt phase rather than the penalty phase is not constitutionally significant. The fact that most states choose to narrow eligibility during the penalty phase through the use of aggravating circumstances is irrelevant. The Court has explained that the use of aggravating circumstances is not an end in itself, but rather one means of genuinely narrowing the class of death-eligible persons.

The Supreme Court accepted this approach when it reviewed the Texas statute in the 1976 case of *Jurek v. Texas*.[21] The Texas statute did not adopt a list of statutory aggravating circumstances for the jury to consider during the penalty phase of the trial. Instead, the Texas legislature created and defined five classes of murder for which the death penalty was an eligible punishment. In defining capital murder, the Texas legislature set forth as elements many of the same factors that Georgia and Florida adopted in their lists of aggravating circumstances, including: 1) murder of a peace officer or fireman; 2) murder committed in the course of kidnapping, burglary, robbery, forcible rape or arson; 3) murder committed for remuneration; 4) murder committed while escaping or attempting to escape from a penal institution; and 5) murder committed by a prison inmate when the victim is a prison employee.[22]

The Supreme Court held in *Jurek* that the Texas scheme was constitutional and that it sufficiently narrowed the class of persons eligible for the death penalty. The Court reasoned that when the jury returned a finding of guilt on capital murder it was equivalent to finding a statutory aggravating circumstance. The capital murder verdict was unanimous and was based upon the government proving each element, including the one that narrowed the class of death eligible defendants, beyond a reasonable doubt. The definition of "capital murder" thus narrowed the pool of death-eligible defendants.

---

[19] Pennsylvania, for example, has 18 aggravating factors.

[20] *See* Sections 11.01 et seq. and 12.01 et seq., *infra*.

[21] 428 U.S. 262 (1976), *reh'g denied*, 429 U.S. 875 (1976).

[22] TEX. PENAL CODE ANN. § 19.03 (Vernon 2011); GA. CODE ANN. § 17-10-30 (2011); FLA. STAT. § 921.141 (2011).

Louisiana, which also uses the guilt phase to narrow the class of persons eligible for death, follows a different approach. The Louisiana statute defines capital murder as murder under certain aggravated situations. However, the statute also has a list of statutory aggravating circumstances for juries to consider during a penalty phase of a capital trial. In a penalty phase, the jury is instructed that it must find at least one aggravating circumstance before it can reach a death verdict. For example, in Louisiana, a defendant can be convicted of capital murder if he committed murder with the specific intent to kill or inflict great bodily injury on more than one person. During the penalty phase, a jury could find a single aggravating circumstance that mirrors the definition of capital murder: that the defendant had the specific intent to kill or inflict great bodily injury on more than one person.

The Supreme Court upheld the Louisiana statute and found that it provided the same type of restrictive definitions of capital murder as the Texas scheme found constitutional in *Jurek v. Texas*. Since the narrowing function was adequately performed during the guilt phase of the trial, no additional narrowing had to occur during the penalty phase.[23]

[C] Hybrid: The California Model

The California death-penalty system presents yet a third variation and takes a hybrid approach. In the guilt phase, a jury must find a defendant guilty of first-degree murder and must also find the existence of at least one enumerated special circumstance. Under the California statute there are twenty-two enumerated special circumstances that encompass at least thirty-three different types of murder. These include murder of a firefighter, a witness, or a juror; murder committed while lying in wait; murder with poison or with torture; murder while escaping from arrest; a killing while committing one of twelve possible felonies; and a catch-all provision that allows death eligibility for any killing that is especially heinous, atrocious, or cruel.[24] Once a defendant is found guilty of first-degree murder with a special circumstance, the case proceeds to the penalty phase, where a jury makes the selection decision of whether to impose a sentence of death.

In California, the jury considers a separate list of factors during the penalty phase to make its selection decision of whether the defendant deserves a sentence of death.[25] These factors include the age of the defendant at the time of the crime, whether the defendant was under emotional or mental distress at the time of the crime, as well as consideration of the "circumstances of the crime."[26] These factors are not separated into a list of mitigating and aggravating factors.[27] Instead, there is a single list of eleven factors (factors a-k) that the jury may consider in deciding

---

[23] Lowenfield v. Phelps, 484 U.S. 231 (1988).

[24] Cal. Penal Code § 190.2(a) (West 2011); People v. Bacigalupo, 862 P. 2d 808, 821-22 (Cal. 1993).

[25] Cal. Penal Code § 190.3 (West 2011).

[26] *Bacigalupo*, 862 P. 2d at 814 (stating that no factor, except factor (k) is exclusively aggravating or mitigating).

[27] *Id.*

whether or not to impose a sentence of death.[28]

In *Tuilaepa v. California*,[29] the Supreme Court reviewed the structure of the California statute. The Supreme Court assumed that California's special circumstances in the guilt phase narrowed the class of persons eligible for the death penalty in the same way that statutory aggravating circumstances narrow under other state statutes during the penalty phase. The Court affirmed that the constitutional narrowing could take place during the guilt phase of the trial as long as two criteria are satisfied: 1) some narrowing process occurs for those eligible for a sentence of death, and 2) the language used to accomplish the narrowing is not unconstitutionally vague.[30] Once these two criteria are satisfied, the Court has no interest in further examining the specific structure employed to accomplish the narrowing.[31]

§ 9.03   SELECTION DECISION IN THE PENALTY PHASE

Once an aggravating circumstance is found, the selection decision remains; the sentencer must decide whether the defendant should be sentenced to death.[32] Most state statutes provide that the selection decision should be made by a jury. Under these statutes, the same jury continues its deliberations and makes the decision whether or not to impose a sentence of death.[33] A few states, including Florida, Alabama, and Delaware, provide that a jury makes a recommendation to the judge, who then makes the final selection decision.[34]

---

[28] People v. Brown, 726 P. 2d 516, 536 (Cal. 1985). The sentencer is given little if any guidance, is not told to make any findings, nor how to weigh aggravating against mitigating factors before deciding whether death is the appropriate penalty.

[29] 512 U.S. 967 (1994).

[30] *Id.* at 972.

[31] In reviewing the California statute, the Court distinguished between what it identified as capital eligibility criteria, the list of special circumstances enumerated in § 190.2 of the statute, from capital selection factors, the criteria listed in § 190.3 of the statute. The issue before the Court in *Tuilaepa* dealt specifically with the constitutionality of the "selection" criteria" in the statute, that is the § 190.3 factors. However, the Court discussed the "special circumstances" eligibility criteria in order to explain the relationship one has to the other.

[32] While the Court, in *Ring v. Arizona*, 536 U.S. 584 (2002), held that the aggravating circumstance, as a basis for death eligibility, must be decided by a jury, the justices left unresolved whether the selection decision must be a jury determination as well: "Accordingly, we overrule *Walton [v. Arizona*, 497 U.S. 639 (1990)] to the extent that it allows a sentencing judge, sitting without a jury, to find an aggravating circumstance necessary for imposition of the death penalty." *Id.* at 609. In *Walton*, the Court had held that it was not a violation of the 6th Amendment for a judge to make a selection decision without a jury recommendation.

[33] TENN. CODE ANN. § 39-13-204 (2011) would be a good example because it goes so far as to include the format of the decision slip that the jury return to the court once a verdict has been reached.

[34] *See* ALA. CODE § 13A-5-46(a) (2011) ("Unless both parties with the consent of the court waive the right to have the sentence hearing conducted before a jury as provided in Section 13A-5-44(c), it shall be conducted before a jury which shall return an advisory verdict as provided by subsection (e) of this section. If both parties with the consent of the court waive the right to have the hearing conducted before a jury, the trial judge shall proceed to determine sentence without an advisory verdict from a jury. Otherwise, the hearing shall be conducted before a jury as provided in the remaining subsections of this

At the selection stage, a sentencer may consider all evidence introduced during the trial, including evidence in aggravation (that argues for death) and evidence in mitigation (that argues for life), before deciding whether life or death is the appropriate sentence.

A sentencer may also consider non-statutory aggravating evidence, evidence that is not enumerated in the statute but that is relevant to the life or death decision. Some statutes specifically provide that non-statutory aggravating evidence may be admitted. Usually, this is predicated on the government providing appropriate notice.[35] Other statutes, like Florida's, specifically provide that non-statutory aggravating evidence may not be introduced or considered by the sentencer.[36]

The defendant must also remain free to present and to have the sentencer consider all of the mitigating evidence about the character, record and crime of the defendant.[37] This includes a wide range of evidence, such as evidence of brain damage or a psychological diagnosis, evidence that a defendant has shown remorse for the killing, or evidence showing his positive adjustment while incarcerated since his arrest.

The way that a sentencer evaluates this evidence varies depending on whether the statute is a weighing statute or a non-weighing statute. In a weighing jurisdiction, the jury is told to balance all of the aggravating evidence against all of the mitigating evidence. A judge instructs the jury on how to balance and consider the evidence. Jurors may be told that they can return a verdict of death only if aggravating evidence outweighs mitigating evidence, that they must return a verdict of death if the aggravating evidence outweighs the mitigating evidence, or even that they may choose to impose life for any reason for no reason at all.[38] The Supreme Court upheld a Kansas statute that instructed the jury that it must impose a sentence of death when aggravating and mitigating circumstances are in equipoise.[39]

---

section."); FLA. STAT. § 921.141(2) (2011) ("After hearing all the evidence, the jury shall deliberate and render an advisory sentence to the court. . . . ").

[35] See 18 U.S.C. § 3592(c) (2011) ("The jury, or if there is no jury, the court, may consider whether any other aggravating factor for which notice has been given exists."). In *Jones v. United States*, 527 U.S. 373, 376 (1999), the Court said that even if allowing the jury to consider non-statutory aggravating circumstances was not proper, it was a harmless error since all indications show that the jury would have reached the same result either way.

[36] See FLA. STAT. § 921.141(5) (2011) ("Aggravating circumstances shall be *limited* to the following. . . .") (emphasis added). In *Barclay v. Florida*, 463 U.S. 939 (1983), the Court held that even though the court allowed the jury to consider a non-statutory aggravating circumstance, this was a harmless error.

[37] See *infra* Chapter 12.

[38] See 42 PA. STAT. ANN. § 9711(c)(iv) (West 2011) ("The verdict must be a sentence of death if the jury unanimously finds at least one aggravating circumstance specified in subsection (d) and no mitigating circumstance, or if the jury unanimously finds one or more aggravating circumstances which outweigh any mitigating circumstances. The verdict must be a sentence of life imprisonment in all other cases."); VIRGINIA MODEL JURY INSTRUCTIONS - CRIMINAL, P33.125 (1998 Replacement Edition) ("If you find from the evidence that the Commonwealth has proved that circumstance beyond a reasonable doubt, then you may fix the punishment of the defendant at death. But if you nevertheless believe from all the evidence, including evidence in mitigation, that the death penalty is not justified, then you shall fix the punishment of the defendant [at a lesser punishment].").

[39] Kansas v. Marsh, 548 U.S. 163 (2006).

In a non-weighing jurisdiction, a jury must still find the presence of at least one aggravating circumstance beyond a reasonable doubt. However, in making the selection decision, it receives little, if any, guidance as to how the evidence should be evaluated. The jury might be instructed simply that it may fix the punishment at death or, if it finds from all the evidence that death is not justified, it may fix the punishment at life.[40]

---

[40] *See* Virginia Model Jury Instructions, *supra* note 38.

Chapter 10

AGGRAVATING CIRCUMSTANCES: ELIGIBILITY OF THE CASE FOR THE DEATH PENALTY

§ 10.01 CONSTITUTIONAL CONSTRAINTS ON AGGRAVATING CIRCUMSTANCES

In the 1972 watershed case of *Furman v. Georgia*,[1] the Supreme Court expressed the need to safeguard the system of capital punishment from caprice and arbitrary administration. For example, Justice Douglas asserted that capital-sentencing laws should be "even handed, non-selective, and non-arbitrary" in their application.[2] Four years later, in *Gregg v. Georgia*,[3] the Court approved a Georgia death penalty statute that created statutory factors called "aggravating circumstances." These aggravating circumstances provided the basis for making a case eligible for a sentence of death.[4] Today, each of the thirty-four states, as well as the federal government, that have death penalty statutes require that at some point in the decision-making process a jury must find at least one statutory aggravating circumstance or its functional equivalent for the defendant to be sentenced to death.[5]

The Supreme Court began reviewing the modern death penalty statutes in 1976. The Georgia, Florida and Texas statutes came before the Court that year. In Georgia and Florida, the death penalty statutes enumerated aggravating circumstances for use in the penalty phase of the trial to determine which crimes were eligible for the death penalty and which individuals should be sentenced to death. The Texas statute did not enumerate separate aggravating circumstances for use during the penalty trial. Instead, the Texas statute defined the crime of "capital murder" such that certain elements of capital murder mirrored the aggravating

---

[1] Furman v. Georgia, 408 U.S. 238 (1972).

[2] *Id.* at 256 (Douglas, J., concurring). "The high service rendered by the "cruel and unusual" punishment clause of the Eighth Amendment is to require legislatures to write penal laws that are evenhanded, non-selective, and non-arbitrary, and to require judges to see to it that general laws are not applied sparsely, selectively, and spottily to unpopular groups."

[3] Gregg v. Georgia, 428 U.S. 153 (1976).

[4] *See, e.g.,* WASH. REV. CODE ANN. § 9.94A.535 (Lexis 2011). The State of Washington lists, among other things, cruelty to the victim and crimes that occurred as a result of the manufacture of controlled substances as aggravating circumstances.

[5] States have varied over whether to require the sentencer in a penalty trial to be a jury, a judge or a three judge panel. Following the Supreme court's decision in *Ring v. Arizona*, 536 U.S. 584 (2002), the defendant has a right to a jury finding that an aggravating circumstance exists.

circumstances in other state statutes.[6]

As part of its review process, the Court identified the constitutional requirements for a death penalty statute to be valid. In deciding to uphold the Georgia, Florida and Texas statutes, the Court held that these new statutes would ensure that the death penalty was not imposed in an arbitrary or capricious manner.

In 1976, the Court also focused on whether each death penalty statute narrowed the class of persons eligible for capital punishment and created a rational system that allowed a jury to extract the few select cases in which the death penalty was appropriate from the many in which it was inappropriate.[7]

As stated in *Gregg*, this narrowing requirement is comprised of three distinct but related criteria. First, the aggravating circumstance cannot apply to every case within the class of crimes defined as capital offenses; it must narrow the class of murderers subject to capital punishment. For example, malice (in statutes that define murder as malice aforethought) cannot be an aggravating circumstance that elevates murder to capital murder, because malice is present in all murders. The second criterion requires that a jury's discretion be guided in a controlled and objective way to produce a non-discriminatory result.[8] Finally, the aggravating circumstance cannot be defined in a manner that is unconstitutionally vague, because vague language fails to adequately inform jurors of what they must find before imposing a sentence of death.[9] Lack of clarity gives a jury the kind of open-ended discretion that was invalidated in *Furman* and that was found to result in the arbitrary infliction of the death penalty.[10]

Since 1976, the Supreme Court has found fault only with the most undefined aggravating circumstances. Generally, the invalidated aggravating circumstances were defined in extremely vague terms, such as "especially heinous."[11] When language was found to be unconstitutionally vague, the Supreme Court looked to see if the highest state court applied a narrowing or limiting construction to the aggravating circumstance.[12]

Over the years, the Supreme Court's review of aggravating circumstances has focused almost exclusively on whether an aggravating circumstance adequately narrows the class of persons eligible for a sentence of death. If this *narrowing function* is properly fulfilled, the aggravating circumstances will be found constitutional.[13]

---

[6] *See* Section 6.05, *supra*; *see also* Section 9.02, *supra*.

[7] *Gregg*, 428 U.S. at 194-95.

[8] *Id.* at 198.

[9] *Id.* at 195 n.46.

[10] *Id.* at 200.

[11] *See, e.g.*, Godfrey v. Georgia, 446 U.S. 420 (1980). In this case, the court found Georgia's statutory aggravating factor requiring that the murder was outrageously or wantonly vile, horrible and inhuman to be too vague. *See* Section 10.03, *infra*, for a more detailed discussion.

[12] *Id.* at 431. The court reversed the death penalty and remanded the case, finding that the Georgia Supreme Court failed to limit the aggravating circumstances.

[13] *See* Zant v. Stephens, 462 U.S. 862, 879 (1983). In this case, the court held that even if an

§ 10.02   AGGRAVATING CIRCUMSTANCES AS "ELEMENTS" OF A CAPITAL CASE

In *Apprendi v. New Jersey*,[14] the Supreme Court held unconstitutional a hate-crime sentencing enhancement based on a factual finding by the trial judge. The Court held that, because the sentencing enhancement acted like an *element* of the offense, the Sixth Amendment mandated that the defendant had a right to a finding by a jury and not by a judge, unless the defendant waived the jury right.[15]

Two years later, in *Ring v. Arizona*,[16] the Supreme Court applied this "elements" rule from *Apprendi* to aggravating circumstances in a capital trial. In *Ring*, the Court held that aggravating circumstances in a death penalty statute are the functional equivalent of the elements of a criminal offense, and therefore, the defendant has a right to have a jury determine whether an aggravating circumstance is present.[17] An aggravating circumstances must be present to elevate the possible punishment to death. For that reason, the Court concluded that an aggravating circumstance is the functional equivalent of an element.[18] Writing for the Court, Justice Scalia emphasized in *Ring* that, as long as a fact is essential to a given statutory punishment, "whether the statute calls them elements of the offense, sentencing factors or Mary Jane,"[19] there is a Sixth Amendment right to a jury determination.

The decision in *Ring* effectively struck down those state death penalty statutes that allowed a judge or a three-judge panel to make the eligibility decision.[20] It also raised questions about whether other findings in penalty trials must be determined by a jury.[21] One unresolved issue is whether *Ring* applies to the selection decision.[22]

---

aggravating circumstance is vague, the sentence will stand so long as the narrowing function was properly achieved by the use of other valid aggravating circumstances.

[14] Apprendi v. New Jersey, 530 U.S. 466, 494 (2000).

[15] *Id.* at 466. The defendant was convicted of three weapon offenses. The court enhanced the sentence pursuant to state statute by finding by a preponderance of the evidence that the defendant acted with a purpose to intimidate because of race. The Supreme Court reversed the sentence and held that the imposition of an enhancement based solely upon findings by the trial court was a violation of the Due Process Clause. The Court held that any findings that provide the basis for an enhanced sentence must be found by a jury beyond a reasonable doubt.

[16] Ring v. Arizona, 536 U.S. 584 (2002).

[17] *Id.* at 609. *See also* Sattazahn v. Pennsylvania, 537 U.S. 101, 111 (2003). Just a year later, Justice Scalia described the underlying offense of murder as a distinct, lesser included offense of murder plus one or more aggravating circumstances.

[18] *Ring*, 536 U.S. at 602.

[19] *Id.* at 610. (Scalia, J., concurring).

[20] *See e.g.*, Ariz. Rev. Stat. § 13-75 (LexisNexis 2011); *compare* Ariz. Rev. Stat. § 13-703 (LexisNexis 2002). *See also* Idaho Code Ann § 19-2515 (2011); *compare* Idaho Code Ann § 19-2515 (1998). *See also* Colo. Rev. Stat. § 18-1.3-1201(2011); *compare* Colo. Rev. Stat. § 18-1.3-1201(2002). Arizona, Idaho and Montana provided for judge trials at the penalty phase. Colorado provided for a three-judge panel. Those states responded by passing new sentencing statutes that provide for jury sentencing at the penalty phase. *See also* Schriro v. Summerlin, 542 U.S. 348 (2004). *Apprendi* and *Ring* did not impact existing death sentences in states with judge penalty trials as the Supreme Court held that this rule was not retroactive.

[21] *See* Adam Thurschwell, *After Ring*, Federal Sentencing Reporter, Vol. 15, No. 2, December 2002.

Defendants argue that facts that support the aggravating evidence for the selection decision also elevate the possible punishment to death.[23] A jury may not be convinced that a defendant deserves the death penalty based solely on the evidence in support of the statutory aggravating circumstance. Rather it may be the culmination of all the aggravating evidence, statutory and non-statutory, that moves a juror to consider a sentence of death.

Prosecutors generally argue that *Ring* does not extend beyond the finding of statutory aggravating circumstances in the eligibility decision. They argue that the only factual finding necessary to elevate the possible sentence to death is the finding of the statutory aggravating circumstance. Once that finding is made, the other aggravating evidence performs a pure sentencing function.

If *Ring* is extended to include the selection decision, it would impact states that allow a judge to make the final selection decision. This process is often called a "judicial override," which allows a judge to impose a death sentence even after a unanimous jury recommendation for life.[24]

§ 10.03   CHALLENGES TO AGGRAVATING CIRCUMSTANCES: VAGUENESS

[A]   Eighth Amendment Vagueness v. Due Process Vagueness

In a number of cases, defendants challenged statutory aggravating circumstances on the grounds that they were unconstitutionally vague. Because these challenges arose in the context of death penalty cases, they were evaluated under the Eighth Amendment rather than under the Due Process Clause.[25] The Supreme Court has determined that when an aggravating circumstance is

---

Thurschwell provides a good discussion on the implications of *Ring*. In a number of cases in the lower courts, defendants argued that the determination of whether the defendant is mentally retarded must be made by a jury under *Ring*. Few, if any judges agreed. *See* Section 8.03[E], note 105, *supra*.

[22] *See* Proffitt v. Florida, 428 U.S. 242, 252 (1976) (noting that it has never been suggested that jury sentencing is constitutionally required). *See also* Clemons v. Mississippi, 494 U.S. 738, 745 (1990) (permitting appellate reweighing of aggravating and mitigating circumstances); Cabana v. Bullock, 474 U.S. 376, 386 (1986) (allowing a factual finding that the defendant met minimum culpability required under *Tison v. Arizona* to be made for the first time on appeal).

[23] *Ring*, 536 U.S. at 610. (Scalia J., and Thomas J., concurring).

[24] *See* Scott. E. Erlich, *The Jury Override: A Blend of Politics and Death*, 45 Am. U. L. Rev. 1403 (1996). Erlich provides a detailed discussion of the judicial override. Florida, Alabama, Delaware and Indiana statutes provide for a judicial override. *See* Fla. Stat. § 921.141(2) (2002). ("After hearing all the evidence, the jury shall deliberate and render an advisory sentence to the court . . . "); Ala. Code § 13A-5-47 (2003) ("In deciding upon the sentence, the trial court shall determine whether the aggravating circumstances it finds to exist outweigh the mitigating circumstances it finds to exist, and in doing so the trial court shall consider the recommendation of the jury contained in its advisory verdict . . . "); Indiana Code 35-50-2-9 ("[t]he jury shall recommend to the court whether the death penalty or life imprisonment without parole, or neither, should be imposed . . . "); 11 Del. Code § 4209(d)(1) (2011) ("The jury's recommendation shall not be binding upon the Court.").

[25] U.S. Const. amend. XIV § 1. (". . . nor shall any State deprive any person of life, liberty, or property, without due process of law; nor deny to any person within its jurisdiction the equal protection of the laws.").

unconstitutionally vague, a death sentence based on that aggravating circumstance alone is invalid. The vagueness of the aggravating circumstance means that it does not necessarily reduce the size of the group subject to the death penalty and, therefore, does not protect against a disproportional death sentence.

When vagueness is evaluated under the due process clause, the standard is less stringent than that applied under the Eighth Amendment.[26] Vagueness is deemed problematic for due process purposes because of the potential for lack of notice to the defendant. Those objections may be overcome in any specific case where it can be shown that a reasonable person would know that his or her conduct was at risk of falling under the statute. In contrast, claims of vagueness analyzed under the Eighth Amendment assert that the challenged provision fails to adequately inform *juries* of what they must find to impose a sentence of death.[27] As a result, juries are left with the kind of open-ended discretion that was held invalid in *Furman v. Georgia*.[28]

[B] Eighth Amendment Vagueness Challenges

[1] "Outrageously or Wantonly Vile, Horrible or Inhuman": Constitutional on Its Face

In the eligibility phase, the Eighth Amendment requires that the class of persons eligible for the death penalty be narrowed, resulting in a smaller, and presumably more heinous or more culpable, group of cases or defendants. This narrowing is usually accomplished by requiring that a jury find at least one statutory aggravating circumstance. These aggravating circumstances must be defined with sufficient clarity that the jury's discretion is sufficiently limited. If the aggravating circumstance is vague or could be applied to almost all murders, it fails to narrow the cases eligible for a sentence of death. The result is that the process of imposing a sentence of death becomes unconstitutionally arbitrary and capricious.[29]

When the Supreme Court reviewed the Georgia statute in 1976 in *Gregg*, part of its analysis included whether the statute was unconstitutionally vague. The Georgia statute had several aggravating circumstances, but one particular aggravating circumstance raised concern. This aggravating circumstance, O.C.G.A. § 17-10-30(b)(7) [hereinafter (b)(7)], authorized the imposition of the death penalty if the

---

[26] Maynard v. Cartwright, 486 U.S. 356, 361-362 (1988). The Supreme Court reversed a death sentence. The state, in *Maynard*, argued that the aggravating circumstance is unconstitutionally vague only if there are no circumstances that could be said with reasonable certainty to fall within the language of the statute. The Supreme Court rejected the state's analysis holding that it presents a Due Process Clause approach to vagueness and fails to recognize the Court's Eighth Amendment vagueness analysis in capital cases.

[27] *Id.*

[28] 408 U.S. 238, 295 (1972) ("[O]ur procedures in death cases, rather than resulting in the selection of 'extreme' cases for this punishment, actually sanction an arbitrary selection. For this Court has held that juries may, as they do, make the decision whether to impose a death sentence wholly unguided by standards governing that decision . . . . [I]n other words, our procedures are not constructed to guard against the totally capricious selection of criminals for the punishment of death.").

[29] *See* Buchanan v. Angelone, 522 U.S. 269, 276 (1998).

murder was "outrageously or wantonly vile, horrible or inhuman in that it involved torture, depravity of mind or an aggravated battery to the victim."

The defendant in *Gregg* argued that the language in (b)(7) was unconstitutionally vague because the words in this provision described circumstances that could apply to every murder. The defendant argued that any sentence of death under this provision would be arbitrary and capricious, as it failed to provide the jury with any guidance on how to make the life and death decision.[30] Although the Court upheld the Georgia statute in *Gregg*, including the (b)(7) provision, it commented that the language of (b)(7) was too broad as it was written. The Supreme Court saw no reason to strike the statute as unconstitutional. Instead, the Justices allowed the state the opportunity to interpret and apply its statute in a constitutionally limited fashion.[31]

[2] "Outrageously or Wantonly Vile": Unconstitutionally Vague as Applied

After the Supreme Court upheld the Georgia statute in 1976, it again reviewed the Georgia statute, and specifically the (b)(7) aggravating circumstance, a few years later, in *Godfrey v. Georgia*.[32] Godfrey was charged with killing his wife and his mother-in-law. At the time of the murder, Godfrey was distraught that his efforts to reconcile with his wife had been rejected. He went to his mother-in-law's trailer, where his wife was staying, and fired his shotgun through the trailer window, killing her instantly. He struck his fleeing daughter with the end of the gun and then shot and killed his mother-in-law. Godfrey called the sheriff and waited for him to arrive.

Godfrey argued that the (b)(7) aggravating circumstance was unconstitutionally vague. The Court agreed that the statute was unconstitutional *as applied* to the facts in Godfrey's case and reversed his sentence of death. The Court emphasized that if the (b)(7) aggravating circumstance applied in Godfrey's case, it could apply in every murder case.[33] The prosecutor had conceded in closing argument that Godfrey's case involved no allegation of torture or aggravated battery to the victim. Accordingly, the jury imposed a sentence of death relying solely on the fact that the murder was outrageously or wantonly vile, horrible, and inhuman. However, the Supreme Court found that there was nothing in the circumstances of the crime or the background of the defendant that showed a consciousness materially more depraved than any other person who commits a murder.

---

[30] *See* Gregg v. Georgia, 428 U.S. 153, 201 n.51, 52 (1976).

[31] *Id.*

[32] Godfrey v. Georgia, 446 U.S. 420 (1980). Godfrey was retried and sentenced to death under the aggravating circumstance of a double murder. That sentence of death was reversed on grounds of double jeopardy and a life sentence was imposed. Godfrey v. Kemp, 836 F.2d 1557 (11th Cir. Ga. 1988).

[33] *Godfrey*, 446 U.S. at 428-29 ("In the case before us the Georgia Supreme Court has affirmed a sentence of death based upon no more than a finding that the offense was outrageously or wantonly vile, horrible and inhuman. There is nothing in these few words, standing alone, that implies any inherent restraint on the arbitrary and capricious infliction of the death sentence. A person of ordinary sensibility could fairly characterize almost every murder as outrageously or wantonly vile, horrible, and inhuman.").

[3] Other "Heinous" Aggravating Circumstances: State Court Narrowing Interpretations

Eight years later, the Court again reversed a death sentence that applied an aggravating circumstance similar to Georgia's. In *Maynard v. Cartwright*,[34] the Court reviewed an Oklahoma statute that allowed a sentence of death if "the murder was especially heinous, atrocious or cruel."[35] Once again, the Supreme Court reversed the death sentence, finding the aggravating circumstance unconstitutional as applied to the facts of the case.

The Court held that the aggravating circumstance of "*especially* heinous, atrocious, or cruel" gave no more guidance than the Georgia statute that required the murder to be "outrageously or wantonly vile, horrible, or inhuman."[36] The Court made clear that the addition of the word *especially* did nothing to narrow the class of cases that were eligible for death. The Court reasoned that an ordinary person could honestly believe that every unjustified, intentional taking of human life is *especially* heinous (which only requires a finding that the murder was something more than heinous).[37]

In *Godfrey* and *Maynard*, the Supreme Court reaffirmed its earlier concern that an aggravating circumstances must adequately narrow the class of persons eligible for the death penalty *and* keep the jury focused on clear and defined criteria. The Court emphasized that it is the responsibility of the state to define the eligibility criteria in a way that obviates standardless sentencing discretion."[38] After *Godfrey* and *Maynard*, it appeared that the Supreme Court was going to hold state courts to a very stringent standard in reviewing their aggravating circumstances.

The Supreme Court consistently maintained that a state court or legislature could save an otherwise vague statute by applying a limiting interpretation of construction to that statute. In *Godfrey* and in *Maynard*, no such limiting had taken place. In *Godfrey*, the Court observed that, although the Georgia Supreme Court had adopted a limiting construction of the (b)(7) aggravating circumstance, the state supreme court failed to apply its own narrow interpretation.[39] In *Maynard*, the Court noted that the Oklahoma courts had failed to apply any limiting interpreta-

---

[34] Maynard v. Cartwright, 486 U.S. 356 (1988).

[35] OKLA. STAT. tit. 21, § 701.12(4) (2002).

[36] *Maynard*, 486 U.S. at 364.

[37] *Id.* "The Oklahoma court relied on the facts that Cartwright had a motive of getting even with the victims, that he lay in wait for them, that the murder victim heard the blast that wounded his wife, that he again brutally attacked the surviving wife, that he attempted to conceal his deeds, and that he attempted to steal the victim's belongings. (citation omitted). Its conclusion that on these facts the jury's verdict that the murder was especially heinous, atrocious, or cruel was supportable did not cure the constitutional infirmity of the aggravating circumstance. The State complains, however, that the Court of Appeals ruled that to be valid the especially heinous, atrocious, or cruel aggravating circumstance must be construed to require torture or serious physical abuse and that this is error . . . We also do not hold that some kind of torture or serious physical abuse is the only limiting construction of the heinous, atrocious, or cruel aggravating circumstance that would be constitutionally acceptable." *Id.* at 364-365.

[38] *Godfrey*, 446 U.S. at 428, *quoting* Gregg v. Georgia, 428 U.S. 153, 196 n.47 (1976).

[39] *Id.*

tion of the statute.[40] Instead, the state court merely concluded that the facts in the case plainly warranted a finding that the killing was especially heinous, atrocious or cruel.

Aggravating circumstances parallel to the ones in *Godfrey* and *Maynard* came before the Supreme Court for review in two more cases, *Walton v. Arizona*[41] and *Arave v. Creech*.[42] Both Arizona (*Walton*) and Idaho (*Creech*) had aggravating circumstances similar to the ones in *Godfrey* and *Maynard*. The Arizona statute stated that the murder had to be especially heinous, cruel, or depraved.[43] The Idaho statute required that a defendant exhibit utter disregard for human life.[44] Both statutes were challenged as unconstitutionally vague for the same reasons that the Supreme Court found Oklahoma's and Georgia's aggravating circumstances to be vague. In both of these cases, the Supreme Court upheld the statutes and the sentences of death, accepting the state high court's narrowing interpretations.

Although the Supreme Court acknowledged that the language in the Arizona statute was unconstitutionally vague (because every murder could be considered especially heinous, cruel, or depraved), the Court upheld Walton's sentence of death by a vote of 5 to 4. The Court reasoned that the Arizona State Supreme Court imposed a constitutionally limited construction of the statute by defining *especially cruel* to mean the infliction of mental anguish or physical abuse before the victim's death and *mental anguish* to include a victim's uncertainty as to his ultimate fate.[45] The Court concluded that these words were unambiguous when applied to Walton's case.

The Court applied essentially the same analysis to the Idaho statute, finding that the Idaho Court had placed a limiting construction on the vague language. The Idaho court concluded that "the phrase "utter disregard" was meant to reflect acts or circumstances surrounding the crime that revealed a "cold-blooded, pitiless slayer."[46] The Supreme Court acknowledged that, while the word "pitiless," standing alone, might not narrow the class of defendants eligible for death, the additional requirement that the murderer be cold-blooded, does provide a sufficiently narrow subclass of defendants.[47]

---

[40] *Maynard*, 486 U.S. at 360. The Oklahoma court simply reviewed all of the circumstances of the murder and decided whether the facts made out the aggravating circumstance. Although the court considered the attitude of the killer and the suffering of the victim to be relevant, it refused to require that any factor be present in a murder to satisfy the statutory factor.

[41] Walton v. Arizona, 497 U.S. 639 (1990).

[42] Arave v. Creech, 507 U.S. 463 (1993).

[43] Ariz. Rev Stat. § 13-703(F)(6) (LexisNexis 2011). ("The defendant committed the offense in an especially heinous, cruel or depraved manner.")

[44] Idaho Code Ann § 19-2515(9)(f) (2011). ("By the murder, or circumstances surrounding its commission, the defendant exhibited utter disregard for human life.")

[45] *Walton*, 497 U.S. at 654.

[46] *Arave*, 507 U.S. at 468.

[47] *Id.* at 471-2. The Court defined these terms according to Webster's dictionary and determined that "pitiless" means "devoid of or unmoved by mercy or compassion," and "cold-blooded" is "one who kills with an absence of warm feelings, without consideration, compunction, or clemency."

Scholars have criticized the holdings in *Walton* and *Arave*. They have argued that the aggravating circumstances in Arizona and Idaho were indistinguishable from those in Oklahoma and Georgia and should have been found unconstitutional as applied. They have argued that the Court abdicated its responsibility when it refused to review state cases to determine whether the professed limiting instructions were, in fact, being applied consistently.[48] Additionally, critics note that the Court failed to inspect the aggravating circumstances to determine if they sufficiently narrowed the class of persons eligible for the death penalty.[49]

Other challenges to the vagueness of statutes have been heard in lower courts. The Ninth Circuit Court of Appeals reviewed several provisions of the California death penalty statute and held that the California special circumstance requiring proof of torture was unconstitutional. The court required evidence that a defendant *intended* to torture and not just that the defendant inflicted extreme physical pain.[50] However, when the Ninth Circuit Court of Appeals reviewed the special circumstance of lying-in-wait, it held that this special circumstance provided a thin but meaningfully distinguishable line between first degree murder lying-in-wait and special circumstances lying-in-wait.[51] To prove the special circumstance, the court held that the government must prove intentional murder plus the three elements of lying-in-wait; waiting, watching and concealment.[52]

§ 10.04   CHALLENGES TO AGGRAVATING CIRCUMSTANCES: DUPLICATIVE OF THE CRIME

Defendants have also challenged aggravating circumstances that are duplicative of one of the essential elements of the offense.[53] This challenge posits that a statute with this duplication fails to narrow the class of persons eligible for the death penalty and is therefore unconstitutional under the Eighth Amendment.

For example, suppose a defendant shoots and kills someone during a robbery and is charged with felony murder. The defendant is found guilty of felony murder, and the case proceeds to the penalty phase of the trial. Suppose the only aggravating circumstance alleged is that the killing was done in the course of a robbery. This aggravating circumstance exactly mirrors one of the elements of felony murder.[54]

---

[48] C. Steiker and J. Steiker, *Sober Second Thoughts: Reflections on Two Decades of Constitutional Regulation of Capital Punishment*, 109 HARV. L. REV. 355, 372-389 (1995).

[49] *Id.*

[50] *See* Wade v. Calderon, 29 F.3d 1312, 1320 (9th Cir. 1994); *see also* Morales v. Woodford, 336 F.3d 1136 (9th Cir. 2003).

[51] Houston v. Roe, 177 F.3d 901, 907 (9th Cir. 1999).

[52] *Morales v. Woodford*, 336 F. 3d 1136 (9th Cir. 2003), *affirmed*, 388 F. 3d 1159 (2004).

[53] *See* Jones v. U.S., 527 U.S. 373 (1999). *See also* U.S. v McCullah, 76 F.3d 1087, 1111-12 (10th Cir. Okla. 1996). A narrowing challenge that an aggravating circumstance is duplicative of an essential element of an offense is different than a challenge that two non-statutory aggravating factors are duplicative and therefore result in an unconstitutional double counting during the selection process.

[54] There is also a related, but separate, claim of double counting, as exemplified in *Woratzeck v. Stewart*, 97 F.3d 329 (9th Cir. 1996). There, the defendant appealed his murder conviction and death

Does the aggravating circumstance in this hypothetical case (killing in the course of a robbery) still narrow the class of cases eligible for a sentence of death as constitutionally required? The answer depends on whether the state statute otherwise narrows the group eligible for the death penalty in the guilt phase.[55] When the Supreme Court upheld state death penalty statutes in 1976, it provided that constitutional narrowing can occur in either of two ways: 1) the legislature may broadly define capital offenses for a guilt phase determination and provide for narrowing in the penalty phase by jury findings of enumerated aggravating circumstances (as most states have done), or 2) the legislature may itself narrow the definition of the capital offenses so that the jury findings during the guilt phase accomplish the narrowing.[56]

If a state death penalty statute narrows the eligible class in the guilt phase, and the language in the penalty phase is duplicative of an element of the offense in the guilt phase, the sentence of death will be upheld.[57] No additional narrowing needs to be accomplished during the penalty phase. Therefore, it is of no consequence that the aggravating circumstance is identical to an element of the offense.

If the statute does not narrow in the guilt phase, the outcome may be different, because no narrowing has occurred. Some state courts have found the duplication in these circumstances to violate the Eighth Amendment. Tennessee and North Carolina courts have held that the duplication between their felony murder statute and an aggravating circumstance in the penalty phase results in a failure of their statutes to constitutionally narrow the class of cases eligible for death.[58] However, as long as some narrowing occurs, duplication will not render a death sentence invalid.[59]

---

sentence, claiming, among other things, that the second aggravating factor used at trial failed to sufficiently channel the sentencer's discretion in felony-murder cases. The court affirmed the sentence, providing that the second factor, that the crime was committed in the expectation of pecuniary gain, did not make all persons convicted of felony-murder and robbery automatically death eligible but required an additional finding of an expectation of gain distinct from the taking in the robbery.

[55] *See* Section 9.03, *supra.*

[56] *See* Jurek v. Texas, 428 U.S. 262 (1976). *See also* Lowenfield v. Phelps, 484 U.S. 231 (1988).

[57] *See* Lowenfield v. Phelps, 484 U.S. 231 (1988) (upholding sentence of death where the sole aggravating circumstance found by the jury at the penalty phase, that "the defendant knowingly created a risk of death or great bodily harm to more than one person," was identical to one category of first-degree murder).

[58] *See* State v. Middlebrooks, 840 S.W.2d 317 (Tenn. 1992) (upheld challenge). The U.S. Supreme Court granted and then dismissed certiorari without deciding the case. *See also* Tennessee v. Middlebrooks, 510 U.S. 124 (1993). *See also* State v. Cherry, 257 S.E.2d 551 (N.C. 1979).

[59] *See* State v. Young, 853 P.2d 327 (Utah 1993) (Defendant argued that the consideration of additional aggravating factors violated the Eighth and Fourteenth Amendments because it failed to properly channel the jury's discretion and to narrow the class of offenders eligible for the death penalty. The court held that the narrowing function required by the Eighth Amendment may occur at either the guilt or the penalty stage of a capital trial. It further held that there was nothing unconstitutional about Utah's scheme which narrowed at the guilt phase.); Oregon v. Wagner, 752 P.2d 1136 (Or. 1988), *cert. denied.*, 498 U.S. 879 (1990). (The court upheld the Oregon statute by comparing it to the Texas statute. The court cited the Supreme Court's opinion in *Jurek, supra*, which upheld the Texas scheme of narrowing at the guilt phase.)

Chapter 11

AGGRAVATING EVIDENCE AND THE SELECTION DECISION

§ 11.01 ELIGIBILITY AND SELECTION DECISION

[A] Overview

Any discussion of aggravating evidence must start with the question: What is the *function* of the aggravating evidence? Is the aggravating evidence being used for the eligibility decision or for the selection decision? Or is it used for both?[1]

The function of the aggravating evidence affects the label given to the evidence as well as how the evidence may be used by the sentencer. First, a jury makes the statutory eligibility decision.[2] The evidence that is considered to make a case eligible for death is called aggravating circumstances. The use of aggravating circumstances in making the eligibility decision was discussed in Sections 10.01-10.04.

Once a case is eligible for the death penalty, a factfinder, in making the selection decision, determines whether the death penalty should be imposed on the defendant.[3] This decision is an individualized one that allows a sentencer to consider the unique facts and circumstances of a specific case and a particular defendant before making a life-or-death decision. The selection decision provides the capital punishment system with the individualized consideration that the Court has concluded is constitutionally required.

There are three categories of evidence that may be considered in making the selection decision. The first is the evidence supporting statutory aggravating circumstances that are the basis for the eligibility decision. That evidence may continue to be part of the sentencer's evaluation of whether death is appropriate at the selection stage.

Second, a sentencer may consider additional aggravating evidence that is introduced by the prosecution. If this evidence is specified in a death penalty statute, it is called statutory aggravating evidence. For example, evidence of a

---

[1] *See* Section 9.01, *supra.*

[2] *See* Ring v. Arizona, 536 U.S. 584 (2002) (holding that Arizona statute that designated that trial judge, sitting alone, shall determine the presence or absence of the aggravating factors required by Arizona law for imposition of the death penalty violated the Sixth Amendment right to a jury trial).

[3] In some states the jury determination is advisory only and the judge makes the final determination as to what the appropriate sentence in the case should be.

defendant's prior record is often listed as evidence that may be considered in the selection decision.[4] Many state statutes allow evidence about the effect of the murder.[5] Additionally, a sentencer may consider non-statutory aggravating evidence that is introduced by the prosecution and relates to the circumstances of the crime or the background of a defendant but is *not* specified in the death penalty statute. This evidence is called non-statutory aggravating evidence. For example, if a state statute does not list a defendant's prior record in its statute as aggravating evidence for the selection decision, the prosecution may still try to introduce that evidence at the penalty phase of the trial. The judge then rules on whether the aggravating evidence should be admitted at trial. In making its decision, a court may consider the nature of the prior conviction, how recently it occurred, and whether it supports other statutory aggravating circumstances (e.g., whether a defendant constitutes a future danger to society). Other non-statutory evidence typically includes evidence that the defendant has no remorse for the crime.

This chapter focuses on the selection decision and the types of aggravating evidence that are introduced in support of a verdict of death.

[B]   Use of the Aggravating Evidence in the Selection Decision: Weighing v. Non-Weighing Statutes

The process by which a sentencer must make the selection decision depends on whether the statute is a *weighing* statute or a *non-weighing* statute. Under a weighing statute, a sentencer must weigh all of the aggravating evidence against all of the mitigating evidence.[6] This process is neither a numerical determination nor a quantitative analysis of the aggravating and mitigating evidence. Rather, it is meant to be a careful, thoughtful evaluation and assessment of all of the evidence presented to determine whether the aggravating evidence outweighs the mitigating evidence. A sentencer is given specific instructions and guidelines as to how to consider the evidence that has been introduced. A typical instruction in a weighing jurisdiction will tell the sentencer that a sentence of death can only be imposed if the aggravating circumstances outweigh the mitigating circumstances.[7]

---

[4] Only a few of the death-penalty states do not list previous convictions as an aggravating circumstance. For an example of a state that does, *see* ALA. CODE § 13A-5-49(2) (2011) ("The defendant was previously convicted of another capital offense or a felony involving the use or threat of violence to the person.").

[5] *See, e.g.*, FLA. STAT., § 921.141 (7) (2011) ("Once the prosecution has provided evidence of the existence of one or more aggravating circumstances as described in subsection (5), the prosecution may introduce, and subsequently argue, victim impact evidence to the jury. Such evidence shall be designed to demonstrate the victim's uniqueness as an individual human being and the resultant loss to the community's members by the victim's death. Characterizations and opinions about the crime, the defendant, and the appropriate sentence shall not be permitted as a part of victim impact evidence.").

[6] Mitigation is any reason why a defendant should not be sentenced to death. *See* Section 12.01, *infra*.

[7] *See, e.g.*, TENN. CODE ANN. § 39-13-204(e)(1) (2011) ("After closing arguments in the sentencing hearing, the trial judge shall include in the instructions for the jury to weigh and consider any of the statutory aggravating circumstances . . . which may be raised by the evidence at either the guilt or sentencing hearing, or both. The trial judge shall also include instructions for the jury to weigh and consider any mitigating circumstances raised by the evidence at either the guilt or sentencing hearing, or both, which shall include, but not be limited to, those circumstances set forth in subsection (j). . . . ").

A weighing jurisdiction may authorize the sentencer to return a verdict of life if the aggravating circumstances outweigh the mitigating ones.[8] In 2006, the Supreme Court upheld a Kansas statute that allowed a jury to return a verdict of death where the aggravating circumstances and mitigating circumstances were in equipoise. In a 5-4 decision, the Court held that such a statute met the constitutional requirements of 1) "rationally narrowing the class of death-eligible defendants" and 2) providing an individual sentencing determination based on a death-eligible defendant's record, personal characteristics and the circumstances of his crime.[9]

Under a non-weighing statute, the decision is more open-ended, and the sentencer has complete discretion to decide between life and death. No specific formula mandates how mitigating evidence and aggravating evidence must be considered. A typical instruction in a non-weighing jurisdiction will only state that the aggravating and mitigating factors should be considered against each other, with no required sentence if one kind of circumstance outweighs another. Since the decision-making process is more open-ended under a non-weighing statute, consideration of additional, non-statutory relevant information may have less impact on the decision-making process.

§ 11.02   EVIDENCE OF FUTURE DANGEROUSNESS

[A]   Overview

A prosecutor introduces evidence of future dangerousness to show that a defendant is likely to commit further acts of criminal violence or poses a continuing danger or threat to society, and therefore, deserves a sentence of death. This type of evidence is allowed under many statutes. In several states, future-dangerousness or continuing-threat evidence has been adopted as a statutory aggravating factor to be considered in making the selection decision.[10] In other states, it has been introduced as non-statutory aggravating evidence.[11] The Texas statute directs a jury to focus on future dangerousness by requiring the sentencer

---

[8] *See e.g.,* N.M. Stat. Ann. § 31-20A-2(b) (2011). "After weighing the aggravating circumstances and the mitigating circumstances, weighing them against each other, and considering both the defendant and the crime, the jury or judge shall determine whether the defendant should be sentenced to death or life imprisonment."

[9] Kansas v. Marsh, 548 U.S. 163, 174 (2006). The Court also noted that weighing is not an end, but a means to reaching a decision, and that Kansas' instructions clearly inform the jury that a determination that the evidence is in equipoise is a decision for death. *See id.* at 179.

[10] Evidence that the defendant will be a future danger or continuing threat to society is enumerated in five state statutes. A typical statute states: "The existence of a probability that the defendant would commit criminal acts of violence that would constitute a continuing threat to society." Okla. Stat. tit. 21, § 701.12(7) (2011). *See also* Idaho Code Ann. § 19-2515(9)(i) (2011) ("The defendant, by his conduct, whether such conduct was before, during or after the commission of the murder at hand, has exhibited a propensity to commit murder which will probably constitute a continuing threat to society."); Wyo. Stat. Ann. § 6-2-102(h)(xi) (2011) ("The defendant poses a substantial and continuing threat of future dangerousness or is likely to commit continued acts of criminal violence.").

[11] For example, future dangerousness is not a statutory aggravating circumstance in Florida but is permitted to be introduced for a jury to consider at the selection stage. *See* Wainwright v. Goode, 464

to respond to a specific question of whether the defendant poses a continuing threat to society.[12]

To support an allegation of future dangerousness, a wide range of evidence has been permitted, including evidence of a defendant's prior criminal record,[13] evidence of the circumstances surrounding the charged offense,[14] evidence demonstrating a defendant's lack of adjustment or violent behavior while incarcerated,[15] evidence of a defendant's lack of remorse,[16] and evidence of threats against others and attempts to prevent the police from being called.[17] Courts have also allowed expert testimony from psychologists and psychiatrists who make predictions as to the dangerousness of a capital defendant.[18]

The Supreme Court upheld the admissibility of future-dangerousness evidence as early as 1976, when it reviewed a Texas statute.[19] The Texas statute required a sentencer to answer three questions, all of which had to be answered "yes" before a sentence of death could be imposed. One question asked whether there was a probability that the defendant would commit criminal acts of violence that would

---

U.S. 78 (1983), (non-statutory aggravating evidence may be considered by the court in making a sentencing decision).

[12] The second special question in the Texas statute asks jurors to decide whether there is a probability that the defendant would commit criminal acts of violence that constitute a continuing threat to society. *See* Tex Code Crim. Proc. Ann. art. 37.071 (2011).

[13] *See, e.g.*, S.C. Code Ann. § 16-3-20(C)(a)(2) (2011) ("The murder was committed by a person with a prior conviction for murder"). *See also* Mo. Rev. Stat. § 565.032(2)(1) (2011) ("The offense was committed by a person with a prior record of conviction for murder in the first degree, or the offense was committed by a person who has one or more serious assaultive criminal convictions."); Va. Code Ann. § 19.2-264.2 (2011) ("In assessing the penalty of any person convicted of an offense for which the death penalty may be imposed, a sentence of death shall not be imposed unless the court or jury shall (1) after consideration of the past criminal record of convictions of the defendant, find that there is a probability that the defendant would commit criminal acts of violence that would constitute a continuing serious threat to society.").

[14] *See, e.g.*, Fla. Stat. Ann. § 921.141(5)(i) (2011) ("The capital felony was a homicide and was committed in a cold, calculated, and premeditated manner without any pretense of moral or legal justification."). *See also* Fla. Stat. Ann. § 921.141(5)(n) (2007) ("The capital felony was committed by a criminal street gang member.").

[15] *See, e.g.*, Ky. Rev. Stat. Ann. § 532.025(2)(a)(5) (2011) ("The offense of murder was committed by a person who was a prisoner and the victim was a prison employee engaged at the time of the act in the performance of his duties.").

[16] *See, e.g.*, Frye v. Commonwealth, 345 S.E.2d 267 (Va. 1986). (Va. Code Ann. § 19.2-264.4 allows juries to consider lack of remorse as part of the prior history of the defendant when deciding whether to impose a death sentence).

[17] *See, e.g.*, Cudjo v. State, 925 P.2d 895 (Okla. Crim. App. 1996).

[18] In *Saldano v. Cockrell*, 267 F. Supp. 2d 635 (E.D. Tex. 2003), aff'd in part, rev'd in part sub nom, *Saldano v. Roach*, 363 F.3d 545 (5th Cir. 2004), the defendant was granted a new penalty phase because of the testimony of an expert witness at trial who testified that race and ethnicity were factors in his conclusion that Saldano would pose a future danger to society. Similar testimony was presented in several other Texas cases, and, for that reason, in most of them, the death sentences were reversed and new penalty hearings were held. *See* Sommer Ingram, *Race-based death sentence challenged*, Dallas Morn. News, Sept. 8, 2011, at A3.

[19] *See* Jurek v. Texas, 428 U.S. 262, 274-275 (1976).

constitute a continuing threat to society.[20]

The defendant challenged the statute, in part, arguing that this question was unconstitutional because future behavior could not be predicted. The Supreme Court rejected this argument and reasoned:

> It is, of course, not easy to predict future behavior. The fact that such a determination is difficult, however, does not mean that it cannot be made. Indeed prediction of future criminal conduct is an essential element in many of the decisions rendered throughout our criminal justice system. . . . The task that a Texas jury must perform . . . is thus basically no different from the task performed countless times each day throughout the American system of criminal justice.[21]

Many lawyers, scholars, and even other psychiatrists have challenged the validity of evidence that predicts future behavior.[22] Despite this controversy, the Supreme Court has not shown any inclination to limit this evidence. In *Dawson v. Delaware*,[23] the Court hinted at a willingness to expand the acceptable evidence of future dangerousness to include "associational evidence," including whether a defendant was a member of a particular organization that engages in violence. In *Dawson*, the prosecutor introduced evidence at trial that Dawson had the words "Aryan Brotherhood" tattooed on his hand. The jury was read a statement that said:

> The Aryan Brotherhood refers to a white racist prison gang that began in the 1960's in California in response to other gangs of racial minorities. Separate gangs calling themselves the Aryan Brotherhood now exist in many state prisons including Delaware.[24]

The Supreme Court reversed Dawson's sentence of death, holding that the stipulation did not adequately link Dawson's membership in the organization to the question of whether he would be a continuing threat to society. However, the Court noted that, under some circumstances, associational evidence might serve a legitimate purpose in showing that the defendant might be a future danger to society.[25]

---

[20] *See* Tex. Code Crim. Proc. Ann. Art. 37.071(b) (Supp. 1975-1976).

[21] *Jurek*, 428 U.S. at 274-76.

[22] *See* Psychiatric News (Nov. 20, 1998) (In March 1983, following the attempt by former psychiatric patient John Hinckley Jr. to assassinate President Ronald Reagan, the American Psychiatric Association, (APA) issued a statement emphasizing its long-held view that "psychiatrists have no special knowledge or ability with which to predict dangerous behavior.") *available at* http://www.psychnews. org/pnews/98-11-20/apa.html (Last visited Dec. 7, 2011).

[23] 503 U.S. 159 (1992).

[24] *Id.* at 162.

[25] *See id.* at 166 ("A defendant's membership in an organization that endorses the killing of any identifiable group, for example, might be relevant to a jury's inquiry into whether the defendant will be dangerous in the future. Other evidence concerning a defendant's associations might be relevant in proving other aggravating circumstances.").

[B]   Can Experts Predict Future Dangerousness?

Evidence of future dangerousness is presented most frequently through the testimony of psychiatrists and psychologists who testify at trial to their expert opinion on whether a defendant is likely to engage in violent behavior in the future. This testimony has been presented in a variety of forms. Sometimes the prosecutor poses a hypothetical question to the expert and asks the expert his or her opinion. Other times expert witnesses base their predictions, at least in part, on interviews conducted with a defendant.

Testimony by expert witnesses on future dangerousness has been challenged on grounds that even psychiatrists are not competent to predict the future dangerousness of an individual. The Supreme Court rejected this argument in *Barefoot v. Estelle*.[26] The Court reasoned that since future dangerousness is a constitutionally acceptable criterion for imposing the death penalty, and a lay jury is allowed to make this decision, psychiatrists should be permitted to express their expert opinion on the issue. The Court noted:

> The suggestion that no psychiatrist's testimony may be presented with respect to a defendant's future dangerousness is somewhat like asking us to disinvent the wheel. . . . If the likelihood of a defendant's committing further crimes is a constitutionally acceptable criterion for imposing the death penalty, which it is, and if it is not impossible for even a lay person sensibly to arrive at that conclusion, it makes little sense, if any, to submit that psychiatrists, out of the entire universe of persons who might have an opinion on the issue, would know so little about the subject that they should not be permitted to testify.[27]

Despite the Court's unambiguous endorsement of the use of expert testimony, evidence of future dangerousness continues to generate a great deal of controversy. The leading national organization of psychiatrists, the American Psychiatric Association[28] (APA), has commented publically and before the Supreme Court that psychiatric predictions of long term future dangerousness are unreliable.[29] Dr. John Monahan, recognized as a leading expert on the issue of predicting behavior, concluded that the "best clinical research currently in existence indicates that psychiatrists and psychologists are accurate in no more than one out of three predictions of violent behavior even among populations of individuals who are mentally ill and have committed violence in the past."[30] Moreover, task forces of

---

[26]   463 U.S. 880 (1983).

[27]   *Id.* at 896-97 (citations omitted).

[28]   American Psychiatric Association, *Governance* (2011) *available at* http://www.psych.org/Resources/Governance.aspx (Last visited Dec. 7, 2011).

[29]   Justice Blackmun noted that the APA had stated that its "best estimate is that two out of three predictions of long term future violence made by psychiatrists are wrong." *Barefoot*, 463 U.S. at 920 (Blackmun, J., dissenting) (quoting from pages 9 and 13 of the American Psychiatric Association amicus brief).

[30]   *Id.* at 920. An example of this inaccuracy is the case of Wilbert Evans who was sentenced to death in Virginia based upon the aggravating circumstance that he posed a future danger. *See* Evans v. Muncy, 498 U.S. 927 (1990). Once incarcerated, he helped restore order after a prison riot, saving the lives of

psychiatric and psychological professional organizations have acknowledged mental health professionals' lack of competence in predicting future dangerousness.[31]

One of the most controversial figures in the predictions of future dangerousness was Dr. James Grigson. Known in the media as Dr. Death, between 1966 and 1994, Grigson testified as an expert for the state of Texas in more than 150 cases predicting the future dangerousness of criminal defendants. By 1989, he testified as to the future dangerousness of one-third of all Texas death-row inmates.[32] Unlike most other psychiatrists who testified to a *probability* that a defendant would be a future danger, Grigson often told juries there was *"no doubt"* a particular defendant would become violent again, and ranked one defendant a "12" on a scale of 1-10 of psychopathic tendencies. The controversy surrounding Dr. Grigson heightened after his testimony in the case of Randall Dale Adams, where he testified that Adams posed a future danger to society and would kill again. The jury sentenced Adams to death. Twelve years later, Adams was exonerated and released.[33] Despite Adam's exoneration, Dr. Grigson continued to assert that Adams was guilty and that he would be violent again. The APA ultimately issued two formal reprimands before finally expelling Grigson from the organization in 1995.[34]

[C]   Constitutional Issues with Psychiatric Interviews

[1]   Overview

Suppose a defendant is charged with murder and appointed a lawyer by the court. While the case is pending, the judge asks a psychiatrist to examine the defendant to see if he is competent to stand trial. The defense counsel has never

---

several hostages and preventing the rape of one nurse. He subsequently filed a Writ of Habeas Corpus asking that his death sentence be overturned on grounds that the finding of the aggravating circumstance that he was a continuing threat to society was unfounded. The petition was denied and on October 17, 1990, Evans was executed.

[31] The American Psychiatric Association Task Force on Clinical Aspects of the Violent Individual has taken the position that neither psychiatrists nor others have demonstrated an ability to predict future violence or dangerousness. *See* APA Task Force Report No. 8, 1974, at 20. The American Psychological Association Task Force on the Role of Psychology in the Criminal Justice system also has concluded that the validity of psychological predictions of violent behavior, at least in the sentencing and release situations, is extremely poor. *33 Am. Psychologist 1099, 1110 (1978), reprinted in* Who is the Client? 1, 14 (J. Monahan, ed. 1980); Aletha M. Claussen-Schulz, Pearce, Marc W. and Robert F. Schopp, *Dangerousness, Risk Assessment and Capital Sentencing.* Vol. 10 Psychology, Public Policy, and Law No. 4, 471 (2004).

[32] *See* Bruce Vincent, *A Dearth of Work for "Dr. Death,"* Texas Lawyer, Dec. 4, 1995; Jeffrey Kirchmeier, *Aggravating and Mitigating Factors: The Paradox of Today's Arbitrary and Mandatory Capital Punishment Scheme,* 6 Wm. & Mary Bill Rts. J. 345, 372 (1998).

[33] Randall Dale Adams was imprisoned for 12 years before he was released in 1989. At one point, he was 72 hours away from execution. His story was the focus of the acclaimed 1988 movie, *A Thin Blue Line,* directed by Errol Morris, which is widely accepted as the impetus behind his release. Adams died in obscurity, but still a free man, on October 30, 2010, at age 61. *See* Douglas Martin, *Randall Adams, 61, Dies; Freed With Help of Film,* N.Y. Times, June 25, 2011, at A24.

[34] The reprimands included one in 1980, after he performed a competency exam on a defendant and used that information to testify to the defendant's future dangerousness, and another, in 1982, after he claimed 100 percent accuracy in predicting future dangerousness of a defendant he had not personally examined.

raised the issue of competency and is not advised that this examination will take place. The expert interviews the defendant and finds him competent. The defendant is found guilty, and, during the *penalty* phase, the prosecution calls that same psychiatrist to testify that, based upon his competency interview with the defendant, he has concluded that the defendant is a severe psychopath who will be a future danger to society. The defendant is sentenced to death.

Did the defendant have a Fifth Amendment right to be warned that any statements made to the psychiatrist could be used against him? Did the defendant have a Sixth Amendment right to have his lawyer present during the interview? If the defendant had raised a defense of insanity, or some other mental state defense, could a psychiatrist who works for the state then interview him? These are some of the questions that have been raised over the years when expert witnesses have interviewed defendants and testified in court. The expert witness's interview and subsequent testimony implicate both the Fifth and Sixth Amendment rights of a defendant.[35] A brief review of these constitutional rights are necessary for an understanding of this issue.

[2] Basic Fifth and Sixth Amendment Analysis

"The Fifth Amendment provides that no person . . . shall be compelled in any criminal case to be a witness against himself."[36] This right, commonly referred to as the right against self-incrimination, not only protects a defendant from being compelled to testify in court but also protects the defendant against the use of his statements in certain pretrial interrogations by a state agent. The existence of a Fifth Amendment privilege is determined not so much by what a defendant says but rather the circumstances under which the statements are made.

There are two aspects to the Fifth Amendment protection. The first protection is from physical coercion, such as an officer beating a defendant to obtain a confession. The second protection is the *Miranda* warnings that are required in any custodial interrogation setting. Thus, critical issues under *Miranda* include whether a defendant is in custody when the psychiatric interview takes place and whether the psychiatrist conducting the interview is acting on behalf of the state.[37]

Miranda requires that the police give an in-custody suspect certain warnings before interrogating him. The purpose is to protect the suspect's Fifth Amendment privilege against self-incrimination.[38] This right to in-custody warnings extends to any interrogation of an in-custody person that is conducted by agents of the government. If police obtain a statement from a criminal defendant in violation of

---

[35] *See Welsh* S. White, *Government Psychiatric Examinations and the Death Penalty*, 37 Ariz. L. Rev. 869 (1995); Thomas Regnier, *Barefoot in Quicksand: The Future of "Future Dangerousness" Predictions in Death Penalty Sentencing in the World of Daubert and Kumho*, 37 Akron L. Rev. 469 (2004); Joanmarie Ilaria Davoli, *Psychiatric Evidence on Trial*, 56 S.M.U. L. Rev. 2191 (2003).

[36] U.S. Const. amend. V, cl. 3.

[37] For more in-depth discussion of 5th amendment right, *see* Joshua Dressler & Alan C. Michaels, 1 Understanding Criminal Procedure: Investigation (5th ed. 2010).

[38] *See* Miranda v. Arizona, 384 U.S. 436 (1966). These warnings include advising a suspect that he has a right to remain silent, that his statements may be used against him at trial, that he has a right to a lawyer during questioning, and that if he cannot afford a lawyer, one will be appointed to him.

the *Miranda* doctrine, the statement is generally not admissible against the defendant in his criminal trial.

The Sixth Amendment guarantees that, in "all criminal proceedings, the accused shall enjoy the right . . . to have the Assistance of Counsel for his defence [sic]."[39] The Sixth Amendment right to counsel attaches at the time that adversarial proceedings are initiated and guarantees a defendant a lawyer at all critical stages of a criminal prosecution.[40] Thus, if a defendant is interviewed by an agent of the state after an indictment or information is filed, the Sixth Amendment applies. If a statement is obtained in violation of a defendant's Sixth Amendment right to counsel, it generally is not admissible at trial against a defendant.[41] The Sixth Amendment may be violated when the government, or one of its agents, deliberately elicits statements from a defendant either without a lawyer present or without a waiver of Sixth Amendment rights from the defendant.

[3] Constitutional Violations and Psychiatric Interviews

Were the defendant's constitutional rights violated in the previous hypothetical?

The Supreme Court said "yes" when it reviewed similar facts in *Estelle v. Smith*.[42] The Court held that once an expert witness interviews the defendant concerning issues of future dangerousness, he becomes an agent of the state. The expert's failure to provide the defendant with *Miranda* warnings at the time of the interview was a violation of the defendant's Fifth Amendment right against self-incrimination. In addition, the failure of the expert witness to notify counsel in advance that an interview was to take place was a violation of the defendant's Sixth Amendment right to counsel. The Court in *Smith* did not address, however, whether the *presence* of counsel at the psychiatric interview was required by the Sixth Amendment. This continues to be a matter of litigation.[43]

---

[39] The Sixth Amendment right was incorporated into the 14th amendment, and, thus, held applicable to the states, in *Gideon v. Wainwright*, 372 U.S. 335 (1963).

[40] For more in-depth information on the right to counsel, *see* JOSHUA DRESSLER & ALAN C. MICHAELS, 1 UNDERSTANDING CRIMINAL PROCEDURE: INVESTIGATION 499-526 (5th ed. 2010); Angela Henson, *Now you have it, Now you don't: The Sixth Amendment Right to Counsel After Texas v. Cobb*, 51 CATH. U. L. REV. 1359 (2002); John E. Spomer, III, *Scared to Death: The Separate Right to Counsel at Capital Sentencing*, 26 HASTINGS CONST. L.Q. 505 (1999).

[41] Massiah v. United States, 377 U.S. 201 (1964) (holding that defendant's Sixth Amendment rights were violated by use in evidence against him of incriminating statements that he made to co-defendant after their indictment and their release on bail and in absence of defendant's retained counsel and that were overheard on radio by government agent without defendant's knowledge that co-defendant had decided to cooperate with government and had permitted agent to install radio transmitter under front seat of co-defendant's automobile).

[42] 451 U.S. 454 (1981).

[43] The court made clear that, in the context of a death penalty case, a psychiatric interview by a representative of the prosecution is a critical stage of the process at which the defendant has a Sixth Amendment right to counsel. Although the Court did not address whether defendant is entitled to counsel's presence during the interview, it acknowledged that testimony of future dangerousness raises issues of life or death and that counsel should be available to assist. *Id.* at 460. *See* Maxwell C. Smith, *Quiet Eyes: The Need for Defense Counsel's Presence at Court-Ordered Psychiatric Evaluations*, 16 CAP. DEF. J. 421 (2004).

[4] Waiver of Constitutional Rights

Although the Supreme Court recognized a defendant's Fifth and Sixth Amendment rights in connection with an interview by a government expert, these rights may be waived if a defendant puts his mental condition in issue.[44] For example, if a defendant raises the defense of severe emotional disturbance or insanity, the government is entitled to hire an expert witness to interview the defendant and testify at trial.[45]

§ 11.03 VICTIM IMPACT EVIDENCE

[A] Overview

Perhaps the most dramatic and powerful form of evidence offered by the prosecution in the penalty phase is "victim impact" evidence.[46] The most common form of victim impact evidence is testimony from a family member of the victim about the impact of the murder on the surviving members of the family. Over the years, prosecutors have introduced, or attempted to introduce a broad range of evidence on the theory that it bears on victim impact, including testimony from surviving victims about feelings of continuing pain and loss, evidence of medical conditions suffered by the victim's loved ones after the murder, photos depicting the life the victim and others had together, testimony from rescue workers about the devastation at the murder scene, and videotaped and narrated movies highlighting the life of the victim.

Although the Supreme Court has held that certain types of evidence about the victim and the loss to the victim's family are admissible,[47] it has not fully resolved the scope of evidence that may be permitted. Many questions remain unanswered by the Court, including whether witnesses other than family members may testify and whether videos or movies depicting a victim's life are permissible. Meanwhile, lower courts around the country are responding to the testimony in a variety of ways.

---

[44] *See* Buchanan v. Kentucky, 483 U.S. 402 (1987). Buchanan was convicted of murder. On certiorari, he contended, among other things, that the admission of findings from a psychiatric examination violated his Fifth and Sixth Amendment rights. The Court held that the introduction of a psychological report for limited rebuttal purposes did not constitute a violation of Buchanan's Fifth or Sixth Amendment rights where he asserted an insanity defense and placed his mental status at issue.

[45] *Id.* at 421-425.

[46] Victim impact evidence is not used as a basis for making a case eligible for a sentence of death. Rather, once a case is eligible, this evidence may be considered in the selection decision to decide whether death is appropriate.

[47] *See* Payne v. Tennessee, 501 U.S. 808 (1991). *See also* Humphries v. Ozmint, 397 F.3d 206 (4th Cir. 2005) (court found prosecutor's closing argument that made victim-defendant comparison of "worth" was not a violation of due process where it was based on evidence at the trial and was not the centerpiece of the argument); United States v. Nelson, 347 F.3d 701 (8th Cir. 2003) (court found no due process violation where witness provided a "tearful and emotional reading" of a poem about the victim, finding it only conveyed the devastating loss they felt and was not unduly long).

The Supreme Court first examined victim impact evidence that was admitted at a capital-sentencing trial in *Booth v. Maryland.*[48] A Maryland statute permitted evidence bearing on three subjects: 1) the personal characteristics of the murder victim, 2) the emotional impact of the killing on the victim's family, and 3) the opinion of family members of the victim about the defendant and the appropriate sentence.[49] The court held that this evidence was not admissible.

Just four years later, in *Payne v. Tennessee,*[50] the Court reconsidered whether victim impact evidence was admissible in a penalty trial. This time, the Court held that the Eighth Amendment did not forbid all victim impact evidence. In *Payne,* the Court ruled that evidence from the first two categories (victim characterization and impact evidence) was allowed. The Court did not address the admissibility of evidence of the family opinion of the defendant and the appropriate sentence, leaving intact the decision in *Booth* that the Eighth Amendment prohibited its admission.[51]

Who qualifies as a victim impact witness? Members of the immediate family? Friends? Co-workers? While the Supreme Court has not explicitly addressed this issue, lower courts have taken widely divergent views. Clearly, members of the immediate family of the victim may testify about the impact of the murder on members of the family. Some courts have expressly limited the testimony to witnesses closely related to the victim.[52] Other courts have taken a broader view, allowing testimony from coworkers and other witnesses who are less closely related.[53]

[B] From *Booth* to *Payne*

The law surrounding the admissibility of victim impact evidence underwent a substantial reversal in a matter of just a few years. In 1987, in *Booth v. Maryland,*[54] the Supreme Court held that victim impact testimony was per se inadmissible in a penalty trial. The Court ruled that this evidence was basically irrelevant and refocused the jury from the defendant and his act to the character and reputation of the victim. In so doing, the Court reasoned, this evidence injected a degree of arbitrariness into the sentencing decision that violated the Eighth Amendment. The Court identified several other concerns that contributed to its unconstitutionality: the evidence was inevitably emotionally charged, making it more difficult for a sentencer to fairly evaluate; the evidence was impossible for the

---

[48] 482 U.S. 496 (1987).

[49] Md. Ann. Code art. 41, § 4-609(c) (1986).

[50] 501 U.S. 808 (1991).

[51] *See, e.g.,* State v. Payne, 2008 Ida. LEXIS 121 (Ida. 2008) (reversing death sentence due to "high volume of victim impact statements" opining about the crime or the defendant's character).

[52] *See, e.g.,* New Jersey v. Muhammad, 678 A.2d 164, 180 (N.J. 1996) (testimony is limited to a single adult family member).

[53] *See, e.g.,* United States v. Whitten, 610 F.3d 168, 188 (2nd. Cir. 2010); United States v. Bolden, 545 F.3d 609, 626 (8th Cir. 2008); United States v. Fields, 516 F.3d 923, 946 (10th Cir. 2008); State v. Byram, 485 S.E.2d 360 (S.C. 1997).

[54] 482 U.S. 496 (1987).

defense to rebut or refute; and the evidence risked creating a hierarchy of victims by making some victims appear more worthy than others.

The Court's holding in *Booth* noted three subjects to which victim impact evidence might be directed: 1) the personal characteristics of the murder victim, 2) the emotional impact of the killing on the victim's family, and 3) family members' opinions and characterizations of the crime and the defendant including their opinion as to whether a defendant should be sentenced to death. The Court prohibited victim impact evidence regarding all three subjects.

Just four years later, in *Payne v. Tennessee*,[55] the Court reversed itself. This time, in a 5-to-4 decision, the Court upheld the admissibility of victim impact evidence in a penalty trial. Payne was convicted of two counts of murder in the brutal stabbing of a mother and her two year-old daughter. At the penalty trial, the grandmother testified about how a surviving two year-old boy had been affected by the murders:

> He cries for his mom. He doesn't seem to understand why she doesn't come home. And he cries for his sister Lacie. He comes to me many times during the week and asks me, Grandmama, do you miss my Lacie. And I tell him yes. He says, I'm worried about my Lacie.[56]

In his closing argument, the prosecutor discussed the impact of the crime by arguing that the little girl would never go to her prom and the mother would never again kiss her son good night. Payne was sentenced to death and appealed, arguing the victim impact evidence violated *Booth*. This time a new majority of the Supreme Court upheld Payne's sentence of death, finding that the Eighth Amendment did not create any per se bar to either victim impact evidence or argument.

Justice Rehnquist wrote the opinion for the Court and found that the testimony was admissible for two reasons. First, a jury is entitled to hear details of the *harm* caused by the crime, and victim impact evidence describes that harm. Second, victim impact evidence serves to "keep the balance true in a capital trial" by presenting evidence that the victim is a unique individual in the same way the defendant presents mitigating evidence that he is a unique individual.

The debate over the admissibility of victim impact evidence reflects the debate on what harm a jury should consider when deciding whether to impose a sentence of death. Should the assessment of harm include specific information about the victim? The Court in *Payne* held that it should.

According to Chief Justice Rehnquist, a sentencer has always considered the harm caused by a defendant when determining an appropriate punishment. Rehnquist posited the example of two individuals who both point a gun at someone and who both pull the trigger. One kills and may be charged with murder and sentenced to death. The other misses and will be charged with a lesser offense with no possibility of death. Both are equally blameworthy but may be guilty of different offenses and punished differently solely because their acts caused differing amounts

---

[55] 501 U.S. 808 (1991).

[56] *Id.* at 814-15.

of harm.[57] Victim impact evidence, he reasoned, allows the sentencer to assess the appropriate punishment for a defendant by evaluating, in part, the harm caused.

Justice O'Connor expressed her concern for the victim and her interest in presenting each victim to a jury as a unique individual. She described murder as "the ultimate act of depersonalization. It transforms a living person with hopes, dreams, and fears into a corpse, thereby taking away all that is special and unique about the person."[58] O'Connor believed that victim impact evidence serves to put a human face and image on the victim.

[C] Limits on Victim Impact Evidence

The decision in *Payne* explicitly overruled portions of the decision in *Booth*.[59] The Court made clear in *Payne* that it did not hold that victim impact evidence was desirable or that it must be admitted. It held only that the Eighth Amendment erects no *per se* bar to its introduction. The admissibility of the evidence depends, in part, on the death-penalty statute in the state.

Payne also only admitted two forms of victim impact evidence: characterization evidence (presenting a characterization of the victim) and impact evidence (showing the impact of the killing on the family). Because the Court never discussed the admissibility of opinion evidence (evidence of the victim's family's opinion of the defendant and the appropriate sentence), that portion of the opinion in *Booth* that held it unconstitutional is still intact.[60]

Should the fact that victim impact evidence is emotional and upsetting affect its admissibility? When the Court in *Payne* held that victim impact evidence was admissible, it made clear that if victim impact evidence becomes too unfair or prejudicial in a particular case, it will violate due process.[61] Many state courts have responded by exercising caution when admitting victim impact evidence.[62] Other states have created rules limiting victim impact evidence. Some state courts have imposed restrictions on the evidence by limiting the testimony to only one adult witness[63] and requiring that accounts be factual, and not unduly emotional.[64]

---

[57] *Payne*, 501 U.S. at 819.

[58] *Id.* at 832 (O'Connor, J., concurring).

[59] *See id.* at 825. The Court did not preclude the possibility if victim impact evidence were unduly prejudicial it could be challenged as a violation of due process.

[60] *See id.* at 830 n.2 (O'Connor, J., concurring) (stating that the Court's holding did not reach Booth's purported limit on sentence opinion testimony); *see also Id.* at 835 n.1 (Souter, J., concurring). *See also* United States v. Brown, 441 F.3d 1330, 1351 (11th Cir. 2006) (concluding that this part of *Booth* "remains good law").

[61] *Id.* at 825.

[62] *See, e.g.*, Wheeler v. State, 4 So.3d 599, 606-09 (Fla. 2009) (stating that victim impact evidence should not be "impermissibly prejudicial," and cautioning trial courts to ensure "the proper balance is struck").

[63] In *New Jersey v. Muhammad*, 678 A.2d 164 (N.J. 1996), the Court stated:

"The greater the number of survivors who are permitted to present victim impact evidence, the greater the potential for the victim impact evidence to unduly prejudice the jury against the defendant. Thus, absent special circumstances, we expect that the victim impact testimony of one survivor will be adequate to provide the jury with a glimpse of each victim's uniqueness

Courts have excluded testimony that the witness has suffered physically[65] or that the witness had to work since the killing.[66] They have disallowed evidence about the impact on neighbors or non-family members.[67] In the Oklahoma City bombing case, the judge prohibited some of the evidence offered as victim impact evidence, including evidence of marriage photos and funeral arrangements.[68]

There are some areas where courts have consistently excluded victim impact evidence offered by the prosecution. For example, most courts will not allow victim impact testimony from victims of other crimes committed by the defendant.[69]

Courts have had more difficulty deciding the admissibility of evidence of information about a particular victim about which the defendant was unaware. For example, one court wrestled with whether evidence that a victim was a nun was admissible when she was not wearing her distinctive religious clothing when she was killed. Some courts that have addressed this kind of question have expressed concern about its admissibility or excluded the evidence.[70] Justice Souter, in *Payne*

---

as a human being and to help the jurors make an informed assessment of the defendant's moral culpability and blameworthiness. Further, minors should not be permitted to present victim impact evidence except under circumstances where there are no suitable adult survivors and thus the child is the closest living relative."

Id. at 180.

The court also noted:

"The limitations that we have placed on the admission of victim impact evidence are not designed to restrict any of the rights afforded to victims by either the Victim's Rights Amendment or the victim impact statute. Rather, these controls are necessary to minimize the possibility that victim impact statements made during the penalty phase of a capital trial will inflame the jury and prevent it from deciding the proper punishment on the basis of relevant evidence."

Id. at 180. *See also* People v. Hope, 702 N.E.2d 1282 (Ill. 1998).

[64] *Muhammad*, 678 A.2d at 180. *See also* United States v. Glover, 43 F. Supp. 2d 1217, 1235-36 (D.Kansas 1999) (noting limitations).

[65] *See, e.g.*, Short v. State, 980 P.2d 1081, 1101 (Okla. Crim. App. 1999) ("Mrs. Yamamoto's statements concerning her feelings and actions upon learning of her son's injury and subsequent death were emotional, but fell within the guidelines set forth in *Cargle* and [statute omitted]. These statements were probative of the emotional, psychological, and physical effects she experienced as a result of the death of her only child. Mrs. Yamamoto's statements concerning her son's desire to study in America, his eventual achievement of that goal and his concern for his mother provided a brief glimpse of the unique characteristics of the individual known as Ken Yamamoto.").

[66] *See, e.g.*, Bowling v. Commonwealth, 942 S.W.2d 293, 302 (Ky. 1997).

[67] *See, e.g.*, State v. Frost, 727 So. 2d 417, 429-430 (La. 1998).

[68] United States v. McVeigh, 153 F.3d 1166, 1221 n. 47 (10th Cir. 1999).

[69] *See, e.g.*, People v. Hope, 702 N.E.2d 1282 (Ill. 1998); Sherman v. State, 965 P.2d 903, 914 (Nev. 1998); State v. Nesbit, 978 S.W.2d 872 (Tenn. 1998); State v. White, 709 N.E.2d 140, 154 (Ohio 1999); People v. Dunlap, 975 P.2d 723, 744-745 (Colo. 1999); Cantu v. State, 939 S.W.2d 627, 637 (Tex. Crim. App. 1997).

[70] *See* People v. Fierro, 1 Cal. 4th 173, 264 (1991) (Kennard, J., concurring and dissenting) (evidence should be limited to those facts known to the defendant); State v. Nesbit, 978 S.W.2d 872 (Tenn. 1998) (probative value of the victim impact evidence is great when a defendant had specific knowledge about the victim's family . . . when defendant lacks such knowledge, the probative value is minimal if nonexistent and the evidence should be excluded); State v. Bernard, 608 So. 2d 966, 972 (La. 1992) (held victim impact evidence admissible to the extent that the murderer knew or should have known that the victim was unique). *But see* People v. Garcia, 52 Cal. 4th 706, 751-52 (2011) (rejecting claim that, to be

wrote that a defendant should know that every victim is unique and that in killing this person, others will be affected. Justice Souter wrote:

> Every defendant knows . . . that the life he will take . . . is that of a unique person like himself, and that the person to be killed probably has close associates, "survivors" who will suffer harms and deprivations from the victim's death. . . . They know that their victims are not human islands, but individuals with parents or children, spouses or friends or dependents. . . . The fact that the defendant may not know the details of a victim's life and characteristics . . . should not in any way obscure the further facts that . . . harm to some group of survivors is a consequence of a successful homicidal act.[71]

Most states have passed statutes specifically authorizing the admissibility of victim impact evidence regarding the selection decision. Other states without express authorization in their statutes have admitted the victim impact evidence under the broad umbrella factor of *circumstances of the crime*.[72] However, when victim impact evidence is admitted as a circumstance of the crime, those courts have generally limited the scope of admissibility to evidence that bears some relation to the crime. For example, in Texas, testimony by a co-worker of the victim about the victim's work with handicapped students did not relate to the crime and was not admissible.[73] However, the same court held that testimony by family members who were present at the shooting and described both the murder scene and its lasting effect on them was admissible.[74]

State and federal courts continue to wrestle with questions on the appropriate scope and form of victim impact evidence. Over the years, the scope and form of the evidence has expanded beyond what was offered in *Payne*.

[D]　Examples of Victim Impact Evidence Admitted at Trial Since *Payne*

Evidence that has been offered under the rubric of victim impact evidence reflects a broad range of information. The most basic form of victim impact evidence, and the form that was clearly allowed in *Payne*, is testimony from family members and close friends concerning the impact that the death has had on their lives. This evidence includes testimony of the financial, emotional, psychological or physical impact of the death on those close to the victim. In *Payne*, the prosecutor

---

admissible under *Payne*, effects of murder must have been known or reasonably apparent to defendant when it occurred).

[71] *Payne*, 501 U.S. at 838.

[72] *See id.* at 827 (no per se prohibition against admission of victim impact evidence). *See also* People v. Russell, 50 Cal.4th 1228, 1264-65 (2010) ("As we have repeatedly held, victim impact evidence is relevant and admissible pursuant to section 19-.3, factor 9(a) as a circumstance of the crime so long as it is not 'so unduly prejudicial' that it renders the trial 'fundamentally unfair.' "); Smith v. State, 919 S.W.2d 96, 102 (Tex. Crim. App. 1996) (victim impact evidence must relate directly to the circumstances of the crime or be necessary for rebuttal).

[73] *See Smith*, 919 S.W.2d at 102.

[74] *See* Ford v. State, 919 S.W.2d 107, 115-116 (Tex. Crim. App. 1996).

offered very limited testimony about the effect of the murders on a surviving son. Subsequent cases have allowed impact evidence that shows the medical condition of family members following the murder. Examples include an aunt who suffered a heart attack[75] and a father who stopped fighting his cancer after learning of the murder.[76] Dramatic testimony was offered in the Oklahoma City bombing trial of Timothy McVeigh, including testimony of a little girl who approached a police officer and hugged his dog, asking, "Mr. Police Dog, will you find my friends?" Only a handful of jurisdictions have limited testimony to those who are close or immediate family members.[77] Otherwise, the tendency of the courts has been to expand the universe of witnesses who may testify. Some courts have concluded, for example, that appropriate witnesses include the community of listeners of a radio call-in talk show,[78] the entire law enforcement community,[79] and a socioeconomically disadvantaged community that had lost a role model.[80]

Although it appeared that the Court in *Payne* left intact the prohibition against any testimony by the victim's family as to the appropriate sentence, some lower courts have also upheld the use of this kind of evidence. Such testimony has included statements from survivors of a murder that "people like the defendant don't deserve to live another day,"[81] from the wife of a murder victim who asked the jury to "show no mercy,"[82] and from the father and brother of a slain police officer who begged the jury to impose death in the name of the victim's family and every police officer.[83]

While *Payne* approved evidence that allows the jury to see the unique nature of the victim, the form in which this evidence has been presented frequently has been far more dramatic and graphic than that introduced in *Payne*. Courts have allowed videotape presentations depicting a victim's life prior to the murder, often narrated

---

[75] *See* Young v. State, 992 P.2d 332, 342 (Okla. Crim. App. 1998).

[76] *See* Griffith v. State, 983 S.W.2d 282, 289 (Tex. Crim. App. 1998) (en banc).

[77] La. Code Crim. Proc. Ann. art. § 905.2(A) (2007); Miss. Code Ann. § 99-19-155(c) (2011); Del. Code Ann. tit. 11, § 9401(7) (2011).

[78] *See* McClain v. State, 477 S.E.2d 814, 824 (Ga. 1996) (When asked about the effect of the victim's death on the community, [witness] responded that the victim's murder was the primary topic of a local radio show in the weeks following the crime and "there was much anger expressed about the crime.").

[79] *See* Hyde v. State, 778 So. 2d 199, 213 (Ala. Crim. App. 1998) (Whitten, the victim's father, testified that he "recommended, on behalf of his son and every law enforcement officer, that the appellant receive the death sentence. Cole, recommended as a police officer, and as the chief investigating officer in this case, that the appellant be sentenced to death.").

[80] *See* Moore v. State, 701 So. 2d 545, 551 (Fla. 1997) ("Here, the judge also found that because of the nature of the specific community in which the victim lived, the evidence was admissible to show a loss to that community.").

[81] *See* People v. Brown, 705 N.E.2d 809, 822 (Ill. 1998).

[82] Witter v. State, 921 P.2d 886, 895 (Nev. 1996).

[83] *See* Whitehead v. State, 777 So. 2d 781 (Ala. Crim. App. 1999). *But see* Ex parte Washington, 2011 Ala. LEXIS 52 (Ala. Sup. Ct. 2011) (reversing death sentence where "victim's parents told the jury that Washington's crime was 'brutal, evil, terrible,' that Washington was 'someone without a conscience,' and that death was the 'appropriate punishment.' ").

by a member of the family.[84] Graphic photos portraying the victims have been shown to a jury, including photos of a stillborn child dressed in the clothes the victim's mother intended for him to wear home from the hospital,[85] and photos of the partially decomposed bodies as they were removed from the woods days after the murders.[86]

The emotional impact of this testimony is obvious. Challenges to this evidence rest, in part, on the overwhelming psychological impact this emotional evidence has on a sentencer. The challenges also question whether, after hearing and seeing this type of evidence, any person can be expected to do what is constitutionally required in a penalty phase of a capital trial: to listen to and consider the individual characteristics of the defendant as well as of the crime itself.[87]

§ 11.04   NON-STATUTORY AGGRAVATING FACTORS AT SENTENCING

[A]   Overview

Once a valid statutory aggravating circumstance is found in the eligibility process, a defendant becomes eligible for the death penalty. The sentencer then moves to the selection decision and considers all the evidence in aggravation and in mitigation to decide whether death is appropriate for this defendant. Courts continue to wrestle with questions of the admissibility of non-statutory evidence at the penalty phase — evidence that is admitted without any express authorization in the statute.

When the Supreme Court approved the death penalty schemes in 1976, the Court indicated that states could create their own individual statutory schemes and that the Court would not issue a general edict requiring a particular structure. The Court left the states free to decide which aggravating circumstances to list in the death penalty statute and to adopt for themselves provisions in their respective sentencing statutes as to the role of non-statutory aggravating evidence.

Non-statutory aggravating evidence includes evidence introduced by the government that was not explicitly covered by the statute and therefore not expressly contemplated by the state's legislature. Once a sentencer is allowed to consider non-statutory evidence, there is a danger that the sentencer will be guided by emotion and caprice rather than by objective standards as mandated in *Furman* and *Gregg*.[88] The question is: once factors outside the contemplation of a

---

[84] *See* Hicks v. State, 940 S.W.2d 855, 857 (Ark. 1997); Whittlesey v. State, 665 A.2d 223, 251 (Md. 1995).

[85] *See* State v. Ard, 505 S.E.2d 328, 331 (S.C. 1998).

[86] *See* State v. Conaway, 453 S.E.2d 824, 849 (N.C. 1995).

[87] *See* Susan Bandes, *Empathy, Narrative, and Victim Impact Statements*, 63 U. Chi. L. Rev. 361, 386 (1996).

[88] Furman v. Georgia, 408 U.S. 238, 294-295 (1972) (Brennan, J., concurring) ("Furthermore, our procedures in death cases, rather than resulting in the selection of 'extreme' cases for this punishment, actually sanction an arbitrary selection.").

statute are allowed into the sentencing process, will courts be able to ensure that death sentences are meted out fairly and not arbitrarily?

The Supreme Court has granted considerable leeway to the states and the prosecutors in the realm of non-statutory aggravating evidence, explaining:

> We have never suggested that the United States Constitution requires the sentencing process to be transformed into a rigid and mechanical parsing of statutory aggravating circumstances. . . . It is entirely fitting for the moral, factual, and legal judgement of judges and juries to play a meaningful role in sentencing.[89]

In evaluating non-statutory evidence, the Supreme Court distinguished between evidence considered for eligibility and that considered in the selection process. Only *statutory* aggravating circumstances may be relied upon for the eligibility process. Once that threshold has been crossed, numerous factors, including non-statutory evidence, may be considered in the selection decision.[90] The selection decision emphasizes the need for an individualized determination based upon the character of the defendant and the circumstances of the crime. A process that allows a sentence of death to be based upon non-statutory aggravating evidence does not necessarily violate this principle.[91]

It is impossible to define all the possible non-statutory evidence without examining a specific statute. Each death penalty statute has its own list of statutory aggravating evidence, and these lists are not the same in every state. One type of evidence may be statutory evidence in one state but non-statutory evidence in a second state.

[B]   Statutory Approaches to Non-statutory Aggravating Evidence

When a prosecutor uses non-statutory aggravating evidence, two fundamental constitutional principles are brought into conflict: the need for heightened reliability and the requirement that the sentence is individualized. In order to ensure reliability, the Court has held that the discretion of the sentencer must be directed and guided. This would seem to argue against the consideration of non-statutory aggravating evidence. At the same time, the sentence should be based upon all of the circumstances of the crime and of the offender. This principle would support introducing relevant information even if it is not enumerated in the statute.

Since non-statutory aggravating evidence lacks the stamp of legislative approval that statutory aggravating circumstances possess, courts must ensure that the proposed non-statutory factor is constitutional before allowing a sentencer to consider it as part of the selection decision. Each proposed non-statutory factor

---

[89]   Barclay v. Florida, 463 U.S. 939, 950 (1983).

[90]   *See* Zant v. Stephens, 462 U.S. 862 (1983). *See also* California v. Ramos, 463 U.S. 992, 1008 (1983) (stating that, once a statutory aggravator is found during the eligibility process, the jury is free to consider a "myriad of factors to determine whether death is the punishment appropriate to the offense and the individual defendant.").

[91]   *See* Barclay, 463 U.S. at 950-51.

must be examined to determine that it is not overly broad, impermissibly duplicative, nor unconstitutionally vague.[92] The factor must also be relevant to the life-or-death decision. While the courts have made clear that their inclination is to provide broad leeway in favor of allowing a sentencer to consider non-statutory aggravating evidence, the constitutional mandate requiring that a sentence of death not be imposed capriciously or in a freakish manner may, at some point, limit what may be admitted.

State and federal death penalty statutes have taken different approaches to the use of non-statutory aggravating evidence. Most jurisdictions allow the introduction and consideration of non-statutory aggravating evidence. Prosecutors in federal court are permitted by statute to introduce non-statutory evidence as long as proper notice is provided to the defense.[93]

Some jurisdictions have prohibited the introduction or consideration of non-statutory evidence. For example, in Alabama, the death-penalty statute states that *"aggravating evidence shall be the following. . . . "* (Emphasis added).[94] Following this language is a finite list of ten statutory aggravating circumstances that a sentencer is allowed to consider.[95] Similarly, Florida's sentencing statute is equally unambiguous in stating that "aggravating circumstances shall be limited to the following. . . . "[96] What follows in the statute is a finite list of fifteen aggravating circumstances that the sentencer is allowed to consider.[97]

Some states, like Georgia, provide specifically for the consideration of non-statutory evidence in their statute. Others are silent on the issue, but the state court has interpreted the statute to allow consideration of non-statutory aggravating evidence. For example, the Kentucky Supreme Court interpreted its statute's silence to mean that a judge is free to consider anything he or she wishes in determining the sentence, including non-statutory aggravating evidence.[98]

---

[92] In *Jones v. United States*, 527 U.S. 373, 398-399 (1999), the Supreme Court found that the introduction of two non-statutory factors was constitutional. The prosecutor introduced evidence of a victim's personal characteristics under one factor and evidence of the victim's vulnerability under a second factor. The Court concluded that these two factors were not overbroad, unnecessarily duplicative nor unconstitutionally vague.

[93] *See* United States v. McCullah, 76 F.3d 1087, 1106 (10th Cir. 1996) (discussing provision).

[94] ALA. CODE § 13A-5-49 (2011).

[95] Despite the proscriptive language in the statute, Alabama has a system of judicial override that allows a trial judge to override a life sentence or recommendation by a jury ostensibly allowing the judge to consider myriad factors, including non-statutory aggravating evidence.

[96] FLA. STAT. ANN. § 921.141(5) (2011).

[97] In Florida, the jury makes a recommendation to the judge, who imposes the ultimate sentence. When a judge imposed a death sentence over a jury recommendation of life and considered evidence not among the fourteen listed in Florida's death penalty statute, the Supreme Court upheld the sentence of death, finding that, since the non-statutory evidence was otherwise valid, and there was no mitigation to be considered in the case, the judge's consideration of the non-statutory evidence was harmless error. *See* Barclay v. Florida, 463 U.S. 939 (1983). *See also* Sawyer v. State, 313 So. 2d 680 (Fla. 1975); Elledge v. State, 346 So. 998 (Fla. 1977).

[98] *See* Matthews v. Commonwealth, 709 S.W.2d 414 (Ky. 1985).

Chapter 12

SELECTION PROCESS: MITIGATION

§ 12.01 OVERVIEW

Offered in the penalty phase, evidence of mitigation provides reasons why the defendant should not be sentenced to death. Mitigating evidence comes in many varieties. For example, the defense might emphasize that the defendant played a minor role in the crime, that he has no prior criminal record, that he has lasting effects from an abusive childhood, that he has an underlying mental disorder, that he is young, that he is remorseful for the crime,[1] or that he can live peaceably in prison. Mitigation evidence enables the sentencer to consider the life and circumstances of the particular defendant in deciding whether death or life is the appropriate sentence.

As the Supreme Court began to develop its post-*Furman* death penalty jurisprudence in 1976, it had to address the permissible scope of mitigation evidence. In two cases decided that year, the Court struck down mandatory death penalty statutes that precluded all mitigation evidence.[2] In subsequent decisions, the Court had to decide what types of evidence were mitigating, and how the states could structure the consideration of the mitigating evidence.

The Court has held that almost all evidence proffered by the defense as mitigating must be permitted in the penalty phase. Relevant mitigation includes any evidence that the defendant offers concerning his character and record or the circumstances of the crime. By enforcing a requirement that the sentencer remain free to reject the death penalty based on any relevant mitigating evidence that the defendant presents, the Court has sought to ensure individualized sentencing consideration for every capital offender.

Although states may not limit the admissibility of relevant mitigating evidence, the Court has permitted latitude in how a state structures the sentencer's use of the evidence. The Court has imposed two basic structural requirements. First, there must be a meaningful way to reject the death penalty based on the mitigating evidence. Second, each juror must be able to decide whether evidence is mitigating. Other than those requirements, the Court has upheld differing statutory structures for the decision process. As a result, states have some freedom to guide the

---

[1] *See* Scott E. Sundby, *"The Capital Jury and Absolution: The Intersection of Trial Strategy, Remorse, and the Death Penalty,"* 83 Cornell L. Rev. 1557 (1998) (documenting jurors' focus on remorse and lack of remorse in making decisions on death or life).

[2] *See* Woodson v. North Carolina, 428 U.S. 280 (1976) (plurality opinion); Roberts v. Louisiana, 428 U.S. 325 (1976) (plurality opinion).

sentencer's use of mitigating evidence. For example, a state may impose a mandatory death sentence if the sentencer answers particular questions affirmatively or finds that aggravation outweighs mitigation. Thus, while the Court has interpreted "individualized consideration" to require admission of the mitigating evidence, there is no standardized formula for the use of mitigation in the actual assessment of the individual's circumstances.

Mitigating evidence is often introduced through expert testimony on the defendant's medical or psychological condition. There is a constitutional right to have the assistance of an expert under certain circumstances. The final section of this chapter discusses the key Supreme Court case regarding expert assistance and lower court cases that have interpreted it.

§ 12.02   THE ADMISSIBILITY OF MITIGATION: THE LEGACY OF *LOCKETT*

[A]   The "No Preclusion" Principle of *Lockett*

[1]   *Lockett v. Ohio:* The Facts

The seminal case on the admissibility of mitigating evidence is *Lockett v. Ohio*.[3] Ohio was one of the states that responded to *Furman* with legislation that provided statutory lists of both aggravating and mitigating circumstances. One of the seven aggravating circumstances focused on whether the capital murder was committed in the course of an aggravated robbery. Another aggravating circumstance focused on whether the capital murder was committed "for the purpose of escaping" from another offense.[4] The statute provided for only three mitigating circumstances. It stated that the death penalty could not be imposed if "considering the nature and circumstances of the offense and the history, character, and condition of the offender, one or more of the following [mitigating circumstances]" was established:[5]

(1) The victim of the offense induced or facilitated it.

(2) It is unlikely that the offense would have been committed, but for the fact that the offender was under duress, coercion, or strong provocation.

(3) The offense was primarily the product of the offender's psychosis or mental deficiency, though such condition is insufficient to establish the defense of insanity.

---

[3] 438 U.S. 586 (1978). Although constitutional principles authorizing the presentation were not yet established, the trial of Leopold and Loeb in 1924 was apparently the first capital case in which an expansive psychological defense was offered in mitigation of the sentence, at least for a heinous murder in which guilt was conceded. Clarence Darrow successfully represented both defendants on the sentencing question after they pled guilty to the indictment. *See generally* Scott W. Howe, *Reassessing the Individualization Mandate in Capital Sentencing: Darrow's Defense of Leopold and Loeb*, 79 IOWA L. REV. 989 (1994) (using the defense in the Leopold and Loeb trial as a basis to explain the need for a broad inquiry into mitigation at the capital sentencing hearing).

[4] OHIO REV. CODE ANN. § 2929.04(A)(1-7) (1975).

[5] *See* OHIO REV. CODE ANN. § 2929.04(B) (1975).

Sandra Lockett was convicted in Ohio of an aggravated murder as an accomplice to a felony murder. Although she remained outside, two acquaintances and her brother entered a pawnshop to commit a robbery.[6] While inside the shop, one of the codefendants loaded bullets into a gun that he had asked to examine.[7] During the robbery attempt, the pawnbroker grabbed the gun, which discharged, killing him.[8] Allegedly, when advised of what had occurred, Lockett drove the codefendants to a home and called a taxicab. Although Lockett denied it, the prosecution also claimed that she placed the gun first in her purse and then under the front seat of the taxi.[9] Lockett also allegedly helped two of the codefendants hide in her parents' home.[10] After his arrest, the codefendant with the gun accepted a plea bargain that allowed him to avoid a death sentence.[11] The other acquaintance codefendant did not receive the death penalty due to the mitigation of "mental deficiency."[12] Lockett's brother received the death penalty, as did Lockett.[13] Under the Ohio statutory scheme, the trial judge found that, " 'whether [he] liked[d] the law or not,' " he had to sentence Lockett to death.[14]

[2] *Lockett v. Ohio: The Constitutional Standard*

Lockett argued that the Ohio statute unconstitutionally precluded the sentencer from considering mitigating aspects of her character, record and crime.[15] The United States Supreme Court agreed, finding it unconstitutional to preclude the sentencer from considering "her character, prior record, age, lack of specific intent to cause death, and her relatively minor part in the crime."[16]

Written by Chief Justice Burger, the plurality opinion[17] held that "the sentencer, in all but the rarest kind of capital case, [may] not be precluded from considering,

---

[6] *Lockett*, 438 U.S. at 590, 592. There was some dispute about whether Lockett knew that the men were going to rob the pawnshop or whether she thought they were merely going to pawn a ring. However, Lockett had apparently suggested earlier that they rob a grocery store and had offered to provide a gun.

[7] *See id.* at 590.

[8] *Id.*

[9] *See id.* at 590-91.

[10] *Id.* at 591.

[11] *Id.* Parker agreed to testify against Lockett, Lockett's brother and Dew.

[12] *Id.*

[13] *See id.* at 591-92 (Lockett turned down several offers to plead to offenses that would have avoided the death penalty).

[14] *See id.* at 594.

[15] Lockett also raised many other issues, including ones that were the subject of later decisions by the Court. Among the issues raised were whether an accomplice must have an intent to kill before the death penalty may be constitutionally imposed (later addressed in *Enmund v. Florida*, 458 U.S. 782 (1982) and *Tison v. Arizona*, 481 U.S. 137 (1987), discussed in Section 8.02) and whether there might be a category of homicides for which a mandatory death penalty was constitutional (later addressed in *Sumner v. Shuman*, 483 U.S. 66 (1987), discussed in Section 6.06).

[16] *See Lockett*, 438 U.S. at 608.

[17] Although only three other justices joined Chief Justice Burger's opinion, a majority of the justices agreed with the plurality's reasoning. In a separate opinion, Justice Marshall concurred in the judgment

as a mitigating factor, any aspect of a defendant's character or record and any of the circumstances of the offense that the defendant proffers as a basis for a sentence less than death."[18] In reaching its decision, the Court noted the long history of individualized consideration in sentencing in American courts. The Court recognized that the practice of individualizing sentencing in non-capital cases was a matter of "public policy," and not constitutionally required. The Court found, however, that individualized consideration in a capital case was constitutionally required because of the qualitative difference between death and non-capital punishment.[19]

The Court analogized to the two mandatory death penalty systems that it had rejected in 1976 in *Woodson v. North Carolina* and *Roberts v. Louisiana.*[20] In light of the general principle from those cases that a death sentence was unreliable without individualized consideration,[21] the Court concluded that states could not preclude the sentencer from rejecting the death penalty based on any relevant mitigating evidence. Although the Ohio statute, in contrast to the mandatory death statutes, allowed for the consideration of some mitigation, the sentencer was still precluded from considering relevant mitigating information.

The plurality distinguished the Georgia, Florida, and Texas statutes held constitutional in 1976. The Court viewed each of those statutes as permitting the consideration of any pertinent mitigating evidence.[22] In contrast, the Ohio statute restricted the consideration of relevant mitigation.

From *Lockett*, we thus draw the "no preclusion" principle. That is, a sentencer cannot be precluded from considering relevant mitigating evidence as a basis to reject the death penalty. Relevant mitigation is evidence that relates to the defendant's "character or record" or "the circumstances of the crime." From Lockett's case, it appeared that those factors included her general character, her lack of a significant prior criminal record, her youth, her lack of an intent to kill, and her accomplice status. The *Lockett* opinion, however, did not specifically provide a list of possible, or even typical, mitigating factors. Thus, subsequent cases developed the parameters of what constitutes relevant mitigating evidence.

[B] The Expansion of the *Lockett* Doctrine

The Supreme Court has generally interpreted the mandate of *Lockett* broadly. The Court has liberally construed when evidence is relevant to the circumstances of the crime or the character and record of the defendant. The Court has specifically upheld the relevancy of the turbulent childhood of a defendant and a defendant's good adjustment to confinement. Although each of the two cases discussed in this section arose in different procedural contexts, the Court

---

and endorsed the plurality's reasoning but also expressed the broader view that the death penalty was always unconstitutional. *See* 438 U.S. at 619.

[18] *Id.* at 604.

[19] *See generally id.* at 602-605.

[20] *Id.* at 603-605.

[21] *See id.* at 601.

[22] *See id.* at 606-07.

reaffirmed the constitutional command of individualized consideration.

In *Eddings v. Oklahoma*,[23] a plurality[24] of the Court found that the state trial and appellate courts erroneously failed to consider the troubled, physically abusive childhood of the defendant as mitigation. Based upon the trial judge's comments, it appeared that he believed he was precluded under the law from taking the defendant's background into account.[25] In reversing, the plurality opinion stated:

> Just as the State may not by statute [as Ohio had done in Lockett] preclude the sentencer from considering any mitigating factor, neither may the sentencer refuse to consider, as a matter of law, any relevant mitigating evidence.[26]

The case was remanded for proper consideration of the mitigating evidence.[27]

In *Skipper v. South Carolina*,[28] all nine justices concurred in reversing and remanding a death sentence where evidence of the defendant's good behavior in jail was excluded. Six of the justices relied upon *Lockett* and the Eighth Amendment as the basis for their opinion. The majority noted that good adjustment to prison related to the defendant's "character and his probable future conduct." The Court found that evidence that was relevant to a defendant's future conduct easily fit within the concept of "mitigating" evidence.[29] In what was perhaps a harbinger of the Court's subsequent limits on the reach of *Lockett* in later cases, the three concurring justices rejected the *Lockett* grounds for the reversal. Instead, they concurred on a due process basis that the defendant had been denied the ability to rebut the prosecution's arguments of future dangerousness.[30]

---

[23] 455 U.S. 104 (1982).

[24] Although only two other justices joined Justice Powell in the plurality opinion, in essence five justices agreed in the reasoning. Justice Brennan concurred in the judgment on the broader basis that the death penalty was unconstitutional in all circumstances. Justice O'Connor concurred on the same *Lockett* reasoning as the plurality, but answered some of the arguments of the dissenters.

[25] *Id.* at 112-113 (The trial judge stated that " 'in following the law' he could not 'consider the fact of this young man's violent background' ").

[26] *Id.* at 113-114.

[27] *Id.* at 121. In *Eddings*, four justices, Burger, White, Blackmun, and Rehnquist, dissented. The dissenters viewed the comments of the trial judge as indicating that, while he considered the evidence of Eddings's troubled youth, he discounted it as entitled to no weight. *See id.* at 125. The dissent correctly characterized the *Lockett* decision as limited: "We did not, however, undertake to dictate the *weight* that a sentencing court must ascribe to the various factors that might be categorized as "mitigating," nor did we in any way suggest that this Court may substitute its sentencing judgment for that of state courts in capital cases." *Id.* at 122.

[28] 476 U.S. 1 (1986).

[29] *Id.* at 5. The Court noted: "Consideration of a defendant's past conduct as indicative of his probable future behavior is an inevitable and not undesirable element of criminal sentencing."

[30] *See id.* at 9 (Powell, J., concurring).

§ 12.03 THE LIMITS OF THE *LOCKETT* DOCTRINE

[A] Irrelevant Evidence

The Court has found or assumed that virtually all proffered mitigating evidence relating to the defendant's character, record or crime is "relevant" and, thus, constitutionally required to be admissible under the *Lockett* principle. In two cases, however, the Court has distinguished information as "irrelevant" and, thus, not constitutionally significant. The first case hinged on the Court's interpretation of a jury instruction involving emotional reactions. The second case, although far from providing a definitive analysis, focused on any "lingering doubts" about the defendant's guilt.

In *California v. Brown*,[31] the Court found no error in giving an "antisympathy" instruction to the jury.[32] In accordance with *Lockett*, a majority of the Court viewed the instruction as the equivalent of telling the jurors to avoid prejudices or emotional responses that were unrelated to the evidence presented.[33] The Court did not believe that a reasonable juror would have interpreted the instruction as precluding consideration of mitigating evidence.[34]

One year later, the Court in essence found that a sentencer's "residual doubt" about a defendant's guilt was not relevant to the penalty consideration of the circumstances of the crime or the character or record of the defendant. In *Franklin v. Lynaugh*,[35] the defendant argued that the jurors should have been instructed in the penalty phase that they could consider in mitigation whether they had any residual doubt about his identification as the perpetrator, his intent, or the cause of death. The plurality stressed the lack of connection between a sentencer's residual doubts about a defendant's guilt and the *Lockett* requirements. The plurality also stressed, however, that the defendant's arguments about residual doubt were given a forum in the sentencer's consideration of causation and of the deliberateness of the defendant's actions, factors required by the Texas death penalty statute.[36] Thus, the decision is somewhat muddled. It is unclear whether

---

[31] 479 U.S. 538 (1987).

[32] *Id.* at 540. The trial court had "cautioned the jury that it 'must not be swayed by mere sentiment, conjecture, sympathy, passion, prejudice, public opinion or public feeling.'"

[33] *Id.* at 542. A majority of the Court found no error in the instructions as a whole, finding that a reasonable juror would "understand the instruction not to rely on 'mere sympathy' as a directive to ignore only the sort of sympathy that would be totally divorced from the evidence adduced during the penalty phase." In concurrence, Justice O'Connor distinguished between a sentence that properly "reflect[s] a reasoned *moral* response to the defendant's background, character, and crime rather than mere sympathy or emotion." *Id.* at 545 (O'Connor, J., concurring). Justice O'Connor viewed the sentencing phase as a "moral inquiry into the culpability of the defendant, and not an emotional response to the mitigating evidence." Due to this distinction, Justice O'Connor agreed that this "anti-sympathy" instruction in and of itself did not violate the Constitution. *See id.* at 546.

[34] *Id.* at 543. In contrast, the dissenters felt that the instruction prohibited constitutionally protected reactions by the jurors to the mitigating evidence. *See id.* at 548 (Brennan, J., dissenting); *id.* at 563 (Blackmun, J., dissenting).

[35] 487 U.S. 164 (1988).

[36] The question posed to the jury was: "'Do you find from the evidence beyond a reasonable doubt

residual doubt is not constitutionally required mitigation or whether this doubt is appropriate mitigation, but adequately considered under the Texas statute.

Part of the confusion arises from a possible difference between residual doubt on identification of the perpetrator and residual doubt on causation and intent. Six members of the Court found that the Eighth Amendment did not require consideration of residual doubt of defendant's guilt of the crime, at least with regard to a claim of misidentification.[37] A different combination of seven members of the Court also found, however, that the jury was adequately able to consider any residual doubt on all three issues relating to defendant's guilt under the questions posed to them in the penalty phase.[38] Most courts and commentators since *Franklin* have assumed that residual doubt on any issue is not constitutionally required mitigation.[39]

---

that the conduct of the Defendant . . . that caused the death of [the victim] was committed deliberately and with the reasonable expectation that the death of the deceased or another would result?' " *Franklin*, 487 U.S. at 169 n.3.

[37] The plurality structured its opinion by separating the discussion of residual doubt on identity from residual doubt on causation and intent. In the first subpart on identity, the plurality noted "that this Court has never held that a capital defendant has a constitutional right to an instruction telling the jury to revisit the question of his identity as the murderer as a basis for mitigation." 487 U.S. at 172-173. In concurrence, Justices O'Connor and Blackmun took the view that the Constitution does not require consideration of residual doubt on any issue relating to guilt. Thus, although taking a broader view than the plurality, they clearly joined the plurality's conclusion on residual doubt on identity. *Id.* at 187-188 (O'Connor, J., concurring).

[38] The seven justices sharing the conclusion that the Texas questions were adequate to provide for consideration of residual doubt were the plurality and the three dissenters. Although on the identity issue, the plurality spoke in terms of no constitutional requirement to allow for residual doubt, they also approached the issue in the alternative. The plurality noted that, even if residual doubt on identity were constitutionally required, there was no infringement in Franklin's case, because he was able to present the argument to the jury and nothing in his requested instruction would have assisted the consideration of the issue.

In a separate subpart on the causation and intent issues, the plurality did not discuss whether the Constitution required consideration of residual doubt on those issues; the plurality simply launched into a discussion of how the Texas questions covered the issues. *Id.* at 166. The jury could have considered residual doubt over "whether the victim would have perished had she received proper medical treatment" under "Special Issue No. One." Special Issue No. One allowed for a determination that "the conduct of the Defendant . . . that caused the death of [the victim] was committed deliberately and with the reasonable expectation that the death of the deceased . . . would result." *Id.* at 167. The jury could have considered intent through this special issue as well as causation. *Id.*

[39] The Supreme Court itself asserted this view in *Penry v. Lynaugh*, 492 U.S. 302 (1989). While discussing *Franklin*, the Court stated, "Moreover, a majority agreed that 'residual doub[t]' as to Franklin's guilt was not a constitutionally mandated mitigating factor." *Id.* at 320.

Lower federal courts: Evans v. Thompson, 881 F.2d 117, 121 (4th Cir. 1989), *cert. denied*, 498 U.S. 927 (1990) (citing *Franklin* for authority that residual doubt is "constitutionally insignificant"); Smith v. Farley, 59 F.3d 659, 666 (7th Cir. 1995), *cert. denied*, 516 U.S. 1123 (1996) (citing *Franklin* for finding that "[t]he sentencing hearing is not an occasion for reexamining the issue of the defendant's guilt"); Grisby v. Blodgett, 130 F.3d 365, 371 (9th Cir. 1997) (finding that *Franklin* explained "lingering doubts are not germane to mitigation because they are 'not over any aspect of petitioner's character, record, or a circumstance of the offense' ").

State courts: Duncan v. State, 831 S.W.2d 115, 120 (Ark. 1992) (stating that the Supreme Court "has rejected this residual doubt mitigation circumstance in *Franklin*"); People v. Staten, 24 Cal. 4th 434, 464 (2000) (stating that the Supreme Court has held that defendants have no federal constitutional right to an instruction on lingering doubt); Shelton v. State, 744 A.2d 465, 496 (Del. 1999), *cert. denied*, 530 U.S.

[B]   Structuring the Use of Mitigating Evidence

Suppose D has evidence of an abusive childhood, substance abuse problems, and a mental disorder. Under *Lockett*, a state cannot preclude D from presenting her mitigating evidence. May the state, however, constitutionally tell the sentencer *how* to use the mitigating evidence?

The Court has approached the *admission* of mitigating evidence quite differently from the *structure for consideration* of the mitigating evidence. The Court has consistently construed the meaning of mitigation broadly and required admission of virtually any evidence that is considered mitigating. Decisions addressing the use of the mitigating evidence, however, have allowed for variation. The sentencing structure must provide a means to give effect to all admissible mitigating evidence. Within the broad framework of some capacity to give effect to mitigation, however, states are free to design their decision-making processes as they choose. Reflecting an underlying federalism theme, the Court tolerates variation in sentencing structure. As long as all permissible mitigating evidence is admitted into evidence and given some type of vehicle for consideration by the sentencer as a basis to reject the death penalty, the Court finds the Eighth Amendment satisfied.

[1]   The Sentencing Structure Must Allow for the Consideration of Mitigation by Individual Jurors

Three principles have emerged from the Court's decisions finding unconstitutional limitations on the consideration of mitigating evidence. The first principle is that mitigating evidence cannot be completely ignored by the sentencer. The second principle is that the decision-making structure must permit the sentencer to give mitigating effect to the mitigating evidence. The third principle is that, if there is a jury, each juror must be able to decide what is mitigating in his or her own mind.

[a]   The Sentencer Must Listen

Suppose the defense offers evidence that D suffered physical abuse throughout his childhood. The jurors hear the evidence, but are instructed only to consider certain listed mitigating factors, which do not allow for the consideration of

1218 (2000) (stating that the *Franklin* Court held "capital defendants do not have constitutional right to demand jury consideration of 'residual doubts' in the sentencing phase"); Bates v. State, 750 So. 2d 6, 9 (Fla. 1999), *cert. denied* 531 U.S. (2000) (following "the holding of the United States Supreme Court that no constitutional right to present 'lingering doubt' evidence exists"); State v. Hartman, 42 S.W.3d 44, 55 (Tenn. 2001) (citing *Franklin* as holding that there is "no constitutional right to have residual doubt considered as a mitigating factor in a capital sentencing hearing").

Scholars: *See, e.g.*, Christina S. Pignatelli, *Residual Doubt: It's a Life Saver*, 13 Cap. Def. J. 307, 312 (2001) (summarizing *Franklin* as leaving "it to the states to determine the role of residual doubt at sentencing"). *But see* Jennifer R. Treadway, *'Residual Doubt' in Capital Sentencing: No Doubt It Is an Appropriate Mitigating Factor*, 43 Case W. Res. L. Rev. 215, 221 (1992) (noting that only "Justices O'Connor and Blackmun *expressly rejected* residual doubt as an Eighth Amendment requirement" and discussing the nuances of actual holding and responses by states).

physical abuse. Is this constitutional? The Supreme Court found it unconstitutional in *Hitchcock v. Dugger.*[40]

Hitchcock exemplifies the first principle — that a sentencer cannot be forced to completely ignore the existence of mitigation, either by virtue of a statute or by sentencing practice. In *Hitchcock*, the jury was told to consider only the statutorily enumerated mitigating factors, which precluded considering factors such as the defendant's deprived background.[41] The Supreme Court held that the inability of the advisory jury and trial judge[42] to consider non-statutory mitigating evidence that had been admitted at trial was constitutional error.

[b]   The Sentencing Structure Must Give Effect to the Mitigation

Consider the facts of *Penry v. Lynaugh,*[43] a Texas case that involved mitigating evidence that D had the developmental disability of mental retardation. *Penry* arose prior to the Court's decision in *Atkins v. Virginia,*[44] where the court held that it was unconstitutional to execute anyone who is mentally retarded. After *Atkins*, a state would be barred from imposing the death penalty on Penry. At the time of Penry's trial, however, it was constitutional to execute a person with mental retardation. Evidence of mental retardation could be offered as mitigating evidence, and the defense offered evidence of Penry's mental retardation in the penalty phase. Under the Texas system at that time, the death or life verdict was based on jurors' answers to two questions, plus a third question in cases involving possible victim provocation.[45] The two questions that were pertinent in Penry's case asked the jurors to decide whether the defendant's actions were deliberate

---

[40] 481 U.S. 393 (1987).

[41] It appeared that the Florida statute at the time allowed only enumerated mitigating factors to be considered, although the state of Florida law on this point was in dispute in the case. The Supreme Court relied on the instructions given to the jury in deciding that they were, in essence, told to ignore some of the mitigation. *Id.* at 398-399. *See also* Parker v. Dugger, 498 U.S. 308 (1991). In *Parker*, the Court held that it was error for the Florida Supreme Court, in the course of reweighing or conducting harmless error analysis on appeal, to fail to consider the existence of non-statutory mitigating evidence that the trial court took into account.

[42] Florida is one of the states that employ an advisory jury in the penalty phase; the trial judge makes the final determination of death or life. For a discussion of the different models of decision-making in the penalty phase, *see* Sections 7.01-7.03, *supra.*

[43] 492 U.S. 302 (1989).

[44] 536 U.S. 304 (2002).

[45] The three questions were:

"(1) whether the conduct of the defendant that caused the death of the deceased was committed deliberately and with the reasonable expectation that the death of the deceased or another would result;

(2) whether there is a probability that the defendant would commit criminal acts of violence that would constitute a continuing threat to society; and

(3) if raised by the evidence, whether the conduct of the defendant in killing the deceased was unreasonable in response to the provocation, if any, by the deceased."

Art. 37.071(b) (Vernon 1981 and Supp. 1989).

and whether the defendant posed a continuing threat to society.[46] The Supreme Court, in *Penry*, addressed whether the deliberateness question and the future dangerousness question adequately permitted the jurors to give effect to the defendant's mental retardation.

In *Penry I*,[47] the Court held that the Texas process was constitutionally inadequate to allow the sentencer to consider the defendant's evidence of mental retardation. The Texas questions concerning the deliberateness of the defendant's actions and concerning his future dangerousness did not provide an adequate forum for assessing his reduced culpability due to a developmental disability. The deliberateness question would only allow the evidence to be used to reject the death penalty if the defendant's condition rendered him extremely disabled. Penry's disability apparently did not strike the jurors as that severe. Likewise, the future dangerousness question would allow the jurors to consider Penry's evidence, but only in an aggravating way. To the degree that retardation helped explain his crime, it also suggested that he could be a future danger. The Court found that Texas had to give a special instruction to allow the jury to draw a mitigating inference from evidence of mental retardation.[48] Thus, *Penry I* represents the second principle of structuring mitigation — that the sentencing structure must allow for the sentencer to give adequate mitigating effect to the mitigating evidence.

In *Penry II*,[49] the Court reaffirmed the requirement that the sentencer must be able to give adequate mitigating effect to mitigating evidence. After *Penry I*, the case was retried, and Penry was again convicted and sentenced to death. At the new trial, the jurors were instructed to consider mitigating evidence, but once again the jurors were asked to answer "yes or no" to the same questions of deliberateness and future dangerousness as in *Penry I*. A majority of the Supreme Court held that the confusing instructions still failed to allow the jury to give "*full* consideration and *full* effect*" to the mitigation.[50] Thus, the Court found that there was still no mechanism by which the jury could provide its "reasoned moral response" to the mitigating evidence.[51]

---

[46] For a description of the unusual Texas system of posing specific questions to the jurors in the penalty phase, *see* Section 6.05, *supra*.

[47] Penry v. Lynaugh, 492 U.S. 302 (1989). *See* discussion of *Penry, supra*, Section 8.03.

[48] *Penry*, 492 U.S. at 328 (finding "in this case, in the absence of instructions informing the jury that it could consider and give effect to the mitigating evidence of Penry's mental retardation and abused background by declining to impose the death penalty, we conclude that the jury was not provided with a vehicle for expressing its 'reasoned moral response' to that evidence in rendering its sentencing decision").

[49] Penry v. Johnson, 532 U.S. 782 (2001).

[50] *Id.* at 797, *quoting from* Johnson v. Texas, 509 U.S. 350, 381 (1993) (O'Connor, J., dissenting) (emphasis in original).

[51] Although the jurors were instructed that they should give "effect and consideration" to the defendant's mitigation, the instruction then told them to give a negative answer to one of the standard questions if they wanted to impose life. The Court considered this too confusing for the jurors. According to the Court, to give effect to the mitigating evidence, the jurors would have to have concluded that they should answer one of the questions negatively even though a negative answer would probably conflict with a truthful answer to the actual question. The problem was that the mitigating evidence, even if

[c]   Mitigation Decisions by Individual Jurors

Suppose the defense presents evidence of D's mental illness, his physically abusive childhood, and his minor role in the crime. Further suppose that nine of the jurors find mental illness mitigating; three do not. Seven of the jurors find the abusive childhood mitigating; five do not. A different combination of six jurors find D's minor role in the crime mitigating; six do not. If a state requires the jurors to reach a unanimous decision on whether evidence is mitigating, they could not consider any of this proffered evidence. However, the Supreme Court has resoundingly declared that the jurors must individually be permitted to decide and consider what is mitigating.

In both *Mills v. Maryland*[52] and *McKoy v. North Carolina*,[53] the Court struck down sentencing schemes that required juror unanimity to consider evidence as a mitigating factor. In *Mills*, the Court believed that jurors could have interpreted Maryland's jury instructions to require a sentence of death where an aggravating circumstance existed and the jurors could not unanimously agree that any particular factor was mitigating. It was possible for the jurors to believe that they could not weigh any mitigating evidence against the aggravating circumstance unless all agreed that the same factor was mitigating.[54] Without any mitigation to weigh, the instructions then mandated death as the punishment.

Similarly, in *McKoy*, the Court struck down the North Carolina sentencing scheme where it was possible that jurors would have believed that they could not consider mitigating evidence unless it was unanimously found to be mitigating by the jury.[55] Unlike the situation in *Mills*, it was possible under the North Carolina instructions for the jury to reject the death penalty even if no mitigating circumstances were found to exist. Nevertheless, the Court felt that the

---

believed, would not logically call for a negative answer. The Court viewed it as capricious to expect the jurors to ignore the actual questions. *Id.* at 797-800.

Based on finding *Lockett* violations, the Court has also in recent years repeatedly reversed death sentences that were imposed under the original post-*Furman* statute. *See* Smith v. Texas, 543 U.S. 37 (2004) (*per curiam*) (*Smith* I) (finding the Texas questions, even with an additional instruction, inadequate to allow sufficient consideration of mitigating evidence focused on defendant's limited mental abilities and troubled childhood); Tennard v. Dretke, 542 U.S. 274 (2004)(concluding that the Texas questions did not allow adequate consideration of mitigating evidence of defendant's low I.Q.); Smith v. Texas, 550 U.S. 297 (2007) (*Smith* II) (concluding that the Texas courts were required to defer to the Supreme Court's conclusion in *Smith* I that the jury could have interpreted the special issues to foreclose adequate consideration of his mitigating evidence); Abdul-Kabir v. Quarterman, 550 U.S. 233 (2007) (holding that the special questions did not allow for consideration of mitigating evidence of rough childhood and possible neurological damage); Brewer v. Quarterman, 550 U.S. 286 (2007) (concluding that the special questions failed to provide a vehicle for consideration of mitigating evidence of childhood abuse and mental illness).

[52]   486 U.S. 367 (1988).

[53]   494 U.S. 433 (1990).

[54]   *Mills*, 486 U.S. at 400 (concluding "that there is a substantial probability that reasonable jurors, upon receiving the judge's instructions in this case, and in attempting to complete the verdict form as instructed, well may have thought they were precluded from considering any mitigating evidence unless all 12 jurors agreed on the existence of a particular such circumstance").

[55]   *McKoy*, 494 U.S. at 444 (finding "that North Carolina's unanimity requirement impermissibly limits jurors' consideration of mitigating evidence and hence is contrary to our decision in *Mills*").

instructions precluded individual jurors from giving effect to the mitigating evidence.

Thus, *Mills* and *McKoy* represent the third principle developed by the Court that limits the structure of the selection process: each juror must be able to give effect to the mitigating evidence, even if other jurors would not.

[2]   State Variation Allowed in Structuring How the Sentencer Uses Mitigating Evidence

Although the Court has rejected statutory schemes that preclude each juror from giving effect to mitigating evidence, other Supreme Court decisions have affirmed state restrictions on how the sentencer may use the evidence. The Court appears to have distinguished between a situation where the sentencer is completely precluded from using the mitigation from one where the sentencer has some mechanism for using the mitigation, *albeit* in a limited fashion.[56] While the former is unconstitutional, the latter is sometimes constitutionally permissible. Some commentators have described the distinction as a "substance-procedure" or "what-how" dichotomy. The states may not restrict the "substance" or "what" mitigating evidence is considered. On the other hand, the states have some freedom to design the "procedure" or "how" the mitigating evidence is used.[57]

[a]   Mitigation Relevant Only to Future Dangerousness

Suppose the defense presents evidence of D's youth as mitigating evidence. Also suppose that the decision-making structure poses two questions to the jurors, only one of which pertains to the mitigating evidence in this case. The question asks if D poses a continuing threat to society.[58] If the jurors answer the questions affirmatively, they must impose death. If the only critical question for the jurors is whether D poses a continuing threat to society, are they able to give effect to D's youth at the time of the crime? The Supreme Court answered this question in the affirmative.

The Texas statutory scheme required the penalty-phase jury to answer

---

[56] *See, e.g.*, the excellent discussion in Scott E. Sundby, *The Lockett Paradox: Reconciling Guided Discretion and Unguided Mitigation in Capital Sentencing*, 38 UCLA L. Rev. 1147 (1991). Professor Sundby commented that the Court began to limit *Lockett* "by drawing a distinction between the substance of mitigating evidence and the procedure for considering such evidence." *Id.* at 1191. He noted that the "substance-procedure" dichotomy is also referred to as the "what-how" dichotomy." *Id.* at 1195. The Court recognizes a "difference between rules that govern what factors the jury must be permitted to consider in making its sentencing decision, and rules that govern how the State may guide the jury in considering and weighing those factors in reaching a decision." *Id.* at 1191.

[57] *Id.*

[58] The two questions posed to the jurors were:

"(1) Was the conduct of [defendant], that caused the death of the deceased, committed deliberately with the reasonable expectation that the death of the deceased or another would result?

(2) Is there a probability that Johnson would commit criminal acts of violence that would constitute a continuing threat to society?"

Johnson v. Texas, 509 U.S. 350, 354 (1993).

questions as in the hypothetical situation. For many years, the instructions limited the sentencer to consideration of mitigating evidence only as it related to answering specified questions.[59] As a result, numerous challenges arose regarding the constitutionality of this type of restriction on the effect of mitigating evidence. In the *Penry* cases discussed earlier, the Court found the Texas questions inadequate to permit consideration of a defendant's mental retardation.[60] More recently, the Court has also repeatedly found the Texas questions inadequate to allow jurors to give mitigating effect to defendants' evidence of low intelligence, mental illness, neurological damage, or childhood abuse.[61] In other cases, however, the Court found that the Texas questions were constitutionally sufficient for consideration of mitigating evidence.

For example, in *Johnson v. Texas*,[62] the Court held that the future dangerousness question adequately allowed the sentencer to give effect to the mitigating circumstance of youth.[63] Although the defendant argued that the sentencer was unable to give effect to his youth at the time of the crime in assessing his overall culpability, the Court found that the assessment of future dangerousness necessarily would involve considering the level of culpability for the crime. The Court concluded that, to the extent that youth helped explain the crime, the defendant's continually advancing age helped support a conclusion that he would be less dangerous in the future. The Court similarly found, in *Franklin v. Lynaugh*,[64] that the Texas question on deliberateness adequately allowed for a consideration of residual doubt about a defendant's guilt.[65]

---

[59] In different versions of the statute, there were either two or three questions posed to the jurors. See discussion of Texas statute in Section 6.05, *supra.*

[60] *See supra* notes 47-48 and accompanying text.

[61] *See* Smith v. Texas, 543 U.S. 37 (2004) (*per curiam*) (*Smith* I) (finding the Texas questions, even with an additional instruction, inadequate to allow sufficient consideration of mitigating evidence focused on defendant's limited mental abilities and troubled childhood); Tennard v. Dretke, 542 U.S. 274 (2004) (concluding that the Texas questions did not allow adequate mitigating consideration of evidence of defendant's low I.Q.); Smith v. Texas, 550 U.S. 297 (2007) (*Smith* II) (concluding that the Texas courts were required to defer to the Supreme Court's conclusion in *Smith* I that the jury could have interpreted the special issues to foreclose adequate consideration of his mitigating evidence); Abdul-Kabir v. Quarterman, 550 U.S. 233 (2007) (holding that the special questions did not allow for mitigating consideration of evidence of rough childhood and possible neurological damage); Brewer v. Quarterman, 550 U.S. 286 (2007) (concluding that the special questions failed to provide a vehicle for mitigating consideration of evidence of childhood abuse and mental illness).

[62] 509 U.S. 350 (1993).

[63] Johnson had argued "that the forward-looking perspective of the future dangerousness inquiry did not allow the jury to take account of how petitioner's youth bore upon his personal culpability for the murder he committed." He urged the Court that "a prediction of future behavior is not the same thing as an assessment of moral culpability for a crime already committed." The Court rejected this argument, reasoning that "it is both logical and fair for the jury to make its determination of a defendant's future dangerousness by asking the extent to which youth influenced the defendant's conduct." *Id.* at 369.

[64] The Court noted that the petitioner did have an opportunity to argue "residual doubt" and the jury was not precluded from considering it. *Franklin*, 487 U.S. at 175-176. *See* discussion of *Franklin* in Section 12.03[A], *supra.*

[65] The Supreme Court also upheld against *Lockett*-type claims the California death-penalty statute (subsequently amended), which required a jury instruction that the sentencer should consider "any other circumstance which extenuates the gravity of the crime even though it is not a legal excuse for the crime."

Thus, although many times holding the Texas statute inadequate to give effect to mitigating evidence, the Court has also found the Texas system of specific questions adequate to give effect to some types of mitigating evidence. The Court is willing to allow states some latitude to structure and restrict the use of the mitigation, although the effect may be to limit the number of ways in which the evidence may be considered mitigating.[66]

[b]   Burden of Persuasion on Mitigation

In *Walton v. Arizona*,[67] a plurality[68] of the Court found it constitutional to impose the burden of persuasion on the defendant to establish mitigating factors by a preponderance.[69] Therefore, if the defendant claims, for example, that he was physically abused as a child, the state can require D to convince the sentencer that he was abused. *Walton* was overruled in part by *Ring v. Arizona*[70] on a separate issue. The Court in *Ring*, however, did not address the viability of the rest of the *Walton* decision. The burden of persuasion holdings of *Walton* are, thus, presently undisturbed, although there are likely to be challenges based on an argument to extend the reasoning of *Ring* to more aspects of the penalty phase. This section discusses the holding of *Walton* on the burden of persuasion on mitigation and possible challenges to the decision.

Petitioners had claimed that the provision implied that only evidence bearing on the offender's level of culpability for the crime was relevant and, thus, failed adequately to allow sentencing juries to consider certain other forms of evidence that is constitutionally relevant under *Lockett*. However, the Supreme Court concluded that the provision allowed sufficient consideration of the evidence in question. *See, e.g.*, Ayers v. Belmontes, 549 U.S. 7 (2006) (evidence of likelihood of future good conduct if given prison sentence instead of death sentence); Boyde v. California, 494 U.S. 370 (1990) (evidence of pre-crime background and character evidence not directly related to culpability for the capital offense).

66 The willingness of the Court to accept variation in structure is also demonstrated by two cases in which the Court upheld jury instructions that did not directly mention mitigating evidence. Despite arguments that the jurors might be confused about whether they could consider mitigating evidence and impose life if they found an aggravating circumstance, the Court found the instruction adequate to permit the consideration of mitigation. *See* Buchanan v. Angelone, 522 U.S. 269 (1998); Weeks v. Angelone, 528 U.S. 225 (2000) (instruction in *Weeks* on selection decision was same as in *Buchanan*, but also included a separate instruction on mitigation that was not given in *Buchanan*). *But see* Stephen P. Garvey, Sheri Lynn Johnson, and Paul Marcus, *Correcting Deadly Confusion: Responding to Jury Inquiries in Capital Cases*, 85 Cornell L. Rev. 627 (2000) (demonstrating confusion among mock jurors with *Weeks* instruction).

67 497 U.S. 639 (1990).

68 Justice Scalia's concurring opinion provided the fifth vote for the affirmance and probably a de facto fifth vote for the reasoning of the Court. In concurrence, Justice Scalia concluded that the *Woodson-Lockett* line of cases has no basis in the Constitution and, thus, mitigation is not constitutionally required at all. Thus, a state restricting a sentencer's discretion regarding mitigation would not be unconstitutional.

69 *Id.* at 649. The actual language of the statute states the standard as a negative, requiring the death penalty if there is an inadequate showing of mitigation. ARIZ. REV. STAT. ANN. § 13-703(E) requires that the court " 'shall impose a sentence of death if the court finds one or more of the aggravating circumstances enumerated in subsection (F) of this section and that there are no mitigating circumstances sufficiently substantial to call for leniency.' "

70 536 U.S. 584 (2002). *See* discussion of *Ring* in Section 10.02, *supra*. *Ring* overruled the aspect of *Walton* that had permitted a non-jury verdict on the aggravating circumstance; in *Ring*, the Court held that the Sixth Amendment requires a jury finding on the aggravating circumstance.

The constitutional argument in *Walton* that a defendant should not bear the burden of persuasion on mitigating evidence relied upon the broad reach of *Lockett*. The defendant argued that, in violation of *Lockett*, the sentencer (the judge alone in Arizona) was unable to consider some of the mitigating evidence or the cumulative effect of mitigating evidence. The defense contended that a particular mitigating factor might not be found by a preponderance and, therefore, would be precluded from consideration.

The Court rejected the defendant's argument in *Walton*. Turning to the fundamental requirement of "no preclusion," a plurality in *Walton* found that no mitigating evidence was precluded from the sentencer's consideration.[71] The plurality additionally distinguished *Mills*, where the Court had struck down a requirement that all jurors agree on the existence of mitigation by a preponderance.[72] Unlike *Mills*, the plurality reasoned that Arizona's statute permitted the sentencer to decide that evidence was mitigating.[73] The burden of proof simply required the sentencer to be convinced of the existence of mitigation by a preponderance. The plurality analogized the mitigation to affirmative defenses in non-capital cases. In the affirmative defense cases, the Court had held that the burden of persuasion could constitutionally fall on a defendant as long as the state retained the burden of persuasion on each element of the crime. The plurality viewed the proof of an aggravating circumstance as the equivalent of the elements of the crime. Thus, as long as the state had the burden of persuasion to establish the aggravating circumstance, as it did in Arizona, the burden of persuasion could constitutionally shift to the defendant for the "defense" of mitigation.[74]

The Court has also recently clarified that states may require the imposition of the death penalty when the sentencer determines that aggravating evidence and mitigating evidence are in equipoise. In *Kansas v. Marsh*,[75] the Court reviewed a decision of the Kansas Supreme Court that the Kansas death penalty statute

---

[71] *Walton*, 497 U.S. at 649.

[72] *See* discussion of *Mills* in Section 12.03[B][1][c], *supra.*

[73] *Walton*, 497 U.S. at 651. The Court distinguished *Mills*, in part, because, in *Walton*, the judge alone was the sentencer. The Court went on to note, however, that "*Mills* did not suggest that it would be forbidden to require each individual juror, before weighing a claimed mitigating circumstance in the balance, to be convinced in his or her own mind that the mitigating circumstance has been proved by a preponderance of the evidence."

[74] *Id.* at 650. Without discussion, the plurality equated proving "the existence of aggravating circumstances" with proving the elements of the crime for constitutional purposes. Others have argued that the entire penalty decision is the equivalent of the elements of the crime for purposes of assessing the constitutional requirements for burden of proof. *See* Linda E. Carter, *A Beyond a Reasonable Doubt Standard in Death Penalty Proceedings: A Neglected Element of Fairness*, 52 Ohio St. L.J. 195 (1991) (arguing that the penalty phase decision is comparable to the guilt phase determination and should require that the state demonstrate beyond a reasonable doubt that aggravation outweighs mitigation). *See also* Beth S. Brinkmann, *Note: The Presumption of Life: A Starting Point for a Due Process Analysis of Capital Sentencing*, 94 Yale L.J. 351 (1984) (arguing for an analogy between the presumption of innocence and a presumption of life, which would require the state to bear the burden of proving the propriety of death); Stephen Kanter, *Confronting Capital Punishment: A Fresh Perspective on the Constitutionality of the Death Penalty Statutes in Oregon*, 36 Willamette L. Rev. 313 (2000) (arguing for a clear beyond a reasonable doubt standard for future dangerousness, rather than one lessened by language of "probable" future dangerousness "beyond a reasonable doubt").

[75] 548 U.S. 163 (2006).

violates the Eighth Amendment because it directs the imposition of the death penalty when aggravating and mitigating circumstances are evenly balanced. In a five-to-four decision, the Supreme Court concluded that the statute was constitutional under *Walton* and under the general principles set forth in the Court's death penalty jurisprudence.[76]

The Court has not yet reconciled the *Walton* and *Marsh* holdings on the burden of persuasion on mitigation at the selection stage with the holding in *Ring*. The *Marsh* decision came after *Ring*, which suggests that the Court will not change course regarding the burden of persuasion on mitigation. However, the implications of *Ring* could raise tensions within the Court's jurisprudence, and these potential tensions were not expressly addressed in *Marsh*. The Court will eventually have to resolve whether only the aggravating circumstances are the functional equivalent of "elements" or whether findings concerning mitigation are to be viewed in the same way. Both elements and their functional equivalent arguably not only merit a jury verdict under the Sixth Amendment but also require the prosecution to bear the burden of persuasion beyond a reasonable doubt under the due process clause.[77] As Justice Scalia has stated, it does not matter if the state calls the facts to be proved "elements of the offense, sentencing factors, or Mary Jane." If a finding of the elements or their functional equivalent is necessary to increase the possible punishment, there is a right to a jury verdict which, in turn, arguably requires the prosecution to bear the burden of persuasion.

The crucial question is whether findings concerning mitigation will be viewed as the functional equivalent of elements in that they are necessary to increase the possible penalty to death. The defense is likely to argue that death cannot be imposed under a capital sentencing system without a finding not only of an aggravating circumstance but also of a weighing or consideration of mitigation against aggravation. If that argument prevails, the defendant would be entitled to a jury verdict at the selection stage, with the prosecution bearing the burden of persuasion. The states are likely to argue in response that mitigation and the ultimate weighing are merely sentencing determinations. This argument will posit that once an aggravating circumstance is found, death could be imposed. Only the aggravating circumstance is necessary to increase the punishment. If that argument prevails, the burden of persuasion could constitutionally be placed on the defendant to prove mitigation.

---

[76] *See id.* at 173.

[77] The Supreme Court has held that the due process clause requires that the prosecution prove each element of the crime beyond a reasonable doubt. *In re* Winship, 397 U.S. 358, 363 (1970).

§ 12.04 CONSTITUTIONAL RIGHT TO ASSISTANCE OF EXPERTS

[A] Overview

The defense in a capital case generally offers mitigation through both lay and expert witnesses. The defendant's family, former teachers, neighbors, and coworkers, among others, may be called to testify to the defendant's background, problems, or character strengths. It is also common to have experts testify if there is psychological evidence or other scientific evidence. However, because many capital defendants are indigent, they cannot afford experts. This reality has forced the Supreme Court to confront questions about a state's obligation to provide a defendant with expert assistance.

Suppose that D is accused of killing a couple and seriously wounding their two children. D believed that he was the "sword of vengeance." The defense in the guilt phase is insanity. Although psychiatrists examined D to determine competency to stand trial, no psychiatrist for either the state or the defense examined D for insanity purposes. The defense moves for a psychiatric evaluation at state expense. The court denies the motion. Suppose further that the jury finds D guilty and rejects the insanity defense. At the penalty phase, the state argues future dangerousness as aggravation. The state relies on the guilt phase testimony of the psychiatrists that D is likely to continue to be dangerous. D has no expert testimony on this issue. D is sentenced to death. D challenges the death sentence on grounds that he had a constitutional right to psychiatric assistance at state expense.

In *Ake v. Oklahoma*,[78] the Supreme Court held that, on these facts, D did have a constitutional right to psychiatric assistance at state expense. The Court set forth a three-part analysis to make this determination. The three parts balance the defendant's interest, the government's interest, and the risk of error in the trial without the expert assistance. Lower courts have wrestled with the parameters of this constitutional doctrine. Some of the most significant issues post-*Ake* are whether the expert must be independent of the state or whether a neutral expert is sufficient, what range of experts are covered, and whether there is a constitutional right to expert assistance in the penalty phase if there is no expert evidence on future dangerousness offered by the state.

[B] *Ake v. Oklahoma*

Ake is the key Supreme Court case on the constitutional right to expert assistance. The Court held that Ake was entitled to psychiatric expertise at state expense under the due process clause. The Court's starting premise was that a fundamentally unfair trial violates due process. If a defendant does not have meaningful access to justice, the proceeding is fundamentally unfair. Meaningful access to justice, in turn, guarantees defendants "an adequate opportunity to

---

[78] Ake v. Oklahoma, 470 U.S. 68 (1985).

present their claims fairly within the adversary system."[79] An adequate opportunity is dependent on providing defendants the "basic tools of an adequate defense."[80]

The Court weighed three factors to decide whether the psychiatric assistance was a basic tool in the *Ake* case. The three factors were: 1) the defendant's interest, 2) the government's interest, and 3) the "probable value" of the safeguard and the "risk of error" if the safeguard is not provided.[81]

Applying the three factors to Ake's case, the Court easily concluded that due process required psychiatric assistance at state expense in the guilt phase. The defendant's interest in presenting a defense of insanity in the guilt phase was very high. In contrast, the state's interest was viewed as financial and not likely to be an overwhelming burden. The probable value of the psychiatric assistance in evaluating the defendant, presenting the defense, and assisting with cross-examination of the state's witnesses was very high. The risk of error without the assistance was also great where the defendant's sanity was crucial to his level of culpability for the crime.[82] The Court further noted that experts were particularly necessary in a field, such as psychiatry, which is not "an exact science," and in which experts will often differ in their diagnoses, and in which the issues are complex and foreign for jurors.[83] When the defendant's sanity is a "significant factor at trial," due process required that the defendant have "access to a competent psychiatrist who will conduct an appropriate examination and assist in evaluation, preparation, and presentation of the defense."[84]

The Court also held that the psychiatric assistance for the defense was constitutionally required when psychiatric evidence of future dangerousness was presented in the penalty phase. Where the state was relying on future dangerousness as an aggravating circumstance, the Court found that due process required psychiatric assistance to present the other side. The Court noted that the burden on the state was slight. The probable value of the psychiatric assistance and risk of error without the assistance was considered very high.[85] Consequently, the Court concluded that due process required "access to a psychiatric examination on relevant issues, to the testimony of the psychiatrist, and to assistance in preparation at the sentencing phase."[86]

---

[79] *Id.* at 77, *quoting* Ross v. Moffitt, 417 U.S. 600, 612 (1974).

[80] Griffin v. Illinois, 351 U.S. 12, 19 (1956).

[81] *Id.* at 77. Based on comments in a later Supreme Court case, *Medina v. California*, 505 U.S. 437, 445 (1992), there is now some doubt about whether the three-factor test remains valid. In *Medina*, the Court noted that "it is not at all clear that [the three factor test] was essential to the results reached [in *Ake* and another case]." The Court further stated that "[t]he holding in *Ake* can be understood as an expansion of earlier due process cases holding that an indigent criminal defendant is entitled to the minimum assistance necessary to assure him 'a fair opportunity to present his defense' and 'to participate meaningfully in [the] judicial proceeding.' " *Ake*, 470 U.S. at 76.

[82] *Ake*, 470 U.S. at 78.

[83] *Id.* at 81.

[84] *Id.* at 83.

[85] *Id.* at 82.

[86] *Id.* at 84.

[C] Post-*Ake* Issues[87]

In *Ake*, the Supreme Court indicated that a defendant did not have a constitutional right to a particular expert, nor did a defendant have a constitutional right to funds to hire an expert of his or her choosing.[88] Although the Court settled the choice-of-expert issue in *Ake*, there are several related issues that lower courts have had to try to resolve. The three key issues are: the constitutional protection, if any, for independence of the expert; the type of expertise to which assistance is constitutionally required and; whether expert assistance is required in the penalty phase in the absence of prosecution expert evidence on future dangerousness.

Courts are divided on whether the defendant has a due process right to an independent expert or, instead, simply to an expert who is neutral but not assigned exclusively to the defense. For example, the Fifth Circuit Court of Appeals has found that a neutral psychiatric expert is sufficient. Despite defense arguments about the need for confidentiality, the court found that a neutral expert who provided a report to both the defense and the prosecution was sufficient under *Ake*. The court emphasized the language from *Ake* that the defendant had no claim to an expert of his choosing. Thus, according to the court, a nonpartisan expert satisfied due process concerns.[89] In contrast, the Ninth Circuit Court of Appeals concluded that a neutral, but not independent, expert violated due process. The Ninth Circuit emphasized the need for an independent expert to allow the defendant to present his defense within an adversary system. This requirement was inconsistent in the court's view with an expert who was merely neutral.[90]

In addition to psychiatric experts, due process requires that states provide other types of experts to assist the defense. Lower courts have found that due process requires expert assistance in such areas as hypnosis,[91] DNA,[92] and fingerprinting.[93] Rather than limiting *Ake*'s application to only a few types of expertise, the courts have focused on how critical the issue is on which the expertise is sought.

---

[87] Another unresolved post-*Ake* issue is whether *Ake* errors are subject to a harmless error analysis.

[88] *Id.* at 83.

[89] White v. Johnson, 153 F.3d 197, 200 (5th Cir. 1998), *cert. denied*, 525 U.S. 1149 (1999) (a "disinterested expert" satisfied *Ake*). *See also* Woodward v. Epps, 580 F.3d 318, 332 (5th Cir. 2009) (holding that, because the Mississippi Supreme Court's interpretation of *Ake* was not "contrary to" or "an unreasonable application of" clearly established Supreme Court precedent, petitioner was not entitled to federal habeas relief based on claim that he was not provided assistance by an "independent" psychiatrist rather than one from state mental hospital). *Cf.* Campbell v. Polk, 447 F.3d 270, 286 (4th Cir. 2006) ("That Dr. Rollins originally provided the court with a neutral opinion that Campbell was competent to stand trial did not disqualify him from later serving as defendant's expert [during the sentencing phase].").

[90] Smith v. McCormick, 914 F.2d 1153, 1158 (9th Cir. 1990), *cert. denied*, 533 U.S. 917 (2001) (holding that, "under *Ake*, evaluation by a 'neutral' court psychiatrist does not satisfy due process.").

[91] *See, e.g.*, Little v. Armontrout, 835 F.2d 1240 (8th Cir. 1987), *cert. denied*, 487 U.S. 1210 (1988).

[92] *See, e.g.*, Polk v. State, 612 So. 2d 381 (Miss. 1992); Cade v. State, 658 So. 2d 550 (Fla. Dist. Ct. App. 1995).

[93] *See, e.g.*, State v. Moore, 364 S.E.2d 648, 657 (N.C. 1988).

For example, the Texas Court of Criminal Appeals found that a forensic pathologist was constitutionally required in a case where the cause of death was disputed.[94] If the cause of death was a heart attack as defendant claimed, he arguably was not death eligible, as the death would not have been "deliberate."[95] The court followed the three-factor approach from *Ake*, emphasizing the importance of the issue and the value of the expert assistance.

On the other hand, expert assistance was constitutionally denied in a case where the defense failed to establish the value of the assistance to the defense. The defense had asked for a "criminologist or other expert witness." The state had experts who had analyzed physical evidence, including bodily fluids and footprints. The court found that the defense "had failed to create a reasonable probability that expert assistance was necessary to the defense and that without such assistance petitioner's trial would be rendered unfair."[96]

This approach comports with the framework from *Ake*. The Court in *Ake* emphasized the need to focus on the value of the expertise to the case and the risk of error that would arise if there was no such assistance. Thus, the greater the significance of the issue on which the expert would testify in the defense case, the more likely it is that the court will find expert assistance constitutionally required.

The lower courts are divided on the constitutional right to expert assistance in the penalty phase when the prosecution does not call expert psychiatric witnesses. The Tenth and Eighth Circuit Courts of Appeals have interpreted *Ake* broadly. For example, in *Liles v. Saffle*,[97] the Tenth Circuit affirmed a grant of habeas corpus where there was non-psychiatric evidence of future dangerousness and the defendant's mental condition could be a "significant mitigating factor."[98] In contrast, the Fifth Circuit Court of Appeals has taken a narrow approach. In *Goodwin v. Johnson*,[99] the court did not conclusively hold that expert assistance to the defense is conditioned on the prosecution using expert evidence of future dangerousness, but emphasized that *Ake* itself referred to the need for expert assistance to contest the "psychiatric" evidence offered by the state.[100]

---

[94] Rey v. State, 897 S.W.2d 333, 338 (Tex. Crim. App. 1995). The state had argued that forensic pathology was based on " 'concrete observation' " and, thus, unlike psychology, there was no need for an independent expert for the defense. The court rejected this argument on two grounds: 1) forensic pathology was not that absolute regarding the cause of death and experts might differ, and 2) the defense was entitled to an independent pathologist in order to ensure fundamental fairness in the adversary system.

[95] *See id.*, at 341-42 (holding that the defendant established the significance of the issue of cause of death; denying his motion for a pathologist unconstitutionally denied defendant a "basic tool" for his defense).

[96] *See* Moore v. Kemp, 809 F.2d 702, 712 (11th Cir. 1987), *cert. denied*, 511 U.S. 1074 (1994). As the court noted, it is unlikely that a "criminologist" would have been the right type of expert to evaluate physical tests on evidence. *Id* at 718.

[97] 945 F.2d 333 (10th Cir. 1991), *cert. denied*, 502 U.S. 1066 (1992).

[98] *Id.* at 341.

[99] 132 F.3d 162, *cert. denied*, 531 U.S. 1120 (2001).

[100] *Id.* at 188. The Fifth Circuit did not take an absolute position that expert assistance was conditioned on expert evidence of future dangerousness. The court cited the *Liles* case and referred to the language that, even if non-psychiatric evidence of future dangerousness were sufficient, the defense

would still have to show that the defendant's mental condition would be a "significant mitigating factor."

Chapter 13

SELECTION PROCESS: THE LIFE OR DEATH DECISION

§ 13.01   OVERVIEW

The previous chapters have covered the proof of aggravating circumstances to establish the *eligibility* of a defendant for the death penalty and the presentation of additional aggravating evidence and mitigating evidence in the penalty phase that begins the *selection* decision of death or life. Ultimately, the sentencer must decide, on the basis of the aggravating and mitigating evidence, whether to impose the death penalty or life imprisonment. It is important to keep in mind several concepts from earlier chapters.

The two key constitutional requirements for imposing the death penalty are *guided discretion* and *individualized consideration*. Both are necessary to ensure a reliable determination of who should live and who should die. In the Supreme Court's current case law, guided discretion is satisfied by narrowing the group of defendants who are death eligible through proof of aggravating circumstances.[1] Individualized consideration is served by the admission of mitigating evidence and the ultimate sentencing decision.[2] As a result, a mandatory death sentence that automatically imposes a death sentence for a particular crime without any consideration of mitigating circumstances is unconstitutional.[3]

The Court's decisions on individualized consideration reflect two principles. First, all relevant mitigating evidence must be admitted in the penalty phase and the sentencer must be free to act on it to reject the death penalty. Second, subject to the first requirement, variation is permitted in how the mitigating evidence is used and in the structure or requirements for the decision of death or life.

Some of the variation in the structure of the decision process is due to the Court's acceptance of both *weighing* and *non-weighing* approaches. In a "weighing" jurisdiction, the sentencer is asked to balance the aggravating and mitigating circumstances.[4] In a "non-weighing" jurisdiction, the decision is open-ended.[5] In the latter system, a sentencer will be instructed to consider the aggravating and mitigating circumstances, but will not be given a balancing formula. Other than

---

[1] *See* Sections 9.01 et seq. and 10.01 et seq., *supra.*

[2] *See* Sections 12.01 et seq. and 13.01 et seq., *supra.*

[3] *See* Section 6.06, *supra.*

[4] *See* discussion in Section 7.03, *supra.*

[5] *See* discussion in Section 7.03, *supra*, and the description of the Georgia statute in Section 6.03, *supra.*

evaluating the evidence, the sentencer has complete discretion to decide between life and death.

Even within weighing jurisdictions, there is considerable variation. A typical weighing instruction will tell the sentencer that *death* can only be imposed if the aggravating circumstances outweigh the mitigating circumstances.[6] On the other hand, many weighing jurisdictions authorize the sentencer to return a judgment of *life* even if the aggravating circumstances outweigh the mitigating circumstances.[7] Thus, in those jurisdictions, the sentencer has wide discretion to impose life. In other weighing jurisdictions, the sentencer is told that death *must* be imposed if the aggravating circumstances outweigh the mitigating circumstances.[8]

Whether weighing or non-weighing, states currently vary in assigning the decision of death or life to a jury, a judge, a panel of judges, or a judge with an advisory jury. After *Ring v. Arizona*,[9] however, a defendant has the right to a jury verdict on aggravating circumstances that establish *eligibility* for the death penalty. It remains unclear what the ramifications of *Ring* are for the *selection* decision, which involves evaluating the aggravating evidence and the mitigating evidence to reach a decision of death or life.

This chapter examines the selection decision and the decision-making process. Section 13.02 provides examples of the sentencing variations accepted by the Court for the consideration and use of aggravating and mitigating evidence. Section 13.03 then discusses whether it is constitutional to impose the burden of persuasion on a defendant to prove that life imprisonment is the appropriate penalty.

Despite the Court's tolerance for wide variation in the structure of the selection decision, there are two major areas where the Court has found constitutional restraints. Section 13.04 describes the Eighth Amendment requirement that the sentencer not be affirmatively misled about its role in a way that diminishes responsibility for the decision of death or life. Section 13.05 considers the circumstances in which the Constitution requires that a sentencer be given information about a defendant's potential release.

When considering the selection process, it is important to keep in mind that the Court increasingly relies on a strong dichotomy between the eligibility decision and the selection decision. The Court views the eligibility decision as satisfying the constitutional requirement of *guided discretion*. The selection process meets the constitutional command of *individualized consideration* of a defendant and the crime. The final section, 13.06, considers whether it is possible to reconcile the two twin mandates of guided discretion and individualized consideration.

---

[6] *See, e.g.*, CALJIC 8.88: "To return a judgment of death, each of you must be persuaded that the aggravating circumstances are so substantial in comparison with the mitigating circumstances that it warrants death instead of life without parole."

[7] *See, e.g.*, Mo. Stat. Ann. 565.030(4)(4).

[8] *See* instruction from *Blystone v. Pennsylvania*, Section 13.02 *infra*.

[9] *See* discussion of *Ring* in Sections 9.02[A] and 10.02, *supra*.

§ 13.02 NO CONSTITUTIONALLY MANDATED FORMULA: VARIATIONS IN DECISION-MAKING STRUCTURE

Although a sentencer must be able to consider mitigating evidence in the decision process, the Court has found sentencing schemes constitutional that are highly structured, open-ended, or somewhere in between. A sentencer may be limited in how it evaluates aggravating and mitigating evidence. Or, a sentencer may have almost complete discretion in deciding how to utilize the aggravating and mitigating evidence. The examples in [A] and [B] show the extremes: the use of specific questions in the Texas system compared with the relatively unstructured Georgia system. Sentencing statutes also differ in the permissible results after a consideration of aggravating and mitigating evidence. Here, too, the Supreme Court has approved completely different approaches. Subsections [C] and [D] contrast statutes that mandate a result from the weighing of aggravating and mitigating evidence and statutes that allow complete discretion after a consideration of aggravation and mitigation.

[A] Highly Structured Format: The Texas System of Specific Questions

When Texas first developed a new capital sentencing scheme after *Furman v. Georgia*,[10] the state legislature devised a system with three specific questions. The directions to the jury were specific and highly structured. The questions were to be answered "yes" or "no." The subjects of the three questions were 1) the deliberate commission of the crime with the expectation that a death would result, 2) the future dangerousness of the defendant, and, if relevant, 3) the unreasonableness of the defendant's response to provocation by the victim.[11] If the jury unanimously answered all three questions affirmatively, the sentence was automatically death. If 10 of the 12 jurors answered any one of the three questions negatively, the sentence was automatically life imprisonment.[12]

The Supreme Court approved the format of the Texas statute on its face in 1976, in *Jurek v. Texas*.[13] The petitioner in *Jurek* challenged the statute as an

---

[10] 408 U.S. 238 (1972). *See* the discussion of *Furman*, the 1972 case that effectively invalidated the death penalty nationwide, in Sections 4.02 and 6.02 *supra*.

[11] *See* the discussion of the Texas statute in Section 6.05, *supra*. Art. 37.071(b) (Supp. 1975-1976) (the statute at the time of *Jurek*) provided the following three questions:

(1) whether the conduct of the defendant that caused the death of the deceased was committed deliberately and with the reasonable expectation that the death of the deceased or another would result;

(2) whether there is a probability that the defendant would commit criminal acts of violence that would constitute a continuing threat to society; and

(3) if raised by the evidence, whether the conduct of the defendant in killing the deceased was unreasonable in response to the provocation, if any, by the deceased.

[12] 428 U.S. 262 (1976). The Court in *Jurek* noted that the Texas statute did not specify what would occur if the jury could not agree either unanimously in the affirmative or 10 out of 12 in the negative. *Id.* at 269 n.5.

[13] 428 U.S. 262 (1976).

unconstitutional mandatory death penalty statute[14] because a death sentence was compelled if the sentencer answered all questions affirmatively. However, the Court found that, despite the dictated result from the answers to the questions, the Texas statute was not unconstitutional, because the content of the questions allowed for an individualized consideration.[15] Since then, many challenges to the original Texas statute have claimed that the narrow scope of the specific questions unconstitutionally precludes a sentencer's consideration of mitigating evidence. The Supreme Court held that the original Texas statute allows for the consideration of a wide scope of mitigating evidence.[16] In particular, the Court found that the question of a defendant's future dangerousness ("continuing threat to society") usually allows a sentencer to reject a death sentence based on the mitigating evidence offered. However, the Supreme Court subsequently held that the statute was unconstitutional as applied in certain cases, particularly those where the defendant offers evidence that he suffers from an impairment that bears on his culpability but that does not reduce his future dangerousness, such as low intelligence, mental illness, neurological damage or childhood abuse.[17] Because of these problems, the Texas legislature revised the questions in 1991 to provide for greater discretion to impose a life sentence based on the consideration of such mitigating evidence.[18] However, affirmative answers to the special issues continue to require a death sentence.

---

[14] *See* the discussion of Supreme Court cases striking down mandatory death sentences as unconstitutional in Section 6.06, *supra.*

[15] *Jurek*, 428 U.S. at 271.

[16] *See, e.g.*, Johnson v. Texas, 509 U.S. 350 (1993) (finding that the Texas system allowed for consideration of youth through the question of future dangerousness); Franklin v. Lynaugh, 487 U.S. 164 (1988) (finding that the Texas statute allowed for adequate consideration of residual doubt). *See also* Blystone v. Pennsylvania, 494 U.S. 299, 303-304 (1990) (finding Pennsylvania statute, like Texas statute, was not unconstitutionally mandatory).

[17] *See, e.g.*, Penry v. Lynaugh, 492 U.S. 302 (1989) (holding that the Texas statute unconstitutionally precluded the consideration of mental retardation, arrested emotional development and childhood physical and sexual abuse); Penry v. Johnson, 532 U.S. 782 (2001) (again finding the Texas questions, even with an additional instruction on mitigation, inadequate to allow consideration of proffered evidence in a mitigating way); Smith v. Texas, 543 U.S. 37 (2004) (*per curiam*) (*Smith* I) (also finding the Texas questions, even with an additional instruction, inadequate to allow sufficient consideration of mitigating evidence focused on defendant's limited mental abilities and troubled childhood); Tennard v. Dretke, 542 U.S. 274 (2004) (concluding that the Texas questions did not allow adequate mitigating consideration of evidence of defendant's low I.Q.) ; Smith v. Texas, 550 U.S. 297 (2007) (*Smith* II) (concluding that the Texas courts were required to defer to the Supreme Court's conclusion in *Smith* I that the jury could have interpreted the special issues to foreclose adequate consideration of his mitigating evidence); Abdul-Kabir v. Quarterman, 550 U.S. 233 (2007) (holding that the special questions did not allow for mitigating consideration of evidence of rough childhood and possible neurological damage); Brewer v. Quarterman, 550 U.S. 286 (2007) (concluding that the special questions failed to provide a vehicle for mitigating consideration of evidence of childhood abuse and mental illness).

[18] *See* discussion of the current Texas statute in Section 6.05, *supra.*

[B]   Unstructured, Open-Ended Format: The Georgia Process of General Consideration of All Evidence

At the other end of the spectrum from the Texas questions is the open-ended process in Georgia. Georgia's statute reflects a "non-weighing" sentencing scheme. The sentencer is given little direction on how to arrive at a verdict of life or death, other than to consider all aggravating and mitigating evidence. In contrast to the specific questions in the original Texas statute, the Georgia sentencer is told to "consider the facts and circumstances, if any, in extenuation, mitigation or aggravation of punishment."[19] Also in contrast to the automatic death sentence in Texas if the questions are answered affirmatively, the Georgia sentencer is instructed that it may find life imprisonment "for any reason satisfactory to you, or without any reason."[20]

Jurors sitting in a Georgia courtroom thus face a very different process than their counterparts in Texas or one of the many weighing states. Unlike the original Texas system of structured questions and result, the sentencer in Georgia has virtually complete discretion to impose death or life. There is no guidance on what to do if the sentencer finds no mitigation, some mitigation, more mitigation than aggravation, or more aggravation than mitigation. This unstructured sentencing was challenged as importing the same unfettered discretion into the process that was considered unconstitutional in *Furman*. The Supreme Court did not agree and upheld the Georgia system.[21]

[C]   Mandatory Results

The Texas approach of using specific questions mandates a sentence of death if the jurors answer each question affirmatively. The Court has also permitted states to require a sentence of death based on the outcome of weighing aggravating and mitigating evidence. In *Blystone v. Pennsylvania*,[22] the Court upheld instructions to jurors that they must impose a sentence of death if they find the existence of an aggravating circumstance (required for eligibility for the death penalty) and no mitigation. Even with some mitigation, a California instruction required a sentence of death if the jury found that aggravating evidence outweighed mitigating evidence. The Court upheld the California instruction in *Boyde v. California*.[23]

The decisions in *Blystone* and *Boyde* reflect the Court's adherence to the notion that, as long as all relevant mitigating evidence is admitted and the sentencer is free to consider it in mitigation, the state is free to structure the sentencer's selection decision. The juries in both cases were able to consider all the mitigating evidence presented. Therefore, the Court was not troubled by the state dictating the result. The Court noted in *Boyde* that "the mandatory language of [the

---

[19] Ga. Pattern Jury Instruction 13(b) Determination of Punishment (on file with authors).

[20] *Id.* at 13(d). May Fix Penalty at Life Imprisonment for any Reason (on file with authors).

[21] *See* Gregg v. Georgia, 428 U.S. 153 (1976).

[22] 494 U.S. 299 (1990).

[23] 494 U.S. 370 (1990). Although constitutional, California courts no longer use the instruction described in *Boyde*.

California instruction] is not alleged to have interfered with the consideration of mitigating evidence."[24]

Furthermore, the Court rejected the idea that the sentencer must always be able to reject the death penalty. As the Court noted in *Boyde*: "States are free to structure and shape consideration of mitigating evidence 'in an effort to achieve a more rational and equitable administration of the death penalty.' "[25]

[D]   Discretionary Results

Many jurisdictions provide the sentencer with the option of imposing life even if aggravating circumstances outweigh mitigating circumstances. The Missouri statute, for example, provides for an option for life at the discretion of the sentencer: The sentencer shall impose life if it "decides under all of the circumstances not to assess and declare the punishment at death."[26] Likewise, the Federal Death Penalty Act provides that jurors must be instructed to decide whether aggravating factors "sufficiently outweigh" the mitigating factors so as to "justify" a death sentence.[27] This instruction allows jurors to return a sentence of life imprisonment even if no mitigating factors are found or aggravating factors are found to outweigh mitigating factors.

§ 13.03   BURDEN OF PERSUASION:[28] PROSECUTION OR DEFENSE?

The Supreme Court has concluded that the Constitution allows states to decide which party should bear the burden of persuasion[29] on the life-or-death decision. Recall that many states instruct the sentencer that death may only be imposed if aggravating circumstances outweigh mitigating circumstances. In these jurisdictions, the prosecution bears the risk of non-persuasion. If the prosecution cannot present sufficient evidence to show that aggravating circumstances outweigh mitigating circumstances, death cannot be imposed. Thus, the prosecution must demonstrate to the sentencer that the balance tips in favor of aggravating circumstances. If the prosecution does not meet this burden, then the sentence must be life.

Assume that the instruction to the sentencer is to impose death unless there is sufficient mitigation to call for leniency. Now the risk of non-persuasion is on the defense. The defense must establish sufficient mitigation or the sentence will be

---

[24] *Id.* at 377.

[25] *Id.*, *quoting from* Franklin v. Lynaugh, 487 U.S. 164, 181 (1988).

[26] *See* Mo. St. Ann. 565.030(4)(4).

[27] 18 U.S.C. § 3593(e).

[28] *See* Section 24.03[B], *infra*.

[29] For discussion on the potential for confusion among jurors about who bears the burden of persuasion, *see* James Luginbuhl and Julie Howe, *Discretion in Capital Sentencing Instructions: Guided or Misguided?* 70 Ind. L.J. 1161 (1995) (documenting confusion of capital jurors about burden of persuasion on mitigation and final sentencing decision in North Carolina).

death.[30]

In *Walton v. Arizona*,[31] a plurality[32] of the Court found it constitutional to impose the burden of persuasion on a defendant to prove mitigating evidence (discussed in Section 12.03[B][2][b], *supra*), and to prove that life was the proper result. Under the Arizona statutory scheme, the defendant has the burden to establish mitigating factors by a preponderance of the evidence. The Arizona statute further places the burden of persuasion on a defendant to demonstrate a basis for a life sentence. The sentencer is to impose death if there are "no mitigating circumstances sufficiently substantial to call for leniency."[33]

The *Walton* plurality appeared to recognize that placing a burden on a defendant in the penalty phase created a "presumption of death."[34] Nevertheless, the Court upheld the constitutionality of requiring death unless the defendant could meet a burden of persuasion to establish "sufficiently substantial" mitigation. Once again, the plurality emphasized that, as long as all mitigating evidence was admitted and given some mechanism for consideration, the states were free to structure different procedures for the use of the mitigation and the actual decision.[35] The plurality relied on its earlier decisions in *Boyde* and *Blystone*, where the Court upheld mandatory language in jury instructions that a death sentence must be imposed if aggravating circumstances outweigh mitigating circumstances.[36]

The opinion of the *Walton* plurality was viewed by some lower courts as not controlling on the question of the constitutionality of a statute that requires death if the sentencer finds that mitigating and aggravating circumstances are in equipoise. The Kansas Supreme Court took this position in a subsequent case.[37] The Kansas court viewed the Arizona statute at issue in *Walton* as allowing the sentencer to have the ultimate discretion regarding whether to impose the death

---

[30] *See* Linda E. Carter, *A Beyond a Reasonable Doubt Standard in Death Penalty Proceedings: A Neglected Element of Fairness*, 52 Ohio St. L.J. 195 (1991) (arguing for burden on state and for standard of beyond a reasonable doubt).

[31] 497 U.S. 639 (1990).

[32] As discussed earlier regarding the plurality's decision on the burden of persuasion for mitigating evidence, Justice Scalia was a de facto fifth vote for the decision that it is constitutional to place the burden of persuasion on the weighing decision on the defendant. In his concurrence, Justice Scalia concluded that the *Woodson-Lockett* line of cases has no basis in the Constitution and, thus, no weighing of mitigation is constitutionally necessary. *Id.* at 670-673 (Scalia, J., concurring).

[33] *Id.* at 649. The actual language of the statute states the standard as a negative, requiring the death penalty if there is an inadequate showing of mitigation. ARIZ. REV. STAT. ANN. § 13-703(E) requires that the court " 'shall impose a sentence of death if the court finds one or more of the aggravating circumstances enumerated in subsection (F) of this section and that there are no mitigating circumstances sufficiently substantial to call for leniency.' " Although the Arizona statute has been modified since the *Walton* decision, the critical burden of proof language remains the same. See ARIZ. REV. STAT. § 13-703(F) (2002).

[34] *Id.* at 651. The plurality acknowledged the defense argument that the statute creates a "presumption of death." The plurality response, however, referred to the mandatory instructions in *Blystone* and *Boyde*, which did not impose a burden of persuasion on a defendant. Thus, it is unclear if the plurality was actually addressing the presumption issue.

[35] *Id.* at 652.

[36] *Id.* at 651-52.

[37] State v. Kleypas, 40 P.3d 139 (Kan. 2001).

penalty.[38] The definition of what constituted "sufficiently substantial" mitigation was left up to the sentencer in the Arizona scheme. Because of that statutory language, the Arizona sentencer arguably could find that aggravating circumstances were equal to or even outweighed mitigating circumstances and still decide to impose life.[39] In contrast, the Kansas court viewed its own statute as mandating death if aggravating and mitigating circumstances were in equipoise.[40] The Kansas court further found that this presumption of death was unconstitutional,[41] but ultimately construed the statute to authorize death only if aggravating circumstances outweighed mitigating circumstances.

The Supreme Court rejected the position of the Kansas Supreme Court. In *Kansas v. Marsh*,[42] a five-Justice majority upheld a presumption of death where mitigating and aggravating circumstances are in equipoise. The Court clarified that, once the prosecution has proved an aggravating circumstance beyond a reasonable doubt, the state's burden of persuasion for death is complete. At that point, a state may impose a burden of persuasion on the defendant to defeat a presumption of death.[43] The Court rejected the contention that a presumption of death in an equipoise situation conflicts with the increased need for reliability in a death sentence.

The *Marsh* decision did not openly address a second argument for disallowing an instruction favoring death in an equipoise situation. In the last few years, the Supreme Court has decided two important cases in which it held that a criminal defendant is entitled to a jury verdict on facts necessary to prove an element, or the functional equivalent of an element, if proof of the element can increase the penalty. In *Apprendi v. New Jersey*,[44] the Court held unconstitutional an increased sentence beyond the statutory limit for the crime on the basis of a hate crime enhancement

---

[38] *Id.* at 226-28.

[39] The decisions in *Boyde* and *Blystone* were even easier to distinguish. In those cases, the Court upheld statutes that required death, but only if aggravating circumstances outweighed mitigating circumstances. The California and Pennsylvania statutes at issue in those cases did not shift the burden of persuasion to the defendant.

[40] *See id.* at 223, quoting K.S.A. 21-4624(e) (emphasis added): "If, by unanimous vote, the jury finds beyond a reasonable doubt that one or more of the aggravating circumstances . . . exist and, further, that the existence of such aggravating circumstances *is not outweighed* by any mitigating circumstances which are found to exist, the defendant *shall* be sentenced to death . . . " The Kansas court viewed the language regarding "outweighed" as giving the sentencer no discretion, unlike the sentencer's judgment call regarding "sufficiently substantial" under the Arizona statute.

[41] Other courts have also found a presumption of death problematic. Colorado addressed the issue under its own state constitution, finding that a presumption of death in an equipoise situation was unconstitutional. *See* People vo Young, 814 P.2d 834 (Colo. 1991). *See also* State v. Biegenwald, 524 A.2d 130, 132 (N.J. 1987), *cert. denied*, 527 A.2d 469 (N.J. 1987) (remanding for resentencing upon finding jurors were not properly instructed to find death only if aggravating factors outweighed mitigating factors beyond a reasonable doubt); Hulsey v. Sargent, 868 F. Supp. 1090, 1101-1104 (E.D. Ark.), *cert. denied*, 493 U.S. 923 (1989) (granting habeas relief where petitioner was sentenced under an unconstitutional statutory regime — earlier Arkansas statute held unconstitutional for requiring death unless mitigating circumstances outweighed aggravating circumstances).

[42] 548 U.S. 163 (2006).

[43] *See id.* at 173.

[44] 530 U.S. 466 (2000).

provision absent a finding beyond a reasonable doubt of the hate crime facts by a jury. Subsequent to *Apprendi*, the Court decided *Ring v. Arizona*,[45] in which it held that an aggravating circumstance under the Arizona death-penalty statute functioned as an "element" that increased the possible penalty to death. As a result, under the reasoning of *Apprendi*, the defendant was constitutionally entitled to a jury verdict on the aggravating circumstance. The Court explicitly overruled a part of the *Walton* decision that had upheld a nonjury determination of the aggravating circumstance.[46] The Court in *Ring* did not address, however, the burden of persuasion on the aggravating circumstance, as all states, including Arizona, impose the burden on the prosecution to establish the aggravating circumstance beyond a reasonable doubt. The prosecution's burden to prove the aggravating circumstance is consistent with the due process requirement of *In re Winship*,[47] which imposed a burden on the prosecution of establishing an "element" of a crime beyond a reasonable doubt. Thus, the defendant is constitutionally entitled to have the prosecution prove all elements of the crime and to have a jury determine the existence of those elements.

The question after *Ring* is whether a finding regarding the weighing of aggravating and mitigating circumstances is also the functional equivalent of an "element" or, instead, merely a sentencing determination. Arguments are likely to be raised that the final decision-making process in the penalty phase fits under the *Apprendi/Ring* reasoning and should require a jury determination.[48] If the Court were to conclude that the final decision-making process requires a jury finding, the presumption of death issue could resurface. To the extent that due process mandates a jury decision on a particular determination, it would also arguably require that the state bear the burden of persuasion beyond a reasonable doubt. Thus, the presumption of death issue could develop into a debate over which "facts" are critical to a determination of death, what is viewed as the "statutory maximum" penalty for the crime, and whether the sentencing determination must be submitted to a jury for proof of facts beyond a reasonable doubt. Defense lawyers will argue, in most states, that death is not an authorized punishment without a factual finding that aggravating circumstances outweigh mitigating circumstances or, in a state like Arizona, that there is insufficient mitigation to outweigh the aggravation. The prosecution will counter that the finding of the aggravating circumstance alone elevates the possible penalty to death, and the weighing process is merely a sentencing determination.

---

[45] 536 U.S. 584 (2002). *See* discussion in Sections 9.02[A] and 10.02, *supra*.

[46] *See id.* at 609.

[47] *Id.* at 609.

[48] *See, e.g.*, State v. Barker (Order on Supplemental Motion to Dismiss Death Penalty, Sept. 10, 2001, Indiana) (trial court holds Indiana death penalty statute unconstitutional on basis of *Apprendi* issue); *rev'd.*, State v. Barker, 826 N.E.2d 648 (Ind. 2005), *cert. denied*, Barker v. Indiana, 546 U.S. 1022 (2005).

§ 13.04 CONSTITUTIONAL LIMITATION ON THE SENTENCING PROCESS: CANNOT AFFIRMATIVELY MISLEAD REGARDING ROLE AND RESPONSIBILITY OF DECISION-MAKER

Suppose that the prosecutor in a capital case tells the jurors in closing argument that no one is going to string D up in front of the courthouse right after their verdict. Indeed, the prosecutor argues, the jury's decision is not final. In fact, the prosecutor continues, the jury's decision goes automatically to the state supreme court. Is there a constitutional problem with emphasizing that the jurors are not the final decision-makers?

In the course of deciding two important cases, the Supreme Court has held that it is unconstitutional under the Eighth Amendment to affirmatively mislead a jury about its responsibility for imposing the sentence. The information given to a jury is not unconstitutional, however, unless it both is inaccurate and misleads the jurors in a way that diminishes their sense of responsibility for the sentencing decision.

Regarding the hypothetical, the Supreme Court has found constitutional error in a prosecutor's argument telling the jury in essence that an appellate court can impose a death or life sentence. In *Caldwell v. Mississippi*,[49] the source of the hypothetical facts, the prosecutor argued in the closing argument that the jury's decision was not final because there was an automatic review in the state supreme court.[50] The Supreme Court interpreted the prosecutor's argument as implying that the decision on the propriety of death would ultimately be made in an appellate court. First, the Court viewed this argument as incorrect, because an appellate court reviews legal issues and does not make factual findings.[51] The Court specifically noted that the element of "mercy," present in the deliberations of the jury, is not a factor in an appellate decision.[52] Second, the Court saw further room for misunderstanding if the jury chose death for inappropriate reasons, such as "sending a message" to the defendant, on the assumption that the sentence would later be set aside by an appellate court.[53]

---

[49] 472 U.S. 320 (1985).

[50] The prosecutor argued:

Now, [the defense] would have you believe that you're going to kill this man and they know — they know that your decision is not the final decision. My God, how unfair can you be? Your job is reviewable.

. . . insinuating that your decision is the final decision and that they're gonna take Bobby Caldwell out in the front of this Courthouse in moments and string him up and that is terribly, terribly unfair. For they know, as I know, and as Judge Baker has told you, that the decision you render is automatically reviewable by the Supreme Court.

Id. at 325-26.

[51] *Id.* 330-31.

[52] *Id.* at 331.

[53] *Id.* at 331-32. The Court further thought that jurors might mistakenly assume that the only way to have the appellate court consider the decision of death or life would be to render a death sentence; that the appellate court could not independently decide life or death if the jurors rendered a life sentence. The jurors would have been correct that the appellate court could not overturn a life sentence and impose a death sentence.

What if the sentencing jury is told that D has already been sentenced to death in an earlier murder case? Assume that it was true at the time of D's trial that he had been sentenced to death in the prior trial, but the conviction was subsequently overturned on appeal. Also assume that, under state law, the prior death sentence is considered irrelevant in the current capital case. Does the information on the prior death sentence diminish the responsibility of jurors? Does the information affirmatively mislead the jurors?

The Court answered these questions in *Romano v. Oklahoma*.[54] The jurors were told that the defendant had previously been convicted of murder and sentenced to death. The jury convicted Romano in the current case and sentenced him to death. Subsequently, the first murder conviction and death sentence were reversed.[55] The defendant claimed that the jury was unconstitutionally misled about the significance of its role in sentencing him to death, and that his conviction should be reversed as in *Caldwell*. The Court rejected the challenge, distinguishing the prior death sentence information in *Romano* from the inaccurate information on appellate review in *Caldwell*. The Court held that the evidence of the prior death sentence did not "affirmatively [mislead] the jury regarding its role in the sentencing process so as to diminish its sense of responsibility."[56] The Court found that the information was neither inaccurate nor did it undermine the jury's sense of responsibility.[57] It was true that the defendant already had a sentence of death at the time of his trial. Moreover, because the information about the prior death sentence, unlike the prosecutor's argument in *Caldwell*, did not speak to the jury's role or responsibility as a decsion-maker, the Court also found that the information would not have misled the jurors about their role or their responsibility.[58]

In addition to his Eighth Amendment claims, Romano also argued that the information about the prior death sentence made the trial fundamentally unfair, in

---

[54] 512 U.S. 1 (1994). The prior conviction and death sentence were introduced as evidence in support of two of four aggravating circumstances, a prior violent felony conviction and a continuing threat to society. On appeal, the Oklahoma Court of Criminal Appeals found that the prior death sentence was irrelevant to those aggravating circumstances. *Id*. at 4-6.

[55] Romano's conviction of the first capital case was overturned while the second case was pending on appeal. Ultimately, Romano was reconvicted and resentenced to death in the first capital case. *Id*. at 5.

[56] *Id*. at 10. Although the prior violent felony aggravating circumstance was invalid without the evidence of the prior murder conviction, the Oklahoma Court of Criminal Appeals had properly reweighed the factors on appeal.

[57] *See id*. at 9. The Court acknowledged the importance of Justice O'Connor's concurrence in *Caldwell* as the fifth vote where she wrote that the information in *Caldwell* was unconstitutional because it was both " 'inaccurate and misleading in a manner that diminished the jury's sense of responsibility.' " *Id.*, *quoting from* Caldwell, 472 U.S. at 342.

[58] The defendant claimed that the evidence was also irrelevant to any of the aggravating circumstances to which the jury's consideration was limited by state law and that the introduction of such evidence prejudiced the jury in violation of the Eighth Amendment. However, the Court concluded that the evidence was not irrelevant under the Eighth Amendment, even if the state had decided to render such evidence inadmissible as a matter of state law. *See id*. at 10-11. Further, the Court also noted that the state appellate court had reweighed the aggravating and mitigating circumstances after exclusion of the aggravating circumstance to which the evidence of the prior death sentence most closely related. The Court had previously upheld the ability of state appellate courts through reweighing to affirm a death sentence after a sentencing jury had considered an invalid aggravating circumstance where the jury had also found at least one other valid aggravating circumstance. *See id*. at 11.

violation of the due process clause of the Fourteenth Amendment. The Court analyzed whether the information "so infected the sentencing proceeding with unfairness as to render the jury's imposition of the death penalty a denial of due process."[59] The Court found that the evidence of the prior death sentence was irrelevant to any of the aggravating circumstances to which the jury was instructed to limit its consideration and, therefore, would not have affected the verdict.[60] Moreover, the Court concluded that, even if the jury considered the prior death sentence, it was impossible to know if the information would have made the jury more likely to impose death or more likely to impose a life sentence.[61]

§ 13.05   INFORMATION ABOUT DEFENDANT'S POTENTIAL RELEASE: COMMUTATION AND PAROLE

[A]   Overview

Where the jury in the penalty phase is instructed that its alternatives are "death" or "life imprisonment," an important question may arise for many jurors over the meaning of "life imprisonment." Jurors may wonder whether it means "life *without* parole" or, instead, "life *with the possibility of* parole." Studies have documented that jurors are concerned about a defendant's potential release.[62] Jurors' concerns are also evident in cases where they have sent questions to the judge about possible release.

Questions have arisen about three types of instructions that relate to a defendant's potential release. The first concerns clemency powers. Defendants have objected to instructions telling the jury that the governor can commute a life sentence to a lesser term. The second type of instruction, as in the opening hypothetical, concerns the meaning of "life without parole." Defendants have objected to the failure to tell the jury that a defendant will never be released from prison if given life without parole. The third concerns instructions on the results of a hung jury. Defendants have objected, for example, to certain instructions on grounds that they imply that the defendant could receive less than life without parole if the jurors cannot reach a verdict.

---

[59] *Id.* at 12.

[60] *See id.* at 13. The Court also noted that other proper evidence supported the death sentence in the case.

[61] *See id.* at 13-14. For studies of the effect of information on juror responsibility, *see* Joseph L. Hoffmann, *Where's the Buck? — Juror Misperception of Sentencing Responsibility in Death Penalty Cases*, 70 IND. L.J. 1137 (1995) (on the basis of interviews with capital jurors, finding tendency to diminish personal responsibility for verdict); Theodore Eisenberg, Stephen P. Garvey, Martin T. Wells, *Jury Responsibility in Capital Sentencing: An Empirical Study*, 44 BUFF. L. REV. 339 (1996) (finding jurors tend to accept "role" responsibility, but not "causal" responsibility for sentence).

[62] *See* Theodore Eisenberg and Martin T. Wells, *Deadly Confusion: Juror Confusion in Capital Cases*, 79 Cornell L. Rev. 1 (1993) (documenting juror confusion over life imprisonment); James Luginbuhl and Julie Howe, *Discretion in Capital Sentencing Instructions: Guided or Misguided?* 70 Ind. L.J. 1161 (1995) (documenting concern over potential release of defendant).

[B]   Commutation Power of Governor

In *California v. Ramos*,[63] the Supreme Court found no constitutional error in instructing a jury that the governor may commute a sentence of life imprisonment to a lesser sentence.[64] The Court also implied that an instruction on possible commutation or pardon from a death sentence would similarly not offend the Constitution.[65] The analysis reflected three considerations: 1) the relevancy of the commutation power to the sentencing decision, 2) whether the information is misleading and diminishes the sentencer's sense of responsibility, and 3) the desirability of state variation in devising death penalty statutes.

The defense in *Ramos* argued that the possibility of a commutation of a life sentence to a lesser sentence was irrelevant to the penalty decision and speculative.[66] However, the Court found that the commutation information was relevant to the issue of the future dangerousness of the defendant. The Court further dismissed the defense argument that a possibility of commutation was so speculative that it injected unreliability into the sentencing process. In the Court's view, reliability was not compromised, because the information was accurate and the defendant had the opportunity to present counter-arguments.[67]

The defense in *Ramos* also contended that an instruction on commutation of a life sentence diminished the reliability of the sentencing decision by "deflect[ing] the jury's focus from its central task."[68] The Court emphasized that the information on commutation was accurate and that it was relevant to the jury's concern about future dangerousness. In the Court's view, the commutation instruction did not divert the jurors' attention from their "central task."[69]

---

[63]   463 U.S. 992 (1983).

[64]   *See id.* at 995-996. The jury in *Ramos* was instructed as follows, " 'You are instructed that under the State Constitution a Governor is empowered to grant a reprieve, pardon, or commutation of a sentence following conviction of a crime. Under this power a Governor may in the future commute or modify a sentence of life imprisonment without possibility of parole to a lesser sentence that would include the possibility of parole.' " This is referred to as the "Briggs Instruction" in California.

[65]   *Id.* at 1010-1011.

[66]   *Id.* at 1001-1002.

[67]   *See id.* at 1004. The Court distinguished *Gardner v. Florida*, 430 U.S. 349 (1977), where a presentence report with information not given to the defense was found to violate the defendant's due process rights. According to the Court, *Ramos* was different because the information about commutation was accurate and the defendant had a chance to respond.

[68]   *See id.* at 1005.

[69]   *See id.* at 1008. The Court distinguished its earlier decision in *Beck v. Alabama*, 447 U.S. 625 (1980). In *Beck*, the Court had held unconstitutional a statute that prohibited giving instructions on lesser-included crimes in capital cases, even where the evidence supported the lesser crime. The Court had found that a jury in Alabama might convict or acquit for improper reasons, unrelated to the proper considerations of guilt or innocence. For instance, the jurors might convict because they felt the defendant was guilty of some level of crime, and had no other choice than convict of a capital crime or acquit. In *Ramos*, the Court noted that the sentencing decision is more open-ended than the guilt-or-innocence issues in *Beck*. According to the Court, there is no "central issue," such as guilt or innocence, in the sentencing phase from which the jury would stray with the commutation information. Thus, the impact of the commutation instruction was much less.

In addition, the defense in *Ramos* contended that, if a court instructs the jury on the possibility of a commutation of a life sentence, the court must also instruct on the possibility of a commutation of a death sentence. The defense argued that, without such an instruction, the jurors would be misled into thinking that a death sentence was final and that only a life sentence could be commuted. The defense contended that, as a result, the jury would be more inclined to impose death as the only way to prevent the possible release of the defendant. The Court rejected this argument, in part because a death commutation instruction would not necessarily work to the defendant's advantage. Jurors might simply view their responsibility as diminished if a decision to impose death could change.[70]

Ultimately, the *Ramos* Court returned to the theme of deferring to state legislatures to decide whether to instruct on a governor's commutation power. Most state courts that had considered the issue had barred commutation instructions. The Supreme Court simply held that the Constitution did not *prohibit* commutation instructions. Individual states were free to choose not to permit such instructions under state law.

Thus, an accurate instruction on the commutation of a life sentence, at least where relevant to a future dangerousness issue, satisfies constitutional constraints. Although a similar instruction that a death sentence could also be commuted is not constitutionally required, it would appear that such an instruction, if accurate, would not offend the Constitution.

It is not clear whether an inaccurate instruction on commutation would violate the Constitution. Suppose, for example, that the jury is told that the governor can commute a death or life sentence when, in fact, only a unanimous decision by the state's parole board could authorize a commutation. The defense would argue that the defendant's release would be much less likely if an entire parole board must agree on a commutation than if the governor alone could authorize it. Under *Ramos*, it seems that the question is whether the jury had been diverted from its "central task."[71] The defense would contend that the jury is diverted from its decision process by thinking about later commutation. However, the prosecution would emphasize that this instruction has no different effect than the constitutional instruction in *Ramos* that advised the jury of the commutation power. Under the later *Caldwell-Romano* approach, discussed in Section 13.04, *supra*, the question would seem to be whether the instruction was inaccurate and misled the jurors about their role in the responsibility for the decision. Although the instruction is inaccurate, the inaccuracy does not seem to mislead the jurors about their role. It is not unconstitutional to give jurors accurate information about a commutation

---

[70] *Id.* at 1011. The Court stated: "In fact, advising jurors that a death verdict is theoretically modifiable, and thus not 'final,' may incline them to approach their sentencing decision with less appreciation for the gravity of their choice and for the moral responsibility reposed in them as sentencers."

[71] Under *Boyde v. California*, 494 U.S. 370, 380 (1990), the standard for deciding this question would be whether there was a "reasonable likelihood" of constitutional error. The reasonable-likelihood approach poses the question of " 'whether there is a reasonable likelihood that the jury has applied the challenged instruction in a way' that violates the Constitution." *Jones v. United States*, 527 U.S. 372, 390 (1999).

power; therefore, providing that same information must not diminish the jurors' sense of responsibility.[72]

[C]   Meaning of "Life With Parole"

Suppose that a state statute provides for "life without parole" that means "no possibility of ever being released on parole." Defendants have argued in this situation that a trial court is constitutionally required to explain the term.

In a series of cases, the Supreme Court has addressed the situation where jurors are told that the choice is death or life without parole but are not told that life without parole truly means that the defendant will be sentenced to live the rest of his or her life behind bars.[73] The possible misperceptions are especially critical when the jurors themselves pose the question to the judge during their deliberations. Courts have wrestled with what constitutes an appropriate instruction in response to the jurors' questions.[74] Defendants have raised arguments under both the Eighth Amendment and the Due Process Clause.

Information that life without parole means there is no possibility of release probably does not constitute mitigating evidence that a defendant is constitutionally entitled to present under the Eighth Amendment. A defendant argued the mitigating-evidence theory in *Simmons v. South Carolina*.[75] A majority of the Court declined to reach this issue under an Eighth Amendment analysis.[76] However, five of the justices, three concurring and two dissenting, commented that states could refuse to give any information about parole, commutation, and sentencing.[77] Although the Justices' comments were not a holding, they relied on

---

[72] The issue of an inaccurate instruction on commutation of a life sentence arose in a case subsequent to *Ramos*, and again involved the same California instruction. In *Calderon v. Coleman*, 525 U.S. 141 (1998), the trial court failed to instruct correctly that the governor could only commute the sentence of the defendant, who was a twice-convicted felon, with the consent of four justices of the California Supreme Court. The Supreme Court did not decide the issue, however, because the state did not seek review of that ruling. Instead, the state argued that the lower court should have conducted a harmless error review. The Supreme Court agreed and remanded the case. The Court made it clear, however, that the unconstitutionality of an inaccurate instruction is still an open issue. The federal district court, however, had found that the inaccuracy of the commutation instruction rendered it unconstitutional, at least where the consequence was misleading the jurors about whether life imprisonment was likely to preclude defendant's release. *Id.*

[73] *See* Julian H. Wright, Jr., *Life-Without-Parole: An Alternative to Death or Not Much of a Life at All?*, 43 VAND. L. REV. 529, 542-43 (1990) (discussing states that use the phrase "life without parole," but set a minimum number of years until parole eligible).

[74] The facts of *Weeks v. Angelone*, 528 U.S. 225, 228 (2000), pose a good example of a jury question and the problems in responding to it. The jury, after being instructed by the trial judge, asked the judge "Does the sentence of life imprisonment in the State of Virginia have the possibility of parole, and if so, under what conditions must be met to receive parole?" The judge responded, "You should impose such punishment as you feel is just under the evidence, and within the instructions of the Court. You are not to concern yourselves with what may happen afterwards." The propriety of the judge's response was not addressed in the Court's opinion.

[75] 512 U.S. 154 (1994).

[76] In *Simmons*, the plurality opinion explicitly stated that the justices "expressed no opinion" on an Eighth Amendment analysis. *Id.* at 162 n.4.

[77] *See id.* at 176 (O'Connor, J., concurring); *id.* at 179 (Scalia, J., dissenting).

the *Ramos* decision's language about the states' choice on whether to instruct on commutation powers. This is a significant indication that those five justices would find no Eighth Amendment requirement to instruct on ineligibility for parole. Of the remaining four Justices in *Simmons*, only two expressly stated that the Eighth Amendment's reliability guarantee would require parole ineligibility information if there was a likelihood of misperception that would diminish the reliability of the decision.[78]

The Court has repeatedly held, however, that there is a due process right to provide information about parole ineligibility when future dangerousness is at issue. The Court acknowledged a common misperception by the public that parole is generally available, even for "life without parole." The Court further reasoned that a defendant was entitled to rebut the prosecution's case of future dangerousness.

In *Simmons*, the prosecutor argued that the future dangerousness of the defendant was a reason to sentence the defendant to death. During their deliberations, the jurors sent out a question asking: "Does the imposition of a life sentence carry with it the possibility of parole?[79] The trial judge responded that the jurors were "not to consider parole or parole eligibility" and that the terms of life imprisonment and death sentence should be viewed in light of their plain meaning.[80] The jury subsequently returned a verdict of death. The Supreme Court by a vote of 7-2 held that, where the prosecutor argued future dangerousness, the defendant had a due process right to rebut that argument with accurate information about parole ineligibility.[81] Thus, at least where the state argues future dangerousness in support of a death sentence, the due process clause will require that the defense have the ability to respond with relevant information about the legal ineligibility of the defendant to be released back into society.

In *Shafer v. South Carolina*,[82] the Supreme Court further examined parole ineligibility instructions. At trial, the prosecution introduced evidence of the defendant's "criminal record, past aggressive conduct, probation violations, and misbehavior in prison," but did not explicitly argue that the defendant would pose a threat of future dangerousness. Shafer argued that the evidence raised a future dangerousness issue and that he was entitled to an instruction on parole ineligibility.[83] There was a better attempt at explaining to the jury that the

---

[78] *See id.* at 172 (Souter, J., concurring).

[79] *Id.* at 160.

[80] *Id.*

[81] *See id.* at 164. The Court rejected the State's argument that the unknown possibility of defendant's future release through "future exigencies such as legislative reform, commutation, clemency" should defeat an instruction on parole ineligibility. The Court said that the parole ineligibility information was "legally accurate." *Id.* at 166.

[82] 532 U.S. 36 (2001).

[83] *See id.* at 54 The South Carolina scheme poses an unusual situation because, at the time of the instruction, which was before the jury found the aggravating circumstance, the jury's choices technically included a sentence less than life and, thus, the jury did not need to be informed about the meaning of life imprisonment. Once the jury found an aggravating circumstance, however, the only choices were death or life imprisonment. *See id.* at 50.

defendant was ineligible for parole than in *Simmons*. The trial court gave a jury instruction that life imprisonment meant "until death of the offender," and the defense counsel argued in closing that a life sentence meant the defendant would "die in prison" after "spend[ing] his natural life there."[84] Even with this information, the jury sent out questions during deliberations about the defendant's eligibility for parole.[85] The trial judge again instructed the jury that life imprisonment meant until the death of the offender and also that "[p]arole eligibility or ineligibility is not for your consideration."[86] The Supreme Court found that the trial court's response failed to cure the jury's confusion about the possibility of parole. The Court remanded the case, however, for a determination of whether future dangerousness was "at issue," which would then mandate an instruction on parole ineligibility.[87]

It took a third case, *Kelly v. South Carolina*,[88] for the Supreme Court to provide guidance on when future dangerousness is "at issue." As in *Shafer*, the prosecution argued that it was not raising future dangerousness.[89] Unlike in *Simmons* and *Shafer*, the jury did not send out a question asking about parole eligibility, although the instructions by the trial court were less clear than in *Shafer*. The trial court instructed the jurors that death and life imprisonment should be given their "plain and ordinary meanings."[90] Defense counsel, however, was more explicit, stating in closing argument that defendant would "be in prison for the rest of his life and would 'never see the light of daylight again'" under a life sentence.[91]

The Supreme Court found that future dangerousness was "at issue" in the case. The prosecution had introduced evidence of an armed attempt to escape from prison with plans to take a hostage. The prosecutor's argument also included calling the defendant a "butcher" and "more frightening than a serial killer."[92] The Court rejected the prosecution argument that this evidence was probative of defendant's character and the propriety of retribution, rather than future dangerousness. The Court defined evidence of future dangerousness as "evidence

---

[84] *Id.* at 52 (italics deleted).

[85] *See id.* at 44.

[86] *Id.* at 45.

[87] *Id.* at 51, 54-55. *See* John H. Blume, Stephen P. Garvey, and Sheri Lynn Johnson, *Future Dangerousness in Capital Cases: Always At Issue*, 86 CORNELL L. REV. 397 (2001) (documenting that future dangerousness is important to jurors regardless of prosecution actions; suggesting that *Simmons* rule is one of reliability, and that information on ineligibility for parole should not be dependent on the "at issue" requirement).

[88] 534 U.S. 246 (2002).

[89] *Id.* at 249. Also, as in *Shafer*, the state argued that *Simmons* was inapplicable because the jury had three options, including a sentence less than life, when they were instructed. *Id.* at 248. Once again, the Supreme Court said that *Simmons* was applicable because the only choices at the time of sentencing were death and life imprisonment. *Id.* at 251-52 n.2. In *Shafer*, the Court left open the issue whether or not *Simmons* would apply if there was a lesser alternative.

[90] *Id.* at 257.

[91] *Id.*

[92] *Id.* at 255-56. The Supreme Court also noted that the jury heard evidence of a brutal crime and defendant's general "propensity for violence." *Id.* at 253-54.

with a tendency to prove dangerousness in the future . . . "[93] Even if there were also other inferences from the evidence, in addition to future dangerousness, the Court held that due process required the parole ineligibility evidence under *Simmons*.

Once the Court found that future dangerousness was at issue in *Kelly*, it easily found that the instructions and defense argument were inadequate to explain parole ineligibility.[94] The dissenters criticized the majority for creating a rule that would require a jury to be instructed on parole ineligibility in all capital cases. However, the majority justices disavowed taking such a broad step. They noted that they were not deciding a case in which the evidence was probative of future dangerousness, but the prosecutor did not argue it,[95] nor were they deciding whether the public misperceptions alone regarding parole eligibility would trigger the need for an instruction.[96]

The Court appears to have taken hesitant steps towards defining the parameters of a constitutional requirement that instructions be given to a jury on parole ineligibility. Perhaps out of concern for the viability of its holding in *Ramos* that it is not constitutionally necessary to instruct on commutation or, perhaps because of a continuing concern expressed by various members of the Court about the Court's intrusion into state criminal procedure, the Court has treaded cautiously. As a result, this area of law is in a state of flux. If there is evidence tending to show that the defendant will be dangerous in the future *and* the prosecution argues the future dangerousness of the defendant, the jury must be instructed that the defendant is parole ineligible under the state system, if that is true. Evidence of future dangerousness includes the unusual violence of the murder and a prior violent record or prior violent behavior. Argument regarding future dangerousness includes references in terms that convey the violent propensities of the defendant. What is undecided is whether an instruction on parole ineligibility is required if the jurors have a third choice of a sentence less than life without parole.[97] Also undecided is what would occur if there was evidence of future dangerousness, but no argument by the prosecution. And finally, it is unclear how the Court would view the due process issue if the general public perception changes to assume that there is no parole eligibility.

---

[93] *Id.* at 254.

[94] *Id.* at 252-58.

[95] *Id.* at 254 n.4.

[96] *Id.* at 256-57 n.7.

[97] The Court has also not squarely decided whether the defense is entitled to introduce evidence or obtain an instruction on the length of time that defendant would serve before becoming parole eligible, although indications in recent decisions are that the Court does not consider a lengthy term of years comparable to information about parole ineligibility. *See* Ramdass v. Angelone, 530 U.S. 156 (2000) (rejecting argument that, under habeas law, there was a contrary or unreasonable application of *Simmons* where state court refused parole ineligibility instruction under circumstances where defendant was not technically parole ineligible until a final judgment was entered on a prior crime; possible post-trial motions could challenge the conviction). *Cf.* Brown v. Texas, 522 U.S. 940 (1997) (Stevens, J., respecting the denial of certiorari) (raising the issue of informing jurors of life sentences with a lengthy minimum).

[D]   Effect of Hung Jury

The Supreme Court has also confronted claims regarding erroneous instructions or the absence of instructions regarding the effect of a hung jury. In *Jones v. United States*,[98] the defendant argued that the jury was misled by erroneous jury instructions about the effect of deadlocking. The defense believed that the jurors might have thought incorrectly that, if they were unable to reach a verdict of death or life imprisonment, the judge would have the option of imposing a prison sentence of even less than a life term. Although the only possible sentences for Jones' crime were death or life imprisonment, the judge erroneously used instructions that were designed for certain other capital cases that had the possibility of a lesser term of years than life imprisonment.[99] The jury returned a verdict of death. The defense believed that the jury might have been pressured to reach a verdict and avoid deadlocking in order to preclude the possibility of a lesser sentence than life imprisonment.

In a 5-4 decision, the Court rejected the constitutional challenge that the instructions violated the Constitution. The majority found no reasonable likelihood that jurors misconstrued the instruction when considered individually or with the instructions as a whole.[100] Moreover, the Court indicated that, even if the jurors had believed that a deadlock would result in a lesser sentence, they would have been just as pressured to agree on life imprisonment as on a death sentence. As in *Romano*, the Court found the possible effect too speculative.[101]

Although the situation in *Jones* is unlikely to be repeated, the issue of hung juries and the broader issue of uncertain effects on jury deliberations are likely to arise again. The Court relied on the traditional approach in criminal trials of not informing juries about the effect of deadlocking to decline to impose such a rule in capital cases.[102] The Court further held that the general failure to instruct on the effects of a hung jury did not violate the Eighth Amendment's commands. The

---

[98] 527 U.S. 373 (1999).

[99] The instruction read:

"If you recommend the imposition of a death sentence, the court is required to impose that sentence.

If you recommend a sentence of life without the possibility of release, the court is required to impose that sentence. *If you recommend that some other lesser sentence be imposed, the court is required to impose a sentence that is authorized by the law. In deciding what recommendation to make, you are not to be concerned with the question of what sentence the defendant might receive in the event you determine not to recommend a death sentence or a sentence of life without the possibility of release. That is a matter for the court to decide in the event you conclude that a sentence of death or life without the possibility of release should not be recommended.*"

Id. at 385 (emphasis added). The problem was compounded by the verdict forms, which included A) no aggravating factor found; B) death; C) life imprisonment; and D) "*some other lesser sentence.*" *Id.* at 387.

[100] The Court analyzed the case under a plain error standard because the issue had not been properly preserved for appeal. *Id.* at 388-89.

[101] Especially under the plain error analysis in *Jones*, the Court stated it could not conclude that any such error affected the substantial rights of the defendant. *Id.* at 394.

[102] *See id.* at 383 (declining to exercise its "supervisory powers to require that an instruction on the consequences of deadlock be given in every capital case").

deadlock did not preclude the consideration of relevant mitigating evidence, nor was the jury "affirmatively misled" about its role in sentencing.[103] Four of the justices, in dissent, however, disagreed with the majority's conceptual approach to the effects of inaccurate instructions. The dissenters viewed the possibility that the jurors felt pressured towards unanimity on death to suffice as a reasonable likelihood of confusion that "tainted the jury deliberations." Although the four dissenters did not disagree with the general proposition that juries are not told the consequences of deadlocking, they found an Eighth Amendment problem with reliability. The issue of how to handle "uncertain" or "speculative" consequences of erroneous instructions is likely to arise in future cases.[104] It is unclear what must be demonstrated to show a reasonable likelihood, rather than a speculative possibility, of an unconstitutional interpretation.

§ 13.06   THE DUAL REQUIREMENTS OF GUIDED DISCRETION AND INDIVIDUALIZED CONSIDERATION

The Supreme Court's famous quintet of decisions in 1976[105] implied that both *guided discretion* and *individualized consideration* are constitutionally required under the Eighth Amendment. Language in the plurality's opinions in the 1976 decisions upholding the Georgia, Florida and Texas statutes suggested that a death penalty statute must guide or channel the discretion of the sentencer in order to avoid the imposition of an arbitrary sentence.[106] The plurality portrayed limitations on sentencer discretion as promoting consistency in capital selection.[107] At the same time, language in the plurality's opinions in the decisions striking down the statutes in North Carolina and Louisiana indicated that a death penalty statute must also allow the sentencer to take into account the circumstances of the crime and the character and record of the individual defendant.[108] The plurality asserted that consideration of individualized circumstances was necessary for a reliable determination that the defendant warranted the death penalty.[109]

The dual goals of guided discretion and individualized consideration have come under attack as irreconcilable. Requiring the sentencer to decide the sentence based only on certain guiding standards seems to contemplate that the sentencer is

---

[103] *See id.* at 382.

[104] *See, e.g., Weeks v. Angelone,* 528 U.S. at 244 (Stevens, J., dissenting) (stating, "[i]n this context, [giving effect to mitigation] even if one finds the explanations of the jury's conduct here in equipoise, a 50-50 chance that the jury has not carried out this mandate seems to me overwhelming grounds for reversal").

[105] *See* Sections 6.02-6.05, *supra.*

[106] *See, e.g.,* Gregg v. Georgia, 428 U.S. 153, 189 (1976) (plurality opinion).

[107] *See* Section 6.03, *supra.*

[108] *See* discussion of these cases in Sections 6.06 and 12.02[A], *supra.*

[109] *See, e.g.,* Woodson v. North Carolina, 428 U.S. 280, 304 (1976) (plurality opinion). *See also* Walton v. Arizona, 497 U.S. at 678-79 (Blackmun, J., dissenting) ("Only if the defendant is allowed an unrestricted opportunity to present relevant mitigating evidence will a capital sentencing procedure be deemed sufficiently reliable to satisfy constitutional standards."). For more on the individualized-consideration requirement, *see* Sections 12.01-02, *supra.*

to restrict its consideration to certain limited issues. On the other hand, individualized consideration contemplates that each offender is unique and that the sentencer should exercise discretion as to whether or not the death penalty is imposed by evaluating a broad array of mitigating evidence. Is the idea of individualized consideration inconsistent with the idea of guided discretion? Both Justice Scalia and Justice Blackmun concluded that the two notions are irreconcilable, but resolved the purported conflict quite differently.

In *Walton v. Arizona*,[110] Justice Scalia described a dichotomy between *"requiring* constraints on the sentencer's discretion to 'impose' the death penalty" and *"forbidding* constraints on the sentencer's discretion to '*decline* to impose' it."[111] In his view, the latter command, from the *Woodson-Lockett*[112] individualized consideration doctrine, entirely undermines any chance of "rationality and predictability" that *Furman* required.[113] Based on his analysis of the conflict and the text of the Eighth Amendment,[114] Justice Scalia took the position that the *Woodson-Lockett* line of cases was not required by the Eighth Amendment.[115] Thus, Justice Scalia would require adherence to guided discretion, but not to individualized consideration.

Justice Blackmun also found the two concepts irreconcilable. Unlike Justice Scalia, however, Justice Blackmun found that both guided discretion and individualized consideration were constitutionally required. In his dissent to the denial of *certiorari* in *Callins v. Collins*,[116] Justice Blackmun stated that both *fairness* based on "the uniqueness of the individual" and *reasonable consistency* based on an evenhanded imposition of the death penalty were necessary.[117] He found, however, that the discretion required for the individualized consideration necessarily imported a degree of arbitrariness into the decision process. In contrast to Justice Scalia's approach, which rejected the individualized-consideration mandate, Justice Blackmun ultimately concluded that the death penalty could not be administered fairly. Thus, the death penalty was unconstitutional and should no longer be tolerated.[118] Moreover, Justice Blackmun criticized specific aspects of death penalty systems. Professor Randall Coyne has identified three primary points in Justice Blackmun's condemnation of the death penalty: 1) racism; 2) the possibility of

---

[110] 497 U.S. 639 (1990).

[111] *Id.* at 661 (Scalia, J., concurring in part and concurring in the judgment).

[112] *See* discussion, of *Woodson* in Section 6.06, *supra*, and *Lockett* in Section 12.02, *supra*. These cases established the individualized consideration requirement.

[113] *Id.* at 661.

[114] *Id.* at 670-72. Justice Scalia interprets the cruel and unusual punishment clause as applicable to punishments, not procedures. He found support for *Furman*, however, in a modified view of the concept of "unusual" punishment. If the death penalty is "random and infrequent," it could be viewed as "unusual." He did not find, however, anything in the history or text that would prohibit a mandatory death sentence and thereby require individualized consideration.

[115] *See id.* at 671-73.

[116] 510 U.S. 1141 (1994).

[117] *Id.* at 1144 (Blackmun, J., dissenting).

[118] *See id.* at 1145 (Blackmun, J., dissenting) (asserting that "no combination of procedural rules or substantive regulations ever can save the death penalty from its inherent constitutional deficiencies").

executing innocent people; and 3) inadequate review in federal court.[119] In Justice Blackmun's view, each of these problems contributes to the inability to administer the death penalty in a nonarbitrary manner.

In the end, the purported conflict can be resolved at the doctrinal level by simply recognizing that the Court has not actually required that a capital sentencing system guide the sentencer to a verdict.[120] Instead, the Court has required that a capital sentencing system require a finding of one aggravating circumstance, which serves merely to slightly reduce the group of death-eligible offenders. What the Court has called "guided discretion" is at best only a slight narrowing of the death-eligible group.[121] After a finding of death eligibility, moreover, a capital sentencing system at the selection stage may allow the sentencer unfettered discretion to decide who lives or dies. The individualized consideration requirement is satisfied at this selection stage as long as the sentencer remains free to reject the death penalty based on any relevant, mitigating evidence proffered by the offender.[122] Recognition that guided discretion actually amounts at most to a slight narrowing of the death-eligible group resolves the seeming doctrinal conflict. Although the requirements of narrowing and individualized consideration may do little to eliminate arbitrariness, they are not at war with one another.[123]

Some justices have acknowledged that the actual requirement is not guided discretion but simply a narrowing of the death-eligible group and that this requirement does not conflict with individualized consideration. For example, Justice Stevens responded to Justice Scalia in *Walton* with a "pyramid" theory.[124] Under the pyramid theory, the base is all homicides. The first level as one moves up the pyramid narrows into those homicides that are murder. The second level narrows into those murders that are death-eligible because an aggravating circumstance exists. The third and final level narrows into those death-eligible murders for which the death penalty is actually imposed. The channeling or guiding function is satisfied by the narrowing into the death-eligible level. The individualized consideration function is satisfied at the apex of the pyramid where the decision of death or life is actually made. By compartmentalizing the functions, both concepts are incorporated into the death penalty process. Justice Stevens wrote that "[a] rule

---

[119] *See* Randall Coyne, *Marking the Progress of a Humane Justice: Harry Blackmun's Death Penalty Epiphany*, 43 U. KAN. L. REV. 367, 413 (1995). Professor Coyne observed three themes: "(1) racism plays an unacceptable role in determining who will be condemned to die; (2) the inevitability of error continues to insure that innocent people will be executed; and (3) federal courts no longer provide meaningful review of the constitutional claims pressed by death row inmates."

[120] *See generally* Scott W. Howe, *Furman's* Mythical Mandate, 40 U. of Mich. J. L. Reform 435, 441-460 (2007) (asserting that "[m]inimal narrowing and expansive individualized consideration are the only Eighth Amendment requirements that the Court has imposed on capital sentencing trials," and arguing that the Court's doctrine is best understood and evaluated as simply an effort to ensure that those who are sentenced to death deserve that sanction rather than as an effort to ensure a meaningful basis for distinguishing cases where the death sentence is imposed from those where it is not).

[121] *See id.* at 447-48.

[122] *See id.* at 459.

[123] *See id.* at 460.

[124] 497 U.S. at 716-18 (Steven, J., dissenting). Justice Stevens used a pyramid theory that was espoused by the Georgia Supreme Court in an earlier case.

that forbids unguided discretion at the base is completely consistent with one that requires discretion at the apex."[125]

However, as Justice Blackmun noted in *Callins*, the narrowing by the aggravating circumstances, with subsequent complete discretion in imposing the death penalty, still allows for arbitrariness. This point is particularly true when the narrowing of the death-eligible group is as minimal as that countenanced by the Court's decisions. Justice Blackmun wrote:

> It is the decision to sentence a defendant to death — not merely the decision to make a defendant eligible for death — that may not be arbitrary. . . . It seems that the decision whether a human being should live or die is so inherently subjective — rife with all of life's understandings, experiences, prejudices, and passions — that it inevitably defies the rationality and consistency required by the Constitution.[126]

The studies that have been conducted to determine the influence of racial bias on capital selection tend to support Justice Blackmun's view that death selection continues to reflect arbitrariness.[127]

The question remains whether the results of the death penalty system, with its narrowing of death eligibility followed by individualized consideration, are *unacceptably* arbitrary and capricious. Professor Scott Sundby has pointed out that *Furman* itself contemplated some discretion in death penalty proceedings.[128] He has further noted that the goals of narrowing the death-eligible group and individualized consideration are the same. Both doctrines are designed to foster a system that decides "which defendants are within the state's power to execute under the eighth amendment."[129] Nonetheless, the doctrines do not necessarily do much to combat arbitrariness in the use of the death penalty if only because many of the most blameworthy murderers may still escape a death sentence through plea bargaining and other decisions made outside of the sentencing hearing.[130] Indeed,

---

[125] *Id.* at 718 (Stevens, J., dissenting).

Justice Kennedy also has viewed the two concepts as reconcilable. In Johnson v. Texas, 509 U.S. 350 (1993), he wrote:

> The reconciliation of competing principles is the function of the law. Our capital sentencing jurisprudence seeks to reconcile two competing, and valid, principles in Furman, which are to allow mitigating evidence to be considered and to guide the discretion of the sentencer.

In *Johnson*, the Court found an appropriate accommodation of the two concepts in the Texas approach of allowing mitigating evidence of youth, but guiding the sentencer's use of the mitigation in answering a question about future dangerousness. *See id.* at 369-70.

[126] *Callins*, 510 U.S. at 1134-35 (Blackmun, J., dissenting).

[127] *See* Section 20.03, *supra*.

[128] *See* Scott E. Sundby, *The Lockett Paradox: Reconciling Guided Discretion and Unguided Mitigation in Capital Sentencing*, 38 U.C.L.A. L. REV. 1147 (1991). *See also* Janet C. Hoeffel, *Risking the Eighth Amendment: Arbitrariness, Juries, and Discretion in Capital Cases*, 46 BOSTON C. L. REV. 771, 786-88 (2005) (asserting that individualized consideration furthers rather than conflicts with *Furman*'s command).

[129] Sundby, *supra* note 128, at 1206.

[130] Because the selection stage of the capital sentencing trial involves substantial discretion by the sentencer, decisions to impose death at that point may also be influenced by seemingly irrational factors.

one commentator has contended that the Supreme Court could have better rationalized the Eighth Amendment rules governing the capital sentencing hearing as an effort to help ensure that each death-sentenced defendant deserves death rather than as an effort to provide a meaningful basis for distinguishing the cases in which a death sentence is imposed from those in which it is not.[131] In any event, a majority of the Justices have concluded that, at the selection stage, providing the capital sentencer with substantial discretion is preferable to narrowly restricting the inquiry and that the results are not unacceptable under the Constitution.

On the other hand, foreclosing individualized consideration by mandating death sentences may also yield arbitrary results. As Professor Sundby has suggested, some death sentences might be unconstitutionally disproportionate if all discretion was removed and mandatory death sentences were employed. *See* Sundby, *supra* note 128, at 1172. *See also* Jeffrey L. Kirchmeier, *Aggravating and Mitigating Factors: The Paradox of Today's Arbitrary and Mandatory Capital Punishment Scheme*, 6 WM. & MARY BILL RTS. J. 345 (1998) (suggesting that even a mandatory death penalty scheme would suffer from arbitrariness through ill-defined and overbroad aggravating factors).

    [131] *See, e.g.*, Scott W. Howe, *Resolving the Conflict in the Capital Sentencing Cases: A Desert-Oriented Theory of Regulation*, 26 GA. L. REV. 323, 337-361 (1992) (contending that the Court's cases prohibiting mandatory capital sentencing and requiring individualized consideration are best justified on this theory, but arguing that an even better approach for resolving offender deserts would involve a two-stage sentencing determination focused separately on culpability and "general deserts").

Chapter 14

DIRECT APPEALS

§ 14.01 OVERVIEW OF STATUTORY APPROACHES

All states that authorize the death penalty and the federal government provide for an appeal from a capital conviction and sentence. In most states, the appeal is to the state supreme court.[1] In a federal capital case, the appeal goes to the circuit court of appeal. In virtually all jurisdictions, the appeal is automatic. Although there are instances where defendants have waived their appeals, there is no clear constitutional law on whether the appeal must be mandatory to fulfill the command of *Furman*.[2]

Many of the issues considered on appeal from a trial in a capital case are similar to those in any criminal trial. Motions to suppress evidence under the Fourth, Fifth, or Sixth Amendments, evidentiary rulings, and jury instructions provide the basis for typical appellate issues from the guilt phase.

Other issues on appeal are unique to a capital case, especially alleged errors from the penalty phase of the trial. The penalty issues may involve challenges, for example, to the aggravating circumstances,[3] to the failure to admit mitigating evidence,[4] or to problems with the jury instructions on the penalty decision.[5]

One of the most significant issues on appeal concerns when and how an appellate court can uphold a conviction or sentence despite a finding of error at trial. The usual analysis in criminal cases is to assess whether the error is harmless. Harmless error analysis does not involve factfinding on appeal; the appellate court is evaluating the effect of the error on a trial jury. The Supreme Court has also upheld a factual determination, unique to capital cases, that calls for reweighing aggravating and mitigating circumstances on appeal. The appellate reweighing has occurred where an appellate court finds that one aggravating circumstance is invalid but also finds that at least one other aggravating circumstance is valid. The Supreme Court's

---

[1] *See, e.g.,* Cal. Const. art. 6, § 11(a) ("The Supreme Court has appellate jurisdiction when judgment of death has been pronounced").

[2] *See* Gilmore v. Utah, 429 U.S. 1012, 1016 (1976) (stating that no one had standing to challenge Gilmore's decision to forego his appeal where there had been no showing that Gilmore was unable to seek relief on his own behalf); Whitmore v. Arkansas, 495 U.S. 149, 165 (1990) (holding that "next friend" lacks standing in federal court when defendant has knowingly and voluntarily waived his right to appeal).

[3] *See* Sections 9.01 and 10.01, 10.03-10.04, *supra.*

[4] *See* Sections 12.01-12.03, *supra.*

[5] *See* Sections 13.03 (burden of persuasion), 13.04-13.05, *supra.*

2002 decision in *Ring v. Arizona*,[6] however, may raise issues about the constitutionality of appellate reweighing.

In the past, death sentences from nonweighing states have also sometimes been affirmed on grounds that the sentences do not violate the Constitution despite an invalid aggravating circumstance, and the Court has now extended this doctrine to weighing states.[7] The Court concluded that, in both kinds of systems, it is constitutional to affirm a death sentence without conducting a harmless error or reweighing analysis if there is at least one valid aggravating circumstance and the evidence supporting any invalid aggravating circumstance could have been given aggravating weight in support of another valid sentencing factor. The applications of harmless error, appellate reweighing, and affirmance despite the finding of an invalid aggravating circumstance are discussed in the sections that follow.

§ 14.02　HARMLESS ERROR IN GENERAL

When an appellate court finds that constitutional error has occurred in a criminal trial or penalty phase, the court must next decide if the error is reversible per se, or if it can be subjected to a harmless error analysis. Some errors are considered so significant to the fairness of the trial that they are never harmless and automatically trigger a reversal for retrial. These errors include: a biased judge, a complete denial of the right to counsel, and a failure to instruct a jury on the beyond a reasonable doubt standard.[8] Most constitutional errors, however, do not automatically result in a reversal. They are only reversible errors if they are not harmless. Thus, the determination of whether the error is harmless is the difference between affirmance and reversal of a guilt or penalty phase.

The test for harmless error of constitutional violations on direct appeal was defined in *Chapman v. California*[9] as whether the error is "harmless beyond a reasonable doubt." Generally, the inquiry is whether the court can find beyond a reasonable doubt that the error did not contribute to the verdict.[10] The burden of persuasion is on the state to demonstrate that the error was harmless. Examples where a court has found errors not to be harmless include erroneous refusal to allow defense to question a key prosecution witness regarding bias;[11] giving a deficient reasonable doubt instruction;[12] and admitting a videotaped confession when the

---

[6] 536 U.S. 584 (2002). *See* discussion of *Ring* in Sections 9.02[A], 10.02, *supra*.

[7] For a discussion of the meaning of "nonweighing" and "weighing" decisions, *see* Sections 7.03, 11.01[B], and 13.01, *supra*.

[8] *See* Neder v. United States, 527 U.S. 1, 8-9 (1999) (citing Arizona v. Fulminante, 499 U.S. 279, 308-308 (1991)) (listing errors that are automatically reversible and not subject to harmless error as complete denial of counsel, biased trial judge, racial discrimination in selection of grand jury, denial of self-representation at trial, denial of public trial, defective reasonable doubt instruction). *But see* Hedgpeth v. Pulido, 555 U.S. 57 (2008) (citing *Neder* and rejecting application of per se reversal in case where jury was instructed on two theories of felony-murder, one of which was invalid).

[9] 386 U.S. 18, 24 (1967).

[10] *Id.* at 26.

[11] Blades v. United States, 25 A.3d 39 (D.C. 2011).

[12] Sullivan v. Louisiana, 508 U.S. 275 (1993).

defendant has clearly invoked his Fifth Amendment right to counsel.[13] Situations in which a court has found errors harmless under the *Chapman* standard include violating the *Bruton* doctrine;[14] the jury's use of a dictionary in violation of the Sixth Amendment;[15] and allowing witnesses to identify defendant's associates while they were dressed in jail clothing.[16]

Constitutional errors raised in postconviction habeas proceedings and nonconstitutional errors are subjected to a less demanding test, and it is easier for the state to demonstrate harmless error.[17] Because there are many federal postconviction habeas petitions in capital cases, the standard for harmless error can be particularly important. In federal habeas corpus cases, the courts apply a standard from *Brecht v. Abrahamson* whether the error "had substantial and injurious effect or influence in determining the jury's verdict."[18] The analysis requires that the court first determine if a constitutional error has occurred of the magnitude required under AEDPA for relief that the decision was contrary to, or an unreasonable application, of federal law, or an unreasonable determination of the facts. If the court finds that the error meets that standard, there is still no relief in habeas unless the error is not harmless. By way of illustration, in *Fry v. Pliler*,[19] the United States Supreme Court assumed that exclusion of a defense witness' testimony in violation of the Constitution was an unreasonable application of a prior precedent, which would satisfy the AEDPA standard for relief. The Court held that, after the determination of error, the *Brecht* standard for harmless error applies.[20] Thus, if there is a constitutional error such as claimed in *Fry* that the defense was precluded from putting on a witness' testimony, the analysis would be a two-step process: 1) Was that error contrary to or an unreasonable application of federal law? and 2) even if the error was unreasonable, did it have a substantial and injurious effect or influence in determining the jury's verdict? To answer the second question, a court would need to consider factors such as what testimony was heard by the jury, whether the precluded witness' testimony duplicated other witnesses, whether the precluded witness would have carried more weight, and other such concerns. In *Fry*, the majority did not reach the issue of harmless error on the merits. The

---

[13] Wood v. Ercole, 644 F.3d 83 (2d Cir. 2011).

[14] Harrington v. California, 395 U.S. 250 (1969).

[15] Bauberger v. Haynes, 632 F.3d 100 (4th Cir. 2011), *cert. denied*, 132 S.Ct 189 (2011).

[16] State v. Ward, 292 Kan. 541, 256 P.3d 801 (2011).

[17] *See* Brecht v. Abrahamson, 507 U.S. 619, 623 (1993) (the harmless error standard for habeas relief is whether the error "had substantial and injurious effect or influence in determining the jury's verdict"). *See also* United States v. Rahm, 993 F.2d 1405, 1415 (9th Cir. 1993) ("Under our test for nonconstitutional error, which we apply to errors as to the admissibility of expert testimony, we must reverse unless it is more probable than not that the error did not materially affect the verdict.").

[18] 507 U.S. 619, 623 (1993). *See* Hedgpeth v. Pulido, 555 U.S. 57 (2008), and Fry v. Pliler, 551 U.S. 112 (2007) for Court's reaffirmation of applicability of *Brecht* standard after AEDPA.

[19] 551 U.S. 112 (2007).

[20] In neither this case nor in Hedgpeth v. Pulido, 555 U.S. 57 (2008), did the Court reach the issue of harmless error on the merits. In *Fry*, the Court indicated that the application of the *Brecht* standard was not before the Court. 551 U.S. at 121. In *Hedgpeth*, the Court remanded the case for an application of *Brecht* to an instructional error in which the jury was instructed on one valid theory and one invalid theory of felony-murder. *Id.*

concurring and dissenting justices, however, would have reached the issue of applying the harmless error standard. They emphasized that the excluded witness was a disinterested witness who would have supported the theory that her cousin, and not the defendant, was responsible for the killings. They further pointed out that the jury was on the fence. They deadlocked initially, as had two prior juries in the case in two previous attempts to try the defendant which ended in hung juries, and deliberated for more than three weeks after the judge asked them to try to reach a verdict.[21] The concurring and dissenting justices also pointed out that the only eyewitness described someone far shorter and lighter in weight than the defendant.[22] In their view, the *Brecht* standard was met.

In developing its harmless error jurisprudence, the Supreme Court has not distinguished between capital and noncapital cases. The same standard is used, even for errors that occur in a penalty phase. The Court established the use of harmless error analysis on direct appeal from the penalty phase of capital cases in *Satterwhite v. Texas*.[23] In *Satterwhite*, a psychiatrist's testimony about the defendant's future dangerousness was erroneously admitted in violation of the defendant's Sixth Amendment right to counsel. Although the Court held that the *Chapman* harmless error test applied on direct appeal, it found that the error was *not* harmless, and reversed and remanded on the death sentence. The Court could not conclude beyond a reasonable doubt that the psychiatrist's testimony on future dangerousness "did not influence the sentencing jury."[24]

§ 14.03   APPELLATE ROLE WHEN AGGRAVATING CIRCUMSTANCE INVALIDATED

Suppose that D is charged with murder and two aggravating circumstances are alleged. The aggravating circumstances are a murder in the course of a robbery and a murder committed in a heinous, atrocious, and cruel manner. The jury convicts D, finds both aggravating circumstances proved beyond a reasonable doubt, and sentences D to death. On appeal, the appellate court finds that the heinousness aggravating circumstance is unconstitutionally vague. Can the appellate court affirm the sentence because one valid aggravating circumstance still applies or must it reverse for a new trial?

The Supreme Court has had several occasions to address the nature of the appellate role when an aggravating circumstance that was relied upon by the sentencer is subsequently invalidated. If the only aggravating circumstance, or all of the aggravating circumstances, are invalidated, the court must reverse. The defendant was not validly determined to be "death-eligible."[25] In many cases, however, only one of several aggravating circumstances is found to be invalid. If one or more valid aggravating circumstances were found by the sentencer, the

---

[21] *Fry*, 551 U.S. at 114 (2007).

[22] *Id.* at 122-127.

[23] 486 U.S. 249, 256 (1988).

[24] *Id.* at 251.

[25] *See* discussion in Section 9.01, *supra*, on death eligibility.

defendant is "death-eligible." The issue on appeal, then, is whether a decision to impose death can be upheld, or whether the case must be reversed and remanded for a new sentencing proceeding. In confronting such questions, the Court for a period distinguished between non-weighing and weighing states, but it has since articulated a single rule to address many of these issues in all jurisdictions.[26]

In *Zant v. Stephens*,[27] the Court first addressed the question of when the consideration by a sentencer of an invalid aggravating circumstance requires reversal in a nonweighing state. One of three aggravating circumstances found by a Georgia jury that sentenced Stephens to death was invalidated on appeal. Nonetheless, the Supreme Court upheld the appellate affirmance of the death sentence. The Court noted that there are multiple reasons why an aggravator might be invalid. Many of those reasons could require reversal of a death sentence in either a nonweighing or a weighing state. For example, if the invalidated aggravating circumstance authorized a jury to consider evidence that otherwise would not have been admitted or to draw adverse inferences from conduct that is constitutionally protected, or if the aggravating circumstance is irrelevant to the sentencing decision or actually should be viewed as mitigating,[28] the sentencing procedure would be unconstitutional. However, the aggravator at issue in *Zant* — that the defendant had "a substantial history of serious assaultive criminal convictions" — was only held invalid by the Georgia court on grounds of vagueness. Also, the Supreme Court noted that the evidence of prior convictions that supported the invalidated aggravator would have been admissible in any event for the jury's consideration as additional aggravating evidence.[29] In Georgia, the aggravating circumstances satisfy the death eligibility requirement, but additional aggravating evidence can be introduced in the penalty phase for consideration in the selection decision. Moreover, in a nonweighing state, such as Georgia, once the jurors find that any aggravating circumstance was proved beyond a reasonable doubt, the aggravating circumstance no longer plays a special role in the selection process. The

---

[26] For an explanation of the differences between "nonweighing" and "weighing" approaches at the selection stage, *see* Sections 7.03, 11.01[B], and 13.01, *supra*.

[27] 462 U.S. 862, 866-67 (1983). The Court noted that there was some confusion about whether there were two or, instead, three aggravating circumstances. One statutory aggravating circumstance that the jury found was that the murder was committed by an escapee. Another statutory aggravating circumstance that the jury found included two parts, a prior conviction of a capital felony and a substantial history of serious assaultive convictions. The verdict included findings that both were present. It was the latter part that was found to be unconstitutionally vague.

[28] The Court noted:

In analyzing [Stephen's] contention it is essential to keep in mind the sense in which that aggravating circumstance is "invalid." It is not invalid because it authorizes a jury to draw adverse inferences from conduct that is constitutionally protected. Georgia has not, for example, sought to characterize the display of a red flag, . . . the expression of unpopular political views, . . . or the request for a trial by jury . . . as an aggravating circumstance. Nor has Georgia attached the "aggravating" label to factors that are constitutionally impermissible or totally irrelevant to the sentencing process, such as for example the race, religion, or political affiliation of the defendant, . . . or to conduct that actually should militate in favor of a lesser penalty, such as perhaps the defendant's mental illness . . . . If the aggravating circumstance at issue had been invalid for reasons such as these, due process of law would require that the jury's decision to impose death be set aside.

Id. at 885.

[29] *Id.* at 878-80.

jurors are not instructed to weigh aggravating and mitigating circumstances, or otherwise to give any particular notice or weight to any required aggravating circumstance.[30] As a result, whether the evidence was viewed as an aggravating circumstance or simply as aggravating evidence was irrelevant. Thus, the error had no effect on the penalty proceeding.

In *Zant*, the Supreme Court noted that it was not deciding what should occur if the sentencer was faced with a "weighing" decision. In a typical weighing state, the sentencer is instructed to weigh aggravating circumstances against mitigating circumstances, and to impose death only if aggravating circumstances outweigh mitigating circumstances.[31] Because the sentencer is specifically told to engage in a balancing process with the aggravating circumstances, the status of the aggravating circumstance is arguably greater than in a nonweighing state. As a result, the effect in a weighing state of invalidating an aggravating circumstance even on grounds of vagueness was for a time thought to warrant a different approach. The Supreme Court articulated this separate approach in *Clemons v. Mississippi*,[32] and again in *Stringer v. Black*.[33]

In *Clemons*, one of two aggravating circumstances relied upon by the jury was found unconstitutionally vague. The Supreme Court determined that such a conclusion in a weighing state like Mississippi rendered the sentencing process unconstitutional.[34] Nonetheless, the Court held that appellate courts in weighing states have two options in such a case. The Court held that such courts may reweigh the aggravating and mitigating circumstances without the invalid aggravator.[35] Although a reweighing approach puts the appellate court in the unusual position of a factfinder, the Supreme Court found appellate reweighing to be constitutional.[36] It was unclear, however, whether the Mississippi court had engaged in a reweighing process in *Clemons*.[37]

As a second option, the Supreme Court held that appellate courts in weighing states could use a harmless error analysis. This approach would require an appellate court to ask whether the evidence and instructions on the invalidated aggravating circumstance were harmless beyond a reasonable doubt. The question was whether, if the aggravating circumstance had been properly defined or narrowed, "beyond a reasonable doubt the result would have been the same

---

[30] *Id.* at 873. *See* Section 6.03, *supra.*

[31] *See* Sections 7.03 and 13.01, *supra.*

[32] 494 U.S. 738 (1990).

[33] 503 U.S. 222 (1992).

[34] *Clemons*, 494 U.S. at 743, 754.

[35] *Id.* at 745.

[36] In fact, the Court found appellate factfinding consistent with Cabana v. Bullock, 474 U.S. 376 (1986), where the Court had indicated that it would be constitutional for appellate courts to determine factually the existence of the threshold *mens rea* for death eligibility under the felony-murder *Enmund-Tison* rule.

[37] As discussed in Sections 9.02[A] and 10.02, *supra*, it is possible that the Court's decision in *Ring* has undermined the reweighing aspect of *Clemons* and the appellate factfinding in *Bullock*.

. . . ."[38] If so, the error is harmless. In *Clemons*, the Mississippi court was too brief and unclear regarding this approach, as well.[39]

In *Stringer*, the Court reiterated the greater significance of an invalidated aggravating circumstance in a weighing jurisdiction. *Stringer* was a habeas case from Mississippi in which one of three aggravating circumstances relied upon by the sentencing jury was alleged to be unconstitutionally vague. The lower federal courts had denied the petition. In reversing and remanding for either reweighing by the state courts or a harmlessness inquiry, the Supreme Court again emphasized the distinction between nonweighing and weighing jurisdictions. The Court noted that "[a] vague aggravating factor used in the weighing process creates the risk that the jury will treat the defendant as more deserving of the death penalty than he might otherwise be by relying upon the existence of an illusory circumstance."[40]

Despite this history of separate approaches for nonweighing and weighing states, the Supreme Court abandoned the distinction in 2006 in favor of a single rule to be applied in all jurisdictions. In *Brown v. Sanders*,[41] two of four aggravating circumstances identified by a California jury that sentenced the defendant to death were deemed unconstitutional by the state appellate court. Nonetheless, the state court, interpreting the California system as nonweighing, affirmed the death sentence under *Zant*. On federal habeas, the Ninth Circuit reversed, concluding that California was a weighing state so that the state appellate court could uphold the death sentence only by independent reweighing or by finding harmless error beyond a reasonable doubt. The U. S. Supreme Court reversed the Ninth Circuit. The Court concluded that California was actually a nonweighing state but that this conclusion should not matter.[42] The Court resolved the case under a single rule that it asserted would henceforth apply in all jurisdictions: "An invalidated sentencing factor (whether an eligibility factor or not) will render the sentence unconstitutional by reason of its adding an improper element to the aggravation scale in the weighing process *unless* one of the other sentencing factors enables the sentencer to give aggravating weight to the same facts and circumstances."[43] In *Sanders*, because all of the facts and circumstances admitted to establish the two invalidated aggravating circumstances were also properly introduced as aggravating facts under a general "circumstances of the crime" sentencing factor, there was no constitutional infirmity in the death sentence. Because the invalidation of the aggravator did not rise to the level of a constitutional error, there was no need for further inquiry.

---

[38] *Clemons*, at 754.

[39] *Id.* 494 U.S. at 751. *See also* Sochor v. Florida, 504 U.S. 527, 540-41(1992) (remanding case to state supreme court because unclear if court had engaged in harmless error analysis).

[40] *Stringer*, 503 U.S. at 235.

[41] 546 U.S. 212 (2006).

[42] *See id.* at 222. In distinguishing between weighing and nonweighing systems, the Court focused on whether, at the selection stage, the aggravating circumstances were discrete and exclusive vessels for the consideration of aggravating evidence rather than on simply whether the jury was instructed to weigh the aggravating circumstances as part of its process for reaching a verdict. Justice Stevens asserted in dissent that this approach departed from the Court's prior method for identifying weighing and nonweighing systems. *See id.* at 225-227 (Stevens, J., dissenting).

[43] *Id.* at 220.

Application of the *Sanders* rule will mean that the invalidation of one or more aggravating circumstances on appeal will not necessarily render a death sentencing process unconstitutional even in states where sentencers are given weighing instructions. For instance, if an aggravating circumstance is found invalid on vagueness grounds, the facts and circumstances that could support a vague aggravating circumstance might also be given aggravating weight under another sentencing factor, regardless whether jurors are told to weigh or balance aggravating factors against mitigating factors. When that is true, the *Sanders* decision will mean that there is no constitutional error in the imposition of a death sentence.

Despite *Sanders*, the invalidation of an aggravating circumstance will sometimes still render a sentencing process unconstitutional, and the question will arise in such cases whether the death sentence must be struck down. Sometimes, the invalidation of an aggravating circumstance identified by a jury will mean that the jury heard facts and circumstances about which it would not otherwise have learned. Similarly, as the Court noted in *Zant*, an aggravating circumstance could be invalidated because it calls for the jury to draw adverse inferences that infringe the Constitution. In such cases, the sentencing process is itself unconstitutional. Can an appellate court nonetheless sometimes uphold the death sentence in these cases? Some language in the *Sanders* opinion indicated that the death sentence under those circumstances must be invalidated.[44] However, the Court may have meant only to indicate that the sentencing process was necessarily unconstitutional but not to require automatic reversal. The Court might allow such a death sentence to stand on a finding that the constitutional error was harmless beyond a reasonable doubt.

In the aftermath of the *Sanders* decision, some lower courts reflect hesitancy in applying, or confusion in how to apply, the case. While the California Supreme Court applied *Sanders*, both the Fifth Circuit Court of Appeals and the Nebraska Supreme Court demonstrate the uncertainty among some courts over the applicability of *Sanders*. In *People v. Lewis*, the California Supreme Court applied *Sanders* and concluded that the evidence supporting the invalidated special (aggravating) circumstances was admissible in support of other, valid special circumstances.[45] However, in *Simmons v. Epps*, the Fifth Circuit Court of Appeals expressed the view that it was unclear whether *Sanders* applied in weighing states.[46] The court held that, in the case at hand, it was error to submit to the jury an aggravating circumstance of "great risk of death to many people" because there was insufficient evidence to support it. However, the court found that it did not have to decide the applicability of *Sanders* because, under the *Brecht* harmless error analysis, the error was harmless. The evidence relating to a great risk of death to many people also was relevant to the valid aggravating circumstance of murder for pecuniary gain.[47] In *State v. Sandoval*, the majority opinion of the Nebraska Supreme Court

---

[44] *See id.* at 219 (asserting that in both categories of cases, the death sentence must "be set aside").

[45] People v. Lewis, 181 P.3d 947, 1022 (Cal. 2008), *cert. denied*, 555 U.S. 1155 (2009).

[46] Simmons v. Epps, 654 F.3d 526 (5th Cir. 2011). The Court noted that the 6th Circuit had found that *Sanders* did not apply to weighing states while the 11th Circuit had noted that it was likely *Sanders* stated a uniform rule for all states, weighing or nonweighing. *Id.* at 538.

[47] *Id.* at 540-542 (evidence included raping and imprisoning a woman in a metal box while the defendant robbed her and the murder victim).

did not even mention *Sanders* in a case in which the court invalidated an aggravating factor relating to "mental anguish."[48] Instead, the court analyzed only whether the error was harmless, concluding that the submission of the invalid aggravator was harmless. Where there were three valid aggravating factors, on balance the court concluded that the sentence would have been the same.[49] As Judge Connolly, concurring in part and dissenting in part pointed out, the majority's analysis failed to take into account the new principles from the *Sanders* case.[50] Judge Connolly's analysis of the cases led to the conclusion that *Sanders* applied and that the evidence of the invalid aggravating factor would not have been otherwise admissible. Moreover, Judge Connolly viewed the majority's harmless error analysis as, in essence, a reweighing and concluded that, under the *Chapman* standard for harmless error, the error was not harmless on these facts.[51] Judge Connolly's analysis would appear to be far more consistent with *Sanders* than the majority's approach. The confusion and different approaches evidenced by these cases among lower courts on the application and interpretation of *Sanders* will probably not be resolved without a future U.S. Supreme Court opinion.

"Reweighing" on appeal, as was approved in *Clemons* and *Stringer*, remains an issue post-*Sanders*. Commentators have criticized the reweighing approach as improper and illogical appellate factfinding. They argue that appellate courts are not traditionally factfinders. When an appellate court simply reads a written record, critics contend that the court is unable to observe witnesses and evaluate credibility.[52] It may be that most appellate courts agree, as it is much more common for the courts to invoke harmless error analysis than to engage in reweighing.

The Supreme Court's decision in *Ring v. Arizona*[53] may affect the continued viability of appellate reweighing. In *Ring*, the Court held that a defendant had a Sixth Amendment right to a jury verdict on the aggravating circumstances that make a defendant death-eligible.[54] The aggravating circumstances were facts that elevated the possible punishment and, thus, were comparable to elements of the crime for which a defendant has a constitutional right to a jury verdict. Does a defendant also have a constitutional right to a jury verdict on the weighing decision? If so, then appellate reweighing would be unconstitutional. The holding in *Ring*, however, was based on finding that aggravating circumstances, which make a defendant death-eligible, were the "functional equivalent" of elements of a crime.[55] It is still an open question whether the "selection" decision, in addition to the

---

[48] State v. Sandoval, 788 N.W.2d 172, 213, 228 (Neb. 2010), *cert. denied*, 131 S. Ct. 2912 (2011).

[49] *Id.* at 213.

[50] *Id.* at 237.

[51] *Id.* at 238.

[52] *See* David McCord, *Is Death "Different" for Purposes of Harmless Error Analysis? Should It Be?: An Assessment of United States and Louisiana Supreme Court Case Law*, 59 LA. L. REV. 1105, 1144 (1999); *see also* Linda E. Carter, *Harmless Error in the Penalty Phase of a Capital Case: A Doctrine Misunderstood and Misapplied*, 28 GA. L. REV. 125, 139-40 (1993).

[53] 536 U.S. 584 (2002).

[54] *Id.* at 609. *See* discussion of *Ring* in Sections 9.02[A] and 10.02, *supra*.

[55] *Id.*

"eligibility" decision, will be viewed in the same way.[56]

§ 14.04 WHAT IS HARMLESS IN A PENALTY DETERMINATION?

Although the Supreme Court has sanctioned the use of harmless error analysis generally in the penalty phase, some commentators have argued that the penalty phase decision is too different from the guilt phase decision to allow for a parallel application of harmless error. They contend that a decision of life or death is a moral decision or a subjective value judgment, rather than a finding of fact such as determining whether the elements of a crime exist. Each individual juror may decide differently what weight to give to aggravating or mitigating evidence, and jurors may come to different conclusions whether death is appropriate. As a consequence, these commentators suggest that it is virtually impossible to determine the effect an error has on individual decision-makers in a penalty decision.[57] On the other hand, the Supreme Court, although acknowledging the difficulty, has indicated that harmless error analysis is appropriate in the penalty phase.[58]

§ 14.05 DOUBLE JEOPARDY

[A] General Principles of Double Jeopardy and Collateral Estoppel[59]

Suppose D has been convicted of a capital crime and sentenced to life imprisonment after the sentencer has rejected the prosecution's request for the death penalty. On appeal, the conviction is reversed and remanded for a new trial. Can the prosecution seek the death penalty when they retry D? Or does the double jeopardy clause preclude the prosecution from seeking a higher penalty than the life imprisonment imposed in the first trial?

The double jeopardy clause of the Fifth Amendment provides "nor shall any person be subject for the same offence to be twice put in jeopardy of life or limb."[60] The purpose of the double jeopardy clause is finality. The defendant is entitled to

---

[56] *See* discussion of *Ring* and the selection decision in Sections 13.01 and 9.02[B], *supra.* The same question is posed with the mens rea requirement of *Enmund* and *Tison* that was at issue in *Cabana v. Bullock.* If the requisite mens rea is necessary to make the defendant death-eligible, *Ring* will probably be interpreted to require a jury verdict on the issue. An appellate decision would not be constitutionally adequate. *See* discussion of *Enmund* and *Tison* in Section 8.02, *supra.*

[57] *See* McCord, *supra*, note 52, at 1144 (stating that ". . . given the highly subjective nature of a death penalty decision, it can never be clear what might have turned the verdict in the opposite direction . . . "); Carter, *supra*, note 52, at 161 (stating that "[b]ecause the 'weighing' decision is so individual to each juror and reflects a value judgment, it is difficult to assess the 'contribution' of any error").

[58] *Satterwhite*, 486 U.S. at 258.

[59] The Supreme Court originally used the term "collateral estoppel," but has indicated in a later case that "issue preclusion" is an interchangeable term. Schiro v. Farley, 510 U.S. 222 (1994).

[60] U.S. Const. amend. V, cl. 2.

have the case end and not be subject to continuing court proceedings.[61]

The double jeopardy clause applies to multiple prosecutions and multiple punishments for the same crime. It does not ordinarily apply to sentencing. Thus, the general rule is that if D's conviction is reversed on appeal, the state may reprosecute and obtain a harsher sentence in a second trial. What the state cannot do is: 1) reprosecute for the same crime after an acquittal; 2) reprosecute for the same crime after a conviction, unless there has been a reversal or mistrial;[62] or 3) impose a punishment more than once for the same offense. Thus, if D is charged with murder and the jury returns a verdict of not guilty, D cannot be recharged with the same murder by that state.[63] Similarly, if D is charged with murder and the jury convicts D of manslaughter, the jury has implicitly acquitted D of murder, and D cannot be reprosecuted by that state on the murder charge. The third protection precludes the state from punishing D twice for the same offense. If D is convicted of robbery for holding up a bank, he cannot subsequently be punished for the lesser-included offense of theft of the funds of the bank.[64]

A related doctrine is collateral estoppel. In *Ashe v. Swenson*,[65] the Supreme Court held that the principle of collateral estoppel was part of the constitutional guarantee of double jeopardy. Collateral estoppel applies when an issue has been decided in the course of a final judgment. The same parties can be precluded from relitigating the issue in subsequent litigation. For example, Ashe was acquitted of the robbery of a poker player. He was subsequently charged with robbing another poker player present at the same time as the first one. The Court found that the jury in the first trial necessarily found that Ashe was not one of the robbers.[66] Thus, the state was precluded from relitigating the issue of Ashe's guilt in a second robbery trial, even though a different victim was involved.

---

[61] *See* United States v. DiFrancesco, 449 U.S. 117, 127-28 (1980), *quoting* Green v. United States, 355 U.S. 184, 187-88 (1957). The Court stated:

> The constitutional prohibition against 'double jeopardy' was designed to protect an individual from being subjected to the hazards of trial and possible conviction more than once for an alleged offense . . . . The underlying idea, one that is deeply ingrained in at least the Anglo-American system of jurisprudence, is that the State with all its resources and power should not be allowed to make repeated attempts to convict an individual for an alleged offense, thereby subjecting him to embarrassment, expense and ordeal and compelling him to live in a continuing state of anxiety and insecurity, as well as enhancing the possibility that even though innocent he may be found guilty.

Id.

[62] *See id.* at 129-30.

[63] *See* Heath v. Alabama, 474 U.S. 82, 88 (1985). Note, however, that separate sovereigns may each prosecute the defendant. Thus, if a murder begins in State #1 and ends in State #2, both states may prosecute the defendant.

[64] *See* United States, 509 U.S. 688, 696-98 (1993) (explaining the "Blockburger", or "same-elements" test, as an inquiry whether each offense contains an element not contained in the other; double jeopardy did not preclude prosecutions of defendants for underlying crimes — drug offense for Dixon and assault for Foster — and prosecutions of them for contempt). Another example where double jeopardy would preclude multiple prosecutions would be for assault and assault with intent to kill for the same conduct.

[65] 397 U.S. 436, 445-46 (1970).

[66] *Id.* at 445.

[B] Double Jeopardy and Collateral Estoppel in Capital Cases

In capital cases, double jeopardy issues arise separately for the guilt and penalty phases. The guilt phase is governed by the same double jeopardy principles outlined above. For example, suppose that D is charged with a capital murder, but is convicted of a lesser-included offense of murder in the second degree. If D subsequently obtains a reversal of the second degree conviction on appeal, the state may not retry her on the capital murder charge. Double jeopardy treats the first verdict as an implied acquittal of the capital murder charge for which D cannot be placed on trial a second time.

The penalty phase raises more controversial double jeopardy issues. Should a sentencer's decision to reject the death penalty in favor of a life sentence be treated as a typical sentence, which can be harsher on retrial, or, instead, as a trial verdict, such that double jeopardy principles would preclude a harsher sentence on retrial? As posed in the hypothetical at the beginning of this section, can the prosecution seek death on remand if the original sentencer rejected death?

When the Supreme Court first faced this problem, it posed the critical question as whether the penalty phase is similar enough to a trial such that a life verdict is an "acquittal" of a death sentence. The Court asked whether the capital sentencer's decision to reject death is comparable to a decision by the factfinder in a regular criminal trial that the state has failed to prove its case.

In *Bullington v. Missouri*,[67] the Court distinguished a capital penalty proceeding from the usual sentencing process and treated it as a trial for double jeopardy purposes. Two major differences from noncapital sentences drove the Court's decision. First, the capital jury was limited by standards and had only two choices of penalty.[68] Conversely, a typical noncapital sentencing involves little in the way of standards, and the precise punishment is usually variable. Second, a capital sentencing proceeding resembled a trial, with the burden on the prosecution to prove specific facts beyond a reasonable doubt. The typical sentencing proceeding does not resemble a trial, and there are no additional facts that the prosecution must prove.[69] As a result of the decision to view the capital sentencing as comparable to a trial, the double jeopardy clause applied.

At Bullington's trial, the jury had found him guilty of capital murder and, in the penalty phase, imposed a sentence of life imprisonment.[70] The trial court then granted Bullington's motion for a new trial on guilt of the crime. The prosecution gave notice of an intent to seek the death penalty again on retrial. The Supreme Court held that the state was precluded from seeking the death penalty because Bullington was in essence acquitted of the death penalty in the first trial.[71]

---

[67] 451 U.S. 430 (1981).

[68] *See id.*

[69] *Id.* at 438-39 (noting the differences between Bullington's case and the Court's prior cases where these "hallmarks of [a] trial" were not present).

[70] *Id.* at 432.

[71] *Id.* at 436-37, 446.

The Court later expanded the application of double jeopardy protections to include sentencing proceedings with a judge alone. In *Arizona v. Rumsey*,[72] the Court again emphasized the limited options for punishment, death or life; guided standards and an evidentiary proceeding that resembled a trial; and the requirement that the state prove certain facts, the aggravating circumstances, beyond a reasonable doubt. A determination of life under these circumstances was an acquittal of the death sentence, and the double jeopardy clause precludes a retrial on the decision.[73]

Subsequently, the Court clarified that there must be a rejection of the death penalty for there to be an acquittal of the death sentence under *Bullington*. The Court also found that there is no collateral estoppel from a sentencer's erroneous rejection at the sentencing trial of an aggravating circumstance where the sentencer imposed the death penalty after finding, although erroneously, another aggravating circumstance. In *Poland v. Arizona*,[74] the trial judge imposed death, finding an aggravating circumstance of the heinousness of the crime. The judge rejected a second aggravating circumstance of pecuniary gain because he incorrectly thought pecuniary gain only applied to contract killings. On appeal, the Arizona Supreme Court found the evidence insufficient to prove the aggravating circumstance of heinousness, but indicated that the aggravating circumstance of pecuniary gain could apply in the case. The Supreme Court agreed with Arizona that double jeopardy did not preclude seeking the death penalty on retrial on the basis of the pecuniary gain aggravating circumstance. The Court concluded that there had been no acquittal of the death sentence under *Bullington*. The trial judge at the first trial had imposed rather than rejected a death sentence,[75] and there had been no acquittal of the death sentence on state appeal.[76] The Court also declined to find that there was collateral estoppel regarding the pecuniary gain circumstance. The Court emphasized that, while the collateral estoppel doctrine is designed to protect a defendant from further litigation, here, it was the defense, not the state, that had sought further litigation regarding the sentence imposed.

The Supreme Court also clarified that the evidence of an acquittal cannot be ambiguous. In *Schiro v. Farley*,[77] the Court held that there was no implied acquittal relevant to sentencing from the jury's failure to complete a verdict form at the guilt phase concerning a factual issue related to sentencing. The jury returned a verdict in the guilt phase of felony-murder and left a verdict form blank that asked if the murder was "knowing and intentional." The defendant argued

---

[72] 467 U.S. 203, 209 (1984).

[73] *Id.* at 210 (observing that "a sentence imposed after a completed . . . capital sentencing hearing is a judgment like the sentence at issue in *Bullington* v. *Missouri*, which this Court held triggers the protections of the Double Jeopardy Clause").

[74] 476 U.S. 147, 149 (1986).

[75] *Id.* at 157.

[76] *Id.* at 154 (explaining that the Arizona Supreme Court had never held that the prosecution had failed to meet its burden on the death penalty, merely that the trial court had mistakenly ruled on the "especially heinous" aggravating circumstance). Note that Arizona's statute providing for a judge decision, rather than a jury verdict, on the existence of an aggravating circumstance is unconstitutional. *See* Sections 9.02[A] and 10.02, *supra* (discussing Ring v. Arizona).

[77] 510 U.S. 222 (1994).

that, since felony-murder does not require a finding of an intent to kill, the jurors had found that he lacked an intent to kill when they left the second "knowing and intentional" form blank in the guilt phase. It was necessary to decide if the killing was "intentional" in the penalty phase. The defendant contended that, because the jury found that he did not intend to kill in the guilt phase, the issue was decided and the court should have been precluded on double jeopardy or collateral estoppel grounds from making a finding of an intentional killing in the penalty phase. However, the Court found that there was no acquittal of the death sentence under *Bullington* because there was no rejection of the death penalty.[78] As for the collateral estoppel claim on the issue of intent to kill, the Court viewed the jurors' actions as ambiguous. The jurors did not necessarily find that the defendant lacked an intent to kill by returning only one verdict; it was possible that the jurors believed they should only fill out one form. As a result, the Court found that there was no collateral estoppel on the issue of an intentional killing.[79]

Double jeopardy and collateral estoppel similarly did not preclude relitigation of a defendant's mental retardation in a case raising the issue post-*Atkins*. In *Bobby v. Bies*,[80] the defendant was tried, convicted, and sentenced to death prior to *Atkins*, the case in which the U.S. Supreme Court held that it is unconstitutional to execute a person who is mentally retarded. In Bies' case, his mental retardation was considered as a mitigating circumstance rather than as a categorical bar to imposing a death sentence.[81] Post-*Atkins*, Bies challenged his death sentence as unconstitutional due to his mental retardation and argued that relitigation of the mental retardation issue was barred under double jeopardy and collateral estoppel.[82] The Court held that there had been no "acquittal" that would call for a double jeopardy bar; in fact, the defendant had been sentenced to death.[83] The Court further rejected Bies' collateral estoppel argument that his mental retardation was already established in the prior proceedings.[84] The Court did not view the use of mental retardation in mitigation as comparable to a finding of an ultimate fact necessary to the decision in the meaning of the *Ashe* case.[85]

---

[78] *See Schiro*, 510 U.S. at 231-32 (stating that "the State did not . . . force [Schiro] to submit to a second death penalty hearing [, but] simply conducted a single sentencing hearing in the course of a single prosecution. The state is entitled to 'one fair opportunity' to prosecute a defendant").

[79] *Id.* at 235 (noting that doctrine was not applicable because "the jury verdict did not necessarily depend on a finding that Schiro lacked an intent to kill . . . Schiro's intent to kill was not a significant issue in the case").

[80] 129 S. Ct. 2145 (2009).

[81] *Id.* at 2148.

[82] *Id.* at 2150.

[83] *Id.* at 2149.

[84] *Id.*

[85] *Id.* at 2153.

[C] Statutorily Imposed Life Imprisonment After a Hung Jury

Another double jeopardy problem that has arisen in capital cases concerns how to view a hung jury on the sentencing question. The general rule is that a hung jury does not terminate jeopardy because there is no decision on guilt.[86] Thus, in a typical trial, the prosecution is free to retry the defendant after a hung jury. There is no decision of "not guilty" of the crime. By analogy, neither does a hung jury on the penalty of death or life represent a verdict on the penalty. Similar to a retrial of a crime, a number of states authorize the court to impanel a new sentencing jury to hear the penalty phase if there is a hung jury on death or life.[87] However, what if the state's law *requires* the court to enter a judgment of life imprisonment if the jury cannot reach a verdict? Suppose there is a hung jury on the sentence, the trial court as required imposes life imprisonment, and then the defendant appeals and the conviction is reversed. Is the state barred under double jeopardy from seeking the death penalty in the new trial? In 2003, the United States Supreme Court answered this question in *Sattazahn v. Pennsylvania*.[88]

The jury in *Sattazahn* deadlocked 9-3 for life in the penalty phase. The judge imposed a life sentence as required by statute in the event of a hung jury.[89] The defendant appealed his conviction, which was reversed for a new trial.[90] The state argued, and the Pennsylvania Supreme Court agreed, that it could seek the death penalty in the second trial.[91] Sattazahn argued that the statutory imposition of life imprisonment, imposed by law, operated as an acquittal of death.[92]

In a 5-4 decision, the Supreme Court agreed with the state that double jeopardy did not bar seeking the death penalty on retrial.[93] Writing for a majority of the Court, Justice Scalia distinguished the *Bullington* and *Rumsey* cases. He emphasized that the correct question was "whether there has been an 'acquittal,'" not simply whether life imprisonment had been imposed as the penalty.[94] An "acquittal" requires a decision on the merits. Unlike the sentencing decisions in *Bullington* and *Rumsey*, the jury in Sattazahn's case had not reached a verdict on

---

[86] *See* Sattazahn v. Pennsylvania, 537 U.S. 101, 118 n.1 (2003) (Ginsburg, J. dissenting) (citing Richardson v. United States, 468 U.S. 317 (1984) and United States v. Martin Linen Supply Co., 430 U.S. 564 (1977)).

[87] *See, e.g.*, CAL. PEN. CODE § 190.4(a) (West 2011).

[88] 537 U.S. 101 (2003).

[89] *Id.* at 104 (discussing the Pennsylvania statute which requires the court to impose a life sentence when further deliberation by the jury will not result in a unanimous agreement).

[90] Commonwealth v. Sattazahn, 631 A.2d 597, 606 (Pa. Super. Ct. 1993) (noting the case was remanded for improper jury instructions).

[91] Commonwealth v. Sattazahn, 763 A.2d 359 (Pa. 2000) (explaining that the Pennsylvania sentencing directive for the judge to enter a sentence of life imprisonment when the jury is deadlocked would be unnecessary if a "hung jury" were to function as the equivalent of an acquittal from the death penalty).

[92] *Sattazahn*, 537 U.S. 101.

[93] *Id* at 116.

[94] *Id* at 107.

the sentence.[95]

The dissenters viewed the statutorily imposed life sentence as a final judgment of life. In their view, the sentence was comparable to a termination of the proceedings, and dissimilar to a mistrial.[96] Where the sentencing decision had been submitted to the jury and the defendant had no choice in the result of a hung jury, the dissenters would have found double jeopardy protection from a retrial on death.[97]

In a section of the opinion joined only by two other justices, Justice Scalia suggested that the critical issue was the existence of the aggravating circumstance and not the final sentence of life.[98] Drawing upon the *Apprendi* and *Ring* cases, discussed *supra* in Sections 9.02[A] and 10.02, Justice Scalia found symmetry between the elements of an "offense" for purposes of the right to a jury trial and the definition of an "offence" for double jeopardy purposes.[99] As Justice Scalia pointed out, *Apprendi* and *Ring* stand for the proposition that "the existence of any fact (other than a prior conviction) [that] increases the maximum punishment that may be imposed on a defendant" must be decided by a jury under a beyond a reasonable doubt standard.[100] *Ring* held that an aggravating circumstance was such a fact that increased the maximum punishment to a possibility of death. Thus, the defendant has a right to a jury verdict beyond a reasonable doubt on the aggravating circumstance.[101] Justice Scalia drew a parallel with double jeopardy. If there is in essence an acquittal of the aggravating circumstance, double jeopardy bars a retrial. If there is no decision on the aggravating circumstance, however, as there was none in *Sattazahn*, Justice Scalia took the position that there would be no double jeopardy problem with a retrial.[102]

Interestingly, neither Justice Kennedy nor Justice O'Connor joined in this part of the opinion, although they joined with Justice Scalia for the other parts. Justice O'Connor disagreed with Justice Scalia on two grounds. First, she rejected the *Apprendi-Ring* cases. In her view, *Apprendi* and *Ring* were incorrectly decided, and a right to a jury should not be required for the facts that increase the maximum penalty.[103] On the double jeopardy issue, however, Justice O'Connor had a more expansive view than Justice Scalia. O'Connor reaffirmed *Bullington* and *Rumsey*, maintaining that there is an "acquittal" of death "when the sentencer 'decide[s] that the prosecution has not proved its case that the death penalty is

---

[95] *Id.* at 109.

[96] *Id.* at 117-18 (explaining that unlike a mistrial, this state-law-imposed life sentence was final and the government could neither appeal the sentence nor retry the sentencing question before a second jury).

[97] *Id.*

[98] *Id.* at 112.

[99] *Id.* at 111-12 (in the Constitution, the word offense is spelled as "offence").

[100] *Id.* at 111.

[101] *See* discussion of *Ring* in Sections 9.02[A] and 10.02, *supra.*

[102] *Sattazahn*, 537 U.S. at 112.

[103] *Id.* at 116-17.

appropriate.' "[104] Thus, in contrast to Justice Scalia's opinion which narrows the jeopardy issue to the aggravating circumstance, Justice O'Connor's position appears to be that the jeopardy issue includes the ultimate decision of death.

Why might the differing positions of Justice Scalia and Justice O'Connor matter? Suppose that a death penalty statute requires a jury to find an aggravating circumstance that puts D in the "death-eligible" category in the *guilt* phase of the trial.[105] In the *penalty* phase, the jury weighs any aggravating evidence, including the aggravating circumstances found to be true in the guilt phase, with mitigating circumstances in order to arrive at a sentence of death or life. Following this statutory scheme, the jury returns a life sentence in D's trial. On appeal, the conviction is reversed, and the state wishes to seek the death penalty in the new trial. Will double jeopardy bar the death penalty in the new trial? Under Justice Scalia's approach, the answer is arguably no. There was no "acquittal" of the aggravating circumstance that allowed the offense to become a death-eligible case. Under Justice O'Connor's approach, however, double jeopardy arguably is a bar. The jury has decided that the state "failed to prove its case for the death penalty."[106]

The Justices' differing views of the function of the capital-sentencing hearing explain their differing interpretations of how double jeopardy applies in capital cases. *Bullington* and *Rumsey* did not draw a distinction between the aggravating circumstance and the life/death decision for double jeopardy purposes.[107] Thus, those cases support the position that the critical finding is the ultimate life imprisonment verdict. Further, a decision of life imprisonment is similar to the decision of guilt or innocence, in that the sentencer listens to evidence and must reject one choice and choose another. Double jeopardy is intended to preserve the finality of a judgment and to protect a defendant from the ordeal of a second trial. Capital penalty proceedings are conducted as trials with a resulting judgment, and thus, arguably, the ordeal and finality are comparable to a guilt/innocence trial. On the other hand, Justice Scalia postulates that *Apprendi* and *Ring* have clarified the

---

[104] *Id.* at 117.

[105] The same issue would arise if, within the penalty phase, there is a special verdict which identifies that the jury found an aggravating circumstance and then imposed life.

[106] At the time of *Sattazahn*, there appeared to be a majority of the court (the four dissenters and Justice O'Connor) who would find a double jeopardy bar in this hypothetical case. Without question, the four dissenters would concur that double jeopardy bars a retrial, since there was a sentence of life imprisonment. It is uncertain how the present Court would resolve the problem. In addition to uncertainty resulting from Justice Alito's replacement of Justice O'Connor, it is unclear what Justice Kennedy would conclude. He did not write a separate opinion in *Sattazahn*, but he also did not join Justice Scalia's opinion that double jeopardy is limited to the aggravating circumstance.

[107] In *Rumsey*, the trial judge found that no aggravating circumstances were present and therefore acquitted defendant by imposing a sentence of life imprisonment. In *Bullington*, "[a]n examination of the jury's finding in this case reveals that a jury could have based its verdict on something other than the absence of aggravating circumstances. There is no requirement in Missouri that a jury make a specific finding that no aggravating circumstance existed to impose a life sentence. Clearly, the first jury might have imposed life imprisonment in response to defendant's plea for mercy rather than a finding of no aggravation. Thus, it cannot be said with any certainty, especially given the nature of this case, that the jury found that no aggravating circumstance existed." Respondents' Brief at 16, Bullington v. Missouri, 451 U.S. 430 (1981) (No. 80-340069).

reasoning behind *Bullington* and *Rumsey*.[108] In his view, the issue is whether the jury acquitted the defendant of the "elements" of murder with an aggravating circumstance.[109] The Court did not have to resolve this issue in *Sattazahn*. *Sattazahn* does reinforce the central notion that double jeopardy applies if there is an "acquittal." The question will be whether an "acquittal" is limited to the aggravating circumstances, or whether the Court will continue to find that there is an "acquittal" of death when the jury renders a verdict of life.

---

[108] *Sattazahn*, 537 U.S. at 110-12.

[109] *Id.* at 111-12.

Chapter 15

POSTCONVICTION PROCEEDINGS: THE WRIT OF HABEAS CORPUS

§ 15.01 OVERVIEW

What is a postconviction proceeding? Let's assume D was convicted and sentenced to death in a state court. Her case was affirmed on her automatic appeal to the state supreme court. She filed a petition for *certiorari* in the United States Supreme Court, but it was denied. At this point, D's *direct* avenues for appellate review for the conviction and sentence are over. D now has the option of pursuing a *collateral* attack on the conviction and sentence. The collateral attack is a *postconviction* proceeding. *Postconviction* proceedings are usually seeking a writ of *habeas corpus*, and the terms will be used interchangeably in this section. There are both state[1] and federal postconviction proceedings for state convictions. Federal convictions are only subject to federal habeas corpus.

Postconviction remedies figure prominently in capital cases. They provide additional avenues of judicial review for the defense, although on limited issues, of the conviction or sentence. In addition, postconviction proceedings are a forum for issues whose existence is not fully evident until after the trial is over. For example, there are cases where evidence about the ineffectiveness of trial counsel is not apparent until much later. Similarly, there may be evidence of the defendant's innocence that only comes to light long after the trial. Moreover, capital cases have been instrumental in developing the law of *habeas corpus*. Many of the rules and policies are reactions to capital cases, and the Supreme Court has interpreted many of the *habeas* statutory provisions in capital cases.

The area of federal *habeas* law is complex, and its intricacies are beyond the scope of this chapter. There are many statutory rules and judicial interpretations of federal *habeas* that are not addressed here; nor are we able to set out fully all of the steps in a *habeas* proceeding. The Antiterrorism and Effective Death Penalty Act

---

[1] State *habeas* proceedings vary and are beyond the scope of this chapter. However, state habeas proceedings, in addition to direct appeals, must have been "exhausted" by a state prisoner pursuing federal *habeas* relief. *See* Section 15.03[B], *infra*, on the exhaustion requirement for federal *habeas* claims.

A prisoner may also sometimes pursue a civil rights action under 42 U.S.C. 1983 rather than a *habeas* petition under 28 U.S.C. 2254 or 2255. The Supreme Court has held that *habeas* is the exclusive remedy for the prisoner who seeks "immediate or speedier" release from confinement but that the prisoner's claim may be brought under § 1983 when it would not "necessarily spell speedier release." Skinner v. Switzer, 131 S. Ct. 1289 (2011) (holding that death-sentenced inmate could pursue claim of unconstitutional denial by state of DNA testing of crime-scene evidence in § 1983 action). Further discussion of the right of an inmate to seek relief under § 1983 is also beyond the scope of this chapter.

(AEDPA) also includes separate rules for capital cases if a state has met the statute's "opt-in" standards.[2] These special rules are an effort to streamline *habeas* proceedings in capital cases to an even greater extent than in noncapital cases. To meet the opt-in requirements, a state must establish a system for appointing and compensating attorneys for indigent petitioners in state *habeas* proceedings. In addition, the state must set up standards for the competency of the attorneys appointed. Only one state has possibly qualified and no cases have been *decided* under the opt-in procedures.[3] Based in part on frustrations over delays in California cases and a desire to assist states in qualifying for the opt-in rules, recent legislation authorizes the U.S. Attorney General, rather than the federal courts, to qualify states as meeting the opt-in provisions.[4] However, while efforts to facilitate the application of the opt-in rules continue, the present state of *habeas* law is still governed almost exclusively by the general provisions. Therefore, the separate opt-in rules are not covered here. Instead, this chapter provides an overview of selected key procedural and substantive aspects of the general provisions that are helpful in understanding the role of federal *habeas corpus* in capital cases.

§ 15.02 THE NATURE OF A *HABEAS* PROCEEDING

Petitions for *habeas corpus* are civil proceedings.[5] The death-sentenced inmate is bringing a cause of action against the state (or federal government). The warden of the prison where he or she is held is named as the respondent. Thus, the inmate is the *petitioner* in the *habeas* proceeding and the warden is the *respondent*. *Habeas*

---

[2] Antiterrorism and Effective Death Penalty Act of 1996 (AEDPA), Pub. L. No. 104-132, 110 Stat. 1214 (1996). For the opt-in provisions, see 28 U.S.C.A. § 2263 et seq. The most striking feature of the opt-in system is the shorter time frame for filing a *habeas* petition in a capital case. There is a 180-day statute of limitations for an opt-in capital *habeas* case, in contrast to the 1-year limitation for non-opt-in capital cases. The federal district court must decide the case within 180 days of the date of the filing of the *habeas* application, with the possibility of only one 30-day extension for specified reasons. The federal court of appeals must decide the case within 120 days of the filing of the reply brief, with a second 120-day period if there is a rehearing *en banc*. The capital amendments also create specific rules for claims that were not raised in state court. Such a claim is only allowed if the failure to raise it was the result of unconstitutional state action, a new federal right recognized by the Supreme Court as retroactive, or the non-discovery of a factual predicate despite due diligence. For an overview of the special capital procedures, *see* Larry W. Yackle, *A Primer on the New Habeas Corpus Statute*, 44 BUFF. L. REV. 381, 393-97 (1996).

[3] *See* Spears v. Stewart, 283 F.3d 992 (9th Cir. 2002) (finding that Arizona has a capital punishment system that facially complies with the opt-in criteria, but not applying the standards in the case because Arizona failed to timely appoint counsel to represent petitioner in state *habeas* proceedings). *See also* John H. Blume, *AEDPA: The "Hype" And the "Bite,"* 91 CORNELL. L. REV. 259, 274-76 (2006) (discussing the failure of states to qualify for opt-in procedures).

[4] *See* USA PATRIOT Improvement and Reauthorization Act of 2005, Pub. L. No. 109-177, 120 Stat. 192 (2006) (codified at 28 U.S.C. 2265(c)). *See also* Carol S. Steiker & Jordan M. Steiker, *A Tale of Two Nations: Implementation of the Death Penalty in "Executing" Versus "Symbolic" States in the United States*, 84 TEX. L. REV. 1869, 1905 (2006) (noting that frustration focused especially on delays in California cases and that supporters of the measure hope that it will assist California in qualifying for the "opt-in" system).

[5] RANDY HERTZ & JAMES S. LIEBMAN, FEDERAL HABEAS CORPUS PRACTICE AND PROCEDURE § 2.2, at 9 (6th ed. 2011).

corpus means "you have the body,"[6] and the petitioner is asking that the warden produce and justify imprisoning the "body" of the petitioner.

Habeas corpus is called the "Great Writ," and has a long history in common law. The framers of the United States Constitution considered the writ so important that they included a provision that the writ of *habeas corpus* could not be suspended. This is referred to as the "suspension clause."[7] The constitutional provision does not prescribe, however, either content or procedure for the writ. In 1789, the Judiciary Act defined the procedures for federal prisoners.[8] It was not until 1867 that Congress passed an act that provided for a writ of *habeas corpus* for state prisoners. It is the 1867 act that provides the basis for today's federal *habeas corpus* statute.[9] However, in 1996, Congress passed significant amendments to the statutory scheme in the Anti-Terrorism and Effective Death Penalty Act (AEDPA).[10]

Habeas proceedings are a check on the criminal justice process. Originally, the *habeas* proceedings were a check on the federal system. Once the writ was expanded to state prisoners, it became a stopgap measure through which the federal courts could review state criminal procedures. Many criticisms were leveled at federal postconviction proceedings as an intrusion on the states. In reaction to this federalism concern, even prior to the 1996 amendments, the courts had imposed various restrictions on granting writs of *habeas corpus*.[11] In addition, some of the major changes reflected in the 1996 amendments are designed to give greater deference to state court decisions. Several provisions restrict the ability of the federal courts to revisit issues decided by the state courts, even on federal constitutional grounds.

Other criticisms of *habeas* proceedings focused on a need for finality.[12] Prior to the 1996 amendments, *habeas* petitioners, and in particular capital petitioners, were

---

[6] Kevin E. Teel, Comment, *Federal Habeas Corpus: Relevance of the Guilt Determination Process to Restriction of the Great Writ*, 37 S.W. L.J. 519, 522 (1983) ("[H]abeas corpus . . . literally means 'you have the body.' . . . In addition to requiring the person at whom the writ was directed to produce the body of the prisoner, it also required the person to state the cause of detention.").

[7] U.S. Const., art. I, § 9, cl. 2 provides: "The Privilege of the Writ of Habeas Corpus shall not be suspended, unless when in Cases of Rebellion or Invasion the public Safety may require it."

[8] Hertz & Liebman, *supra* note 5, § 2.4d, at 47-48.

[9] Act of February 5, 1867, c. 28, § 1 (1867); Fay v. Noia, 372 U.S. 391, 402 n.9 (1963) (describing the 1867 Act as extending *habeas* to prisoners in state custody). For an overview of the historical development of the *habeas* statutes, see Andrea A. Kochan, *The Antiterrorism and Effective Death Penalty Act of 1996: Habeas Corpus Reform?* 52 Wash. U. J. Urb. & Comtemp. L. 399, 400-02 (1997); Limin Zheng, *Actual Innocence as a Gateway Through the Statute-of-Limitations Bar on the Filing of Federal Habeas Corpus Petitions*, 90 Cal. L. Rev. 2101, 2108-11 (2002).

[10] Antiterrorism and Effective Death Penalty Act of 1996 (AEDPA), Pub. L. No. 104-132, 110 Stat. 1214 (1996).

[11] These limitations included doctrines on exhaustion of state remedies, non-retroactivity, procedural default, presumption of correctness for state factual findings, and abuse of the writ with successive petitions.

[12] As Justice Stevens stated in *Williams v. Taylor*, 529 U.S. 362, 386 (2000), "Congress wished to curb delays, to prevent 'retrials' on federal habeas, and to give effect to state convictions to the extent possible under law." In a portion of the majority opinion in the same case, written by Justice O'Connor, she too noted these concerns in stating "[t]hat acknowledgement [made by Justice Stevens regarding Congress's

criticized for abusing the writ by filing multiple, or *successive*, petitions. A concern for finality, especially in capital cases, led to changes reflected in the 1996 law that restrict the timing of petitions, limit the grounds on which *habeas* may be granted, and virtually foreclose successive petitions. These changes are discussed in Section 15.04[B], *infra*.

§ 15.03   THE *HABEAS* PROCESS

Suppose that D was tried, convicted, and sentenced to death in a state court in 1997, after the passage of AEDPA. The state trial judge refused to allow the defense to put on evidence of D's problems with mental illness, ruling that it was irrelevant in the penalty phase. The trial judge was incorrect on the law. As discussed in Section 12.02, *supra*, the Supreme Court has held that it is unconstitutional to preclude the introduction by the defense at the penalty phase of any evidence concerning the defendant's character, record or crime, and evidence of mental illness would meet that standard. Assume that defense counsel made an offer of proof, and the argument on the issue is in the record. On direct appeal, appellate counsel raised the error. The state supreme court incorrectly affirmed the trial court's ruling that the evidence of mental illness was irrelevant and also denied a state *habeas* petition on the claim. What must D do to proceed in federal *habeas* corpus?

[A]   Statute of Limitations and Basis of Claim

D must file a timely petition. For the first time in the history of the writ, the AEDPA amendments provide for a statute of limitations on the filing of a writ of *habeas corpus* in federal court.[13] Responding to complaints that too many petitioners waited many years or until the eve of execution to file, Congress passed a provision that a petitioner only has one year, which ordinarily runs from the conclusion of the direct appeal.[14] The time limit is tolled while a "properly filed"

---

wishes] is correct and significant to this case. It cannot be disputed that Congress viewed § 2254(d)(1) as an important means by which its goals for habeas reform would be achieved." Williams, 529 U.S. at 404.

[13] HERTZ & LIEBMAN, *supra* note 5, § 5.2, at 248-49 (stating that there was no statute of limitations prior to 1996); James S. Liebman, *An "Effective Death Penalty"? AEDPA and Error Detection in Capital Cases*, 67 BROOK. L. REV. 411, 416 (2001) (noting that "time bar was unprecedented in the history of habeas corpus").

[14] 28 U.S.C. § 2244(d)(1) provides:

A 1-year period of limitation shall apply to an application for a writ of habeas corpus by a person in custody pursuant to the judgment of a State court. The limitation period shall run from the latest of —
(A) the date on which the judgment became final by the conclusion of direct review or the expiration of the time for seeking such review;
(B) the date on which the impediment to filing an application created by State action in violation of the Constitution or laws of the United States is removed, if the applicant was prevented from filing by such State action;
(C) the date on which the constitutional right asserted was initially recognized by the Supreme Court, if the right has been newly recognized by the Supreme Court and made retroactively applicable to cases on collateral review; or
(D) the date on which the factual predicate of the claim or claims presented could have been discovered through the exercise of due diligence.

application for state postconviction review is pending.[15] Thus, it is possible for a federal *habeas* petition to be filed in compliance with the rules more than a year after the end of the direct appeal if a state *habeas* case is ongoing. However, absent extraordinary circumstances justifying equitable tolling, the courts will adhere to the AEDPA statute of limitations.[16] To be timely then, D must file the petition within a year of the latest of four possible triggering dates in the statute, usually the completion of *certiorari* proceedings on direct review.[17]

D's claim must be based on a violation of the Constitution, a federal law, or a treaty.[18] The vast majority of habeas claims are for constitutional error and, of those, the most common claim is Sixth Amendment ineffective assistance of counsel error.[19] In our case, D is claiming constitutional error for a violation of her Eighth Amendment right to present all relevant mitigating evidence.

---

[15] *See, e.g.*, Allen v. Siebert, 552 U.S. 3, 4-5 (2007) (holding that a state postconviction petition that is untimely under state law does not toll the time limit for filing a federal petition under § 2244(d)); Artuz v. Bennett, 531 U.S. 4, 8-9 (2000) (indicating when a state petition for *habeas corpus* is "properly filed" for purposes of tolling the statute of limitations); Carey v. Saffold, 536 U.S. 214, 217, 227(2002) (concluding that the word "pending" includes the time period between a lower state court's decision and filing a notice of appeal to a higher state court, and includes California's unusual system for state habeas that, instead of a notice of appeal, requires a filing of an original state habeas petition in the appellate court "within a reasonable time"; remanding case for determination whether 4½ months was a reasonable time such that state habeas was "pending").

[16] *See* Holland v. Fla., 130 S. Ct. 2549, 2562-65 (2010) (holding that *habeas* petitioner is entitled to equitable tolling if he can show: 1) that he has pursed his rights with reasonable diligence, and 2) that some extraordinary circumstance stood in his way and prevented timely filing). *See also* Day v. McDonough, 547 U.S. 198 (2006) (holding that a federal district court, although without power to override a State's deliberate waiver of a time-limitations defense, may, nonetheless, correct a State's evident miscalculation of the elapsed time and dismiss a petition as untimely under AEDPA's one-year limitation).

[17] *See supra* note 14; HERTZ & LIEBMAN, *supra* note 5, § 5.2[b], at 273.

[18] Both federal and state prisoners must allege that they are held "in custody in violation of the Constitution or laws or treaties of the United States." 28 U.S.C. §§ 2241, 2254-55. A federal prisoner must allege "that the sentence was imposed in violation of the Constitution or laws of the United States, or that the court was without jurisdiction to impose such sentence, or that the sentence was in excess of the maximum authorized by law, or is otherwise subject to collateral attack." 28 U.S.C. § 2255. A state prisoner must allege "that he is in custody in violation of the Constitution or laws or treaties of the United States." 28 U.S.C. § 2254. Other sources of error do not give rise to cognizable claims in *habeas* proceedings. *See, e.g.*, Wilson v. Corcoran, 131 S. Ct. 13 (2010) (reversing grant of habeas relief for purported failure of state courts to follow state law). Even some constitutionally based claims, such as the Fourth Amendment exclusionary rule for search and seizure error, are not cognizable claims except in limited circumstances. *See* Stone v. Powell, 428 U.S. 465, 494 (1976) (exclusionary rule for Fourth Amendment violations).

[19] Kathleen M. Ridolfi, *Not Just an Act of Mercy: The Demise of Postconviction Relief and a Rightful Claim to Clemency*, 24 N.Y.U. REV. L. & SOC. CHANGE 43, 72 (1998), *citing* National Center For State Courts-State Justice Institution, Habeas Corpus In State And Federal Courts 1, 46 (1994) (ineffective assistance of counsel most common claim).

[B] Exhaustion of State Remedies

Even if D's petition is within the statute of limitations, she may not proceed in federal *habeas* until she has exhausted all of her possible remedies on the claim in state court.[20] In addition to a direct appeal, state remedies are not exhausted unless available state *habeas* proceedings are completed through the highest state court with jurisdiction to hear the claims, including any discretionary state review.[21] Petitions can be sent back from federal court until the claims are resolved in state court first. The AEDPA amendments provide for a quicker end to the process. A federal court may dismiss a federal *habeas* claim on the merits without sending it back for exhaustion in state court.[22] In addition, the AEDPA amendments provide that a waiver of exhaustion requirements by the state may not be implied; it must be an affirmative waiver.[23] Thus, exhaustion is a stronger requirement under the revised statute. In our hypothetical, D has exhausted her state remedies by pursuing both a direct appeal and a state *habeas* claim in the state supreme court.

[C] Adequate and Independent State Grounds: Procedural Default of Constitutional Claims

Even though D has exhausted her state remedies in the direct appeal and state *habeas* actions, her claim may not be considered in a federal *habeas* proceeding if it is *procedurally defaulted.* In many cases, a petitioner has failed to raise the

---

[20] 28 U.S.C. § 2254(b)(1)(A)-(B) provides: "An application for a writ of habeas corpus on behalf of a person in custody pursuant to the judgment of a State court shall not be granted unless it appears that — (A) the applicant has exhausted the remedies available in the courts of the State; or (B)(i) there is an absence of available State corrective process; or (ii) circumstances exist that render such process ineffective to protect the rights of the applicant." *See also* Baldwin v. Reese, 541 U.S. 27 (2004) (holding that petitioner failed to exhaust federal claim of ineffective assistance of appellate counsel by failing to present it in his state habeas petition).

[21] O'Sullivan v. Boerckel, 526 U.S. 838, 842, 847 (1999) (stating that "[b]efore a federal court may grant habeas relief to a state prisoner, the prisoner must exhaust his remedies in state court" and announcing a rule "requiring state prisoners to file petitions for discretionary review when that review is part of the ordinary appellate review procedure in the State"). *See also* Kirk J. Henderson, *Thanks, But No Thanks: State Supreme Courts' Attempts To Remove Themselves from the Federal Habeas Exhaustion Requirement,* 51 CASE W. RES. L. REV. 201, 201-02 (2000) (discussing holding in *O'Sullivan* and possibility that it may not always be necessary to exhaust discretionary review).

[22] 28 U.S.C. § 2254(b)(2) provides: "An application for a writ of habeas corpus may be denied on the merits, notwithstanding the failure of the applicant to exhaust the remedies available in the courts of the State." *See also* Larry W. Yackle, *The American Bar Association and Federal Habeas Corpus,* 61 LAW & CONTEMP. PROBS. 171, 179 (1998). Professor Yackle noted that § 2254(b)(2) "permits a federal court to deny relief 'on the merits,' despite a prisoner's failure to exhaust state remedies. Courts have taken that provision to establish a discretionary authority to sacrifice the values ordinarily associated with exhaustion (comity and federalism) to the competing goals of speed and efficiency."

Regarding federal petitions that contain both exhausted and unexhausted claims, or "mixed" petitions, the Supreme Court held in *Rhines v. Weber,* 544 U.S. 269 (2005), that a federal district court under some conditions has discretion to hold the petition in abeyance to allow for exhaustion of unexhausted claims. Dismissal of a mixed petition would potentially prevent the offender from subsequently meeting the time limit for filing a federal petition and invoke the additional obstacles imposed on a successor federal petition.

[23] 28 U.S.C. § 2254(b)(3).

constitutional, treaty, or federal law claim in state court, and is now barred under a state procedural rule from pursuing the claim in state court. In this situation, the claim may be *procedurally defaulted*, and the petitioner barred from raising the claim in federal court, if the state court's procedural rule is viewed as an *adequate and independent* ground for rejecting the federal claim.[24]

For example, Angel Breard's claim of a treaty violation was procedurally defaulted because he did not raise the claim regarding consular notification until federal *habeas*.[25] Under the treaty, which is discussed *infra* in Section 23.04[D], any detained foreign national whose country is a party to the treaty has a right to be told that he or she may contact the country's consular office. At the time of Breard's case, the treaty was virtually unheard of in the defense community and, not surprisingly, Breard's attorneys in state court failed to recognize and raise the issue. By the time of the federal *habeas* action, Breard could no longer bring his claim in state court because of state rules. The federal courts, including the Supreme Court, viewed his claim as procedurally defaulted and, thus, not reviewable in habeas.[26]

The AEDPA amendments do not directly address procedural default in the sections applicable to all *habeas* actions.[27] The courts are continuing to apply the case law developed under the previous statutory scheme on procedural default.[28]

The effect of the procedural default rule is that petitioners ordinarily must raise issues at the trial level or on direct appeal to have those issues considered in a federal habeas case. There are exceptions to a procedural default preclusion in federal habeas, however, if the petitioner can show either 1) cause and prejudice for the default or 2) a fundamental miscarriage of justice.[29] Cause is often premised on

[24] *See* HERTZ & LIEBMAN, *supra* note 5, at § 26.1 (describing five points that must be established to show adequate and independent state procedural rule).

In *Cone v. Bell*, 129 S. Ct. 1769, 1781 (2009), the Court made clear that the question of adequacy of the state procedural bar to the assertion of the federal claim is itself a federal question. In *Cone*, the Court concluded that a state court's refusal to adjudicate a claim on the ground that the claim had been previously determined did not create a procedural default for purposes of federal *habeas* review. *See also* Wellons v. Hall, 130 S. Ct. 727, 730 (2010) (reiterating the *Cone* holding that a state court refusal to review the merits of a claim on the ground that it has already been addressed does not create a procedural default for purposes of federal *habeas*).

The Court held in *Beard v. Kindler*, 130 S. Ct. 612, 618 (2010), that a discretionary state procedural rule can serve as an adequate ground to bar federal *habeas* review. The Court reaffirmed this conclusion in *Walker v. Martin*, 131 S. Ct. 1120 (2011).

[25] *See* discussion of the *Breard* case and the Vienna Convention on Consular Relations in Section 23.04[D], *infra*.

[26] Breard v. Greene, 523 U.S. 371 (1998).

[27] The opt-in provisions for capital cases, *see supra* text at note 2, address procedural default and are more restrictive than the general development of the law outlined above. Under the opt-in provisions, the only claims that can be considered if they were not decided on the merits in state court are those that were precluded due to illegal action by the state, a new retroactive right recognized by the Supreme Court, or a factual basis that was not discoverable previously with due diligence. 28 U.S.C.A. § 2264.

[28] *See* discussion of procedural default in HERTZ & LIEBMAN, *supra* note 5, at § 26.1.

[29] *Id.*

ineffective assistance of counsel.[30] Cause can also be a new legal argument that was not discoverable at the time. Cause is not easily established under these standards. For example, in *Breard*, the defense argued that the failure to recognize and raise the consular notification treaty right was cause because it had never been raised in a criminal, rather than an immigration, matter at the time of Breard's case. The Fourth Circuit Court of Appeals, however, found that the attorneys' ignorance of the consular notification treaty right was insufficient to constitute cause because the treaty had been in existence since 1969 and was accessible through legal research.[31] Even if cause is established, prejudice must also be demonstrated.[32] The Court has indicated that there must be "actual prejudice" which affected the outcome of the case.[33]

The second exception to the procedural default rule requires a defendant to show that a fundamental miscarriage of justice will occur if the claim is not reviewed. This exception has come to be equated with the situation where petitioner claims innocence of the crime[34] or "innocence" of the death penalty.[35] "Innocence" of the death penalty means *ineligibility* for the death penalty, not an incorrect judgment in deciding to impose the death penalty.[36] Ineligibility would typically include any categorical bar to the death penalty, such as mental retardation, or failure to establish an aggravating circumstance.[37] The burden on the petitioner is lower if the claim is actual innocence of the crime as opposed to death ineligibility. In *Schlup v. Delo*,[38] where the defendant claimed he was innocent of the crime, the Court found that the standard was a *preponderance* — that "it is more likely than not that no reasonable juror would have convicted him in light of the new evidence."[39] The Court recently reaffirmed this standard in

---

[30] *See also* Banks v. Dretke, 540 U.S. 668, 698 (2004) ("cause" found to justify reaching merits of claim that prosecution suppressed exculpatory evidence despite finding of procedural default for failure to fully develop claim in state habeas).

[31] Breard v. Pruett, 134 F.3d 615, 620 (4th Cir. 1998).

[32] *See, e.g., Banks*, 540 U.S. at 703 (finding prejudice sufficient to justify reversal on procedurally defaulted claim that prosecution suppressed exculpatory evidence).

[33] *See* HERTZ & LIEBMAN, *supra* note 5, at § 26.3c (discussing unclear status of what "prejudice" means in this context). *See* discussion of standard for harmless error in Section 15.04[C], *infra*.

[34] *See* Schlup v. Delo, 513 U.S. 298 (1995) (Schlup claimed both that he was innocent of the crime and that other constitutional violations occurred at trial). *See also* HERTZ & LIEBMAN, *supra* note 5, at § 26.4 (discussing Court's failure to give a definitive statement of the meaning of the term, but indicating miscarriage of justice includes actual innocence).

[35] Sawyer v. Whitley, 505 U.S. 333 (1992).

[36] In *Sawyer v. Whitley*, Chief Justice Rehnquist noted that, while the phrase is not a natural usage of the words, it is helpful in characterizing those circumstances in which a capital defendant is not eligible for a sentence of death. 505 U.S. at 341 (citing importance of honing in on those objective factors or conditions that must be shown to exist before a defendant is eligible to have the death penalty imposed). *Id.* at 346-47.

[37] *See* discussion of categorical bars to death-eligibility in Sections 8.01-8.05, *supra*.

[38] 513 U.S. 298 (1995).

[39] For a criticism of the *Schlup* test as too demanding of defendants and inconsistent with the public concern for substantive justice, *see* Todd E. Pettys, *Killing Roger Coleman: Habeas, Finality, and the Innocence Gap*, 48 WM. & MARY L. REV. 2313, 2362-63 (2007).

House v. Bell,[40] in which it concluded that consideration of the inmate's claims was warranted despite procedural default, since "this is the rare case where — had the jury heard all the conflicting testimony — it is more likely than not that no reasonable juror viewing the record as a whole would lack reasonable doubt."[41] In contrast, the Court has imposed a *clear and convincing* burden on the petitioner if the claim was innocence of the death penalty.[42]

In our hypothetical, D is not procedurally defaulted, as she raised her claim at trial, on direct appeal and in state *habeas*. If she had not raised it in the state courts, she would be facing a procedural default bar to the claim, if she were now precluded from seeking a state remedy.[43]

[D]   Evidentiary Hearings

Assuming D's claim is not procedurally defaulted, the next question is whether she will obtain an evidentiary hearing on her claim. Unlike a typical criminal or civil proceeding, evidentiary hearings are not automatic in *habeas* proceedings. *Habeas* petitions are often submitted on the basis of the pleadings and attachments, and federal courts decide the merits on the basis of the record. Nevertheless, D will usually prefer to have an evidentiary hearing if possible. D must evaluate whether she is entitled to a mandatory hearing,[44] whether the hearing is discretionary, or whether she is precluded from having a hearing.[45] The answer will be based on a complex set of standards, largely governed by case law. The AEDPA amendments only address when the court is prohibited from holding an evidentiary hearing.[46]

---

[40]   547 U.S. 518 (2006).

[41]   *Id.*, at 2087. For further discussion of *House*, see Section 17.02[B][2], *infra*.

[42]   Sawyer v. Whitley, 505 U.S. 333, 336 (1992). In *Sawyer*, the Court stated: "We . . . hold that to show 'actual innocence' one must show by clear and convincing evidence that, but for a constitutional error, no reasonable juror would have found the petitioner eligible for the death penalty under the applicable state law."

[43]   The procedural default bar would also apply if previously applied by a state court. The bar would apply, for example, if D had not raised the claim at trial, and the state appellate court had subsequently ruled the claim barred on procedural grounds when D raised it on direct appeal. Likewise, the bar would apply if D had raised the claim at trial but had not raised it on direct appeal in state court, and the state courts had subsequently ruled the claim procedurally barred for that reason in state postconviction proceedings.

[44]   Generally, an evidentiary hearing is mandatory if a petitioner has been precluded in some manner that is not the petitioner's fault from receiving a "full and fair" hearing in the state court and an evidentiary hearing could enable the petitioner to prove the petition's factual assertions, which, if established, would entitle the petitioner to relief. *See generally* HERTZ & LIEBMAN, *supra* note 5, at § 20.3.

[45]   The AEDPA amendments expanded upon the pre-AEDPA case law restrictions on evidentiary hearings. The AEDPA provision is discussed in this section.

[46]   Before the passage of AEDPA, district courts conducted evidentiary hearings in only 1.17% of all federal habeas cases. *See Report to the Federal Courts Study Committee of the Subcommittee on the Role of the Federal Courts and their Relation to the States* (Mar. 12, 1990) (Richard A. Posner, Chair), in 1 FEDERAL COURTS STUDY COMMITTEE, WORKING PAPERS AND SUBCOMMITTEE REPORTS 468-515 (July 1, 1990). Justice Stevens has asserted that "[t]his figure makes it abundantly clear that doing justice does not always cause the heavens to fall." Schriro v. Landrigan, 127 S. Ct. 1933, 1954-55 (2007) (Stevens, J., dissenting).

A petitioner will be precluded from having an evidentiary hearing by specific language in AEDPA if she "has failed to develop the factual basis" in state court.[47] In *M. Williams v. Taylor*,[48] the Supreme Court interpreted "failed" to mean a "lack of diligence, or some greater fault, attributable to the prisoner or the prisoner's counsel."[49] Thus, a petitioner who could not have discovered the factual basis for the claim prior to federal *habeas* proceedings is not barred from an evidentiary hearing for having failed to develop the factual record in state court.

In *M. Williams*, for example, the Court held that the petitioner had not "failed" to develop claims of juror bias and prosecutorial misconduct regarding relationships between the juror and both a key prosecution witness as well as a prosecutor. According to the Court, there was no lack of diligence on petitioner's part in uncovering the misrepresentations of the juror and prosecutor.[50] On the other hand, the Court found that petitioner had failed to exercise diligence in discovering a psychiatric report about a prosecution witness that would have aided the defense.[51]

If there has been a lack of diligence, and thus a failure to develop the factual basis of the claim, the petitioner must satisfy one of two conditions to avoid the statutory bar to an evidentiary hearing.[52] The first situation is if there is a retroactive decision from the Supreme Court on "a new rule of constitutional law."[53] The second requires facts that could not have been discovered through "due diligence"[54] and that would establish by clear and convincing evidence that, but for a constitutional error, a reasonable factfinder would not have found the petitioner guilty of the "underlying offense."[55]

Even when the specific statutory bar does not apply, however, the federal district court often will not hold an evidentirary hearing. In *Cullen v. Pinholster*,[56] the Supreme Court recently held that, for claims that have been adjudicated on the merits in state court, federal *habeas* review "is limited to the record that was

---

[47] 28 U.S.C.A. § 2254(e)(2).

[48] 529 U.S. 420 (2000).

[49] *Id.* at 432.

[50] *Id.* at 440-43.

[51] *Id.* at 437-40.

[52] These provisions impose a greater restriction on gaining a hearing than existed under prior case law. *See* HERTZ & LIEBMAN, *supra* note 5, § 20.2b (discussing AEDPA's effect of superseding the cause and prejudice and miscarriage exceptions on procedural default under prior law). *See also* Yackle, *supra* note 2, at 388-90 (describing the AEDPA amendment as replacing the cause and prejudice and miscarriage exceptions with a more stringent standard).

[53] 28 U.S.C.A. § 2254(e)(2)(A)(ii) describes "a new rule of constitutional law, made retroactive to cases on collateral review by the Supreme Court, that was previously unavailable."

[54] *Id.*

[55] 28 U.S.C.A § 2254(e)(2)(B). Note that the standard of factual innocence comes up in three places. Here, it is part of the standard for excusing the failure to develop a factual record and still merit an evidentiary hearing. Factual innocence is also a basis for establishing an exception to procedural default. *See* Section 15.03[C], *supra*. Factual innocence is also part of the standard to allow a successive petition. *See* Section 15.05, *infra*.

[56] 131 S. Ct. 1388 (2011).

before the state court that adjudicated the claim on the merits."[57] Thus, the Court reversed a grant of relief by the District Court, which was affirmed by the Court of Appeals, on an ineffective assistance claim that was based in part on additional evidence developed at a federal hearing after the state courts had rejected the claim based on the evidence developed in state court.

Despite the rule articulated in *Pinholster,* federal evidentiary hearings on *habeas* claims will remain necessary in some circumstances. For example, the state court may have rejected a claim on an inadequate state ground rather than on the merits, or may have erroneously rejected a claim based on an unreasonable interpretation of federal law after assuming that petitioner's facts were true or may otherwise have denied the petitioner a full and fair hearing on a claim.[58] In such cases, the federal judge will need to consider whether a hearing might enable the petitioner to establish his "factual allegations, which, if true, would entitle the applicant to . . . relief."[59]

In our case, D established a factual record through raising the constitutional right to present relevant mitigating evidence of mental illness at trial and on appeal. Thus, she would not fall into the category of petitioners who are barred by the specific language of AEDPA from an evidentiary hearing.[60] Because the state trial court heard the argument on the issue, it is also unlikely that an evidentiary hearing would be mandatory. D probably falls into the category in which the federal district court has discretion whether to grant a hearing. Thus, she may be proceeding solely on the basis of written submissions or she may have an evidentiary hearing at the discretion of the judge.[61] Although the Supreme Court stated in *Pinholster* that federal *habeas* review, where the state court has ruled on the merits, "is limited to the record that was before the state court,"[62] a federal district judge might want to hear D's excluded mitigating evidence before deciding her petition.

---

[57] *Id.* at 1398. In reaching this decision, the Court pointed to the language in AEDPA. Under 28 U.S.C. 2254(d)(2), a federal court may not grant a state prisoner's habeas petition based on a claim resolved on the merits in state court unless the decision "was based on an unreasonable determination of the facts in light of the evidence presented in the State court proceeding." For more on the *Pinholster decision, see* Justin Marceau, *Challenging the Habeas Process Rather Than the Result,* 69 Wash. & Lee L. Rev. ___ (2012) (Part I.B.2.).

[58] *Id.* at 1412 (Breyer, J., concurring in part and dissenting in part).

[59] Schriro v. Landrigan, 550 U.S. 465, 474 (2007).

[60] If she had failed to develop a factual record, D would have had to argue that the failure was not due to a lack of diligence or that the failure should be excused because it represents a "new rule" or was not discoverable through due diligence and would show that she was not guilty of the offense. In our hypothetical, D would have had a hard time meeting this standard. The constitutional right to present mitigating evidence is not new; nor is it a standard that was not discoverable through due diligence. Finally, it may be difficult to establish that the evidence would show D is innocent of the crime.

[61] *See* Schriro v. Landrigan, 550 U.S. 465, 474 (2007).

[62] 131 S. Ct. at 1398.

§ 15.04 GROUNDS FOR GRANTING A WRIT OF *HABEAS CORPUS*

If D has surmounted the procedural hurdles of the statute of limitations, exhaustion of state remedies, and procedural default, she is now at the point of convincing the court that she is entitled to prevail on her petition. Whether or not she has had an evidentiary hearing, the court must evaluate three factors: 1) the retroactivity of the constitutional rule that she is claiming, 2) whether her claim satisfies the statutorily-defined grounds for relief, and 3) a harmless error analysis.

[A] Non-retroactivity

D is claiming a violation of the Eighth Amendment based on Supreme Court cases from the 1970s and 1980s. An issue that frequently arises in *habeas* litigation is whether decisions of the Supreme Court are retroactive to the pending *habeas* case. The *habeas* court must do a *"Teague"* analysis of the non-retroactivity of the constitutional rule at issue.[63]

In *Teague v. Lane*,[64] decided prior to AEDPA, the Court held that "new constitutional rules" are not generally applicable in postconviction proceedings.[65] *Habeas* proceedings are to be based on the law in existence at the time the petitioner's conviction became "final."[66] In *Horn v. Banks*,[67] the Supreme Court addressed this issue in a post-AEDPA case involving an error of juror unanimity on mitigation. Banks argued that the jury instructions impermissibly implied, under *Mills v. Maryland*,[68] that the jurors had to be unanimous on mitigating circumstances in order to consider them.[69] Although the Third Circuit Court of Appeals found grounds to grant the *habeas* petition, the Supreme Court reversed. Without analyzing whether relief was warranted, the Supreme Court remanded for a determination of the retroactivity of the *Mills* decision in *habeas* proceedings.[70]

---

[63] *See generally* Lyn S. Entzeroth, *Reflections On Fifteen Years Of The* Teague v. Lane *Retroactivity Paradigm: A Study Of The Persistence, The Pervasiveness, And The Perversity Of The Court's Doctrine*, 35 NEW MEX. L. REV. 161 (2005).

[64] 489 U.S. 288 (1989).

[65] *Teague*, 489 U.S. at 310 (stating that "we now adopt Justice Harlan's view of retroactivity for cases on collateral review. Unless they fall within an exception to the general rule, new constitutional rules of criminal procedure will not be applicable to those cases which have become final before the new rules are announced").

[66] *Id.* at 306. A conviction becomes final when the Supreme Court "affirms a conviction on the merits on direct review or denies a petition for a writ of certiorari, or when the time for filing a certiorari petition expires." Clay v. United States, 537 U.S. 522, 527 (2003) (applying this rule "long-recognized, clear meaning" to federal prisoner filing habeas petition under 28 U.S.C § 2255).

[67] 536 U.S. 266 (2002).

[68] 486 U.S. 367 (1988). *See* discussion of *Mills* in Section 12.03[B][1][c], *supra*.

[69] *Horn v. Banks*, 536 U.S. at 269.

[70] *Id.* at 2151. The Court stated that "in addition to performing any analysis required by AEDPA, a federal court considering a habeas petition must conduct a threshold *Teague* analysis when the issue is properly raised by the state."

After remand, the Court of Appeals again granted Banks' habeas petition, but the Supreme Court again reversed. *See* Beard v. Banks, 542 U.S. 406 (2004). The Supreme Court concluded that the *Mills*

Although the AEDPA amendments do not incorporate the precise language of the *Teague* rule in the statutory language for relief, the Supreme Court has indicated that the AEDPA language that based relief on a finding of a contrary or unreasonable application of *clearly established Federal law* is comparable to the *Teague* non-retroactivity rule.[71] The one statutory change is an additional restriction that the clearly established law must be promulgated by the Supreme Court.[72] *Horn v. Banks* reaffirmed that the non-retroactivity analysis is a necessary and separate part of the basis for relief. Since the Court is continuing to use the *Teague* non-retroactivity analysis, this also means that the two exceptions to non-retroactivity are still applicable.[73] Although, in general, "new rules" are not retroactive, they will be given retroactive effect if they fall within the exception of 1) a type of conduct that cannot be constitutionally punished or a "substantive categorical guarantee" against punishment or 2) a "watershed" rule that concerns the "fundamental fairness and accuracy" of the trial.[74]

In our hypothetical, D is in luck. The Court's decisions on a constitutional right to present relevant mitigating evidence were decided before her conviction became final. The Eighth Amendment requirement that prohibits a Court from restricting the admission of relevant mitigating evidence is not a "new rule;" it was established federal law. Thus, she is not prohibited by the non-retroactivity doctrine from continuing to press her petition.

[B]   Contrary To or Unreasonable Applications of the Law or Unreasonable Determinations of Facts

D is now ready to argue her claim that the Eighth Amendment was violated by the preclusion of her evidence on mental illness. It is not enough, however, to establish a violation of the Constitution. The 1996 AEDPA amendments provide

---

holding was announced after Banks' conviction and sentence became final and that the Court of Appeals erred in concluding that *Mills* applied retroactively to Banks. *See id.* at 410. Given this conclusion, the Supreme Court did not reach the question whether the Court of Appeals also erred in concluding that relief was permissible under AEDPA. *See id.* at 410 n.2.

[71] T. Williams v. Taylor, 529 U.S. 362, 412 (2000). The Court stated that "[w]ith one caveat, whatever would qualify as an old rule under our *Teague* jurisprudence will constitute 'clearly established Federal law, as determined by the Supreme Court of the United States' under § 2254(d)(1). The one caveat, as the statutory language makes clear, is that § 2254(d)(1) restricts the source of clearly established law to this Court's jurisprudence." *See also* Greene v. Fisher, 504 U.S. ___, 181 L.Ed.2d 336 (2011) (confirming that the *Teague* retroactivity rules are distinct from the relitigation bar imposed by AEDPA).

[72] *See id.*

[73] *See Horn*, 536 U.S. at 272 n.5. Moreover, *Teague* is inapplicable to "the meaning of a criminal statute enacted by Congress"; it is applicable to "procedural" rules. *See* Bousley v. United States, 523 U.S. 614, 620 (1998).

[74] *Teague*, 489 U.S. at 311. *See also* Beard v. Banks, 542 U.S. 406, 410 (2004) (concluding that the holding in *Mills* did not fall within the exceptions).

After the Court ruled in *Ring v. Arizona*, 536 U.S. 584 (2002), that a jury, rather than a judge, must find an aggravating circumstance necessary to make a defendant death-eligible, uncertainty existed about whether the holding fell within one or the other of the *Teague* exceptions. The Court later ruled that the *Ring* holding was not retroactive to cases that were final when *Ring* was decided. *See* Schriro v. Summerlin, 542 U.S. 348 (2004).

that no relief may be granted from a state decision[75] unless the decision is:

(1) . . . contrary to, or involved an unreasonable application of clearly established Federal law, as determined by the Supreme Court of the United States; or

(2) . . . was based on an unreasonable determination of the facts in light of the evidence presented in the State court proceeding.[76]

Since 1996, several significant Supreme Court opinions have interpreted the standards for relief. The first part of the statutory standard, defining what is "contrary to" or an "unreasonable application" of established federal law has gained the most attention. Recent cases also have addressed the "unreasonable determination of fact" prong of the statute. Both subparts of the statute are discussed below.

It is important to note that, in the first subpart, the Court has separated the concepts of "contrary to" and "unreasonable application." A decision is contrary to clearly established law if it either applies an incorrect rule or it reaches a result that is different based on facts that are "materially indistinguishable" from facts in a Supreme Court case based on the same law. An unreasonable application of established law arises if the court uses correct law, but applies it in an "objectively unreasonable" manner. A decision contrary to established law is thus wrong on the legal principle. A decision that is an unreasonable application of established law, on the other hand, is correct on the legal principle, but unreasonably wrong on the application.

[1] Contrary To or an Unreasonable Application of Clearly Established Federal Law

Can D establish that her claim of error in precluding evidence of mental illness is contrary to or an unreasonable application of clearly established federal law? What is *contrary to* clearly established federal law? As discussed in Sections 12.01-12.02, a defendant is constitutionally entitled to present all relevant mitigating evidence. Thus, the appellate court's decision to affirm the trial court's position would be *contrary to* clearly established federal law, as determined by the Supreme Court.

What is an *unreasonable application* of clearly established federal law? Suppose that the trial judge recognizes that the Supreme Court held that mental illness is relevant mitigation. The trial judge does not allow it in D's case, however, because he believes that D's mental illness from 10 years ago is too remote. This is arguably *contrary to* clearly established federal law, which is based on a constitutional right

---

[75] The standard for federal convictions provides that "[i]f the court finds that the judgment was rendered without jurisdiction, or that the sentence imposed was not authorized by law or otherwise open to collateral attack, or that there has been such a denial or infringement of the constitutional rights of the prisoner as to render the judgment vulnerable to collateral attack, the court shall vacate and set the judgment aside and shall discharge the prisoner or resentence him or grant a new trial or correct the sentence as may appear appropriate." 28 U.S.C. § 2255.

[76] 28 U.S.C. § 2254(d)(1)-(2).

to present *any* relevant mitigating evidence, which often includes even childhood abuses and problems. It is also arguably an *unreasonable application* of the Supreme Court's decisions. Although the Supreme Court's decisions did not directly reach a holding on remoteness of mental illness, and the trial court's ruling is not literally inconsistent with holdings of the Court, the underlying principle in the Court's decisions was to allow a defendant to present all relevant mitigating evidence. Because a history of mental illness could have a causal or explanatory effect on later conduct or blameworthiness, and thus would be relevant, the application of the law in this case would probably be *objectively unreasonable*.

T. Williams v. Taylor[77] provides a good example where the Court addressed both the *contrary to* and the *unreasonable application* prongs as grounds for *habeas* relief.[78] Williams had alleged that the lower court misapplied the prejudice standard for ineffective assistance of counsel under the Sixth Amendment. The Supreme Court first held that the Virginia court used the wrong legal principle when it required an overarching fundamental unfairness rather than using the established standard for assessing the prejudice prong that analyzes whether there was a reasonable probability that the sentence would have been different.[79] Thus, the decision was *contrary to* clearly established federal law based on decisions from the Supreme Court. The Court further found that, even if the Virginia court had used the correct legal standard for part of its analysis, the decision was an *unreasonable application* of clearly established law by adding on an additional fundamental fairness requirement.[80]

The *unreasonable application* prong involves two steps. First, although using the correct legal principle, the decision must reflect an incorrect application. Second, the incorrect application must also be *unreasonable*. The Court clarified this standard in *Price v. Vincent*.[81] In *Vincent*, the Court suggested that, even if the lower court had incorrectly applied the Court's double jeopardy cases to the facts, the application was not *objectively* unreasonable because other lower courts had reached a similar conclusion.[82] If there is any possibility that fair-minded jurists

---

[77] 529 U.S. 362 (2000).

[78] *See also* Mitchell v. Esparza, 540 U.S. 12 (2003) (application of harmless error standard to failure to charge essential fact in indictment was correct and application of that standard was not unreasonable); Bell v. Cone, 535 U.S. 685 (2002) (correct law applied for ineffective assistance of counsel, and no unreasonable application of the standard); Ramdass v. Angelone, 530 U.S. 156 (2000) (correct law applied denying LWOP instruction because, at time of trial, defendant not parole ineligible, and no unreasonable application of Supreme Court precedent as instruction only required if no possibility of).

[79] *Id.* at 393-97.

[80] *Id.* at 397-98. The Court also noted that the Virginia court was "unreasonable" in not analyzing all of the mitigation when conducting a reweighing of aggravation and mitigation on appeal. *Id.*

The Supreme Court recently clarified that "clearly established Federal law" does not "include decisions of the Supreme Court that are announced after the last adjudication of the merits in state court but before the defendant's conviction becomes final." Greene v. Fisher, 504 U.S. ___, 181 L. Ed. 2d 336 (2011).

[81] 538 U.S. 634 (2003).

[82] In *Vincent*, the defense counsel moved for a verdict of acquittal. In response, the trial court made a statement that "what we have at the very best is Second Degree Murder. . . . " *Id.* at 637. However, the trial court agreed to hear the prosecutor on first-degree murder the next day. In the end, the trial

could have supported the state ruling, the Court will not find the particular application to be *objectively* unreasonable.[83] In contrast, it is likely that the Court would find that the exclusion of evidence of mental illness in the hypothetical case is *objectively unreasonable*, because the reasoning of the mitigation cases clearly mandate the admission of relevant mitigating evidence.[84]

---

court allowed first-degree murder to go to the jury. The defense claimed that the trial court had granted their motion and jeopardy had terminated as to the first-degree murder charge. *Id.* The Supreme Court viewed the issue about whether the trial court's statement had sufficient "finality" to trigger double jeopardy protection as debatable, but thought the state court's reasoning logical and not *objectively unreasonable. Id.* at 887.

The Supreme Court also has explained that the law upon which a petitioner relies must not only have been *established* at the time of the state-court decision but *clearly* so. *See, e.g.,* Abdul-Kabir v. Quarterman, 550 U.S. 233, 253 n.14 (2007) (finding that a rule requiring special instructions in certain Texas cases to enable the sentencing jury to give mitigating effect to proffered evidence had been "clearly established" before petitioner's conviction and sentence became final and justified habeas relief in petitioner's case). The level of generality at which existing law is deemed to have been clear will affect the perceived reasonableness of the state court decision. *See, e.g.,* Lockyer v. Andrade, 538 U.S. 63, 74 (2003) (affirming state-court rejection of Eighth Amendment disproportionality challenge to sentence of two consecutive 25-year terms for petty thefts under three-strikes law because then existing Supreme Court precedent was clear only at a very general level); Yarborough v. Alvarado, 541 U.S. 652, 665 (2004) (affirming state-court rejection of claim that petitioner was in custody for *Miranda* purposes because "[t]he custody test is general" so that the state-court application of it was not unreasonable). For more on the requirement that the law be "clearly established," *see* Melissa M. Berry, *Seeking Clarity in the Federal Habeas Fog: Determining What Constitutes "Clearly Established" Law Under The Anti-Terrorism and Effective Death Penalty Act,* 54 CATH. L. REV. 747, 755-88 (2005).

[83] Recently, in *Harrington v. Richter*, 131 S. Ct. 770 (2011), the Court emphasized that "only extreme malfunctions in the state criminal justice systems" justify relief under § 2254(d)(1). *Id.* at 786. Federal relief is precluded unless "there is no possibility fair-minded jurists could disagree." *Id.* On this basis, the Court overturned the decision of the Court of Appeals, which had "conducted a de novo review, and after finding a Strickland violation, [had] declared, without further explanation, that the 'state court's decision to the contrary constituted an unreasonable application of Strickland.' " *Id. See also* Brown v. Payton, 544 U.S. 133, 147 (2005) (holding that California Supreme Court had not applied prior Supreme Court precedent in an "objectively unreasonable" manner when it rejected petitioner's claim that evidence of post-crime religious conversion and good behavior had been precluded from mitigating consideration).

In *Richter*, the Court also clarified what significance a state-court summary denial without statement of reasons should have under § 2254(d). The Court concluded that there is no requirement in the statute that "a state court . . . give reasons before its decision can be deemed" entitled to deference. 131 S. Ct. at 785. Thus, even if the state-court denial does not clarify that it is on the merits, federal courts are to presume that it was, absent contrary indications, and to defer to it, unless there is no possibility fair minded jurists could have reached such a decision on the merits. *See id.* at 784-85. For more on *Richter*, see Marceau, *supra* note 58, at Part I.B.1.

[84] For two recent cases in which the Supreme Court found that the Texas courts had unreasonably applied prior mitigation cases by upholding the trial court's refusal to give special instructions, see Abdul-Kabir v. Quarterman, 550 U.S. 233 (2007), and Brewer v. Quarterman, 550 U.S. 286 (2007).

In *Panetti v. Quarterman*, 551 U.S. 930 (2007), the Supreme Court also indicated that "[w]hen a state court's adjudication of a claim is dependent on an antecedent unreasonable application of federal law, the requirement set forth in § 2254(d)(1) is satisfied" and that "[a] federal court must then resolve the claim without the deference AEDPA otherwise requires." In *Panetti*, the Supreme Court concluded that the Texas courts had unreasonably applied the procedural requirements of *Ford v. Wainwright*, 477 U.S. 399 (1986), regarding adjudication of a claim of incompetency to be executed, and, thus, that there was no basis for deference to the state court's finding of competency.

[2] Unreasonable Application and Unreasonable Determination of Facts

A federal court may sometimes apply both subparts of Section 2254. In *Wiggins v. Smith*,[85] for example, the Supreme Court first held that the state court had *unreasonably applied* the first prong of the Sixth Amendment analysis of ineffective assistance of counsel, which assesses the reasonableness of the defense counsel's conduct.[86] The details of the *Wiggins* case are addressed in more detail in Section 16.04[B], *infra*. The defense counsel had failed to conduct an adequate investigation to support a decision not to present mitigating evidence. In addition, the Court found, under Section 2254(d)(2), that the state court had incorrectly found that social services records, which defense counsel had reviewed, described defendant's abusive background. The abusive background was not in the records, and thus defense counsel was not aware of the background from those records. It was an *unreasonable determination of the facts* to find that the abusive background was in the records.[87]

[C] Harmless Error

D is now at a point where the federal court has found that the appellate decision to affirm the trial court's ruling to exclude evidence of mental illness is either *contrary to* or an *unreasonable application* of clearly established law. The court has also found that the critical Supreme Court decisions were not new law. Thus, the decisions may be applied to D's case. Does this mean that the court will grant D's *habeas* petition? Not yet. The court must also determine if the error is subject to *harmless error* analysis and if so, whether or not the error was harmless.

Even if the federal court finds that the petitioner has established that a state court decision is erroneous under the contrary to, unreasonable application, or unreasonable determination standards discussed above, reversal is usually conditioned on a finding that the error is not harmless. Although there are some egregious errors, such as a complete denial of counsel or a biased judge, that are reversible per se,[88] most errors are subject to a harmless error analysis. If the error is deemed harmless, there is no reversal on that basis. The standard for harmless constitutional error in habeas proceedings is lower than the standard for

---

[85] 539 U.S. 510 (2003).

[86] *Id.* at 528-29. In *Rompilla v. Beard*, 545 U.S. 374 (2005), the Supreme Court also held that a state court was objectively unreasonable in concluding that defense counsel's investigation was reasonable. *See id.* at 389.

[87] *See id.* at 532. The state court had found that defense counsel had adequately investigated defendant's background and viewed counsel's decision as a strategic choice not to present mitigating evidence. That conclusion was, in part, based on the state court's incorrect finding that defense counsel was aware of defendant's abusive background from the social services records.

For a Supreme Court case holding that state courts engaged in unreasonable determinations of facts relating to defense claims of racial discrimination in the use of peremptory challenges, *see Miller-El v. Dretke*, 545 U.S. 231, 266 (2005).

[88] *See* Arizona v. Fulminante, 499 U.S. 279 (1991) (describing errors that are reversible per se as "structural" error that affects the framework of the trial). *See also* discussion of harmless error in Section 14.04, *supra*.

harmless constitutional error on direct appeal. In a direct appeal, a constitutional error is harmless only if the court can find that the error is harmless beyond a reasonable doubt, which means that the court finds beyond a reasonable doubt that the error did not contribute to the verdict.[89] As a result of a 1993 Supreme Court decision, a constitutional error in a *habeas* proceeding is harmless unless the error "had substantial and injurious effect or influence in determining the jury's verdict."[90]

As with much of *habeas* law, the justification for a lower standard for the state to demonstrate harmless error in a *habeas* proceeding rests on a determination to show deference to state court rulings. This deference stems from a recognition by the Supreme Court of the "State's interest in the finality of convictions that have survived direct review within the state court system" and that "Federal intrusions into state criminal trials frustrate both the States' sovereign power to punish offenders and their good-faith attempts to honor constitutional rights."[91] However, commentators have been critical of the second-class status of constitutional error in *habeas* proceedings as a result of the lesser standard in *habeas*.[92]

Whether the error in D's case is subject to harmless-error analysis and, if so, is harmless will be the final battleground between D and the state. The error in preclusion of mitigating evidence is subject to harmless-error analysis, as the admission and exclusion of evidence is not viewed as a structural error.[93] The final determination of whether there is harmless error will depend on many of the other facts in the case. D will certainly argue that precluding her from presenting evidence of her history of mental illness had a "substantial and injurious . . . influence on the jury's verdict." She will argue that the jury, if weighing aggravating and mitigating evidence, could have been swayed by the additional mitigation to impose life instead of death. The state is likely to counter that there was significant aggravating evidence, and the additional mitigating evidence of mental illness years earlier would not have had a substantial and injurious effect on the jury's decision to reach a death verdict. Whether the federal court would find this error harmless would depend on the federal court's assessment of the effect of excluding the evidence on the decision process of the jurors.

---

[89] *See* Section 14.04, *supra*.

[90] Brecht v. Abrahamson, 507 U.S. 619 (1993) *citing* Kotteakos v. United States, 328 U.S. 750, 776 (1946) (holding that "the standard for determining whether habeas relief must be granted is whether the . . . error 'had substantial and injurious effect or influence in determining the jury's verdict.' ").

[91] *Id.* at 635.

[92] *See, e.g.*, James A. Carey, Jr., *Habeas Corpus — Harmless-Error Rule — Proper Harmless-Error Standard on Habeas Review of Fifth Amendment Violations Is Whether the Error Had "Substantial or Injurious Effect" on the Jury's Determination of Petitioner's Guilt — Brecht v. Abrahamson, 113 S. Ct. 1710 (1993)*, 24 SETON HALL L. REV. 1636, 1670 (1994) (stating that "the Court's decision to distinguish direct and collateral review by establishing an easily satisfied harmless-error standard is a significant step in the evisceration of habeas corpus . . . ").

[93] *See, e.g.*, Smith v. Singletary, 61 F.3d 815 (11th Cir. 1995), *cert. denied*, 516 U.S. 1140 (1996) (case was remanded from Supreme Court for application of *Brecht* harmless error standard; on remand, Eleventh Circuit found error in precluding mitigating evidence was not harmless).

§ 15.05 SUCCESSIVE PETITIONS

If D's petition was not her first federal habeas petition, would she still be able to obtain federal *habeas* relief? An area of great controversy, successive petitions by capital defendants triggered one of the most restrictive AEDPA amendments. Fueled by a hostility to multiple *habeas* petitions by capital defendants, AEDPA restricts the filing of a second or successive petition. There must be a claim that was not presented in a prior petition that either is based on a "new rule of constitutional law" from the Supreme Court that is made retroactive by the Court to collateral review[94] or that involves a factual predicate that was not discoverable through "due diligence," where the facts would establish by clear and convincing evidence that "no reasonable factfinder would have found the applicant guilty of the underlying offense."[95] Thus, a successive petition is permissible if it either raises 1) a new rule or 2) an unknown factual predicate and an innocence claim.

There are also open issues about precisely what constitutes a successive petition that will affect capital and noncapital cases.[96] For example, in *Stewart v. Martinez-Villareal*,[97] the Court held that a *Ford*[98] claim that the petitioner was incompetent to be executed, which had been raised in the first petition and dismissed as unripe, did not constitute a successive petition when later reasserted. More recently, in *Panetti v. Quarterman*,[99] the Court held that a *Ford* claim did not constitute a successive petition although the claim had not been raised in Panetti's first federal petition. The Court concluded that interpreting the petition as successive would only encourage defendants to include unripe and often factually unsupported *Ford* claims in their first federal petition. The Court also recently concluded that a federal *habeas* petition challenging the constitutionality of a resentencing proceeding that produced a new sentencing judgment is not successive to a previous federal *habeas* petition that challenged the underlying conviction and original sentence.[100]

---

[94] 28 U.S.C.A § 2244(b)(2)(A); *Tyler v. Cain*, 533 U.S. 656, 663 (2001). In *Tyler*, the Court stated: "The new rule becomes retroactive not by the decisions of the lower court or by the combined action of the Supreme Court and the lower courts, but simply by the actions of the Supreme Court. . . . We thus conclude that a new rule is not 'made retroactive to cases on collateral review' unless the Supreme Court holds it to be retroactive."

[95] 28 U.S.C.A § 2244(b)(2)(B). *See* discussion of new successive petition provision in Bryan A. Stevenson, *The Politics of Fear and Death: Successive Problems in Capital Federal Habeas Corpus Cases*, 77 N.Y.U. L Rev. 699, 737-40 (2002) (describing split among lower courts about whether the "innocence" provision includes death-ineligibility; suggesting that prior case law including "innocence of death" should still prevail).

[96] *See e.g.*, Calderon v. Thompson, 523 U.S. 538 (1998) (Motion to recall a mandate would be a second petition, but in this case, Ninth Circuit acted *sua sponte* so not considered a second petition); Abdur'rahman v. Bell, 537 U.S. 88 (2003) (Court dismissed *certiorari* as *improvidently granted*, but issue raised involved status of a motion under F.R.C.P. 60(b) for relief of judgment; Justice Stevens, dissenting from dismissal, would not find Rule 60(b) motion is a successive petition). *See also* Stevenson, *supra* note 95, at 791-92 (contending that Rule 60(b) motion should not be treated as a successive petition).

[97] 523 U.S. 637 (1998).

[98] *Ford v. Wainwright*, 477 U.S. 399 (1986). *See* discussion in Section 19.01[A][2], *infra.*

[99] 551 U.S. 930 (2007).

[100] *See* Magwood v. Patterson, 130 S. Ct. 2788 (2010).

In our hypothetical, it is unlikely that D could bring a successive petition. Her claim that mitigating evidence was unconstitutionally excluded is not a new rule, nor is it a claim that was not discoverable by due diligence. There is even a question as to whether or not she could satisfy the "innocence" requirement. Thus, D will only be able to seek federal habeas corpus relief on this claim if it is contained in her first habeas petition.

Chapter 16

INEFFECTIVE ASSISTANCE OF COUNSEL

§ 16.01   OVERVIEW

[A]   The Role of Defense Counsel in Capital Cases

Because a capital trial is two separate trials with a guilt phase and a penalty phase, the law that governs each phase is different. So too is the investigation and preparation necessary for each.[1] The differences between a guilt phase and a penalty phase are so fundamental that a lawyer who is quite skilled and able to try a complex civil or criminal case may be unable to adequately prepare and effectively present a penalty trial.[2] The defendant is no longer presumed innocent, and there is no comparable presumption of life. The jury was *death qualified* during *voir dire*, which means that each juror told the judge that he or she could impose a sentence of death on the defendant.[3] One scholar argues that an added difficulty for counsel is the fact that jurors come to their task with a bias that those who commit violent crimes do so because they have "no personal history, no human relationships, and no social context, there was no explanation for what they did except their own personal evil."[4] One experienced capital litigator described defense counsel's job at the penalty phase as an effort to tell the life story of the defendant, explain the significance of that life to the jury, and convince the jury that this person should not be sentenced to death.[5] The life story of the defendant is told through mitigating evidence. Ultimately, the mitigating evidence introduced by the defense is evaluated by the jurors along with aggravating evidence introduced by the prosecutor.

---

[1] As one scholar described: "The guilt trial establishes the elements of the capital crime. The penalty trial is a trial for life. It is a trial *for* life in the sense that the defendant's life is at stake, and it is a trial *about* life, because a central issue is the meaning and value of the defendant's life." Gary Goodpaster, *The Trial for Life: Effective Assistance of Counsel in Death Penalty Cases*, 58 N.Y.U. L. Rev. 299, 303 (1983). For an excellent account of the task of representing a capital defendant, *see* Welsh S. White, Litigating in the Shadow of Death: Defense Attorneys in Capital Cases, University of Michigan Press (2005).

[2] Goodpaster argues that "counsel . . . who presents a seemingly skilled, but unsuccessful, defense at the guilt phase may have tried and lost the issue of his client's worthiness to live before the penalty trial has even begun." Goodpaster, *supra* note 1, at 304.

[3] *See* Chapter 7, *supra*.

[4] Craig Haney, *The Social Context of Capital Murder: Social Histories and the Logic of Mitigation*, 35 Santa Clara L. Rev. 547, 550 (1995) (systematically analyzing information about crime and criminals that was disseminated by television crime drama, newspaper reporting, film and works of fiction).

[5] Stephen B. Bright, Presenting the Theme For Life Throughout A Capital Case (on file with author).

Given this task, the investigation necessary to prepare for a penalty phase is very different from the investigation for the guilt phase.[6] In the guilt phase, defense counsel focuses primarily on the prosecutor's evidence and witnesses, examining historical facts, forensic evidence, and eyewitness accounts. In contrast, the evidence that must be gathered and presented by defense counsel in the penalty phase is a social and medical history of the defendant, including "educational history, employment and training history, family and social history, prior adult and juvenile correction experience, and religious and cultural influences."[7] This work is similar to that traditionally performed by a social historian or social worker, not a lawyer. Experienced capital lawyers and scholars have long argued that the penalty phase investigation "require[s] perceptions, attitudes, preparation, training, and skills that ordinary criminal defense attorneys may lack."[8]

[B] Ineffective Assistance of Counsel in a Capital Case

The Supreme Court established a two prong test to evaluate the performance of counsel. First, a defendant must show that his lawyer was *deficient* in his performance. Second, a defendant must show that he was *prejudiced* because of the lawyer's failings.[9] In a guilt phase, the court usually looks to whether a defendant is in fact guilty to determine whether he was prejudiced by counsel's failings. Prejudice in the context of a penalty phase requires a showing that the outcome of the sentencing phase would have been different.

The decision process in a penalty phase differs from that in a guilt phase. There are no clear criteria that define exactly which defendant should be selected for death. It is an individualized determination made by all of the jurors, based not only on the circumstances of the crime but also on the background of the offender. It is often impossible to predict what evidence will move a juror from death to life. During deliberations, each individual juror is entitled to decide what evidence is mitigating and what weight to give it.[10] A defendant who has committed even the most egregious crime may, in the view of some jurors, be entitled to a life sentence.[11] In some states, if even one juror votes for life, a life sentence will be

---

[6] "A substantial mitigating case may be impossible to construct without this kind of life-history investigation, which is a very different inquiry from an investigation of facts relating to an offense." GOODPASTER, *supra* note 1, at 321.

[7] Wiggins v. Smith, 539 U.S. 510, 524 (2003) (citing, with approval, the American Bar Association, *Guidelines for the Appointment and Performance of Defense Counsel in Death Penalty Cases* (rev. ed. 2003), *reprinted in* 31 HOFSTRA L. REV. 913 (2003), *available at* http://www.americanbar.org/content/dam/aba/migrated/2011_build/death_penalty_representation/2003guidelines.authcheckdam.pdf (last accessed 01/12/2011) [hereinafter *ABA Guidelines*]).

[8] Goodpaster, *supra* note 1, at 303-04.

[9] Strickland v. Washington, 466 U.S. 668, 677 (1984).

[10] *See* Chapter 12, *supra*.

[11] *See, e.g.*, Alex Kotlowitz, *In the Face of Death*, N.Y. TIMES MAGAZINE, July 6, 2003, at 50 (discussing how twelve jurors, each of whom was convinced that some people, given the cruelty of their acts, deserve to die, chose to spare the life of Jeremy Gross).

imposed.[12] In other states, counsel must convince all twelve jurors to vote for life before a life sentence is imposed.[13]

[C] Raising a Claim of Ineffective Assistance of Counsel

A claim of ineffective assistance of counsel may be raised in several ways. A defendant can file a motion for a new trial, direct appeal, or a petition for a petition for a writ of habeas corpus in state or federal court. The most common stage is a petition for a writ of habeas corpus.[14] Because claims of ineffective assistance of counsel are fact specific, a defendant will typically support his claim with detailed information and evidence as to the acts and omissions of trial counsel that provide the basis for the ineffectiveness claim. With a petition for habeas corpus, a defendant may request an evidentiary hearing to present evidence to support his or her claims. When a defendant alleges ineffective assistance of counsel, trial counsel will usually testify at the evidentiary hearing as a witness for the prosecution. He or she will testify as to efforts made in the case to prepare the case for trial.

§ 16.02 RIGHT TO COUNSEL

[A] Introduction

It is now accepted that every defendant charged with a felony or facing actual incarceration on a misdemeanor has a Sixth Amendment right to counsel. This right includes a right to have counsel appointed if a defendant cannot afford one and the right to have an effective lawyer.[15] It is important to examine the journey the courts have taken in defining a defendant's right to counsel, especially in capital cases. Many scholars argue that even today, enforcement of any substantive standards for competent counsel, even in a capital case, remains more elusive than real.[16]

---

[12] *See, e.g.*, MD. CODE ANN. CRIM. LAW § 2-303(j)(2) (2002) ("If, within a reasonable time, the jury is unable to agree as to whether a death sentence shall be imposed, the court may not impose a death sentence."). The Federal court system requires that a jury "by unanimous vote" return a sentence of death. 18 U.S.C. § 3593(e) (2002). *See also* Section 24.03[B], *infra*.

[13] *See* Cal. Penal Code § 190.4(b), "If the trier of fact is a jury and has been unable to reach a unanimous verdict as to what the penalty shall be, the court shall dismiss the jury and shall order a new jury impaneled to try the issue as to what the penalty shall be. If such new jury is unable to reach a unanimous verdict as to what the penalty shall be, the court in its discretion shall either order a new jury or impose a punishment of confinement in state prison for a term of life without the possibility of parole."

[14] *See* Chapter 15, *supra*.

[15] "In all criminal prosecutions, the accused shall . . . have the Assistance of Counsel for his defense." U.S. CONST. Amend. VI.

[16] *See, e.g.*, Stephen B. Bright, *Counsel for the Poor: The Death Sentence Not for the Worst Crime but for the Worst Lawyer*, 103 YALE L. J. 1835 (1994); Ellen Kreitzberg, *Death Without Justice*, 35 SANTA CLARA L. REV. 485 (1995). For standards for appointment of counsel in capital cases, see American Bar Association, *Guidelines for the Appointment and Performance of Defense Counsel in Death Penalty Cases* (October 12, 2003), *available at* http://www.americanbar.org/content/dam/aba/migrated/2011_build/death_penalty_representation/2003guidelines.authcheckdam.pdf (last accessed 01/12/2011).

[B] The Scottsboro Case: A Failure to Provide Effective Representation

The right to counsel evolved slowly, in cases that span almost half a century. It began with the 1932 landmark case of *Powell v. Alabama.*[17] *Powell* was the Supreme Court's first significant statement about a defendant's right to counsel. This case underscored the need for pretrial preparation by a lawyer on issues relating to both guilt and punishment.

In *Powell,* two women from Tennessee claimed they were raped by nine black youths, ranging in age from 13 -20, on a train from Tennessee to Alabama. The youths were arrested and indicted for this rape only five days later. The government announced that it was seeking the death penalty.

The day the young men were brought to the courthouse, the judge announced he was appointing "all the members of the bar" to defend the youths. This included seven lawyers, three of whom were later retained to assist the prosecution.[18] The trial began one week later. When the case was called, there was great confusion over who would be counsel for the youths. No one had taken responsibility for the case or taken any steps to prepare it. Finally, two lawyers were appointed to represent all nine defendants. The first was described as a lawyer whose modest legal talents were further limited by his inability to remain sober.[19] The second lawyer was 69 years old, and described as a "doddering, extremely unreliable, senile individual who was losing whatever ability he once had."[20] No investigation, no preparation and almost no consultation with their clients took place prior to the trial.

The scene in and around the courthouse was described as resembling a fort under siege. Several thousand people arrived early, and the National Guard was called to maintain order. Four machine guns guarded the doors of the courthouse. The first trial against two of the young men began in the afternoon. A sentence of death was returned by the following afternoon. By Thursday evening, after four days, eight of the young men had been convicted and sentenced to death in three separate trials.

The Supreme Court reversed the convictions and sentences by a vote of 7-2. Justice George Sutherland wrote for the Court:

> The right to be heard would be, in many cases, of little avail if it did not comprehend the right to be heard by counsel. Even the intelligent and educated layman has small and sometimes no skill in the science of law . . .
> He lacks both the skill and knowledge adequately to prepare his defense, even though he have a perfect one. He requires the guiding hand of counsel

---

[17] 287 U.S. 45 (1932) (often referred to as the "Scottsboro Boys" case). For an excellent report on this case, *see* DAN T. CARTER, SCOTTSBORO: A TRAGEDY OF THE AMERICAN SOUTH (Louisiana State University Press 1979). Many of the details about the Scottsboro case in this chapter are taken from Carter's account.

[18] *Powell,* 287 U.S. at 56.

[19] CARTER, note 17, at 19, 22, *supra.*

[20] *Id.* at 18.

at every step in the proceedings against him. Without it, though he be not guilty, he faces the danger of conviction because he does not know how to establish his innocence.[21]

Since all of the defendants in the case had, at least technically, been appointed counsel, *Powell v. Alabama* was not just a case about the right to counsel; it was about the right to *effective* counsel. The Supreme Court was struck by the fact that the lawyers did not meet with their clients until the day of trial, foreclosing any possibility of pretrial preparation. Justice Sutherland emphasized the problem of denying counsel *prior* to trial, stating:

> [D]uring perhaps the most critical period of the proceedings against these defendants, that is to say, from the time of their arraignment until the beginning of their trial, when consultation, thorough-going investigation and preparation were vitally important, the defendants did not have the aid of counsel in any real sense, although they were as much entitled to such aid during that period as at the trial itself.[22]

Although the Court's opinion underscored the importance of pretrial investigation and preparation as a basis for evaluating the effective performance of counsel, no specific standards were set by the Court to judge a lawyer's performance. Since the lawyers in *Powell* did nothing prior to trial, the bar to determine whether counsel was effective began at a very low level.

[C] *Gideon*: Recognition of a Fundamental Need for Counsel in Criminal Cases

Although *Powell* was limited to providing a right to counsel in capital cases, the Supreme Court appeared committed to providing counsel to criminal defendants. The right to counsel began to expand and trickle down from federal capital cases, to all federal cases,[23] to state cases where unique or special circumstances were identified as requiring counsel,[24] and finally, in the landmark case of *Gideon v. Wainwright*,[25] in all state felony cases.

In *Gideon*, the Supreme Court recognized that a lawyer was indispensable to the fairness of a criminal trial. In a unanimous opinion, the Court in *Gideon* held that the Sixth Amendment right to counsel is a fundamental right and therefore applies to the states. Justice Black wrote:

---

[21] *Powell*, 287 U.S. at 68-69.

[22] *Id.* at 57. Despite the Supreme Court reversal, the case continued for more than eighteen years before the last Scottsboro defendant was released from prison in 1950.

[23] *See* John E. Spomer, III, *Scared to Death: The Separate Right to Counsel at Capital Sentencing*, 26 Hastings Const. L.Q. 505, 513 (1999) ("[Powell v. Alabama's] narrow holding guaranteed capital defendants the right to counsel in federal cases under the Sixth Amendment, empowered by those 'fundamental principles of liberty and justice' which constitute due process." (citation omitted)).

[24] Betts v. Brady, 316 U.S. 455 (1942) (holding that the right to counsel applies to state cases where the court identifies special or unique circumstances warranting a lawyer).

[25] 372 U.S. 335 (1963).

[R]eason and reflection require us to recognize that in our adversary system of criminal justice, any person hauled into court, who is too poor to hire a lawyer, cannot be assured a fair trial unless counsel is provided for him. This seems to us to be an obvious truth . . . The right of one charged with crime to counsel may not be deemed fundamental and essential to fair trials in some countries, but it is in ours.[26]

The Supreme Court in *Gideon* looked back 30 years to the words of Justice Sutherland in *Powell* and stated, "[i]n returning to these old precedents, sounder we believe than the new, we but restore constitutional principles established to achieve a fair system of justice."[27]

§ 16.03   STRICKLAND: DEVELOPMENT OF A TEST FOR INEFFECTIVE ASSISTANCE OF COUNSEL

[A]   Introduction

The Supreme Court in *Powell* found that under some circumstances, a lawyer can be so ineffective that it is tantamount to having no lawyer at all. In *Gideon*, the Court focused on the presence of counsel to insure that the proceedings were constitutional and fair. But still no specific test had been devised to evaluate counsel's performance in a criminal case. By 1970, federal courts applied a vague standard of whether a proceeding was a "farce or a mockery of justice" to decide whether counsel was ineffective.[28] While expressing concern in its opinions that poor defendants not be left to the mercies of incompetent counsel, the Supreme Court still failed to provide clear standards on how to evaluate a lawyer's performance during trial.[29]

The years that followed saw the lower state and federal courts continue to struggle to define an appropriate test. The Supreme Court finally stepped in to clarify the standards in 1984.

---

[26] *Id.* at 344. When Gideon's petition to the Supreme Court was filed, 23 attorneys general filed an amicus brief supporting Gideon's request.

[27] *Id.*

[28] *See, e.g.,* Trapnell v. United States, 725 F.2d 149, 151 (2d Cir. 1983); Bottiglio v. United States, 431 F.2d 930, 931 (1st Cir. 1970) (per curiam); Williams v. Beto, 354 F.2d 698, 704 (5th Cir. 1965); Frand v. United States, 301 F.2d 102, 103 (10th Cir. 1962); O'Malley v. United States, 285 F.2d 733, 734 (6th Cir. 1961); *In re* Ernst, 294 F.2d 556, 558 (3d Cir. 1961), *cert. denied,* 368 U.S. 917 (1961); Cofield v. United States, 263 F.2d 686, 689 (9th Cir. 1959), *vacated on other grounds,* 360 U.S. 472 (1959) (per curiam); Snead v. Smyth, 273 F.2d 838, 842 (4th Cir. 1959); Johnston v. Unites States, 254 F.2d 239, 240 (8th Cir. 1958); United States *ex rel* Feeley v. Ragen, 166 F.2d 976, 980-81 (7th Cir. 1948); Diggs v. Welch, 148 F.2d 667, 670 (D.C. Cir. 1945), *cert. denied,* 325 U.S. 889 (1945). For a complete list of cites, *see* Jeffrey L. Kirchmeier, *Drink, Drugs, and Drowsiness: The Constitutional Right to Effective Assistance of Counsel and the Strickland Prejudice Requirement,* 75 Neb. L. Rev. 425 (1996).

[29] *See, e.g.,* McMann v. Richardson, 397 U.S. 759 (1970) (holding that a lawyer's advice to a client to plead guilty was reasonably professional and not ineffective).

[B]   The Case: *Strickland v. Washington*

In *Strickland v. Washington*,[30] the Supreme Court established a more specific test to measure whether the performance of counsel was constitutionally adequate. Washington was charged with three brutal murders over the course of a 10 day crime spree. Once arrested, he confessed and, contrary to the advice of counsel, decided to plead guilty. During the plea, Washington accepted full responsibility for his crimes, and was complemented on that fact by the judge.[31] Washington waived his right to a jury sentencing, and let the judge decide his sentence. The judge sentenced Washington to death.

Washington claimed on appeal that his lawyer was ineffective in the investigation, preparation and presentation of the penalty phase of his trial. The lawyer's preparation was minimal. He did not introduce any evidence. He spoke with Washington's wife and mother on the phone, but never met with them or prepared them to testify. He conducted no additional investigation to uncover, prepare, or present mitigating evidence. He prepared no social history, and conducted no psychological assessment of Washington.

Washington's lawyer testified that he experienced a sense of hopelessness about the case after Washington confessed to all three murders. He indicated it was his *strategy* at the sentencing hearing to persuade the judge to spare Washington's life based upon Washington's sincerity and frankness in his pleas of guilty.[32] The Supreme Court held that Washington's lawyer was not ineffective. In upholding Washington's sentence of death, the Court created a two-pronged test that a defendant must satisfy to prevail on a claim of ineffective assistance of counsel.

[C]   The Two-Prong Test

First, a defendant must show that counsel's performance was *deficient*. Deficient means the attorney was not functioning effectively as counsel. In applying this test, courts were instructed to presume that the performance of counsel was constitutionally adequate with "a heavy measure of deference to counsel's judgments."[33]

Second, a defendant must establish *prejudice*. Even if counsel's performance was deficient, a defendant must show that counsel's failures were so serious that the sentence of death was not reliable.

When the Court in *Strickland* created a test for ineffective assistance of counsel, it did not distinguish between a penalty phase of a capital trial and any other ordinary trial. The same test and the same standards were to apply in all cases. This approach has been criticized by courts and scholars.[34] Justice Marshall

---

[30] 466 U.S. 668 (1984).

[31] Washington v. Strickland, 693 F.2d 1243, 1247 (5th Cir. 1982) (en banc), *rev'd on other grounds*, 466 U.S. 668 (1984).

[32] *Id.* at 1249.

[33] *Strickland*, 466 U.S. at 690-91.

[34] *See, e.g.*, Jeffrey Levinson, *Don't Let Sleeping Lawyers Lie: Raising the Standard for Effective*

argued that, in failing to hold lawyers in capital cases to a *higher* standard, the Court was abdicating its responsibility to apply greater constitutional safeguards in a capital case. Marshall reiterated his belief that "death is . . . different" and, as such, requires a greater need for reliability.[35] Even before Strickland was decided, one scholar argued:

> A higher level of particularized judicial scrutiny is constitutionally mandated in [the penalty phase of capital cases]. Specific standards of attorney competence, tailored to the requirements of the penalty phase of capital trials, are proposed. If capital case defense attorneys are held to these standards, capital defendants will be less likely to receive death sentences because counsel did not know how to try a capital case. Ineffective assistance might no longer be a significant cause of arbitrariness in the imposition of death sentences.[36]

Another scholar argued that the low standard from *Strickland* allowed indigent defendants to be tried and sentenced to death not for committing the "worse crime," but for having the "worst lawyer."[37] Nevertheless, the Court's stated goal was to insure that the overall process was fair, not to necessarily improve the quality of legal representation within the criminal system. The Court believed that by establishing the standard in *Strickland*, it would remove much of the arbitrariness in the imposition of sentences of death.

[D] Applying the Two Prong Test

The Court applied the two-prong test to Washington's case and found his lawyer was not ineffective. Applying the first prong, the Court found his lawyer was not deficient in his performance. Although the Court acknowledged there was a duty by counsel to investigate a case, the Court held that Washington's lawyer had a reasonable and sound strategy that justified his decision not to investigate. Washington's lawyer testified that his strategy was two-fold: 1) to argue that Washington was suffering from extreme emotional distress, and 2) to show that Washington had taken full responsibility for his crimes. Because Washington had made his emotional troubles known to the court at the plea colloquy, his lawyer testified that he decided not to introduce additional evidence, in order to limit the rebuttal by the government. The Court concluded that although unsuccessful, this was a reasonable, professional decision.[38]

Although a finding that a lawyer was not deficient should end the inquiry, the Court next examined the second prong to determine whether Washington suffered

---

Assistance of Counsel, 38 Am. Crim. L. Rev. 147 (2001); Amy R. Murphy, *The Constitutional Failure of the Strickland Standard in Capital Cases Under the Eight Amendment*, 63-SUM Law & Contemp. Probs. 179 (2000).

[35] *Strickland*, 466 U.S. at 715 (Marshall, J., dissenting) (quoting Woodson v. North Carolina, 428 U.S. 280 (1976)). *See* Kirchmeier, note 28 *supra*, at 438 n.74, for a scholarly criticism of the Strickland standard.

[36] Goodpaster, *supra* note 1, at 305.

[37] Bright, *supra* note 16, at 1835.

[38] *Strickland*, 466 U.S. at 699.

any prejudice. The Court found even less merit in this claim. The Court reviewed the affidavits from numerous witnesses who detailed Washington's life, and who indicated they would have testified on Washington's behalf had they been asked. The Supreme Court concluded that none of this evidence, standing alone or taken together, would have affected the sentencing judge's decision to impose death. All of the evidence "would barely have altered the sentencing profile presented to the sentencing judge."[39] The Court concluded that no amount of mitigating evidence would have outweighed the horrible nature of the crimes.

It is unclear why the Supreme Court allowed such minimal preparation by trial counsel to be constitutionally sufficient. The capital punishment system was recently resurrected in 1976 and professional norms for the preparation and presentation of a penalty trial were just beginning to develop.[40] The Court also seemed interested in bringing finality to these cases. Whatever the reason, the Court's decision in *Strickland* set a low bar for acceptable performance by trial counsel in capital cases.

§ 16.04 INEFFECTIVE ASSISTANCE OF COUNSEL: THE FIRST PRONG: DEFICIENT PERFORMANCE

[A] Overview

The first prong of the test in *Strickland* presented criminal defendants with several difficult hurdles. First, the Court placed the burden of persuasion on a defendant to prove, by a preponderance of the evidence, that counsel's performance was deficient.[41] To meet this standard, a defendant has to point to specific and identifiable acts or omissions by counsel at the guilt or penalty phase of the trial as being outside the wide range of professional conduct.[42] Second, the Court imposed a strong presumption in favor of a trial lawyer's competence. This included an assumption that counsel made all significant decisions within the limits of reasonable professional judgment until a defendant proved otherwise. Third, the Court showed great deference to trial counsel once the lawyer described his acts, omissions, or decisions as *strategic*. A tactical or a strategic decision was virtually unchallengeable.[43]

---

[39] *Id.* at 700.

[40] The *Strickland* Court warned, "[t]he availability of intrusive post-trial inquiry into attorney performance . . . would encourage the proliferation of ineffectiveness challenges. Criminal trials resolved unfavorably to the defendant would increasingly come to be followed by a second trial, this one of counsel's unsuccessful defense . . . Intensive scrutiny of counsel and rigid requirements for acceptable assistance could dampen the ardor and impair the independence of defense counsel, discourage the acceptance of assigned cases . . . ." *Id.* at 690.

[41] *Id.* at 687.

[42] *See, e.g.*, Chandler v. United States, 218 F.3d 1305, 1334 (11th Cir. 2000). The court found that trial counsel did not act out of the range of professional standards where he had no more than 40 days to prepare for the penalty phase. *Id.* at 1340.

[43] Writing for the Court in Wood v. Allen, 558 U.S. ___, 130 S. Ct. 841 (2010), Justice Sotomayor agreed the Court should afford "great deference" to the strategic decisions of counsel in investigating their clients' claims, but held "counsel's unconsidered decision to fail to discharge that duty cannot be

There are two separate but related questions that arise repeatedly when examining the performance of counsel in a penalty phase of a capital case that were not directly addressed in Strickland. First, when is a lawyer's duty to investigate the penalty phase satisfied? Second, when is a lawyer's failure to present any mitigating evidence at the penalty phase ineffective assistance of counsel?

[B] Duty to Investigate and Present Penalty Phase Evidence

A lawyer has a duty to investigate a case for trial. In a capital trial, this includes not only information and evidence relating to guilt or innocence, but also information relating to a penalty phase of the trial.[44] In the context of a penalty phase, this responsibility includes seeking out and discovering relevant mitigating evidence, including evidence relating to the life and background of a defendant. Although the Court acknowledged this responsibility in Strickland, they qualified counsel's obligation by allowing a lawyer to make a reasonable strategic decision that investigation is not necessary.[45] In Strickland, trial counsel testified he made a strategic decision not to present any evidence at the penalty phase and the Supreme Court, by a vote of 7-2, accepted this decision as a reasonable trial strategy.

In the years following Strickland, lower courts around the country were frequently faced with ineffective assistance of counsel claims where lawyers conducted minimal or no investigation for penalty phase evidence. Not surprisingly, in these cases, counsel also presented no mitigating evidence at the penalty phase of the trial. Some courts found that a failure to conduct any investigation was constitutionally deficient.[46] Others, however, were willing to find even minimal

---

strategic. The only conceivable strategy that might support forgoing counsel's ethical obligations under these circumstances would be a reasoned conclusion that further investigation is futile and thus a waste of valuable time." In Wiggins v. Smith, 539 U.S. 510 (2003), Justice O'Connor, writing for the Court, affirmed the principle that " 'strategic choices made after less than complete investigation are reasonable precisely to the extent that reasonable professional judgments support the limitations on investigation.' " Id. at 521 (quoting Strickland, 466 U.S. at 690-91) Lower Courts had frequently found that a lawyer's failure to present mitigating evidence was a reasonable trial strategy and not deficient. In Riley v. Cockrell, 215 F. Supp. 2d 765 (E.D. Tex. 2002), the defense counsel decided *not* to argue that his client was mentally retarded and did not introduce a report that placed the defendant's IQ at 67). In Hunt v. Lee, 291 F.3d 284, 289 (4th Cir. 2002), the lawyers decided simply to argue for mercy and did not introduce any mitigating evidence, which included evidence that the defendant's father and mother were physically abusive to the defendant, and that the father had the children fight each other for his amusement.

[44] ABA STANDARDS FOR CRIMINAL JUSTICE § 4-4.1 (3d ed. 1993) (stating that an attorney has a duty to investigate "the circumstances of the case and explore all avenues leading to facts relevant to the merits of the case and the penalty in the event of conviction."). *See also* GOODPASTER, *supra* note 1, at 320 (arguing that a capital defender must start thinking about and planning for the penalty phase the moment he accepts a capital case); Bruce A. Green, *Lethal Fiction: The Meaning of "Counsel" in the Sixth Amendment*, 78 IOWA L. REV. 433, 497 (1993) (arguing the capital defenders' responsibility for a penalty phase starts with an investigation prior to trial into the life of the client in order to uncover information to be presented in mitigation).

[45] *Strickland*, 466 U.S. at 691 ("counsel has a duty to make a reasonable investigation or to make a reasonable decision that makes particular investigations unnecessary.").

[46] *See, e.g.*, Brownlee v. Haley, 306 F.3d 1043, 1045 (11th Cir. 2002) (counsel was found to be ineffective due to their failure to investigate, obtain, or present any evidence of mitigation); Karis v. Calderon, 283

investigation by a lawyer constitutional.[47] Three years after *Strickland*, the Supreme Court demonstrated even greater deference to defense counsel's judgment and professed strategy in the case of *Burger v. Kemp*.[48]

Counsel for Burger was generally aware of some, although not all, of the family history. He had spoken to Burger's mother with an out-of-state lawyer who had been a "big brother" to his client, and to a psychiatrist who had conducted a pre-trial examination. Counsel knew that Burger was 17 years old at the time of the offense, had an IQ of 82, and was functioning at the level of a 12-year-old. Burger also showed evidence of brain damage that may have been caused by beatings from his father. Burger's mother was 14 years old when he was born and remarried several times. One stepfather beat Burger's mother, and another introduced Burger to marijuana. In spite of this turmoil, at the time of his capital trial Burger had only a minor shoplifting charge. The jury who sentenced Burger to death did so without being told anything about his childhood or psychological problems.

Trial counsel for Burger testified that he made a strategic decision not to present this evidence because he believed it would contribute little to the chances of a life verdict.[49] The Supreme Court agreed. *Burger* reaffirmed that the standard for acceptable conduct by defense counsel was driven, in large part, by the lawyer's own testimony that decisions were strategic or tactical ones.

For twelve years following *Strickland*, lower courts continued to evaluate the performance of counsel against these standards and, not surprisingly, more often

---

F.3d 1117, 1133 (9th Cir. 2002) (counsel was ineffective where counsel failed to adequately investigate the defendant's troubled childhood, the abuse he suffered, and the abuse of his mother); Silva v. Woodford, 279 F.3d 825 (9th Cir. 2002) (counsel completely abandoned the investigation and failed to present the substantial and compelling mitigation available including evidence of childhood, mental illnesses, organic brain disorders and substance abuse); Caro v. Woodford, 280 F.3d 1247, 1254 (9th Cir. 2002) (ineffective assistance of counsel where counsel failed to investigate and introduce evidence that defendant suffered brain damage as a result exposure to neurotoxins and head trauma); Ainsworth v. Woodford, 268 F.3d 868 (9th Cir. 2001) (counsel was ineffective by failing to investigate defendant's background, present mitigating evidence, give an opening statement, or question aggravating witnesses); Skaggs v. Parker, 235 F.3d 261 (6th Cir. 2000) (counsel failed to present even a marginally competent expert where the defendant's one chance to avoid death was his diagnosis of borderline mental retardation and clinical psychiatric disorders); Austin v. Bell, 126 F.3d 843, 848-49 (6th Cir. 1997) (counsel's failure to present any mitigating evidence was not a strategic decision, but an abdication of advocacy). *See also* Bill Cristman, *Chandler v. United States: Does the Defense Attorney Have a Legal Obligation to Present Mitigation Evidence In Eleventh Circuit Death Penalty Cases?*, 18 GA. ST. U. L. REV. 563 (2001).

[47] *See, e.g.*, Hunt v. Lee, 291 F.3d 284, 290-92 (4th Cir. 2002) (counsel's investigation was sufficiently complete to support his decision not to put on mitigating evidence, and counsel's decision to rely on argument that death penalty was barbaric and immoral, though considered by some to be a desperate appeal, was an appeal nonetheless); Fox v. Ward, 200 F.3d 1286, 1295 (10th Cir. 2000) (counsel was not ineffective where he failed to present mitigating evidence for fear it would lead to questions about the defendant's sexual background); Brecheen v. Reynolds, 41 F.3d 1343, 1366-70 (10th Cir. 1994) (no absolute duty to present mitigating evidence where there was sufficient investigation to the base decision); Bunch v. Thompson, 949 F.2d 1354 (4th Cir. 1991) (counsel's decision not to investigate further was reasonable when balancing time demands and overall usefulness of search); Smith v. Dugger, 840 F.2d 787, 793-795 (11th Cir. 1988) (counsel's investigation and hiring of a psychologist was sufficient, and the strategic decision to not present evidence of mental illness was done to prevent loss of credibility).

[48] 483 U.S. 776 (1987). In *Burger*, the Court was more closely divided and decided the case by a vote of 5-4.

[49] *Id.* at 790.

than not, found the performance of counsel to be effective.[50] In 2000, the Court, for the first time since *Powell*, reversed a sentence of death based on a claim of ineffective assistance of counsel.[51] The Court established standards and expectations that counsel would investigate and present mitigating evidence in a capital case.[52] The Court, for the first time, incorporated the ABA Guidelines as a benchmark to measure and evaluate counsel's performance.[53] Scholars began to discuss whether the Court was beginning a new era of vigilance over the performance of counsel in death penalty cases since it was difficult to discern the difference between the performance of counsel in these cases that was deemed to be deficient, and the performance of counsel in *Strickland* and *Burger* that was deemed effective.[54]

In the first case, *Williams v. Taylor*,[55] the Supreme Court applied the two prong test of *Strickland* and found not only that counsel's performance was deficient, but that Williams was prejudiced as a result of that failure.[56] Trial counsel for Williams called three witnesses at the penalty phase. They basically testified that Williams was a nice boy and not violent. The lawyer, however, failed to locate or introduce other mitigating evidence that was readily available. Counsel never learned that Williams suffered a childhood of mistreatment, abuse and neglect, was borderline mentally retarded and had organic mental impairments. Counsel failed to obtain Williams' institutional records that showed that he had an exemplary record in prison, helped crack a prison drug ring, and was described by prison guards as being among the inmates least likely to act violently, dangerously, or provocatively.

This time, the Supreme Court rejected counsel's argument that his decision not to present mitigating evidence was a tactical one. Instead, the Court held that counsel's performance fell below the range expected of reasonable, professional, competence, and reversed William's sentence of death.[57]

---

[50] *See supra*, note 47.

[51] *See* Williams v. Taylor, 529 U.S. 362 (2000).

[52] " 'It is the duty of the lawyer to conduct a prompt investigation of the circumstances of the case and to explore all avenues leading to facts relevant to the merits of the case and the penalty in the event of conviction . . . The duty to investigate exists regardless of the accused's admissions or statements to the lawyer of facts constituting guilt or the accused's stated desire to plead guilty.' " Rompilla v. Beard, 545 U.S. 374, 387 (2005) (quoting ABA STANDARDS FOR CRIMINAL JUSTICE § 4-4.1 (2d ed. 1982 Supp.)).

[53] *ABA Guidelines supra*, note 7.

[54] *See, e.g.*, Charles Lane, *Death Penalty of Maryland Man is Overturned*, WASH. POST, June 27, 2003, at A01. John H. Blume & Stacey D. Neumann, *"It's Like Deja Vu All Over Again": Williams v. Taylor, Wiggins v. Smith, and Rompilla v. Beard And a (Partial) Return To the Guidelines Approach To the Effective Assistance of Counsel*, 34 Am. J. Crim. L. 127 (2007).

[55] 529 U.S. at 362. This case addressed many procedural issues under the Antiterrorism and Effective Death Penalty Act (AEDPA) of 1996, 28 U.S.C.A. §§ 2254(d)(1)-(2) (West 2002), which limits the availability of review on appeal and in habeas corpus. *See supra* Chapter 15. However, in that context, the Court clarified its standard for ineffective assistance of counsel claims.

[56] *Williams*, 529 U.S. at 420.

[57] *Id.* at 371. The Court went on to find that Williams was prejudiced by these deficiencies, influenced in large part by the fact that when the trial judge heard the possible mitigation evidence, he declared that if the evidence had been introduced at trial, the result of the trial would have been different. *Id.* at 396-97.

What was the difference between the performance of William's counsel, who was deemed deficient, and Washington's or Burger's lawyers, who were not? Perhaps it was the "nightmarish" childhood of Williams that was never presented to a jury. Maybe it was the fact that William's lawyer misunderstood the law and erroneously believed he could not get access to certain records and documents when, in fact, he could. In *Williams*, the Supreme Court appeared to return to its earlier theme that was heralded in *Powell* and *Gideon* of evaluating the overall fairness of the trial. The Court turned a more critical eye towards evaluating counsel's pretrial investigation and preparation prior to making any strategic decision.

In the second case, *Wiggins v. Smith*,[58] the Court discussed a lawyer's duty to investigate possible mitigation before any strategic decision can be made about how to proceed in a penalty phase. In 1989, Wiggins was convicted of murder in Maryland. On appeal, Wiggins claimed his lawyer was ineffective; the lawyer conducted a limited investigation, and failed to present any mitigating evidence. Trial counsel testified that these decisions were tactical and reflected his trial strategy. The Supreme Court reversed Wiggins' sentence of death and rejected the lawyer's claim that any failure to investigate or present evidence was strategic. The Court found that the investigation by counsel was so woefully lacking that it could not provide an adequate basis for a reasoned professional decision. Quoting from its earlier opinion in *Strickland*, the Court stated:

> [S]trategic choices made after thorough investigation of law and facts . . . are virtually unchallengeable; and strategic choices made after less than complete investigation are reasonable precisely to the extent that reasonable professional judgments support the limitations on investigation.[59]

The third case was *Rompilla v. Beard*,[60] where the Court, in a more closely divided 5-4 decision, reversed the defendant's death sentence.[61] The lawyers in *Rompilla*, did interview several family members, conduct some investigation, and hire mental health experts. The Court even remarked that "[t]his is not a case in which defense counsel simply ignored their obligation to find mitigating evidence . . . ."[62] During the preparation of the case, both Rompilla and his family indicated to counsel that no mitigation evidence was available and even, at times, obstructed counsel's ability to find helpful information.[63]

---

[58] 539 U.S. 510 (2003). In a 7-2 decision, the Court held that the lawyer's failure to investigate the penalty phase was ineffective.

[59] *Id.* at 521 (quoting *Strickland*, 466 U.S. at 690-691).

[60] 545 U.S. 374 (2005).

[61] The majority opinion is written by Justice Souter and joined by Ginsberg, Stevens, and Breyer, with Justice O'Connor concurring separately. Justice Kennedy wrote the dissenting opinion, which was joined by Rehnquist, Scalia and Thomas.

[62] *Rompilla*, 545 U.S. at 381 (2005). The Court has previously found trial counsel to be effective even where little or no investigation took place and few if any witnesses were called during the penalty phase. *See Strickland*, 466 U.S. at 668 (counsel was effective where he presented no evidence, spoke minimally to his client's wife and mother, obtained no psychological assessment and conducted no additional independent investigation). *See also Burger*, 483 U.S. at 776 (counsel was effective where he conducted some investigation but failed to present any evidence in mitigation during the penalty phase).

[63] *Rompilla*, 545 U.S. at 381-83. However, in his dissent, Justice Kennedy described the lawyer's

The Court focused on the failure of Rompilla's lawyers to make any effort to obtain or review a court file of Rompilla's prior rape conviction that the prosecutor alerted them they would introduce during the penalty trial.[64] It was this failure, in particular, that the Court found fell below the standard of reasonable performance. The Court observed that the prior rape conviction went to the heart of the prosecution aggravation case and the file would have provided important mitigation leads for counsel portraying a very different picture of Rompilla's childhood that was presented to the jury at trial.[65] Once the Court found the performance of counsel was deficient, the Court went on to find that Rompilla was prejudiced by this failure.[66]

Rompilla is important in another respect. Justice Souter, writing for the majority, cited the American Bar Association (ABA) Guidelines for the Representation of Criminal Defendants in Death Penalty Cases (hereinafter ABA Guidelines) as a point of reference for evaluating the conduct of the lawyer.[67] The Court stopped short of holding that the ABA Guidelines establish a minimum standard below which a lawyer may not fall in order to be effective. Nonetheless, *Rompilla* marked the third case where the Court cited the ABA Guidelines as a benchmark to determine whether counsel's conduct fell below the level of reasonable performance.[68]

With three reversals on grounds of ineffective assistance of counsel in five years, it appeared that the Court was returning to a heightened concern for the performance of counsel in capital cases. But that was short-lived as subsequent cases seemed to retreat from this concern. In reviewing cases, the Court went to great lengths to limit its earlier holdings in *Williams, Wiggins,* and *Rompilla* or to

---

preparation as "not only adequate but also conscientious." *Id.* at 397 (Kennedy, J., dissenting).

[64] *Id.* at 381-83 (majority opinion).

[65] O'Connor identifies three circumstances that provide the basis to find that Rompilla's lawyers were ineffective. First, O'Connor posits that the attorneys knew that Rompilla's prior conviction was the basis of the prosecution case for death. The prosecutors told the lawyers they planned to use it to prove that Rompilla was dangerous and deserved the death penalty. Second, the prior conviction eviscerated the defense theory in the penalty phase which was to appeal to any lingering doubts that jurors may have had about Rompilla's guilt in the case as a reason to impose a life sentence. Because the two cases were reasonably similar, this undermined any possible success of a "lingering doubt" argument. Third, the decision not to get the file was not the result of an informed decision or because efforts were placed elsewhere. It was the result of inattention. *Id.* at 394-96 (O'Connor, J., concurring).

[66] *Id.* at 390 (majority opinion). The Court observed that had counsel examined the file, they would have seen reports that demonstrated not only Rompilla's serious learning disorders, but also information that would have provided a basis for a diagnosis of schizophrenia and organic brain damage and problems associated with fetal alcohol syndrome. This childhood picture was dramatically different from the one presented to the jury at trial, which was based on "pleas for mercy" with nothing remarkable noted in the childhood to explain the violent crimes. *Id.* at 393.

[67] *See Id.* at 387 n.7 (quoting *ABA Guidelines, supra* note 44). The ABA Guidelines were first promulgated in 1989, and revised and adopted in February 2003. The Court in *Rompilla* cited the section 11.4.1.D.4, the 1989 guideline that requires counsel to make efforts to secure information in the possession of the prosecution or law enforcement authorities. The Court also cited the more recent version of the Guideline that requires counsel to "investigate prior conviction that could be used as aggravating circumstances or otherwise come into evidence."

[68] *See, e.g., Wiggins,* 539 U.S. at 524-525 (referring to the ABA Guidelines without explicitly holding them to be binding). *See also Williams,* 529 U.S. at 396 (referring to the ABA Standards as a guide).

differentiate the facts of the new cases from the three reversals.[69]

In 2009, the Court issued two *per curiam* opinions in cases alleging ineffective assistance of counsel; in one it found counsel was not ineffective and in the second it found he was. In *Bobby v. Van Hook*,[70] the Court found counsel was *not* ineffective and carefully distinguished his performance from counsel's performance in *Wiggins* and *Rompilla*.[71] The Court compared Van Hook's counsel to Strickland's counsel and found counsel's decision in *Van Hook* 'not to seek more' mitigating evidence from the defendant's background 'than was already in hand' fell 'well within the range of professionally reasonable judgments.' "[72]

The same year, in *Porter v. McCollum*, the Court reversed Porter's sentence of death finding that counsel's performance was clearly deficient.[73] Trial counsel failed to obtain "any of Porter's school, medical, or military service records or interview any members of Porter's family," Did the fact that Porter was a wounded and decorated veteran from the Korean war make the difference? Or was the court drawing other distinctions that are more subtle and difficult to discern? Some suggest the Court will find counsel's performance sufficient as long as counsel investigates potentially mitigating evidence and elects not to use it at trial, but insufficient where counsel fails to investigate entire areas of mitigating evidence.[74]

Two years after Porter, in *Cullen v. Pinholster*, the Court denied the claim of ineffective counsel. Justice Thomas, writing for the majority, seemed to return the court to a very deferential treatment of trial counsel's strategic decisions. Justice Thomas reaffirmed "the constitutionally protected independence of counsel . . . the wide latitude counsel must have in making tactical decisions . . . . [and] the strong presumption of competence that *Strickland* mandates."[75]

---

[69] One interesting twist is that *Rompilla* reversed a Third Circuit Court of Appeals opinion that denied relief. (*Rompilla v. Horn*, 355 F.3d 233 (3rd Cir. 2005)). This opinion was written by then Judge Samuel Alito, who went on to replace Justice O'Connor on the Supreme Court several months after *Rompilla* was decided. Justice O'Connor was the fifth vote for reversal in Rompilla.

[70] 558 U.S. __, 130 S. Ct. 13 (2009). Van Hook's defense counsel presented eight mitigating witnesses and an unsworn statement by Van Hook. The Sixth Circuit granted Van Hook claim of ineffective assistance of counsel based on a showing of additional evidence that could have been presented but was not. The Supreme Court reversed. Id. at 16.

[71] The Court in *Van Hook* described *Wiggins* as a case where "the defendant's attorneys failed to act while potentially powerful mitigating evidence stared them in the face.", 558 U.S. __, 130 S. Ct. 13, 19 (2009), citing Wiggins, 539 U.S., at 525, 123 S.Ct. 2527. The Court called *Rompilla* as case where mitigating evidence "would have been apparent from documents any reasonable attorney would have obtained." Id. citing *Rompilla v. Beard*, 545 U.S. 374, 389-393, 125 S. Ct. 2456 (2005).

[72] Id., quoting *Strickland v. Washington*, 466 U.S., at 699, 104 S. Ct. 2052.

[73] Porter v. McCollum, 558 U.S. ___, 130 S. Ct. 447, 453 (2009) The Court directly contrasted Porter with *Van Hook*, characterizing Van Hook's attorney as reasonable decision not to pursue additional sources." Id.

[74] Renee Newman Knake, *The Supreme Court's Increased Attention to the Law of Lawyering: Mere Coincidence or Something More?*, 59 Am. U. L. Rev. 1499, 1544 (2010), arguing that performance is deficient where "an entire category of mitigation evidence goes unconsidered (i.e., Porter's military history), but not when more evidence falling into the same category is omitted (i.e., Van Hook's . . . evidence on childhood abuse)."

[75] Cullen v. Pinholster, 563 U.S. ___ (2011), 131 S. Ct. 1388, 1407. Pinholster represented himself during the guilt phase of a capital trial. Following Pinholster's conviction, Pinholster's attorneys only

With the Supreme Court seeming to go in different directions on the issue of effective counsel, lower courts responded in different ways. Many continue to find counsel effective even where counsel conducts minimal investigation and presents little or no evidence during the penalty phase by distinguishing the facts of each case they review from *Wiggens*, *Williams* and *Rompilla*.[76] Given the Supreme Court's recent rulings, these fact-specific distinctions and assessments will likely continue. Perhaps more significantly, the changes in habeas corpus legislation in 1996 under AEDPA, created significant barriers in a federal court's ability to review claims of ineffective assistance of counsel.[77] In any case, it remains difficult to distinguish those cases in which counsel was found to be ineffective from those in which he was not.[78]

---

presented his mother in mitigation despite having a report by a psychiatrist that diagnosed the defendant with antisocial personality disorder. The Court applied the "doubly deferential" standard from *Richter* (infra) in order to consider whether *Strickland's* "reasonableness" standard had been applied "unreasonably" under AEDPA. In finding the Ninth Circuit had improperly heard the case, it affirmed the California Supreme Court's "reasonable" application and decision under *Strickland*.

[76] For example, in Emmett v. Kelly, 474 F.3d 154, 168 (4th Cir. 2007), counsel was found not to be ineffective where counsel failed to investigate siblings or obtain juvenile mental health records which would have portrayed defendant as raised in poverty, neglect, hunger and physical abuse — a very different picture than the one presented to the jury. The court distinguished *Williams*, *Wiggins*, and *Rompilla*, stating "[t]his is not a case in which counsel ignored his duty to investigate background information . . . ." The Court found that even if the representation was deficient, there was no prejudice because the nature of the crime was so heinous. *See also* Coble v. Quarterman, 496 F.3d 430 (5th Cir. 2007) (distinguishing *Williams*, where counsel began investigation a week before penalty trial, distinguished *Wiggins*, where there was no attempt to compile a social history, and distinguished *Rompilla*, where counsel failed to obtain material he knew the prosecutor would use and found counsel to be effective); Clark v. Mitchell 425 F.3d 270 (6th Cir. 2005) (holding that counsel not ineffective where he failed to discover organic brain damage, and distinguished *Rompilla*, where the state did not contest prejudice); Conner v. McBride 375 F.3d 643 (7th Cir. 2004) (distinguished *Wiggins* by noting that the evidence uncovered here was more a question of degree, while in *Wiggins* there was no information on the issue at all).

[77] *See* AEDPA, *supra* note 55. *See also* Section 15.02, *supra*. This legislation changed the standard of review by federal courts of state court findings. In Schriro v. Landrigan, 550 U.S. 465 (2007), the Court held, in a 5-4 decision, that the District Court did not err in refusing to grant the defendant a hearing on the issue of whether counsel was ineffective at trial. The dissent pointed out that counsel failed to discover defendant had a serious organic brain disorder, his mother used drugs and alcohol during pregnancy, his adoptive parents inflicted physical and emotional abuse, and he overdosed in the 8th or 9th grade and was in a psychiatric ward for a period of time. In light of these facts, "the Court's decision can only be explained by its increasingly familiar effort to guard the floodgates of litigation." *Schriro*, 550 U.S. at 499 (Stevens, J., dissenting).

[78] *See, e.g.*, Outten v. Kearney 464 F.3d 401 (3d Cir. 2006) (counsel was ineffective despite presenting family members in mitigation where counsel failed to investigate child protective services records, mental health records, or school records, and presented no theme or theory in mitigation); Smith v. Dretke, 422 F.3d 269 (5th Cir. 2005) (counsel was ineffective when he failed to investigate the defendant's drug and alcohol use, his abusive upbringing, and his prison records showing positive institutional adjustment); Carter v. Bell, 218 F.3d 581, 596-97 (6th Cir. 2000) (counsel was ineffective when he failed to investigate defendant's family, social and psychological history).

§ 16.05   ABA GUIDELINES FOR THE REPRESENTATION OF CRIMINAL DEFENDANTS IN DEATH PENALTY CASES

The American Bar Association (ABA) is the national organization representing the legal profession and providing initiatives to improve the legal system for the public.[79] Although the ABA has never taken a position on the constitutionality of the death penalty, it opposed the imposition of the death penalty on offenders who committed their crimes when they were under the age of 18 or on the mentally retarded before the Supreme Court similarly ruled.[80] Additionally, the ABA has adopted policies that address the administration of the death penalty and, in particular, the performance of counsel in representing defendants charged in a capital case.

In 1989, the ABA promulgated Guidelines for the Appointment and Performance of Counsel in Death Penalty Cases. In February, 2003, the ABA formerly adopted these guidelines and recommended adoption of these by all death penalty jurisdictions.[81] These guidelines are designed to insure that competent counsel will be provided to all defendants in a capital case. It sets out basic requirements for counsel to follow in preparing and presenting their case for trial. They include efforts to secure information in possession of prosecution and law enforcement authorities, to investigate prior convictions, and to find other mitigating evidence or evidence rebutting aggregating factors.[82] While states have not moved quickly to adopt these guidelines for the appointment of counsel in their own states, the Supreme Court now refers to the guidelines in decisions that evaluate the effective assistance of counsel.

The Court's endorsement of the guidelines seems to fluctuate depending on the facts of a particular case or on which Justice writes the opinion. In *Williams v Taylor* the Court referenced the ABA guidelines when finding that counsel did not fulfill their obligation to conduct a thorough investigation of the defendant's background.[83] In *Wiggins*, Justice O Connor, writing for the Court, invoked the guidelines as a measure of whether or not the performance of counsel was reasonable, stating, "the American Bar Association [guidelines are] standards to which we long have referred as 'guides to determining what is reasonable.' "[84] Many

---

[79] *See* American Bar Association, http://www.americanbar.org/utility/about_the_aba.html (last visited January 17, 2011).

[80] *See ABA Guidelines, supra,* note 7. Arizona adopted the ABA Guidelines in Rule 6.8 of the Arizona Rules of Criminal Procedure.

[81] *See ABA Guidelines, supra.* Note 7.

[82] *See ABA Guidelines, supra.* Note 7.

[83] 529 U.S. 362 (2000).

[84] Wiggins v. Smith, 539 U.S. 510, 524 (2000), quoting *Strickland v. Washington,* 466 U.S. at 688. But Justice Scalia's dissent in *Wiggins* criticized the majority's use of the ABA guidelines, arguing "[t]here was nothing . . . in any of our 'clearly established' precedents . . . to support *Williams*" statement that trial counsel had an 'obligation to conduct a thorough investigation of the defendant's background.' That is why the citation supporting the statement is not one of our opinions, but rather standards promulgated by the American Bar Association." 539 U.S. at 543, citations omitted. *See also Rompilla v. Beard,* 545 U.S. 374, 375 (2005), quoting *Wiggins v. Smith, supra* at 524.

believed that the Court's reference to the ABA guidelines in this way seemed to suggest that the ABA's standards were the *de facto* measure for deficient performance.[85]

The Court's endorsement of the ABA Guidelines was short lived. In *Bobby v. Van Hook*[86] the Court chastised the 6th Circuit for treating "the ABA's 2003 Guidelines not merely as evidence of what reasonably diligent attorneys would do, but as inexorable commands with which all capital defense counsel must fully comply."[87] Van Hook's trial took place before adoption of the Guidelines leaving open the question of what deference might be afforded the guidelines in a later case. In *Pinholster*, the Court relegated the guidelines to mere advisory in holding that "specific guidelines are inappropriate," and that lower courts should not "attribute a strict set of rules" to the *Strickland* standard.[88]

Some states have promulgated their own standards for counsel in capital cases without specifying how these standards should be used to evaluate the performance of counsel.[89] Other states specifically provide that failure to meet the standards is not evidence that counsel was ineffective.[90]

§ 16.06 INEFFECTIVE ASSISTANCE OF COUNSEL: THE SECOND PRONG: PREJUDICE

[A] Overview

Once a defendant is able to show that the performance of his lawyer is deficient, a second, and perhaps even more difficult, hurdle remains. A defendant has to prove prejudice — that because of the performance of his lawyer, he was deprived of a fair trial. To succeed, a defendant must show that there is a "reasonable probability that, but for counsel's unprofessional errors, the result of the proceedings would have been different."[91] It is not sufficient to merely show that

---

[85] See: Blume and Neumann, *"It's Like Déjà Vu All Over Again"*, supra; Robert R. Rigg, *The T-Rex Without Teeth: Evolving Strickland v. Washington And The Test for Ineffective Assistance of Counsel*, 35 PEPP. L. REV. 77, 104 (Dec. 2007), arguing the Court had begun using the ABA standards as "an evaluative tool rather than mere guidelines." (Internal quotations omitted.)

[86] 558 U.S. __, 130 S.Ct. 13 (2009). Van Hook's trial had been held 18 years prior to the ABA's creation of their guidelines. While the facts of the case may limit the applicability of the ruling to similar cases, the Court's strongly worded caution about the weight to be given the ABA guidelines indicates otherwise.

[87] Id. at 17, internal quotations omitted.

[88] Cullen v. Pinholder, 131 S.Ct. at 1406-1407. Emily Chiang, *Indigent Defense Invigorated: A Uniform Standard For Adjudicating Pre-Conviction Sixth Amendment Claims*, 19 TEMP. POL. & CIV. RTS. L. REV. 443 (Spring 2010), arguing "Commentary contending that Strickland 'has teeth' to strengthen criminal defense counsels' obligations to their clients is rather less persuasive in light of this decision." Id., fn. 160.

[89] *See, e.g.*, FLA. R. CRIM. P. 3.112; IL. SUP. CT. R. 714.

[90] *See* CAL. R. CT. 4.117(a) (2003) ("Nothing in this rule is intended to be used as a standard by which to measure whether the defendant received effective assistance of counsel."). *See also* TENN. SUP. CT. R. 13(a)(2) ("The failure of appointed counsel to meet the qualifications set forth in this rule shall not be deemed evidence that counsel did not provide effective assistance of counsel in a particular case.").

[91] *Strickland*, 466 U.S. at 694. States that have rejected the requirement of a showing of prejudice

the lawyer's acts or omissions had some conceivable impact on the case.

The Court's analysis in *Strickland* raised more questions than answers. When will a lawyer's deficient performance be prejudicial and warrant a reversal of a sentence of death?[92] Under what circumstances will the performance of counsel be deemed deficient but no prejudice will be found?[93] How does a court determine what piece of evidence or how much evidence in total will affect a juror in making a decision between life or death? Should the court apply a different standard of prejudice when the penalty trial is in front of twelve jurors instead of one judge? Although these issues arise frequently in capital cases, very few of these cases have been reviewed by the Supreme Court.

[B] Prejudice in a Penalty Phase

What is prejudice in the context of a penalty phase? What failure of counsel could result in a *reasonable probability* that the outcome would have been different?

Even though a penalty phase is different from a guilt phase in many ways, the Supreme Court applies the same test to decide whether or not a defendant is prejudiced based upon the ineffective performance of his lawyer.

In a guilt phase, a court generally looks at whether a defendant is guilty of the offense to determine whether she was prejudiced by her lawyer's failings. In a penalty phase, the decision is more individualized. It is based upon a jury determining whether, given a particular defendant's background and experiences, that person should be given a sentence of death. A single fact, witness, or piece of evidence may carry more weight in a decision of life or death than in any determination of guilt. In order for jurors to make an informed decision, they must be given the opportunity to consider the entire life of a defendant in order to evaluate whether it is a life worth saving. The jury must hear all aspects of a life — the positive family connections, as well as any emotional or mental problems of the defendant and his family.

In *Strickland*, the Court looked at the evidence of Washington's life and concluded that his life and his background could not offset the heinousness of his crimes. However, in juxtaposing the crime with Washington's life, the Court

---

include Alaska and Hawaii. *See, e.g.,* Risher v. State, 523 P.2d 421 (Alaska 1974); State v. Smith, 712 P.2d 496 (Haw. 1986). Neither of these states have a death penalty.

[92] *See, e.g.,* Brownlee v. Haley, 306 F.3d 1043, 1070 (11th Cir. 2002) (prejudice exists where counsel's failure to investigate and present powerful mitigating evidence of defendant's borderline mental retardation, psychiatric disorders, and history of drug and alcohol abuse undermines the confidence in the sentence of death); Glenn v. Tate, 71 F.3d 1204, 1206-10 (6th Cir. 1995) (defendant was denied effective assistance of counsel and prejudiced where lawyers did not begin penalty preparation until the guilty verdict, and failed to present any information about defendant's background, character or organic brain disorder which would show have explained his participation in the crimes).

[93] In Fortenberry v. Haley, 297 F.3d 1213 (11th Cir. 2002), the court found deficient performance where there was no tactical reason for a lawyer's failure to investigate and discover mitigating evidence. However, there was no finding of prejudice because the court was unable to consider affidavits of witnesses who might have testified, as this was not presented in a state court proceeding and therefore waived.

arguably misrepresented the nature of mitigating evidence. As one scholar explained:

> Mitigating evidence is not presented in order to "offset," "explain," or "justify" the underlying crime. Mitigating evidence is presented to persuade a jury that the defendant is somehow deserving of mercy because his character or background indicates that he will be rehabilitated, will be harmless in prison, or does not deserve to die for some other reason.[94]

After *Strickland*, the Court has rarely addressed the question of when the deficient performance of counsel is prejudicial.[95] Most of the decisions have been in the lower courts. However, in resolving these issues, these courts often cite to *Strickland* and hold that prejudice exists when there is a reasonable probability that, absent the errors, the sentencer would have concluded that the balance of aggravating and mitigating circumstances did not warrant death.[96]

§ 16.07 INEFFECTIVE ASSISTANCE OF COUNSEL: PRESUMPTION OF PREJUDICE

[A] Overview

The test in *Strickland* required a determination of whether the performance of the lawyer was deficient and, if so, whether the defendant was prejudiced. However, the Court also identified certain limited circumstances where, once a lawyer is found to be deficient, prejudice can be presumed and does not have to be proved by the defendant. The Court in *Strickland* identified those narrowly defined circumstances where this would be the case. These include where there is a "complete breakdown of the adversarial process" due to an actual or constructive denial of counsel or an actual conflict of interest.[97]

---

[94] LEVINSON, *supra* note 34, at 171.

[95] Although the Court discussed this issue in Lockhart v. Fretwell, 506 U.S. 364 (1993), the facts in Fretwell were sufficiently unique that Justice O'Connor wrote separately to state that the decision should have no effect on the prejudice inquiry in the vast majority of cases under *Strickland*. Fretwell's lawyer failed to object at trial that the aggravating circumstance (robbery for pecuniary gain) was duplicitous of an element in the underlying felony (murder in the course of a robbery). Because the Eighth Circuit had found this duplicity to be unconstitutional in a previous case, if Fretwell's lawyer had objected, Fretwell's sentence of death would have been reversed. By the time Fretwell's case reached the Supreme Court, the Eighth Circuit had reversed itself and upheld the aggravating circumstance. Although the Supreme Court found the performance of Fretwell's lawyer to be deficient, it found no prejudice arguing that Fretwell should not receive a windfall solely because of the timing of his trial.

[96] *See* Strickland v. Washington, 466 U.S. 668, 696 (1984). *See also* Caro v. Woodford, 280 F.3d 1247, 1256 (9th Cir. 2002) (finding prejudice where counsel failed to investigate or present evidence of defendants childhood exposure to toxic chemicals and resulting brain damage); Bean v. Calderon, 163 F.3d 1073 (9th Cir. 1998) (finding prejudice where counsel called expert witnesses, but failed to provide experts with adequate background information from which they could testify effectively, including information about defendant's sadistic treatment by his father who inflicted beatings that left a permanent indentation in his head).

[97] *Strickland*, 466 U.S. at 692.

[B] Complete Breakdown of Adversary System

In *United States v. Cronic*,[98] the Supreme Court acknowledged the principal that prejudice may be presumed where there is a complete breakdown of the adversary system.[99] Nonetheless, in *Cronic* and the cases that follow, the Court failed to find any factual scenario that satisfies this standard. Instead, the Court sent each case back for review under the two-prong test set forth in *Strickland*.[100]

In *Cronic*, the defendant was charged with mail fraud and his hired counsel withdrew before trial. The court then appointed an attorney to the case, and gave the new counsel only 25 days to prepare for trial (despite the fact that the government had taken over four years to prepare their case). The defendant was convicted on 11 out of the 13 counts and sentenced to 25 years in prison. Deciding the case the same day as *Strickland*, the Court held that Cronic's lawyer should be evaluated under the two-prong *Strickland* test, and that prejudice should not be presumed. What happened to Cronic, the Court held, did not reach the level of a complete breakdown of the adversarial system as in *Powell v. Alabama*. The Court recounted the earlier case:

> The [*Powell*] defendants, young, ignorant, illiterate, surrounded by hostile sentiment, haled back and forth under guard of soldiers, charged with an atrocious crime regarded with especial horror in the community where they were to be tried, were thus put in peril of their lives within a few moments after counsel for the first time charged with any degree of responsibility began to represent them.[101]

The Court thus distinguished the facts in *Powell* as much more egregious than those presented in *Cronic*. The Court steadfastly adhered to the view that a court may presume prejudice only in cases where counsel fails *entirely* to test the prosecutor's case.

In 2002, the Court reaffirmed this narrow interpretation in *Bell v. Cone*.[102] Cone's lawyer called no witnesses and waived closing argument during the penalty trial of his case.[103] The Supreme Court held, by a vote of 8-1, that Cone was not entitled to a presumption of prejudice because there was not a *complete* breakdown of the adversarial system. The Court held that the performance of Cone's lawyer should be evaluated under the two-prong test of *Strickland*.[104]

---

[98] 466 U.S. 648 (1984).

[99] *Id.* at 659 (holding a presumption of prejudice should apply where "counsel entirely fails to subject the prosecution's case to meaningful adversarial testing . . . [creating] a denial of Sixth Amendment rights that make the adversary process itself presumptively unreliable.").

[100] *See* Section 16.03[D], *supra*.

[101] *Cronic*, 466 U.S. at 660 (quoting Powell v. Alabama, 287 U.S. 45, 57-58).

[102] 535 U.S. 685 (2002).

[103] *Id.* at 692, 700.

[104] Cone's lawyer testified that he decided not to call any witnesses based upon how the jury viewed the evidence during the guilt trial. He waived closing argument to keep the prosecutor from presenting a rebuttal argument. The Court found, under *Strickland*, that the lawyer was not deficient as he had legitimate strategic reasons for his actions.

The Court addressed this presumption of prejudice again in 2004, in *Florida v. Nixon*.[105] Nixon's attorney conceded his client's guilt during the guilt/innocence phase of his capital trial without the express consent of his client. The Florida Supreme Court found that prejudice should be presumed because the failure of counsel to obtain his client's consent constituted a complete breakdown of the adversary system. The Supreme Court disagreed and, in a unanimous opinion, reversed.[106] The Court observed that counsel's strategy was to concede guilt and focus on persuading the jury to impose a life sentence rather than a sentence of death.[107] This strategy, the Court found, was adequately disclosed and discussed with Nixon, and express consent was not required. The Court held that no presumption of prejudice applied, and the case should be decided under the two prong *Strickland* test.[108] Despite the Supreme Court's reluctance to presume prejudice in cases of ineffective assistance of counsel, some federal appellate courts have found facts that warranted a finding of presumption of prejudice.[109]

For example, the Sixth Circuit Court of Appeals has granted relief and found a presumption of prejudice where the lawyer failed to object to the composition of the jury when it contained seven jurors that had just a few months earlier convicted a codefendant who was tried separately.[110] The Court of Appeals held that "counsel's acquiescence in allowing [these] seven jurors . . . to sit in judgment of his case amounted to an abandonment of 'meaningful adversarial testing' *throughout* the proceeding, making 'the adversary process itself presumptively unreliable.' "[111]

---

[105] 543 U.S. 175 (2004).

[106] *Id.* Justice Rehnquist took no part in the decision of this case.

[107] *Id.* at 188. The Court distinguished a concession of guilt from an actual guilty plea by a defendant. Here, with a concession of guilt, Nixon retained all his trial rights including the right to cross examine witnesses and to object to the admission of evidence.

[108] The United States Supreme Court sent the case back for a hearing before the Florida Supreme Court. On remand, the Florida Supreme Court found that the performance of counsel was not deficient, and the defendant was not entitled to relief. Nixon v. State, 932 So. 2d 1009, 1013-14 (Fla. 2006).

[109] *See* Bell v. Quintero, 535 U.S. 1109 (2002). *See also* Jones v. French, 540 U.S. 1018 (2003); Mason v. Mitchell, 536 U.S. 901 (2002). The Supreme Court vacated three cases and remanded them back to the Sixth Circuit Court of Appeals. Ironically, in all three cases, the Sixth Circuit reinstated the writ. *See, e.g.,* Bell v. Cone, 535 U.S. 685 (2002). In *Cone*, after the Supreme Court remanded the case, the Sixth Circuit granted relief on other grounds.

[110] Quintero v. Bell, 368 F.3d 892 (6th Cir. 2004), *cert. denied*, 544 U.S. 936 (2005). When the Supreme Court denied certiorari (which allowed the grant of relief to stand), Justice Thomas and the Chief Justice dissented, asserting that *Cronic* requires a "complete failure" of the adversary system in order to grant relief and that was simply not the case in *Quintero*. They also noted, with obvious displeasure, that Quintero's case was one of three that the Supreme Court vacated and remanded following the decision in Bell v. Cone 535 U.S. 685 (2002). In all three cases the Sixth Circuit reinstated its previous opinion and again ordered that a writ of habeas corpus be granted. *See* Mitchell v. Mason, 325 F.3d 732 (6th Cir. 2003) (finding *Cronic* error); French v. Jones, 332 F.3d 430, 436 (6th Cir. 2003) (finding *Cronic* error). The Sixth Circuit also granted relief in cases following *Bell*. *See, e.g.,* Valentine v. United States, 488 F.3d 325 (6th Cir. 2007); United States v. Brika, 416 F.3d 514 (6th Cir. 2005); Caver v. Straub, 349 F.3d 340 (6th Cir. 2003).

[111] *Quintero*, 368 F.3d at 893 (quoting *Cronic*, 466 U.S. at 659).

[C] Conflict of Interest

A defendant's Sixth Amendment right to effective assistance of counsel includes a defendant's right to undivided loyalty from a lawyer who is free from any conflicts of interest. For Sixth Amendment purposes, an *actual* conflict of interest is one that adversely affects counsel's performance.[112] When an actual conflict exists, a defendant is entitled to a presumption of prejudice. These actual conflicts can arise in a variety of ways, but arise most often in cases where a lawyer represents multiple clients whose interests are adverse to each other.

When a lawyer represents codefendants for trial, the likelihood that a conflict of interest exists is very high. Because of this, joint representation is constitutionally suspect, although not completely forbidden, and not necessarily an actual conflict of interest.[113]

Courts are hesitant to find a conflict of interest between a lawyer and his client. However, what if the court appoints one lawyer to represent codefendants and denies defense counsel's request for separate lawyers? Under these circumstances, a trial court must hold a hearing to assess whether or not a conflict exists. If no inquiry is made, prejudice will be presumed and an "automatic reversal" rule will apply.[114]

What if a lawyer is appointed to represent a defendant in a capital case where the murder victim was the lawyer's former client? Is there an actual conflict of interest and a presumption of prejudice? The Supreme Court said "no." In *Mickens v. Taylor*, the trial court appointed counsel to represent 17-year-old Timothy Hall in a criminal assault case.[115] When Hall was murdered, the same judge appointed the lawyer to represent Mickens, who was charged with Hall's murder. Mickens faced a sentence of death. Mickens argued that because of this conflict, his lawyer did little during the penalty phase to bring out evidence of the victim's background that may have spared his life. The lawyer testified that he had no conflict. He testified that he met Hall only once for less than an hour, learned no confidential information, and that any allegiance to Hall ended when Hall died.[116] The Supreme Court, in a 5-4 decision, found no constitutional violation.[117] Writing for the Court, Justice Scalia argued that the automatic reversal rule did not apply simply because the judge failed to initiate an inquiry; automatic reversal was limited to cases where defense counsel brings a conflict to the court's attention and is forced to

---

[112] *See* Mickens v. Taylor, 535 U.S. 162, 172 (2002).

[113] The Court's analysis on this subject evolved in a series of cases involving multiple representation. *See* Cuyler v. Sullivan, 446 U.S. 335, 345-50 (1980); Holloway v. Arkansas, 435 U.S. 475, 487-91 (1978).

[114] *See Holloway*, 435 U.S. at 482.

[115] *Mickens*, 535 U.S. at 164-65.

[116] The lawyer's belief that he no longer had any duty to his deceased client Hall was mistaken. However, Justice Kennedy argued this mistaken belief confirmed that the prior representation did not influence the lawyers choices during Mickens trial. *Id.* at 177 (Kennedy, J., concurring) ("Indeed, even if [the attorney] had learned relevant information, the District Court found that he labored under the impression he had no continuing duty at all to his deceased client.").

[117] *Id.* at 175-76 (majority opinion).

represent codefendants over objection.[118] The bottom line was that *Strickland's* two-prong test applied, and Mickens had to show prejudice.

What if a lawyer makes a book deal based upon his client's story without his client's knowledge? Is there a conflict of interest? While these facts have never provided a basis for reversal of a sentence of death, this scenario has occurred. Appellate lawyers for Timothy McVeigh raised this issue after learning that trial counsel signed a book deal not after McVeigh's trial, but while he was still representing him.[119]

[D]   The Mentally Impaired, Drug Addicted, or Alcoholic Lawyer

Will there be a constructive denial of counsel and a presumption of prejudice if the lawyer is a drug addict? An alcoholic? Suffering from a mental disease or mental disorder? The answer in most of these cases has been "no." As a result, when a lawyer is found to suffer from any of these conditions, courts have required a defendant to show prejudice. Most courts have rejected an argument that prejudice should be presumed even when lawyers are shown to have these disabilities during trial.[120]

The examples of lawyers in capital cases who have problems with drug or alcohol abuse are legion. In evaluating a lawyer's performance, however, courts continue to apply the two-prong test from *Strickland.* As a result, courts rarely find ineffective assistance of counsel because a defendant must still prove prejudice.[121]

Much of the harshest criticism of the *Strickland* test as too low a standard has come from cases involving lawyers who suffer substance abuse or mental illness problems. One of the more egregious examples is Ronald Frye's case from North

---

[118] *Id.* at 168.

[119] *See* Howard Pankratz, *Leaks Cited in McVeigh Case Lawyers Argue for a New Trial,* THE DENVER POST, August 18, 2000, at B-02 ("In attacking lead defense lawyer Stephen Jones, appellate attorneys Nathan Chambers and Dennis Hartley said Jones put his personal and financial interests above those of his client."). *See also* United States v. McVeigh, 118 F. Supp. 2d 1137 (D. Colo. 2000); Alan Berlow, *Lethal Injustice,* AMERICAN PROSPECT MAGAZINE, Mar. 27-Apr. 10, 2000, at 54 (describing the story of death row inmate Betty Lou Betts, whose lawyer had evidence of her innocence but withheld it deliberately because he had the movie and book rights to her movie and did not want to lose those rights by withdrawing from the case in order to testify on her behalf).

[120] *See, e.g.,* McFarland v. Scott, 512 U.S. 1256, 1259 (1994) (Blackmun, J., dissenting) ("Capital defendants have been sentenced to death when represented by counsel who never bothered to read the state death penalty statute . . . ."); Gardner v. Dixon, 966 F.2d 1442 (4th Cir. 1992); Young v. Zant, 727 F.2d 1489, 1493 (11th Cir. 1984) (concluding there was no evidence that counsel's handling of the trial was affected by his drug usage); People v. Garrison, 765 P.2d 419, 440 (Cal. 1989) ("Although it is uncontested that [counsel] was an alcoholic at the time of trial and that he has since died of the disease, defendant has failed to prove that [counsel's] performance was deficient. His reliance on a per se rule of deficiency for alcoholic attorneys is contrary to settled law.").

[121] *See, e.g.,* Young v. Zant, 727 F.2d 1489 (11th Cir. 1984), *cert. denied,* 470 U.S. 1009 (1985). Young's lawyer was addicted to drugs and a few weeks after Young's trial was incarcerated on federal drug charges. The 11th Circuit rejected Young's ineffective assistance of counsel claim. Young was executed in 1985.

Carolina. Frye argued that his lawyer's alcohol dependency made it impossible for the lawyer to provide effective assistance of counsel. The depth of the lawyer's dependency was described as follows:

> Every night after trial, instead of preparing for the next day, the lawyer went home and drank a bottle of rum. According to his own testimony, Frye's counsel consumed at least 12 shots of 80-proof rum every evening, beginning around 5 and continuing until he fell asleep or passed out. He drank a good deal more on the weekends . . . When the lawyer was involved in a car wreck during the same time period, his blood-alcohol level was a near-lethal 0.436 percent — even though it was 11 in the morning and he hadn't had anything to drink in hours.[122]

The lawyer failed to present any evidence of Frye's childhood which was replete with abuse and neglect. Frye and his brother were given up by their mother to strangers she met in a restaurant. The new "father" beat Frye with a bullwhip and ordered Frye to whip his brother. Frye's scars were so striking that photographs of them were used at the police training academy as examples of severe child abuse. The jury never heard any of this evidence before sentencing him to death. The court rejected Frye's claim of ineffective counsel.[123] Frye's sentence of death was upheld and he was executed on August 31, 2001.

[E] The Sleeping Lawyer

Although dozing by lawyers is not new,[124] when it has occurred in a capital murder trial it has captured the attention of the public and the media. The courts, however, do not always find a sleeping lawyer to be ineffective. Courts have distinguished between a lawyer who sleeps for limited periods of time (whose performance could then be evaluated under the two-prong test from *Strickland*) from a lawyer who sleeps for extended periods of time (where prejudice could be presumed.).[125] At some point, the court reasoned, a sleeping lawyer is the equivalent of no lawyer, and prejudice must be presumed. The question is, where do we draw the line? How much sleeping is too much? The line also seems to move depending on which court is drawing it.

In *Burdine v. Johnson*,[126] the defendant argued his death sentence should be reversed because his lawyer repeatedly dozed through substantial portions of his trial. Burdine argued that a sleeping lawyer is like no lawyer at all, and constitutes a complete breakdown of the adversarial system. Ultimately, the Fifth Circuit

---

[122] Gene R. Nichol, *Justice Undone by Liquor*, THE NEWS AND OBSERVER, Aug. 22, 2001, at A15.

[123] *Id.*

[124] In Javor v. United States, 724 F.2d 831 (9th Cir. 1984), a non-death penalty drug trial, Javor's lawyer was found by a judge to be asleep, dozing, or not alert during substantial portions of the trial. The Ninth Circuit Court of Appeals reversed his conviction, concluding that when an attorney sleeps through substantial portions of a trial, it is like having no lawyer at all.

[125] *See* Stephen B. Bright, *The American Bar Association's Recognition of the Sacrifice of Fairness for Results: Will We Pay the Price for Justice?*, 4 GEO. J. ON FIGHTING POVERTY 183, 184-85 (1996). *See also* Tippins v. Walker, 77 F.3d 682 (2d Cir. 1996).

[126] 262 F.3d 336 (5th Cir. 2001).

Court of Appeals agreed. The court concluded that Burdine's lawyer was repeatedly asleep, and hence "unconscious," while adverse evidence was introduced. It was, the court reasoned, as if Burdine had no counsel at all, and therefore prejudice should be presumed. The court observed that an unconscious lawyer does not analyze, object, listen, or in any way exercise judgment on behalf of a client.[127] The court distinguished a sleeping lawyer from lawyers who were drunk, drugged, mentally impaired, or suffering from Alzheimer's.[128] All of these lawyers could, the court reasoned, exercise judgment, unlike a lawyer who was unconscious or absent.

Other capital defendants whose lawyers slept through their trials did not fare as well. Carl Johnson argued that his lawyer slept through portions of his trial. The court declined to presume prejudice, and he was executed by Texas on September 18, 1995. George McFarland argued that his lawyer also slept through portions of his trial. The trial was described as follows:

> Seated beside his client — a convicted capital murderer — defense attorney John Benn spent much of Thursday afternoon's trial in apparent deep sleep. His mouth kept falling open and his head lolled back on his shoulders, and then he awakened just long enough to catch himself and sit upright. Then it happened again. And again. And again. Every time he opened his eyes, a different witness was on the stand describing another aspect of the November 19, 1991, arrest of George McFarland in the robbery killing of grocer Kenneth Kwan. When State District Judge Doug Shaver finally called a recess, Benn was asked if he truly had fallen asleep during a capital murder trial. "It's boring," the 72-year-old longtime Houston lawyer explained.[129]

§ 16.08   CONCLUSION

Recently, the issue of the competence of lawyers in capital cases has begun not only to appear in the popular media,[130] but has also been mentioned in almost unprecedented public statements by sitting Supreme Court Justices. As early as

---

[127] On June 19, 2003, Burdine pleaded guilty to three charges: aggravated assault with a deadly weapon, felony possession of a weapon, and capital murder. The 50-year-old defendant received consecutive life sentences.

[128] See, e.g., Dows v. Wood, 211 F.3d 480 (9th Cir. 2000) (concluding there was no showing of prejudice where the defendant's lawyer was diagnosed with advanced Alzheimer's disease subsequent to the end of the trial).

[129] John Makeig, Asleep on the Job? Slaying Trial Boring Lawyer Says, Hous. Chron., Aug. 14, 1992, at 35. See also McFarland v. Texas, 928 S.W.2d 482, 527 (Tex. 1996), cert. denied, 519 U.S. 1119 (1997). McFarland's second counsel, Melamed, testified that his preparation of the case consisted of only a seven-hour review of the state's files, one visit to McFarland, and some motions. Neither lawyer interviewed any witnesses. Benn decided which witnesses he would cross-examine, informing Melamed of his decision only after the State concluded its direct examination. The Supreme Court denied a writ of certiorari. The Texas appellate court denied a writ of habeas corpus and held that since McFarland's second attorney was a present and an active advocate at all times he was not burdened by Mr. Benn's behavior. Ex Parte McFarland, 163 S.W.3d 743, (2005).

[130] See, e.g., Richard Willing, Bill Would Expand Access to DNA Tests, USA Today, July 28, 2001, at 11A (discussing proposed legislation to create a national counsel on competency).

1994, Justice Harry Blackmun wrote in dissent that "[w]ithout question, 'the principal failings of the capital punishment review process today are the inadequacy and inadequate compensation of counsel at trial and the unavailability of counsel in state post-conviction proceedings.' "[131] In the summer of 2001, Justice O'Connor spoke publicly about the troubling standard of representation in capital cases, and observed that some assessment for the standards of counsel in death cases should be examined.[132] That same summer, Justice Ginsberg went even further and observed "I have yet to see a death case among the dozens coming to the Supreme Court on the eve of execution in which the defendant was well represented at trial."[133]

Evaluating the representation received by a defendant is a difficult and complex task. On the one hand, the Court's interest in finality weighs in favor of affording significant deference to the performance of counsel. On the other hand, the interest in fairness looks to insure that any sentence of death is reliable. In the end, it is sometimes difficult to tell which fact tilts the balance one way or the other. As one scholar opined, "[w]hat is most striking in examining these cases . . . is the factual similarity between the winners and losers."[134]

---

[131] McFarland v. Scott, 512 U.S. 1256, 1256 (1994) (Blackmun, J., dissenting) (quoting Ira P. Robbins, *Toward a More Just and Effective System of Review in State Death Penalty Cases*, 40 Am. U. L. Rev. 1, 16 (1990)).

[132] Bob Herbert, *In America; Death Penalty Dissenters*, N.Y. Times, July 9, 2001, at A15.

[133] Anne Gearan, *Supreme Court Justice Backs Proposed Death Penalty Freeze*, The Record, Apr. 10, 2001, at A18.

[134] Amy R. Murphy, *The Constitutional Failure of the Strickland Standard in Capital Cases Under the Eighth Amendment*, 63 Law & Contemp. Probs. 179, 199 (2000).

Chapter 17

INNOCENCE

§ 17.01 OVERVIEW

[A] What is Innocence?

The question, "What is innocence?" is a seemingly obvious question. Yet, in the context of death penalty law, it can be a complex factual question involving even more difficult questions about appropriate relief.[1] *Factual or actual innocence* is when a defendant claims he is *innocent of the crime*.[2] The defendant claims he did not commit the capital offense for which he is charged, convicted, and sentenced to death. While this concept is easy to understand, the difficulty lies in the complex legal standards required for a defendant to get a hearing to prove his innocence.

[B] Facts and Figures

The evidence over the last few years shows that innocent people are being sentenced to death.[3] Since 1973,[4] 140 men and women have been released from death rows in more than 25 states based upon evidence of their innocence.[5] These exonerations have given rise to a new measure often cited for evaluating the death penalty — the ratio of the number of exonerations to the number of executions.

---

[1] *See* Richard Rosen, *Innocence and Death*, 82 N.C. L. Rev. 61, 73 (2003), for an in-depth discussion of the intersection between innocence and the death penalty. *See also* Randall Coyne, *Dead Wrong in Oklahoma*, 42 Tulsa L. Rev. 209 (2006) (for the compelling story of three men who were convicted and sentenced to die by lethal injection in Oklahoma and only many years later to finally be exonerated) John Grisham, The Innocent Man: Murder and Injustice in a Small Town (2006), Scott Christianson, Innocent: Inside Wrongful Conviction Cases (NYU Press 2004); Stanley Cohen, The Wrong Men:America's Epidemic of Wrongful Death Row Convictions (Carroll and Graf 2003) Alan Berlow, *The Wrong Man*, The Atlantic Monthly, Nov. 1999.

[2] There is a second concept sometimes referred to as *innocent of the death penalty*. This is when a defendant is not eligible for a sentence of death. *See* Chapter 8, *supra*; Ellen Kreitzberg & Linda Carter, *Innocent of a Capital Crime: Parallels Between Innocence of a Crime and Innocence of the Death Penalty*, 42 Tulsa L. Rev. 437 (2006). *See also* Section 15.03[C], *supra*.

[3] Samuel R. Gross, Kristen Jacoby, Daniel J. Matheson, Nicholas Montgomery & Sujata Patil, *Exonerations in the United States 1989 through 2003*, 95 J. Crim. L. & Criminology 523 (2005).

[4] In 1972, the Supreme Court struck down the death penalty as unconstitutional in the case of *Furman v. Georgia*, 408 U.S. 238 (1972). Following that decision, legislatures around the country passed new death penalty statutes and began to sentence people to death again. This marks the beginning of what is known as the modern death penalty era. *See* Chapter 6, *supra*.

[5] The states with the highest numbers of exonerations: Florida with 23, Illinois with 20, Texas with 12, Oklahoma with 10, and Arizona and Louisiana both have 8. *See* Death Penalty Information Center http://www.deathpenaltyinfo.org/documents/FactSheet.pdf (last visited on October 11, 2011).

Nationally, that number has stayed fairly constant at one exoneration to nine executions.[6] However, some states have a far more troubling ratio. For example, in 2003, Illinois had 13 death row exonerations and 12 executions.[7] Pennsylvania's ratio was 6 exonerations for 3 executions.[8]

An examination of the cases of those who have been exonerated gives rise to more questions than answers. There is no particular pattern to these cases or similarity among the defendants. Those who were wrongfully convicted and sentenced to death include those with extensive prior criminal records and those who had never been arrested prior to the capital charge.[9] The methods by which the 140 persons were exonerated also varied. Slightly over 12 percent[10] were released on the basis of DNA evidence and testing.[11] Others were proven innocent based upon the work of Northwestern University undergraduate journalism students.[12] Still others had their innocence established through the work of movie

---

[6] The exact numbers are 140 exonerations to 1279 executions. Taken from http://www. deathpenaltyinfo.org/documents/FactSheet.pdf (last visited on January 31, 2012).

[7] On January 31, 2000, former Governor George Ryan declared a moratorium in Illinois citing the troubling number of death row exonerations as an impetus for the action. *See* Steve Mills & Ken Armstrong, *Chicagoland Final Edition*, CHI. TRIB., Jan. 31, 2000, at 1. In 2011, the Illinois legislature passed and Governor Quinn signed into law the abolition of the death penalty.

[8] Robert Moran and Lou Yi, *Pa. Death Penalty Faces Protested at Independence Hall Against the State Death Penalty*, PHILA. INQUIRER, Apr. 14, 2007, at B05.

[9] For example, Madison Hobley, who was exonerated in 2003 as part of Governor Ryan's clearing of death row, had no criminal record prior to his arrest and wrongful conviction. Conversely, Rudolph Holton, who was released from Florida's death row in January of 2003, had prior convictions for burglary and various drug-related offenses. Death Penalty Information Center, Innocence Cases: 1994-2003, http://www.deathpenaltyinfo.org/article.php?did=2340 (last visited February 11, 2012).

Cory Maye who was exonerated in 2011 had no criminal record prior to his arrest and wrongful conviction for the death of a police officer. *See* http://www.huffingtonpost.com/2011/07/22/cory-maye-radley-balko-live-chat_n_907120.html (last visited November 2, 2011).

Michael Roy Toney was exonerated in 2009 had prior convictions for burglary. *See* Alex Branch, *Death Row inmate whose conviction was overturned maintains that he is innocent, Overturned conviction revives inmate's claim of innocence, victims' pain from 23 years ago* STAR TELEGRAM http:// truthinjustice.org/toney.htm (last visited November 2, 2011).

[10] In 17 out of 140 exonerations, which is 12.1%, DNA played a substantial factor in establishing innocence. http://www.deathpenaltyinfo.org/innocence-list-those-freed-death-row (last visited January 31, 2012).

[11] Earl Washington of Virginia, and Ray Krone of Arizona were released after 19 years and 11 years respectively as a result of DNA testing. See WELSH S. WHITE, LITIGATING in the SHADOW of DEATH: DEFENSE ATTORNEYS in CAPITAL CASES (University of Michigan Press) (2005), for a full account of Earl Washington's case. After Governor Gilmore's pardon, the Chief prosecutor in Earl Washington's case continued to believe that he played a role in the murder. *Id.* at 38 n.10. Michael Blair of Texas was released after 13.5 years as a result of DNA testing. *See* Innocence Project http://www.innocenceproject.org/Content/ Michael_Blair.php (last visited November 1, 2011). Kennedy Brewer of Mississippi who was convicted for the rape and murder of his girlfriend's three year old daughter, was released after 12 years as a result of DNA testing. *See* Death Penalty Information Center http://www.deathpenaltyinfo.org/innocence-cases-2004-present#137-138 (last visited November 1, 2011).

[12] Anthony Porter of Illinois was released after a group of Northwestern University journalism students, working with a private investigator, proved that Porter was innocent, and obtained a videotaped confession from the actual murderer. Alan Berlow, *The Wrong Man*, THE ATLANTIC MONTHLY, Nov. 1999, at 66.

directors or producers.[13]

As with every issue surrounding the death penalty, there is a great deal of controversy about the accuracy of many of the claims of innocence.[14] Many pro-death penalty organizations and supporters have disputed both the number and the validity of these "exonerations" and have countered that many on the list of "innocents" were falsely exonerated and not actually innocent.[15] Other scholars have argued that there are risks associated with any justice system, and that we should accept that risk of error.[16] Supreme Court Justice Antonin Scalia wrote, "This court has never held that the Constitution forbids the execution of a convicted defendant who has had a full and fair trial but is later able to convince a habeas court that he is 'actually' innocent."[17]

The debate over the number of innocent persons released from death rows continues. While it does, more exonerations occur. What all of this will mean in the larger death penalty debate remains to be seen. As a legal matter, the question of what it means to be innocent and the legal consequences of a finding of innocence must be addressed.

[C]   Direct Appeal and Claims of Innocence

When a defendant is arrested, charged with a crime and claims he is innocent, he has the opportunity to go to trial, present evidence and prove his innocence to a jury. However, there are cases where a defendant is convicted and sentenced to

---

[13] Randall Dale Adams of Texas was sentenced to death for the murder of a Dallas police officer. His exoneration was due in large part to interest by a movie director. The movie, THE THIN BLUE LINE (Miramax Films 1988) tells the story of his arrest, conviction, and ultimate exoneration. Adams was released in 1989 after spending 13 years in prison. The 2010 movie, CONVICTION, highlights the real life story of Betty Ann Waters who became an attorney to assist her wrongfully convicted brother. After 18 years of work, Waters obtained her brother's freedom and a civil award for wrongful conviction.

[14] HUGO ADAM BEDAU, MICHAEL L. RADELET & CONSTANCE E. PUTNAM, IN SPITE OF INNOCENCE, (Northeastern University Press) (May 1994); Gross, *supra*, note 3.

[15] *See* Ward A. Campbell, *Critique of DPIC List of "Innocence" Freed from Death Row*, http://www.prodeathpenalty.com/DPIC.htm (last visited February 11, 2012). Ward Campbell, Supervising Attorney General for the State of California, lamented the lack of perspective exhibited by the concern for innocents on death row. He posited that the true comparison should be between the "true innocents," who are brutally murdered in their homes, with the remote possibility that an innocent person may be executed despite the most elaborate protracted and sympathetic legal review procedures in the world. In 1985, Kirk Bloodsworth was sentenced to death for the rape and murder of a nine year old girl in Maryland. In 1993, new testing eliminated Bloodsworth as a suspect, and he was exonerated in 1994. Despite the exoneration, the Maryland attorney general was unwilling to clear Bloodsworth's name saying "I believe that he is not guilty. I am not prepared to say that he is innocent." Ultimately the DNA was matched to the actual perpetrator who was charged with this offense. *See* Dan Rodricks, *Bloodsworth and prosecutor to move on to new things*, The Baltimore Sun, http://articles.baltimoresun.com/2009-12-07/news/bal-rodricksonlinedec07_1_bloodsworth-case-mr-bloodsworth-dna-testing (last visited January 31, 2012) Tim Junkin, Bloodsworth: *The True Story of the First Death Row Inmate Exonerated by DNA*, (Shannon Ravenel Books 2004).

[16] Ernest van den Haag, *Why Capital Punishment?*, 54 ALB. L. REV. 501, 512 (1990) (noting this liability to grave error [of executing those who might be innocent] does not outweigh the deterrence or moral benefits of the death penalty).

[17] In re Troy Anthony Davis 557 U.S. ___, 130 S.Ct. 1, 3 (2009).

death, but still maintains that he is innocent of the crime.[18] At this point, his legal recourse is complicated because the question of his guilt or innocence has already been decided once by a jury. He is not automatically entitled to a second trial on the mere assertion that he is innocent.

After a conviction and sentence of death, a defendant's first appeal is called a direct appeal.[19] On direct appeal a defendant raises claims of legal errors that occurred during trial. The court, on appeal, does not directly reevaluate whether or not a defendant is guilty or innocent. Nonetheless, the issue of innocence frequently becomes part of the court's analysis on appeal. For example, a defendant may claim that his lawyer was ineffective at trial.[20] In order to prevail on this claim, a defendant has to show not only that his lawyer's performance was deficient, he must also show prejudice that the deficiencies affected the outcome of the case.[21] In order to evaluate whether a defendant was prejudiced at the guilt phase of a trial by his lawyer's failings, a court will look at the evidence of the defendant's guilt or innocence.

A defendant may also claim that a prosecutor failed to disclose potentially exculpatory evidence.[22] Recently, prosecutorial misconduct has been the subject of many internet articles, news stories, and reports.[23] In 2011, a group of former state prisoners sued the prosecutors and prosecutor's office in New Orleans for *Brady* violations; they argued that the prosecutor failed to turn over exculpatory evidence to the defense. When a court evaluates a claim of prosecutorial misconduct, it looks to see whether the evidence would have affected the outcome of the case.[24] In doing so, a court has to evaluate the strength of the evidence of guilt or innocence of a defendant. Despite these avenues where questions of innocence are raised, a court on direct appeal never directly reevaluates the factual guilt or innocence of a defendant.

---

[18] Rosen, *supra* note 1.

[19] *See* Section 14.01, *supra*.

[20] *See* Chapter 16, *supra*.

[21] See Chapter 16, *supra*. *See also* Strickland v. Washington 466 U.S. 668 (1984).

[22] Brady v. Maryland, 373 U.S. 83 (1963). The suppression by the prosecution of evidence favorable to an accused upon request violates due process where the evidence is material either to guilt or to punishment, irrespective of the good faith or bad faith of the prosecution.

[23] *See* PREVENTABLE ERROR: A REPORT ON PROSECUTORIAL MISCONDUCT IN CALIFORNIA, 1997-2009 by Kathleen M. Ridolfi and Maurice Possley, available at http://www.veritasinitiative.org/our-work/ prosecutorial-misconduct/pm-preventable-error-a-report-on-prosecutorial-misconduct-in-california/ pm-research-report-highlights/#download/. *See* Editorial from the New York Times, *Justice and Prosecutorial Misconduct* published on December 28, 2011. *See* http://www.nytimes.com/2011/12/29/ opinion/justice-and-prosecutorial-misconduct.html?_r=1 (last visited January 31, 2012). *See* Jack Leonard, *Report details prosecutorial misconduct, pushes for transparency*, LOS ANGELES TIMES, April 4, 2011, http://articles.latimes.com/2011/apr/04/local/la-me-prosecutor-misconduct-20110404 (last visited on January 31, 2012).

[24] Arizona v Youngblood 488 U.S. 51 (1988) (Court held no due process violation where police failed to preserve some semen samples for testing since it would not have changed the outcome of the case). Eighteen years later, Youngblood had other evidence tested with new DNA technology and it excluded Youngblood as the assailant. In August 2000, Youngblood was exonerated and released.

[D] Habeas Corpus and Claims of Innocence

When a defendant decides to raise a post-conviction claim of innocence, it is usually in federal court by filing a petition for a writ of habeas corpus.[25] A writ of habeas corpus is filed by a person in custody who claims that he is being held in prison in violation of the Constitution, federal law or treaty. In a habeas corpus proceeding, a defendant may ask a court to review evidence of his actual innocence.

There are numerous procedural rules and requirements that must be satisfied in order for a defendant to receive a hearing in federal court. Three of these limitations directly affect the filing of a claim of innocence; 1) procedural default,[26] 2) restrictions on second or successive habeas corpus petitions[27] and 3) limitations on the ability to present new evidence of innocence at an evidentiary hearing.[28]

Because evidence that supports a defendant's claim of innocence is often not discovered until years after the trial is over and a sentence of death has been imposed, claims of innocence are often filed years after a defendant has been sentenced to death.[29] At this point, a defendant has already begun, and in some case may have finished, litigation on his first habeas corpus petition. Over the years, Congress and the courts became increasingly concerned that prisoners, particularly in death penalty cases, were filing repeated petitions of habeas corpus seeking relief from the courts.[30] This led to a heightened concern for finality. Congress and the courts responded by fashioning procedural rules to limit the scope of habeas corpus review and to restrict the ability of a defendant to file a habeas corpus petition.[31]

---

[25] *See* Chapter 15, *supra.*

[26] If a habeas corpus petition fails to comply with a state procedural rule (i.e. time limits within which a petition must be filed), a defendant may be prevented from filing his claim. Kreitzberg and Carter, note 2, at 114-55, *supra.*

[27] A successive petition raises claims that are identical to those that have been heard and decided on the merits in a previous petition. *See supra* Chapter 15. Generally, a defendant is required to bring all claims in a single habeas corpus petition so that a second or successive petition may be barred by the court. Jordan Streiker, *Innocence and Federal Habeas*, 41 UCLA L. Rev. 303, 303-04 (1993); Kreitzberg & Carter, *supra*, note 6, at 115.

[28] A petitioner may be permitted to present evidence if he is granted a federal hearing. *Id.*

[29] For example, Timothy Howard and Gary Lamar James spent 26 years in prison in Ohio before using the Freedom of Information Act to gain access to conflicting witness statements and fingerprint evidence that was unavailable at the time of their trial in 1973. *See* Death Penalty Information Center, note 10, *supra.*

[30] John Scalia, U.S. Department of Justice, Office of Justice Programs, Bureau of Justice Statistics Special Report: Prisoner Petitions Filed in U.S. District Courts, 2000, with Trends 1980-2000 (January 2002), *available at* http://www.ojp.usdoj.gov/bjs/pub/pdf/ppfusd00.pdf. Although the Antiterrorism and Effective Death Penalty Act (AEDPA) was passed to limit the number of habeas petitions filed since the date of its enactment in 1996, the numbers have increased. Between 1995 and 2000, the total number of habeas corpus petitions filed increased from 20,958 to 31,556. *Id.* John H. Blume et. al., *In Defense of Noncapital Habeas: A Response to Hoffmann and King*, 96 Cornell L. Rev. 435 (2011).

[31] *See* Chapter 15, *supra*. In 1996. Congress passed the Antiterrorism and Effective Death Penalty Act (AEDPA), Pub. L. No. 104-132, 110 Stat. 1214 (1996). It addresses habeas corpus petitions in several ways including: 1) requiring inmates to exhaust direct appeals at the state level prior to filing a petition in federal court, 2) establishing a one year statute of limitations so that inmates have one year from the time their conviction becomes final (after all direct appeals of the conviction and/or sentence have been

Courts have struggled to find the appropriate balance between the often conflicting principles of finality and fairness, and to reach a consensus as to when a defendant is entitled to a hearing on innocence. The Court's commitment to finality places the emphasis on the trial as the main event and the place where questions of guilt or innocence are best resolved. At the same time, the Court has recognized that in appropriate cases, even the principle of finality must yield to fundamental fairness and the need to correct a fundamental miscarriage of justice. No one wants to sentence an innocent person to death. But, the courts have been divided on how best to correct such a sentence when it occurs.

[E] Freestanding Claim of Innocence v. Innocence as a Gateway Claim

There are two principal ways in which claims of innocence are raised in a habeas corpus petition. When a claim of innocence is raised as a substantive issue, it is called a *freestanding claim of innocence*. When an inmate files a petition alleging that he is factually innocent of the capital crime for which he was sentenced to death but acknowledges there were no constitutional violations before or during his trial, it is called a freestanding claim of innocence. When filed, a defendant is asking a court to re-evaluate the evidence of his guilt or innocence. Since a freestanding claim of actual innocence is based on the assumption that the trial was free of constitutional error, a reviewing court affords significant deference to the verdict and sentence imposed at trial. As a consequence, when a defendant raises a freestanding claim of innocence, he must make a *truly persuasive* showing of his innocence before he is entitled to a hearing.[32] Freestanding claims of innocence are discussed in Section 17.02[B], *below*.

A claim of innocence may also be used as a procedural device that allows a court to review a defendant's constitutional claim that is otherwise barred from being heard in court.[33] A defendant who raises both a claim of innocence and an underlying constitutional violation at trial is required to make a *lesser* showing of innocence than a defendant who raises a freestanding claim of innocence in order to get a hearing. With an allegation of constitutional error at trial, courts afford less respect to the trial and its verdict. These claims of innocence are used as a *gateway* to allow a court to review an underlying constitutional violation. Once a

---

exhausted) to file a habeas petition in Federal Court. A court will ordinarily not reach the merits of a successive petition absent of showing of cause and prejudice. Wainwright v. Sykes, 433 U.S. 72 (1977). *See* Section 15.03, *supra*.

[32] House v. Bell 547 U.S. 518 (2006) House raised both a freestanding claim of innocence and innocence as a gateway claim. Herrera v. Collins, 506 U.S. 390 (1993). Caroline Livett, 28 U.S.C. S 2254(j): Freestanding Innocence As A Ground for Habeas Relief: Time for Congress to Answer the Court's Embarrassing Question, 14 Lewis & Clark L. Rev. 1649 (2010). David R. Dow et. al., *Is It Constitutional to Execute Someone Who Is Innocent (and If It Isn't, How Can It Be Stopped Following House v. Bell)?*, 42 Tulsa L. Rev. 277 (2006).

[33] A claim of innocence may be barred based on a finding of procedural default, restrictions on the filing of a second or successive petition, or failure to comply with the limitations on evidentiary hearings. In *Maples v. Thomas*, the Supreme Court held that post-conviction attorneys' abandonment of Maples in state court was good cause to excuse procedural default in federal court and allow Maples to pursue his claim. Maples v. Thomas, 132 S. Ct. 912 (U.S. 2012).

defendant makes a sufficient showing of innocence, he passes through the gateway and is permitted to present his constitutional claims to the court.[34] A defendant must present enough evidence of innocence to show that refusing to allow him to present his claims in habeas would be a *miscarriage of justice*.[35] Innocence as a "gateway" claim is discussed in Section 17.02[C], *below*.

While most people agree that executing an innocent person is not acceptable, there is no unanimity on how to ensure this does not occur. There is also disagreement as to the extent of the problem of "innocence" in death penalty cases.[36] The courts and the legislatures continue to struggle to balance the competing interests of finality and fairness. They must find a way to ensure that a truly innocent person gets a hearing in federal court while keeping the door closed to the many who are not.

§ 17.02   INNOCENT OF THE CRIME

[A]   Is it Unconstitutional to Execute an Innocent Person?

Suppose ten years after an inmate is sentenced to death, he files a petition for habeas corpus. Instead of claiming that various constitutional errors occurred at the trial, D makes only one claim — that he is factually innocent of the charge and would like a hearing in federal court to present the new evidence he now has to prove it. Is innocence, by itself, enough to entitle D to a hearing to present his evidence? Is it unconstitutional to execute D if he is innocent of the crime? These questions were raised in *Herrera v. Collins*.[37]

The Court voted 6-3 to deny Herrera a hearing in federal court. They held he was not entitled to present his evidence of innocence to the court to be evaluated and reviewed.[38] Chief Justice Rehnquist, writing for the Court, emphasized the Court's concern for federalism and finality. Federalism dictated that the federal courts defer to the state system (even though Herrera had no additional state court review), and finality dictated that federal courts defer to the trial verdict, where questions of guilt and innocence were best resolved. In a constitutionally fair trial,

---

[34] *Herrera*, 506 U.S. at 404. House v. Bell 547 U.S. 518 at 537.

[35] *Id.* at 409.

[36] Kansas v. Marsh 126 S. Ct. 2516 (2006). Justice Scalia rejects the dissent's concern with executing the innocent and argues, "It should be noted at the outset that the dissent does not discuss a single case — not one — in which it is clear that a person was executed for a crime he did not commit. If such an event had occurred in recent years, we would not have to hunt for it; the innocent's name would be shouted from the rooftops by the abolition lobby . . . . *Id.* at 2533. Like other human institutions, courts and juries are not perfect. One cannot have a system of criminal punishment without accepting the possibility that someone will be punished mistakenly . . . . But with regard to the punishment of death in the current American system, that possibility has been reduced to an insignificant minimum. *Id.* at 2539.

[37] *Herrera*, 506 U.S. at 390. In *House v. Bell*, 547 U.S. 518(2006) House alleged both a free standing claim of innocence as well as innocence as a gateway to the underlying constitutional violations. *See* Section 17.02[B][2].

[38] This evidence was not presented to the jury during Herrera's trial, but was discovered subsequent to his conviction and sentence of death.

the Court reasoned, Herrera was convicted and sentenced to death.

Rehnquist underscored that the purpose of a writ of habeas corpus was not to review the evidence presented at trial independent of a separate constitutional claim. Generally, habeas corpus petitions must claim a violation of the Constitution, federal law, or a treaty.[39] Therefore, a claim of actual innocence, Rehnquist wrote, without an allegation of a specific constitutional violation, does not *necessarily* entitle a defendant to a hearing in federal court. He concluded that few rulings would be more disruptive of our federal system than to provide for federal habeas review of freestanding claims of actual innocence.[40] The Court was concerned that if they provided a death row prisoner the right to apply for habeas review solely on the grounds of innocence, numerous habeas petitions would be filed by death row inmates long after their cases had undergone an initial review by the federal courts.

The Court was splintered on the more fundamental question raised in *Herrera:* Was it unconstitutional to execute a factually innocent person? Two Justices held it was not. Justices Scalia and Thomas were unequivocal that no constitutional violation occurs if an innocent person is executed. Scalia argued that the Constitution requires that a defendant be afforded certain procedures and processes during his criminal trial. When these constitutional minimums are satisfied, the Constitution is satisfied. The question of *injustice*, Scalia reasoned, is different from the question of *constitutionality*:

> There is no basis in text, tradition or even in contemporary practice, for finding in the Constitution a right to demand judicial consideration of newly discovered evidence of innocence brought forward after conviction . . . . I can understand, . . . the reluctance of the present Court to admit publicly that Our Perfect Constitution lets stand any injustice, much less the execution of an innocent man who has received, though to no avail, all the process that our society has traditionally deemed adequate.[41]

Chief Justice Rehnquist never directly answered this question. Instead, he assumed, for purposes of deciding Herrera's case, that it *was* unconstitutional to execute an innocent person. He found, however, that Herrera failed to make a sufficient showing that he was innocent and was not, therefore, entitled to a

---

[39] 22 U.S.C. § 2254(a) (2006).

[40] *Herrera*, 506 U.S. at 390. Justice Rehnquist wrote, "We may assume, for the sake of argument in deciding this case, that in a capital case a truly persuasive demonstration of "actual innocence" made after trial would render the execution of a defendant unconstitutional, and warrant federal habeas relief if there were no state avenue open to process such a claim. But because of the very disruptive effect that entertaining claims of actual innocence would have on the need for finality in capital cases, and the enormous burden that having to retry cases based on often stale evidence would place on the States, the threshold showing for such an assumed right would necessarily be extraordinarily high". Herrera, 506 at 417.

[41] *Id.* at 428 (Scalia, J., concurring). "This Court has never held that the Constitution forbids the execution of a convicted defendant who has had a full and fair trial but it is later able to convince a habeas court that he is 'actually' innocent." In re Davis, 557 U.S. ___, 130 S. Ct. 1, 3 (2009) (mem.) (Scalia, J., dissenting).

hearing.[42]

Six justices ultimately agreed that it was unconstitutional to execute an innocent person. They took very different positions on the showing needed for a defendant to be entitled to present his evidence of innocence in a habeas corpus proceeding. Three of the six justices (Justices O'Connor, Kennedy, and White) voted to deny Herrera a hearing, finding that he had not met the requisite burden of proof (without specifying what the burden was). According to O'Connor, Herrera was an individual who received a fair trial, was properly convicted and, after ten years, still refused to accept the verdict, continuing to seek another judicial proceeding to have his guilt determined yet again.[43] Justice White made clear that Herrera had not made a truly persuasive showing of his innocence to entitle him to a hearing.[44]

The last three justices (Justices Blackmun, Stevens, and Souter) voted in dissent to grant Herrera a hearing. Justice Blackmun characterized the execution of a person who can show that that he was innocent as "perilously close to murder."[45] With uncharacteristic bluntness, the dissent argued that the Supreme Court's first priority must be to ensure that each state's death penalty scheme is administered in a fair and constitutional manner.[46] This responsibility, they argued, must trump even the need for finality. The dissent urged the Court to acknowledge that a constitutionally perfect trial could still result in a conviction and sentence of death to an innocent person. When this happens, they reasoned, the Constitution must provide an opportunity for that defendant to prove his innocence.

[B] Freestanding Claims of Actual Innocence

[1] *Herrera v. Collins*

In *Herrera*, the Court distinguished between freestanding claims of actual innocence and claims of innocence that are linked to constitutional violations that tainted the trial. Herrera raised only a freestanding claim of innocence and alleged

---

[42] *Id.* Herrera was executed in Texas on May 12, 1993.

[43] *Id.* at 419 (O'Connor, J., concurring). "In petitioner's case, that paramount event occurred 10 years ago. He was tried before a jury of his peers, with the full panoply of protections that our Constitution affords criminal defendants. At the conclusion of that trial, the jury found petitioner guilty beyond a reasonable doubt. Petitioner therefore does not appear before us as an innocent man on the verge of execution. He is instead a legally guilty one who, refusing to accept the jury's verdict, demands a hearing in which to have his culpability determined once again."

[44] *Id.* at 429 (White, J., concurring). "To be entitled to relief, however, petitioner would at the very least be required to show that based on proffered newly discovered evidence and the entire record before the jury that convicted him, 'no rational trier of fact could [find] proof of guilt beyond a reasonable doubt.' " *Id.* at 420 (citation omitted). For the reasons stated in the Court's opinion, petitioner's showing falls far short of satisfying even that standard, and I therefore concur in the judgment."

[45] "In voting to affirm, I assume that a persuasive showing of 'actual innocence' made after trial . . . would render unconstitutional the execution [of Herrera] in this case." *Id.* at 429 (Blackmun, J., dissenting).

[46] *Herrera*, 506 U.S. at 404. In striking this balance [between "the State's interest in the finality of its criminal judgments and the prisoner's interest in access to a forum to test the basic justice of his sentence"], the Court adopted the view of Judge Friendly that there should be an exception to the concept of finality when a prisoner can make a colorable claim of actual innocence.

that although his trial was fundamentally fair, he was innocent of the crime. Chief Justice Rehnquist argued that there was no historical basis in habeas corpus jurisprudence that provided a constitutional right to a hearing *solely* on a freestanding claim of actual innocence. Nonetheless, Rehnquist assumed, for purposes only of deciding *Herrera*, that the execution of a truly innocent person would be unconstitutional and that some standard must be set to determine when this *hypothetically* innocent defendant is entitled to a hearing. Chief Justice Rehnquist posited that a defendant may get a hearing in federal court on a freestanding claim of actual innocence only if he can make a *truly persuasive* showing of innocence.[47] In addition, Rehnquist argued, this person must also show there are no state avenues available to present this claim.[48] Rehnquist found that Herrera failed in both respects.

The Court provided little guidance as to what a *truly persuasive* showing of innocence would include, except to say that this threshold would necessarily be *extraordinarily* high. The cases seem to turn on the specific facts presented.[49]

Herrera argued that he had no state remedy because Texas law allowed only sixty days from the date of judgment for a defendant to file a motion for a new trial. More than eight years had passed since he had been sentenced to death. Although Rehnquist acknowledged that Texas law barred Herrera from filing any motion in state court, he found he had a state remedy based on Herrera's right to file a clemency petition with the governor.[50] Clemency, Rehnquist argued, was designed to provide exactly this type of fail-safe mechanism and ensure that a miscarriage of justice does not occur. At the clemency hearing, he added, Herrera could present his evidence of innocence for the governor to review.[51]

The effect of *Herrera* was to virtually close the door on a defendant's ability to obtain habeas corpus relief on a freestanding claim of actual innocence. Defendants have been unable to meet their burden of a "truly persuasive showing of inno-

---

[47] *Id.* at 417.

[48] *Id.* at 417.

[49] House v. Bell, 547 U.S. 518 (2006); Stafford v. Saffle, 34 F.3d 1557 (10th Cir. 1994), *cert. denied*. 514 U.S. 1099 (1995) (noting that the federal court found that Stafford failed to meet the extraordinarily high showing of actual innocence and that his evidence only raised *questions* about his guilt). Noel v. Norris, 322 F.3d 500, 504 (8th Cir. 2003), *reh'g denied*, 2003 U.S. App. LEXIS 8443 (8th Cir. 2003). This extraordinarily high showing only applies to freestanding claims of actual innocence, not to newly discovered mitigating evidence and ensuing challenges to the imposition of the death penalty. *See also* Tania Nelson, *House v. Bell: A Second Chance for Procedurally Barred Claims*, 8 Loy. J. Pub. Int. L 225 (2007). Andre Mathis, *A Critical Analysis of Actual Innocence After House v. Bell: Has the Riddle of Actual Innocence Finally Been Solved?*, 37 U. Mem. L. Rev. 813, 814 (2007).

[50] *See* Section 18.03, *infra*.

[51] Very few clemency petitions are granted in Texas where state law requires 18 members of the parole board to recommend clemency before a governor may grant a petition. From 1995-2001, 68 death row inmates in Texas have asked for clemency and only once has the Texas Board of Pardon and Paroles granted it. Sara Rimer, *Pending Execution in Texas Spotlights a Powerful Board*, N.Y. Times, June 21, 2000, at A1. In Georgia, clemency may be granted only by the Board of Pardon and Parole. In the case of Troy Davis, the defense presented the Board with affidavits from seven of the nine witnesses whose original trial testimony had identified Davis as the murderer, but who now had changed or recanted their previous testimony. The Board denied Davis clemency and he was executed on September 21, 2011 amid extensive controversy of his guilt or innocence.

cence,"[52] Even when they do, most defendants, like Herrera, still have the opportunity to petition for clemency, which, according to Justice Rehnquist, provides an adequate remedy and forecloses their ability to get into federal court.

The decision in *Herrera* was controversial and generated a great deal of attention and criticism.[53] From 1972 until 1993 when *Herrera* was decided, 52 former death row inmates had been exonerated or acquitted (an average of 2-3 per year).[54] In the 14 years since *Herrera*, approximately another 72 have been exonerated. This is double the previous rate. At the time *Herrera* was decided, the question of a factually innocent defendant was a far more remote possibility than it is today. It was more than twelve years after *Herrera* before the Court addressed this issue again.

[2]　*House v. Bell*[55]

Twelve years after *Herrera* was decided, Paul House argued to the Supreme Court that he should be granted relief based upon his freestanding claim of actual innocence.[56] House urged the Court to finally articulate the standard to apply when Courts review freestanding claims of innocence. In *Herrera*, the Court declined to articulate a test and suggested, without deciding, that any showing would have to be "extraordinarily high."[57] House argued that the lower courts need guidance on how to assess claims of innocence. To underscore this need, House pointed out that no federal habeas petitioner has ever succeeded in obtaining relief for a free standing claim of actual innocence,[58] that lower courts are applying different standards when they review these claims,[59] and some courts even question whether these claims provide a basis for relief at all.[60] Finally, House argued that the numerous exonerations that had occurred in the years since *Herrera* was decided underscore

---

[52] *House*, 547 U.S. at 518; *Stafford*, 34 F.3d at 1557.

[53] Editorial, *Lethal Expediency*, THE PROGRESSIVE, March, 1993, at 10. "The U.S. Supreme Court has plunged to a new depth of barbarity surprising even to its harshest critics." Editorial, Nat Hentoff, *When Guilt or Innocence 'Doesn't Matter,'* THE WASH. POST, Feb. 12, 1993, at A31. "I would expect that Thurgood Marshall would have vigorously disagreed. Like William Brennan, Marshall often cited 'the evolving standards of decency that mark the progress of a maturing society.' But when the Supreme Court utterly disregards the probable innocence of a man sentenced to death, that as Justice Harry Blackmun said in dissent comes 'perilously close to simple murder.' "

[54] The Supreme Court found the death penalty unconstitutional in 1972 in *Furman v. Georgia*, 408 U.S. 238 (1972), and upheld new death penalty statutes in 1976 in a series of cases, including *Gregg v. Georgia*, 428 U.S. 153 (1976).

[55] *House*, 547 U.S. at 518.

[56] Brief of the Petitioner-Appellant at 31-32, House v. Bell, No. 04-8990 (6th Cir. Jan. 4, 2006), 2006 WL 26089. *See also* David R. Dow, Jared Tyler, Francis Bourliot, Jennifer Jeans, *Is it Constitutional to Execute Someone Who is Innocent (And if it Isn't, How Can it Be Stopped Following House v. Bell)* 42 TULSA L. REV. 277 (2006).

[57] *Herrera*, 506 U.S. at 429 (White, J., concurring).

[58] Brief of the Petitioner-Appellant, note 56, at 33, *supra.*

[59] Carriger v. Stewart, 132 F. 3d 463, 476 (9th Cir. 1997) (noting that a habeas petitioner asserting a freestanding innocence claim must go beyond demonstrating doubt about his guilt and must affirmatively prove that he is probably innocent).

[60] Royal v. Taylor, 188 F.3d 239, 243 (4th Cir. 1999) (noting that *Herrera* held that a claim of actual innocence alone is not a basis for habeas relief); Lucas v. Johnson, 132 F.3d 1069, 1075 (5th Cir.1998)

the need for courts to have a framework from which to review claims of innocence.[61]

The Supreme Court in *House* declined to articulate any specific test to evaluate a freestanding claim of actual innocence. Writing for the Court, Justice Kennedy stated, "We conclude here, much as in *Herrera*, that whatever burden a hypothetical freestanding innocence claim would require, this petitioner has not satisfied it."[62] The Court observed that earlier decisions seem to imply there is a higher burden for a freestanding claim of innocence than is required for a claim of innocence as a "gateway" claim.[63] The Court in *House* then reasoned that since they found House's "gateway" claim was "a close one," his showing clearly fell short for a free standing claim of innocence. If *Herrera* appeared to close the door on freestanding claims of innocence, then *House* failed to pry it open. House presented significant evidence of innocence, which was still deemed insufficient by the Court to entitle him to pursue a free standing claim of actual innocence.[64]

[C] Innocence as a Gateway to Consideration of Constitutional Error

The more typical scenario for claims of actual innocence occurs when claims of innocence are used as a "gateway" or threshold to obtain review of constitutional violations that occurred during the trial. When this occurs, the test from *Herrera* no longer applies. Instead, the Court applies a lesser standard than *Herrera's* exceptionally high or "truly persuasive" showing.

Suppose D is convicted and sentenced to death. In a second habeas petition, D claims that he was factually innocent. D also argues that there were two constitutional violations at his trial. He claimed that his lawyer was ineffective and that the government withheld significant exculpatory evidence at trial. D would like a hearing in federal court to prove his claims. The prosecutor argues the claims are barred and cannot be heard because they were not raised earlier in state court.

(noting that *Herrera* does not overrule previous holding . . . that a claim of actual innocence based on newly discovered evidence fails to state a claim in federal habeas corpus).

[61] From 1999-2010 there were 69 exonerations from death row. *See* Death Penalty Information Center, *supra* note 5. *See* http://www.deathpenaltyinfo.org/innocence-and-death-penalty (last visited January 31, 2012).

[62] *House*, 547 U.S. at 553 (citing *Herrera*, 506 U.S. at 417).

[63] Schlup v. Delo, 513 US 298 (1995). *See* Section 17.02[C] (discussing when claims of innocence are used as a "gateway" to obtain review of other constitutional violations that occurred at trial).

[64] House presented significant evidence in support of his innocence including a DNA test showing that the semen found on the victim's clothes belonged to the victim's husband, not to House; credible forensic evidence to show that the blood stains on Mr. House's jeans, identified as the victim's blood, came from blood collected from the victim during the autopsy and not from blows that were inflicted during her attack; and new testimonial evidence implicating the victim's husband in the murder. *House*, 547 U.S. at 557 (Roberts, C.J., dissenting)."The new body of evidence as a whole so completely undermines the case against House and establishes a persuasive case against Muncey that, had it been presented at trial, no rational juror could have found evidence sufficient for conviction. The new evidence so completely turns the case around that the proof is no longer constitutionally sufficient to warrant a conviction or imposition of the death penalty. Thus House should be immediately released." *House v. Bell*, 386 F.3d 668, 708 (6th Cir. 2004) *rev'd and remanded*, 547 U.S. 518 (2006). House's petition for relief was granted, and he was released from prison several months later.

This issue was raised in *Schlup v. Delo*.[65]

When a defendant like Schlup raises these claims for the first time in federal court, he is usually procedurally barred from having a hearing unless he falls within one of two exceptions. A defendant must show either 1) cause and prejudice for the failure to raise the claim, *or* 2) that a fundamental miscarriage of justice will result.[66] Schlup argued that his claim of innocence placed him squarely within the *miscarriage of justice* exception. His claim of innocence, Schlup argued, was like a *gateway* through which he could pass to have his otherwise barred constitutional claims considered on the merits. Schlup argued that once he made his showing of innocence, the court had to review his other constitutional claims as well.

Again, the Supreme Court was divided on how to balance both finality and fairness when evaluating claims of actual innocence. This time, the Court held 5-4 that a defendant who claims both innocence *and* a constitutional error at trial must show only that it is *more likely than not* that no reasonable juror would have found the defendant guilty beyond a reasonable doubt.[67] The Court held that Schlup met that standard and granted him a hearing.

The rule in *Schlup* was thrown into question when Congress amended the Habeas Corpus statute in 1996 with the Anti-terrorism and Effective Death Penalty Act. (AEDPA).[68] Although AEDPA did not directly address how a court

---

[65] *Schlup*, 513 U.S. at 298. Schlup's first petition was filed in 1989. Schlup v. Armontrout, No 89-0020C(3), 1989 U.S. Dist. LEXIS 18285, at *1-2 (E.D. Mo May 31, 1989). His second writ was filed in 1993. Schlup v. Delo, 11 F.3d 738 (8th Cir. 1993). Schlup argued that he was factually innocent, his lawyer was ineffective, and that the government had failed to disclose exculpatory evidence at his trial.

[66] *See* Section 15.03[C], *supra*. The Courts have equated the miscarriage of justice exception with actual innocence, and have held that this narrow exception allows an otherwise barred claim to be heard where a defendant makes an adequate showing of innocence. Kreitzberg & Carter, note 2, at 115, *supra*. Jordan Steiker, *Innocence and Federal Habeas*, 41 UCLA L. Rev. 303, 338 (1993). "Injustice occurs if an innocent person remains in jail when the "hook" of a federal claim could provide the occasion for his release" Matthew J. Mueller, *Handling Claims of Actual Innocence: Rejecting Federal Habeas Corpus As the Best Avenue for Addressing Claims of Innocence Based on DNA Evidence*, 56 Cath. U. L. Rev. 227 (2006).

Sarah A. Mourer, *Gateway to Justice: Constitutional Claims to Actual Innocence*, 64 U. Miami L. Rev. 1279 (2010).

[67] *Schlup*, 513 U.S. at 321. In 1999, Schlup pled guilty to second-degree murder and was sentenced to life imprisonment. Tim O'Neil, *Killer Who Escaped Execution Over New Evidence Pleads Guilty*, St. Louis Post-Dispatch, March 25, 1999, at A15.

[68] By adopting the probability standard the court returned to an earlier test set out in *Murray v. Carrier*, 477 U.S. 478, 496 (1986). However, the AEDPA rejected this test and required a defendant to show by clear and convincing evidence that no juror would have found him guilty beyond a reasonable doubt. *See supra* [Section] 15.03[C]; Antiterrorism and Effective Death Penalty Act of 1996, Pub. L. No. 104-132, § 735, 110 Stat. 1214 (1996). The AEDPA amendments included an "innocence proviso" as an exception to the general rules prohibiting second or successive petitions or the granting of an evidentiary hearing where the petitioner failed to develop the factual basis for the claim in state court. The exception for second or successive petitions requires a two-part showing: (A) the factual predicate for the claim could not have been discovered previously through the exercise of due diligence; and (B) the facts underlying the claim, if proven and viewed in light of the evidence as a whole, would be sufficient to establish by *clear and convincing evidence* that, but for constitutional error, no reasonable factfinder would have found the applicant guilty of the *underlying offense*. Kreitzberg & Carter, *supra*, note 2, at 117.

should review a claim that was procedurally defaulted, the government argued that *Schlup* no longer applied and these claims should be decided under AEDPA. This was significant because AEDPA had raised the standard of review for evidentiary hearings and successive petitions to require a showing of *clear and convincing evidence* before a court could review a claim. These questions were not resolved until a decade later in *House v. Bell.*[69]

The Supreme Court in *House* acknowledged that AEDPA did not specifically address claims that were procedurally defaulted. Since House's petition was his first federal habeas petition of a procedurally defaulted claim, AEDPA did not apply and *Schlup's* "preponderance" standard did apply.[70] The Court held that House presented sufficient evidence of innocence to allow his habeas petition to go forward for review even on the procedurally defaulted claims. The Court reaffirmed that *Schlup* recognized a "miscarriage of justice" exception to claims that have been deemed to be procedurally defaulted.

The Court in *House* underscored two important aspects of the "gateway" test set out in *Schlup*. First, a defendant is not required to demonstrate innocence with absolute certainty. Rather, a defendant must show that "in light of the new evidence, it is more likely than not that no reasonable juror would find the defendant guilty beyond a reasonable doubt".[71] Essentially, the role of the Court is to assess what the impact of the new evidence will be on potential jurors.

Second, the Court makes clear that a federal court reviewing the "gateway" claim must assess how reasonable jurors would react to the entire record in the case — both old and new evidence collectively.[72] A Court may not reject a claim simply by finding that there was sufficient evidence to support the outcome in the case.[73]

---

[69] *House*, 547 U.S. at 518.

[70] House filed a second state post conviction petition. The state Supreme Court held that his claims were barred under a state statute that provided that claims not raised in a prior post-conviction proceeding are presumptively waived. House v. State, 911 S.W. 2d 705 (Tenn. 1995). House filed a federal post conviction petition and was granted a hearing. The Federal District Court found that House had not demonstrated actual innocence under *Schlup* nor demonstrated that he was ineligible for the death penalty under *Sawyer*. The Court of Appeals affirmed this denial in an 8-7 split. Six dissenters argued that House was entitled to immediate release pursuant to his showing of actual innocence. House v. Bell, 386 F.3d 668 (6th Cir. 2004).

[71] Interestingly, Justice Kennedy goes on to clarify this test by stating, "to remove the double negative, that more likely than not any reasonable juror would have reasonable doubt." *House*, 126 S.Ct. At 2077.

[72] *House*, 547 U.S. ____ 126 S. Ct. at 2077. Schlup discusses three categories of new reliable evidence that can form the basis for a claim of actual innocence: exculpatory scientific evidence, trustworthy eyewitness accounts, and critical physical evidence. *Schlup*, 513 U.S. at 324.

[73] In this way, the Court distinguishes the gateway test from the test set out in *Jackson v. Virginia*, 443 U.S. 307 (1979), that is used to govern claims of insufficient evidence.

[D] The Effect of the Antiterrorism and Effective Death Penalty Act (AEDPA)

In 1996, Congress passed the Anti-Terrorism and Effective Death Penalty Act (AEDPA).[74] This legislation was designed to streamline the process of habeas corpus review, including limiting the filing of second or successive petitions[75] and restricting the availability of evidentiary hearings.[76] In addressing claims of innocence, AEDPA raised the showing required for a court to hear a second or successive habeas petition even when a claim of innocence is used as a gateway for an underlying constitutional claim. AEDPA rejected the "preponderance of the evidence" test of *Schlup*, and instead required defendants raising claims of innocence to show by *clear and convincing* evidence that but for the constitutional error, no reasonable fact-finder would have found the defendant guilty had the newly discovered evidence been presented at the original trial.[77]

AEDPA did not specifically address the standard courts should apply when deciding whether to hear a claim that has been procedurally defaulted. But with the passage of AEDPA, the status of *Schlup* was called into question.

The Court in *House* discusses when a court should apply the "gateway" test from *Schlup* (preponderance of the evidence) and when they should apply the stricter gateway test from AEDPA (clear and convincing). AEDPA applies in two distinct circumstances: 1) when a defendant seeks an evidentiary hearing on claims that were not fully developed in state court,[78] and 2) when a defendant files a second or successive federal petition for review of new claims.[79] AEDPA did not apply in House's case because House was seeking review in his first federal habeas petition for claims that were deemed to be procedurally defaulted.

§ 17.03   EVIDENCE OF INNOCENCE

[A] DNA Evidence

Although most of the exonerations from death row were supported by nonscientific evidence, it is DNA cases that captured the attention of the public. DNA cases act as a window, and allow us to examine the shortcomings and fallibility of our system in all cases, including those in which DNA is not present. From DNA cases, we know that factually innocent people have been arrested,

---

[74] *See* Section 15.03 *supra.*

[75] 28 U.S.C. § 2244(d)(1) (2007).

[76] 28 U.S.C. § 2254(e)(2) (2007).

[77] 28 U.S.C.A. § 2244(b)(2)(ii) (2007); *see* Section 15.04[B][1], *supra.*

[78] The Supreme Court in *House* noted that the District Court had already held an evidentiary hearing that was not challenged by the state. They, therefore, declined to elaborate on the test to apply when a defendant seeks a hearing. The Court only observed that *Schlup* provided that a court should "consider how the timing of the submission and the likely credibility of the affiants bear on the probable reliability of that evidence." *House*, 547 U.S. at 537 (quoting *Schlup*, 513 U.S. at 331-32).

[79] The applicable statutory provisions for those two types of claims are 28 U.S.C. Sections 2244(b)(2)(B)(ii) and 2254(e)(2).

convicted, and sentenced to death, that their cases have withstood state and federal court review, and in some cases, that the individuals have come perilously close to being executed. What DNA does not tell us is what went wrong in the system. It has, however, encouraged a more careful examination of the system in an effort to determine the causes of wrongful convictions.[80]

Since the death penalty was reinstated in 1976, there have been 140 exonerations in 26 states from death row.[81] It was not until the recent spate of exonerations based upon DNA evidence that any real debate about whether there are innocent persons on death row reached the forefront of public discourse. Although DNA evidence accounts for only slightly more than 12 percent of the total number of death row exonerations, it is these cases, instead of the many other exonerations, that are most frequently covered by the media.[82] DNA testing focuses solely on the question of "who did it" rather than more nuanced questions of a defendant's intent, motive, or other circumstances of the killing. When the exoneration is based upon DNA testing, few dispute that a defendant was actually innocent.[83]

What is DNA and how does it prove innocence? DNA (deoxyribonucleic acid) is the genetic material present in the cells of all living organisms. Structurally, about 99% of DNA is identical from one person to the next. However, there are certain regions of DNA that are different and make each person unique. It is this unique component of DNA that is useful as an identification tool in criminal investigations. These segments can be examined in labs and compared to other DNA samples to determine whether or not they match; that is, whether the DNA samples came

---

[80] *See* BARRY SCHECK, PETER NEUFELD, & JIM DWYER, ACTUAL INNOCENCE: 5 DAYS TO EXECUTION AND OTHER DISPATCHES FROM THE WRONGLY CONVICTED (Signet Books 2001), for a more in depth discussion on the causes of wrongful convictions. Scheck's book identifies several causes of wrongful conviction including: 1) mistaken eyewitness identification, 2) coerced confessions, 3) unreliable forensic work, 4) false testimony by jailhouse informants and other cooperating government witnesses, 5) law enforcement and/or prosecutorial misconduct, and/or 6) ineffective representation by counsel.

[81] David Keaton was the first exoneration from death row in 1973. http://www.deathpenaltyinfo.org/innocence-cases-1973-1983 (last visited January 31, 2012) Kirk Bloodsworth was the first person exonerated from death row through DNA testing. In 1993, he was convicted for the murder and rape of a 9 year old girl. Ten years later, DNA linked the man who occupied the cell directly above Bloodsworth as the true perpetrator. Tim Junkin, BLOODSWORTH: THE TRUE STORY OF THE FIRST DEATH ROW INMATE EXONERATED BY DNA (Shannon Ravenel Books, 2004) http://www.law.northwestern.edu/wrongfulconvictions/exonerations/mdBloodsworthSummary.html (last visited January 31, 2012).

[82] Don Terry, *After 18 Years In Prison, 3 Are Cleared Of Murders*, N.Y. TIMES, July 3, 1996, at A14. Dennis Williams and two others were exonerated and released from death row in Illinois after being convicted of murdering a white couple. New DNA evidence, witness recantations and the jailhouse confession of a man who said that he and his brother had committed the crime led to the exonerations. *Id.* John Grisham, THE INNOCENT MAN: MURDER AND INJUSTICE IN A SMALL TOWN (2006) Random House Publishing Group. In a non-fiction book Grisham tells the story of Ron Williamson of Ada Oklahoma, a minor league baseball player who was convicted of rape and murder and sentenced to death. After 11 years in prison, Williamson is exonerated by DNA evidence and released in 1999.

[83] *See* Jennifer Thompson-Cannino, Ronald Cotton, and Erin Torneo, PICKING COTTON: OUR MEMOIR OF INJUSTICE AND REDEMPTION (St. Martins Press, 2006) (a moving account of how Jennifer Thompson was certain of her identification of Ronald Cotton as her rapist until DNA evidence showed her he was innocent).

from the same source.[84]

DNA testing has been a powerful tool for law enforcement only since the 1990s. DNA is found only in biological material; This includes a person's fluids and tissue (i.e. blood, semen, saliva, bone, teeth, and hair).[85] Police labs compare samples that are collected at a crime scene and samples that are collected from a suspect. If DNA patterns match, a suspect may have contributed to the evidence left at a crime scene. If samples do not match, the answer is often not as simple. It does not automatically exclude a defendant as the perpetrator of the crime. For example, the sample may have been left by anyone who was at the scene, including other perpetrators, police officers, or bystanders. The defendant may have been at the scene but left no biological evidence.

One of the earliest tests for analyzing and comparing DNA samples was Restriction Fragment Length Polymorphism (RFLP). This test requires a relatively large DNA sample and loses its reliability when the sample suffers any degradation from dirt, mold or other environmental factors.[86]

More recently, Polymerase Chain Reaction analysis (PCR) has begun to replace RFLP testing because it requires much smaller amounts of DNA and is not as affected by degradation of samples. While RFLP required samples about the size of a quarter, PCR allows DNA analysis on samples as small as a few skin cells. PCR has reliability problems, however, if there is any contamination with other material during identification, collection or storage. It is, therefore, sometimes considered less precise than RFLP results.[87]

In 1996, The United States Department of Justice published "Convicted by Juries, Exonerated by Science,"[88] This report collected statistics on roughly 10,000 sexual assault cases that occurred between 1989 and 1996 and documented that subsequent DNA testing ruled out the person arrested as the perpetrator in approximately 20% of the cases (about 2,000 people).[89] The 20% error rate was fairly consistent each of the seven years for which data was collected. The consistency of error underscores how frequently mistakes are made in identifying, prosecuting, and convicting suspects in criminal cases. The report raises serious concerns that these errors frequently go undetected.

The drawback of DNA technology rests in its ability to give the public a false sense of security that our system can now determine who is or is not guilty. DNA testing is only helpful in a very small percentage of cases. Most crimes do not involve biological evidence at a crime scene, so there is no genetic material left at

---

[84] U.S. DEP'T OF ENERGY: OFFICE OF SCI., DNA FORENSICS (April 19, 2003), *available at* http://www.ornl.gov/sci/techresources/Human_Genome/elsi/forensics.shtml (last visited February 11, 2012).

[85] *Id.*

[86] *Id.*

[87] Restriction Fragment Length Polymorphism in DNA testing, *see* http://www.dnajunction.com/technology/rflp.php (last visited February 11, 2012).

[88] EDWARD CONNORS ET AL, CONVICTED BY JURIES, EXONERATED BY SCIENCE: CASE STUDIES IN THE USE OF DNA EVIDENCE TO ESTABLISH INNOCENCE AFTER TRIAL (Dep't of Justice, Nat'l Inst. of Justice 1996).

[89] *Id.* at xxviii.

In most cases, DNA testing was not available at the time of the original arrest.

the scene to compare to a suspect. DNA is most frequently found in cases of rape, because semen is a source of DNA. Murder cases often do not have genetic material that can be tested and compared to a suspect.

For the 3,242 men and women currently on death rows around the country, DNA testing is even less likely to be helpful, because evidence samples from their cases may no longer be available for testing.[90] Many persons on death row were sentenced to death before DNA testing was used by law enforcement or available to criminal defendants. Those who have been exonerated from death row thus far on the basis of DNA testing were able to have testing done only after waiting years on death row. For many, evidence in their cases has long since been destroyed. Even where evidence was preserved, there are additional obstacles. A defendant has no absolute right to DNA testing of evidence and district attorneys are often unwilling to allow testing of the evidence. In some cases, biological samples are contaminated which compromises the accuracy of any results.[91] DNA testing is only as reliable as the methods used for collecting, identifying, and preserving the evidence.[92]

[B] Non DNA Forensic Evidence and Crime Labs

While DNA evidence has shown to be an effective tool to both exonerate innocent individuals and identify guilty parties to a crime, other forensic evidence has led to wrongful convictions and executions.[93] A study of wrongful convictions in the U.S. revealed that 11% of these convictions were attributed to "false or misleading science."[94] In some areas of forensic science, innovations or new technology transformed what had been accepted principles of science into unreliable "junk science." There are now significant questions of the legitimacy of bite mark analysis, fiber comparisons, shoe print comparisons, and firearm tool mark analysis all of which have been used at trial to support a conviction or sentence of death.[95] Arson investigation has undergone significant change and

---

[90] Cynthia E. Jones, *Evidence Destroyed, Innocence Lost: The Preservation of Biological Evidence Under Innocence Protection Statutes*, (hereinafter *Evidence Destroyed*) 42 Am. Crim L. Rev. 1239 (2005).

[91] This point was made in the O.J. Simpson trial, the former football star who was tried for the murder of his former wife, Nicole Brown Simpson, and her friend, Ronald Goldman. The first samples in Simpson's case were collected from the crime scene at 7:00 A.M., but were not taken to the laboratory to begin testing procedures until 7:00 P.M. For twelve hours, these samples were stored in the back of a police van, without refrigeration, "cooking like a stew in the sunshine of a warm June day." Simpson's lawyers argued that testing by even the most sophisticated laboratory could not be trusted if the samples tested were contaminated, compromised, and corrupted even before it arrived; the principle of "garbage in; garbage out." Gerald Uelman, Lessons from the Trial: The People v. O.J. Simpson, at 116-2 (Andrews and McMeel 1996).

[92] Ryan M. Goldstein, *Improving Forensic Science Through State Oversight*, 90 Tex. L. Rev. 225 (2011).

[93] Lupe S. Salinas, *Is It Time to Kill the Death Penalty?: A View from the Bench and the Bar* (2006) 34 Am. J. Crim. L. 39, 64-65.

[94] http://www.aclunc.org/issues/criminal_justice/death_penalty/fact_sheet_on_wrongful_convictions_in_ca.shtml?ht=wrongful%20convictions%20wrongful%20convictions.

[95] Report by the National Academy of Sciences Urges Comprehensive Reform of U.S. Forensic Sciences *available at* http://www.innocenceproject.org/Content/National_Academy_of_Sciences_Urges_

today's experts reject old protocols and methodologies in favor of new, more reliable analysis. In the last few years, scandals and accusations of improprieties plagued many state crime labs.[96] Forensic labs faced greater scrutiny revealing inadequate resources, poor training for experts and increased caseloads.[97] The public pressure to produce results is heightened by juries' romanticized notions, based on popular television, of the type of forensic science available.[98] There is evidence of significant error in these cases.[99]

Recent developments in the science of analyzing fires changed the method of determining whether or not a fire should be classified as arson or accidental. Two defendants in Texas challenged the arson science from their trials with dramatically different outcomes; Ernest Ray Willis was exonerated and released from Texas death row while Cameron Todd Willingham was executed by Texas.

In 1986, Ernest Ray Willis lived in Pecos County, Texas when two women were found dead in a home consumed by fire. Willis was charged with arson. At trial, experts testified that there was an "accelerant" in the carpet that led them to conclude the fire was an arson. Willis was convicted and sentenced to death[100] After 17 years, Willis' conviction was reversed and a new prosecutor hired an arson expert to review the evidence.[101] The expert concluded there was no evidence of arson; the accelerant was actually "flashover burning" consistent with electrical fires. Willis was exonerated and released.

Cameron Todd Willingham was not as lucky. Willingham was convicted and sentenced to death for killing his three children in their home with a house fire.[102] At trial fire investigators and experts testified that the fire was arson. More than ten years later, new experts reviewed the evidence applying modern protocols and procedures. They concluded that the original arson ruling "could not be

Comprehensive_Reform_of_US_Forensic_Sciences.php

[96] Problems and scandals at dozens of crime labs across the nation led to full or partial closures, reorganizations, investigations or firings at city or county labs in Baltimore; Boston; Chicago; Colorado Springs, Colorado; Dallas; Detroit; Erie County, New York; Houston; Los Angeles; Monroe County, New York; Oklahoma City; San Antonio, Texas; San Diego; San Francisco; San Joaquin County, California; New York City; Nashville, Tennessee; and Tucson, Arizona, as well as at state-run crime labs in Illinois, Montana, Maryland, New Jersey, New York, Oregon, Pennsylvania, Virginia, Washington, North Carolina, West Virginia and Wisconsin, plus the federally-run FBI and U.S. Army crime labs. *See* https://www.prisonlegalnews.org/(S(oy0shv4520stu555aljzwpyh))/displayArticle.aspx?articleid= 22698&AspxAutoDetectCookieSupport=1 (last visited January 31, 2012).

[97] Craig M. Cooley, *Forensic Science and Capital Punishment Reform: An "Intellectually Honest" Assessment* (2007) 17 Geo. Mason U. Civ. Rts. L.J. 299, 306-08.

[98] *Id.* at 308-09.

[99] Paul C. Giannelli, *Wrongful Convictions and Forensic Science: The Need to Regulate Crime Labs* (2007) 86 N.C. L. Rev. 163.

[100] *See After 17 Years on Death Row, Texas Inmate Walks Free* — New York Times, Maureen Balleza, October 8, 2004 (last visited February 2, 2012).

[101] Willis v Cockrell, 2004 U.S. Dist. LEXIS 15950 (W.D. Tex Aug. 9 2004) (Willis' conviction was initially reversed on a *Brady* violation where prosecution failed to disclose that its mental health expert had evaluated Willis regarding future dangerousness and had written a report that would have led to favorable testimony for Willis.)

[102] *See* Willingham v. State, 897 S.W. 2d 351 (Tex. Crim. App. 1995).

substantiated."[103] Willingham was executed in 2004.[104]

In response to these two cases, in May, 2005, the Texas legislature created the Texas Forensic Science Commission (FSC) to investigate the forensic science used in Willis' and Willingham's case. The FSC report outlines many changes in the manner that arson investigators classify a fire as arson. In the Willingham case, arson investigators relied on an alleged "V-pattern" on a wall to determine the point of origin of the fire. The report states, "Scientists now know that the 'V-pattern' simply points to where something was burning at some stage of the fire, not necessarily the origin." The report discusses that pour pattern, flashover indication, burn intensity, and other factors previously used to classify a fire as arson are "subject to numerous variables that require study and evaluation."

There are numerous examples of problems in crimes labs throughout the country. One county in Texas is reviewing cases identified as having "major problems" with the reliability of crime lab work.[105] Some of those cases were death penalty cases in which inmates were already executed. In a capital case in Oklahoma, one forensic chemist falsified records and testimony in several cases; she deliberately delayed sending reports and samples to defense counsel and omitted critical information from her report.[106] In another Oklahoma death case, the same chemist testified that semen recovered on the victim's bed at the crime scene was consistent with that of the defendant when, in fact, there was no semen recovered from the bed.[107] The defendant in the case, Malcom Rent Johnson, had already been executed and the chemist had received a certificate of achievement for her work.[108]

In response to the ongoing problems, some states have created independent bodies to review the findings of crime labs.[109] A large number of labs remain unaccredited; only three states require accreditation.[110] Oversight, accreditation and rigorous scientific review are all necessary to stem the tide of wrongful convictions caused by forensic labs.

---

[103] *See* http://articles.cnn.com/2011-04-14/justice/texas.arson.review_1_texas-forensic-science-commission-cameron-todd-willingham-arson-investigation?_s=PM:CRIME) (last visited February 2, 2012).

[104] For a full account of this case *see* David Grann, *Did Texas Execute an Innocent Man?* The New Yorker, September 7, 2009. The Innocent Project Report concludes: "The State's expert witnesses in both cases [Willis and Willingham] relied on interpretations of "indicators" that they were taught constituted evidence of arson . . . each and every one of the indicators relied upon have since been scientifically proven to be invalid. *See* http://gritsforbreakfast.blogspot.com/2008/05/many-arson-convictions-based-on-invalid.html (last visited February 2, 2012). Report of the Texas Forensic Science Commission, Willingham/Willis investigation, April 15, 2011 *available at* http://www.newenglandinnocence.org/wp-content/uploads/2011/07/TFSC-Final-Report-Willingham-and-Willis.pdf.

[105] 4 No. 2 Quinlan, Computer Crime and Technology in Law Enforcement art. 4.

[106] Paul C. Giannelli, *Wrongful Convictions and Forensic Science: The Need to Regulate Crime Labs* (2007) 86 N.C. L. REV. 163, 175. The case was reversed on appeal.

[107] Id. at 179-80.

[108] Id.

[109] Brandon L. Garrett, *Judging Innocence* (2008) 108 COLUM. L. REV. 55, 123-25.

[110] Paul C. Giannelli, *Wrongful Convictions and Forensic Science: The Need to Regulate Crime Labs* (2007) 86 N.C. L. REV. 163, 211-13.

[C]   Police and Prosecutorial Misconduct.

Prosecutorial misconduct continues to gain attention from legal scholars, the media, and the Supreme Court.[111] As one scholar observed, "Prosecutors are the most powerful officials in our criminal justice system."[112] The misconduct leading to wrongful conviction arises most often when prosecutors fail to disclose exculpatory evidence to the defense. In *Brady v. Maryland*, the Supreme Court imposed a constitutional duty on prosecutors to disclose any evidence material to a defendant's guilt. Almost fifty years later cases continue to emerge where clearly exculpatory evidence was in the possession of a prosecutor that was purposefully never disclosed to the defense.[113] Prosecutorial misconduct has contributed to a number of wrongful convictions of person who ended up on death row.[114] The real concern, however, is the misconduct that has not yet been disclosed or uncovered. These defendants may still be sitting on death row or waiting to be executed with evidence of innocence in the hands of a prosecutor.

Louisiana has had eight exonerations from death row. John Thompson was one of them. Thompson spent 14 years on death row even though the prosecutor had evidence that he knew showed the Thompson was not guilty. In 1999, just five weeks before his scheduled execution, Thompson's attorney discovered crucial blood analysis evidence and crime lab report that proved Thompson was innocent.[115]

In 1987, Michael Ray Graham and Albert Ronnie Burrell were convicted of murder and sentenced to death in Union Parish, Louisiana. Thirteen years later,

---

[111] *See* Preventable Error: A Report on Prosecutorial Misconduct in California 1997-2009, Kathleen M. Ridolfi and Maurice Possley, Northern California Innocence Project at Santa Clara School of Law, A Veritas Initiative report, *available at* http://law.scu.edu/ncip/file/ProsecutorialMisconduct_BookEntire_online%20version.pdf.

[112] Robert Barnes, *Supreme Court to take another look at prosecutorial misconduct*, Washington Post October 30, 2011, Quoting Angela Jordan Davis. http://www.washingtonpost.com/politics/supreme-court-to-take-another-look-at-prosecutorial-misconduct/2011/10/28/gIQAnBvoWM_story.html (last visited February 2, 2012).

[113] Brady v. Maryland, 373 U.S. 83 (1963) *Smith v. Cain*, 132 S. Ct. 627 (2012) (Although now a death penalty case, Smith's conviction for murder was overturned where the only evidence against Smith at trial was the testimony of a single eyewitness account. The police files contained statements from other witnesses who contradicted and impeached that witnesses' testimony. The court held 8-1 that *Brady* requires Smith conviction to be reversed.

[114] Natasha Minsker, *Prosecutorial Misconduct in Death Penalty Cases*, 45 CAL. WESTERN L. REV. 373 (2009).

[115] For a compelling account of the John Thompson case, *see* John F. Hollway and Ronald M Gauthier, Killing Time: An 18 Year Odyssey from Death Row to Freedom (Skyhorse Publishing 2010) In 1999, a private investigator hired by his lawyer found a blood test in the police lab that exonerated Thompson of the carjacking that was the basis for making the murder charge a death case. The judge ordered a new trial on the murder where additional exculpatory evidence was finally disclosed that clearly pointed to another man as the killer. Thompson was quickly acquitted of all the charges in the murder. Once released, Thompson sued the district attorney's office, run by Harry Connick Sr. (the father of the famous singer). He won $14 million in a civil rights judgment based on the jury's finding that Mr. Connick had been "deliberately indifferent" to the need to train his prosecutors about their legal obligation to turn over evidence that could be favorable to the defense. In a 5-4 decision, the Supreme Court reversed the civil judgment and held he was not entitled to sue. *See also* http://motherjones.com/mojo/2011/03/supreme-court-rules-against-exonerated-death-row-prisoner-who-sued-prosecutors.

Graham was granted a new trial when the judge found that the district attorney failed to provide key pieces of evidence to the defense.

Among the many exonerations from Illinois death row, several were due, at least in part, to prosecutorial or police misconduct. Defendants Rolando Cruz and Alejandro Hernandez provide a compelling example. Both were charged with the 1983 kidnaping, rape, and murder of a 10-year-old girl. The lead detective in the case resigned just prior to the trial believing they were prosecuting innocent men. During trial police officers testified falsely leading to the conviction and sentence of death. Ultimately, DNA evidence excluded Cruz and Hernandez as possible rapists in the case.[116]

§ 17.04 LEGISLATIVE RESPONSE

The public debate about the death penalty has increased as a result of the death row exonerations. There is currently discussion about the fairness and the effectiveness of the death penalty, not just about the appropriate method of execution. State legislatures from New Hampshire to Texas have introduced legislation addressing a wide range of death penalty issues, including proposals providing access to DNA testing. Although many DNA testing bills have been introduced, most include numerous restrictions on an inmate's access to testing. No statute to date provides absolute access to DNA testing for persons already convicted of a crime.[117]

New York and Illinois were the first states to pass DNA testing legislation; there were serious limitations in what the provided. Both statutes apply only to cases that were tried before DNA testing was readily available. A defendant must also show that the outcome would have been different had DNA testing been available.[118] Forty-eight states now have bills allowing for some form of DNA testing if evidence is also presented that the testing could lead to an exoneration.[119]

The Justice for All Act of 2004 (HR 5107) was signed into law (Public Law 108-405) by President Bush on October 30, 2004, providing a Federal Innocence

---

[116] http://articles.chicagotribune.com/2009-07-29/news/0907280606_1_brian-dugan-jeanine-nicarico-rolando-cruz (last visited February 11, 2012). In an unusual step, a special grand jury indicted four sheriff's deputies and three former prosecutors for perjury and obstruction of justice for their misconduct in the Cruz case. Although a jury acquitted the police and prosecutors, the County later paid $3.5 million to settle the civil rights claims filed by Cruz and Hernandez.

[117] Jones, *supra*, note 90, at 1241. Jones reviews all existing DNA statutes to show how most of the statutes do not mandate that the government preserve the biological evidence needed for DNA analysis. She argues that, as a result, the right to post conviction testing is "purely illusory". She also demonstrates that even those statutes that impose a duty provide for no remedy when testable evidence is destroyed.

[118] New York requires a defendant to show that it is reasonably probable that a more favorable outcome would have resulted while Illinois requires a defendant to show that any new evidence is "materially relevant" and would probably change the outcome.

[119] The Innocence Project, *Access to DNA Testing*, http://www.innocenceproject.org/fix/DNA-Testing-Access.php (last visited November 9, 2011). Cynthia E. Jones, *supra*. Note 84. at 1249 (for a list of current DNA testing statutes) Karen Christian, *And the DNA Shall Set You Free: Issues Surrounding Post-Conviction DNA Evidence and the Pursuit of Justice*, 62 Ohio St. L.J. 1195 (2001).

Protection Act.[120] The Justice For All Reauthorization Act of 2010 provides funding to assist both state and local government's ability to use DNA evidence to help convict the guilty and exonerate the innocent.[121]

Individuals who try to prove their innocence still face enormous hurdles to obtain access to biological evidence in their cases, to obtain testing of the evidence and to admit any test results in a court.[122] These statutes allow greater access to post-conviction DNA testing.[123] Unfortunately, the statutes fail to impose any duty on the government to preserve the biological evidence for testing and fail to provide a remedy when the government intentionally destroys the evidence sought.[124]

§ 17.05   NEW VOICES ON INNOCENCE AND THE DEATH PENALTY

In the summer of 2002, Judge Jed S. Rakoff of the Southern District of New York held the federal death penalty to be unconstitutional because of the likelihood that an innocent person would be convicted, sentenced to death, and executed.[125] Judge Rakoff reasoned:

> This unacceptable high rate at which innocent persons are convicted of capital crimes, when coupled with the frequently prolonged delays before such errors are detected (and then often fortuitously or by the application of newly developed techniques) compels the conclusion that execution under the Federal Death Penalty Act, by cutting off the opportunity for exoneration, denied due process and, indeed, is tantamount to foreseeable, state sponsored murder of innocent human beings.[126]

Although the decision was reversed in the Second Circuit Court of Appeals,[127] it placed the issue of the execution of innocent persons at the forefront of public debate.[128] Judge Rakoff rejected the government's argument that the federal death

---

[120] 18 U.S.C.A. 3600 (2004).

[121] *See*   http://www.leahy.senate.gov/press/press_releases/release/?id=a550d868-fe4d-4e76-a3d0-e920bd6ba6a3) (last visited February 12, 2012). The bill requires that the Nation Institute of Justice "create practices and protocols for the collection of DNA evidence." The bills also provides funding for DNA evidence grant programs for state and local government and eliminates the requirement that individuals who plead guilty waive their rights to post-conviction DNA testing.

[122] California, Penal Code 1405, provides an inmate access to DNA testing, but only after that inmate shows a reasonable probability that their sentence would have been more favorable if the testing was available at the time of the conviction.

[123] Jones, *supra*, note 90 at 1250-1252.

[124] For a good discussion of remedies for destruction of evidence before DNA testing can occur see Cynthia E. Jones, *The Right Remedy for the Wrongly Convicted: Judicial Sanctions for Destruction of evidence* 77 Fordham L. Rev. 2893 (2007).

[125] United States v. Quinones, 205 F. Supp. 2d 256 (2nd Cir. 2002).

[126] *Id.* at 268.

[127] *Quinones*, 313 F.3d at 49, *reh'g denied* 317 F.3d 86 (2nd Cir. 2003).

[128] *See, e.g.*, Neftali Bandavid, *Ending A Decline, Executions Rose Slightly in 2002*, CHI. TRIB., Dec. 25, 2002, at 18; Lyle Denniston, *Death Penalty Law is Upheld by Court Says Chance of Error is Not Reason Enough to Challenge Statute*, THE BOSTON GLOBE, Dec. 11, 2002, at A2.

penalty did not present a high risk of executing an innocent person. None of the thirty-one persons who had been sentenced to death under the Federal Death Penalty Act at that time had been exonerated. Rakoff observed that of the thirty-one federal death sentences, five had already been reversed on appeal and one had been commuted by President Clinton (in part due to a claim of actual innocence).[129] The rest, Rakoff added, represented too small a sample to conclude that the system is working. In addition, the sentences of death were still relatively recent with no sentence more than seven years old. In state court proceedings, he observed, the time lag between conviction and exoneration averaged somewhere between 7-10 years after conviction. Since Rakoff's decision, other judges have begun to comment publicly and in their opinions their concerns whether innocent defendants may be convicted and sentenced to death.[130]

Many staunch supporters of capital punishment have changed their views and now publicly oppose capital punishment. Noted conservative columnist George Will read the book Actual Innocence[131] that documents defendants who were exonerated and concluded, "Conservatives, especially, should draw this lesson [from the cases of actual innocence]: Capital punishment, like the rest of the criminal justice system, is a government program, so skepticism is in order."[132] The Honorable William S. Sessions, former federal prosecutor, federal judge, and director of the FBI, joined other distinguished former judges and prosecutors in March 2003 in asking the Supreme Court to halt the execution of Texas inmate, Delma Banks, Jr., to review what they alleged were serious questions about the reliability of Mr. Banks' guilty verdict and sentences of death.[133]

---

[129] Michael Beach, *Clinton Pardons 140 as His Final Act*, THE ADVERTISER, Jan. 22, 2001, at 23. David Chandler was sentenced to death in 1991. After his sentence, the government's star witness, the man who said Chandler had hired him to kill the informant, recanted his testimony as a lie. Clinton commuted his sentence on his last day in office in January of 2002.

[130] Adam Liptak, *U.S. Judge Sees Growing Signs That Innocent are Executed.* N.Y. TIMES, Aug. 12, 2003, at A10 A federal judge in Boston declined to rule that the death penalty was unconstitutional, but voiced alarm today that imposing the death penalty "will inevitably result in the execution of innocent people." Judge Mark L. Wolf wrote, "In the past decade, substantial evidence has emerged to demonstrate that innocent individuals are sentenced to death, and undoubtedly executed, much more often than previously understood."

[131] BARRY SCHECK ET AL., ACTUAL INNOCENCE (Signet Books 2001) (documentation of actual cases of persons exonerated from death row).

[132] George F. Will, *Innocent on Death Row*, WASHINGTON POST, Apr. 6, 2000, at A23. Reverend Pat Robertson, founder and Chairman of the Christian Broadcast Network, also expressed his doubts about capital punishment and called for a moratorium on executions. Brooke A. Masters, *Pat Robertson Urges Moratorium on U.S Executions*, WASHINGTON POST, Apr. 8, 2000, at A1, *available at* 2000 WL 2295691.

[133] Delma Banks, Jr. was scheduled to be executed on March 12, 2003 in Texas. An African-American man, he was convicted and sentenced to death for the murder of a young white man by an all-white jury after the prosecutor excluded all African-American jurors from the panel. In a highly unusual move, the Supreme Court issued a stay just minutes before the execution was to take place. The Court granted certiorari on April 21, 2003 to determine whether Bank's lawyer was ineffective. The case was scheduled to be heard in the fall of 2003. Briefs were filed on July 11, 2003. Banks v. Dretke, 540 U.S. 668 (2004). The Court found that prosecution's misrepresentations of the evidence prevented Banks from investigating informant's status, and that the Brady standard should have been applied. The case was reversed and remanded to the U.S. Court of Appeals, who remanded to the district court in *Banks v. Dretke*, 383 F.3d 272 (5th Cir. 2004) to make a determination of whether the Brady claim was tried by implied consent of the parties. As of May 2011, Banks is still in prison, and the prosecutor who charged him the first time

§ 17.06   CURRENT DEBATE AND CONTROVERSY

Concern about the very real possibility of executing an innocent person has ignited a debate about the wisdom of a system of capital punishment more than any other time since 1976. The enormity of this issue was summed up in the words of former Supreme Court Justice William Brennan, who wrote "perhaps the bleakest fact of all is that the death penalty is imposed not only in a freakish and discriminatory manner but also in some cases upon defendants who are actually innocent."[134]

North Carolina responded to wrongful convictions and sentences of death in its state by creating the North Carolina Innocence Inquiry Commission.[135] The first, and at the moment only one of its kind in this country,[136] this commission reviews cases of alleged innocence. A creation of the Chief Justice of the North Carolina Supreme Court, this bipartisan group of judges, the attorney general, police officers, sheriffs, defense attorneys, victim advocates and academics evaluates ways to improve crime investigations and trials.[137]

In 2010, Gregory Taylor became the first person exonerated by the Commission after he had already served seventeen years in prison for a murder that he did not commit.[138] In September 2011, the Commission exonerated Kenneth Kagonyera and Robert Wilcoxson based on DNA evidence that eliminated them as participants in the case. They had both pled guilty eleven years earlier to second degree murder to avoid a sentence of death.[139]

The execution of Troy Davis on September 21, 2011, in Georgia, generated a reaction around the country that has been unprecedented. Davis was convicted in 1991 for the murder of an off duty police officer in Savannah, Georgia. Davis always maintained his innocence. Although at trial several witnesses identified him as the shooter, no physical evidence linked him to the crime.[140] In the years following Davis' conviction, witnesses began to recant their testimony and some stated that the police pressured them to identify Davis as the shooter. Re-creations of the scene raised serious questions of whether or not witnesses could actually see what they claimed especially since the shooting took place at night, As the execution

---

30 years ago is still prosecuting him. The original prosecutor, James Elliott says "he will pursue Banks until he gets what he deserves."

[134] Justice W. Brennan, Jr., *Neither Victims nor Executioners*, 8 Notre DAME J.L. ETHICS & PUBLIC POLICY 1, 4 (1994).

[135] North Carolina Innocence Inquiry Commission Rules and Procedures, Revised August 24, 2007, available at http://www.aoc.state.nc.us/www/ids/Other%20Manuals/Innocence%20Inquiry/innocence%20commission%20rules%20and%20procedures,%20rev.%208-24-07.pdf (last visited November 8, 2011).

[136] *See* http://news.yahoo.com/2-nc-men-walk-free-murder-exoneration-222600983.html) (last visited January 31, 2012).

[137] *See* http://www.innocencecommission-nc.gov/ (last visited January 31, 2012). Henry Weinstein, *N.C. to Weigh Claims of Innocence*, L.A. TIMES, Aug. 4, 2006, at A18.

[138] *See* http://www.innocencecommission-nc.gov/ (last visited January 31, 2012).

[139] *See* http://www.usatoday.com/news/nation/story/2011-09-22/innocence-prisoners-freed/50519198/1 (last visited January 31, 2012).

[140] *See* http://www.time.com/time/nation/article/0,8599,2094103,00.html (last visited February 12, 2012).

approached, Pope Benedict XV and former President Jimmy Carter joined other voices both home and abroad supporting Davis' claim of innocence and his request for clemency.[141] Ultimately, Davis was executed, but a national conversation about innocence had taken off.

Governor George Ryan, a death row supporter while in the Illinois state legislature, called for a moratorium on executions in Illinois after the thirteenth person was exonerated and released from Illinois death row. He stated, "Until I can be sure with moral certainty no innocent man or woman is facing a lethal injection, no one will meet that fate."[142] There were no more executions in Illinois while Ryan was governor, and before leaving office he pardoned four defendants and granted clemency to the rest of the men and women on death row.[143]

Sitting Supreme Court justices have publicly expressed their views about innocent people on death row. Some have expressed their concern in speeches to the public,[144] others have written their concern in Supreme Court opinions.[145] Since retiring from the Court, Justice Stevens, has spoken out about his concern for the death penalty. In 2010, he wrote an essay "On the death sentence," where he urged author David Garland to conclude that the death penalty should be abolished.[146] In September 2011, George Stephanopoulous interviewed Stevens and asked about

---

[141] http://www.washingtonpost.com/blogs/post-partisan/post/troy-davis-guilty-as-charged/2011/03/04/gIQAh23BoK_blog.html (last visited Febuary 12, 2012).

[142] Governor Ryan also stated in his speech: Yes, it is right that I am here with you, where, in a manner of speaking, my journey from staunch supporter of capital punishment to reformer all began. But I must tell you — since the beginning of our journey — my thoughts and feelings about the death penalty have changed many, many times . . . We then had the dubious distinction of exonerating more men than we had executed. Thirteen men found innocent, 12 executed . . . As I reported yesterday, there is not a doubt in my mind that the number of innocent men freed from our Death Row stands at 17, with the pardons of Aaron Patterson, Madison Hobley, Stanley Howard and Leroy Orange. That is an absolute embarrassment. See http://www.nytimes.com/2003/01/11/national/11CND-RTEX.html (last visited February 12, 2012). Eric Slater, The Nation, A Matter of Life and Death, L.A. TIMES, Nov. 8, 2002, at 1.

[143] "I cannot say it more eloquently than Justice Blackmun. The legislature couldn't reform it. Lawmakers won't repeal it. But I will not stand for it. I must act. Our capital system is haunted by the demon of error, error in determining guilt, and error in determining whom among the guilty deserves to die. Because of all of these reasons today I am commuting the sentences of all death row inmates . . . There have been many nights where my staff and I have been deprived of sleep in order to conduct our exhaustive review of the system. But I can tell you this: I will sleep well knowing I made the right decision." Speech by Governor Ryan of Illinois at Northwestern University College of Law www.deathpenaltyinfo.org/article.php?scid=13&did=551 (last visited November 8, 2011).

[144] In a speech to a Minnesota women lawyers group, death penalty supporter Sandra Day O'Connor said that there are "serious questions" about whether the death penalty is being fairly administered in the United States. "If statistics are any indication, the system may well be allowing some innocent defendants to be executed." Ken Armstrong and Steve Mills, O'Connor Questions Fairness of Death Penalty, CHI. TRIB., July 4, 2001, at 1.

[145] Gina Hollad, Justice Stevens Calls Attention to 'Serious Flaws' in Death Penalty, ASSOC. PRESS, Aug. 9, 2005. Justice Stevens said DNA evidence has shown "that a substantial number of death sentences have been imposed erroneously." "It indicates that there must be serious flaws in our administration of criminal justice." Id.

[146] This essay is a book review for Peculiar Institution: America's Death Penalty in an Age of Abolition by David Garland who stopped short of advocating abolition. Stevens argues "Professor Garland identifies arguably relevant purposes without expressly drawing the conclusion that I think they

any regrets from his time on the bench. Stevens replied with the Texas case in 1976 where he upheld the death penalty under the new Texas statute.[147]

The public debate about innocence and the death penalty is even being played out in Supreme Court opinions, most recently between Justices Souter and Scalia.[148] Justice Scalia, however, expressed the view that the "possibility [of executing an innocent person] has been reduced to an insignificant minimum."[149]

As this book goes to print, a book-length study was released claiming to present evidence that in 1989, Texas executed Carlos DeLuna, who was, in fact, innocent.[150]

---

dictate."   (http://www.politicsdaily.com/2010/11/29/john-paul-stevens-book-reviewer-death-penalty-opponent/) (last visited February 12, 2012).

[147] *Id.* "My vote in the Texas death case. And I think I do mention that in that case. I think that I came out wrong on that" . . . I was rather disappointed, because it — maybe one believes, and certainly a lot of people sincerely do, that [the death penalty] is an effective deterrent to crime . . . I don't happen to share that view.

[148] Kansas v. Marsh, 548 U.S. 163 (2006). Justice Souter expressed his concern for the number of death row exonerations "in numbers never imagined before the developments of DNA tests." Justice Scalia disagreed and replied, "It should be noted at the outset that the dissent does not discuss a single case-not one-in which it is clear that a person was executed for a crime he did not commit. If such an event had occurred in recent years, we would not have to hunt for it; the innocents name would be shouted from the rooftops." Others echoing Scalia's skepticism include former Florida congressman, Bill McCullom, who announced that executing the innocent is an acceptable trade-off for the public's increased sense of security. Assistant Attorney General in Missouri, Frank Jung, recently told the Missouri Supreme Court that it should not concern itself with mounting evidence that death row inmate Joseph Amrine might be innocent.

[149] Kansas v. Marsh, *Id.*

[150] James S. Liebman, Shawn Crowley, Andrew Markquart, Lauren Rosenberg, Lauren Gallo White, and Daniel Zharkovsky, *Los Tocayos Carlos, available at* http://www3.law.columbia.edu/hrlr/ltc/print-version.html also available (without footnotes) in 43 COLUM. HUM. RTS. L. REV. 711 (2012).

Chapter 18

CLEMENCY

§ 18.01 OVERVIEW

Governor Ryan of Illinois made the news in 2003 for the unusual step of commuting the sentences of all 167 individuals on death row in that state.[1] While for years clemency petitions were only occasionally the subject of any significant press coverage and were routinely denied, the blanket grant of clemency in Illinois brought issues about clemency into sharp focus.[2] What is clemency? Who grants or denies clemency? Why is clemency granted or denied? Does it always mean that the inmate walks out of the prison walls? Do the courts have any role in clemency? This chapter will look at how clemency operates in states with the death penalty.

Clemency is the ultimate recourse for a death row inmate. Clemency includes a pardon, a reprieve, and a commutation. A pardon absolves the defendant of the conviction and sentence.[3] Pardons are rare in capital cases, but have occurred in

---

[1] Governor George Ryan commuted the sentences of 167 death row inmates on January 11, 2003. Almost all the sentences were commuted to life imprisonment, but three were commuted to 40 years incarceration. Eleven of the inmates had sentencing or resentencing pending. *See* Death Penalty Information Center, *Clemency: Commutations in Capital Cases on Humanitarian Grounds* (2007), available at http://www.deathpenaltyinfo.org/article.php?did=126&scid=13; Maurice Possley & Steve Mills, *Clemency for All; Ryan Commutes 164 Death Sentences to Life in Prison Without Parole*, CHI. TRIB., Jan. 12, 2003, § 1, at 1 (describing number as 164 with commutations to life without parole; other three were commuted to 40 years). The Illinois Supreme Court has upheld the commutations against several challenges, such as that some of the inmates had not requested commutations and some had already received judicial reversals of their death sentences. *See* People el rel Madigan v. Snyder, 804 N.E.2d 546 (Ill. 2004). That court has also more recently rejected the state's effort to pursue the death penalty against one of the inmates whose conviction was reversed after the commutation. *See* People v. Morris, 848 N.E.2d 1000 (Ill. 2006).

[2] While Governor Ryan had the legal authority to grant the blanket commutations, the question whether it was an appropriate use of that authority has been debated by scholars. *See, e.g.*, David A. Wallace, *Dead Men Walking — An Abuse of Clemency in Illinois*, 29 DAYTON L. REV. 379 (2004) (calling Ryan's blanket commutation a "grave injustice"); Stephen P. Garvey, *Is it Wrong to Commute Death Row? Retribution, Atonement, and Mercy*, 82 N. C. L. REV. 1319, 1322-23 (2004) (arguing that the blanket commutation was unjustified as an act of mercy under a retributive theory of punishment although it might have been justifiable under a theory of punishment as atonement); Dan Markel, *State, Be Not Proud: A Retributivist Defense of the Commutation of Death Row and the Abolition of the Death Penalty*, 40 HARV. C. R. — C. L. L. REV. 407, 410 (2005) (explaining why a retributivist "not only *can* but *should* accommodate the blanket commutation").

[3] James R. Acker & Charles S. Lanier, *May God — Or the Governor — Have Mercy: Executive Clemency and Executions in Modern Death-Penalty Systems*, 36 CRIM. L. BULL. 200, 204 (2000) ("A pardon effectively nullifies both a conviction and a sentence. The recipient of a pardon normally is not exonerated of wrongdoing; the more common interpretation is that guilt is not erased but the offender is simply forgiven.").

situations where the inmate was believed to be innocent of the crime. For instance, in addition to the 167 commutations, Governor Ryan pardoned four death row inmates on the basis of innocence.[4] Those individuals no longer must serve time on that crime. A reprieve is a temporary delay of the sentence.[5] For example, the execution might be delayed for 30 days to allow time to conduct DNA testing. A commutation is a reduction in the sentence.[6] Commutations are the most common form of clemency in capital cases. The inmate typically seeks to have the death sentence commuted to life imprisonment (usually without parole). Most of the death row inmates whose sentences were commuted by Governor Ryan were commuted to life imprisonment without parole.[7] They will have to serve the life sentence. In this chapter, the terms commutation and clemency will be used interchangeably.

Although considered part of the overall criminal justice system, clemency is unique. The power to grant clemency is given to the executive branch. The judicial branch is only rarely involved in any issue that affects granting or denying clemency. In most states, the governor has the authority to grant clemency.[8] In a few states, an administrative board is given the exclusive authority.[9] Some states combine an administrative board with the governor's authority. In several states, an administrative board makes a nonbinding recommendation to the governor.[10] In other states, the governor may only grant clemency if the administrative board recommends it.[11] Thus, a negative decision by the administrative board is binding.

---

[4] Death Penalty Information Center, *supra*, note 1.

[5] For example, TEX. CODE CRIM. PROC. ANN. art. 48.01 (West 2012) states: "The Governor shall have the power to grant one reprieve in any capital case for a period not to exceed 30 days; and he shall have power to revoke conditional pardons."

[6] *See* Michael L. Radelet & Barbara A. Zsembik, *Executive Clemency in Post Furman Capital Cases*, 27 U. RICH. L. REV. 289, 289 (1993) (describing clemency as including a commutation "which reduces the severity of punishment"). *See also* Acker & Lanier, *supra* note 3, at 205 (describing commutation as occurring when "a lesser punishment is substituted for a more severe one").

[7] Death Penalty Information Center, *supra*, note 1.

[8] *See* Mary-Beth Moylan and Linda E. Carter, *Clemency in California Capital Cases*, 14 BERKELEY J. CRIM. L. 37, 88 (2009) (describing five different types of clemency authority); Alyson Dinsmore, *Clemency in Capital Cases: The Need to Ensure Meaningful Review*, 49 U.C.L.A. L. REV. 1825, 1838 n.66 (2002), *citing* Acker & Lanier, supra note 3, at 217. The 13 states in which the governor has sole authority to grant clemency are California, Colorado, Kentucky, Mississippi, New Mexico, North Carolina, Oregon, South Carolina, South Dakota, Tennessee, Virginia, Washington, and Wyoming.

[9] *See* Death Penalty Information Center, *supra*, note 1. The states in which a board or advisory group make the sole determination are Connecticut, Georgia, Nebraska, Nevada, and Utah. In some of the states that give clemency authority to an administrative board, the governor sits on the board as one of its members. *See* Michael Heise, *Mercy by the Numbers: An Empirical Analysis of Clemency and Its Structure*, 89 VA. L. REV. 239, 257 (2003) (describing clemency actions taken by boards with and without governor sitting on the board); Dinsmore, *supra*, note 8 (noting that, in Florida, the governor sits on the board).

[10] *See* Acker & Lanier, *supra* note 3, at 217. There are nine states in which an administrative board makes a nonbinding recommendation to the governor, but the ultimate power lies with the governor. Those states are Alabama, Arkansas, Indiana, Kansas, Maryland, Missouri, Montana, New Hampshire, and Ohio.

[11] *See id.* The eight states in which the governor may grant clemency only after a recommendation by an administrative board are Arizona, Delaware, Florida, Idaho, Louisiana, Oklahoma, Pennsylvania, and Texas.

California has a unique model. The governor ordinarily has exclusive authority. When the defendant is a twice-convicted felon, however, the governor may only grant clemency with the concurrence of four members of the state supreme court.[12] For federal crimes, the authority is granted to the President by the United States Constitution.[13]

Clemency in the United States is an historical legacy from the use of clemency in England.[14] The King or Queen had the power to grant clemency. Those sentenced to death might receive a commutation based on "benefit of the clergy,"[15] youth, or insanity.[16] The idea of reposing the authority to grant clemency in the executive was transferred to governors in the early development of the United States.[17] Part of the legacy of clemency is the unfettered discretion to grant it as an act of "grace."[18] Our modern day system of clemency follows the historical pattern and places virtually complete discretion in the hands of the executive authority to decide whether or not to grant clemency, on what grounds, and by what procedure.[19]

---

[12] Cal. Const. art. V, § 8(a) provides: "Subject to application procedures provided by statute, the Governor, on conditions the Governor deems proper, may grant a reprieve, pardon, and commutation, after sentence, except in case of impeachment. The Governor shall report to the Legislature each reprieve, pardon, and commutation granted, stating the pertinent facts and the reasons for granting it. The Governor may not grant a pardon or commutation to a person twice convicted of a felony except on recommendation of the Supreme Court, 4 judges concurring."

[13] *See* U.S. Const. art. II, §§ 2, cl. 1.: "(The President) shall have Power to grant Reprieves and Pardons for Offenses against the United States, except in Cases of Impeachment."

[14] *See* Michael Korengold, et al., *And Justice for Few: The Collapse of the Capital Clemency System in the United States*, 20 HAMLINE L. REV. 349, 353 (1996) (describing the history of clemency in England and its continued use in the colonies). The concept of clemency has ancient roots. *See* Daniel Kobil, *Chance and the Constitution in Capital Clemency*, 28 CAP. U. L. REV. 567, 569 (2000) (describing the history of clemency; giving example of clemency granted in ancient Rome if the condemned man happened to cross the path of vestal virgins).

[15] *See* Daniel Kobil, *The Quality of Mercy Strained: Wresting the Pardoning Power from the King*, 69 TEX. L. REV. 569, 586 n.97 (1991) (describing the "benefit of the clergy" as originally exempting "clerics and their associates").

[16] *See* Kathleen M. Ridolfi, *Not Just an Act of Mercy: the Demise of Post-Conviction Relief and a Rightful Claim to Clemency*, 30 N.Y.U. REV. OF L. & SOC. CHANGE 43, 48 n.23 (1998) (describing the use of clemency in England for situations that would be covered today by defenses: "self-defense, lack of intent, insanity, and age"); Korengold, et al., *supra* note 14, at 353 (describing clemency grants as early as the thirteenth century for capital crimes committed "accidentally or in self-defense"); Acker & Lanier, *supra* note 3, at 206 (describing the lack of defenses at common law and the role of clemency to adjust sentences).

[17] *See* Kobil, *supra* note 14, at 570-71 (noting that originally many of the states did not trust the executive and gave clemency authority to the legislature; eventually the clemency authority was transferred to the governor); Beau Breslin & John J.P. Howley, *Defending the Politics of Clemency*, 81 OR. L. REV. 231, 248-249 (2002) (describing fear of abuse of power by the executive as reason for giving pardon power to legislature; also describing eventual change to impose clemency authority in executive).

[18] Samuel T. Morrison, *The Politics of Grace: On the Moral Justification of Executive Clemency*, 9 BUFF. CRIM. L. REV. 1 (2005).

[19] *See* Linda E. Carter, *Lessons From Avena: The Inadequacy of Clemency and Judicial Proceedings for Violations of the Vienna Convention on Consular Relations*, 15 DUKE J. COMP. & INT'L. L. 259, 267 (2005) (noting that, in most states, "the only oversight of clemency rest[s] with voters who elect the governors").

§ 18.02   THE FUNCTION OF CLEMENCY

Clemency contemplates that, despite meticulous attention to legal standards and procedures in the courts, a governor or administrative board can modify the decision of the court system. The United States Supreme Court has referred to clemency as "a matter of grace."[20] Scholars provide a number of different descriptions of the purposes of clemency. Key among the definitions is the idea of "mercy."[21] A second significant purpose identified by most scholars is to remedy an incorrect or unjust result in the criminal justice system.[22] For example, Professor Ridolfi has capsulized the purposes as: "(1) to dispense mercy when the system is too harsh in an individual case and, (2) to ensure justice when the system proves itself incapable of reaching a just result."[23]

One of the most classic examples of clemency occurred in *Regina v. Dudley and Stephens*,[24] a case that is included in most textbooks on Criminal Law. Three sailors stranded at sea killed and consumed a fourth sailor, a 17 year-old boy.[25] Two of them were convicted of murder and sentenced to death. The court rejected their claim of a necessity defense. Ultimately, however, their death sentences were commuted to six months incarceration.[26] This could be viewed as both a "mercy" commutation as well as correcting an unjust result in the legal system. These individuals were arguably less blameworthy due to the extraordinary pressures of facing death at sea. Moreover, the legal system had no defense that covered their situation.[27]

---

[20] *See, e.g.*, Ohio Adult Parole Auth. v. Woodard, 523 U.S. 272, 285 (1998).

[21] *See* Radelet and Zsembik, *supra* note 6, at 289, 290 (describing clemency as "a free gift of the executive, needing no justification or pretense of fairness"); Acker & Lanier *supra* note 3, at 206 (describing clemency "at one level as an act of mercy, unencumbered by the assumption that the offender somehow earned or deserved the particular dispensation"); Morrison, *supra* note 18, at 132 (describing clemency as "a mechanism for smoothing out the unavoidably rough edges of the system").

[22] *See, e.g.*, Heise, *supra* note 9, at 252 (describing the goals of clemency to "include the amelioration of miscarried justice and the correction of legal errors").

[23] Ridolfi, *supra* note 16, at 77-78. *Compare* Breslin & Howley, *supra* note 17, at 246 (defending the political influences on the clemency process). Breslin and Howley define the two major uses of clemency as "(1)as a grant of mercy, and (2)as a political measure aimed at gaining the favor of particular groups." *See also*, Radelet and Zsembik, *supra* note 6, at 299 (identifying two categories of clemency as "1) judicial expediency, in cases where the court has vacated or likely to vacate a sentence and a commutation would save the time and expense of a new sentencing proceeding . . . and 2) humanitarian reasons, because of a governor's opposition to the death penalty, or because of unique characteristics of the crime or offender. such as mental illness or doubt about guilt."); Kathleen (Cookie) Ridolfi and Seth Gordon, *Gubernatorial Clemency Powers Justice or Mercy?*, Crim. Just. 26, 27 (Fall 2009) (arguing that the clemency power is flexible enough to be used as both an act of mercy and to correct an imperfect criminal justice system, noting that the clemency power rationale does not have to be understood as an "either/or" proposition).

[24] 14 Q.B.D 273 (1884).

[25] One of the three sailors did not assist in killing the boy, but did partake in eating the body. *Id.* at 274.

[26] Joshua Dressler, Understanding Criminal Law § 22.04[B] (5th ed. 2009).

[27] *See also* Ridolfi, *supra* note 16, at 79 (discussing clemency for incarcerated women who were victims of a battered women's syndrome as example of lesser culpability and a legal system that was inadequate to take into account the special circumstances of these women); Elizabeth Rapaport, *Straight is the Gate: Capital Clemency in the United States from Gregg to Atkins*, 33 N. M. L. Rev. 349, 372 (2003) (noting that clemency serves an important function as an "incubator and laboratory for defenses and mitigation" that have not yet been embodied in the law).

§ 18.03 HOW CLEMENCY WORKS

[A] How Often is Clemency Granted?

Studies have compared how often clemency was granted before and after the modern era of capital punishment, which began in 1972 with the Supreme Court decision in *Furman v. Georgia*.[28] There is a noticeable decline in grants of clemency after *Furman* when compared with the number of executions.[29] For example, in California, between 1943-1966, there were 34 commutations and 162 executions, or about a 17% commutation rate.[30] After 1976 in California, there have been no commutations and 13 executions. Nationally, there were 900 commutations and 2,861 executions between the years of 1903 and 1976, equating to a commutation rate of about 20%.[31] In contrast, prior to Governor Ryan's blanket commutations, there had only been 49 commutations nationally between 1976 and 2002, compared with 820 executions, about a 6% commutation rate.[32]

The percentage of commutations to executions has recently increased, however, to approximately 20% due to blanket commutations in a few states. As of January 2012, which includes the Illinois commutations, 270 individuals on death row had received clemency nationwide since 1976, compared with 1,279 executions.[33] In addition to Governor Ryan, who commuted 167 death sentences, other governors have also granted multiple commutations at the end of their terms. Governor Anaya of New Mexico commuted the sentences of all five individuals on death row in that state in 1986. Governor Celeste of Ohio commuted eight death sentences (but left 101 on death row) in 1991.[34] More recently, in 2007, Governor Corzine of New Jersey commuted the death sentences of all eight individuals on death row in conjunction with signing a bill abolishing the death penalty in the state. Illinois has also now abolished the death penalty and, in 2011, Governor Quinn commuted the death sentences of the 15 individuals on death row.[35] If the blanket commutations are put to one side, however, the percentage of commutations to executions post-

---

[28] Furman v. Georgia, 408 U.S. 238 (1972). *Furman* effectively invalidated the death penalty in the United States. After *Furman*, however, states reenacted death penalty statutes that were approved by the Court beginning in 1976. *See* discussion of *Furman* in Sections 4.02 and 6.02, *supra*.

[29] *See* Kobil, *supra* note 14, at 572 (noting that before *Furman*, 25% or more of death sentences were commuted compared with 7.5% after 1976); Acker & Lanier, *supra* note 3, at 215 (calculating the ratio of executions to commutations as 13.8 to one post-*Furman*, which is significantly higher [3-9 times higher depending on the state] than before *Furman*).

[30] Moylan & Carter, *supra* note 8, at 45.

[31] Acker & Lanier, *supra* note 3, Table 1, at 212-213 (state by state comparison of commutations to executions prior to 1976).

[32] Death Penalty Information Center, *supra* note 1.

[33] *Id.* at http://www.deathpenaltyinfo.org/clemency (last visited January 27, 2012), and at http://www.deathpenaltyinfo.org/documents/FactSheet.pdf (last visited January 27, 2012).

[34] *See* Kobil, *supra* note 14, at 572; Acker & Lanier, *supra* note 3, at 215. For a criticism of blanket commutations, *see* Robert Blecker, *Changes in the Law Since 9/11: The Death Penalty: Where Are We Now?* 19 N.Y. L. Sch. J. Hum. Rts. 295 (2003) (arguing that clemency should be granted on a case by case basis; can be instrument to impose death only on the "worst of the worst").

[35] Death Penalty Information Center, *supra* note 1, at www.deathpenaltyinfo.org/clemency (last visited January 27, 2012).

1976 remains low compared to the pre-1976 statistics.

[B] How is Clemency Decided?

[1] The Process

When we think of courts and the judicial process, we immediately look for the standards to be applied and the procedures to follow. Here, too, clemency is very different from other proceedings in the criminal justice system. It is rare for a state to have any standards on granting or denying clemency. In fact, a hallmark of clemency is that a governor or administrative board may grant clemency for any reason it chooses and, similarly, may deny it despite arguments for mercy or injustice in the system. Nor does the governor or administrative board need to be consistent from one case to the next. Thus, unlike any judicial proceeding imaginable, clemency is purposely standardless. The lack of standards is perceived as both a weakness and a strength.[36]

Prescribed procedures are also rare. Moreover, there is almost no law governing what is required for procedure.[37] Consequently, procedures are as variable as reasons for granting or denying clemency. Some states conduct hearings, others do not. In the course of a hearing, some states permit the inmate to appear, others do not. Some permit counsel to appear, and others do not.[38] Even within one state, the procedures may vary from governor to governor. For instance, in California, each governor has designed procedures for clemency for that particular administration. Some governors held hearings; others did not. Some governors accepted evidence at a hearing; others did not.[39]

[2] Reasons to Grant Clemency

With the varied decision-making models, lack of set standards, and different procedures, one might not expect any common characteristics in grants of clemency. There most certainly is no guarantee, for example, that an inmate granted clemency due to a mental illness in one state would have received clemency in the next state. There are, however, some identifiable reasons why inmates have received commutations.

Of the 270 commutations since 1976, 203 were those who received clemency as part of blanket commutations by governors leaving office or in the wake of state repeal of the death penalty. Of the 67 other individuals whose sentences were commuted, the reasons for commutations included doubts about their guilt, questions about their mental illness or severe childhood deprivations, exemplary behavior or remorse, inadequate representation, and concerns that their sentences

---

[36] *See* Section 18.05[C], *infra.*

[37] *See* Section 18.04, *infra.*

[38] *See* Acker & Lanier, *supra* note 3, at 224.

[39] Moylan & Carter, *supra* note 8, at 54-67 (describing the processes in California administrations for 5 governors).

were unequal to those received by codefendants.[40] For example, an inmate in Ohio was granted clemency in 2003 when new DNA evidence proved that the blood on his shoes introduced as trial evidence was actually his own and not the victim's.[41] An Indiana inmate was granted clemency in 2004 after his apparently equally culpable co-defendant was spared the death penalty.[42] Another inmate in Indiana received a commuted sentence to life imprisonment without parole from the governor in early 2005 because that sentencing option was not available when he was tried and he suffered from severe mental illness.[43] In late 2005, the governor of Virginia commuted a death sentence to life imprisonment without parole because a court clerk had illegally destroyed trial evidence that the inmate could have used in his appeals.[44] An inmate in Ohio was granted clemency in 2009 for several reasons, including the victim's family's opposition to the death penalty, inadequate legal representation, remorse, a disproportionate sentence compared to other similar cases, and the views of two justices of the Ohio Supreme Court.[45] More recently, in 2012, Governor Markell of Delaware followed the recommendation of the parole board to grant clemency to an inmate based on the inmate's highly abusive and neglected family background.[46] Given the nature of clemency, however, there is no consistency within a state or between states on when clemency is granted.

Questions have arisen about whether clemency is granted or denied in a discriminatory manner. In a 2003 study, Professor Heise isolated a number of variables, including race and ethnicity, gender, age, and region of the country. He did not find that race and ethnicity were statistically significant variables in who

---

[40] *See* Radelet & Zsembik, *supra* note 6, at 300-01 (identifying five subcategories of humanitarian commutations). These categories are described as mercy ("unqualified by any characteristics of the crime or offender); "lingering doubts about the defendant's guilt;" blameworthiness (especially mental capacity); equity ("equally or more culpable codefendant was not sentenced to death"); and "other" (miscellaneous reasons). *See also* Death Penalty Information Center, *supra* note 1 (noting humanitarian reasons of doubts about guilt and doubts about the death penalty system); NINA RIVKIND & STEVEN F. SHATZ, CASES AND MATERIALS ON THE DEATH PENALTY 744 (2001) (identifying "lingering doubt about the condemned person's guilt, mental problems that reduced the condemned person's blameworthiness, and disproportionate punishments among equally culpable codefendants" as primary reasons for clemency since 1976). *See* Daniel T. Kobil, *How to Grant Clemency in Unforgiving Times*, 31 CAP. U. L. REV. 219, 225-226 (2003) (reviewing reasons for granting clemency and finding that the grants were based largely on retributive reasoning (e.g., innocence or problems in the judicial system), rather than redemptive reasoning (e.g., exemplary behavior or remorse)).

[41] *See* Death Penalty Information Center, *supra* note 1 (Jerome Campbell). The Ohio Parole Board stated that the defense had "presented credible evidence for the majority of the board to question any sustained confidence or reliability in the jury's recommendation." Governor Bob Taft commuted Campbell's death sentence to life imprisonment without parole.

[42] *Id.* (Darnell Williams).

[43] *Id.* (Arthur P. Baird, II).

[44] *Id.* (Robin Lovitt).

[45] *See* "Ohio Governor Grants Death Row Inmate Clemency," http://www.deathpenaltyinfo.org/ohio-governor-grants-death-row-inmate-clemency. The Ohio Parole Board had unanimously recommended clemency in the case. *Id.*

[46] *See* "Statement of Governor Jack Markell Regarding the Commutation of Sentence of Robert Gattis." http://news.delaware.gov/2012/01/17/statement-of-governor-jack-markell-regarding-the-commutation-of-sentence-of-robert-gattis/ (calling the inmate's family background "the most troubling [the Governor had] encountered").

received clemency, but being female was a statistically significant plus in seeking clemency. He also found that younger defendants were more likely to get clemency. Defendants in southern states were less likely to receive clemency.[47]

§ 18.04 DUE PROCESS RESTRICTIONS ON CLEMENCY

The courts in general have maintained a "hands off" policy regarding clemency. In a major case, however, a slim majority of the United States Supreme Court found a "minimal" due process requirement in clemency proceedings. The case of *Ohio Adult Parole Authority v. Woodard*[48] and its progeny are discussed in this section.

[A] "Minimal" Due Process: The *Woodard* Case

Suppose a state requires its parole board to conduct a clemency hearing whenever an execution is 45 days away. D is told that he may have an interview with the board three days from today's date. D is further told that the hearing on clemency will be held in 10 days, and that neither he nor his attorney may appear, nor may D submit any evidence to the board. The board will then make a recommendation to the governor, who has the ultimate authority to grant or deny clemency. Is D entitled to any due process of law in a clemency proceeding? If so, is D denied due process because of the short period to prepare for the interview, because he cannot have an attorney appear on his behalf, or because he cannot submit evidence to the board?

These due process questions were posed to the Supreme Court in *Woodard*.[49] Four of the justices, in an opinion authored by Justice Rehnquist, stated that Woodard's life interest had already been adjudicated in the trial and appeal.[50] For the Rehnquist plurality, there was no interest to which due process would apply. Moreover, the Rehnquist plurality emphasized that it is not the province of the courts to interfere with clemency decisions.[51] Five of the justices, however, believed that "some minimal procedural safeguards apply to clemency proceedings."[52]

---

[47] *See* Heise, *supra* note 9, at 295, 301 (noting that regional components factor into whether a state imposes the death penalty; also noting that the structure of a state's clemency procedure was not a significant factor; nor were political factors such as an election year). *Cf.* Sections 18.05[B] and [D], *infra*, on assumed political effect. *See also* John Kraemer, *An Empirical Examination of the Factors Associated with the Commutation of State Death Row Prisoners' Sentences Between 1986 and 2005*, 45 AM. CRIM. L. REV. 1389 (2008) (analyzing and evaluating factors associated with commutation decisions, finding that women's death sentences are substantially more likely to be commuted than men's).

[48] 523 U.S. 272 (1998).

[49] Eight justices agreed that Woodard should not prevail on his § 1983 claim, but those justices split 4-4 on whether Woodard had any due process rights in the clemency proceeding.

[50] *See id.* at 281. Justice Rehnquist did concede that there was a "residual life interest" of some kind, such as "not being summarily executed by prison guards."

[51] *Id.* at 280, *quoting from* Connecticut Bd. of Pardons v. Dumschat, 452 U.S. 458, 464 (1981) (noting that "pardon and commutation decisions have not traditionally been the business of courts; as such, they are rarely, if ever, appropriate subjects for judicial review").

[52] Ohio Adult Parole Auth. v. Woodard, 523 U.S. 272, 289 (1998) (O'Connor, J., concurring). Justice O'Connor's concurrence was joined by Justices Souter, Ginsburg, and Breyer. Justice Stevens in concurrence and dissent was the fifth voice finding some level of due process.

In her concurring opinion, Justice O'Connor gave examples of what might violate "minimal" procedural safeguards:

> Judicial intervention might, for example, be warranted in the face of a scheme whereby a state official flipped a coin to determine whether to grant clemency, or in a case where the State arbitrarily denied a prisoner any access to its clemency process.[53]

Because Ohio had basic procedures, Justice O'Connor found no due process violation in Woodard's case.

The five-justice majority in *Woodard* has opened the door to due process claims in clemency proceedings. The scope of the "minimal" due process right is, however, undeveloped. It is clear that Justice O'Connor was treading cautiously into judicial involvement in clemency proceedings. The concurring justices found that Woodard's due process rights were not violated where there were few of the usual procedural mechanisms. These justices also did not suggest overruling prior case law. In two prior cases, the Supreme Court had found no due process rights in release on parole or commutation of a life sentence.[54] Thus, the concurring justices were distinguishing a "liberty" interest, which had been extinguished by the sentence, from a "life" interest, which continued despite the sentence.

Barring a governor who admits to flipping a coin, will a clemency procedure ever violate due process? *Woodard* has opened the door to various claims, discussed in the next section.

[B] Post-*Woodard* Cases

Despite the window of due process rights opened by the *Woodard* decision, courts are routinely rejecting challenges to clemency proceedings. Defendants post-*Woodard* have claimed bias on the part of the members of the administrative board;[55] a blanket policy by a governor not to commute death sentences;[56] political

---

[53] *Id.* In his dissent, Justice Stevens gave examples that, in his view, would result in unconstitutional clemency proceedings. He referred to "procedures infected by bribery, personal or political animosity, or the deliberate fabrication of false evidence." Justice Stevens also wrote that the equal protection clause would prohibit "race, religion, or political affiliation as a standard for granting or denying clemency." *Id.* at 290 (1998) (Stevens, J., concurring in part and dissenting in part).

[54] The Court concluded in Connecticut Bd. Of Pardons v. Dumschat, 452 U.S. 458, 464 (1981), "that an inmate has "no constitutional or inherent right" to commutation of his sentence." But note in Greenholtz v. Inmates of Neb. Penal and Correctional Complex, 442 U.S. 1, 12 (1979), a Nebraska statute was found to "create a presumption that a parole release will be granted, and that in turn creates a legitimate expectation of release absent the requisite finding that one of the justifications for deferral exists." The Court in *Greenholtz* accepted that the statute created an entitlement to some measure of constitutional protection but emphasized that the Nebraska statute has a unique structure and language and that a case by case analysis is necessary to determine a protected entitlement.

[55] *See* Parker v. Georgia State Bd. of Pardons & Paroles, 275 F.3d 1032 (11th Cir. 2001), *cert. denied* 543 U.S. 1072 (2001) (rejecting a due process claim by a capital defendant who had raised bias due to statement by chairman of parole board that "no one on death row should ever receive clemency;" statement, if made, was several years old and chairman indicated an "open mind"); Gilreath v. State Bd. of Pardons & Paroles, 273 F.3d 932, 934 (11th Cir. 2001) (holding that the "appearance of impropriety and bias in proceedings that are not judicial proceedings do not necessarily violate due process").

[56] *See* Anderson v. Davis, 279 F.3d 674, 676 (9th Cir. 2001) (rejecting claim that Governor Davis'

pressure on the governor from running for office not to commute sentences;[57] no hearing, no reasons for denial, and no records or public proceedings;[58] refusal to allow counsel to interview prison inmates and staff about defendant's mental health;[59] and false testimony at the clemency proceeding.[60] The courts typically distinguish these claims from Justice O'Connor's extreme example of "flipping a coin" or Justice Stevens' example of "race, religion, political affiliation . . ." . Thus, "minimal" due process is satisfied in these circumstances.

In two situations, however, courts have not foreclosed a claim on due process grounds, although there was no decision on the merits. In one instance, the defense claimed that it was misled by the governor's agents about what would be considered in the clemency proceeding. As a result, the defense did not present evidence of a lack of culpability for the crime. The defense claimed that the governor denied clemency because there was no such evidence.[61] In a second case, the court reversed a summary judgment for the state in a § 1983 case where the defense claimed that a prosecutor did not give favorable information to the governor in the clemency proceeding because of a threat of losing her job if she did so. The information related to ineffective assistance of counsel and racially based use of peremptory challenges.[62]

Would either of the undecided cases be likely to raise meritorious due process claims? In each case, the state argued that there was no misleading of the defense and no blocking of evidence to the governor, but those arguments are only necessary if the courts find that the claims raise a cognizable due process issue. Thus, the first step is to identify whether the actions complained of, if true, would deprive the defendant of "minimal" due process. It is unlikely that either situation would be viewed as capricious as "flipping a coin." The governor can decide whether or not to grant clemency on any basis he or she chooses. However, it may

---

blanket policy of refusing clemency violated due process); *In re* Sapp, 118 D.3d 460 (6th Cir.1997) (stating that "courts have uniformly rejected allegations that due process is violated by a governor who adopts a general policy of not granting clemency in capital cases").

[57] *See* Roll v. Carnahan, 225 F.3d 1016 (8th Cir. 2000).

[58] *See* Faulder v. Texas Bd. of Pardons & Paroles, 178 F.3d 343, 344 (5th Cir. 1999), (holding that the "minimal due process requirements" in light of the "low threshold of judicial reviewability" set forth in *Woodard*, had been satisfied). The defendant in *Faulder* alleged that the Board acted in secrecy, refused to hold hearings, and gave no reasons for its decisions, and kept no records of its action, describing the Board's action as "an arbitrary exercise of administrative power." *Id.*

[59] Baze v. Thompson, 302 S.W.3d 57 (Ky. 2010), *cert. denied* 131 S. Ct. 111 (2010). *See also* Johnston v. State, 27 So. 3d 11 (Fla. 2010), *cert. denied* 131 S. Ct. 459, 178 L. Ed. 2d 292 (U.S. 2010) (rejecting argument that clemency proceedings were inadequate due to failure to fully develop life history and mental health information).

[60] *See* Workman v. Bell, 245 F.3d 849, 852 (6th Cir. 2001) (stating that the court does not sit as a "super appeals courts over state commutation proceedings", and is "not authorized to review the substantive merits of a clemency proceeding").

[61] *See* Wilson v. United States Dist. Court, 161 F.3d 1185 (9th Cir. 1998) (denying the State's writ of mandamus, leaving in place a temporary restraining order issued by the District Court). The issue was ultimately moot when a new governor took office and conducted a second clemency proceeding.

[62] *See* Young v. Hayes, 218 F.3d 850, 853 (8th Cir. 2000) (holding that conduct on the part of a state official is fundamentally unfair when it "unconscionably interferes with a process that the State itself had created").

be that both situations would be tantamount to a denial of "access" to the clemency process. If the defense is told not to present evidence on lack of culpability and the decision is based on that issue, the defendant arguably did not have access to the process. Similarly, if due to the job-loss threat, the defense is unable to present important evidence to the governor, there is a possible denial of access claim.

§ 18.05   CRITICISMS AND DEFENSE OF THE CLEMENCY PROCESS

[A]   Misguided Reliance on Clemency to Justify Limiting Judicial Review

Many of the commentators on clemency criticize the Supreme Court's reliance on clemency as a reason to limit judicial review at a time when clemency is infrequently granted and provides no guarantee of review.[63] They point to the Court's decision in *Herrera v. Collins*[64] as the paradigm of this breakdown in logic. In *Herrera*, the Court set a high threshold standard for a defendant to meet in order to prevail on an actual innocence claim in federal habeas corpus.[65] In the course of explaining why habeas proceedings were not designed for innocence claims, Justice Rehnquist indicated that clemency proceedings were the proper forum for consideration of post-trial innocence claims. He wrote that "[e]xecutive clemency has provided the fail safe in our criminal justice system."[66] The commentators contend that the reliance on clemency is misplaced because it is so rarely granted. In addition, the commentators criticize the reliance on clemency, which is a nonjudicial proceeding, unregulated and unreviewable.[67] The commentators agree with Justice Blackmun, dissenting in *Herrera*, who commented:

> Whatever procedures a State might adopt to hear actual-innocence claims, one thing is certain: The possibility of executive clemency is not sufficient to satisfy the requirements of the Eighth and Fourteenth Amendments.

---

[63] *See, e.g.*, Victoria J. Palacios, *Faith in Fantasy: The Supreme Court's Reliance on Commutation to Ensure Justice in Death Penalty Cases*, 49 VAND. L. REV. 311, 341, 349 (1996) (commenting on parole authority's mistaken reliance on justice in the judicial system at a time when the Supreme Court is limiting review of capital cases); Kobil, *supra* note 14, at 572 (discussing *Herrera* and noting greater reliance on clemency for innocent defendants at same time that there are fewer grants of clemency); Ridolfi, *supra* note 16, at 73-74 (noting several limitations on the availability of habeas relief).

[64] 506 U.S. 390 (1993).

[65] For further discussion of *Herrera*, see Section 17.02, *supra*.

[66] 506 U.S. at 415.

[67] *See* Hugo Adam Bedau, *The Decline of Executive Clemency in Capital Cases*, 18 N.Y.U. REV. LAW & SOC. CHANGE 255, 257 (1990-91) (describing executive clemency proceedings as "standardless in procedure, discretionary in exercise, and unreviewable in result"); Ridolfi & Gordon, *supra* note 23, at 29-30 (criticizing the Court's decision in *Herrera* for presuming that a governor would in fact hear evidence and grant clemency); Moylan & Carter, *supra* note 8, at 96-97 (noting that clemency is inadequate to guarantee review of specific issues where governor has no obligation to act).

. . . The vindication of rights . . . has never been made to turn on the unreviewable discretion of an executive official or administrative tribunal.[68]

This ongoing debate, on and off the Court, about the significance of the availability of clemency proceedings when evaluating the need for judicial remedies, is likely to continue to arise in capital cases. In addition to habeas cases, the federal government argued before the International Court of Justice that the availability of a clemency proceeding satisfied the need for a "review and reconsideration of the conviction and sentence" of death when there has been a violation of the consular notification provision of an international treaty. In this case, brought by Mexico against the United States, the attorneys for Mexico responded that clemency was an inadequate proceeding to provide a substantive review. The Court found in favor of Mexico and found that clemency was too unregulated a process to satisfy the requirement of a review and reconsideration.[69] The consular notification treaty and standards are discussed in Section 23.04[D], *infra*.

[B]   Political Chilling Effect

Commentators have also criticized the political nature of and influences on clemency. Some of the criticism focuses on the governors' fears of not being reelected, or of being perceived as soft on crime, if they commute death sentences.[70] The only governors who have granted large-scale commutations were those who were leaving office.[71] As noted earlier, some governors have been quoted as stating a policy that they would not commute the sentences of those on death row. One scholar has advocated a selection procedure for a board that would minimize the political influence. Professor Victoria Palacios has proposed that the governor appoint a citizen selection board that then would choose the members of the clemency authority. She suggested that the members of the selection board should be unpaid; some members should be representative of the community, and others should have some knowledge or experience in the criminal justice system, but not be associated with criminal justice agencies.[72] In another article, three co-authors have also suggested a clemency authority appointed by a board.[73] They suggest that the board be comprised of "the Attorney General, a justice from the

---

[68]   506 U.S. at 440-41 (Blackmun J., dissenting).

[69]   Avena and Other Mexican Nationals (Mex. v. U.S.), 2004 I.C.J. No 128, ¶¶ 139-43 (Mar. 31). *See* discussion in Carter, *supra* note 19, at 265-71.

[70]   *See* Palacios, *supra* note 63, at 350 (stating that "[c]ommuting a death sentence can pose 'serious political consequences' "); Ridolfi & Gordon, *supra* note 23, at 33 (noting the effect of "tough-on-crime" stances towards clemency combined with the AEDPA's limitations on federal habeas petitions). *But see* Heise, *supra* note 9, at 295 (finding no statistical significance between grants of clemency and pending elections); Korengold, *supra* note 14, at 363-4 (finding that the "belief that granting clemency is certain political suicide is not well-founded").

[71]   *See* Section 18.03[A], *supra*. Korengold, *supra* note 14, at 363 (stating that "the only widespread use of executive clemency has been by individuals who are leaving office and thus immune from reelection pressures").

[72]   *See* Palacios, *supra* note 63, at 371.

[73]   Korengold, *supra* note 14, at 368.

state supreme court, and a current or past member of the state parole board."[74] As an innovative suggestion to remove political influence, the co-authors advocated that the members of the clemency authority be appointed for life in order to further insulate them from outside pressures.[75]

[C]   Lack of Procedures

Yet another criticism of clemency proceedings is the lack of any standardized procedures. Without any regulations, the grant or denial of clemency is subject to claims of arbitrariness.[76] One writer has suggested that the arbitrariness of clemency decisions warrants establishing guidelines. The procedure would include notice to the defendant of the factors that will be considered. She also proposed substantive statutory guidelines on factors that could be considered.[77]

The American Bar Association (ABA) has similarly advocated for establishing standards and procedures in clemency. Both the report of the ABA Justice Kennedy Commission,[78] with a focus largely on noncapital cases, and the ABA Death Penalty Moratorium Project[79] urge adoption of standards and procedures. The latter report specifically makes recommendations. The recommendations include substantive factors to consider in clemency, such as the circumstances of the crime, racial or geographic disparity, serious mental illness, lingering doubt, and rehabilitation.[80] The recommendations further include procedural protections, such as representation by counsel and a public hearing before the decision-maker.[81]

[D]   The Response: In Defense of Clemency as Political and Unregulated

The existence of clemency as a politically influenced decision is not without its defenders. In a 2002 article, Beau Breslin and John J.P. Howley emphasized that clemency is not part of the judicial process and should remain within the exclusive province of an elected executive.[82] They suggested that problems in the judicial

---

[74] *Id.*

[75] *Id.*

[76] *See, e.g.,* Radelet and Zsembik, *supra* note 6, at 305, (concluding that "the exercise of executive clemency in post-*Furman* cases is idiosyncratic at best, and arbitrary at worst").

[77] *See,* Dinsmore, *supra* note 8, at 1855 (suggesting substantive guidelines "reflecting the value judgements of each individual state" to be decided upon by elected lawmakers").

[78] ABA Justice Kennedy Commission, Reports with Recommendations to the ABA House of Delegates, 3   (2004),   *available   at*   http://www.abanet.org/crimjust/kennedy/JusticeKennedyCommission ReportsFinal.pdf.

[79] ABA, Death without Justice: A Guide for Examining the Administration of the Death Penalty in the United States, *available at* http://www.abanet.org/irr/finaljune28.pdf.

[80] *Id. See also* discussion in Moylan & Carter, *supra* note 8, at 90-93.

[81] *Id.*

[82] Breslin & Howley, *supra* note 17, at 246-53. *But see* Joanna M. Huang, *Correcting Mandatory Injustice: Judicial Recommendation of Executive Clemency,* 60 Duke L.J. 131, 153-55 (2010) (arguing for increased judicial involvement through judicial recommendations for clemency in particular cases as

system should be corrected without invading the separate status of clemency by imposing procedural requirements. They further pointed out that the unregulated clemency process has, in fact, allowed governors or administrative boards the prerogative to grant clemency, as well as to deny it.[83] This prerogative, unfettered by judicial constraints, gives the clemency authority the ability to commute a sentence for reasons not legally recognized. Professor Rapaport described this role of clemency as "an incubator and laboratory for defenses and mitigation not yet developed to the point of being accepted legal doctrines."[84] For example, prior to the admissibility of the battered woman syndrome as evidence of self-defense in homicide cases, some governors commuted sentences based on the syndrome.[85] In an earlier article, written before her appointment to the bench, Judge Janice Rogers Brown also defended the concept of clemency as a means to dispense mercy outside of the constraints of the legal process.[86] Judge Brown captured the essence of the ongoing debate between prescribing procedures to regularize the clemency process and retaining clemency as a nonlegal, moral judgment. She wrote: "Law is narrower than justice. Mercy is broader than both. Justice can be merciless, but mercy must be just."[87]

---

a way to combat harsh sentences and decrease arbitrary influences in clemency decisions).

[83] *Id.* at 253.

[84] Rapaport, *supra*, note 27, at 372.

[85] *See*, Sarah M. Buel, *Effective Assistance of Counsel for Battered Women Defendants: A Normative Construct*, 26 HARV. WOMEN'S L.J. 217, 320-23 (2003) (analyzing battered woman syndrome with a focus on the need for effective counsel, including a discussion on post-conviction remedies such as clemency reform and advocacy efforts based on battered woman syndrome defenses).

[86] Janice Rogers Brown, *The Quality of Mercy*, 40 U.C.L.A. L. Rev. 327 (1992) (at the time of the article, Judge Brown was Legal Affairs Secretary to the Governor).

[87] *Id.* at 335.

Chapter 19

DEATH ROW ISSUES: INSANITY AND DEATH ROW PHENOMENON

§ 19.01 INSANITY OR INCOMPETENCY AT THE TIME OF EXECUTION

[A] Eighth Amendment Prohibition Against Executing the Insane

[1] The Nature of the Issue

Consider the following situation: D is convicted of a capital murder and sentenced to death. The automatic appeal to the state supreme court is completed and the court has upheld the conviction and sentence. State and federal habeas petitions have been denied. An execution date is set. While on death row during the several years of post conviction proceedings, D's mental state has deteriorated. D develops delusions that there is a conspiracy by various prison authorities and political figures to hold D's relatives hostage and force D to commit suicide. D states to a psychiatrist that he cannot be executed "because he own[s] the prisons and [can] control the Governor through mind waves." Ultimately, D speaks only in phrases using the word "one," such as "Hands one, face one. Mafia one. God one, father one, Pope one. Pope one. Leader one."[1]

In *Ford v. Wainwright*,[2] the Supreme Court held that it violated the Eighth Amendment to execute a person who is "insane" or "incompetent" at the time of execution. Why does it violate the Constitution to execute an insane person? Is the person in the opening hypothetical insane? How does insanity at the time of execution differ from incompetency to stand trial or an insanity defense to the crime? What kind of procedure is necessary to decide whether or not a person is insane at the time of execution? Who should make that determination?

This section examines these questions about the basis for the constitutional bar to executing the insane, the definitional issues, and the procedural requirements.

---

[1] Ford v. Wainwright, 477 U.S. 399, 402-403 (1986). In this chapter, the terms "insane" and "incompetent" and their derivatives are used interchangeably as they relate to a capital inmate's mental state at the time of execution.

[2] *Id.* at 410.

[2] The *Ford* Opinion

In a 5-4 decision, the Supreme Court held that the Eighth Amendment prohibits the execution of a person who is insane at the time of execution. Citing both Blackstone and Coke, the Court found support in early common law doctrine that a "lunatic" or a "mad man" should not be executed.[3]

The common law prohibited executing the insane for various reasons. The Court noted that they included: 1) a concept of "humanity," (2) a lack of deterrent purpose, 3) a religious concern that a person be able to prepare for death, and 4) a concept that "madness" was a sufficient punishment in itself. The Court included a fifth reason of more recent conception: a lack of retributive purpose.[4]

In addition to the common law heritage, the Court looked to evolving standards of decency as a means to interpret the current meaning of the Eighth Amendment. Although some state statutes were more explicit than others, the Court found no state that allowed the execution of the insane. The Court specifically pointed to two of the long-standing reasons: 1) a lack of a retributive purpose when the person cannot understand why the punishment is being imposed and 2) a sense of humanity for a person who cannot understand what is occurring.[5]

[3] What is Meant by "Insane" or "Incompetent" at Time of Execution?

It is clear that insanity at the time of execution is not identical to either incompetency to stand trial or the insanity defense to the commission of a crime. On the other hand, all three legal concepts, all based on a defendant's mental state, are related. Each concept pertains to a different point in time.

Although definitions vary, in general a defendant is viewed as *incompetent to stand trial* if he or she does not understand the charges or cannot assist counsel. The due process clause prohibits proceeding with the prosecution of the defendant unless and until competency is restored. The critical point is the time of the trial.[6]

The *insanity defense* is raised as an affirmative defense to the commission of the crime itself. The critical point is when the crime occurred. Thus, a defendant may be sane or competent at the time of trial and yet have been insane at the time of the crime. Here, too, states use different definitions. A typical definition, derived from common law, provides for an insanity defense only if, because of a mental illness or

---

[3] *See id.* at 406-407 (stating that the doctrine bears "impressive historical credentials," and quoting Blackstone: "if, after judgement, he becomes of nonsane memory, execution shall be stayed: for peradventure . . . he might have alleged something in stay of judgement or execution").

[4] *See id.* at 408 (finding that more recent commentaries have reasoned that, because it is of a "lesser quality," the execution of an insane person does not serve "the need to offset a criminal act by a punishment of equivalent moral quality").

[5] *See id.* at 409 (concluding that "the ancient and humane limitation upon the State's ability to execute its sentences has as firm a hold upon the jurisprudence of today as it had centuries ago in England").

[6] Medina v. California, 505 U.S. 437, 440, 448 (1992) (explaining that the focus of a competency hearing "is on [the defendant's] capacity to consult with counsel and to comprehend the proceedings, and . . . this is by no means the same test as those which determine criminal responsibility at the time of the crime.") (internal quotes omitted).

disorder, the defendant either did not know the nature and quality of the act or did not understand the difference between right and wrong.[7] If the defendant is found insane as a defense, in most jurisdictions, he is deemed "not guilty by reason of insanity."[8] The result is typically commitment to a state mental institution until such time as the defendant is no longer considered mentally ill or a danger to himself or others. At that point, the defendant would be released as he was not guilty of the crime itself.[9]

The Eighth Amendment prohibition against executing an insane person, or *incompetency at the time of execution*, designates the critical point as right before execution. Thus, the defendant was convicted and sentenced and was competent to stand trial; any insanity defense, if raised, was rejected. Like Alvin Ford, the defendant described in the opening hypothetical, the defendant has developed severe psychological problems while sitting on death row. In the *Ford* opinion, the Court did not define "insane." Writing for a four-justice plurality, Justice Marshall stated that the Eighth Amendment proscribes the execution of "one whose mental illness prevents him from comprehending the reasons for the penalty or its implications."[10] Justice Powell, concurring to provide the fifth vote for the holding that the Eighth Amendment prohibited the execution of the insane, tackled the definition in his separate opinion. Based on both history and the reasons for barring the execution of the insane, Justice Powell found that the Eighth Amendment ban should prohibit the execution of "those who are unaware of the punishment they are about to suffer and why they are to suffer it."[11] In deciding on this approach, Justice Powell rejected a definition that would have precluded the execution of a defendant who was unable to "assist his defense."

Since the *Ford* decision in 1986, most states followed a version of the "awareness" definition from Justice Powell's concurrence. Two states specifically identified an inability to assist the defense as qualifying for insane or incompetent at the time of execution.[12] Under the awareness standard, very few defendants were found insane.

---

[7] *See, e.g.,* CAL. PENAL CODE § 25(b) (West 2011) (stating that the insanity defense "shall be found by the trier of fact only when the accused person proves by a preponderance of the evidence that he or she was incapable of knowing or understanding the nature and quality of his or her act and of distinguishing right from wrong at the time of the commission of the offense").

[8] *See* JOSHUA DRESSLER, UNDERSTANDING CRIMINAL LAW § 25.02[C] (5th ed. 2009) (describing not guilty by reason of insanity verdict). Approximately 22 states have adopted a "guilty but mentally ill" verdict in place of or in addition to a "not guilty by reason of insanity" defense. *See id.* at § 25.07. A few states have attempted to abolish the insanity defense entirely, while allowing mental illness to negate the *mens rea* of the crime. *See id.* at § 25.06; Daniel J. Nusbaum, *The Craziest Reform of Them All: A Critical Analysis of the Constitutional Implications of "Abolishing" the Insanity Defense*, 87 CORNELL L. REV. 1509 (2002) (describing and criticizing the efforts in four states to abolish an affirmative defense of insanity and replace it with only a "mens rea" defense).

[9] *See, e.g.,* CAL. PENAL CODE § 1026 (establishing a procedure once a defendant has been found not guilty by reason of insanity); DRESSLER, *supra* note 8, at § 25.05.

[10] 477 U.S. at 417.

[11] *See id.* at 422 (stating that the defendant's perception of the connection between the crime and the punishment satisfies the retributive goal of criminal law).

[12] *See* John L. Farringer, IV, *The Competency Conundrum: Problems Courts Have Faced in Applying Different Standards for Competency to be Executed*, 54 VAND. L. REV. 2441, 2456 (2001) (indicating Mississippi and Missouri follow "the broader two-prong test endorsed by the ABA," which

A defendant who believed that his "protective genes" would prevent him from dying was found incompetent to be executed.[13] However, defendants who believed that they were Jesus Christ,[14] Julius Caesar,[15] or believed that a deceased relative would protect them from death despite a lethal injection[16] were found to possess a minimal level of awareness of their impending executions and the reasons for it.

[4] The *Panetti* Opinion

The Supreme Court modified the *Ford* decision by concluding that the correct test of competency at the time of execution is not whether a defendant is simply aware that the state has identified his crime as the rationale for his impending execution but whether he has a "rational understanding" of the reasons for his execution. In *Panetti v. Quarterman*,[17] the petitioner, Scott Panetti, was severely mentally ill at the time of his scheduled execution. He was aware that he had committed two murders, that he was to be executed, and that Texas's stated reason for executing him was his commission of the murders. At the same time, because of gross delusions resulting from schizophrenia, Panetti reportedly believed that the articulated reason for the execution was a "sham" and that the state actually wanted to kill him to prevent him from preaching the word of God. The lower courts determined that this information was irrelevant to whether Panetti had the basic awareness seemingly required by *Ford*. However, a five-justice majority of the Supreme Court disagreed, concluding that a competency determination requires a deeper inquiry than merely whether the defendant is aware that the State has identified a link between his crime and his execution. The Court did not attempt to set forth a clear rule defining competency for execution. However, the Court stated that the inmate must have not simply an "awareness of the state's rationale" for the execution but rather a "rational understanding of it."[18] The Court remanded the case for reconsideration by the District Court after further development of the evidentiary record regarding Panetti's mental illness.

While the *Panetti* opinion clarifies that use of the simple "awareness" test is no longer proper, it also creates new uncertainty about the Eighth Amendment rule for determining sanity for execution. The opinion will spawn litigation that will benefit some death-row inmates. However, it is unlikely that *Panetti* will greatly expand the number of death-row inmates who are ultimately spared from execution. The *Panetti* majority underscored that its concern was not with inmates whose possibly bizarre understandings of their situations stems from "a misanthropic personality" or "an amoral character," but, instead, with inmates who suffer from "a severe, documented mental illness that is the source of gross delusions."[19] Moreover, the

---

considers both a defendant's ability to understand the proceedings and his capacity to participate in his defense by communicating facts or arguments indicating why his sentence should not be carried out).

[13] Singleton v. State, 437 S.E.2d 53, 58 (S.C. 1993).

[14] Provenzano v. State, 760 So. 2d 137, 140 (Fla. 2000), *cert. denied* 481 U.S. 1024 (2000).

[15] Billiot v. State, 655 So. 2d 1, 8 (Miss. 1995), *cert. denied* 516 U.S. 1095 (1996).

[16] Garrett v. Collins, 951 F.2d 57 (5th Cir. 1992).

[17] 551 U.S. 930 (2007).

[18] *Id.* at 959.

[19] *Id.* at 960.

majority emphasized that these delusions must actually prevent the inmate "from comprehending the meaning and purpose of the punishment to which he has been sentenced."[20] It remains doubtful that most mentally ill death-row inmates will meet the insanity standard, even after *Panetti*.[21] Both the justification for and criticism of using a narrow standard of insanity are based on the reasons for prohibiting the execution of the insane. Those who advocate for a narrow standard focus on the procedural protections that the defendant has already received in the trial and postconviction proceedings. The retributive benefit of punishing an individual who was sane at the time of the crime is also cited as justifying the execution of an individual, even though the individual is severely mentally ill. Those favoring a broader standard focus on the human dignity concept. The heart of this position is that it is inhumane and uncivilized to execute an individual who is seriously disadvantaged due to a mental illness.[22]

[5]   What Procedure is Required?

Once it is decided that the Eighth Amendment provides a right not to be executed if insane, the next issue is what type of procedure is required to protect the right. How should the issue of the defendant's insanity be decided? Should there be an evidentiary proceeding like a trial? Should the decision be made by a judge or a jury? Should the proceeding be solely before the governor as in clemency?

In the *Ford* decision, by a 7-2 vote, the Supreme Court held that Florida's procedure failed to meet due process standards. Under Florida law, the sanity decision was made by the governor. The governor appointed psychiatrists (often referred to as "alienists" in the statutes) to examine the defendant and report to the Governor. The defense was not able to question the psychiatrists, and it was unclear whether the governor would consider written materials from the defense. A four-justice plurality of the Court found the Florida procedures inadequate on three major grounds: the defendant's lack of opportunity to present information; the defendant's inability to challenge the state-appointed psychiatrists' reports; and the conferral of the decision-making authority on the governor, who, as the chief executive of state prosecutions, was not in a neutral position.[23]

Three justices, Powell, O'Connor, and White, concurred with the plurality that Florida's procedures failed to meet due process standards. Justice Powell, who also agreed that the Eighth Amendment prohibited the execution of an insane person, found due process required an opportunity to present information on the defendant's sanity and an impartial decision-maker.[24] Justices O'Connor and White, who dissented on the Eighth Amendment issue but found a state-created expectation that an insane person would not be executed, also found due process problems with

---

[20] *Id.*

[21] Thompson v. Bell, 580 F. 3d 423 (6th Cir. 2009) (applying *Panetti* standard and remanding for an evidentiary hearing that would take into account the defendant's delusions and mental history).

[22] *See* discussion in Jeffrey L. Kirchmeier, *The Undiscovered Country: Execution Competency & Comprehending Death*, 98 Ky. L. J. 263 (2010).

[23] *Ford*, 477 U.S. at 413-416.

[24] *Id.* at 427.

Florida's procedure. Their focus was on the inability to be heard. Thus, they were in agreement with the plurality and Justice Powell that due process required the opportunity to present and have considered by the decision maker the defendant's information about his sanity.[25]

In his concurrence, Justice Powell made it clear that he did not believe that due process required extensive trial-type protections. Thus, in his view, the defendant could be required to meet a "substantial threshold showing of insanity . . . to trigger the hearing process," and would not necessarily be entitled to cross-examination and other adversarial protections. The plurality similarly, although in a less defining manner, indicated that less than a "full trial" would be adequate and that a "high threshold showing" might be appropriate. The plurality suggested looking to procedures for competency to stand trial and involuntary commitment by analogy.[26]

In the *Panetti* case, a majority of the justices reaffirmed that Justice Powell's concurring opinion in *Ford* set forth certain minimum procedures a state must provide to an inmate who has made "a substantial threshold showing" of incompetency. These basic requirements include a "fair hearing" that provides an opportunity to submit "evidence and argument from the prisoner's counsel, including expert psychiatric evidence that may differ from the State's own psychiatric examination."[27] The Court found that Panetti, despite having met the threshold showing, had not been afforded such an opportunity by the Texas courts.[28] As a result, the determination of competency by the Texas courts was invalid and entitled to no deference by federal courts in addressing Panetti's claim of incompetency on habeas review. Because the case was remanded to the federal District Court, which had already provided a much more expansive, adversarial hearing, the Supreme Court did not address what procedures beyond those specified by Justice Powell in *Ford* would in some cases be required under the Due Process Clause.[29]

The procedures in states today provide death row inmates with an opportunity to be heard, but vary in format. Most states satisfy the impartiality issue by giving the decision to a court.[30] The typical procedure includes appointment of alienists,

---

[25] *Id.* at 429-430.

[26] *Id.* at 417 n 4.

[27] 551 U.S. at 949-950.

[28] The Supreme Court noted that the state trial court may have violated state law by failing to provide a competency hearing. *See id.* at 950.

[29] For discussion concerning what minimum procedures should be required, see Richard J. Bonnie, *The Death Penalty and Mental Illness: Mentally Ill Prisoners on Death Row: Unsolved Puzzles for Courts and Legislatures*, 54 Cath. L. Rev. 1169, 1174 (2005) ("The prisoner is entitled to state-subsidized counsel and expert assessment once evidence raising a significant doubt about his competence is discovered. The issue should be adjudicated at a hearing before a judge at which the prisoner bears the burden of proving his incompetence by a preponderance of the evidence.").

[30] *See, e.g.*, Ariz. Rev. Stat. §§ 13-4021-13-4024; Ga. Code Ann. §§ 17-10-60 to 17-10-63, 17-10-71; Md. Code Ann., Correctional Services § 3-904; Mo. Rev. Stat. § 552.060; N.Y. Correct. Law § 656; N.C. Gen. Stat. § 15A-1001; Ohio Rev. Code Ann. §§ 2949.28-2949.29; Tenn. Code Ann. § 39-13-204(c) (this is for sentencing for 1st degree murder). California and Oklahoma provide for a jury decision on incompetency to be executed. *See*, e.g., Cal. Penal Code §§ 3703-3704.5; Okla. Stat. tit. 22, §§ 1005-1008.

presentation of evidence, and the ability to contest the evidence.[31] The burden is generally on the inmate to demonstrate incompetency.[32]

[B]   "Medicate-to-Execute" Issues

[1]   The Nature of the Issue

Suppose that D, who is incompetent to be executed, regains an awareness of his impending execution and an understanding of the reasons for it when he is placed on antipsychotic drugs. Is D now competent to be executed? Suppose further that D refuses the medication. Is it constitutional to medicate D involuntarily? Can the use of involuntary medication render D competent to be executed?

Consider the case of Charles Laverne Singleton.[33] Convicted of capital murder and sentenced to death in 1979, Singleton's mental state deteriorated while he was on death row. At various points in time, he thought he was either God or the Supreme Court, had hallucinations about a demon in his cell and his food turning into worms, behaved destructively and belligerently, thought Sylvester Stallone and Arnold Schwartzenegger would save him, and believed he could not be killed.[34] Although Singleton was on some medication almost immediately on his arrival on death row, beginning in 1987 he was treated consistently for his schizophrenia. During much of the time from 1987-2001 the medication was administered involuntarily, interspersed with periods of no medication and voluntary medication.[35] The case raised the issues of: 1) the constitutionality of involuntary medication if it rendered him competent for execution, and 2) the constitutionality of executing a person who is competent only because of medication.

[2]   Overview of the Legal Issues

The "medicate-to-execute" situation is more complicated legally than the situation in *Ford* and *Panetti*, discussed in the previous section. In *Ford* and *Panetti*, the Supreme Court held that the Eighth Amendment prohibited the execution of an incompetent inmate and that the due process clause required a certain level of procedural protections for the determination of competency. The medicate-to-execute situation includes the *Ford/Panetti* issues and invokes a second set of cases involving involuntary medication. One type of case arises in a *noncapital* context of involuntarily medicating prison inmates. Inmates had argued that involuntarily medicating them violated their substantive due process liberty interests. With

---

[31] *See, e.g.,* OHIO REV. CODE ANN. §§ 2949.28-2949.29 (describing procedure in which judge may appoint psychiatrists/psychologists and then conduct a hearing at which the prosecutor, defendant, and defense attorney are present and may call witnesses and cross-examine the other side's witnesses).

[32] *See, e.g.,* ARIZ. REV. STAT. §§ 13-4021-13-4024 (placing burden of clear and convincing evidence on defendant); OHIO REV. CODE ANN. § 2949.29 (placing burden of a preponderance of the evidence on defendant).

[33] Singleton v. Norris, 267 F.3d 859 (8th Cir. 2001), *vacated* 319 F.3d 1018 (8th Cir. 2003). *See* discussion of the *Singleton* decisions in Section 19.01[B][6][a], *infra.*

[34] *Id.* at 864.

[35] *Id.* at 865.

certain requirements, the Supreme Court upheld the involuntary medication of noncapital inmates in *Washington v. Harper*.[36] A second type of involuntary medication case arises in capital or noncapital cases in the context of medicating before trial to induce competency to stand trial.[37] The Supreme Court has provided a balancing test of the defendant's interests and the state's interests to determine the constitutionality of involuntarily medicating a defendant for competency to stand trial.[38] In the medicate-to-execute context, the inmates argue that, in a *capital* case, *Ford/Panetti* prohibits the involuntary medication and execution. The states argue that the reasoning of *Harper* controls the involuntary medication issue and that, once the inmate is constitutionally medicated into competency, the execution does not contravene *Ford/Panetti*.

This section considers the confluence of the due process and Eighth Amendment issues, unresolved by the Supreme Court.

[3] Constitutionality of Involuntary Medication in Prison or for Competency to Stand Trial

As death row inmates are incarcerated at the time of their pending executions, the case law that is most directly implicated is the involuntary medication of prison inmates. A second, related area of case law is the involuntary medication of pretrial detainees who are otherwise incompetent to stand trial. Both areas of jurisprudence are described in the next subsections.

[a] *Washington v. Harper*: Involuntary Medication of Prison Inmates

Harper was a significant case for both inmates and prison authorities. The Supreme Court held that an inmate has a liberty interest under the Due Process Clause to be free from involuntary antipsychotic drugs.[39] At the same time, the Court held that an inmate's liberty interest was not violated by involuntary antipsychotic medication if the inmate suffered from a "serious mental illness" and "the inmate is dangerous to himself or others and the treatment is in the inmate's medical interest."[40] The Court additionally upheld the state of Washington's procedural protections that involved a hearing before a three-person committee and the right to seek state court review of the committee's decision.[41]

---

[36] Washington v. Harper, 494 U.S. 210 (1990).

[37] *See* Riggins v. Nevada, 504 U.S. 127 (1992); Sell v. United States 539 U.S. 166 (2003).

[38] *See Sell*, 539 U.S. at 180.

[39] *See Harper*, 494 U.S. at 221-222 (although the Court states that the due process clause creates a liberty interest, it noted that because state policy allowed an inmate to challenge forced medication in a hearing before a Department of Corrections committee, the State had also created a significant liberty interest).

[40] *Id.* at 227.

[41] *Id.* at 231-232.

[b]   Involuntary Medication for Competency to Stand Trial

Although the involuntary medication of prison inmates and death row inmates arises after trial, conviction, and sentencing, there is also an involuntary medication issue that arises at the beginning of the criminal proceedings. It is unconstitutional to try a defendant who is "incompetent" to stand trial.[42] While incompetency to stand trial is a different standard[43] from incompetency to be executed, there are still potential parallels in assessing the constitutionality of involuntary medication. Thus, it is helpful to understand the Supreme Court's reasoning on the competency to stand trial cases.

The constitutionality of involuntarily medicating a defendant to induce competency to stand trial is dependent on a delicate balancing test. In *Sell v. United States*,[44] the Supreme Court held that a defendant could be involuntarily medicated in order to make the defendant competent to stand trial under the following circumstances:

> . . . if the treatment is medically appropriate, is substantially unlikely to have side effects that may undermine the fairness of the trial, and, taking account of less intrusive alternatives, is necessary significantly to further important governmental trial-related interests.[45]

The Court acknowledged that the state or federal government had an important governmental interest in being able to prosecute the defendant for a crime. The Court made it clear, however, that it was less likely to be constitutional to medicate involuntarily for the sole purpose of rendering the defendant competent to stand trial than it would be to medicate involuntarily under a *Harper*-type analysis of danger to the defendant or others.[46] Among other concerns, the Court reiterated Justice Kennedy's admonition from an earlier case[47] that the medication could interfere with the fairness of the trial by affecting the defendant's demeanor at trial.[48]

---

[42] *See* discussion in Section 19.01[A][3], *supra.*

[43] *Id.*

[44] 539 U.S. 166 (2003). Sell's case was remanded to the Eighth Circuit because the lower courts focused on the dangerousness of the defendant rather than on whether trial competency warranted the forced medication. As the Court noted:

> The failure to focus upon trial competence could well have mattered. Whether a particular drug will tend to sedate a defendant, interfere with communication with counsel, prevent rapid reaction to trial developments, or diminish the ability to express emotions are matters important in determining the permissibility of medication to restore competence.

Id. at 185.

[45] *Id.* at 179.

[46] *Id.* at 181-82.

[47] *Riggins*, 504 U.S. at 142 (Kennedy, J., concurring).

[48] *Id.* In *Riggins*, Justice Kennedy also raised a concern about a medicated defendant's ability to assist counsel.

[4] Questions from the Confluence of *Ford/Panetti* and *Harper/Sell*

A number of interrelated questions arise in capital cases when a death row inmate is involuntarily medicated and the medication brings the inmate from incompetency into a state of awareness of the impending execution. The following sections will look at each of these questions:

1) Is it constitutional to medicate a death row inmate involuntarily for the express purpose of making her competent for execution?

2) Is it constitutional to medicate a death row inmate involuntarily because she poses a danger to herself or others and it is in her best medical interests?

3) If it is permissible to medicate a death row inmate involuntarily under *Harper* standards and she appears to meet the *Ford/Panetti* criteria of competency while medicated, is it constitutional for a state to proceed with the execution?

4) Although not a legal issue,[49] there is an intertwined medical ethical issue: Is it ethical for physicians to prescribe medication that will facilitate the inmate's execution?

[5] Medication for the Purpose of Competency for Execution

Consider the following situation: The state has followed its procedures and D is found to be incompetent under the state standard. If D is medicated, however, she will meet the state standard for competency. May the state constitutionally medicate D involuntarily for the purpose of making her competent to be executed?

Two state supreme courts have held that to "medicate to execute" under these circumstances is unconstitutional. In both *State v. Perry*[50] and *Singleton v. State*,[51] the courts found that forcible medication for the purpose of execution violated state constitutional provisions on the right to privacy. Without a medical and safety rationale, the state's interest was not sufficient to justify the medication. In *Perry*, the Louisiana Supreme Court explicitly rejected the rationale that the state had a compelling interest in carrying out the execution that surmounted the inmate's privacy interest. In addition, *Perry* held that medicating to execute violated the state constitutional provision on cruel and unusual punishment. The court viewed forcible medication for the purpose of inflicting a punishment as degrading the human dignity of the inmate in contravention of the underlying principles of the

---

[49] There is an argument that the medical ethics should be considered in assessing the constitutionality of involuntary medication. The dissent in *Singleton*, *see* discussion in Section 19.01[B][6][a], *infra*, noted that the "ethical dilemma" of the medical profession was "an appropriate consideration." *Singleton*, 267 F.3d at 1037.

[50] State v. Perry, 610 So. 2d 746 (La. 1992).

[51] Singleton v. State, 437 S.E.2d 53 (S.C. 1993).

prohibition of cruel and unusual punishment.[52]

The holdings of the *Perry* and *Singleton* cases seem sound. *Harper* required that any involuntary medication be in the best medical interest of the inmate as well as to prevent harm to the inmate or others. When the expressed purpose is to render an inmate competent for execution, the state fails to satisfy either prong of *Harper*. Thus, assuming *Harper* applies in a capital context, a true "medicate to execute" plan would violate the due process rights of the inmate.

[6]   Medication for the Purposes of the Inmate's Medical Interest and Prison Safety

[a]   Changing the Focus to Medical and Safety Needs

In *Perry*, the Louisiana Supreme Court noted that the state had not demonstrated that involuntarily medicating the inmate was for any purpose other than executing him. In contrast, Arkansas state officials asserted in *Singleton v. Norris*[53] that they had legitimate reasons to medicate Singleton based on medical need and prison safety. Singleton was seriously mentally ill. Arkansas procedures were followed and involuntary medication was approved. The state argued that they had complied with *Harper* and the forcible medication was valid. The Arkansas Supreme Court agreed, and further found that the "collateral effect" of the involuntary medication, which made Singleton competent for execution, did not violate the due process clause.[54] The Arkansas court, however, did not explicitly address the Eighth Amendment issues raised by the *Ford* decision.

When Singleton's case wound its way into federal court, more inquiry was made into his competency. Findings were made that Singleton was incompetent prior to being medicated and would possibly revert to incompetency within a number of months if taken off medication. In addition, the evaluating psychiatrist reported that he was not sure he could verify that Singleton was competent even when medicated.[55] The state renewed its argument that the primary purposes for involuntary medication were medical and safety, and not for execution.[56] The state further maintained its position that, if the medication was constitutional under

---

[52] *Perry*, 610 So. 2d at 763 (stating "[t]he principal hallmark of any punishment that is degrading to the dignity of human beings is that it treats members of the human race as non-humans. . . . [E]ven the vilest criminal remains a human being both possessed and deserving of common human dignity"). *See also* Bonnie, *supra* note 27, at 1175 (agreeing with the decision in *Perry* and asserting: "There is only one sensible solution to this dilemma: a death sentence should be automatically commuted to a lesser punishment after a prisoner has been found incompetent for execution.").

[53] 992 S.W.2d 768, 770 (Ark. 1999).

[54] *Id.*

[55] *See* Singleton, 267 F.3d at 866 (The Eighth Circuit's earlier remand order did not ask the district court to make a determination on whether Singleton, under medication, was competent to be executed, so the district court made no finding on the issue).

[56] *See id.* at 867 (The state also argued that the controversy was moot because, at the time the petition was taken by the Court of Appeals, Singleton was voluntarily taking his medication. However, both the State and the Court agreed that this case fell within an exception to the mootness doctrine as it was highly possible that Singleton would refuse his medication in the future).

Harper, any resulting competency would render an execution valid under *Ford*.[57]

Although a divided panel of the Eighth Circuit initially reduced Singleton's sentence to life imprisonment, the court *en banc* reversed.[58] The panel had found that, because it was unclear if Singleton would be competent off medication and, more importantly, unclear if Singleton would be competent on the day of execution even while medicated, they could not conclude that Singleton had the requisite awareness to be found competent for execution. As a result, the panel ordered Singleton's sentence reduced to life without parole.[59] The court *en banc* assumed Singleton's competence on medication.[60] Drawing on the standards of earlier cases on involuntary medication, the *en banc* court first held that it was constitutional under the due process clause to medicate a death row inmate involuntarily if the requirements were otherwise met.[61] Thus, the court rejected the argument that it was not in the defendant's "best medical interests" to be medicated into competency. Instead, the court viewed the medical interest issue as solely related to treatment of the mental disorder. The court further held that it was constitutional under the Eighth Amendment to execute a death row inmate who was competent solely because of the medication.[62]

The dissenters disagreed with both conclusions. They did not view medicating the inmate to treat the disorder with the result of competency for execution as in the inmate's best medical interest.[63] The dissenters further did not consider a "drug-induced sanity" as comparable to "true sanity."[64] As a result, they considered *Ford* controlling, barring the execution of an inmate with " 'artificial' or 'synthetic' sanity."[65]

The Eighth Circuit's majority and dissenting opinions in *Singleton* reflect the uncertain resolution of the constitutional issues surrounding involuntary medication of death row inmates. The "medicate for treatment with resulting competency for execution" situation remains a difficult issue, unresolved by the Supreme Court. The Sixth Circuit Court of Appeals also addressed the Eighth

---

[57] *Id.* at 869.

[58] Singleton v. Norris, 319 F.3d 1018 (8th Cir. 2003) (most circuit court decisions are made by three-judge panels; an *en banc* court is a review by the full court).

[59] *Singleton*, 267 F.3d at 871.

[60] *Singleton*, 319 F.3d at 1022 (Noting "[a]lthough the district court did not make a specific finding as to Singleton's present competence, Singleton does not argue that under medication he is unaware of his punishment and why he is to be punished").

[61] *Id.* at 1027.

[62] *Id.* (concluding that "[a] State does not violate the Eighth Amendment as interpreted by *Ford* when it executes a prisoner who became incompetent during his long stay on death row but who subsequently regained competency through appropriate medical care").

[63] *Id.* at 1036 n.11 (Heaney, J., dissenting) (stating "[u]nlike the majority, I am not convinced that forced medical treatment is in Singleton's best medical interest when it may ultimately result in his execution").

[64] *Id.* at 1034. Judge Heaney commented: "I am left with no alternative but to conclude that drug-induced sanity is not the same as true sanity. Singleton is not "cured;" his insanity is merely muted, at times, by the powerful drugs he is forced to take. Underneath this mask of stability, he remains insane."

[65] *See id.* at 1024.

Amendment issue, but found it unnecessary to decide the issue in the case before them. In *Thompson v. Bell*,[66] the defendant was not presently medicated involuntarily. As a result, his challenge to "chemical competency" as sufficient for competency to execute was not currently an issue. The Court noted, however, that "[i]f forced medication reduces a prisoner's delusions and controls his outward behavior, but does not improve his understanding of his impending death or his ability to prepare for it, it is quite possible that the prisoner cannot be executed under the principles of *Ford*."[67] A concurring opinion took the opposite view. Thus, similar to the 8th Circuit in *Singleton*, the division in the 6th Circuit panel reflects the difficulty of the legal issues when a person on death row is involuntarily medicated, with the result of at least "chemical" competence. The next section discusses the arguments of both sides on the due process and Eighth Amendment issues.

[b]   Is It Constitutional to Execute an "Artificially" Competent Death Row Inmate?

Part of the division on the Eighth Circuit centers on whether *Harper* was the correct framework for the decision. One approach looks at *Harper* without attaching any significance to the death penalty aspects of the case. Under this view, if involuntary medication is in the medical interest of the inmate and necessary for the safety of the inmate or others, then forced medication is constitutional. The fact that the "byproduct" is competency for execution is irrelevant to the due process analysis.[68]

What Singleton argued, and commentators have raised, is whether *Harper's* due process analysis, developed in a noncapital situation, is appropriate in a capital case.[69] *Harper* represented a balancing of the inmate's liberty interest with the state's interest in prison security. These interests, and the balance, are different with a death row inmate. Now it is more than an interest in freedom from unwanted medication — the inmate's interest in life is at stake. The tension arises in weighing the defendant's interest in life and liberty against the state's interest in

---

[66] 580 F. 3d 423 (6th Cir. 2009).

[67] *Id.* at 440.

[68] Both the Arkansas Supreme Court and the Eighth Circuit *en banc* took this position.

[69] *See* Lester Dupler, *The Uncommon Law: Insanity, Executions, and Oklahoma Criminal Procedure*, 55 OKLA. L. REV. 1, 54 (2002) (suggesting that "applying the Harper analysis to capital prisoners facing forced medication and possibly execution invites prosecutors and courts to engage in disingenuous assessments of governmental intent and pretextual appraisals of medical interest"); Rebecca A. Miller-Rice, *The "Insane" Contradiction of Singleton v. Norris: Forced Medication in a Death Row Inmate's Medical Interest which Happens to Facilitate His Execution*, 22 U. ARK. LITTLE ROCK L. REV. 659, 677 (2000) (concluding the Arkansas Supreme Court's analysis in *Singleton* is contrary to the United States Supreme Court's mandates for forcible medication and should be examined); Bruce A. Arrigo & Jeffrey J. Tasca, *Right to Refuse Treatment, Competency to be Executed, and Therapeutic Jurisprudence: Toward a Systematic Analysis*, 23 LAW & PSYCHOL. REV. 1, 43-44 (1999) (asking "whether the coercive treatment of incompetent death row inmates is therapeutic or anti-therapeutic; . . . in violation of the Eighth Amendment" and suggesting legislatures should consider the "various therapeutic implications of treatment refusal" before granting or denying death row inmates such a right).

prison security or carrying out the execution.[70]

Even assuming that it is constitutional to medicate a death row inmate into awareness of the impending execution, is it constitutional to proceed with the execution? Some judges and commentators have argued that it is unconstitutional to execute someone in a state of "artificial competency."[71] Proponents of this view assert that the inmate must be competent under *Ford* without medication. Otherwise, the inmate and the treating medical professionals may be placed in an unfair position of choosing between madness and death. These commentators also argue that the underlying reasons for not executing the insane in *Ford* apply equally to an inmate who is competent only by virtue of the medication. The inhumanity of executing a mentally disturbed individual remains, as does the lack of deterrent or retributive purpose in carrying out the execution.[72]

Others argue that as long as the inmate is medicated into competency, the Constitution is satisfied.[73] Whether the awareness is natural or due to medication

---

[70] *See, e.g., Singleton,* 319 F.3d at 1036 (Heaney, J., dissenting) (noting that where "the welfare of the prisoner, and the execution of the prisoner's sentence" are in conflict, in the least, the state's motivation for continued forcible medication of the prisoner should be called into question); Dupler, *supra* note 69, at 54 (arguing that "the long-term health (or 'medical interest') of the insane capital prisoner is not the concern of the State that seeks to forcibly medicate him"); Miller-Rice, *supra* note 69, at 677 (explaining "forcibly medicat[ing] an inmate contrary to his medical interest[,]" so as to render him competent for execution, violates the principle set out in *Washington v. Harper*).

[71] *See Singleton,* 319 F.3d at 1037 (Heaney, J., dissenting) (explaining that, despite his treatments, Singleton remains insane and that his execution would violate *Ford*); Singleton v. Norris, 992 S.W.2d 768, 770 (1999), *cert. denied,* 528 U.S. 1084 (2000) (Thornton, J., dissenting) (disagreeing "that forcible medication [enabling] a mentally ill prisoner to become competent to be executed can be in the inmate's medical interest"); Arrigo & Tasca, *supra* note 69, at 43 (questioning whether forced medication "of incompetent death row inmates is therapeutic or anti-therapeutic; that is, in violation of the Eighth Amendment's cruel and unusual punishment clause"); Roberta M. Harding, *"ENDGAME": Competency and the Execution of Condemned Inmates — a Proposal to Satisfy the Eighth Amendment's Prohibition Against the Infliction of Cruel and Unusual Punishment,* 14 St. Louis U. Pub. L. Rev. 105, 123 (1994) (questioning whether the use of psychotropic drugs to "render [an] inmate 'artificially competent' or 'synthetically sane' . . . is sufficient to reactivate the inmates's eligibility to be executed without violating Ford" and suggesting such a determination may depend on "whether the restoration is designated as a 'cure' or as a 'treatment' "); Ptolemy H. Taylor, *Execution of the "Artificially Competent": Cruel and Unusual?,* 66 Tul. L. Rev. 1045, 1065 (1992) (concluding "the execution of the 'artificially competent' must be recognized as a violation of the Eight[h] Amendment's prohibition on the execution of the insane").

[72] *See Ford,* 477 U.S. at 409-10 (questioning the deterrent and "retributive value of executing a person who has no comprehension of why he has been singled out and stripped of his fundamental right to life"); Bruce Ebert, *Competency to be Executed: A Proposed Instrument to Evaluate an Inmate's Level of Competency in Light of the Eighth Amendment Prohibition Against the Execution of the Presently Insane,* 25 Law & Psychol. Rev. 29, 32-33 (2001); Farringer, *supra* note 12, at 2445-48 (presenting a sixth, more modern rationale against execution of the insane, that to do so denies the inmate an opportunity to assist in his defense, and concluding the rule established in *Ford* "is now ingrained in the American legal system and accepted almost universally"); Eric M Kniskern, *Does Ford v. Wainwright's Denial of Executions of the Insane Prohibit the State from Carrying Out its Criminal Justice System?,* 26 S.U. L. Rev. 171, 180-84 (1999).

[73] *Singleton,* 267 F.3d at 870 (stating that where "an inmate has been administered antipsychotic medication that has resulted in his reachieving competency and maintaining that status over a long period . . . it could be said, consistent with the Supreme Court decision in *Ford,* that the inmate was aware of the punishment he was about to suffer and why he was about to suffer it").

is irrelevant. If it is legitimate to medicate the inmate, even involuntarily, and the result is the competency of the inmate, then the execution should proceed. Proponents of this point of view argue that the underlying reasons for not executing the insane in *Ford* are inapplicable here. They assert that the deterrent and retributive purposes are met if the medicated inmate is competent.[74]

[c] Is It Ethical for Physicians to Participate in Medicating a Death Row Inmate into Competency?

The competency of a medicated inmate for execution purposes has raised medical ethics questions in addition to the legal issues. When doctors take the Hippocratic Oath, they pledge to "never do harm to anyone" and to not "give advice which may cause death."[75] The American Medical Association's Code of Medical Ethics more specifically provides that a physician should not restore a death row inmate to competency for purposes of execution. The Code allows an exception for some medical treatment to alleviate "extreme suffering" of the individual.[76] The American Psychiatric Association similarly prohibits participation in competency evaluations for purposes of execution.[77] As a result, psychiatrists face a dilemma about whether or not to medicate a death row inmate into a state of "competency" that will then make the inmate, who was otherwise incompetent for execution, eligible.

The case of Claude Maturana[78] in Arizona illustrates the problem. The treating psychiatrist refused to prescribe a greater dosage of medication for Maturana that

---

[74] *Id. see Singleton*, 319 F.3d at 1027 (holding that "[a] state does not violate the Eighth Amendment . . . when it executes a prisoner who . . . subsequently regained competency through appropriate medical care").

[75] The Hippocratic Oath in the relevant portion states "I will prescribe regimens for the good of my patients according to my ability and my judgment and never do harm to anyone. . . . I will not give a lethal drug to anyone if I am asked, nor will I advise such a plan . . . " *American Medical Association, The Hippocratic Oath*, translated by Michael North, *available at* http://www.nlm.nih.gov/hmd/greek/greek_oath.html (last visited Jan. 23, 2012).

[76] The American Medical Association's Code of Medical Ethics provides: "When a condemned prisoner has been declared incompetent to be executed, physicians should not treat the prisoner to restore competence unless a commutation order is issued. However, if the incompetent prisoner is undergoing extreme suffering as a result of psychosis or any other illness, medical intervention intended to mitigate the level of suffering is ethically permissible . . . "

[77] Alfred M. Freedman, *Commentary: The Doctor's Dilemma: A Conflict of Loyalties*, PSYCHIATRIC TIMES (Jan. 2001). *See also* THE PRINCIPLES OF MEDICAL ETHICS, Section 1(4) (2001 ed.) (last visited July 23, 2007) *available at* http:www.psych.org/psych_pract/ethics/medicalethics2001_42001.cfm (stating: "A psychiatrist should not be a participant in a legally authorized execution"). *Compare* Donald P. Judges, *The Role of Mental Health Professionals in Capital Punishment: An Exercise in Moral Disengagement*, 41 HOUS. L. REV. 515, 610 (2004) ("Involvement in a process aimed at killing does appear to be at odds with mental health professionals constitutive ethical commitment to beneficence and harm-avoidance . . . .") *with* Julie D. Cantor, *Of Pills and Needles: Involuntary Medicating the Psychotic Inmate When Execution Looms*, 2 IND. HEALTH L. REV. 117, 149 (2005) ("Physicians are ethically bound to treat a patient's illness — not what awaits him when he recovers.").

[78] Claude Maturana died in prison.

would have restored Maturana's ability to understand the impending execution.[79] The state of Arizona searched until they found the medical director for Georgia inmates who was willing to reevaluate Maturana. The Georgia doctor concluded that Maturana was competent for execution without further medication.[80] The willingness of one psychiatrist and the unwillingness of the other to participate in declaring Maturana competent for execution illustrates the medical ethics debate forming the backdrop for the legal issues.

[d]   Legal, Medical, and Legislative Responses

The medical and legal issues frame an ongoing debate. At this point, the courts are just beginning to explore the Eighth Amendment implications in medicating death row inmates into competency. The medical profession appears to prohibit participating in medicating defendants for execution, but the parameters of a physician's involvement in the process are still being defined. The potential exists for legal decisions to be inconsistent with medical ethics. Clearly, Arizona tried to proceed with the execution of an incompetent death row inmate who had been restored to competence through medication. On the other hand, the Maryland legislature decided that, once an inmate is found incompetent for execution, the death sentence is permanently commuted to life without parole.[81]

§ 19.02   DEATH ROW PHENOMENON

[A]   The Nature of the Issue

Consider the following situation from *Moore v. Nebraska*:[82] D is convicted of a capital crime and sentenced to death in 1980. While on death row, D pursues a direct appeal and state collateral postconviction remedies. Those proceedings last through 1984. D then pursues post-conviction relief in federal court. In 1988, the federal district court finds that the state's procedures violated the Constitution. The Circuit Court of Appeal affirms and the United States Supreme Court denies certiorari. It is now 1992. In 1995, the state conducts a new sentencing proceeding and D is sentenced to death for a second time. D pursues his right to direct appeal

---

[79] Lindsay A. Horstman, *Commuting Death Sentences of the Insane: A Solution for a Better, More Compassionate Society*, 36 U.S.F. L. Rev. 823, 827 (2002). *See also* Carol Morello, *'Healthy' would be a fatal diagnosis for prisoner*, USA Today, November 9, 1999, at 4A.

[80] Horstman, *supra* note 79, at 828-29.

[81] Md. Code Ann. § 3-904(h) (2011) provides:

(1) If the court finds the inmate to be incompetent, the court shall:

(i) stay any warrant of execution . . . . and

(ii) remand the case to the court in which the sentence of death was imposed.

(2) The court in which the sentence of death was imposed shall strike the sentence of death and enter in its place a sentence of life imprisonment without the possibility of parole.

(3) The sentence of life imprisonment without the possibility of parole imposed under paragraph (2) of this subsection is mandatory and may not be suspended wholly or partly.

[82] Moore v. Nebraska, as companion case to Knight v. Florida, 528 U.S. 990, 993-94 (1999) (Breyer, J., dissenting from denial of certiorari in both *Knight* and *Moore*) (recounting the nineteen-year delay in Moore's execution in *Moore v. Nebraska*).

and state collateral review. In 1999, when D loses in the state proceedings, he files a petition for certiorari in the U.S. Supreme Court. Among other issues, D claims that it is cruel and unusual punishment to have kept him on death row for 19 years and 4 months. A lengthy period awaiting execution on death row is referred to as the *death row phenomenon*. The issue also directly or indirectly includes the restrictive conditions under which death row inmates live and the psychological effects of living under a sentence of death.[83]

American courts have faced the issue of the death row phenomenon in two rather different situations. First, defendants have claimed that a lengthy delay in execution constitutes cruel and unusual punishment in violation of the Eighth Amendment.[84] Second, foreign jurisdictions have refused to extradite defendants wanted for trial in the United States on the grounds that the death row phenomenon would violate human rights treaties or the rights guaranteed to persons within their borders under that country's laws. The Eighth Amendment claim is considered in this section, and the extradition issues are considered in Section 23.05, *infra*.

[B]   Cruel and Unusual Punishment?

The Supreme Court has yet to address the constitutionality of a prolonged delay on death row before execution. In eight cases, however, justices have dissented from or commented on denials of certiorari where the constitutionality of the death row phenomenon was raised.[85]

Does a lengthy delay make a subsequent execution cruel and unusual? Is it excessive punishment? Justice Stevens suggested that if the lengthy delay deprives the execution of serving the purposes of punishment, then the punishment is unconstitutional. Arguably, retribution has already been satisfied by the incarceration and the psychological agony of expecting death for many years. Deterrence may also be amply served by the death row experience and life imprisonment. If the actual execution no longer serves the purposes of punishment, the imposition of death becomes an excessive penalty, which violates the Eighth Amendment.[86]

---

[83] *See, e.g.*, Soering v. United Kingdom, 11 Eur. Ct. H.R. 439 (1989) (discussing how the psychological trauma, extreme conditions, sexual abuse, and other factors associated with death row constitute the "phenomenon").

[84] *See, e.g.*, Lackey v. Texas, 514 U.S. 1045, 1045 (1995) (Stevens, J., respecting denial of certiorari).

[85] *See* Johnson v. Bredesen, 130 S. Ct. 541 (2009) (Stevens, J., dissenting); Thompson v. McNeil, 129 S. Ct. 1299 (2009), (Breyer, H., dissenting); Allen v. Ornoski, 546 U.S. 1136 (2006) (Breyer, J., dissenting); Foster v. Florida, 537 U.S. 990 (2002) (Breyer, J., dissenting); Knight v. Florida, 528 U.S. 990 (Breyer, J., dissenting); Moore v. Nebraska 127 S.Ct. 1134 (2007) (Breyer, J., dissenting); Elledge v. Florida, 525 U.S. 944 (1998) (Breyer, J., dissenting); Lackey, 514 U.S. 1045 (Stevens, J., respecting denial of certiorari).

[86] *See Lackey*, 514 U.S. 1045, 1045 (1995) (Stevens, J., respecting denial of certiorari) (suggesting state and federal courts serve as laboratories to examine the issue; also suggesting that framers of Constitution would not have anticipated a long stay on death row; and commenting that retribution and deterrence are not served once an inmate has spent an extended time on death row).

The primary counter-argument advanced is that delays are inevitable if defendants pursue their legal remedies. Although the direct appeal from the conviction may be automatic, subsequent post-conviction remedies are optional. Justice Thomas pointed out the tension between defendants insisting on post-conviction proceedings, and then claiming that the delays are too great while the proceedings are heard in the courts.[87] Many lower courts have agreed that there is no Eighth Amendment violation if the delay is due to court proceedings.[88]

Does the reason for the delay make a difference? What if the case is reversed for a new trial based on the state's errors? In *Lackey v. Texas*, Justice Stevens suggested that courts could distinguish between valid and invalid reasons for delays. He posed three situations: the defendant's abuse of the system, the defendant's legitimate use of the system, and the state's negligence or intentional action to delay. Defendants have argued that a delay is the state's fault if the case is reversed because of constitutional error. For example, in *Moore*, described at the beginning of the section, post-conviction proceedings resulted in a reversal of the penalty phase and a retrial on the sentence. The defense argued that the time spent on death row was due to the state's failure to adhere to constitutional requirements and thus, the state should be held responsible for the delay.[89] Most courts, however, have focused on the lack of any purposeful delays by the state, and have rejected the defendant's claims.[90]

If a lengthy period on death row violates the Eighth Amendment, one unanswered question is how long an inmate must be on death row before a constitutional violation would arise. In the eight cases commented on by Supreme Court justices, the time on death row was quite extensive, between 17 and 32

---

[87] *Knight*, 528 U.S. at 990 (Thomas, J., concurring). Justice Thomas commented that "[i]t is incongruous to arm capital defendants with an arsenal of 'constitutional' claims with which they may delay their executions, and simultaneously to complain when executions are inevitably delayed." *Id.* at 991. *See also* Foster v. Florida, 537 U.S. 990, 123 S. Ct. 470 (2002) (Thomas, J., concurring in denial of certiorari) (restating position that delay in execution is meritless).

[88] *See, e.g.*, People v. Frye, 18 Cal. 4th 894, 1031 (Cal. 1998) (asserting that delays caused by satisfying the Eighth Amendment cannot violate it); *see also* People v. Massie, 19 Cal. 4th 550, 574 (Cal. 1998) (explaining that delay in carrying out a death sentence is a "constitutional safeguard," not a "constitutional defect"); *see also* People v. Simms, 736 N.E.2d 1092, 1141 (Ill. 2000) (stating that "delay, in large part, is a function of the desire of our courts, state and federal, to get it right, to explore exhaustively, or at least sufficiently, any argument that might save someone's life").

[89] Elledge v. Florida, 525 U.S. 944, 944 (1998) (Breyer, J., dissenting) (summarizing Elledge's argument that "he has experienced . . . delay because of the State's own faulty procedures and not because of frivolous appeals on his own part," based upon errors at the sentencing stage at trial that caused three subsequent reversals of his sentence by reviewing courts); Knight, 528 U.S. at 998 (summarizing the petitioners' argument that the cases before the court "involve delays which resulted in large part from the States' failure to apply constitutionally sufficient procedures at the time of initial sentencing"); *Foster*, 537 U.S. at 993 (indicating that delay in part due to state's procedural errors).

[90] *See* McKenzie v. Day, 57 F.3d 1461, 1466-67 (9th Cir. 1995) (noting that, despite McKenzie's death sentence being vacated twice, the court is "not confronted with a situation where the State of Montana has set up a scheme to prolong the period of incarceration, or rescheduled the execution repeatedly in order to torture McKenzie"); *see also* Chambers v. Bowersox, 157 F.3d 560, 570 (8th Cir. 1998) (asserting that, even after three retrials, in which all three juries convicted him and three judges sentenced him to death, there is "no evidence, not even a claim, that the State has deliberately sought to convict Chambers invalidly in order to prolong the time before it could secure a valid conviction and execute him").

years.[91] In 2009, the average time nationally spent on death row before execution was 12.6 years.[92] Two of the justices and litigants have turned to decisions of foreign tribunals for guidance on the length of time.[93] The case of *Pratt v. Attorney General for Jamaica* is often cited. In 1993 the Privy Council of the United Kingdom invalidated a Jamaican death sentence after the defendants spent 14 years on death row.[94] Moreover, the Privy Council indicated that a death row stay of more than five years would be excessive.[95] The European Court of Human Rights, in an extradition case discussed in Section 23.05, *infra*, also found a fairly short period of time by U.S. death row standards, six to eight years, problematic.[96] Justice Thomas, on the other hand, has protested the use of decisions from foreign or international tribunals as irrelevant to the interpretation of the Eighth Amendment.[97] This debate in the courts thus leaves us not only with unanswered legal questions regarding the constitutionality of a death sentence after a lengthy

---

[91] Johnson (29 years), Thompson (32 years), Allen (23 years), Foster (27 years), Knight (24 years), Elledge (23 years), Moore (19 years), and Lackey (17 years).

[92] *See* U.S. DEPARTMENT OF JUSTICE, OFFICE OF JUSTICE PROGRAMS, *Bureau of Justice Statistics Bulletin, Capital Punishment 2009*, at 12, Dec. 2009, *available at* http://bjs.ojp.usdoj.gov/content/pub/pdf/cp09st. pdf (stating that the prisoners executed in 2009 were under a sentence of death an average of 12 years and 8 months).

[93] *See Foster*, 123 S.Ct. at 471-72 (Breyer, J., dissenting from denial of certiorari). Justice Breyer cites *Pratt* (Privy Council); *Soering* (European Court of Human Rights), and *Burns* (Canadian Supreme Court). In *Knight*, 528 U.S. at 995-996 (Breyer, J., dissenting from denial of certiorari), Justice Breyer cites *Pratt*, *Soering*, and cases from India and Zimbabwe; Justice Breyer contrasts those decisions with decisions from Canada and the United Nations Human Rights Committee, but indicates that those bodies were not dealing with delays of the magnitude in *Knight* and *Moore*.

[94] Pratt & Morgan, 2 A.C. 1, 33 (British Privy Council 1993) (*en banc*) (stating that "[t]o execute these men now after holding them in custody in an agony of suspense for so many years would be inhuman punishment within the meaning of section 17(1) [of the Jamaican Constitution]"). The result for the prisoners in *Pratt & Morgan* was that their sentence was commuted from death to life imprisonment. *Id.* at 34. *Pratt & Morgan* is perhaps even more significant than decisions from other tribunals because the law is based on the 1689 English Bill of Rights, which is also the precursor to the Eighth Amendment of the U.S. Constitution.

[95] *Id.* at 35 (concluding that "in any case in which execution is to take place more than five years after sentence there will be strong grounds for believing that the delay is such as to constitute 'inhuman or degrading punishment or other treatment' ").

[96] Soering v. United Kingdom, 11 Eur. Ct. H.R. 439, 478 (1989) (deciding that, "having regard to the very long period of time spent on death row in such extreme conditions, with the ever present and mounting anguish of awaiting execution of the death penalty, and to the personal circumstances of the applicant, especially his age and mental state at the time of the offence, the applicant's extradition to the United States would expose him to a real risk of treatment going beyond the threshold set by Article 3 [of the European Convention on Human Rights]").

[97] *See Foster*, 123 S.Ct. at 470 n.* (Thomas, J., concurring in denial of certiorari) (commenting that "this Court's Eighth Amendment jurisprudence should not impose foreign moods, fads, or fashions on Americans."). *See also Chambers*, 157 F.3d at 570 (distinguishing the American legal system from the legal systems in commonwealth countries and concluding that "the essential point for [the court's] purposes . . . is whether or not the Eighth Amendment is being violated"); White v. Johnson, 79 F.3d 432, 439 (5th Cir. 1996) (rejecting White's arguments that "binding norms of international law" compel the court "to follow *Pratt & Morgan* and strike down his death sentence as a violation of his human rights" on the ground that the United States Senate filed reservations with respect to both the International Covenant on Civil and Political Rights and the Convention Against Torture and Other Cruel, Inhuman or Degrading Treatment or Punishment to the effect that punishments are only prohibited as cruel and unusual punishment as defined by the Eighth Amendment).

time on death row, but also what sources are relevant to the determination.[98] The issue of the death row phenomenon is likely to continue to arise as those sentenced to death spend lengthy periods of time on death row.

---

[98] Some have suggested dividing the claim based on whether the state itself is responsible for the delay or whether the delay can be attributed to the defendant's own mental infirmity. *See* Jennifer McHugh, *International Law and the Mortal Precipice: a Legal Policy Critique of the Death Row Phenomenon*, 17 Tul. J. Int'l & Comp. L. 77 (2008).

Chapter 20

RACE AND THE DEATH PENALTY

§ 20.01 HISTORICAL BACKGROUND

Although our nation has an historical commitment to equal justice under the law, the administration of our criminal justice system in general, and of the death penalty specifically, has often raised questions and concerns about its fairness on the question of race. The early history of our country is marred by the adoption of slavery in many states and the acceptance of that institution by others. This history institutionalized a clear message that race made a difference under the law. Although the Emancipation Proclamation and the Thirteenth Amendment ended the legal institution of slavery (except as punishment for crime), extralegal violence against African-American people in particular continued both on an individual scale as well as in the form of lynchings by groups of vigilantes.

The legal systems in many states even formalized the disparate treatment of African-Americans and whites with the passage of "Black Codes." These statutes provided different punishments for crimes based upon the race of the victim and the defendant.[1] Ultimately, the Fourteenth Amendment was enacted in large part to prohibit this differential treatment:

> The 14th Amendment was framed and adopted . . . to assure to the colored race the enjoyment of all the civil rights that under the law are enjoyed by white persons, and to give to that race the protection of the General Government, in that enjoyment, whenever it should be denied by the states.[2]

Discriminatory views led to the enactment in many states of a body of law that was intensely hostile to African-American people, including a comprehensive code of civil law that segregated the races in most aspects of life. For example, in Georgia, it was a misdemeanor to confine white and African-American convicts together or to work them chained together.[3] Many of these states had criminal statutes that made the severity of punishment explicitly dependent upon racial factors.

---

[1] LEON LITWACK, BEEN IN THE STORM SO LONG: THE AFTERMATH OF SLAVERY 276-277, 285-286 n.8 (Leon F. Litwack ed., Vintage Books 1980) (1979); Stuart Banner, *Traces of Slavery; Race and the Death Penalty in Historical Perspective*, in FROM LYNCH MOBS TO THE KILLING STATE 96, 98-100 (Charles J. Ogletree & Austin Sarat, eds., 2006).

[2] Strauder v. W. Virginia, 100 U.S. 303, 306 (1886) (discrimination in jury selection based on race amounted to a denial of equal protection).

[3] GA. CODE ANN. § 77-9904 (repealed 1950).

There has been significant public debate concerning whether the death penalty is administered in a racially neutral fashion. Initially, this debate focused on African-American defendants who were executed for the crime of rape. Numerous scholars attempted to determine whether the race of the victim or of the defendant affected the way in which the death penalty was imposed.[4] Many of these studies were conducted with complex statistical models. Each time, these studies showed a correlation between rape, race, and the death penalty.[5] These studies were used in court to challenge the constitutionality of the death penalty on the basis of its discriminatory effect. The challenges to the death penalty based on race expanded to include the imposition of the death penalty in cases of murder. The most significant case that raised this issue in the modern era was *McCleskey v. Kemp*.[6] Despite the comprehensive nature of these studies, statistics have never provided defendants with a successful legal challenge.

Perhaps the complexity of the problem makes it difficult to resolve. Rubin "Hurricane" Carter stated that it was "impossible to speak about race and the death penalty without speaking about habeas corpus, politics, and popular culture and fear."[7]

This chapter identifies issues of race and its interrelationship with the imposition of the death penalty.

§ 20.02   THE CRIMINAL JUSTICE SYSTEM

[A]   Overview

The criminal justice system operates, in large part, with police officers, prosecutors, judges and juries all exercising discretion in the myriad of decisions that are made during the course of a case. Because of this broad discretion, there are significant opportunities for an individual's bias or prejudice, conscious or unconscious, to affect each decision and the ultimate outcome of a case. At every stage in the system, suspects and defendants can be treated differently because of

---

[4] U.S. General Accounting Office, *Death Penalty Sentencing: Research Indicates Pattern of Racial Disparities*, (GGD-90-57) Feb. 26, 1990 *available at* www.gao.gov; (noting that among 28 relevant studies of acceptable research quality and statistical competence, 82% found that race of the victim influenced the outcomes of cases); Judiciary Subcommittee on Civil and Constitutional Rights, Racial Disparities in Federal Death Penalty Prosecutions 1988-1994, March 1994 *available at* http://www.deathpenaltyinfo. org.

[5] Marvin E. Wolfgang, *Racial Discrimination in the Death Sentence for Rape*, in EXECUTIONS IN AMERICA (1974) at 115; Robert J. Hunter, Paige Heather Ralph, and James Marquet, *The Death Sentencing of Rapists n Pre-Furman Texas (1942-1971): The Racial Dimension*, 20 AMERICAN JOURNAL OF CRIMINAL LAW (Spring 1993) (examining historical research on the relationship between race, rape and the death penalty in Texas from 1942-1971).

[6] 481 U.S. 279 (1987).

[7] Rubin Carter, *Death Penalty Symposium Keynote Address*, in 35 SANTA CLARA L. REV. 426 (1995). Rubin Carter was a middleweight boxer who was arrested in 1966 and charged with a triple murder. Although the government sought the death penalty, he received a life sentence. After Carter had been incarcerated for nearly twenty years, Judge H. Lee Sarokin granted his writ of habeas corpus, releasing Carter and calling his trial an appeal to racism rather than reason.

their own race or the race of the victim — from initial contacts with the police, to charging and bail decisions by prosecutors, to evaluations of appropriate sentences by juries or judges.[8] From the police, prosecutors, lawyers, judges, and other officials who run the system to the defendants and victims who are drawn into it unwillingly, the behavior and treatment of almost everyone in the criminal justice process reflects the complex social mechanisms of race and class.[9]

Over the years, questions about the impact of race in the system have given rise to numerous legal challenges based upon claims of racial discrimination and racial bias. Courts have most often acknowledged the influence of race in focusing on the harm to potential jurors from racial discrimination in jury selection.[10] Even in those cases, the response from the courts has been mixed. Courts have historically avoided questions of whether racial bias in decision-making harms criminal defendants so as to violate the constitution.

[B] Rape, Race and the Death Penalty

The question of the interrelationship between rape, race and the death penalty has long been a source of discussion and debate.[11] In 1949, the defendants in the case of the "Martinsville Seven" challenged their sentences of death, arguing that there was systemic discrimination against African-Americans in Virginia in capital rape cases. Seven African-American men were convicted and sentenced to death for the rape of a white woman. There was no question about their guilt or the competence of their appointed counsel. There was also no evidence of overt racial prejudice during the trial by either the prosecutor or the judge.[12] However, the defendants, on appeal, argued that they were sentenced to death in part because of their race. In pursuing this broad systemic challenge to the death penalty in Virginia, the defendants introduced statistical evidence and attempted to document the racial discrimination in the Virginia death penalty system.[13] The defense, headed by the National Association for the Advancement of Colored People - Legal Defense Fund ("NAACP-LDF"), argued that there was a persistent pattern of racial discrimination in rape cases in Virginia that violated the equal protection clause of the Fourteenth Amendment. The court rejected their statistics and their arguments, denied their appeal, and the seven defendants were executed in 1951.[14]

Challenges based on the issue of rape, race and the death penalty continued over the years with no success. From 1930-1967, out of a total of 455 persons around the country who were executed for rape, 48 defendants were white and 405

---

[8] Angela J. Davis, *Prosecution and Race: The Power and Privilege of Discretion*, 67 FORDHAM L. REV. 13, 16 (1998); Erwin Chemerinsky, *Eliminating Discrimination in Administering the Death Penalty: The Need for the Racial Justice Act*, 35 SANTA CLARA L. REV. 519 (1995).

[9] Angela J. Davis, *supra* note 8, at 17 n.12.

[10] *See* Section 7.05[C], *supra*.

[11] Carol S. Steiker, *Remembering Race, Rape, and Capital Punishment*, 83 VA. L. REV. 693 (1997) (reviewing THE MARTINSVILLE SEVEN: RAPE, RACE, AND CAPITAL PUNISHMENT (1995)).

[12] Hampton v. Commonwealth, 190 Va. 531, 542-544, 58 S.E.2d 288, *cert. denied*, 339 U.S. 989 (1950).

[13] Steiker, *supra* note 11.

[14] Hampton, 190 Va. at 554-557.

defendants were African-American.[15] Despite these numbers, courts were unwilling to acknowledge the impact of race on sentences of death even in cases of rape. Scholars argue that the Supreme Court has historically tried to avoid the issue of race.[16]

For example, in 1977, in *Coker v. Georgia*,[17] the Supreme Court addressed whether the death penalty was unconstitutional for the charge of rape. Although the Court accepted certiorari in three cases, the Court held two of the cases in which the defendant was black and chose instead, to issue a decision in *Coker*, in which the defendant was white.[18] The Court reversed the sentence of death, and a plurality held that death was excessive for the crime of rape. There was no discussion of whether race was a factor in the selection of who would be sentenced to death in cases of rape.

[C] The Modern Era of Death Penalty Trials and Race

The Supreme Court has struggled with the constitutional impact of racial disparities in the imposition of the death penalty. However, the Court has shown great reluctance to find a constitutional flaw in a death penalty scheme based solely on racial discrimination. In 1972, in *Furman v. Georgia*,[19] the Supreme Court declared the death penalty unconstitutional due, in part, to the arbitrary and capricious manner in which it was imposed. In *Furman*, several of the Justices discussed the effect that race played in the imposition of the death penalty. Justice Douglas cited the President's Commission on Law Enforcement and Administration of Justice, which concluded that the death sentence was disproportionately imposed and carried out on minorities.[20] Justice Stewart observed that the selection process of who should die appeared to be affected by race.[21] Justice Marshall cited statistical evidence demonstrating racial bias against persons who had been executed.[22]

Four Justices dissented and voted to uphold the death penalty statutes.[23] These justices acknowledged the racially discriminatory application of the death penalty in the past, but argued that racial bias no longer pervaded the system. Times had changed. Society had changed. Segregation, and the attitudes that accompanied it,

---

[15] Furman v. Georgia, 408 U.S. 238, 364 (1972) (Marshall, J., concurring).

[16] *See* Charles J. Ogletree, *Making Race Matter in Death Matters*, in FROM LYNCH MOBS TO THE KILLING STATE; RACE AND THE DEATH PENALTY IN AMERICA 55, 63 (Charles J. Ogletree & Austin Sarat, eds. 2006); RANDALL KENNEDY, RACE CRIME AND THE LAW (1997); Steiker, *supra* note 11.

[17] 433 U.S. 584 (1977).

[18] *Eberheart v. Georgia*, 206 S.E.2d 12 (1974) (African-American defendant) and *Hooks v. Georgia*, 210 S.E.2d 668 (1974) (African-American defendant), were held and then vacated after *Coker v. Georgia*, 433 U.S. 584 (1977). *See* Eberheart v. Georgia, 433 U.S. 917 (1977). *See generally* Sheri Lynn Johnson, Coker v. Georgia: *Of Rape, Race, and Burying the Past*, in DEATH PENALTY STORIES 171 (John Blume & Jordan Steiker, eds., 2009).

[19] 408 U.S. 238 (1972).

[20] *Id.* at 249 (Douglas, J.).

[21] *Id.* at 309 (Stewart, J.).

[22] *Id.* at 373 (Marshall, J.).

[23] *Id.* at 389 n.12 (Burger, C.J., dissenting), 449-50 (Powell, J., dissenting).

were no longer prevalent. Juries around the country were more representative of the minority populations, and legal safeguards corrected any improper bias that appeared. These changes, the dissenters argued, assured that the death penalty would be applied fairly.

A few years later, in 1976, the Supreme Court reviewed several new death penalty statutes and found them to be constitutional. The Court acknowledged the earlier concerns that the death penalty was imposed in a racially biased manner. However, a majority of the Court now believed that, under the new sentencing schemes, discrimination on the basis of race would not occur.

The new death penalty statutes did not allow juries to exercise the unfettered discretion that they had exercised previously. The Court characterized these statutes as satisfying two seemingly conflicting principles.[24] On the one hand, jurors had to be guided and directed so that their decisions were not random or arbitrary. On the other hand, jurors had to be given sufficient discretion so that they could look at the unique facts and circumstances each case presented and provide "individualized consideration." The discretion given to the juries, however, continued to provide the opportunity for the racial bias of a juror to influence that juror and her decision-making process.

The Supreme Court acknowledged this danger when it held that a defendant had a right to question potential jurors about racial attitudes and views. In *Turner v. Murray*, the Court observed:

> Because of the range of discretion entrusted to a jury in a capital sentencing hearing, there is a unique opportunity for racial prejudice to operate but remain undetected. . . . [This] risk of racial prejudice infecting a capital sentencing proceeding is especially serious in light of the complete finality of the death sentence.[25]

Although Supreme Court justices have come to very different conclusions about the fairness of the capital punishment system, most agree that race continues to influence the imposition of capital sentences in some fashion. Some, like Justice Scalia, have decided that the influence of race is inevitable, but that it does not affect the constitutionality of the sentence.[26] Others, like Justices Brennan and Marshall, believed that the role of race in death penalty sentences is constitutionally unacceptable. Still others, like Justice Blackmun, struggled for years to impose sufficient safeguards to insure that race was not an unfair factor — only to conclude that the system could not work.[27]

---

[24] For more on this purported conflict, *see* Section 13.06, *supra*.

[25] Turner v. Murray, 476 U.S. 28, 35 (1986).

[26] *See infra* note 53.

[27] *See* Callins v. Collins, 510 U.S. 1141 (1994) (Blackmun, J., dissenting from denial of cert.).

§ 20.03   MEASURES OF RACIAL DISCRIMINATION

How does a criminal defendant prove discrimination on the basis of race? Is it sufficient to show that there is a disparity in the way people of different races are treated? Or does something more have to be shown? What other type of evidence is available?

For many years, challenges that the death penalty was applied in a discriminatory manner relied extensively on statistical studies. These studies examined cases in which the death penalty was imposed and tried to identify and quantify the impact that race (and other variables) had on the outcome of the cases. At best, studies were able to show a *correlation* between race and imposition of the death penalty. None could show causation.

The statistical studies had clear limitations. The outcome of a capital case is affected in large part by discretionary decisions. The attitudes and beliefs of the decision-makers (the judge, the prosecutor, the jury, and even the defense attorney) are difficult, if not impossible, to quantify. The race, ethnicity, background, and life experiences of these individuals affect their decisions, often in unconscious ways.[28] Even when specific incidents of racial misconduct by one of these actors are identified, they rarely provide a basis for constitutional error; and yet, the attitudes of these individuals are critical when evaluating the overall fairness of the death penalty system.

Numerous studies conducted over the years have concluded that race is a factor in the ultimate decision of who receives a death sentence and who is executed.[29] Repeatedly, the single most statistically significant factor that determines who is sentenced to death and who is executed is the race of the *victim*.[30] Nationally, about

---

[28] *See, e.g.*, Charles R. Lawrence III, *The Id, the Ego, and Equal Protection: Reckoning with Unconscious Racism*, 39 STAN. L. REV. 317 (1987); Sheri Lynn Johnson, *Symposium: Criminal Law, Criminal Justice, and Race, Racial Imagery in Criminal Cases*, 67 TUL. L. REV. 1739 (1993) (discussing how racial imagery affects views and decision process of jurors); Davis, *supra* note 8 (discriminatory treatment of defendants and victims may be based on unconscious racism and institutional bias rather than on discriminatory intent).

[29] For a recent statistical study that found evidence of racialized decision-making by prosecutors in Harris County (Houston) capital cases from 1992 to 1999, *see* Scott Phillips, *Racial Disparities in the Capital of Capital Punishment*, 45 HOUS. L. REV. 807, 830 & 834 (2008). For a discussion of many prior studies, *see* Scott W. Howe, *The Futile Quest for Racial Neutrality in Capital Selection and the Eighth Amendment Argument for Abolition Based on Unconscious Racial Discrimination*, 45 WM. & MARY L. REV. 2083, 2106-2123 (2004). *See also The Federal Death Penalty System: A Statistical Survey* (1988-2000), Sept 12, 2000 *available at* http://www.usdoj.gov/dag/pubdoc/dpsurvey.html (study found that more than 80% of the cases sent for death penalty review involved racial minorities); FINAL REPORT OF THE PA. SUP. CT. COMM. ON RACIAL AND GENDER BIAS IN THE JUSTICE SYSTEM (2003), *available at* http://www. courts.state.pa.us/NR/rdonlyres/EC162941-F233-4FC6-9247-54BFE3D2840D/)/FinalReport.pdf (chapter 6 "Racial and Ethnic Disparities in the Imposition of the Death Penalty" reports that race plays a major if not an overwhelming role in the imposition of the death penalty).

[30] McCleskey v. Kemp, 481 U.S. 279 (1987) (the Baldus study relied upon by the defendants concluded, *inter alia*, that defendants whose victims were white faced odds of receiving the death penalty that were 4.3 times higher than defendants whose victims were African-American); Glenn L. Pierce & Michael L. Radelet, *The Impact of Legally Inappropriate Factors on Death Sentencing for California Homicides, 1990-1999*, 46 SANTA CLARA L. REV. 1 (2005); David C. Baldus, George Woodworth, et. al., *Arbitrariness and Discrimination in the Administration of the Death Penalty: A Legal and Empirical*

50% of all murder victims are white. But of the more than 3000 men and women who are on death row, almost 80% killed a white victim. When examining those defendants who have been sentenced to death since 1976 for an interracial murder, 249 African-Americans were executed for killing white victims. At the same time, only fifteen white defendants were executed for killing African-American victims.[31]

Studies have also shown that the race of the *defendant* sometimes influences the outcome of a death penalty case. For example, a recent report by a committee appointed by the Pennsylvania Supreme Court noted that researchers studying Philadelphia capital cases found, after controlling for numerous non-racial factors, that African-American defendants were sentenced to death at a significantly higher rate than similarly situated non-African-Americans."[32]

Studies and statistics are often difficult to evaluate. Critics of the claims of racial discrimination have argued that a large percentage of African-American victims die in "hot-blooded" homicides in the streets or bars, or in domestic altercations. These cases are rarely the subject of capital prosecutions. Conversely, it is argued that white victims are more often killed in "cold blooded" killings by strangers — the type of case more likely to be charged as a death case.[33]

§ 20.04   *McCLESKEY v. KEMP*

[A]   The Case

Eleven years after the Supreme Court upheld the death penalty in *Gregg v. Georgia*[34] it was asked to examine whether the death penalty in Georgia was being imposed in a racially neutral fashion. This challenge was raised in *McCleskey v. Kemp*.[35]

McCleskey was a young African-American man who was involved in an armed robbery in which a white police officer was killed. McCleskey went to trial before a jury of eleven whites and one African-American. He was convicted and sentenced to death.

The basis of McCleskey's argument was that he was condemned to die, in large part, because of race. He asserted that, in Georgia, the odds that a killer of a white victim would be sentenced to death were 4.3 times higher than the odds that a

---

Analysis of the Nebraska Experience (1973-1999), 81 NEB. L. REV. 486 (2002); David C. Baldus et al., *Racial Discrimination and the Death Penalty in the Post-Furman Era: An Empirical and Legal Overview, with Recent Findings from Philadelphia*, 83 CORNELL L. REV. 1638 (1998); U.S. General Accounting Office, *Death Penalty Sentencing: Research Indicates Pattern of Racial Disparities*, (GGD-90-57) Feb. 26, 1990, *available at* www.gao.gov.

[31] Death Penalty Information Center, *National Statistics on the Death Penalty and Race, available at* http://www.deathpenaltyinfo.org/race-death-row-inmates-executed-1976#deathrowp (last visited Nov. 8, 2011).

[32] PA. SUP. CT. COMM., *supra* note 29, at 201.

[33] Dennis Dorin, *Far Right of the Mainstream: Racism, Rights, and Remedies From the Perspective of Justice Antonin Scalia's McCleskey Memorandum*, 45 MERCER L. REV. 1035, 1043-1044 (1994).

[34] 428 U.S. 153 (1976).

[35] 481 U.S. 279 (1987).

similarly situated killer of an African-American victim would receive a death sentence. Had the officer been African-American, McCleskey argued, he would likely have been sentenced to life imprisonment.

McCleskey challenged his sentence under the equal protection clause of the Fourteenth Amendment and the cruel and unusual punishments clause of the Eighth Amendment. McCleskey argued that race was still a significant factor in the determination of who received the death penalty. McCleskey's case was unique because of the sophisticated and comprehensive study that he presented to support his claim. This evidence has become known as the Baldus study.

[B] The Baldus Study: Statistical Evidence of Sentencing Disparities in Georgia

In the early 1980s, the NAACP Legal Defense Fund commissioned the largest empirical study to date to examine the impact of race in the administration of the death penalty.[36] Conducted by David Baldus, George Woodworth, and Charles Pulaski, Jr., this study analyzed the relationship between the sentencing outcome and race characteristics in 2484 homicide cases in Georgia that occurred between 1973 and 1979.[37]

Professor Baldus examined the death penalty in Georgia to determine, from a statistical perspective, whether "racial or other illegitimate or suspect case characteristics influenced the flow of cases from the point of indictment up to and including the penalty-trial sentencing decision."[38] Professor Baldus concluded that the statistical evidence tended to show that racial bias skewed the capital-selection process in Georgia. Baldus looked for alternative explanations for the huge racial disparities that were apparent in the cases. Despite sophisticated research techniques and analysis, no other factor could fully or even substantially account for the racial disparities.[39] Baldus concluded that, on a statewide basis, the death sentencing outcomes correlated significantly with the race of the victim. Specifically, he determined that defendants charged with killing a white person rather than an African-American person faced odds 4.3 times higher of receiving

---

[36] For a description of the study, see David C. Baldus et al., *Equal Justice and the Death Penalty*, 40-228 (1990) [Hereinafter Baldus Study]; *see also* Baldus, Pulaski, Woodworth & Kyle, *Identifying Comparatively Excessive Sentences of Death*, 33 Stan. L. Rev. 601 (1980); Baldus, Pulaski & Woodworth, *Comparative Review of Death Sentences: An Empirical Study of the Georgia Experience*, 74 J. Crim. Law & Criminology 661 (1983). Other articles include: Baldus, Woodworth & Pulaski, *Monitoring and Evaluating Contemporary Death Sentencing Systems: Lessons From Georgia*, 18 U.C. Davis L. Rev. 1374 (1985); Baldus, Pulaski & Woodworth, *Arbitrariness and Discrimination in the Administration of the Death Penalty: A Challenge to State Supreme Courts*, 15 Stetson L. Rev. 133 (1986).

[37] The Baldus Study was actually two studies, one that examined the application of the death penalty on a state-wide basis during that period and a second that examined the application of the death penalty in Fulton County, Georgia, where McCleskey was sentenced to death.

[38] Baldus Study, *supra* note 36, at 45.

[39] To test whether other factors accounted for the apparent racial disparities, Baldus collected information from the Georgia Board of Pardon and Parole and the records of the Georgia Supreme Court on approximately 230 variables for each case and each defendant.

the death penalty.[40] In addition, within the category of white-victim cases, an African-American defendant faced odds 2.4 times higher of receiving the death penalty than a white defendant solely because of the race factor.[41]

The Baldus study concluded that the racial disparities in capital sentencing in Georgia could not be explained by any of the other 230 case characteristics for which Dr. Baldus controlled. Those factors included the viciousness of the killing, the number of victims, and the prior record of the defendant. In fact, Baldus found that the race of the victim in the case affected the outcome as much as the fact that the defendant had a prior murder conviction or that the defendant was the primary actor in the killing.

The study also concluded that the observed race-of-victim disparity was due primarily to decisions made by prosecutors, rather than juries. Prosecutors decided whether to charge the death penalty in any given case and whether to pursue a sentence of death or allow a defendant to plead guilty.

McCleskey submitted the data and the evidence to the Supreme Court. He asked the Court to find that, because the statistical study demonstrated a risk that racial considerations played a role in death penalty decisions, his death sentence was unconstitutional under either the equal protection clause of the Fourteenth Amendment or the cruel and unusual punishments clause of the Eighth Amendment.

McCleskey pointed out that the equal protection clause was specifically drafted to prohibit the unequal enforcement of a state's criminal laws based upon the race of the victims (a practice followed in the early 1900s in Georgia as well as other states). The Georgia capital-punishment system, McCleskey noted, allowed broad discretion to prosecutors and juries in deciding a case, which, in turn, afforded ample opportunity for discrimination. McCleskey urged that, regardless of the reasons or the source, the findings of the Baldus study required the Court to find discrimination on the basis of race and to strike down the Georgia death penalty statute.

The Eighth Amendment was implicated, according to McCleskey, because the prohibition against imposing the death penalty in an arbitrary or capricious manner includes a prohibition against any capital-selection system that is affected by race. If race helps determine those who will die, the statute must be unconstitutional.[42]

---

[40] *See id.*, at 316.

[41] *See id.*, at 328.

[42] McCleskey's submissions to the Supreme Court included: 1) two multifaceted social scientific studies of the actual application of Georgia's capital sentencing system from 1973-1979, each comprising information on hundreds of relevant items on each case; 2) a statistical study of capital sentencing in Fulton County, where McCleskey was tried and sentenced to death; 3) two non-statistical "cohort" studies, one investigating all police homicides in Fulton County since 1973, the other examining those "near neighbor" homicides in Fulton County similar to McCleskey's; and 4) the deposition testimony of the Fulton County District Attorney concerning the sentencing policies and procedures of his office in homicide cases. *See* McCleskey, 481 U.S. at 286; Brief for Petitioner, McCleskey v. Kemp, 481 U.S. 279 (1986) (No. 84-6811).

The prosecutor's response to McCleskey's arguments focused on challenging the validity of the methodology and the statistics presented. If the study was flawed, then its conclusions linking race to the outcome of the cases could not be relied upon. The prosecution flatly rejected the Baldus study, and maintained that capital cases were sufficiently complex and unique so that multiple regression analysis could not provide the court with any insight into the decision-making process.

[C] The Five-Justice Majority

The Supreme Court rejected McCleskey's arguments and held that statistical evidence of systemic discrimination in the imposition of the death penalty, no matter how compelling, failed to prove that McCleskey himself was a victim of discrimination. In rejecting McCleskey's claim, the Court suggested that legislative authorization would be necessary before statistical evidence of systemic bias would be sufficient as a basis to overturn a death penalty statute.[43]

In making its ruling, the Court assumed that the statistics were accurate and the methodology employed was valid.[44] Nonetheless, the majority opinion, written by Justice Lewis Powell, held that there was insufficient evidence to satisfy the equal protection claim or the Eighth Amendment claim.

The Court concluded that discriminatory impact was insufficient for an Equal Protection claim. Although the Court found that Professor Baldus' study established a discrepancy that appeared to correlate with race, the justices "refused to assume that what is unexplained is invidious."[45] To prevail on his claim, the Court indicated, McCleskey needed to show that the prosecutor or the jury in his case acted with a discriminatory *intent or purpose*. The Court held that the equal protection claim failed because McCleskey did not establish "exceptionally clear proof . . . that any of the decision makers in McCleskey's case acted with a discriminatory purpose."[46]

The Court set a high burden for a defendant in a capital case to meet to prevail on a claim that the death penalty was imposed in a racially discriminatory manner. This showing was greater than the showing required in racial discrimination claims in the areas of employment discrimination, jury composition or voting redistricting challenges.[47]

McCleskey's Eighth Amendment claim was also rejected. The Court reasoned that the statistics failed to establish a constitutionally significant risk that racial factors had influenced McCleskey's death sentence. The Court said that evidence that other defendants who might appear similarly situated to McCleskey did not

---

[43] 481 U.S. at 319.

[44] *Id.* at 292 n.7.

[45] *Id.* at 312-13.

[46] *Id.* at 297.

[47] *Id.* at 293-294. *See also* Ogletree, *supra* note 16, at 63; Hon. Julian A. Cook Jr. & Mark S. Kende, *Color-Blindness in the Rehnquist Court: Comparing the Court's Treatment of Discrimination Claims by a Black Death Row Inmate and White Voting Rights Plaintiffs*, 13 T. M. COOLEY L. REV. 815 (1996) *and* Shaw v. Reno, 509 U.S. 630 (1993) (plaintiff need only allege that a reapportionment scheme is "so irrational on its face" to state a claim of political gerrymandering).

receive the death penalty was insufficient to establish an Eighth Amendment violation. In fact, the Court found that some statistical disparity was inevitable given the Court's directive that a jury must be given discretion in making a penalty decision.

The viability of any claim successfully using statistics in a future Eighth Amendment challenge was left unclear in the *McCleskey* opinion, although it appeared that the door was almost closed. While the Court hinted that statistics might be sufficient if they showed an even greater disparity than the one documented in the Baldus study, the Court also suggested that statistics could never provide a basis for an Eighth Amendment challenge as long as the process was otherwise constitutional.[48]

The fact that the Court accepted the validity of the statistics in the Baldus study while rejecting McCleskey's claim has been the subject of much discussion and debate. The Court has been accused of validating racially oppressive official conduct.[49] Scholars have compared the opinion in *McCleskey* to other notorious decisions of the Supreme Court, such as *Dred Scott v. Stanford*,[50] *Plessy v. Ferguson*,[51] and *Korematsu v. United States*.[52]

Supporters of the decision in *McCleskey* are quick to point out that the challenges raised by McCleskey to the Georgia statute in no way diminish his culpability or alter the fact that he deserved the death penalty. If anything, they argue, his evidence supports an argument that the death penalty should be imposed on a larger pool of defendants.[53]

Others who support the decision in *McCleskey* share the view expressed by Justice Powell that McCleskey's claim, "if taken to its logical conclusion, throws into serious question the principles that underlie our entire criminal justice system."[54] Several of the justices questioned what the remedy would be if

---

[48] 481 U.S. at 308, 313.

[49] Randall Kennedy, *McCleskey v. Kemp: Race, Capital Punishment and the Supreme Court*, 101 HARV. L. REV. 1388, 1389 (1988); DAVID COLE, NO EQUAL JUSTICE: RACE AND CLASS IN THE AMERICAN CRIMINAL JUSTICE SYSTEM 141 (1999).

[50] 60 U.S. 393, 407 (1857) (holding that African-Americans were altogether unfit to associate with the white race, either in social or political relations, and so far inferior that they had no rights that the white man had to respect).

[51] 163 U.S. 537, 552 (1896) (maintaining a separate but equal doctrine and holding that if one race is inferior to the other socially, the Constitution cannot put them on the same plane).

[52] 323 U.S. 214 (1944) (upholding Japanese petitioner's conviction for violating internment order since the order was justified by exigencies related to national security).

[53] Kennedy, *supra* note 49, at 1436 (discussing, although not supporting, the theory that states may "level-up," by increasing the number of death penalty prosecutions in those categories where it has previously been pursued less frequently).

[54] 481 U.S. at 282. The debate surrounding the decision in *McCleskey* gained even more fuel when, after the death of Justice Marshall, the Library of Congress released some of his papers, including an internal Court memo written on January 6, 1987, and signed by "Nino." This memo, written by Justice Scalia, demonstrated that Scalia felt that no statistical showing would have been sufficient to satisfy an equal protection or Eighth Amendment claim. The memo stated:

I plan to join Lewis' opinion in this case with two reservations. I disagree with the argument

McCleskey was granted relief. Would the death penalty system be invalid? Would the entire criminal justice system be subject to the same attack? Still others believed that to the extent that there was a disparate racial impact, the legislatures, rather than the courts, should address the issue.

McCleskey is a decision that haunted at least one member of the Court. When Justice Lewis Powell was interviewed by his biographer and asked whether he would change any vote on the Court, Powell's answer was *"McCleskey v. Kemp."*[55] Powell's biographer explained that Powell ultimately came to believe that the death penalty should be barred, not because it was intrinsically wrong, but because it could not fairly and expeditiously be enforced.

[D] An Impassioned Dissent

Justices Blackmun and Brennan each wrote a dissent joined by three other justices. Justice Blackmun addressed the equal protection claim and Justice Brennan the Eighth Amendment claim. While Justice Marshall joined their opinions, surprisingly, he did not write a separate dissent. Because he usually wrote separately in cases that raised important issues of race or death penalty sentences, some scholars have hypothesized that this break with tradition was purposeful and meant to convey the depth of his discouragement and alienation with the *McCleskey* decision.[56]

While Justice Blackmun agreed that a defendant must show that there was purposeful discrimination to prevail on a claim of racial discrimination under the equal protection clause, he argued that the Court should apply the same test used in claims of racial bias in jury selection. This test requires a defendant to make a prima facie showing of discrimination, at which time the burden shifts to the prosecution to show that any racial disparity was based upon permissibly neutral criteria.

Justice Brennan disagreed with the Court's Eighth Amendment analysis that rejected McCleskey's claim because it only showed a risk of discrimination, rather than actual racial discrimination, in his case. Brennan pointed out that, since *Furman*, the Court had been concerned with the *risk* of an arbitrary sentence rather than the proven fact that one had occurred. He argued:

> This emphasis on *risk* reflects the fact that concern for arbitrariness focuses on the rationality of the system as a whole and that a system that

---

that the inferences that can be drawn from the Baldus study are weakened by the fact that each jury and each trial is unique, or by the large number of variables at issue. And I do not share the view, implicit in the opinion, that an effect of racial factors upon sentencing, if only it could be shown by sufficiently strong statistical evidence, would require reversal. Since it is my view that unconscious operation of irrational sympathies and antipathies including racial upon jury decisions and (hence) prosecutorial decisions is real, acknowledged in the decisions of this court, and ineradicable, I cannot honestly say that all I need is more proof.

See generally Dennis D. Dorin, *Far Right of the Mainstream: Racism, Rights and Remedies from the Perspective of Justice Antonin Scalia's McCleskey Memorandum*, 45 MERCER L. REV. 1035, 1037-38 (1994).

[55] JEFFRIES, JUSTICE LEWIS F. POWELL JR. 451-452, (1994).

[56] Kennedy, *supra* note 49, at 1417 n.2.

features a significant probability that sentencing decisions are influenced by impermissible considerations cannot be regarded as rational.[57]

Justice Brennan accused the majority of being afraid of "too much justice"[58] and rejected the notion that racial discrimination was a relic of the past. Justice Brennan wrote:

> [I]t has been scarcely a generation since this Court's first decision striking down racial segregation, and barely two decades since the legislative prohibition of racial discrimination in major domains of national life. These have been honorable steps, but we cannot pretend that in three decades we have completely escaped the grip of a historical legacy spanning centuries . . . [W]e remain imprisoned by the past as long as we deny its influence on the present.[59]

§ 20.05   POST-*McCLESKEY*: JUDICIAL RESPONSE

After *McCleskey* it was unclear what kind of showing, if any, would be sufficient to prevail on a claim of racial discrimination. What followed was a general refusal by the federal courts to even hold hearings on claims of racial bias in capital sentencing.

There are only a handful of cases in state or federal court that have held evidentiary hearings on the issue of whether racial bias rendered the sentence of death unconstitutional. In each instance, defendants tried to identify evidence that proved that the death sentence was a result of racial discrimination. The Court, in *McCleskey*, had made it clear that statistical evidence was not enough. Therefore, some defendants also presented evidence of the actions and attitudes of the decision-makers in capital cases to show that their individual and collective racial bias affected the outcome.[60]

Could evidence of racial prejudice on the part of the prosecutor, jury, judge, or defense attorney support a constitutional challenge? What if most of the jurors in a case testified that they were raised in segregated schools and churches, had reservations about intermarriage, and referred to African-Americans as colored and other more derogatory terms while maintaining that they meant no disrespect? What if the jurors found Martin Luther King, Jr. "intrusive"? Would this evidence be enough to show racial bias? What if, in addition, the judge in a case was also raised in the segregated South and denounced integration when it was started? Finally, what if the defense counsel believed that African-Americans were uneducated and would not make good teachers, but made good basketball players, and referred to his clients jokingly in racially derogatory terms?

---

[57] McCleskey v. Kemp, 481 U.S. at 323 (Brennan, J., dissenting) (emphasis added).

[58] *Id.* at 339 (Brennan, J., dissenting).

[59] *Id.* at 344 (Brennan, J., dissenting).

[60] *See* Stephen Bright, *Will the Death Penalty Remain Alive in the Twenty-First Century?: International Norms, Discrimination, Arbitrariness, and the Risk of Executing the Innocent*, 2001 WISCONSIN LAW REVIEW 14-15 (describing hearing on racial discrimination held in Georgia where evidence was presented of disparate treatment of cases based upon the race of the victim).

The answer, so far, is "no." These views by trial participants do not support a finding of constitutional error. The scenario presented here mirrors the facts in *Dobbs v. Zant*.[61] The federal court in *Dobbs* held that the racial attitudes of the jurors, the judge, and the prosecutor did not affect the sentencing deliberations, because there was no evidence that they communicated their views among themselves. Although the court recognized that some jurors possessed more racial animus than others, the showing was deemed insufficient to establish a constitutional violation.[62]

Most of the state supreme courts have followed the lead of the federal courts and have denied claims of racial discrimination without holding a hearing.[63] New Jersey was a notable exception before it abolished the death penalty by legislation in December, 2007. The New Jersey Supreme Court rejected the *McCleskey* decision. It refused to accept that racial disparities were an inevitable part of the criminal justice system. The New Jersey court held that under its *state* constitution, racial disparities are unconstitutional and would not be tolerated.[64] Between 1989 and 2007, under the supervision of the state supreme court, the New Jersey Administrative Office of the Courts collected data on capital cases pursuant to mandatory reporting requirements to determine whether race was a factor in sentencing. History has shown that the courts are hesitant to address the issue of race in the criminal justice system. However, as more studies and reports collect data and statistics on the impact of race and sentences of death, courts may feel they need to take up this issue.

§ 20.06 POST-*McCLESKEY*: LEGISLATIVE RESPONSE

Responding to the Supreme Court's call for legislative action in *McCleskey*, several members of Congress introduced the Racial Justice Act.[65] This legislation would have allowed a defendant to use statistics to prove racial discrimination in his sentence of death to the same extent that statistics are used to prove racial discrimination in employment, public benefits, use of peremptory challenges, and composition of grand juries. Although hearings were held, and a great deal of support was voiced for this bill, it did not gain approval. Since that time, similar legislation has been introduced in both houses of Congress and has also failed to pass into law.

---

[61] 720 F. Supp. 1566 (1989). Postconviction affidavits were collected from almost every juror. One juror stated that "I believe in blacks marrying blacks and whites marrying white . . . Its because of the children . . . I just don't believe in mixing people. Now, you can have them as friends, . . . that child somewhere down the line is going to suffer. *Id.* at 1575 n.14.

[62] This decision was affirmed by the Court of Appeals in Dobbs v. Zant, 963 F.2d 1403 (11th Cir. 1991). *cert. granted*, 506 U.S. 357 (1993) (rev'd on other grounds). The appellate court held that Dobbs failed to prove that the decision-makers in his case acted with discriminatory purpose. *Id.* at 1408 n.4.

[63] *See* Foster v. State, 614 So. 2d 455 (Fla. 1992), *cert. denied*, 510 U.S. 951 (1993) (refusing to require a hearing on racial disparities) *and* Jones v. State, 440 S.E.2d 161 (Ga. 1994) (upholding the quashing of defendant's subpoena of the district attorney to testify in response to a claim of racial discrimination in his selection of juries and hiring of staff).

[64] State v. Marshall, 130 N.J. 109, 207 (1992).

[65] H.R. 4442, 100th Cong. (1988).

The state legislative response has been similar. Although several state legislatures introduced a "Racial Justice Act," Kentucky and North Carolina are the only states that have signed one into law. The Kentucky Racial Justice Act provides:

> No person shall be subject to or given a sentence of death that was sought on the basis of race . . . A finding that race was the basis of the decision to seek a death sentence may be established if the court finds that race was a significant factor in decisions to seek the sentence of death in the Commonwealth [Kentucky] at the time the death sentence was sought.[66]

The Act provides that statistical and other evidence may be presented to prove that race was a factor in making the decision to seek death. The difficulty for defendants in gaining relief under the Kentucky statute, however, is that it requires the defense to raise the claim before trial and state with particularity how the statistical evidence proves that racial considerations played a significant part in the decision to seek a death sentence in the defendant's case. The effect apparently is to allow defendants only to challenge charging decisions and only where there is evidence of discrimination in the particular prosecutorial district. Moreover, the statute requires the defendant to prove his claim "by clear and convincing evidence."

The North Carolina Act, adopted in 2009, is more favorable toward capital defendants.[67] Although originally very similar to the Kentucky statute, changes were made to promote its effectiveness in limiting the influence of race on capital selection. For example, the North Carolina Act 1) allows statistical evidence that does not focus on the specific prosecutorial district, 2) covers not merely charging decisions but also prosecutorial peremptory challenges and decisions by juries, and 3) imposes no burden of proof on the defendant higher than the normal preponderance standard.[68] Future litigation will reveal the degree to which the North Carolina statute affects capital selection in the state.

§ 20.07 RACIAL ISSUES

[A] Racial Attitudes of the Decision Makers

As a capital case proceeds through the criminal justice system, decision-makers often exercise discretion in ways that are not reviewed in any organized manner. The decision-making is also highly decentralized, which generally reduces the sense of responsibility experienced by individual decisionmakers along the way.[69] However, even when the evidence of racial bias is overt, courts have been reluctant to act.[70] One death penalty scholar argues:

---

[66] Ky. Rev. Stat. Ann. § 532-300.

[67] *See* N.C. Gen. Stat. § 15A-2011-12.

[68] *See* Seth Kotch & Robert P. Mosteller, *The Racial Justice Act and the Long Struggle with Race and the Death Penalty in North Carolina*, 88 N. C. L. Rev. 2031, 2116-18 & nn. 380 & 381 (2010).

[69] Howe, *supra* note 29, at 19.

[70] A stark example is Andrews v. Shulsen, 485 U.S. 919 (1988). Justice Marshall's dissent from the denial of certiorari reports: "[A] mid-trial incident in which a juror handed the bailiff a napkin with a drawing of a man on a gallows above the inscription, 'Hang the Niggers.' The District Court in this case

Racial discrimination not acceptable in any other area of American life is tolerated in criminal courts. The use of a racial slur may cost a sports announcer his job, but there have been capital cases in which judges, jurors and defense counsel have called African American defendants [racially derogatory names] with no repercussions for anyone except the accused.[71]

One of the most important decision-makers in a case is the prosecutor.[72] The prosecutor decides whom to charge, what charges to bring, whether to offer a plea bargain, whether to proceed to trial, and in which cases, of the many that are death-eligible, the death penalty will be pursued. These decisions are, for the most part, unreviewable, and often made without articulated, objective guidelines.[73]

Defendants in death penalty cases have challenged the neutrality with which prosecutors exercise their discretion. Professor Jeffrey Pokorak examined the race of the district attorneys who had the ultimate decision-making power in capital cases. In a study covering October 1993-February 1998, Pokorak determined that, in the 38 states that had death penalty statutes, the district attorneys were almost entirely white. Of the 1838 total district attorneys in death penalty states, 1794 were white (97.5%), 22 were African-American (1.2%), and 22 were Hispanic (1.2%). In 18 of these states, 100% of the district attorneys who made these decisions were white.[74] Based on this data, Pokorak questioned the effect unconscious racial bias might have on a prosecutor's decision-making:

> This study thus suggests two ways in which unconscious bias might enter the system. The first and most obvious channel for this bias arises from the racial disparity between the prosecutors and the death row population. The predominantly white prosecutors are more likely to have absorbed the 'cultural stereotype' of black inferiority and thus perceive black defendants as more 'violent' and more 'dangerous' than their white counterparts. . . . The second and more subtle expression of unconscious bias may result from the similarity between the prosecutor and the victim populations. The victim population's racial makeup, 83.2% white . . . resembles the prosecutor's population more closely than it resembles the death row prisoner's population. As a result, unconscious bias may creep into the prosecutor's decision to seek the death penalty.[75]

---

refused even to undertake an evidentiary hearing to investigate petitioner's substantial allegations of racial prejudice." Andrews was executed in Utah in July, 1992.

[71] Stephen B. Bright, *Discrimination, Death and Denial: The Tolerance of Racial Discrimination in Infliction of the Death Penalty*, 35 SANTA CLARA L. REV. 433, 446-447 (1995).

[72] *See* ANGELA J. DAVIS, ARBITRARY JUSTICE: THE POWER OF THE AMERICAN PROSECUTOR 77 (2007).

[73] *See, e.g.*, PA. SUP. CT. COMM., *supra* note 28, at 216 (noting that no county prosecutors office in PA employs public guidelines defining standards and procedures for seeking the death penalty and that the PA District Attorneys Association advised member counties not to cooperate with the committee on this issue). *See also* DAVIS, *supra* note 72, at 89 ("Like so many other prosecutorial decisions, the death penalty decision is far too arbitrary, often depending on the philosophy and proclivities of the chief prosecutor instead of on legal principles, standards, or guidelines.").

[74] Jeffrey J. Pokorak, *Probing The Capital Prosecutor's Perspective: Race of the Discretionary Actors*, 83 CORNELL L. REV. 1811 (1998).

[75] *Id.* at 1818-1819. *See also* Davis, *supra* note 8, at 35. (A prosecutor may unconsciously consider a case involving a white victim as more serious than a case involving a black victim. This unconscious view

The courts, for the most part, have dismissed claims of racial bias of prosecutors in a perfunctory manner and have rarely granted a hearing on the subject. Great deference is shown to a prosecutor's decisions. This is true whether the decision is to charge a case with the death penalty or whether a plea agreement is offered or allowed. There are no reported cases of a court granting relief on a claim that the prosecutor exercised his discretionary decisions in a racially biased manner.[76]

The judge in a death penalty case also exercises discretion on issues such as the jury-selection procedure used, the evidence admitted at trial, and the instructions given to a jury. While most judges conduct death penalty trials in a fair and impartial manner, there are cases in which judges have made comments during a trial that suggest they view minorities as inferior. The question remains whether a racial bias of a judge makes a sentence of death unconstitutional.[77]

The racial attitude of jurors has often been the subject of challenging a sentence of death. Jurors are also afforded a great deal of discretion that is neither reviewed nor controlled for conscious or unconscious racial bias. One scholar argues that the sentencer discretion afforded to juries exacerbates the tendency of prosecutors to consider race in deciding when to pursue the death penalty:

> Prosecutors know that capital sentencers have expansive discretion. They will also recognize that this discretion allows the racial preconceptions of sentencers to influence sentencer choices. Because prosecutors often weigh the odds that a sentencer will vote for death, their perceptions of sentencer biases will tend to influence their decisions about when to pursue death.[78]

Juries in capital cases may have few, if any, jurors of color.[79] During the "death qualification" process, the numbers of minority jurors may be reduced further, and

---

may influence not only the charging decision, but related decisions as well.).

[76] Edwards v. Scroggy, 849 F.2d 204, 207 (5th Cir. 1988) (rejecting defense claim that included showing that prosecutor had been quoted in a local newspaper that his philosophy regarding blacks on jury panels was to "get rid of as many" as he could); Bright, *supra* note 60 (noting that, in Georgia's Chattahoochee Judicial Circuit between 1973-1990, although African-American were the victims of 65% of the homicides, 85% of the capital cases in that circuit were cases in which the homicide victims were white).

[77] One of the more dramatic examples was a judge in Polk County, Florida who referred to the defendant's parents in racially derogatory terms. Although the trial judge was disqualified for the penalty trial, he was not sanctioned nor was the conviction reversed. *See* Peek v. State, 488 So. 2d. 52, 56 (1986).

[78] Howe, *supra* note 29, at 28.

[79] A significant proportion of potential jurors of color can be eliminated through the use of peremptory challenges by the prosecution. Despite efforts by the Supreme Court to prevent racially discrimination in jury selection, the racial motivations for peremptory challenges are not always easy to uncover. For example, in Miller-El v. Dretke, 545 U.S. 231 (2005), the Supreme Court reversed a capital conviction and death sentence obtained after the prosecution used peremptory challenges to exclude ten of eleven black venire panelists. Miller-El's claim of discrimination had been rejected by the Texas trial court, the Texas Court of Appeals, the U.S. District Court and the U.S. Court of Appeals for the Fifth Circuit. *See also* Snyder v. Louisiana, 128 S. Ct. 1203 (2008) (reversing capital conviction and sentence based on prosecution's improper use of peremptory challenge to strike African-American person from jury after the defense claim was rejected by the Louisiana courts). For more on the Court's effort to regulate racial discrimination in the use of peremptory challenges, *see* Section 7.05[c], *supra*.

a prosecutor might be able to remove all of them through peremptory challenges.[80] Most scholars agree that racial diversity makes a difference where either conscious or unconscious stereotypes and assumptions may influence a decision.[81]

[B]   Racial Attitudes of the Defense Attorney

What if the defense counsel holds attitudes that are racially biased? Should this have any impact on the constitutionality of a death sentence? For the most part, the courts say no.

Capital defendants have claimed that their sentences of death are unconstitutional based upon the racism of their lawyers. These cases are usually dismissed by the courts with little discussion. Courts generally maintain that, because defense counsel is not a decision-maker in the trial, his views and attitudes towards minorities do not affect the legitimacy of a sentence of death. This view has been criticized for its failure to recognize the role defense counsel plays in a penalty trial. As one capital defense expert argues:

> A lawyer defending an accused in a capital case has the obligation to investigate the life and background of the client in order to introduce mitigating evidence. To fulfill this constitutional and ethical obligation, a lawyer must be comfortable working with the client, the client's family, and the client's friends. If the appointed lawyer regards the client, his family or his friends in a demeaning way, the lawyer cannot possibly obtain and present the needed information and fulfill the role as an advocate for the client's life. In addition, the defendant who is assigned a lawyer who shares the racial prejudices of the jurors, judges, and prosecutors is left without an advocate to expose and challenge such biases.[82]

When cases with evidence of racial bias are reversed, it is usually on grounds other than the claim of racial prejudice. One stark example is a California lawyer who had two clients appeal their sentences of death on the grounds of ineffective assistance of counsel.[83] In support of their claims, each presented numerous affidavits alleging the racist attitudes of the lawyer.[84] Both clients' sentences were reversed, but without any mention of the evidence of racism presented to the

---

[80]   Bright, *supra* note 71, at 455; *see also* Section 7.05[B], *supra.*

[81]   *Id.* at 458. For a discussion of the psychological tendencies of white decision-makers to sympathize more with whites than with blacks; *see* Samuel H. Pillsbury, *Emotional Justice: Moralizing the Passions of Criminal Punishment,* 74 Cornell L. Rev. 655, 708 (1989).

[82]   Bright, *supra* note 71, at 459-60.

[83]   Mayfield v. Woodford, 270 F.3d 915 (9th Cir. 2001); Wade v. Calderon, 29 F.3d 1312 (9th Cir. 1994), *cert. denied,* 513 U.S. 1120 (1995).

[84]   In one affidavit, Professor Kim Taylor of Stanford University School of Law, described the relationship between Ames and his client:

> Mr. Wade was represented by a man who viewed blacks with contempt, and this evidence is supported by the manner in which that attorney conducted himself at trial. Trial counsel failed to take any steps to impeach the state's injection of racial stereotyping and race-based misinformation into the case . . . and counsel comported himself in his argument to the jury in a manner as to convey his race-based contempt.

Affidavit of Kim A. Taylor, (Sept. 30, 1991), filed in Wade v. Calderon, 29 F.3d 1312 (9th Cir. 1994).

court.[85] In one of the cases, however, when the Ninth Circuit Court of Appeals heard the case *en banc,* four of the eleven judges supported the reversal but dissented from the opinion, arguing that the lawyer's racial bias constituted an actual conflict of interest that should have required an automatic reversal of the *conviction* as well as the sentence of death. They wrote that the defense lawyer harbored "deep and utter contempt for African-Americans."[86]

[C]   Race and Future Dangerousness

Suppose an expert witness testifies for the government that the racial background of a defendant is a factor in determining whether he will be a future danger to society? Is this evidence permissible? Or is a sentence of death based upon this evidence unconstitutional?

This issue was presented in the *Saldano v. Cockrell.*[87] At Saldano's penalty trial, the government called Dr. Walter Quijano, a clinical psychologist, who testified that one of the factors that he used in his assessment of an individual's future dangerousness was that person's race or ethnicity. Dr. Quijano testified that ethnicity should be considered in Saldano's case since Saldano, as an Argentinean, would be considered Hispanic.[88] In the Supreme Court, the Attorney General for the State of Texas confessed error and the Court sent the case back to Texas, only to have the Texas Court of Criminal Appeals reinstate Saldano's sentence of death.[89] In June 2003, the Federal District Court held that this testimony was improper and ordered a new sentencing hearing.[90] The Texas Attorney General did not appeal the decision. Although the local district attorney attempted to intervene, the District Court denied the application for intervention, and the U.S. Court of Appeals for the Fifth Circuit upheld the District Court's ruling.[91]

---

[85] This same lawyer also represented Stephen Wayne Anderson, whose case came before the Ninth Circuit during the same period. Anderson's sentence of death was upheld, and he was executed on January 29, 2002. *See* Anderson v. Calderon, 276 F.3d 483 (9th Cir. 2001).

[86] The dissent quotes the lawyer's daughter who testified that: "[The lawyer's] contempt for [his family] was exceeded only by his contempt for people of other races and ethnic groups. He especially ridiculed black people referring to them with racial invectives." Mayfield, 270 F.3d at 939-940.

[87] Saldano v. Cockrell, 267 F. Supp. 2d 635 (2003).

[88] This testimony also raises interesting questions about the meaning of the word Hispanic. Although Argentineans are Spanish speaking, 85% are of European descent (mostly Spanish and Italian) and do not consider themselves to be Hispanic. *See generally Argentina,* Microsoft Encarta Online Encyclopedia 2003, *available at* http://encarta.msn.com.

[89] Similar testimony was presented in several other Texas cases, and, for that reason, in most of them, the death sentences were reversed and new penalty hearings were held. *See* Sommer Ingram, *Race-based death sentence challenged,* DALLAS MORN. NEWS, Sept. 8, 2011, at A3. *See, e.g.,* Avalos-Alba v. Johnson, 232 F.3d 208 (5th Cir. 2000); Garcia v.Johnson, 232 F.3d 209 (5th Cir. 2000); Blue v. Johnson, No. H-99-0350 (S.D. Tex. Oct. 2, 2000); Broxton v. Johnson, No. H-00cv1034 (S.D. Tex. Mar. 28, 2001).

[90] Saldano v. Cockrell, 267 F. Supp. 2d 635 (2003).

[91] *See* Saldano v. Roach, 363 F.3d 545 (2004), *cert. denied,* Roach v. Saldano, 543 U.S. 820 (2004).

Chapter 21

GENDER BIAS AND THE DEATH PENALTY

§ 21.01 OVERVIEW

We've all heard the stereotype: weak, dependent, submissive, nurturing, and home-maker. Women have been characterized as the more passive sex and are often portrayed in the role of the damsel in distress. If capital punishment is about portraying people as devils to make it easier for a juror to impose death, then stereotypes of women may play a part in decreasing the likelihood a woman will be sentenced to death.[1] The disparity in the number of death sentences imposed on men over women was cited by Justice Thurgood Marshall when the death penalty was struck down in 1972. In his concurring opinion, he wrote:

> There is also overwhelming evidence that the death penalty is employed against men and not women. Only 33 women have been executed since 1930, while 3,827 men have met a similar fate. It is difficult to understand why women have received such favored treatment since the purposes allegedly served by capital punishment seemingly are equally applicable to both sexes.[2]

There is an ongoing debate over whether the gender of a defendant will impact the likelihood that a sentence of death will be imposed or that an execution will occur. Most agree that the numbers do not tell the entire story. Several theories have been developed, each of which provides some understanding to when and how women end up on death row.

§ 21.02 STATISTICS

Statistics appear to support the idea that there is a disparity in the ways in which the death penalty is administered against men relative to women. As of December 31, 2011, there were 58 women on death row. This constitutes only 1.8% of the total death row population of about 3,250 persons and less than 0.1% of the approximately 9,031 women in prisons in the United States.[3]

---

[1] For more discussion on issues of women and the death penalty see VICTOR STREIB, THE FAIRER DEATH: EXECUTING WOMEN IN OHIO, (Paul Finkelman ed., 2006); Death Penalty Information Center (DPIC), *Women and the Death Penalty*, (last visited Jan. 31, 2012), http://www.deathpenaltyinfo.org/women-and-death-penalty#facts; Elizabeth Rapaport, *Some Questions About Gender and the Death Penalty*, 20 GOLDEN GATE U. L. REV. 501 (1990); Thad Rueter, *Why Women Aren't Executed: Gender Bias and the Death Penalty*, 23 HUM. RTS. 10 (1996).

[2] Furman v. Georgia, 408 U.S. 238, 365 (1972) (Marshall, J., concurring) (footnotes omitted).

[3] Victor L. Streib, *Death Penalty For Female Offenders, January 1973 through December 31, 2011*

A total of 174 death sentences were imposed on women from 1973 through 2011, which constitutes 2% of all death sentences in that time.[4] Six states (California (21), Florida (20), Texas (19), North Carolina (16), Ohio (12) and Alabama (11) account for over half of all sentences of death for women.[5] California, Texas and Florida have consistently led states in sentencing women to death.[6] In 2011, women constituted 6.4% (five of seventy-eight sentences of death) of all persons sentenced to death. This constitutes the highest percentage in the modern era (1973-2011).[7]

As of December 31, 2011, twelve of these death sentences resulted in executions.[8] Seven different states have executed women with Texas and Oklahoma executing three women each.[9] Of the twelve women who have been executed, only three murdered someone who was a stranger to them; the others killed family members or those with whom they were in a relationship.

Velma Barfield of North Carolina was executed in 1984.[10] She was the first woman to be executed under the modern post-1972 statutes. After she was executed, another 407 executions took place around the country before another woman was executed. This time it was Karla Faye Tucker of Texas in February, 1998.[11]

§ 21.03 THEORIES OF GENDER DISCRIMINATION

Scholars and others have espoused various theories about why women are not sentenced to death with the same frequency as men. A discussion of some of these theories follows.

(2011), http://www.deathpenaltyinfo.org/documents/femaledeathrow.pdf. *Also available at* www.deathpenaltyinfo.org/article.php?did=230&scid=24#facts (last visited October 10, 2011).

[4] Tracy L. Snell & Laura M. Maruschak, U.S. Dept. of Justice, *Capital Punishment 2001*, p. 8, Table 7 (2002), www.ojp.gov/bjs/pub/pdf/cp01.pdf (last visited Sept. 24, 2007); *see also* DPIC, *supra* note 1.

[5] These five states account for seventy-eight of the 160 sentences of death. Ohio, in fifth place with 11 women sentenced to death has not executed a women since 1954 and only has one woman on death row. The other ten sentences of death were either reversed or commuted. The state of Virginia, a leading death penalty state, has sentenced one woman to death since 1976 and she was executed on September 23, 2010. Previously Virginia last executed a woman in 1912. Streib, *supra* note 3.

[6] Victor L. Streib, *Death Penalty For Female Offender, January 1, 1973 – December 31, 2011*, Issue #66, *available at* http://www.deathpenaltyinfo.org/documents/FemDeathDec2011.pdf.

[7] Id.

[8] Death Penalty Information Center, *supra*, note 1.

[9] http://www.deathpenaltyinfo.org/women-and-death-penalty#facts (last visited January 10, 2011). States that have executed women include Alabama (1), Arkansas (1), Florida (2), North Carolina (1), Oklahoma (3), Texas (3), and Virginia (1).

[10] William E. Schmidt, *First Woman is Executed in U.S. Since 1962*, N.Y. Times, Nov. 3,1984, at A1.

[11] Sam Verhovek, *Execution in Texas: The Overview; Divisive Case of a Killer of Two Ends as Texas Execution*, N.Y. Times, Feb. 4, 1998, at A1 (discussing the controversy surrounding the execution of Karla Faye Tucker, the born again Christian who had murdered a couple with a pickax).

[A]　Chivalry Theory

The chivalry theory attributes the relative scarcity of women on death row to the stereotype of women as more passive and more submissive. This stereotype, coupled with the stereotypical standards of the "western gentleman," creates a more protective attitude towards women, and makes women less likely to be sentenced to death.[12] Professor Elizabeth Rapaport[13] describes this phenomenon as one that creates "[d]eep cultural inhibitions against the deliberate killing of women, even women who have been convicted of heinous murders.[14]

[B]　Evil Woman Theory

The evil woman theory attempts to identify and define why certain women are sentenced to death while others are not. It posits that the women on death row have not been accorded the same deference given to other women because their crimes include unusually violent or "shockingly unlady-like behavior." This allows the sentencing judges and juries to put aside their traditional stereotypes of women as "the gentler sex" and view them as "crazed monsters." Once this transformation takes place, these women are viewed as "deserving of nothing more than extermination."[15]

[C]　Legislative Selection of Death Eligible Crimes

Other scholars, including Professors Victor Steib and Elizabeth Rapaport, attribute the disparate treatment of women, in part, to the manner in which death penalty statutes have been written. Most statutes define specific types of murders that are eligible for sentences of death by enumerating aggravating circumstances that define one murder as worse than another. Streib argues that men and women tend to commit different kinds of murders. The murders committed by women are less likely to fall within one of the statutory circumstances that make a crime "eligible for death."[16] Streib identifies a number of aggravating circumstances typically found in death penalty statutes that are committed more frequently by men than women. These include:

1) A defendant with a previous record of violent crimes; (Streib argues that research reveals that women convicted of murder are generally less likely than men to have prior convictions for murder, attempted murder, or other violent

---

[12]　Jenny E. Carroll, *Images of Women and Capital Sentencing Among Female Offenders: Exploring the Outer Limits of the Eighth Amendment and Articulated Theories*, 75 Tex. L. Rev. 1413, 1418 (1997).

[13]　Elizabeth Rapaport is a Professor of Law at the University of New Mexico.

[14]　Elizabeth Rapaport, *Some Questions About Gender and the Death Penalty*, 20 Golden Gate U. L. Rev. (1990), http://digitalcommons.law.ggu.edu/ggulrev/vol20/iss3/3; *see also* Ilene H. Nagel & John Hagan, *Gender and Crime: Offense Patterns and Criminal Court Sanctions*, 4 Crime and Just. 91, 113 (M. Tonry & N. Morris eds. 1983).

[15]　Victor L. Streib, *Death Penalty for Female Offenders*, 58 U. Cin. L. Rev. 845, 878 (1990); *see also* Melinda O Neil, *The Gender Gap Argument: Exploring the Disparity of Sentencing Women to Death*, 25 New Eng. J. on Crim & Civ. Confinement 213, 221 (1999); Carroll, *supra* note 12, at 1439.

[16]　Streib, *supra* note 1, at 459.

crimes)[17] 2) Felony-murder; (Streib argues that most felony murders occur during the commission of a rape, kidnaping, or armed robbery and that men are more likely than women to be convicted of a killing during the course of one of these violent felonies), 3) Planned or premeditated murder; (Elizabeth Rapaport and Victor Streib agree that women who kill are more likely than men to kill in anger or fear rather than for a predatory purpose).[18]

At the same time that women are less likely to kill according to certain aggravating factors, they are more likely to murder family members or other relatives. Nearly one quarter (12/49) of the women on death row in 2007 killed their husbands or boyfriends. Nearly another one-quarter (11/49) killed their children. Two others killed both husbands and children.[19] Despite the large proportion of women on death row for killing family members, these cases are often classified as "domestic violence" and prosecutors frequently do not seek the death penalty in these types of murders.[20]

[D]   Retribution

Victor Streib argues that a significant reason the death penalty is applied more often against men has more to do with our feelings of appropriate retribution than other specific factors. He writes:

> My three decades of research on this and similar issues have led me to conclude that the death penalty system is the most extreme refuge for macho men. . . . Our most highly touted system of justice appears to be more about insecure middle-age male egos needing to reassure themselves and others of their continuing manhood than it is about the more commonly heard principles of deterrence: justice, retribution, and incapacitation. To bolster their manliness, they need to dispatch the toughest of male opponents; zapping the skinny little guy just doesn't deliver. Needless to say, executing a woman does not give them that masculine rush. To the contrary, it stains them as "guys who hit girls," the ultimate wimps on the playground.[21]

---

[17] *Id.* at 461.

[18] Elizabeth Rapaport, *The Death Penalty and Gender Discrimination*, 25 Law & Soc'y Rev. 367, 370 n.5, (1991) (citing data from FBI Supplementary Homicide Reports that are compiled from the FBI's Uniform Crime Reporting section based upon information from local law enforcement agencies. Data was collected covering the years 1976-1987); *see also* Victor L. Streib, *Sentencing Women to Death*, 16-SPG Crim. Just. 24 (2001).

[19] Streib, *supra* note 3.

[20] *See* Rapaport, note 14, at 370, *supra* (pointing out that since women are more often the victims of domestic violence cases, the attitude that diminishes the seriousness of these offenses work more often to a woman's disadvantage).

[21] Streib, *supra* note 1, at 28.

§ 21.04   CASE STUDIES

[A]   Velma Barfield

Velma Barfield was a plump, 46-year-old white woman. She appeared to be a devoutly pious Christian, and also was known as a loving and caring mother of a son.[22] Velma was hardly the typical image of a murderer; however, she was the first female to be executed after 1972.[23]

In 1978, Velma Barfield was sentenced to death for the arsenic poisoning death of her boyfriend, Stewart Taylor.[24] Although Barfield had no prior convictions, she admitted to the fatal poisoning of an elderly couple for whom she was employed as nurse and caretaker, as well as the poisoning death of her own mother.[25] Barfield also was a suspect in the poisoning death of her husband some years earlier.[26] It was not until four days before her scheduled execution that the issue of her lack of competence due to bipolar disorder was raised.[27]

By the time of her execution, Barfield claimed to be a new woman; she had changed into a drug-free, born-again Christian, beloved by inmates and staff at her prison and supported by Ruth Graham, wife of evangelist Billy Graham.[28]

Many attribute Barfield's execution more to politics than personality.[29] Barfield's execution was scheduled just four days before election day when Governor Jim Hunt, a Democrat, was attempting to win a senate seat from Republican Jesse Helms.[30] Granting clemency was a political risk that Hunt was unwilling to take. At the time, North Carolina was a state where 70% of the electorate was in favor of capital punishment and nearly 80% favored executing Barfield.[31]

---

[22] TruTV Crime Library, *Stuart Taylor's Agony*, *available at* http://www.crimelibrary.com/notorious_murders/women/velma_barfield/1.html (last visited Jan. 31, 2012).

[23] In 1972, the Supreme Court struck down all death penalty statutes. States then passed new statutes beginning what is called the modern death penalty era.

[24] State v. Barfield, 259 S.E. 2d 510, 522 (N.C. 1979).

[25] Rapaport, *supra* note 14, at 539.

[26] *Barfield*, 259 S.E. 2d at 521-22.

[27] Joseph Ingle, *Final Hours: The Execution of Velma Barfield*, 23 Loy. L.A. L. Rev. 221, 232 (1989) (describing Velma Barfield's lawyer, Dick Burr, assertion that she was not competent to stand trial).

[28] William E. Schmidt, *Woman Executed in North Carolina*, N.Y. Times, Nov. 2, 1984, at A1.

[29] *See* Rapaport, *supra* note 14, at 540.

[30] *See* Schmidt, *supra* note 10 (noting that Hunt's election bid was heated and that Hunt's reluctance to grant Barfield clemency may have been politically motivated).

[31] Rapaport, *supra* note 14, at 540.

[B] Karla Faye Tucker

In 1984, Tucker was convicted and sentenced to death for the brutal murders of her ex-lover, Jerry Lynn Dean, and his companion, Deborah Thornton.[32] Tucker not only admitted she and her boyfriend took a pickax and hacked Dean and Thornton to death while they were sleeping, she boasted of the orgasm it provided her. At the murder scene, investigators found the pickax still embedded in Thornton's chest. Tucker was a drug addict and prostitute who seemed unrepentant, and even proud, of her actions.

In various pleas to save her life, Tucker, then 38, claimed she was not the same woman who committed those brutal murders nearly 15 years earlier. She, too, was a born-again Christian with a virtually spotless disciplinary record while in prison. Tucker received extensive media coverage, in part because she was an attractive, telegenic, articulate, white woman, and in part because she received support from pro-death penalty celebrities as Pat Robertson who argued that Tucker should be permitted to live because she had found Jesus.[33] Tucker was scheduled to die in Texas where then Governor George W. Bush was seeking reelection and examining his potential as a presidential candidate. Governor Bush refused to grant clemency to Tucker and she was executed.[34]

[C] Susan Smith

Susan Smith was spared the death penalty by a jury, but for some time that did not appear to be possible. She became perhaps the most loathed woman in American after she confessed to drowning her two boys, Michael aged 3 and Alex 14 months.[35] She had strapped them into their car seats and let her car roll into John D. Long Lake. For 10 days, she appeared on national television claiming that a black man had car-jacked her car and taken her children. She cried and pleaded for their safe return, knowing that they were in the bottom of the lake. Once she confessed to the murder, the prosecutor sought the death penalty.

There was no question of her guilt. The only question for the jury was her punishment. In less than 2½ hours, a jury of nine men and three women rejected the death penalty and returned a life verdict. Even the four African Americans on her jury felt sympathy for her.[36] This was surprising to many since Smith's choice

---

[32] For an interesting account of Karla Faye Tucker's life and death, see Joan Howarth, *Review Essay: Feminism, Layering, and Death Row*, 2 S. Cal. Rev. L. & Women's Stud. 401 (1992) (in which Howarth reviews *Crossed Over: A Murder, A Memoir* by Beverly Lowry).

[33] Teresa Malcolm, *Tucker Death Affected Robertson Views*, National Catholic Reporter, April 23, 1999, quoting Robertson as saying after the execution of Karla Faye Tucker, "This was a different person. To execute her was an act of barbarity that was totally unnecessary".

[34] Sister Helen Prejean, Death in Texas, *See* http://www.nybooks.com/articles/archives/2005/jan/13/death-in-texas/?pagination=false (last visited January 31, 2012).

[35] Mike Dorning, *Susan Smith's Jurors Felt Her Pain: Quiet End Sought to Public Ordeal*, Chicago Tribune, July 30, 1995, at 3.

[36] Michael Young, *Where's the Danger? Tensions Between Whites and Blacks Rest On A Basis of Widespread Stereotypes of Criminality*, Sun Sentinel, July 9, 1996, at 9A.

of a black perpetrator for her fictitious car-jacking had antagonized race relations in her town.

What was it about Susan Smith that made jurors choose life while for Karla Faye Tucker and Velma Barfield they chose death? As a mother who was able to kill her small children, she easily fit within the description of an "evil woman." What accounted for the difference in outcome?

There is no question that Susan Smith had excellent legal counsel for her trial. She effectively demonstrated her remorse for the killing during her trial. It was difficult for the prosecutor to portray Smith as a stranger or a monster in a small town where the 12 jurors had known her, seen her walk around town and passed her family every day.[37] Whatever the reason, Susan Smith lives while other women do not.

§ 20.05   THE FUTURE OF EXECUTING WOMEN

Although the media hype surrounding the execution of Karla Faye Tucker was almost unprecedented, many now wonder whether the perceived reluctance of the public to execute women was misunderstood or exaggerated.[38] Governor Bush suffered no political backlash for allowing Tucker's execution to proceed; in fact he was reelected governor that year and made a successful bid for the presidency two years later. A few weeks after Tucker's execution in 1998, Florida executed Judi Buenoano with almost no public or media interest. The execution of Betty Lou Beets in 2000 came next.[39] These two executions garnered little attention and no outcry by the public. They also demonstrated a renewed effort to create the "evil woman" through characterizations of both women as "black widows"[40] This comparison was to an insect that kills its spouse as each of these women were charged with doing.[41]

Since Beet's death, eight executions of women have followed including: in 2000, Christina Riggs in Arkansas; in 2001, Wanda Jean Allen, Marilyn Plantz, and Lois Nadean Smith in Oklahoma; and 2002, Lynda Lyon Block in Alabama and Aileen Wuornos in Florida, in 2005 Francis Newton in Texas and in 2010 Theresa Lewis in Virginia.[42] None of these cases generated publicity or created public outcry.

---

[37] Elizabeth Gleick, *No Casting of Stone: After hearing heart wrenching testimony, A jury sentences Susan Smith to Life imprisonment*, Time, August 7, 1995, at 31.

[38] Elizabeth Rapaport, *Equality of the Damned: The Execution of Women on the Cusp of the 21st Century*, 26 Ohio N. U. L. Rev. 581, 596 (2000).

[39] For a moving account of the execution of Betty Beets, *see* Joseph Margulies, *Memories of an Execution*, 20 Law & Ineq. 125 (2002).

[40] Rapaport, *supra* note 38, at 600.

[41] Diane Jennings, *Beets Executed for Husband's Murder: Woman is Second to be Put to Death in Texas Since Civil War*, Dallas Morning News, Feb. 25, 2000, at A1; Wendy Spriaduso, *A Frightened Buenoano Dies in Florida's Electric Chair*, Sun Sentinel, Mar. 31, 1998, p. A1; Michael Kellerher, Murder Most Rare (Praeger Publishers 1998).

[42] DPIC, *Women Executed in the U.S. 1900-2003*, http://www.deathpenaltyinfo.org/article.php?scid=24&did=229. (last visited Jan. 31, 2012).

Not surprisingly, many of the same issues and controversies that arise in death penalty cases generally appear in cases of women on death row including evidence of ineffective assistance of counsel, allegations of arbitrariness and claims of innocence. Two cases of innocence, both in Texas, have reached very different results.

The first is Cathy Henderson. Since her arrest in 1994, Henderson has maintained that the death of Brandon Baugh, an infant she was babysitting, was an accident from a fall. Just weeks before her scheduled execution in June 2007, the Texas Court sent her case back to the trial court for a review of the scientific evidence. This review was largely the result of an affidavit submitted by the former Travis County medical examiner who recanted his original trial testimony and stated that new scientific evidence suggests that the injuries to the infant could have been the result of an accidental fall.[43]

The other woman is Frances Newton.[44] Charged with killing her husband and children, Newton maintained her innocence until the end. As her execution date approached, new evidence continued to emerge, raising questions about her guilt including evidence of a possible second gun at the scene and questions whether the wrong gun was tested for trial.[45]

---

[43] Former Travis County Medical examiner, Bayardo submitted an affidavit that states: "Since 1995, when I testified at Cathy Henderson's trial, the medical profession has gained a greater understanding of pediatric head trauma and the extent of injuries that can occur in infants as a result of relatively short distance falls . . . I cannot determine with a reasonable degree of medical certainty whether Brandon Baugh's injuries resulted from an intentional act or an accidental fall. In fact, had the new scientific information been available to me in 1995, I would not have been able to testify the way I did about the degree of force needed to cause Brandon Baugh's head injury." DPIC, http://deathpenaltyinfo.org/news/past/31/2007 (last visited Jan. 31, 2012).

[44] Newton was executed in Texas on September 14, 2005. The night of her execution, about 50 demonstrators chanted outside but the crowd paled in comparison to the group of hundreds that assembled in 1998 to protest the execution of Karla Faye Tucker, who was the first woman executed in Texas since the Civil War. Allan Turner, Cynthia Lenor Garza, *Newton is Executed for Slaying Her Family*, HOUSTON CHRONICLE, Sept. 15, 2005, at A1.

[45] Significant questions were raised about Newton's innocence and her ineffective trial counsel. Her attorney at trial was the notorious Ron Mock, whose shoddy work in capital murder trials is well known in legal circles. He has been repeatedly disciplined by the State Bar of Texas, and has since been disqualified from handling capital cases. No less than 16 people whom Mock represented were sent to death row. Mock apparently did no investigation of Newton's claims of innocence. When asked by a trial judge, he could not name a single witness he had interviewed on Newton's behalf. Ralph Blumenthal, *Report of Second Gun is Used in Defense of a Texas Woman Facing Death*, N.Y. TIMES, Aug. 25, 2005, at A17.

Chapter 22

VOLUNTEERS: DEFENDANTS WHO WANT TO DIE

§ 22.01 NATURE OF THE ISSUES

Defendants who want to die, or "volunteers" as they are frequently called, pose unique problems for the criminal justice system. The first person executed in the post-*Furman* era, Gary Gilmore, was a volunteer. At Gilmore's trial, adversary proceedings were conducted in both the guilt and penalty phases. At the appellate level, however, Gilmore insisted that he did not want to appeal to the Utah Supreme Court and wished to be executed immediately.[1] Many other volunteers have followed in the years since Gilmore's execution. According to the Death Penalty Information Center, between 1976 and May 2011, 133 individuals were executed who were considered "volunteers."[2] Some have tried to abandon court proceedings at the appellate level, like Gilmore. Others have proceeded through a state court appeal, but have then tried to forgo postconviction remedies. Still others have tried to relinquish all rights and have advocated for death at the trial level. For instance, Thomas Akers pleaded guilty to capital murder, told his attorneys not to present any mitigating evidence, and argued for death to the court.[3] Not surprisingly, he then indicated that he did not want an appeal. Defendants like Akers, who wish to forego all adversary proceedings, are the most problematic for the courts.

Volunteers pose a variety of constitutional, statutory, and ethical issues. Is mitigating evidence required under the Eighth Amendment even if the defendant does not want to offer it? Does the Constitution require appellate review of death sentences? What does the Sixth Amendment require for effective assistance of counsel? What should a defense attorney do ethically, argue for death? Present mitigating evidence or an appeal against the wishes of the client? If a state has an automatic appeal, can the defendant waive it? What if the defendant is incompetent to make a decision? How and when should the courts decide if the defendant is competent? When does a "next friend" have standing to raise issues on the defendant's behalf? These issues are discussed in the sections that follow.

---

[1] Gilmore v. Utah, 429 U.S. 1012, 1015 n.4 (1976).

[2] http://www.deathpenaltyinfo.org/information-defendants-who-were-executed-1976-and-designated-volunteers (last visited July 19, 2011).

[3] *See* Akers v. Commonwealth, 535 S.E.2d 674, 676-77 (Va. 2000), *cert. denied*, 531 U.S. 1205 (2001). *See also* Ross E. Eisenberg, *The Lawyer's Role When the Defendant Seeks Death*, 14 CAP. DEF. 55, 64 (2001) (stating that capital defendants "in Virginia have at times directe[d] counsel not to brief or argue the case on appeal or have attempted to waive their rights to appeal altogether").

§ 22.02   DEFENDANT ADVOCATES DEATH AT TRIAL LEVEL

[A]   Overview

Defendants are generally permitted to waive their constitutional rights. Thus, a defendant may waive a jury[4] and try a case to the judge, waive counsel and represent him or herself, waive a trial and plead guilty, or waive an appeal and accept the trial judgment. In noncapital cases, there are many instances in which defendants have waived juries, waived a trial and pleaded guilty, and represented themselves. In the instances where defendants in noncapital or capital cases decide to plead guilty to a murder charge, there is, of course, no trial on guilt or innocence at all.

In a capital penalty proceeding, however, where the defendant decides to argue for death over life as the sentence and wishes to waive any constitutional rights in the penalty phase, the defendant's "plea" does not end the proceedings. The penalty phase is still conducted, even though the defendant is in essence "pleading guilty" to death. However, the penalty phase proceeds in a somewhat unusual fashion. In most instances, the prosecutor introduces aggravating circumstances and argues for death; the defense introduces no mitigating evidence and argues for death.[5] Thus, there is no adversarial argument with one side advocating death and the other side advocating life. As a result, this situation has raised a barrage of

---

[4] *See* Singer v. United States, 380 U.S. 24, 34 (1965) (asserting that "a defendant can . . . in some instances waive his right to a trial by jury"). However, the Court also noted that there is "no constitutional impediment to conditioning a waiver of [the] right [to a jury trial] on the consent of the prosecuting attorney and the trial judge when, if either refuses to consent, the result is simply that the defendant is subject to an impartial trial by jury — the very thing that the Constitution guarantees him." *Id.* at 36. Under Florida law, the trial judge may exercise her discretion to require an advisory jury recommendation despite a capital defendant's voluntary and intelligent waiver of such a recommendation. Muhammad v. State, 782 So. 2d 343, 361 (Fla.), *cert. denied*, 534 U.S. 836 and 534 U.S. 944 (2001).

[5] *See, e.g.*, Morrison v. State, 373 S.E.2d 506, 508-09 (Ga. 1988), *cert. denied*, 490 U.S. 1012(1989) (concluding upon review of Morrison's sentencing phase at which no evidence was presented by the defense, that Morrison's attorney "[did] not violate any right of the defendant" by arguing for the death penalty where Morrison was properly informed, competent, and insisted on death over life in prison out of a fear that he would "break out and kill again"); Vargas ex rel. Sastegui v. Lambert, 159 F.3d 1161, 1163 (9th Cir. 1998) (staying defendant's execution and remanding for evidentiary hearing where "next friend" provided new evidence questioning defendant's competence to waive introduction of mitigating evidence at penalty phase that resulted in a sentence of death), *stay vacated by*, 525 U.S. 925; Singleton v. Lockhart, 962 F.2d 1315, 1316 (8th Cir. 1992) (holding defendant's competent waiver of mitigating evidence during penalty phase foreclosed challenge to constitutionality of death penalty statute); Durocher v. Singletary, 623 So. 2d 482, 483 (Fla. 1993) (ordering trial judge to determine defendant's competency to waive assistance of "next friend" following defendant's waiver of mitigating evidence in penalty phase). Commonly, a volunteer defendant will represent himself and waive his right to counsel during the sentencing phase. During the sentencing phase, he will then present no mitigating evidence and argue to the jury for death. *See, e.g.*, People v. Bradford, 939 P.2d 259, 344-45 (Cal. 1997), *cert. denied*, 523 U.S. 1118 (1998) (holding trial court did not abuse its discretion in allowing defendant to proceed pro se though defendant would offer no mitigating evidence in penalty phase); People v. Stansbury, 846 P.2d 756, 783-85 (Cal. 1993), *cert. denied*, 516 U.S. 923 (1995) (same); People v. Clark, 833 P.2d 561, 595 (Cal. 1992), *cert. denied*, 507 U.S. 993 (1993) (same); People v. Bloom, 774 P.2d 698, 709-10 (Cal. 1989), *cert. denied*, 523 U.S. 1145 (1998) (same); Commonwealth v. Appel, 689 A.2d 891, 896, 905-06 (Pa. 1997) (holding standby counsel not ineffective for failing to present evidence of defendant's mental illness

arguments and criticisms. Those arguments raise the issues of whether the sentencer must have mitigating evidence in order to render a constitutional death sentence, who should present mitigating evidence if it is required, whether the defendant should have the right to preclude mitigating evidence, whether the defendant's right to self-representation conflicts with a mandatory mitigation requirement, and what the ethical and constitutional roles of the defense attorney are in a voluntary situation.

For example, contrast the situations in the Florida case of *Klokoc v. State*[6] and the Washington case of *State v. Elledge.*[7] Klokoc pleaded guilty to first degree murder, waived the penalty phase jury,[8] and insisted that no mitigation be presented. Despite Klokoc's plan for no mitigation, the trial court appointed an independent counsel to present mitigating evidence. As a result, after the state introduced aggravating evidence, both the state and Klokoc rested. The independent counsel then called witnesses to present mitigating evidence. The trial court proceeded to weigh aggravating and mitigating evidence and rendered a death sentence. The death sentence was reversed on appeal in part because the record reflected mitigating evidence that outweighed the aggravating evidence.[9] Elledge similarly pleaded guilty to capital murder and made it clear that he wanted the death penalty. During a jury penalty phase, the prosecution offered aggravating evidence and Elledge made a statement to the jury asking for the death penalty. No independent counsel was appointed and no mitigation was presented. The jury sentenced Elledge to death. The Washington court affirmed after considering the four mandatory review issues, one of which was based on the insufficiency of mitigating circumstances.[10] There was, of course, no mitigating evidence in the record.

Some defendants may even wish to supplement the aggravating evidence presented by the prosecution. Many defendants in this situation also ask to argue for death to the jury.[11] If the defense counsel will not cooperate with the defendant's decision to fight for death, it is likely that the defendant will seek to represent him or herself.

The stark contrast between the responses of the Florida and Washington courts define the debate. Must mitigating evidence be presented? Is there ineffective assistance of counsel if no mitigation is presented? Is the defendant's right of self-

---

where defendant repeatedly waived right to counsel and offered only his gainful employment and lack of prior felony record as mitigating circumstances).

[6] 589 So. 2d 219 (Fla. 1991).

[7] 26 P.3d 271 (Wash. 2001).

[8] *See Klokoc*, 589 So. 2d at 220.

[9] *Id.* at 222.

[10] *See Elledge*, 26 P.3d at 280, 285. *See also* Mary Pat Treuthart et al., *Mitigation Evidence and Capital Cases in Washington: Proposals for Change*, 26 SEATTLE U. L. REV. 241-42 (2002) (indicating Elledge's jury was not presented evidence of Elledge's brutal childhood, his marriage, children, and grandchildren, his friends at church and in the community, his insanity plea in a previous murder trial, and his saving of a prison guard's life during his incarceration).

[11] *See, e.g., Morrison*, 373 S.E.2d at 508 (indicating Morrison's counsel argued for death on his behalf).

representation violated if mitigation is presented over his or her protest? What is the proper ethical duty of the defense attorney in these circumstances? These Eighth Amendment, Sixth Amendment, and ethical issues will be discussed below.

[B] Eighth Amendment: Is Mitigation Required?

As discussed in earlier chapters, a constitutionally valid death sentence requires individualized consideration of the defendant.[12] Thus, mandatory death sentences are unconstitutional, as is any exclusion of relevant mitigating evidence.[13] The question raised in the volunteer circumstance is whether the individualization requirement is satisfied if the defendant has the *opportunity* to present mitigation or whether *actual* mitigation must be considered by the sentencer.

Most courts have applied a waiver principle and have found that the opportunity to present mitigation is sufficient to satisfy the constitutional mandate. In these cases, the defendant typically refuses to present mitigating evidence. The sentencer hears the aggravating evidence, is charged with weighing aggravating and mitigating evidence, and renders a decision.

Both the *Elledge* and *Akers* cases followed this pattern. In *Elledge*, the defendant pleaded guilty to capital murder, declined to present any mitigating evidence, and asked the sentencing jury for death. The prosecutor proved the aggravating circumstance of a murder in the course of a kidnapping and presented evidence of Elledge's extensive criminal record.[14] The *Akers* case from Virginia, described in the introduction to this section, followed a similar format. Akers, too, pleaded guilty and told his lawyers not to present any mitigating evidence. The state relied on aggravating factors of "vileness" and future dangerousness and additional evidence of prior criminal history and current violent behavior in jail.[15] In each case, the sentencer (jury in *Elledge* and judge in *Akers*) "weighed" the aggravating and mitigating circumstances.[16] Needless to say, in each case the aggravating circumstances outweighed the mitigating circumstances, which, if they existed, were never brought to the attention of the sentencer.

A few courts have required the introduction of mitigating evidence even though a defendant wanted to waive the right to present it. The two primary approaches

---

[12] *See* Section 12.03[B][1], *supra.*

[13] *See* Section 6.06, and Section 12.02, *supra.*

[14] *See Elledge*, 26 P.3d at 279-80.

[15] *See Akers*, 535 S.E.2d at 676.

[16] In Washington, sentencing juries are asked whether, "[h]aving in mind the crime of which the defendant has been found guilty, are you convinced beyond a reasonable doubt that there are not sufficient mitigating circumstances to merit leniency?" WASH. REV. CODE § 10.95.060(4) (2011).

The charge in Virginia is whether the sentencer:

. . . having found the defendant guilty of [murder] and that (after consideration of his prior history that there is a probability that he would commit criminal acts of violence that would constitute a continuing serious threat to society) or his conduct in committing the offense is outrageously or wantonly vile, horrible or inhuman in that it involved (torture) (depravity of mind) (aggravated battery to the victim), and having considered the evidence in mitigation of the offense, unanimously fix his punishment at death." VA. CODE ANN. § 19.2-264.4(D)(1) (Michie 2011).

that courts have used to promote the presentation of mitigating evidence in such cases are an order to the relevant department to prepare a presentence report with mitigation information or the appointment of an independent counsel, who is charged with presenting mitigation. Initially, some courts tried to require the defense counsel to present mitigating evidence against the defendant's wishes.[17] This approach failed because defense counsel believed that ethically they could not work against the client's decision.[18]

The courts that require mitigation base their decisions on both constitutional and statutory concerns that death sentences be reliable and not arbitrary. In Florida cases, an advisory jury makes a recommendation to the trial court after weighing aggravating and mitigating evidence. In its decision that information on mitigation was required, the Florida court focused on the inability of the trial court to satisfy the statutory requirement to give "great weight" to the recommendation of the advisory jury with no mitigation in the record. The court found that a presentence report was necessary if the defendant chose not to present mitigation, and gave the lower courts the discretion to appoint an independent counsel.[19] Prior to abolishing the death penalty in 2007, the New Jersey court also had held that mitigating evidence was required, emphasizing the need for reliability and the ability to conduct a weighing determination as required by statute.[20]

The independent counsel approach appears to accommodate the defendant's advocacy of death and the individualized consideration that the Eighth Amendment contemplates. In 2002, however, the Fifth Circuit Court of Appeals held that the appointment of independent counsel to present mitigation unconstitutionally infringed on the defendant's right of self-representation when the defendant was arguing for death.[21]

The 2007 decision of the Supreme Court in *Schriro v. Landrigan*[22] raises questions about whether a majority of the current justices would interpret the Eighth Amendment to prohibit a defendant from waiving the right to present mitigating evidence. The Arizona courts had concluded that Landrigan had waived the right by instructing his attorney not to bring any such information to the

---

[17] *See, e.g.,* People v. Deere, 710 P.2d 925, 933 (Cal. 1985), *overruled by* People v. Bloom, 774 P.2d 698 (1989) (stating that the defense attorney was "an officer of the court [citation omitted] with a duty to assure that the court has all relevant information to be able to perform its mandatory consideration of mitigating circumstances").

[18] *See* People v. Deere, 808 P.2d 1181, 1185 (Cal. 1991) (indicating defense counsel entered a guilty plea, waived a jury trial, and withheld mitigating evidence " 'based on [defendant's] desires and [counsel's] conclusion that [he had] no right whatsoever to infringe upon [defendant's] decisions about his own life' ").

[19] *See* Muhammad v. State, 782 So. 2d 343, 363 (Fla. 2001) (requiring "the preparation of a [presentence report] in every case where the defendant is not challenging the imposition of the death penalty and refuses to present mitigation evidence").

[20] *See* State v. Koedatich, 548 A.2d 939, 994 (N.J. 1988), *cert. denied,* 488 U.S. 1017 (1989). The New Jersey court even stated that the sentencing jury would have problems conducting its "moral duty" without mitigating evidence.

[21] *See* United States v. Davis, 285 F.3d 378, 381 (5th Cir. 2002), *cert. denied sub nom.* White v. United States, 537 U.S. 1066 (2002). *See* discussion, *infra,* Section 22.02[C].

[22] 127 S. Ct. 1933 (2007).

attention of the trial court. On this basis, a five-justice majority upheld the decision of the federal district judge not to grant an evidentiary hearing on petitioner's habeas petition alleging ineffective assistance of trial counsel.[23] The majority concluded that the state courts' finding that Landrigan did not want his counsel to present mitigating evidence was not an unreasonable determination of fact. Moreover, the Court assumed that a defendant could validly decide to foreclose the presentation of mitigation. The Court noted that "we have never required a specific colloquy to ensure that a defendant knowingly and intelligently refused to present mitigating evidence."[24]

Because it is a decision based on a Sixth Amendment ineffective assistance of counsel issue and is decided under the deferential habeas standard, *Landrigan* does not definitively resolve the Eighth Amendment issue. The Court did not directly confront a claim that the Eighth Amendment forecloses or limits the ability of a defendant to waive, and the Court did not discuss the issue. The Court addressed the waiver question in the context of a claim of ineffective assistance under the Sixth Amendment. The case also came before the Court on federal habeas in which deference is due state court interpretations of law. Nevertheless, both the majority and the dissent assumed that the defendant could validly foreclose the presentation of mitigating evidence, and none of the Justices suggested that there was an unresolved question about whether the Eighth Amendment would pose a bar to waiver.

Which view of the Eighth Amendment is more valid? Some commentators have argued that the defendant should have a right of autonomy that allows him or her to make the decision on death or life. Others have countered that society's interest in a fair, reliable administration of the death penalty requires consideration of mitigating evidence. As one commentator stated, the dilemma is that "[t]he prisoner's dignity stands against the dignity of the law."[25] The autonomy argument is premised on the idea that the rights in the Constitution are personal rights that are the defendant's to relinquish.[26] The system is generally designed to respect the dignity of the individual.

Many commentators on both sides have analogized a defendant's advocacy for the death penalty to a request for an unauthorized punishment. A defendant is not entitled to demand a punishment that is not authorized by law.[27] Thus, a defendant cannot demand to be boiled in oil as a consequence for his crime. The autonomy

---

[23] *Id.* at 1944.

[24] *Id.* at 1943. For an insightful critique of the application of the waiver standard in the context of foregoing mitigating evidence, *see* Dale E. Ho, *Silent at Sentencing: Waiver Doctrine and a Capital Defendant's Right to Present Mitigating Evidence after Schriro v. Landrigan*, 62 Fla. L. Rev. 721 (2010) (criticizing the ambiguity in the record in *Landrigan* and arguing for greater procedural safeguards, including an on-record colloquy, to ensure that the waiver is knowingly done based on information about mitigation and its role).

[25] *See* Richard J. Bonnie, *The Dignity of the Condemned*, 74 Va. L. Rev. 1363, 1377 (1988).

[26] *See* Welsh S. White, *Defendants Who Elect Execution*, 48 U. Pitt. L. Rev. 853, 864-65 (1987) (arguing that "protecting a capital defendant's individual autonomy is . . . an important consideration" and that "the major arguments in favor of circumscribing the capital defendant's autonomy may not be able to withstand analysis").

[27] *See, e.g.*, Jeffrey L. Kirchmeier, *Let's Make a Deal: Waiving the Eighth Amendment by Selecting*

proponents argue that, since the death penalty is authorized by law, a defendant is entitled to argue for it. The only constitutional requirement that a defendant could not relinquish would be the elements that elevate the murder to a death-eligible crime.[28]

Other commentators have contended that the procedures, including the individualized consideration of the defendant, are necessary to ensure a death sentence is constitutionally imposed.[29] The Eighth Amendment embodies society's interest in preventing a cruel and unusual punishment. A death sentence violates this provision if the process for imposing it does not distinguish those deserving to die from those deserving to live. Individualized consideration of the circumstances of the crime and the background of a defendant, presented through mitigating evidence, is designed to satisfy this constitutional command. As Justice Marshall stated in his dissent in *Whitmore v. Arkansas*,[30] the defendant's consent could not make a barbaric punishment, such as "being drawn and quartered or burned at the stake," a constitutional sanction; nor could the defendant's consent make the execution of an innocent person constitutional; nor could the defendant's consent to forego an appeal make a death sentence without appeal constitutional. By the same reasoning, proponents of this position argue that the defendant should not be able to choose the death penalty when the constitutionally required individualized consideration of mitigation has not occurred.[31]

---

a *Cruel and Unusual Punishment*, 32 CONN. L. REV. 615, 642-51 (2000) (explaining why a defendant cannot waive the right not to be subjected to cruel and unusual punishment).

[28] *See* Bonnie, *supra* note 25, at 1389-91. Professor Bonnie takes this position. Generally, this would be aggravating circumstances. *See* Sections 9.01 et seq. and 10.01 et seq., *supra*. *See* John H. Blume, *Killing the Willing: "Volunteers," Suicide and Competency*, 103 MICH. L. REV. 939, 943 (2005) (proposing a standard for assessing waiver that seeks to distinguish between the inmate who tries "to use the death penalty as a means to commit state-assisted suicide" and one who merely accepts "the justness of his punishment."

[29] *See* Linda E. Carter, *Maintaining Systemic Integrity in Capital Cases: The Use of Court-Appointed Counsel to Present Mitigating Evidence When the Defendant Advocates Death*, 55 TENN. L. REV. 95, 106-07 (1987) (arguing that the defendant should not be allowed to waive the presentation of mitigating evidence because consideration of such is indispensable to a constitutionally imposed death penalty); Martin Sabelli & Stacey Leyton, *Criminal Law: Train Wrecks and Freeway Crashes, An Argument for Fairness and Against Self-Representation in the Criminal Justice System*, 91 J. CRIM. L. & CRIMINOLOGY 161, 205 (2000) (quoting Lockett v. Ohio, 438 U.S. 586, 603 (1978), that "[p]ossession of the fullest information possible concerning the defendant's life and characteristics is highly relevant — if not essential — [to the] selection of an appropriate sentence"); *see also* Treuthart, *supra* note 10, at 248 (arguing that without mitigation, the imposition of the death penalty is tantamount to an unconstitutional mandatory sentence).

[30] 495 U.S. 149, 173 (1990) (Marshall, J., dissenting).

[31] *See Lenhard v. Wolff*, 444 U.S 807, 814-15 (1979) (Marshall, J., dissenting) (asserting that, by the sentencing court allowing the defendant to refuse to put on mitigating evidence and acquiescing to the defendant's request not to allow standby counsel to present mitigating evidence, it "deprived itself of the very evidence that this Court has deemed essential to the determination whether death was the appropriate sentence").

[C]   Sixth Amendment: What is Effective Assistance of Counsel for a Volunteer?

When a defendant volunteers to be executed, the Sixth Amendment is also implicated. Initially, courts faced the dilemma of whether the defense counsel was ineffective for failing to present mitigating evidence or, alternatively, for presenting mitigating evidence against the defendant's wishes. Virtually all courts found that there is no ineffective assistance of counsel if the attorney followed or acquiesced in the defendant's wishes to forego mitigation and advocate death.[32] The Supreme Court's opinion in *Schriro v. Landrigan*,[33] discussed in the previous section, supports this position.

The Sixth Amendment also includes a right of self-representation. If a defendant invokes his or her right to self-representation, should the defendant be able to preclude efforts to present mitigating evidence? From a defendant's perspective, any mitigation presented by standby or independent counsel interferes with his goals and strategy. On the other hand, regardless of evidence presented by an independent counsel, a defendant is able to proceed with his evidence and argument. Thus, arguably, the defendant's right of self-representation is preserved even with the presentation of unwanted mitigation evidence.

Although some courts have addressed a defendant's right to represent himself to advocate death,[34] very few have directly decided how to resolve the tension between the right to self-representation and the right to be free from cruel and unusual punishment.

In 2002, the Fifth Circuit Court of Appeals tackled the tension in *United States v. Davis*,[35] In a 2-1 split, the court viewed the independent counsel's presentation of mitigating evidence as depriving the defendant of the ability to control the content of the defense case. Moreover, the court found little or no authority for a trial court to appoint an independent counsel for the purpose of presenting mitigation. The two-judge majority placed great weight on the argument that the trial judge's limited ability to question witnesses or appoint amicus had to be conducted in an

---

[32] *See Singleton*, 962 F.2d 1315; Wallace v. Ward, 191 F.3d 1235 (10th Cir. 1999), *cert denied*, 530 U.S. 1216 (2000); State v. Cowans, 717 N.E.2d 298 (Ohio 1999), *cert. denied*, 529 U.S. 1102 (2000); Kirksey v. State, 923 P.2d 1102 (Nev. 1996); People v. Kirkpatrick, 874 P.2d 248 (Cal. 1994), *cert. denied*, 514 U.S. 1015 (1995); *Morrison*, 373 S.E.2d 506; *Koedatich*, 548 A.2d 939; *Bloom*, 774 P.2d 698, 690 n.9 (disapproving the decision in People v. Deere, 710 P.2d 925, to the extent the court suggested that failure to present mitigating evidence was sufficient to render a death penalty judgment unreliable).

[33] 127 S. Ct. 1933 (2007).

[34] *See e.g.*, Chapman v. Commonwealth, 265 S.W.3d 156 (Ky. 2007) (defendant's self-representation and argument for death precluded presentation of mitigation by standby counsel); *Bradford*, 939 P.2d 259, 339 (finding defendant has a right to represent himself even if he confesses and asks for death); *Stansbury*, 846 P.2d 756 (noting that a court does not necessarily abuse its discretion if it allows self-representation when a defendant wants death); *Clark*, 833 P.2d 561 (granting a midtrial request for self-representation may be proper); *Appel*, 689 A.2d 891 (noting various reasons why a defendant might choose death); *Durocher*, 623 So. 2d 482 (finding self-representation proper if defendant is found competent).

[35] *See Davis*, 285 F.3d 378.

impartial manner, without giving support to one side over the other. The majority viewed the trial judge as compromising her impartiality by injecting the independent counsel into the trial.[36]

The counterargument, as presented in the dissenting judge's opinion in *Davis*, emphasized the need to reconcile the two competing constitutional provisions, the right to self-representation, and the right to be free from cruel and unusual punishment. This argument does not view self-representation as an absolute right. Courts can deny defendants the right to represent themselves at trial if, for example, a defendant is disruptive.[37] Moreover, the dissent found the right to self-representation less compelling in the penalty phase than in trial. The dissenting judge analogized this situation to *Martinez v. Court of Appeal of California*,[38] where the Supreme Court held that there was no right of self-representation on appeal. As with an appeal, sentencing occurs after there is a conviction and, therefore, the right to self-representation is less significant.[39]

[D] Ethical Issues for Defense Counsel

The adversary balance of the penalty proceeding is skewed when the defendant wants the same outcome as the prosecution. The constitutional issues are complicated because of the imbalance, and there are ethical issues faced by the defense attorneys involved in the case. Although prosecutors might have some concerns about seeking "justice" in a one-sided proceeding,[40] it is the defense attorneys who must resolve conflicts with the client and decide how to proceed.

Many defense attorneys find themselves in an ethical or moral dilemma. They often believe on a personal level that the death penalty is wrong. Thus, the thought of advocating for death is abhorrent. Even if the defense attorneys do not feel that the death penalty is always wrong, they may well believe that there are viable legal arguments against the death penalty in the current case.[41] The dilemma is heightened by the recognition that many capital clients at times want to stop

---

[36] *Id.* at 381-82.

[37] *See* Faretta v. California, 422 U.S. 806, 834 n.46 (1975) (". . . the trial judge may terminate self-representation by a defendant who deliberately engages in serious and obstructionist misconduct.").

[38] 528 U.S. 152 (2000).

[39] *See Davis*, 285 F.3d at 397 (Dennis, J., dissenting) (arguing that "the autonomy interests that survived Davis's conviction are now outweighed by the public's interest in the fair and faithful administration of justice, an interest that is even more acute in a death penalty case").

[40] *See* Ronald D. Rotunda, Legal Ethics — The Lawyer's Deskbook on Professional Responsibility Appendix J § 3-1.2 (b)-(c) (2002-03 ed.) [hereinafter Legal Ethics]. "(b) The prosecutor is both an administrator of justice, and an advocate, and an officer of the court; the prosecutor must exercise sound discretion in the performance of his or her functions. (c) The duty of the prosecutor is to seek justice, not merely to convict."

[41] *See* White, *supra* note 26, at 861 n.29. *See also* Treuthart, *supra* note 10, at 278. Professor Treuthart states: "When defendants volunteer for execution, their lawyers are placed in an unfair predicament. Most lawyers who choose to represent capital defendants are opposed to capital punishment; thus, in the case of a volunteer, there is a forced choice between the attorney's own interests in opposing the death penalty and counsel's obligation to 'seek the lawful objectives of her client.' ").

proceedings and die but then generally change their minds.[42]

The rules, standards, and guidelines of the American Bar Association serve as the template for most states' rules of professional conduct. The defense counsel's role is discussed in a general sense in the overall Model Rules;[43] in greater detail in the standards for the Defense Function;[44] and in specific terms for capital cases in the Guidelines for the Appointment and Performance of Defense Counsel in Death Penalty Cases.[45] Despite the overall thoroughness of the ABA's guidance, there is very little to guide the defense attorney in the situation where the defendant wants to seek death.

The ABA rules contemplate a defense attorney working to achieve the client's substantive goals. The rules rather specifically state that the client is in charge of the "objectives of representation."[46] The examples given in the general rule state that the client is to decide ". . . a plea to be entered, whether to waive jury trial and whether [to] testify." The commentary to the rules refers to the client's decisions on "the *purposes* to be served by legal representation . . . "[47] It is sometimes stated as a division between the objectives and the means or tactics.[48] The Defense Function similarly divides the control of the case between major decisions by the client on matters such as pleas[49] and the "strategic and tactical decisions" of the defense counsel. These provisions do not, however, specifically address the volunteer situation in a capital case.

---

[42] *See* White, *supra* note 26, at 855, 860; *see* Christy Chandler, Note, *Voluntary Executions*, 50 Stan. L. Rev. 1897, 1919-20 (1998) (explaining the abject conditions on death row encourage inmates to pursue death).

[43] *See generally* ABA Model Rules of Prof'l Conduct R. (2002) (hereinafter Model Rules).

[44] *See generally* Legal Ethics, *supra* note 40, at § 4-1.2.

[45] *See generally* American Bar Association, Guidelines for the Appointment and Performance of Defense Counsel in Death Penalty Cases (Revised Edition, February 2003) [hereinafter ABA Guidelines].

[46] *See* Model Rules 1.2 (stating that "a lawyer shall abide by a client's decisions concerning the objectives of representation").

[47] *See* Model Rules 1.2 cmt. (emphasis added). The complete point made is: "Paragraph (a) confers upon the client the ultimate authority to determine the purposes to be served by legal representation, within the limits imposed by law and the lawyer's professional obligations." *Id.*

[48] *See* Sabelli & Leyton, *supra* note 29, at 182-83. *See also* Carter, *supra* note 29, at 130 (stating that "[a]lthough the attorney maintains control of how to present the client's case, it is the client who determines the objectives"); John R. Mitchell, Comment, *Attorneys Representing Death Row Clients: Client Autonomy Over Personal Opinions*, 25 Cap. U.L. Rev. 643, 647-48 (1996) (relying on Standard 4-5.2 of the ABA Standards of Criminal Justice in explaining "substantive" matters, such as what plea to enter, whether to accept a plea agreement, whether to waive jury trial, whether to testify in his or her own behalf, and whether to appeal, are decisions that should be made the client, whereas "strategic and tactical" decisions, such as which witnesses to call, whether and how to conduct cross-examination, the selection and dismissal of jurors, the trial motions to be made, and the evidence that will be introduced at trial, are within the decision-making ability of the attorney).

[49] *See* American Bar Association, Standards Relating to the Administration of Criminal Justice, The Defense Function, Standard 4-5.2 (3rd ed. 1993) ((i) what pleas to enter; (ii) whether to accept a plea agreement; (iii) whether to waive jury trial; (iv) whether to testify in his or her own behalf; and (v) whether to appeal"; strategic and tactical decisions made by counsel after consulting with client).

The ABA Guidelines and commentary for defense counsel in capital cases more directly suggest a course of conduct for the attorney, but do not go so far as to advise on the ultimate professional position if a client insists on advocating death. The emphasis in the Guidelines is on dissuading a client from pursuing a result of death. For instance, the commentary recognizes that capital defendants may want to die at some point during the representation.[50] The approach of the commentary is to suggest ways for defense counsel to dissuade a defendant from choosing to die. The commentary emphasizes establishing a relationship with the client, drawing on family members and others in the community who are important to the client, and actively dissuading the client from actions that would increase the chance of death.[51] One guideline that specifically addresses a volunteer issue mandates that the attorney conduct an investigation for the penalty phase regardless of the client's wishes at the time.[52] Another guideline addresses pleas of guilty and states that it is the client's decision to enter a plea of guilty to a crime.[53] The commentary provides that counsel should try to dissuade the client from a plea that would likely result in death and suggests that, without a guarantee of life, "counsel should be extremely reluctant to participate in a waiver of the client's trial rights."

If efforts at dissuading a defendant from advocating death are unsuccessful, the defense attorney faces a quandary. Most capital defense attorneys try every tactic they know to persuade the defendant to contest the death penalty.[54] Because most courts honor a defendant's decision not to challenge a death sentence, in the end, the defense attorney ethically must either represent the client's decision or attempt to withdraw.[55] In many cases involving volunteers, the defendants invoke their right to represent themselves, undoubtedly in part because of the recalcitrance of the defense attorneys to actively promote the death of the client.

Defense attorneys face a particularly incongruous task where the courts have asked them to present mitigating evidence against the defendant's wishes. A defense attorney in these circumstances is caught between an ethical duty to the

---

[50] *See* ABA Guidelines, *supra* note 45, at Commentary to 10.5 (commenting that it is ineffective assistance of counsel "to simply acquiesce" in a client's desire to die; counsel should work with client and enlist aid of others to persuade client to pursue life).

[51] *Id.* at Commentary to 10.5 and 10.9.2.

[52] *Id.* at 10.7(A)(2), which provides: "The investigation regarding penalty should be conducted regardless of any statement by the client that evidence bearing upon penalty is not to be collected or presented."

[53] *Id.* at 10.9.2.

[54] *See* White, *supra* note 26, at 857-58; *see* Eisenberg, *supra* note 3, at 74 (stating that a capital defense attorney faced with a client who wants to die "should operate, from start to finish, on the assumption that the defendant will in fact change his mind"); Treuthart, *supra* note 10, at 279 (quoting from Christy Chandler, *Voluntary Executions*, 50 Stan. L. Rev. 1897, 1913 (1998): "First, the attorney can try to have her client deemed incompetent, thereby eliminating the client's authority to decide what is in his best interests. Second, the attorney can acquiesce to the client's wishes by complying with his requests or withdrawing from the case. Third, the attorney can outright defy her client's wishes and act without the client's consent, which will likely lead to discharge. Lastly, the attorney can use persuasive or coercive tactics to try to convince her client to change his mind."

[55] *See* Eisenberg, *supra* note 3, at 67-69; Michael Mello, *A Letter on a Lawyer's Life of Death*, 38 S. Tex. L. Rev. 121, 170 (1997).

client and a professional obligation to the court. The courts may, nonetheless, conclude that a zealous presentation is important, especially if there is a nonwaivable mitigation requirement. The argument for an independent counsel to present mitigation is, in part, designed to alleviate the ethical tension for the defense attorney.

§ 22.03 DEFENDANT ADVOCATES DEATH ON APPEAL OR IN POSTCONVICTION PROCEEDINGS

Most states do not permit the defendant to waive an automatic appeal. Patterned after the early Florida, Georgia, and Texas statutes, all states provide for an appeal from a death sentence.[56] In most states, the appeal goes directly to the highest court in the state.[57] In the first volunteer case, Gary Gilmore successfully waived his automatic appeal to the Utah Supreme Court. In several subsequent cases, the courts found that their state statutes required a review, regardless of the defendant's position.[58] The purpose of the appellate review is typically defined as assuring that the sentence is legal, proportional, or constitutional,[59] which the states appear to view as at least a statutory, if not a constitutional, requirement.[60]

Appellate review of a record from a penalty proceeding, in which the defendant refused to present any mitigation, is subject to the same criticism as the actual penalty proceeding. If the appellate court is charged with assuring proportionality, it is doing so on the basis of a one-sided record.[61] Similarly, critics argue that the constitutionality of the sentence cannot be assessed without evaluating mitigating evidence.[62] The defenders of the constitutionality of the process counter that the appellate court is merely assessing proportionality by comparing this case as it

---

[56] *See* Joan M. Fisher, *Expedited Review of Capital Post-Conviction Claims: Idaho's Flawed Process,* 2 J. App. Prac. & Process 85, 89-90 (2000) (noting that "[a] majority of the thirty-eight states which authorize the death penalty rely on a direct appeals process that includes an automatic sentence review by the state court of last resort and direct appellate review of trial and sentencing error, followed by a state habeas corpus or post-conviction process").

[57] *See id.* at 90.

[58] *See* Marks v. Superior Court, 38 P.3d 512 (Cal. 2002); Akers, 535 S.E.2d 674; State v. Brewer, 826 P.2d 783 (Ariz. 1992).

[59] *See, e.g.,* Akers, 535 S.E.2d at 677 (stating that "the purpose of the review process is to assure the fair and proper application of the death penalty statutes in this Commonwealth and to instill public confidence in the administration of justice).

[60] *See* Sara L. Golden, Comment, *Constitutionality of the Federal Death Penalty Act: Is the Lack of Mandatory Appeal Really Meaningful Appeal?,* 74 Temple L. Rev. 429, 457-58, 467-68 (2001) (arguing that mandatory review of all death sentences is a constitutional requirement and allowing a defendant to waive such appellate review violates the Constitution).

[61] One-sided records are especially likely to develop where the defendant not only refuses to introduce mitigating evidence but also argues for death. *See, e.g., Morrison,* 373 S.E.2d at (stating that the defendant refused to present mitigating evidence and had his attorney argue for death during the penalty phase).

[62] *See supra* note 29 and accompanying text; Treuthart, *supra* note 10, at 251-53 ("In the absence of mitigating evidence at the trial level, on mandatory review the Supreme Court must always determine that the jury finding was correct — that there was not sufficient evidence to merit leniency. Thus, the principal issue for the court on review is predetermined. Just as the jury could answer the question presented to it in only one way, the court is also forced to answer the question regarding the sufficiency

stands on its record with other cases.[63] The defenders further argue that the constitutionality of the sentence is satisfied by the opportunity to present evidence.[64]

There is also a problem of who briefs the issues on appeal. In *Akers*, the court required the defense attorneys, over Akers' objection, to brief certain issues that the court was statutorily required to review.[65] The court sidestepped the defense counsel's ethical dilemma by declaring that the "duty to assist the Court . . . as officers of the Court does not conflict with their concomitant duty to represent the defendant in the manner he desires."[66] The court acknowledged that counsel were in an "ethically difficult" position, but insisted that the "interest of the defendant" and the "interests of justice" were both satisfied.[67] The Virginia court's position is certainly open to attack. If a defendant does not want to argue that his sentence is disproportionate, and the defense attorney is required to raise the issue, there is inevitably a conflict.

§ 22.04   RAISING THE ISSUE: "NEXT FRIEND" AND INDIVIDUAL STANDING

Intertwined with the constitutional issues raised by volunteers are *standing* issues. Generally, standing requires that a party identify an injury to him or herself, not to another person.[68] Thus, if the defendant does not want mitigation or an appeal, who can challenge the courts' rulings on these issues? In many of the volunteer cases, a defense attorney or a family member has filed a *next friend* petition.[69] The "next friends" often have difficulty, however, establishing standing to challenge rulings that affected the defendant. Unless a defendant is incompetent, only the defendant has standing to raise the issues.[70] As a result, volunteer cases

---

of the evidence one way and uphold a death sentence. The court's function to ensure the reliability of the jury's decision is meaningless, and the legislature's system for mandatory review is useless.").

[63] *See* State v. Elledge, 26 P.3d 271, 281-83 (Wash. 2001) (holding that Elledge's sentence was not "wantonly and freakishly[,]" and therefore not disproportionately, imposed where Elledge's demonstrated record of brutality exceeded that of other defendants similarly sentenced to death).

[64] *Id.* at 279-81; *see Bloom*, 774 P.2d at 719 (stating that "[a] rule *requiring* a pro se defendant to present mitigating evidence would be unenforceable" and that a death penalty verdict is not unconstitutional where the "trier of penalty has duly considered the relevant mitigating evidence, if any, which the defendant has *chosen* to present") (emphasis added).

[65] 535 S.E.2d at 677.

[66] *Id.*

[67] *Id.*

[68] *See* Whitmore v. Arkansas, 495 U.S. 149, 155 (1990) (stating that, in order to establish standing, a person must establish the following: 1) injury in fact; 2) the injury must "be concrete in both a qualitative and temporal sense;" 3) the "alleged harm must be actual or imminent, not 'conjectural' or 'hypothetical.' " and 4) "causation" and "redressability").

[69] *See, e.g.,* Whitmore. 495 U.S. 149 (fellow inmate); Evans v. Bennett, 440 U.S. 1301 (1979) (defendant's mother); Gilmore, 429 U.S. 1012 (defendant's mother); West v. Bell, 242 F.3d 338 (6th Cir. 2001) (defendant's attorneys); Vargas, 159 F.3d 1161 (defendant's mother); White v. Horn, 112 F.3d 105 (3d Cir. 1997) (defendant's daughter); Franz v. State, 754 S.W.2d 839 (Ark. 1988) (priest).

[70] *See* Whitmore, 495 U.S. 149, 163-64 (summarizing the two "firmly rooted prerequisites" for next-friend standing: "First, a 'next friend' must provide an adequate explanation — such as

typically involve a heavy emphasis on competency determinations. Moreover, because most volunteers are not found to be incompetent, many trial-level judgments in volunteer cases are not reviewed.

Gary Gilmore's case is a good illustration of the inability of a next friend to gain review of any of the issues once the defendant is found competent to waive the proceedings. After contesting guilt and the death sentence at the trial level, Gilmore insisted that he wanted to waive his appeal to the Utah Supreme Court and be executed immediately. The Utah Supreme Court accepted Gilmore's waiver. Gilmore's mother then filed a petition as a next friend to stay the execution. Ultimately, the United States Supreme Court accepted the findings that Gilmore was competent to waive his rights and found that Gilmore's mother lacked standing to bring the claim.[71]

In addition to next friend status, some litigants have claimed individual standing to challenge the capital convictions and death sentences of others based on alleged injury to themselves. These petitions have not been successful. For example, the courts have rejected claims of standing as a citizen with an interest in upholding the Eighth Amendment's guarantees of no cruel and unusual punishment and claims of standing as a death row inmate whose comparative appellate review would be compromised if undeserving volunteers receive the death penalty.[72]

The practical effect of the standing cases is that the volunteer issue is rarely reviewable beyond the direct appeal unless a defendant is incompetent. Thus, the definition and determination of competency, discussed in the final section, are critical issues in volunteer cases.

§ 22.05 COMPETENCY OF THE DEFENDANT

As noted in the earlier sections in this chapter, competency of the defendant to acquiesce in the death penalty, whether by choosing not to present mitigating evidence in the penalty phase or by deciding not to pursue appeals or postconviction remedies, is a threshold determination. The competency of a defendant affects his or her ability to waive rights and also is determinative of next friend standing.

Although there are variations on the definition of competency,[73] most courts refer to a standard from *Rees v. Peyton*.[74] In the context of competence to waive

---

inaccessibility, mental incompetence, or other disability — why the real party in interest cannot appear on his own behalf to prosecute the action" and "[s]econd, the 'next friend' must be truly dedicated to the best interest of the person on whose behalf he seeks to litigate[] . . . and must have some significant relationship with the real party in interest.") (citations omitted).

[71] *See Gilmore*, 429 U.S. at 439.

[72] *See Whitmore*, 495 U.S. at 156-57 (rejecting Whitmore's individualized standing as a fellow inmate to appeal Simmons' sentence of death as too speculative, concluding that no factual basis existed to find "that the sentence imposed on a mass murderer like Simmons would even be relevant to a future comparative review of Whitmore's sentence").

[73] *See* Matthew T. Norman, Note, *Standards and Procedures for Determining Whether a Defendant is Competent to Make the Ultimate Choice — Death, Ohio's New Precedent for Death Row "Volunteers,"* 13 J.L. & HEALTH 103, 119-122 (1998-99) (summarizing four different standards for competency to waive further death sentence appeals: (1) the *Rees* standard, (2) the *Gilmore* standard, (3) the *Rumbaugh*

federal habeas review, the Supreme Court in *Rees* defined the standard as:

> [W]hether [the petitioner] has capacity to appreciate his position and make a rational choice with respect to continuing or abandoning further litigation or on the other hand whether he is suffering from a mental disease, disorder, or defect which may substantially affect his capacity in the premises.[75]

Another commonly cited definition is the one from Arkansas. Although the Supreme Court neither approved nor disapproved of the standard, the Arkansas definition is often referenced by lower courts because it was cited in the Supreme Court's decision in *Whitmore*.[76] The Arkansas standard is:

> [I]f [the defendant] has been judicially determined to have the capacity to understand the choice between life and death and to knowingly and intelligently waive any and all rights to appeal his sentence.[77]

Most states provide for an adversary proceeding to decide competency. Experts evaluate the defendant, a report or live testimony is submitted, and the court makes a determination of competency.[78] Typically, the burden is on the party trying to establish that the defendant is incompetent.

It is rare that a defendant is found incompetent to waive rights in the volunteer context.[79] The defendants who opt for death are generally mentally ill,[80] but not irrational.[81] As a result, it is rare to see next friend petitions permitted. Thus,

---

version of the *Rees* standard, and (4) the *Arkansas* standard).

[74] 384 U.S. 312, 313 (1966). In *Rees*, a series of appeals followed the defendant's death sentence, ultimately culminating in filing a petition with the U.S. Supreme Court seeking review of a federal court judgment denying habeas corpus relief. The Court denied his petition. Thereafter, the defendant decided to withdraw his petition and forego any further challenges to his conviction and sentence.

[75] *Id.* at 314.

[76] *See Norman, supra* note 73, at 121-22, 124.

[77] *See Whitmore*, 495 U.S. at 152.

[78] *See* Vargas, 159 F.3d 1161, 1163 (9th Cir. 1998) (describing the trial court's determination of Sagastegui's competency). In *Vargas*, the defendant underwent a fifteen-day examination at a mental hospital before trial. The examination panel included a competency therapist, a clinical psychologist, and a psychiatrist. The panel concluded that he was competent to stand trial, and the trial court accepted the panel's findings. The defendant was thereafter sentenced to death and sought to waive his right to appeal. When considering whether the defendant was competent to waive his appellate rights, the trial court questioned the defendant orally and reviewed his response to a written questionnaire. In making its competency determination, the trial court also considered the findings of the examination panel at the mental hospital.

[79] *See* Richard J. Bonnie, *The Death Penalty and Mental Illness: Mentally Ill Prisoners on Death Row: Unsolved Puzzles for Courts and Legislatures*, 54 Cath. L. Rev. 1169, 1185 (2005) (asserting that "[n]o more than five to ten percent of volunteers are found incompetent); Treuthart, *supra* note 10, at 279. ("It is next to impossible to find that a defendant is incompetent."). Nevertheless, a hearing should be conducted if there is "substantial evidence" of incompetency. State v. Marshall, 27 P.3d 192 (Wash. 2001) (remanding case for a hearing on competency where there was "substantial evidence" of incompetency).

[80] *See* Blume, *supra* note 28, at 962 (noting that 88% of the 106 first post-*Gregg* volunteers "had documented mental illness or severe substance-abuse disorders).

[81] *See* White, *supra* note 26, at 854-55 (suggesting that a significant proportion of capital defendants

volunteers are usually successful in precluding efforts, at trial, on appeal, or in postconviction proceedings, to contest the death penalty.

§ 22.06   FUTURE ISSUES

As the population on death row grows in the United States, there is likely to be an increase in the number of volunteers. When these defendants are deemed competent, there is unlikely to be standing for anyone else to raise issues of the constitutionality of foregoing mitigation or appeals. As a consequence, future issues will probably be concentrated in the legislative and executive branches rather than in the courts. Thus, policy and statutory decisions may determine how volunteers are handled on a state-by-state basis. Each state has the potential to approach the issues differently.

For example, in one law review article, the authors propose a novel approach for the state of Washington.[82] They take a comprehensive constitutional, statutory, and policy approach to volunteers. They also recognize that volunteers have an effect on multiple levels in capital proceedings. As a result, the authors suggest the appointment of an independent "mitigation specialist," who could be consulted or invoked at the stage of the charging decision, the penalty proceeding, on appeal, or at the time of a clemency petition.[83]

---

elect execution); *see* Chandler, *supra* note 42, at 1902-03 (explaining that "[t]he capital defendant who chooses to waive his appeals and expedite his execution is not as anomalous as one might think" and "capital defendants often express a desire to concede to the State at some point during their criminal proceedings").

[82] *See* Treuthart, *supra* note 10, at 286. The proposal includes:

> First, for the purpose of assisting both in the collection and presentation of mitigation evidence, the court should appoint a mitigation specialist in every case where the death penalty is a possible sentence. . . . Second, after a person is charged with aggravated first-degree murder, there should be a mandatory period where mitigation evidence is collected to assist the prosecution in deciding whether to seek the death penalty. . . . Third, if a competent defendant refuses to present mitigation evidence, the mitigation specialist should present that evidence under the court's direction. . . . Fourth, the language of the statute, rather than a separate jury instruction, should include a provision that sets forth the jury's responsibility to assess any information presented about the defendant or the crime that suggests that life without parole is the appropriate disposition. . . . Fifth, the clemency board should be vested with specific authority to receive information on mitigation that bears on commutation of a death sentence. . . . Finally, in the sentencing phase of a capital trial, defense counsel, or independent counsel on behalf of the court, should be held to a duty to argue for the defendant's life. *Id.* at 286-89.

[83] *Id.* The authors' proposal goes beyond volunteers. They further suggest that a mitigation specialist would also alleviate many concerns about ineffective assistance of counsel in failing to develop or present adequately mitigating evidence.

Chapter 23

INTERNATIONAL TREATY RIGHTS AND THE USE OF FOREIGN LAW IN DEATH PENALTY CASES

§ 23.01 OVERVIEW

The United States is a party to many treaties, conventions, and other international agreements.[1] These agreements bind the United States to certain obligations. Some of these treaties and agreements guarantee basic civil and human rights for individuals within the country's borders. Many of the basic rights mirror the fundamental due process rights in a criminal trial. For instance, the International Covenant on Civil and Political Rights (ICCPR) provides, *inter alia*, for a presumption of innocence, the right to legal assistance, a double jeopardy protection, and a fair and public hearing.[2] In addition, some of the treaties either prohibit the death penalty or greatly restrict its use.[3] The United States has generally taken a "reservation" to provisions that affect the death penalty, in an effort to preserve the use of the death penalty as it is applied under the U. S. Constitution.[4] Nevertheless, there are an increasing number of cases in which defendants are raising possible treaty violations as grounds for relief in capital and noncapital criminal cases. The first part of this chapter focuses on the basic principles of treaties and issues surrounding their applicability in a capital case in a U.S. court. As an analog to litigating treaty rights in U.S. courts, the chapter also indicates how the issues have been raised in international tribunals.

There are other rights based on international law that are beyond the scope of this chapter. For example, in some cases, defendants have argued that there are violations of customary international law and peremptory norms that cannot be derogated under any circumstances.[5] There are also additional treaties that could

---

[1] Other terms include pacts, protocols, or accords. In each case, there is an agreement between or among countries. In this chapter, we will use the term "treaty" to refer to all forms of these international agreements.

[2] International Covenant on Civil and Political Rights, 999 U.N.T.S. 171, 6 I.L.M. 360, 372-3, *entered into force* Mar. 23, 1976. *See* discussion of the ICCPR, *infra*, Section 23.04[A].

[3] For example, the ICCPR, art. 6 (1) provides for an "inherent right to life" and that "[n]o one shall be arbitrarily deprived of his life." Art. 6(2) provides that, for those countries with the death penalty, a "sentence of death may be imposed only for the most serious crimes" and (5) provides that there shall be no death penalty for those below 18 years old or pregnant women. *See* William A. Schabas, *International Law and Abolition of the Death Penalty*, 55 Wash. & Lee L. Rev. 797 (1998) (describing international agreements and norms that prohibit or limit the use of the death penalty).

[4] *See* discussion of reservations for each treaty, *infra*, Section 23.04.

[5] The Restatement (Third) of the Foreign Relations Law of the United States § 102 (1987) provides that a rule of international law includes customary law, international agreement, or as derived from

be raised by capital defendants.[6] Although all sources of international law are important and could be relevant in capital cases, this chapter focuses only on rights under selected treaties, as examples of the use of international law in capital litigation.

The treaties covered in this overview of international law are the: 1) ICCPR; 2) Convention Against Torture and Other Cruel, Inhuman or Degrading Treatment or Punishment (Convention Against Torture);[7] 3) Convention on the Elimination of All Forms of Racial Discrimination (CERD);[8] and 4) Vienna Convention on Consular

---

"general principles common to the major legal systems of the world." These rules include peremptory norms, referred to as *jus cogens*. Some of the cases described in the notes in Section 23.04 involved arguments based on customary law and *jus cogens*. The reference to the case indicates if those sources of law were raised.

[6] Relevant to the United States, among others, are 1) the *American Declaration of the Rights and Duties of Man*, [hereinafter Declaration] adopted May 2, 1948, Ninth Int'l Conference of American States, reprinted in Inter-American Commission on Human Rights, Organization of American States, Basic Documents Pertaining to Human Rights in the Inter-American System, *available at* http://www.oas.org/en/iachr/mandate/basic_documents.asp and 2) the *American Convention on Human Rights*, [hereinafter Convention] Nov. 22, 1969, 1144 U.N.T.S. 123, 9 I.L.M 99. Claims that the death penalty or death penalty trials violate the Declaration or the Convention can be brought before the Inter-American Commission on Human Rights (IACHR) and the Inter-American Court of Human Rights (IACtHR). For example, the IACHR recommended compensation to the next of kin of William Andrews, who was executed in Utah, for violations of the right to life, equality, an impartial hearing, and no cruel, infamous, or unusual punishment under the American Declaration. IACHR, Report No. 57/96, December 6, 1996. The IACHR recommended an effective remedy, including commutation of sentence of death, for Michael Domingues, because of his status as a juvenile, for a violation of the right to life of the American Declaration. IACHR, Report No. 62/02, October 22, 2002. *See also* Roberto Moreno Ramos, IACHR, Report No. 1/05, January 28, 2005 (finding Ramos was denied due process in Texas on the basis of inadequacy of counsel, a violation of his consular notification right, and discriminatory comments by the prosecutor; recommending new sentencing hearing on death penalty); Javier Suarez Medina, IACHR, Report No. 91/05 (October 24, 2005) (finding due process violations and a violation due to a failure to abide by precautionary measures issued by the Commission to keep Medina alive until the Commission decided the merits; Medina was executed in Texas prior to the decision on the merits, but the Commission recommended compensation to his family). Although there is a growing body of decisions, especially from the IACHR, it is not common to see recommendations from the IACHR or advisory opinions from the IACtHR cited in U.S. cases. The United States does not recognize the decisions of the IACHR as binding, and has not ratified the Convention which authorizes the IACtHR. Thus, even though an IACHR recommendation of a stay of execution was mentioned in Garza v. Lappin, 253 F.3d 918, 925-26 (7th Cir. 2001), *cert. denied*, 533 U.S. 924 (2001), the court noted that the recommendation was not binding. Similarly, in Thompson v. State, 134 S.W.3d 168 (Tenn. 2004), *overruled on other grounds by* State v. Irick, 320 S.W.3d 284 (Tenn. 2010), the court viewed precautionary measures from the IACHR requesting that defendant not be executed before the Commission considered the case as nonbinding and not justifying a stay of execution. *See* discussion of advisory opinion of IACtHR on VCCR violations in Section 23.04[D], *infra*. For a general overview of cases recently before the IACHR, *see* Rick J. Wilson & Jan Perlin, *The Inter-American Human Rights System: Activities from Late 2000 Through October 2002*, 18 AM. U. INT'L L. REV. 651 (2003).

[7] Convention Against Torture and Other Cruel, Inhuman or Degrading Treatment or Punishment, G.A. res. 39/46, annex, 39 U.N. GAOR Supp. (No. 51) at 197, U.N. Doc. A/39/51 (1984), *entered into force* June 26, 1987 [hereinafter Convention Against Torture].

[8] International Convention on the Elimination of All Forms of Racial Discrimination, *opened for signature* Mar. 7, 1966, Article 5, 660 U.N.T.S. 195, 5 I.L.M. 350 *entered into force Jan. 4, 1969* (hereinafter CERD).

Relations (VCCR).[9] The first three apply to any defendant, American or foreign national, who is being tried in the United States. The fourth treaty, the VCCR, is applicable only to defendants who are foreign nationals in the United States.

In addition to the treaty issues, the final section in the chapter discusses the relevance and use of foreign law in U.S. capital cases.

§ 23.02   THE NATURE OF THE ISSUE

How do treaty issues arise in capital cases? Let's revisit the issue of the "death row phenomenon" that was presented in Section 19.02, *supra*, as an example. Suppose D is convicted in a state court of a capital crime that she committed in 1992 and is sentenced to death. An appeal to the state supreme court is automatic, but there is no appellate counsel available to represent D until 1994 due to a shortage of death penalty lawyers in the state. Once counsel is appointed, the appeal proceeds. On appeal, the defense argues for reversal of the sentence, claiming that one of the aggravating circumstances, that the crime was "heinous, atrocious, and cruel," was vague. In 1996, the conviction is affirmed, but the sentence is reversed for error in relying on a vague aggravating circumstance. New defense counsel requests, and is granted, a 10-month delay in order to prepare for the new sentencing hearing. The sentencing phase is reheard in 1997 before a new jury without the vague aggravating circumstance. The trial court, however, refuses to admit mitigating evidence on organic brain damage. D once again appeals to the state supreme court, raising the claim that it was error to refuse the mitigating evidence of organic brain damage. In 1998, the state supreme court issues an opinion in which they affirm the sentence. D then files a state habeas corpus petition, which is denied. D next files a habeas corpus petition in 1999 in federal district court, continuing to claim constitutional error in the sentencing on the basis of a refusal to admit relevant mitigating evidence. The federal district court denies the habeas petition in 1999 and D appeals to the federal circuit court. In 2000, the federal circuit court reverses D's sentence on the basis of the refusal to admit the mitigating evidence of organic brain damage. The United States Supreme Court denies the petition for a writ of *certiorari* filed by the state. In 2000, a third sentencing hearing is held with the additional mitigating evidence. D is again sentenced to death. She again goes through a state appeal, state habeas, and federal habeas processes. All the courts affirm the conviction and sentence, and the U.S. Supreme Court denies *certiorari*. It is now 2012 and D, 20 years after her initial conviction, is scheduled to be executed.

D may have challenges based on provisions of the U.S. Constitution that could arise in any capital case — inadequate consideration of mitigation, ineffective assistance of counsel, or faulty jury instructions. In addition, because D has been on death row for many years, she might challenge the constitutionality of executing her at this point on the basis of the Eighth Amendment. As discussed in more detail in Section 19.02, *supra*, defendants have raised claims that a long period of time on death row under the restrictive conditions typical of such confinement, the "death

---

[9] Vienna Convention on Consular Relations, 21 U.S.T. 77 *entered into force* Dec. 1969 [hereinafter VCCR].

row phenomenon," is cruel and unusual punishment that violates the Eighth Amendment. So far, D's arguments are all based on provisions of the U.S. Constitution.

D could also raise legal arguments based on the provisions of the ICCPR and the Convention Against Torture. The United States is a party to both treaties. As a party to a treaty, the United States and all of its subsidiary states are bound by the provisions. One provision of the ICCPR prohibits "cruel, inhuman or degrading treatment or punishment." The Convention Against Torture similarly prohibits "severe pain or suffering, whether physical or mental," and, like the ICCPR, prohibits "cruel, inhuman or degrading treatment or punishment," even if it does not constitute "torture." D will argue that her execution would violate the legal obligation of the United States pursuant to the treaties and, therefore, the court must find her death sentence invalid. The state will argue that, although the United States signed the treaties, the treaties are not enforceable in court because the United States attached a "declaration" to each treaty that the U.S. did not consider the treaty "self-executing." Additionally, the state will argue that, because the United States Senate attached a "reservation" that "cruel, inhuman, or degrading treatment or punishment" has an identical meaning to the Eighth Amendment's "cruel and unusual punishment" clause, the meaning under the U.S. Constitution controls the case.

D might also draw on decisions from foreign courts as support for her arguments that a lengthy time on death row either violates the treaties or should be viewed as a violation of the Eighth Amendment. The state will likely respond that foreign law is not relevant to a determination of U.S. constitutional law and should not be accorded any significant weight in interpreting a treaty.

How are the courts likely to resolve these issues? Is the execution of a person under "death row phenomenon" conditions a violation of the ICCPR and the Convention Against Torture? Is the treaty enforceable in a capital case? What is the effect of the "reservation" that the guarantee under the treaties is limited to the Eighth Amendment's guarantee? How much weight, if any, should be placed on decisions from foreign courts? The following sections of this chapter will address the significance of a treaty right in either a U.S. court or an international tribunal and the effect of foreign decisions in U.S. courts.

§ 23.03 INTERNATIONAL TREATIES IN GENERAL

Most international law issues raised in capital cases are based on a treaty. Treaties are authorized by Art. II § 2 of the United States Constitution.[10] Pursuant to Art. VI of the Constitution, treaties are included as part of the "supreme law of the land."[11] Under constitutional law, treaties have a status equivalent to statutory

---

[10] U.S. Const. art. II, §§ 2, cl. 2:

"He shall have Power, by and with the Advice and Consent of the Senate, to make Treaties, provided two thirds of the Senators present concur . . . "

[11] U.S. Const. art. VI, cl. 2 (emphasis added):

"This Constitution, and the Laws of the United States which shall be made in Pursuance

law.[12]

The Constitution authorizes the President to enter into treaties on behalf of the United States. Although the President may sign the treaty, the treaty is not "ratified," or binding, until two-thirds of the Senate give their "advice and consent." For instance, President Clinton signed the Rome Treaty which establishes the International Criminal Court, but the United States is not a party to the treaty because the Senate has yet to ratify it.[13]

Sometimes a nation will enter into a treaty, but attach a "reservation," "understanding," or "declaration" (RUD) to one or more provisions. A qualification, such as a reservation, ordinarily exempts the country from the particular provision. For example, the United States signed the Convention Against Torture, but attached a reservation intended to clarify that the United States did not consider the death penalty prohibited as cruel, inhuman, or degrading treatment or punishment by the Convention.[14] A reservation is considered invalid, however, if it is contrary to the

---

thereof; *and all Treaties made,* or which shall be made, under the Authority of the United States, *shall be the supreme Law of the Land*; and the Judges in every State shall be bound thereby, any Thing in the Constitution or Laws of any State to the Contrary notwithstanding."

[12] "By the Constitution a treaty is placed on the same footing, and made of like obligation, with an act of legislation. Both are declared by that instrument to be the supreme law of the land, and no superior efficacy is given to either over the other." Whitney v. Robertson, 124 U.S. 190, 194 (1888). Similarly, in Reid v. Covert, 354 U.S. 1, 18 (1957), the Court stated: "[A]n Act of Congress, which must comply with the Constitution, is on a full parity with a treaty, and that when a statute which is subsequent in time is inconsistent with a treaty, the statute to the extent of conflict renders the treaty null." Note, however, that the Court has also indicated that conflicts should be resolved if possible: "It has also been observed that an act of Congress ought never to be construed to violate the law of nations if any other possible construction remains, and consequently can never be construed to violate neutral rights, or to affect neutral commerce, further than is warranted by the law of nations as understood in this country." Murray v. Charming Betsy, 6 U.S. 64, 118 (1804). *See also,* Richard J. Wilson, *Defending a Criminal Case with International Human Rights Law,* 24 CHAMPION 28, 29 (2000) (quoting NOWAK AND ROTUNDA, CONSTITUTIONAL LAW 217 (5th ed. 1995)) (noting treaties are equal in status to congressional legislation).

[13] *See* Diane A. Holcombe, *Comment: The United States Becomes a Signatory to the Rome Treaty Establishing the International Criminal Court: Why are so Many Concerned by this Action?* 62 MONT. L. REV. 301 (2001) (quoting William Jefferson Clinton, President of the United States, Statement on Signature of the International Criminal Court Treaty, Washington, D.C., at 1 (Dec. 31, 2000) *available at* http://www.state.gov/www/global/swci/001231clintonicc.html. For further discussion of the concerns of the United States in signing the treaty, *see* Elizabeth C. Minogue, *Increasing the Effectiveness of the Security Council's Chapter VII Authority in the Current Situations Before the International Criminal Court,* 61 VAN. L. REV. 647, 676-79 (2008); Cheryl Moralez, *Article and Essay: Establishing an International Criminal Court: Will it Work?* 4 DEPAUL INT'L L.J. 135 (2000); Matthew A. Barrett, *Note: Ratify or Reject: Examining the United States' Opposition to the International Criminal Court,* 28 GA. J. INT'L & COMP. L. 83 (1999).

[14] Reservation (1) provides: "That the United States considers itself bound by the obligation under article 16 to prevent 'cruel, inhuman or degrading treatment or punishment', only insofar as the term 'cruel, inhuman or degrading treatment or punishment' means the cruel, unusual and inhumane treatment or punishment prohibited by the Fifth, Eighth, and-or Fourteenth Amendments to the Constitution of the United States."

Understanding (4) provides: "That the United States understands that international law does not prohibit the death penalty, and does not consider this Convention to restrict or prohibit the United States from applying the death penalty consistent with the Fifth, Eighth and-or Fourteenth Amendments to the Constitution of the United States, including any constitutional period of confinement prior to the imposition of the death penalty."

basic purpose of the treaty.[15]

The effect of treaties under American law may be dependent on implementing legislation. Some treaties are viewed as "self-executing" and others are not. If a treaty is self-executing, there is no need for implementing legislation, and the treaty constitutes enforceable law in U.S. courts.[16] If a treaty is not self-executing, then the use of the treaty is more problematic. A non-self-executing treaty is generally viewed as not judicially enforceable.[17] A number of scholars, however, take the position that even non-self-executing treaties can be raised defensively or as an underlying civil right in a statutory cause of action.[18] Although a non-self-executing treaty does not create a cause of action enforceable in a U.S. court, the United States is bound by the treaty. As a result, some scholars contend that the rights under the treaty can be raised as a defense in a criminal case. Capital defendants argue that even if a treaty is not self-executing, the provisions apply as a defense in a criminal case.[19] Decisions from courts on treaty issues in capital cases appear to

[15] Vienna Convention on the Law of Treaties, art. 19, May 23, 1969, 1155 U.N.T.S. 331, 8 I.L.M 679 provides that reservations may be taken to treaties unless the reservation is prohibited by the treaty, not within limitations on reservations, or is "incompatible with the object and purpose of the treaty."

[16] See Restatement § 111(3): "Courts in the United States are bound to give effect to international law and to international agreements of the United States, except that a 'non-self-executing' agreement will not be given effect as law in the absence of necessary implementation." See discussion in Curtis A. Bradley, International Delegations, the Structural Constitution, and Non-Self-Execution, 55 Stan. L. Rev. 1557, 1587 (2003) (noting that "[o]nly self-executing treaties, courts have held, constitute judicially enforceable federal law").

[17] Bradley, supra note 16, at 1589 (describing non-self-executing treaties as binding on the United States, but "not enforceable in U.S. courts . . . "). See also Commonwealth v. Judge, 916 A.2d 511, 526 (Pa. 2007), cert. denied, 552 U.S. 1011 (2007), (finding that ICCPR, as non-self-executing treaty, is not enforceable in state court); Poindexter v. Nash, 333 F.3d 372 (2nd Cir. 2003), cert. denied, 540 U.S. 1210 (2004) (noting that the ICCPR is non-self-executing, precluding defendant's claim in federal habeas). But see Carlos Manuel Vazquez, The Four Doctrines of Self-Executing Treaties, 89 Am. J. Int'l L. 695 (1995) (explaining that there are four separate situations where it is logical that a treaty is not judicially enforceable without legislation, including where a treaty is raised as creating a private cause of action; distinguishing those situations where the treaty rights are judicially enforceable, such as through federal statutes on habeas corpus or Section 1983 civil rights actions).

[18] For example, although the Senate declared that the ICCPR was not self-executing, some scholars conclude that this language does not preclude a party from using the treaty defensively. See Kristen Carpenter, The International Covenant on Civil and Political Rights: A Toothless Tiger?, 26 N.C.J. Int'l Law & Com. Reg. 1 (2000); John Quigley, Judge Bork Is Wrong: The Covenant Is the Law, 71 Wash.U.L.Q. 1087, 1097-98 (1993) ("Even if the Covenant was found not to create a private cause of action in U.S. courts, the Covenant could nonetheless be invoked defensively by an individual against whom legal action is being taken") See generally David Sloss, The Domestication of International Human Rights: Non-Self-Executing Declarations and Human Rights Treaties, 24 Yale J. Int'l L. 129, 152 (1999) ("The statement that a treaty is not self-executing, in the sense that it does not create a private cause of action, does not mean that the treaty cannot be applied directly by the courts. . . . Furthermore, there are a number of possible federal statutory bases for rights of action to enforce treaties, the most important being section 1983 and the APA"). But see Curtis A. Bradley, Intent, Presumptions, and Non-Self-Executing Treaties, 102 Am. J. Int'l L. 540, 547-550 (2008) (noting the ambiguity in the U.S. Supreme Court's Medellin decision regarding whether non-self-executing treaties are only not judicially enforceable or whether they lack any status in domestic law; further commenting that the interpretation of non-self-executing treaties as not judicially enforceable, rather than lacking domestic status, is more consistent with the Supremacy Clause; and noting that the decision precludes the defensive use of treaties).

[19] Another complicating factor is that it is not always clear when a treaty is or is not self-executing.

reflect the uncertainty over the effect of a non-self-executing treaty raised as a defense. Some courts dismiss a defense based on a treaty on the ground it is non-self-executing and cannot be raised in a court. Other courts proceed to consider the merits of the defense.[20] The U.S. Supreme Court's 2008 decision in *Medellin v. Texas*[21] has further thrown the analysis of the effect of non-self-executing treaties into disarray. Scholars are wrestling with the meaning of the Court's statement that non-self-executing treaties are not "binding domestic law" and whether this usurps the Supremacy Clause, which provides that treaties are the "law of the land."[22] Prior to *Medellin*, the more typical language used was that non-self-executing treaties were not "judicially enforceable," which according to the commentators is potentially qualitatively different from not "binding domestic law."[23]

Even if the treaty applies, the remedy in a criminal case in a U.S. court[24] when the federal or state government violates a treaty is unclear. The remedies vary and are evolving through litigation.[25] For instance, lower courts almost uniformly have

---

Prior to Medellin v. Texas, 552 U.S. 491 (2008), the courts had developed an analysis using multiple factors to determine the status. *See, e.g.*, People of Saipan v. U.S. Department of the Interior, 502 F.2d 90, 97 (9th Cir. 1974), *cert. denied*, 420 U.S. 1003 (1975). The Ninth Circuit established various factors to consider in determining if a treaty is self-executing. "The extent to which an international agreement establishes affirmative and judicially enforceable obligations without implementing legislation must be determined in each case by reference to many contextual factors: the purposes of the treaty and the objectives of its creators, the existence of domestic procedures and institutions appropriate for direct implementation, the availability and feasibility of alternative enforcement methods, and the immediate and long-range social consequences of self- or non-self-execution." The test was clarified in Islamic Republic of Iran v. Boeing Co., 771 F.2d 1279, 1283 (9th Cir. 1985), *cert. dismissed*, 479 U.S. 957 (1986). "The purposes of the treaty and the objectives of its creators" is "critical to determine whether an executive agreement is self-executing, while the other factors are most relevant to determine the extent to which the agreement is self-executing." *See also* discussions of treaties, whether self-executing or non-self-executing in John Quigley, *The Rule of Non-Inquiry and Human Rights*, 45 Cath. U.L. Rev. 1213, 1236 (1996); Vazquez, *supra* note 17, at 715; Richard J. Wilson, *Feature: Defending a Criminal Case with International Human Rights Law*, 24 Champion 28 (2000). After *Medellin*, it appears that the analysis will be a treaty-by-treaty approach, rather than a factor-based approach. *See* Bradley, *supra* note 18, at 541.

[20] *See* cases in notes 42-45, *infra*.

[21] 552 U.S. 491 (2008).

[22] *See, e.g.*, Carlos Manuel Vazquez, *The Separation of Powers as a Safeguard of Nationalism*, 83 Notre Dame L. Rev. 1601, 1613-1624 (2008) (criticizing the *Medellin* decision for the language on "domestic law" that arguably conflicts with the Supremacy Clause); Bradley, *supra* note 18, at 547-550 (noting the ambiguity in the *Medellin* decision whether a non-self-executing treaty is simply not judicially enforceable or whether it more broadly is not domestic law which could conflict with the Supremacy Clause; suggesting that narrower reading is more likely).

[23] *Id.*

[24] In an international tribunal, the remedy is "reparation." Reparation includes restitution of the *status quo ante*, compensation, and satisfaction, such as an apology. Restatement (Third) of the Foreign Relations Law of the United States § 901 (1987) (stating principle of reparation for breaches of international law). *See also* William J. Aceves, *The Vienna Convention on Consular Relations: A Study of Rights, Wrongs, and Remedies*, 31 Vand. J. Transnat'l L. 257, 312 (1998) (discussing restitution, compensation, and satisfaction).

[25] A potential remedy in civil cases may be monetary damages. *See* Standt v. City of New York, 153 F. Supp. 2d 417 (S.D.N.Y. 2001) (denying motion for summary judgment on a VCCR claim brought pursuant to 42 U.S.C. § 1983); Jogi v. Voges, 480 F.3d 822, 836 (7th Cir. 2007) (finding that the VCCR grants private rights to aliens from countries that are a party to the Convention who are in the United

found that suppression of evidence is not a valid remedy for a violation of the VCCR,[26] and recently the U.S. Supreme Court confirmed that suppression of evidence was not required by the treaty.[27] On the other hand, the Ninth Circuit Court of Appeals dismissed an indictment in a case charging illegal entry after deportation. The prior involuntary deportation, which was an element of the crime, arguably would not have occurred but for the violation at the time of the VCCR treaty.[28] Thus, in that context, the court provided a remedy, *albeit* indirectly, in a criminal case. Other arguments for remedies for a violation of VCCR have included dismissal or reversal of a death sentence.[29]

States, and that § 1983 provides a remedy). *See also* Jordan J. Paust, *Agora: Breard: Breard and Treaty-Based Rights Under the Consular Convention*, 92 Am. J. Int'l.L. 691, 694 (1998) ("Since the treaty [VCCR] is supreme federal law under the Constitution, a consular officer's treaty-based rights fit within the language of 42 U.S.C. § 1983 . . . "). *But see* Sorensen v. City of New York, 2000 U.S. Dist. Lexis 15090 (S.D.N.Y. 2000) (finding no civil cause of action for VCCR violation under § 1983); Bieregu v. Ashcroft, 259 F. Supp. 2d 342, 353-54 (D.N.J. 2003) (holding that the VCCR does not create a duty enforceable in tort); Cornejo v. County of San Diego, 504 F.3d 853, 863-64 (9th Cir. 2007) (holding that the VCCR does not confer a privately enforceable right under § 1983); Gandara v. Bennet, 528 F.3d 823, 826-30 (11th Cir. 2008) (declining to follow *Jogi*, and holding that the VCCR does not contemplate private rights and remedies enforceable through § 1983 claim).

[26] *See* cases cited in note 69, *infra. See also* Lopez v. State, 274 Ga. 663, 665 (Ga. 2002); United States v. Cisneros, 397 F. Supp. 2d 726, 734-35 (E.D. Va. 2005) (holding that since a violation of the VCCR does not violate a constitutional right, suppression is not a viable remedy).

[27] Sanchez-Llamas v. Oregon, 126 S. Ct. 2669 (2006).

[28] *See* United States v. Rangel-Gonzales, 617 F.2d 529 (9th Cir. 1980). The defendant proved that INS regulations, which mirror the VCCR, were violated because he was not notified of his right to contact his national consulate during a deportation proceeding. The defendant demonstrated that he was prejudiced by this violation because had he contacted the Mexican Consulate, he may have been able to establish his eligibility for a voluntary departure. A voluntary departure would have precluded the current charge of illegal entry after deportation. As a result of the violation, the Ninth Circuit Court dismissed the indictment for illegal entry.

Both the Ninth Circuit and other courts require that there be a showing of prejudice before a remedy will be provided with a violation of the INS regulations that embody the VCCR guarantees. *See, e.g.*, Sango-Dema v. District Dir., INS, 122 F. Supp. 2d 213, 222 (D.Mass. 2000) (no remedy for VCCR violation where no showing of prejudice). Note, however, that one court has also rejected suppression of evidence as a remedy in the context of an INS case. United States v. Chaparro-Alcantara, 226 F.3d 616 (Ill. 2000) (no suppression where statements were made after an INS agent had read defendants their Miranda rights, but had not given them the required warnings under the VCCR).

[29] *See* United States v. Bin Laden, 126 F. Supp. 2d 290, 296 (S.D.N.Y. 2001) (rejecting the defendant's argument that his death sentence should be dismissed for a violation of VCCR). *See also* Villegas v. State, 546 S.E.2d 504, 507 (Ga. 2001) (rejecting either dismissal of the indictment or application of the exclusionary rule to VCCR violation; finding that VCCR violation did not "rise to the level of a constitutional right protected by the judicially created remedies sought by [Villegas]."). Courts have also indicated a likely need to show prejudice from a violation. *See, e.g.*, Darby v. Hawk-Sawyer, 405 F.3d 942, 946 (11th Cir. 2005) (commenting that, even if a VCCR claim were properly raised, it is unlikely that overturning a final judgment would be a remedy without showing "that the violation had an effect on the trial.").

§ 23.04   SPECIFIC TREATIES

[A]   International Covenant for Civil and Political Rights

The treaty with the most comprehensive statement of rights for those accused of crimes is the International Covenant for Civil and Political Rights (ICCPR). Ratified by the United States in 1992, the ICCPR provides, *inter alia*, that "[n]o one shall be arbitrarily deprived of . . . life;"[30] that the death penalty will only be imposed "for the most serious crimes;"[31] that no one will be subjected to "cruel, inhuman or degrading treatment or punishment;"[32] the right to be presumed innocent;[33] to prepare for trial;[34] have legal assistance;[35] to review by a higher court;[36] and to not be tried or punished twice for an offense."[37] Although accommodating those countries that authorize the death penalty for certain crimes, the ICCPR states unequivocally: "Sentence of death shall not be imposed for crimes committed by persons below eighteen years of age and shall not be carried out on pregnant women."[38]

When it ratified the ICCPR, the United States Senate attached various reservations, understandings, and declarations (RUDs). With regard to juvenile executions, the United States specifically reserved the right to impose the death penalty on persons under eighteen years of age.[39] The Senate also made a reservation that "cruel, inhuman or degrading treatment or punishment" was synonymous with "cruel and unusual treatment or punishment" as defined by the Eighth Amendment to the U.S. Constitution.[40] The United States further attached a declaration that it did not consider the Covenant self-executing.[41]

---

[30] International Covenant on Civil and Political Rights, 999 U.N.T.S. 171, *entered into force* Mar. 23, 1976.

[31] *Id.* at Article 6(2).

[32] *Id.* at Article 7.

[33] *Id.* at Article 14(2).

[34] *Id.* at Article 14(3)(b).

[35] *Id.* at Article 14(3)(d).

[36] *Id.* at Article 14(5).

[37] *Id.* at Article 14(7).

[38] *Id.* at Article 6(5).

[39] The reservation states:

"(2) That the United States reserves the right, subject to its Constitutional constraints, to impose capital punishment on any person (other than a pregnant woman) duly convicted under existing or future laws permitting the imposition of capital punishment, including such punishment for crimes committed by persons below eighteen years of age."

Note that the reservation to allow the execution of juveniles is now moot since the U.S. Supreme Court has held that the execution of persons who were juveniles at the time of the crime is unconstitutional under the Eighth Amendment. *Roper v. Simmons*, 543 U.S. 551, 567 (2005). *See* discussion of the prohibition in the *Roper* case in Section 8.04, *supra*.

[40] Reservation (3).

[41] Declaration (1).

Despite the RUDs attached by the United States, capital defendants have raised alleged ICCPR violations in cases involving issues of clemency,[42] unequal, harsher punishment than a codefendant,[43] double jeopardy,[44] the punishment of death itself,[45] and execution after a lengthy stay on death row.[46] Most courts to date have either found that the treaty is not binding because it is not "self-executing," or they have found that the reservation limiting the meaning to the Eighth Amendment's provisions precludes relief.[47] Some scholars, however, contend that the declaration of non-self-execution may be invalid or that the defensive use of a treaty does not conflict with the non-self-executing provision.[48] Although the *Medellin* decision,

---

[42] In Lagrone v. Cockrell, 2003 U.S. App. Lexis 18150, 35, 36 (5th Cir. 2003), *cert. denied*, 540 U.S. 1172 (2004) the defendant argued that the "State's failure to provide any real or meaningful process for commutation violates Article 6, §§ 1 and 4 of the ("ICCPR"), which requires that anyone sentenced to death have the right to seek pardon or commutation." The 5th Circuit upheld the district court's determination that "LaGrone failed to show how the Texas clemency process violates international law, because Senate has declared Articles 1-27 of the ICCPR not self-executing." *See also* Roach v. Quarterman, 220 Fed. App'x. 270 (5th Cir. 2007) (unpublished) (challenge to clemency under the ICCPR rejected on grounds treaty is inapplicable because not self-executing; challenge to clemency under customary international law rejected on basis no violation).

[43] People v. Caballero, 794 N.E.2d 251 (Ill. 2002) (rejecting claim that co-defendant's life sentence created a disparity compared with defendant's death sentence that violated ICCPR in part because no violation of U.S. Constitution and treaty reservation precludes further reach of the treaty).

[44] In State v. Carpenter, 69 S.W.3d 568 (Tenn. Crim. App. 2001), *cert. denied*, 535 U.S. 995 (2002), the defendant argued that he could not be tried in state court after he had been convicted for the same homicide in federal court under the ICCPR provision prohibiting multiple prosecutions. The Tennessee court rejected the argument on the grounds that the Senate had adequately limited the ICCPR to preserve the right under the U.S. Constitution to multiple prosecutions if done by separate sovereigns, such as two different states or the federal government. This was affirmed recently by State v. Thomas, 158 S.W.3d 361, 392 (Tenn. 2005).

[45] *See* Buell v. Mitchell, 274 F.3d 337 (6th Cir. 2001) (finding ICCPR not binding as non-self-executing treaty and rejecting claims that death penalty violated ICCPR, on basis of U.S. reservation; also finding no violation of customary international law or peremptory norm, *jus cogens*, on basis of current state of international norms); *People v. Taylor*, 48 Cal. 4th 574 (2010), *cert. denied*, 131 S. Ct. 529 (2010) (death penalty does not violate ICCPR when imposed in accordance with federal and state law); People v. Ramirez, 39 Cal. 4th 398 (Cal. 2006), *cert. denied*, 550 U.S. 970 (2007) and People v. Brown, 33 Cal. 4th 382 (Cal. 2004), *cert. denied*, 543 U.S. 1155 (2005) (death penalty does not violate ICCPR because of U.S. reservation preserving right to impose death penalty subject only to U.S. constitutional restrictions and also finding that death penalty is not violative of international norms).

[46] *See, e.g.*, State v. Davis, 2011 Ohio 787 (Ohio Ct. App., Butler County Feb. 22, 2011) (rejecting defendant's argument that twenty-six year stay on death row violates Article 7 of the ICCPR when there is no constitutional violation).

[47] *See* cases cited in notes 42-45, *supra*.

[48] *See* Jordan J. Paust, *Symposium: The Ratification of the International Covenant on Civil and Political Rights: Avoiding "Fraudulent" Executive Policy: Analysis of Non-Self-Execution of the Covenant on Civil and Political Rights*, 42 DePaul L. Rev. 1257 (1993) (describing scholars' position that this Senate declaration of non-self-execution is in conflict with express articles of the Covenant); John Quigley, *Human Rights Defenses in U.S. Courts*, 20 Hum. Rts. Q. 555 (1998) (asserting that a defendant may be able to invoke his ICCPR treaty rights defensively in a criminal proceeding despite its non-self-execution); M. Shah Alam, *Enforcement of International Human Rights law by Domestic Courts in the United States*, 10 Ann. Surv. Int'l & Comp. L 27 (2004) (arguing that declarations that treaties are non-self-executing are unconstitutional). *But see* Bradley, *supra* note 18, at 547-548 (commenting that the *Medellin* decision precludes a defensive use of a non-self-executing treaty).

This issue also arose in cases where defendants were challenging the execution of those who were

discussed *supra* in § 23.03, casts doubt on the defensive use of treaties, until there is great clarification, it is likely that the status of reservations taken by the United States to treaties will continue to be raised in litigation under the ICCPR as the case law develops.

[B] Convention Against Torture and Other Cruel, Inhuman or Degrading Treatment or Punishment

The United States ratified the Convention Against Torture and Other Cruel, Inhuman or Degrading Treatment or Punishment (Convention Against Torture) in 1994. The Convention Against Torture defines torture in terms of the intentional infliction of "severe pain or suffering, whether physical or mental" as a means to gain information or as a punishment.[49] Parties to the Convention agree to prohibit and prevent torture within their territories, and also to preclude any "cruel, inhuman or degrading treatment or punishment", even if it does not rise to the level of "torture."[50]

In ratifying the Convention, the Senate attached reservations similar to those attached to the ICCPR. One reservation limits the terminology of "cruel, inhuman or degrading treatment or punishment" to the meaning of similar language under the U.S. Constitution.[51] Another reservation states that the United States does not consider the Convention to "restrict or prohibit" the death penalty as applied in the United States.[52] Once again, the Senate also added a declaration that the Convention was not self-executing.

---

juveniles at the time of their crimes as violative of the ICCPR despite a reservation preserving the right to execute the juvenile defendants. For example, in Domingues v. State, 961 P.2d 1279 (Nev. 1998), *cert. denied*, 528 U.S. 963 (1999), the juvenile defendant argued that the reservation was invalid because it defeated the "object and purpose" of the Covenant and that, as a result, the state of Nevada was in violation of the ICCPR in seeking to execute him. This argument was rejected by the Nevada Supreme Court, and the United States Supreme Court denied *certiorari*. The status of juvenile executions under the ICCPR is moot today since the Supreme Court has held that executions of those who were minors at the time of the crime are unconstitutional. Roper v. Simmons, 543 U.S. 551 (2005). *See* discussion of the unconstitutionality of executing those who were juveniles at the time of their crimes in Section 8.04, *supra*.

[49] Convention against Torture and Other Cruel, Inhuman or Degrading Treatment or Punishment, G.A. res. 39/46, annex, 39 U.N. GAOR, 39th Sess., Supp. (No. 51) at 197, U.N. Doc. A/39/46 (1984), *entered into force* June 26, 1987. Article 1 provides:

"1. For the purposes of this Convention, the term "torture" means any act by which severe pain or suffering, whether physical or mental, is intentionally inflicted on a person for such purposes as obtaining from him or a third person information or a confession, punishing him for an act he or a third person has committed or is suspected of having committed, or intimidating or coercing him or a third person, or for any reason based on discrimination of any kind, when such pain or suffering is inflicted by or at the instigation of or with the consent or acquiescence of a public official or other person acting in an official capacity. It does not include pain or suffering arising only from, inherent in or incidental to lawful sanctions."

[50] *Id.* at Article 16, which provides:

"1. Each State Party shall undertake to prevent in any territory under its jurisdiction other acts of cruel, inhuman or degrading treatment or punishment which do not amount to torture as defined in article I, when such acts are committed by or at the instigation of or with the consent or acquiescence of a public official or other person acting in an official capacity."

[51] *Id.* at Reservation (1).

[52] *Id.* at Reservation (4).

In several capital cases, as in our hypothetical defendant's case at the beginning of the chapter, defendants have argued that a lengthy delay between sentence and execution, the "death row phenomenon," violates the Convention Against Torture and the ICCPR. D, in our opening hypothetical, could make these arguments. In cases decided to date in U.S. courts, however, the courts have rejected the treaty claims on the grounds that the delay did not constitute "cruel and unusual" punishment under either the U.S. Constitution or the treaties.[53] Some of the courts further noted that the United States had attached reservations to both treaties which limited the nature of "cruel, inhuman, or degrading treatment or punishment" to the definition under the U.S. Constitution.[54] Thus, the resolution of the Eighth Amendment constitutional issues also resolved the treaty issue.[55] Nevertheless, as interpretations of the treaties develop in international and foreign forums or courts, it is likely that there will be arguments made in future cases to revisit the issue of violations of both the treaties and the Constitution.

[C] Convention on the Elimination of All Forms of Racial Discrimination

Another treaty that has implications for capital cases is the International Convention on the Elimination of All Forms of Racial Discrimination (CERD), which the United States ratified in 1994. As with the ICCPR and the Convention Against Torture, the United States attached a declaration that the treaty was not self-executing.[56] CERD imposes an obligation on the parties ". . . to prohibit and

---

"4) That the United States understands that international law does not prohibit the death penalty, and does not consider this Convention to restrict or prohibit the United States from applying the death penalty consistent with the Fifth, Eighth and-or Fourteenth Amendments to the Constitution of the United States, including any constitutional period of confinement prior to the imposition of the death penalty."

[53] White v. Johnson, 79 F.3d 432, 440 n.2 (5th Cir. 1996), *cert. denied*, 519 U.S. 911 (1996) (finding White's claims barred under *Teague*, but indicating his argument would fail due to the reservation). *See also* Faulder v. Johnson, 99 F. Supp. 2d 774, 777 (S.D. Tex. 1999), *cert. denied*, 527 U.S. 1018 (1999); Booker v. State, 773 So.2d 1079 (Fla. 2000), *cert. denied*, 532 U.S. 1033 (2001) (rejecting arguments that a delay constitutes cruel and unusual punishment); Murray v. Schriro, 2005 U.S. Dist. LEXIS 22296 (D. Ariz.) (Order of Sept. 29, 2005) (noting that circuit courts have held that a delay in execution does not violate the Eighth Amendment). *See* discussion of the death row phenomenon in Section 19.02, *supra*.

[54] *See, e.g.*, Ralk v. Lincoln County, 81 F. Supp. 2d 1372 (S.D. Ga. 2000); Faulder v. Johnson, 99 F. Supp. 2d 774 (S.D. Tex. 1999); People v. Brown, 33 Cal. 4th 382 (Cal. 2004), *cert. denied*, 543 U.S. 1155 (2005) (noting the reservation limits the meaning to the understanding of the terms in the U.S. Constitution).

[55] The Supreme Court has declined to grant certiorari in a death row phenomenon case. *See* Lackey v. Texas, 514 U.S. 1045 (1995) (Stevens. J., dissenting from denial of certiorari); Elledge v. Florida, 525 U.S. 944 (1998) (Breyer, J., dissenting from denial of certiorari); Knight v. Florida, 528 U.S. 990 (1999) (Breyer, J., dissenting from denial of certiorari); Foster v. Florida, 537 U.S. 990 (2002) (Breyer, J., dissenting from denial of certiorari); Allen v. Ornoski, 546 U.S. 1136 (2006) (Breyer, J., dissenting) (in each case, discussing the need for the Court to consider the claim that a lengthy delay of execution violates the Eighth Amendment). *See also* Wilson and Perlin, *supra* note 6, at 726-27 (describing U.S. death row phenomenon cases before the Inter-American Commission on Human Rights).

[56] As with the ICCPR, it is debatable whether or not the United States can make a treaty, such as CERD, non-self-executing. *See* David Sloss, *Article: The Domestication of International Human Rights: Non-Self-Executing Declarations and Human Rights Treaties*, 24 YALE J. INT'L L. 129, 133 (1999).

to eliminate racial discrimination in all its forms and to guarantee the right of everyone, without distinction as to race, colour, or national or ethnic origin, to equality before the law."[57] One of the specific areas where racial discrimination should be eliminated is in the judicial system.[58]

Although racial discrimination claims based on constitutional rights are difficult to prove under the standards established in *McCleskey v. Kemp*,[59] CERD may sweep more broadly. In *McCleskey*, the United States Supreme Court found that a constitutional violation required a showing of *purposeful* discrimination. In contrast, the treaty defines racial discrimination in terms of a discriminatory purpose or *effect*.[60] As a result, the statistics of systemwide discrimination that were inadequate to demonstrate purposeful discrimination in violation of the Constitution in *McCleskey* might violate the treaty as a discriminatory effect. In one reported case, the defendants argued that their death sentences were impermissibly tainted by racial discrimination in violation of both the U.S. Constitution and CERD.[61] Although the court did not reach the treaty issue because it found no racial discrimination, a number of scholars suggest that CERD should apply in some situations where the discrimination might not rise to the level of a violation of the U.S. Constitution.[62]

[D]   Vienna Convention on Consular Relations

Ratified by the United States in 1969, the Vienna Convention on Consular Relations (VCCR) only became an issue in capital cases in the mid-1990s. The treaty provides that authorities must notify any detained foreign national of the right to contact his or her consulate; must contact the consulate if requested; and must allow consular officials access to the prisoner. Unlike the ICCPR, Convention Against Torture, and CERD, which conceivably apply to any defendant, the VCCR is limited to defendants who are *foreign nationals*. The VCCR also differs from the other treaties discussed in that there is no declaration that the treaty is non-self-executing.

---

[57] CERD, Article 5.

[58] CERD, Article 5(a).

[59] *See* Section 20.04, *supra*.

[60] CERD, art. 1. "In this Convention, the term "racial discrimination" shall mean any distinction, exclusion, restriction or preference based on race, colour, descent, or national or ethnic origin which has the purpose or effect of nullifying or impairing the recognition, enjoyment or exercise, on an equal footing, of human rights and fundamental freedoms in the political, economic, social, cultural or any other field of public life."

[61] United States v. Bin Laden, 126 F. Supp. 2d 256 (S.D.N.Y. 2000). For a case raising CERD generally, *see In re Shinnecock Smoke Shop*, 571 F.3d 1171, 1174-75 (Fed. Cir. 2009), *cert. denied*, 130 S. Ct. 1156 (2010) (finding no violation under CERD and no private cause of action where CERD is a non-self-executing treaty).

[62] *See, e.g.*, Gay J. McDougall, *Toward a Meaningful International Regime: The Domestic Relevance of International Efforts to Eliminate All Forms of Racial Discrimination*, 40 How. L.J. 571, 585-586 (1997) (discussing the scholarly commentary on the "effect" standard in CERD); Nkechi Taifa, *Codification or Castration? The Applicability of the International Convention to Eliminate All Forms of Racial Discrimination to the U.S. Criminal Justice System*, 40 How. L. J. 641, 670 (1997) (noting possible violations of CERD, even without discriminatory intent).

Although consular notification rights are embodied in the regulations of the Immigration and Naturalization Service and have been litigated in deportation-related cases since the 1970s, the first reported capital case raising the issue did not occur until 1996. In 1996, a Canadian defendant, Stanley Faulder, argued in a habeas petition that his conviction and sentence were invalid on the basis of the VCCR violation.[63] The defendant had not been notified that he could contact his consulate, and Canada had never been notified that he was in custody.[64] The Fifth Circuit Court of Appeals affirmed the denial of the habeas petition on the grounds that, although the VCCR was violated, there was no prejudice from the violation.[65]

Although pertaining only to a subset of capital defendants who are foreign nationals, VCCR violations have been raised in many capital cases since 1996, and as of October 2011, there are 136 foreign nationals on death row in the United States.[66] The United States Supreme Court has issued three important decisions regarding the VCCR.[67]

The issues surrounding the VCCR claims reflect the uncharted parameters of the treaty in criminal cases. One issue that is still unresolved in U.S. courts is whether the treaty provides for an individual right that can be claimed in a criminal case. Most cases, including the 2006 U.S. Supreme Court decision, *Sanchez-Llamas v. Oregon*,[68] assume without deciding that there is an individual right to raise a claim.[69] Another legal battleground has been what, if any, remedy exists for

---

[63] *See* Faulder v. Johnson, 81 F.3d 515 (5th Cir. 1996), *cert. denied*, 519 U.S. 995 (1996).

[64] *Id.* at 520. "Assistant Attorney General of Texas could find no evidence that Faulder had been advised of his rights under the Convention."

[65] *Id.* "While we in no way approve of Texas' failure to advise Faulder, the evidence that would have been obtained by the Canadian authorities is merely the same as or cumulative of evidence defense counsel had or could have obtained. The violation, therefore, does not merit reversal."

[66] Death Penalty Information Center, "Foreign Nationals and the Death Penalty in the United States," *available at* www.deathpenaltyinfo.org [Foreign Nationals], current as of October 2, 2011 (last visited January 14, 2012). The 136 foreign nationals on death row are citizens of 36 different countries.

[67] *See* Breard v. Greene, 523 U.S. 371 (1998); Sanchez-Llamas v. Oregon, 126 S. Ct. 2669 (2006); Medellin v. Texas, 552 U.S. 491 (2008).

[68] Sanchez-Llamas v. Oregon, 126 S. Ct. 2669 (2006).

[69] Sanchez-Llamas v. Oregon, 126 S. Ct. 2669 (2006) (stating that even assuming that the VCCR creates individually enforceable rights, the courts must follow procedural default rules.) *See also* Breard v. Greene, 523 U.S. 371, 376 (1998) (explaining that the Vienna Convention "arguably confers on an individual the right to consular assistance following arrest"). Some courts are more convinced that there is no individual right under the VCCR. *See* Rocha v. Thaler, 619 F.3d 387, 407 *clarified on denial of reconsideration*, 626 F.3d 815 (5th Cir. 2010), *cert. denied*, 132 S. Ct. 397 (U.S. 2011) (affirming circuit precedent that the VCCR does not create an individually-enforceable right and denying a COA for en banc consideration). Most courts, however, have avoided the issue of determining whether the VCCR creates individual rights by deciding that, even if there was an individual right, it was not violated in the instant case. *See, e.g.*, United States v. Lombera-Camorlinga, 206 F.3d 882, 884 (9th Cir. 2000) *cert. denied*, 531 U.S. 991 (2000); United States v. Li, 206 F.3d 56 (1st Cir. 2000), *cert. denied*, 531 U.S. 956 (2000); United States v. Salameh, 54 F. Supp. 2d 236, 279 (S.D.N.Y. 1999), *cert. denied*, 537 U.S. 847 (2002); United States v. Page, 232 F.3d 536, 540 (6th Cir. 2000), *cert. denied*, 532 U.S. 1056 (2001); *Emuegbunam*, 268 F.3d at 391 ("Confronted in recent years with numerous claims based upon the Vienna Convention without the benefit of a definitive statement from the Supreme Court, federal courts whenever possible have sidestepped the question of whether the treaty creates individual rights — typically by concluding that remedies such as suppression of evidence or dismissal of an indictment are

a violation of the VCCR. The lower courts had almost uniformly rejected suppression of evidence as a remedy for a violation,[70] and the Supreme Court affirmed in *Sanchez-Llamas* that suppression of evidence is not mandated by the treaty.[71] The lower courts have also rejected dismissal of the death penalty charge.[72] In some of the cases, the VCCR issue is a significant part of a clemency petition. The U.S. Department of State has added its voice in a few of the cases, recommending an investigation of the VCCR claim before clemency is decided.[73] As with all issues in clemency, which is almost entirely without judicial oversight, the reaction to a VCCR violation by the executive authority is quite varied. For example, the governor of Oklahoma commuted Osvaldo Torres' death sentence in 2004 in part on the basis of a VCCR violation in his case. However, earlier in 2004, Hung Thanh Le was denied clemency by the same governor in Oklahoma, despite raising a VCCR violation, and was executed.[74]

---

not available even if the treaty creates individual rights"); Green v. Apker, 153 Fed. Appx. 77, 79 (3rd Cir. 2005) (noting that it is unclear whether there are privately enforceable rights or claims under the VCCR). *But see* Standt v. City of New York, 153 F. Supp. 2d 417 (S.D.N.Y. 2001) (finding VCCR is self-executing, creating an individual right that allows an individual to pursue a civil rights claim under § 1983); Osagiede v. United States, 543 F.3d 399, 409-10 (7th Cir. 2008) (finding individual right for claim in a criminal case).

[70] *See, e.g.*, United States v. Lombera-Camorlinga, 206 F.3d 882 (9th Cir. 2000), *cert. denied*, 531 U.S. 991 (2000); United States v. Li, 206 F.3d 56 (1st Cir. 2000), *cert. denied sub nom.* Mao Bing Mu v. United States, 531 U.S. 956 (2000); United States v. Chaparro-Alcantara, 226 F.3d 616 (7th Cir. 2000), *cert. denied*, 531 U.S. 1026 (2000); United States v. Cordoba-Mosquera, 212 F.3d 1194 (11th Cir. 2000), *cert. denied sub nom.* Zuniga v. United States, 531 U.S. 1131 (2001); United States v. Chanthadara, 230 F.3d 1237 (10th Cir. 2000), *cert. denied*, 534 U.S. 992 (2001); United States v. Jimenez-Nava, 243 F.3d 192 (5th Cir. 2001), *cert. denied*, 533 U.S. 962 (2001); State v. Issa, 752 N.E.2d 904 (Ohio, 2001), *cert. denied*, 535 U.S. 974 (2002); United States v. Ortiz, 315 F.3d 873, 886 (8th Cir. 2002), *cert. denied*, 540 U.S. 1073 (2003). *But see* State v. Reyes, 740 A.2d 7 (Del. Super. 1999) (Court granted defendant's motion to suppress statements obtained in violation of the VCCR. Note, however, that in a subsequent unpublished case, the court indicated it was unlikely to follow *Reyes.*)

[71] Sanchez-Llamas v. Oregon, 126 S. Ct. 2669 (2006). For a decision post-*Sanchez-Llamas* that denies suppression as a remedy, *see* Gomez v. Quarterman, 529 F.3d 322, 330 (5th Cir. 2008), *cert. denied*, 555 U.S. 1050 (2008).

[72] *See, e.g.*, United States v. Bin Laden, 126 F. Supp. 2d 290, 296 (S.D.N.Y. 2001) (noting that "dismissal of the Government's death penalty notice is not a remedy that may be imposed by the Court for violations of the Vienna Convention"). *See also* United States v. Li, 206 F.3d 56, 62 (1st Cir. 2000) (concluding that dismissal of an indictment is not warranted for a remedy of the VCCR); United States v. Emuegbunam, 268 F.3d 377, 391 (6th Cir. 2001) *cert. denied*, 535 U.S. 977 (2002) (holding dismissal of the indictment as a remedy is inappropriate "even if Defendant has suffered a violation of his rights under the Vienna Convention and even if he can enforce those rights in federal court"); United States v. Ortiz, 315 F.3d 873, 886 (8th Cir. 2002), *cert. denied*, 540 U.S. 1073 (2003) (holding that even if the VCCR confers individual rights, the VCCR does not provide that the death penalty is excluded if the VCCR is violated).

[73] *See, e.g., United States of America: A Time for Action — Protecting the Consular Rights of Foreign National Facing the Death Penalty, available at* http://www.prisonpolicy.org/scans/amr511062001.pdf (last visited Jan. 28, 2012) (Oklahoma Governor Frank Keating noted that the U.S. Department of State had "asked that I take [the treaty violation] into consideration when determining whether to grant clemency"); *Breard*, 523 U.S. at 378 (noting that Secretary of State sent a letter to Virginia Governor requesting a stay).

[74] Torres v. State, 120 P.3d 1184 (Okla. Crim. App. 2005). *See also* http://www.internationaljusticeproject.org/nationalsTLe.cfm detailing the case of Hung Thanh Le. Hung Thanh Le was denied clemency even though the Oklahoma Pardon and Parole board recommended that Governor Henry commute his sentence.

The VCCR issue is not only a matter for domestic courts. There are also international tribunals that have addressed the issue. The Inter-American Court of Human Rights issued an advisory opinion in 1999 at the request of Mexico and other Central and South American countries.[75] The IACtHR is a regional human rights tribunal created by the American Convention on Human Rights. Decisions from the IACtHR are advisory, and not binding on the United States.[76] However, the U.S. State Department appeared and argued the case before the court. In its opinion, the IACtHR found that a failure to advise a foreign national of consular notification rights under the VCCR was a violation of due process under the ICCPR.[77] The nature of the violation, denying the defendant access to information, was prejudicial and, under such circumstances, the imposition of the death penalty would be arbitrary in violation of the ICCPR.[78]

The International Court of Justice (ICJ) also issued two opinions on the VCCR in the context of death penalty sentences. The ICJ was created by the United Nations, and the United States originally agreed to submit to the jurisdiction of the court for disputes under the VCCR.[79] That agreement to the resolution of application and interpretation conflicts by the ICJ was withdrawn by the United States in reaction to the ICJ decisions in these cases.

In the first VCCR case to be decided on the merits[80] before the ICJ, Germany brought an action against the United States for violations of the VCCR in the capital cases of two German nationals in Arizona. Although both defendants were executed by Arizona before the Court's decision was handed down, the ICJ judgment in *LaGrand Case (Germany v. United States)*[81] made several important determinations. The Court found that there was an individual right under the treaty;[82] that the efforts of the United States to secure compliance by Arizona with

---

[75] Advisory Opinion OC-16/99, Oct. 1, 1999 Inter-Am. Ct. H.R (Ser A) No. 16. The countries bringing the case included Mexico, El Salvador, Dominican Republic, Honduras, Guatemala, Paraguay, and Costa Rica.

[76] The United States has yet to ratify the American Convention on Human Rights, which created the IACtHR. Even of those countries that have ratified the Convention, only Columbia recognizes the IACtHR decisions as binding. Christina M. Cerna, *International Law and the Protection of Human Rights in the Inter-American System*, 19 Hous. J. Int'l L. 731, 752-54 (1997).

[77] Advisory Opinion OC-16/99, Oct. 1, 1999 Inter-Am. Ct. H.R (Ser A) No. 16.

[78] *Id.* The Court noted that depriving a foreign national of his rights under VCCR may constitute "a violation of the right not to be arbitrarily deprived of one's life" and thus in violation of the ICCPR and the American Convention on Human Rights.

[79] In the case of the VCCR, the treaty provides that parties to its Optional Protocol will submit to the ICJ for resolution of disputes. Optional Protocol Concerning the Compulsory settlement of Disputes, art. I (stating that disputes lie within compulsory jurisdiction of ICJ).

[80] There was a case involving the VCCR that preceded Germany's action, but that first case did not proceed to a decision on the merits. The initial case was brought by Paraguay against the United States and raised a VCCR violation regarding a Paraguayan national on death row. When the Paraguayan, Angel Breard, was executed prior to a decision on the merits, Paraguay withdrew its action in the ICJ. Vienna Convention on Consular Relations (Para. v. U.S.), 1998 I.C.J. 248 (Apr. 9).

[81] LaGrand Case (Germany v. U.S.), 2001 I.C.J. 466 (Order of June 27) [hereinafter LaGrand Case].

[82] *Id.* at ¶ 77. "Based on the text of these provisions, the Court concludes that Article 36, paragraph 1, creates individual rights, which, by virtue of Article I of the Optional Protocol, may be invoked in this Court by the national State of the detained person."

the provisional measures ordered by the ICJ to delay the execution were inadequate;[83] that the use of a doctrine, such as procedural default, to defeat judicial consideration of the VCCR issue failed to give "full effect" as required by the treaty;[84] and that the United States had to "allow for the review and reconsideration of the conviction and sentence" in future cases where a VCCR violation occurred.[85]

The ICJ again interpreted the VCCR in a case brought by Mexico against the United States, *Avena and Other Mexican Nationals (Mexico v. U.S.)*.[86] In early 2003, Mexico sought the jurisdiction of the ICJ on behalf of 51 Mexican nationals on death rows in the United States, for violations of the VCCR.[87] Mexico obtained provisional measures that required the United States to "take all measures necessary to ensure that [three of the death row inmates with the greatest likelihood of having execution dates set in the near future] are not executed pending final judgment in these proceedings."[88] Unlike in the *LaGrand* case, this time the defendants were not executed prior to a decision on the merits.

The *Avena* decision reiterated some points from the *LaGrand* decision and also further developed what would satisfy the requirement of a "review and reconsideration." One of the primary issues in the litigation was whether clemency proceedings were an adequate "review and reconsideration" of the conviction and sentence when there is a VCCR violation. The United States argued that clemency proceedings were a sufficient review and reconsideration.[89] Mexico contended that there had to be a remedy at law, which would exclude the nonjudicial, executive clemency process.[90] The ICJ found in favor of Mexico in its judgment. The Court

---

[83] *Id.* at ¶ 115. Another significant finding of the ICJ was that its provisional measures are binding on the parties. *See* discussion of import of binding nature of provisional orders in Howard S. Schiffman, *The LaGrand Decision: The Evolving Legal Landscape of the Vienna Convention on Consular Relations in U.S. Death Penalty Cases*, 42 SANTA CLARA L. REV. 1099, 1116-18 (2002).

[84] LaGrand Case at ¶ 91. Procedural default is a doctrine in federal habeas cases that precludes a hearing on an issue that was not litigated in state court and is now procedurally barred from a hearing under state procedural rules. Many of the death row inmates failed to raise the VCCR issue until they were in federal habeas and were declared to be procedurally defaulted, which resulted in an inability to have the claim heard. *See, e.g.*, Breard v. Greene, 523 U.S. 371 (1998); LaGrand v. Stewart, 133 F.3d 1253, 1261 (9th Cir.), *cert. denied*, 525 U.S. 971 (1998); United States v. Emuegbunam, 268 F.3d 377, 394-94 (6th Cir. 2001), *cert. denied*, 535 U.S. 977 (2002).

[85] LaGrand Case at ¶ 125. The ICJ further provided that compliance by the United States with the review and reconsideration could be by "means of its own choosing."

[86] 2004 I.C.J. 12 (March 31).

[87] Avena and Other Mexican Nationals (Mexico v. U.S.), Application Instituting Proceedings of January 9, 2003 [hereinafter Avena Application], available at http://www.cij-icj. Originally, there were 54 named individuals, but three were granted clemency by Governor Ryan of Illinois.

[88] Avena and Other Mexican Nationals (Mexico v. U.S.), 2003 I.C.J. 96 (February 5) (Order of Provisional Measures).

[89] Verbatim Record ¶ 32, I.C. J. Order in Avena, 2003 I.C.J. 128.

[90] Avena Application, *supra* note 87, at ¶ 281(5)(3). *See* Linda E. Carter, *Avena and Other Mexican Nationals (Mexico v. United States) in the International Court of Justice: Compliance with Provisional Measures and the Meaning of Review and Reconsideration under the Vienna Convention on Consular Relations*, 25 MICH. J. INT'L L. 117 (2003) (arguing that clemency is an inadequate review and reconsideration).

further found that clemency was inadequate to satisfy the review and reconsideration requirement and that a *judicial* hearing was necessary.[91] Clemency was too unregulated and unpredictable a process to be a review and reconsideration of the conviction and sentence.[92] The Court also reconfirmed that the United States would be in violation of the treaty if they failed to provide a hearing that would take into account the effect of the violation. Once again, the Court indicated that the application of a procedural default rule in habeas that precludes a hearing on the VCCR violation was inconsistent with the treaty obligations.[93] The Court did not, however, mandate any particular process for the hearing.[94]

After the ICJ's *Avena* decision, the U.S. Supreme Court decided another case that is significant in the ongoing development of the application of the VCCR in capital cases. In *Sanchez-Llamas v. Oregon* (and consolidated case of *Bustillo v. Johnson*),[95] the Court considered the cases of two foreign nationals in noncapital cases. Although Sanchez-Llamas is a Mexican national, neither he nor Bustillo (a Honduran national) were directly covered by the *Avena* litigation. Assuming, without deciding, that individual defendants could raise VCCR claims, the Supreme Court went on to hold that suppression of evidence was not required as a remedy for a VCCR violation;[96] that the ICJ's decisions deserved "respectful consideration," but were not binding interpretations of the treaty in U.S. courts;[97] and that a state was not required to set aside its rules of procedural default in order to conduct a review and reconsideration.[98] Although recognizing the inconsistency of its decision allowing procedural default to preclude a hearing with the contrary decisions of the ICJ in *LaGrand* and *Avena*, the reasoning of the Supreme Court relied on the nonbinding status of the ICJ decisions and the nature of an adversarial system in which parties, not the court, must raise issues under the rules.[99]

---

[91] Avena and Other Mexican Nationals (Mex. v. U.S.), 2004 I.C.J. 12, ¶¶ 140-41 (Mar. 31).

[92] *Id. at* ¶¶ 139-43 (Mar. 31). *See also* Linda E. Carter, *Lessons from Avena: The Inadequacy of Clemency and Judicial Proceedings for Violations of the Vienna Convention on Consular Relations*, 15 DUKE J. COMP. ¶ INT'L L. 259 (2005) (discussing the problems with relying on clemency as a forum for a hearing on the effect of a VCCR violation).

[93] Avena and Other Mexican Nationals (Mex. v. U.S.), 2004 I.C.J. 12, ¶¶ 133-34 (Mar. 31).

[94] *Id. at* ¶¶ 141-52 (Mar. 31).

[95] Sanchez-Llamas v. Oregon, 548 U.S. 331 (2006).

[96] *Id.* at 347-350.

[97] The Court stated: "Nothing in the structure or purpose of the ICJ suggests that its interpretations were intended to be conclusive on our courts. The ICJ's decisions have 'no binding force except between the parties and in respect of that particular case.' Any interpretation of law the ICJ renders in the course of resolving particular disputes is thus not binding precedent even as to the ICJ itself; there is accordingly little reason to think that such interpretations were intended to be controlling on our court." *Id.* at 353-355 (footnotes and citations omitted). The Court went on to state: "*LaGrand* and *Avena* are therefore entitled only to the 'respectful consideration' due an interpretation of an international agreement by an international court." *Id.* at 355. However, in dissent, Justice Breyer was critical of the majority's approach to "respectful consideration." Breyer stated that " 'respectful consideration' reflects the understanding that uniformity is an important goal of treaty interpretation." *Id.* at 382-383.

[98] *Id.* at 356-360.

[99] The Court noted: "Procedural default rules generally take on greater importance in an adversary

After *Sanchez-Llamas*, yet another VCCR case went to the U.S. Supreme Court. This time, unlike in *Sanchez-Llamas*, the petitioner was a Mexican national who was directly covered by the *Avena* decision. In *Medellin v. Dretke*,[100] a case involving one of the Mexican nationals who was named in the ICJ litigation, a key issue was the effect of the ICJ decision in U.S. courts. The United States Justice Department was an *amicus curiae* in the case. In a surprise move in their brief before the Court, the Justice Department revealed a memorandum from President Bush on compliance with the ICJ decision. The memorandum was addressed to the Attorney General and indicated that President Bush had decided to comply with the ICJ decision as a matter of comity through hearings in state courts in the cases of the 51 Mexican nationals from the *Avena* litigation.[101] As a result of this development, Medellin's attorneys filed a new state habeas petition in Texas state court and the U.S. Supreme Court dismissed *certiorari* as improvidently granted.

The Texas courts refused to hold a hearing on the VCCR violation. In *Ex Parte Medellin*,[102] the Texas Court of Criminal Appeals held that President Bush's memorandum exceeded his constitutional authority to bind the states; that the decisions of the ICJ were not binding on the Texas court; and that Medellin could not surmount the procedural default necessary to obtain a state habeas hearing.[103]

The *Medellin* case was back before the Supreme Court in its 2007-2008 term. The issues before the Supreme Court were whether the state courts had to give effect to the *Avena* judgment in Medellin's case and whether the President acted within his constitutional and statutory authority in deciding that the states would give effect to the ICJ judgment.[104] In its opinion, the Court rejected the arguments

---

system such as ours than in the sort of magistrate-directed, inquisitorial legal system characteristic of many of the other countries that are signatories to the Vienna Convention. . . . In an inquisitorial system, the failure to raise a legal error can in part be attributed to the magistrate, and thus to the state itself. In our system, however, the responsibility for failing to raise an issue generally rests with the parties themselves." *Id.* at 357. In dissent, Justice Breyer disagreed with the Court's holding, even in an adversary system. He noted that in the case of a *state* procedural rule, a treaty would have primacy under the Supremacy Clause. He also questioned whether the holding from *Breard* that *federal* habeas default rules have primacy over the treaty is still valid after the ICJ's decisions in *Avena* and *LaGrand* that were decided after *Breard. Id.* at 388-390. Breyer also noted that *Breard* was a per curiam decision reached in a highly compressed timetable due to Breard's impending execution. He would have found that state procedural default rules must give way if there has been a failure of the state or federal authorities to provide notification of the VCCR rights and where the failure to raise the claim is due to the underlying violation by those authorities, and there is no other effective way (such as ineffective assistance of counsel) to raise the VCCR claim. *Id.*

[100] 544 U.S. 660 (2005) (writ dismissed as improvidently granted).

[101] "I have determined, pursuant to the authority vested in me as President by the Constitution and the laws of the United States of America, that the United States will discharge its international obligations under the decision of the International Court of Justice in the Case Concerning Avena and Other Mexican Nationals (Mexico v. United States of America) (Avena), 2004 ICJ 128 (Mar. 31), by having State courts give effect to the decision in accordance with general principles of comity in cases filed by the 51 Mexican nationals addressed in that decision."

George W. Bush, Memorandum for the Attorney General (Feb. 28, 2005), App. 2 to Brief for United States as Amicus Curiae 9a.

[102] Ex parte Medellin, 223 S.W.3d 315 (Tex. Crim. App. 2006).

[103] *Id.*

[104] Medellin v. Texas, 552 U.S. 491 (2008).

that either the ICJ's decision or the President's action were binding on the state of Texas. The Court first found that, although the VCCR is a self-executing treaty, neither the Optional Protocol nor the U.N. Charter is a self-executing treaty. The Court viewed the Optional Protocol, through which the ICJ had jurisdiction, and the U.N. Charter, with which the U.S. as a party to the U.N. Charter "undertakes to comply" with decisions of the ICJ, as the controlling treaties. As a result, the Court held that the decision of the ICJ is not "binding federal law."[105] The Court additionally held that President Bush's memorandum was outside the President's authority to bind the states; instead, such authority falls to Congress as the legislative branch.[106] The case has proved to be controversial. Not only did three justices dissent,[107] but scholars have also criticized the majority's analysis. The major thrust of the criticism is that the majority's approach, which in their view potentially eviscerates the effect of non-self-executing treaties, is inconsistent with the U.S. Constitution's Supremacy Clause phrase that treaties are the "law of the land."[108]

Despite the controversy over the *Medellin* decision, as would be expected, lower courts are following *Medellin* and rejecting claims that raise the ICJ decision. For example, in *Leal Garcia v. Quarterman*,[109] the Fifth Circuit Court of Appeals dismissed the petitioner's habeas claim based on the *Avena* decision on the grounds that *Medellin* foreclosed the claim. According to the court, pursuant to *Medellin*, neither the ICJ decision nor President Bush's memorandum compelled a hearing.[110]

---

[105] *Id.* at 522-523.

[106] *Id.* at 523-532.

[107] *Id.* at 538-567 (dissenting opinion of Justice Breyer, joined by Justices Souter and Ginsburg).

[108] *See* Vazquez, *supra* note 22 at 1613-1624 (criticizing Court's failure to distinguish among types of non-self-executing treaties as creating an inconsistency with Supremacy Clause).

[109] 573 F.3d 214 (5th Cir. 2009), Leal Garcia subsequently moved for a stay of his execution and a motion to reopen his judgment, raising pending legislation in Congress that would grant hearings on VCCR claims. Relief was denied in Garcia v. Thaler, 793 F. Supp. 2d 894 (W.D. Tex. 2011) and both a stay and a certificate of appealability were denied in Garcia v. Thaler, 440 Fed. Appx. 232 (5th Cir. 2011). The U.S. Supreme Court also denied a stay of execution and a petition for writ of habeas corpus. Garcia v. Texas, 131 S.Ct. 2866 (2011).

[110] *Id.* at 224. Prior to *Sanchez-Llamas* and *Avena*, lower courts varied in their assessment of the effect of the ICJ decisions in U.S. courts. For example, a federal district court in Illinois recognized the ICJ's decision as a binding interpretation of the treaty. U.S. *ex rel* Madej v. Schomig, 223 F. Supp. 2d 968 (N.D. Ill. 2002) (acknowledging the binding effect, but deciding case on other grounds). On the other hand, a Massachusetts court referred to the effect of the decision as "unclear." Com. v. Diemer, 785 N.E.2d 1237 (Mass. App. Ct. 2003) *cert. denied* by Diemer v. Massachusetts, 124 S. Ct. 1144 (2004). *See also* Bell v. Com., 563 S.E.2d 695 (Va. 2002), *cert. denied*, 537 U.S. 1123 (2003) (discussing *LaGrand* decision, but not deciding effect of decision; finding no violation in notification delay of 36 hours and distinguishing *LaGrand* as not deciding individual rights in domestic courts and not mandating a suppression remedy). Other courts generally treated decisions of the ICJ as at least a persuasive, if not binding, interpretation of a treaty. *See* David M. Reilly and Sarita Ordonez, *Effect of the Jurisprudence of the International Court of Justice on National Courts*, 28 N.Y.U.J. INT'L L. & POL. 435, 454-455 (1995-1996) (discussing the various ways domestic courts could treat ICJ decisions and suggesting that most often courts treat ICJ decisions as "persuasive authority on questions of international law"). *See also* Roger P. Alford, *Federal Courts, International Tribunals, and the Continuum of Deference*, 43 VA. J. INT'L L. 675 (2003) (describing a continuum of effect given to decisions from international tribunals from "full faith and credit" to a "no deference" model). One effect commonly advocated is what Professor

While judicial action regarding VCCR violations and the effect of the ICJ decisions may be waning, Congress appears to be stepping into the void. In 2011, a bill was introduced in the Senate called the "Consular Notification Compliance Act of 2011."[111] The bill provides for a hearing in federal court for violations of the VCCR arising in capital cases. Subject to various procedural restrictions, relief can be granted if the violation is proved and actual prejudice is shown. The bill is an attempt to comply with the *Avena* decision and to act on the effect of the *Medellin* decision, which repeatedly indicated that implementation of the treaty through U.S. courts was a legislative matter. While future passage of the bill would provide capital defendants with a hearing in some cases, the Supreme Court, in a *per curiam* decision, denied a stay of execution to a defendant who raised the proposed legislation as a basis to stay his execution while the legislation is under consideration.[112] At the time this book was going to press, the bill was pending in Judiciary Committee.[113]

§ 23.05 RELEVANCE OF FOREIGN LAW

Another issue that is related to the use of treaties and to the interpretation of U.S. constitutional provisions is the use of foreign law and decisions. For example, courts around the world have faced issues of "death row phenomenon," similar to the facts of our opening hypothetical. Sometimes the issue arises in the context of extradition proceedings. Extradition is discussed *infra* in Chapter 26. The death row phenomenon issue also arises in direct challenges to an execution in a foreign country.

The Supreme Court of Uganda and the Caribbean Court of Justice are two of the foreign courts that have rendered decisions related to the death row phenomenon in recent years. In 2009, the Ugandan Supreme Court decided the case of *Attorney General v. S. Kigula & 417 Others*,[114] holding that a 3-year delay on death row was unconstitutional. In 2006, the Caribbean Court of Justice similarly reaffirmed earlier Privy Council cases that holding prisoners for too long under a death sentence is inhumane treatment.[115]

Are these decisions relevant in litigation in U.S. courts? The decisions from the foreign courts would not be binding in a U.S. court, just as a decision from the California Supreme Court is not binding on the Florida Supreme Court. Neverthe-

---

Alford called the "Paquete Habana" model of the international decision as "persuasive authority."

[111] http://www.govtrack.us/congress/billtext.xpd?bill=s112-1194 (last visited January 13, 2012).

[112] Garcia v. Texas, 131 S. Ct. 2866, 2867 (2011) (suggesting that it is doubtful that it is ever appropriate to stay a lower court judgment in light of proposed legislation because it is the Court's task "to rule on what the law is, not what it might eventually be.").

[113] http://www.govtrack.us/congress/bill.xpd?bill=s112-1194 (last visited January 13, 2012).

[114] *Available online at* http://www.ulii.org/ug/cases/UGSC/2009/6.html (last visited January 21, 2012) [hereinafter *Kigula*].

[115] *Id.* at 138. The Court affirmed the principle from *Pratt v. Attorney General for Jamaica*, 98 I.L.R. 335 (P.C. 1993), that more than 5 years on death row is likely to be inhumane, but also noted that the time in which a petition is pending before an international human rights body, such as the Inter-American Human Rights Commission, should not be part of the 5-year calculation, assuming that the time before the Commission is not attributable to delays occasioned by the Government.

less, some justices and commentators maintain that decisions from foreign courts on similar issues to those under consideration are relevant in the same way that decisions from California provide helpful information to the decisional process in Florida or that scholarly articles inform the reasoning of a court.[116] On the other hand, others counter that, at least in interpreting the U.S. Constitution, foreign law and decisions are irrelevant.[117]

Death row phenomenon issues raise both U.S. constitutional claims as well as treaty claims. The argument for relevance of foreign decisions is similar, but not identical with the two claims. The meaning of "cruel and unusual punishment"

---

[116] *See, e.g.*, Ronald A. Brand, *Judicial Review And United States Supreme Court Citations To Foreign And International Law*, 45 DUQLR 423, 430-31 (2007) (pointing out that the Court has used references to foreign law only for a limited purpose of support, and has not viewed it as binding or persuasive authority; as support, foreign law is appropriately used in the same way that the Court uses any sources); Harold Hongju Koh, *International Law as Part of Our Law*, 98 AM. J. INT'L L. 43 (2004) (tracing the history and relevance of using foreign and international law in constitutional cases); Ganesh Sitaraman, *The Use and Abuse of Foreign Law in Constitutional Interpretation*, 32 Harv. J.L. & Pub. Pol'y 653 (2009) (evaluating the uses of foreign law and finding that most uses are not problematic); Holly Arnould, *Lawrence v. Texas and Roper v. Simmons: Enriching Constitutional Interpretation with International Law*, 22 ST. JOHN'S J. LEGAL COMMENT 685 (2008) (arguing that the Court's use of international law as persuasive authority in determining "evolving standards of decency" is appropriate). *See also* Roper v. Simmons, 543 U.S. 551, 575-76 (2005). Justice Kennedy noted that: "Our determination that the death penalty is disproportionate punishment for offenders under 18 finds confirmation in the stark reality that the United States is the only country in the world that continues to give official sanction to the juvenile death penalty. This reality does not become controlling, for the task of interpreting the Eighth Amendment remains our responsibility. Yet at least from the time of the Court's decision in *Trop*, the Court has referred to the laws of other countries and to international authorities as instructive for its interpretation of the Eighth Amendment's prohibition of "cruel and unusual punishments." *See also Atkins*, 536 U.S. at 317, n. 21, where the Court recognized that "within the world community, the imposition of the death penalty for crimes committed by mentally retarded offenders is overwhelmingly disapproved."

[117] *See, e.g.*, John Yoo, *The Supreme Court's Use of Foreign Precedents in Constitutional Cases*, 26 HAW. L. REV. 385 (2004) (noting that use of foreign decisions to support a decision without affecting the outcome (ornamental use) is not a concern; commenting, however, that deference to foreign decisions conflicts with the American constitutional structure through which the power is delegated from the American people to the Constitution and from the Constitution to the courts; as such, the relevant reference group for interpreting constitutional norms is the American people; and arguing that the Court's emphasis on European views is misplaced where they reflect different documents and political systems); Roger P. Alford, *Misusing International Sources to Interpret the Constitution*, 98 AM. J. INT'L L. 57 (2004) (arguing that foreign law is not appropriate for constitutional interpretation in the context of constitutional provisions that rely on national community standards and criticizing the selective use of foreign law); Kenneth W. Starr, *The Court of Pragmatism and Internationalization: A Response to Professors Chemerinsky and Amann*, 94 GEO. L.J. 1565 (2006) (discussing the misuse of international and foreign sources); Zachary Larsen, *Discounting Foreign Imports: Foreign Authority in Constitutional Interpretation & the Curb of Popular Sovereignty*, 45 WILLAMETTE L. REV. 767 (2009) (arguing that the use of international law in construing constitutional provisions should be rejected). *See also Atkins*, 536 U.S. at 325 (Rehnquist, C.J., dissenting): "While it is true that some of our prior opinions have looked to 'the climate of international opinion,' Coker, 433 U.S. at 596, n. 10, to reinforce a conclusion regarding evolving standards of decency, see Thompson v. Oklahoma, 487 U.S. 815, 830, 108 S. Ct. 2687, 101 L. Ed. 2d 702 (1988) (plurality opinion); *Enmund*, 458 U.S. at 796-797, n. 22 (1982); Trop v. Dulles, 356 U.S. 86, 102-103, 78 S. Ct. 590, 2 L. Ed. 2d 630 (1958) (plurality opinion); we have since explicitly rejected the idea that the sentencing practices of other countries could 'serve to establish the first Eighth Amendment prerequisite, that [a] practice is accepted among our people.' Stanford v. Kentucky, 492 U.S. 361, n. 1 (1989) (emphasizing that "American conceptions of decency are dispositive").

under the U.S. Constitution relies on an analysis of "evolving standards of decency" and proportionality.[118] This is where the most heated debate occurs over the relevance of foreign law. For example, the majority opinions in the U.S. Supreme Court cases in *Atkins* and in *Roper* referred to foreign law as additional support for holding that the execution of mentally retarded individuals and of juveniles was unconstitutional.[119] Further, the dissenting opinions to denials of *certiorari* in death row phenomenon cases have also referred to foreign decisions.[120] Even these peripheral references to foreign law, however, were disputed by other justices in the cases.[121]

While not without controversy, there would seem to be some relevance to the foreign law in reaching a decision on the interpretation of "cruel and unusual punishment." If the wording of another country's constitution is similar, the interpretation of that language might be informative, even if not binding. For example, the language at issue in the Ugandan Constitution was a prohibition of "torture or cruel, inhuman or degrading treatment or punishment,"[122] which is similar, although not identical to, the U.S. constitutional language and to other national constitutions. Looking to similar constitutions, the Constitutional Court of Uganda, whose decision was affirmed by the Supreme Court of Uganda, referred to decisions of courts from Zimbabwe and the Privy Council (regarding a death sentence in Jamaica) in considering the constitutionality of executions after a long

---

[118] *See supra* § 4.04[C].

[119] Atkins v. Virginia, 536 U.S. 304, n. 21 (2002) (commenting that, ". . . within the world community, the imposition of the death penalty for crimes committed by mentally retarded offenders is overwhelmingly disapproved."); Roper v. Simmons, 543 U.S. 551, 576 (2005) (noting that the United States was the only country to officially sanction the death penalty for those who commit crimes while under the age of 18). More recently, in Graham v. Florida, 130 S.Ct. 2011, 2033-2034 (2010), the Court again referred to foreign and international law to confirm its interpretation of the 8th Amendment as prohibiting life without parole for a juvenile offender on a non-homicide case. The Court noted that the United States was the only country that presently imposed life without parole on juvenile non-homicide offenders and noted that the international treaty on the Right of the Child, which also prohibits life without parole for juvenile offenders, was signed by all countries except the United States and Somalia.

[120] *See* Knight v. Florida, 528 U.S. 990 (1999) (Breyer, J., dissenting) (acknowledging that foreign authority does not bind the United States, but that it does show trends such as India's practice of taking into account delay when deciding on whether to impose a death sentence.); Elledge v. Fla., 525 U.S. 944 (1998) (Breyer, J., dissenting) (noting that "British jurists have suggested that the Bill of Rights of 1689, a document relevant to the interpretation of our own Constitution, may forbid, as cruel and unusual, significantly lesser delays."); Lackey v. Texas, 514 U.S. 1045 (1995) (Stevens, J., respecting denial of certiorari) (noting both British and Privy Council decisions on death row phenomenon.). *See also* discussion in Section 19.02(B), *supra*.

[121] *See, e.g.*, Foster v. Florida, 537 U.S. 990, 991 (2002) (Thomas, J., concurring in denial of *certiorari*): "While Congress, as a legislature, may wish to consider the actions of other nations on any issue it likes, this Court's Eighth Amendment jurisprudence should not impose foreign moods, fads, or fashions on Americans."

[122] *See Kigula, available online at* http://www.ulii.org/ug/cases/UGSC/2009/6.html. The Constitution of Uganda art. 24. The *Kigula* Court also considered whether the death penalty itself was unconstitutional. The Court noted that Uganda has a *qualified* right to life in its Constitution, as opposed to South Africa which has an *unqualified* right to life. With a qualified right to life, the Court concluded that the death penalty itself is constitutional under the Ugandan Constitution. The Court found, however, that a mandatory death sentence was unconstitutional under the Uganda Constitution as a denial of a fair trial.

delay on death row.[123] Ultimately, the Supreme Court of Uganda found that the calculation of the period should begin from the point at which a conviction and sentence is affirmed by the highest appellate court and that longer than 3 years was unconstitutional.[124] Similar to the Ugandan Constitutional Court's use of the decision from Zimbabwe and the Privy Council, one can argue that the decision of the Ugandan Court and other foreign decisions on the death row phenomenon at least form part of the body of relevant information available to a court in the U.S. that must interpret the meaning of "cruel and unusual punishment." The foreign decisions are not binding, but arguably useful in the way that decisions of California are relevant in Florida and that law review articles are relevant.

Moreover, if the issue under consideration is the interpretation of a treaty provision, the foreign law may be of greater significance if the foreign court was interpreting the identical treaty provision, not just similarly-worded constitutional language. The ICCPR and Convention Against Torture, for example, are treaties that were signed by many countries. While a national constitution may be viewed as unique to the country within which it was adopted, multilateral treaties pertain to every country that is a signatory. Because of the nature of a treaty, there is likely to be a stronger argument that foreign law interpreting a treaty is relevant.

Thus, D in our opening hypothetical might use the decisions of the Ugandan Court and the Caribbean Court of Justice to support her argument that the 20-year period that she has spent on death row should be viewed as cruel and unusual punishment under the U.S. Constitution. Whether or not the court accepted her argument that the delay violates the U.S. Constitution, she could also contend that the delay is in violation of the ICCPR and Convention Against Torture, and again use the foreign decisions as support for her argument that the delay is violative of the treaties. Recall, though, the difficulties in prevailing upon treaty arguments in U.S. courts. To make the argument that her rights under the treaties are violated by the delay, D would have to assert that the declaration that the treaties are not self-executing does not bar raising the claim defensively. Moreover, if the court finds that the Eighth Amendment is not violated, then D must claim that the reservation that limits the treaty provisions to the meaning of the Eighth Amendment is invalid as contrary to the "object and purpose" of the treaties. The state would likely contend that the treaties cannot be raised because of the non-self-executing status, and that the reservations are valid that limit the meaning of the treaties to the parameters of the U.S. Constitution. The state might also argue that, in interpreting the U.S. Constitution, the Ugandan and Caribbean Court decisions should not be considered relevant. As indicated in the cases cited in this chapter, the applicability of the treaties and their reservations as well as the propriety of using foreign law are far from being resolved in court decisions to date. The arguments posed by D and the state are indicative of the developing nature of treaty rights and the use of foreign law, a debate that is likely to continue in the future.

---

[123] *Available at* http://www.ulii.org/ug/cases/UGCC/2005/8.html. In affirming the Constitutional Court's decision, the Supreme Court of Uganda also cited to the decision from Zimbabwe, which had found that a delay of enforcing a death sentence beyond two years was unconstitutional. *Kigula*, at 48.

[124] *See Kigula* at 54.

Chapter 24

THE FEDERAL DEATH PENALTY

§ 24.01 OVERVIEW[1]

Capital punishment has always been part of federal criminal law, and more than forty federal crimes now carry a possible death penalty. However, the federal death penalty has been imposed sparingly in the modern era. The vast majority of capital crimes have always been prosecuted in the state courts.[2] After the decision in *Furman v. Georgia*,[3] Congress also did not act quickly to create new death-sentencing procedures. In 1988, the federal government finally promulgated death-sentencing procedures for certain drug-related murders, and, in 1994, it created those procedures for federal capital crimes generally. Due largely to this delay, there were no *post-Furman* executions for federal crimes until 2002, when Timothy McVeigh was executed for the murders associated with the bombing of the federal building in Oklahoma City. Two more federal prisoners have been executed since McVeigh, and as of October, 2011, there were 58 federal prisoners on death row.[4]

Although the Supreme Court in 1999 upheld federal death-sentencing procedures promulgated after *Furman*,[5] the pursuit of death sentences by federal prosecutors has continued to cause some controversy. The Department of Justice has imposed procedures to help ensure even-handed decisions about when to pursue the federal death penalty. Despite these efforts, questions have arisen about racial and geographic disparities. Pursuit of the federal death penalty in jurisdictions that do not provide for the death penalty also has created political tensions and raised constitutional questions. Nonetheless, one knowledgeable commentator has observed that "unless Congress repeals the statutory structure . . . the federal death penalty is here to stay."[6]

---

[1] For an excellent discussion of the history and administration of the federal death penalty, *see* Rory K. Little, *The Federal Death Penalty: History and Some Thoughts About the Department of Justice's Role*, 26 Fordham Urb. L. J. 347 (1999).

[2] Between 1930 and 2009, the federal government executed only 36 defendants while state governments executed more than 5,000 defendants. *See* U.S. Department of Justice, *Capital Punishment, 2009 — Statistical Tables* 18, tbl. 17 (Dec. 2010), *available at* http://www.deathpenaltyinfo.org/article.php?scid=29&did=193, http://bjs.ojp.usdoj.gov/index.cfm?ty=pbdetail&iid=2215.

[3] 408 U.S. 238 (1972).

[4] *See* Death Penalty Info. Ctr., Federal Death Row Prisoners, *available at* http://www.deathpenaltyinfo.org/federal-death-row-prisoners#list (last updated Oct. 21, 2011).

[5] *See, e.g.,* Jones v. United States, 527 U.S. 373, 375-76 (1999).

[6] Rory K. Little, *The Future of the Federal Death Penalty*, 26 Ohio N. U. L. Rev. 529, 5 34 (2000).

§ 24.02 HISTORICAL BACKGROUND

[A] From The First Congress Through Furman

The crime bill passed by the first Congress in 1790 provided for a death penalty for various offenses.[7] The death penalty applied to treason, murder, piracy[8] and also some less serious crimes, such as counterfeiting "any certificate, indent, or other public security of the United States."[9] As was customary at the time, the death penalty was mandatory upon conviction. Because capital punishment played an accepted role in the criminal law in the late 18th century, these provisions generated only minor controversy.[10]

In 1829, however, a report prepared by the President at the behest of the Congress, raised questions about society's acceptance of the mandatory federal death penalty.[11] Over a period of 36 years, 118 federal death sentences had been imposed after 138 federal capital trials.[12] However, only 42 federal capital offenders had been executed. Of the remaining group of 76 convicts, 64 had been pardoned, one committed suicide, three died, two escaped and six were unaccounted for.[13] The overwhelming proportion of pardons suggested that the mandatory death penalty was frequently viewed as unduly harsh.

The federal death penalty remained applicable to various crimes and in most cases mandatory throughout most of the nineteenth century, but a movement began in the states during the early to middle part of the century to narrow the application of the sanction and to make it discretionary. Many states reduced the number of crimes to which the death penalty applied, and many also passed legislation dividing murder into degrees and making the mandatory death penalty applicable only to murder in the first degree.[14] However, even this reform proved inadequate to solve the problem of juries failing to convict seemingly guilty defendants of the mandatory capital offense. Racist sentiments favoring white capital defendants often played a role in the tendency of juries to conclude in some

---

[7] See 1 Stat. 112-19.

[8] See id. at 112 (treason); id. at 113 ("willful murder" on federal lands); id. at 113-14 (piracy).

[9] See id. at 115.

[10] Two aspects of the death penalty provisions, however, produced some disagreement. One section authorized the court after a conviction for murder to direct that the body of an offender "be delivered to a surgeon for dissection." Id. at 113. Some members of Congress argued that this mandate was inappropriate, but it was ultimately retained. Some members also argued unsuccessfully against the imposition of the death penalty for the counterfeiting offenses on grounds of disproportionality. Although the Supreme Court later interpreted the Eighth Amendment to require proportionality in the use of the death penalty, the argument at the time was not based on the Constitution. See generally DAVID P. CURRIE, THE CONSTITUTION IN CONGRESS: THE FEDERALIST PERIOD 1789-1801, 95-96 (1997). The Eighth Amendment was not even ratified by a sufficient number of states until 1791. See Little, supra note 1, at 361.

[11] See H.R. EXEC. No. 20-146 (1829), reprinted in H.R. REP. No. 53-545, app. at 6, table 1.

[12] See id.

[13] See id.

[14] See Woodson v. North Carolina, 428 U.S. 280, 289-90 (1976) (joint opinion of Stewart, J., White, J., and Stevens, J.).

cases that the death penalty would be unduly harsh.[15] "[A]lmost certainly to allow juries to take race into account,"[16] a trend began with Tennessee in 1838, followed by Alabama in 1841 and Louisiana in 1846, of making the death penalty discretionary even for first-degree murder.[17] By the beginning of the 20th century, 23 states had made the death penalty discretionary in all cases.[18]

In the late 1890s, reform of the federal death penalty reflected this movement toward narrowing the number of capital offenses and making the death penalty discretionary.[19] Representative Newton Curtis, from New York, introduced a bill in 1892, supported by a report published two years later, seeking the total abolition of the federal death penalty.[20] Although total abolition was not achieved, Curtis's efforts spurred passage of a law in 1897 that eliminated the death penalty for many federal offenses and that rendered capital punishment discretionary for those that were not already discretionary.[21]

Two years later, in *Winston v. United States*,[22] which involved three separate murder cases from the District of Columbia, the Supreme Court implicitly approved of the 1897 law.[23] The Court also clarified that the statute was intended to give capital juries discretion to impose a prison sentence whether or not there were "palliating or mitigating circumstances."[24] Because the trial judges in each of the cases had instructed the juries that they were required to reach a death verdict absent mitigation, the Supreme Court reversed the death sentences.[25]

From 1897 until the *Furman* decision in 1972, Congress re-expanded the federal death penalty to cover more federal crimes but continued to provide for absolute discretion in the capital sentencing jury. Congress provided for a discretionary death penalty for violent kidnapping, train-wrecking involving the death of passengers, providing narcotics to a minor, certain espionage crimes related to the Atomic Energy Act, airplane bombing and hijackings and, finally, killings with explosives.[26] As is evident from this list, Congress continued to believe that the death penalty was potentially appropriate for a number of crimes that did not result in death. However, the conferral of unfettered sentencing discretion allowed the capital jury to decide in each case whether the appropriate punishment was death.

---

[15] *See* Stuart Banner, *Traces of Slavery: Race and the Death Penalty in Historical Perspective*, in FROM LYNCH MOBS TO THE KILLING STATE: RACE AND THE DEATH PENALTY IN AMERICA 96, 100 (2006).

[16] *Id.*

[17] *See id.* at 291.

[18] *See id.*

[19] *See* Little, *supra* note 1, No. 99-282, at 2-3 (1986).; at 367.

[20] *See id.*

[21] *See id.*

[22] 172 U.S. 303 (1899).

[23] *See id.* at 312-13.

[24] *Id.* at 313.

[25] *See id.* at 313-14.

[26] *See* Little, *supra* note 1, at 371.

There were relatively few federal executions in the decades leading up to *Furman*. From 1927 to 1963, only 34 occurred, an average of less than one per year.[27] Six of these were for sabotage by a group of German men during World War II, and two others were for espionage by Ethel and Julius Rosenberg.[28] After the hanging of Victor Feguer in 1963 for kidnaping, there were no further federal executions before the Supreme Court struck down the discretionary death penalty in *Furman*, a decision that appeared to invalidate existing federal death-penalty procedures.

[B] The Post-*Furman* Era Through 1988

Between *Furman* and 1988, the federal death penalty was moribund because the federal government generally failed to enact new death-penalty procedures. Initially, Congress was stymied, as were many state legislatures, by a failure to discern how the Supreme Court would later interpret the *Furman* mandate. In 1974, the federal government passed a death-penalty provision, applicable only to those convicted of the capital crime of aircraft piracy, that provided for a separate sentencing hearing at which jurors could consider aggravating and mitigating circumstances.[29] However, the statute also made the death penalty mandatory if the jury found at least one aggravating factor but no mitigating factors. Only two years later, the Supreme Court concluded in *Woodson v. North Carolina*[30] and *Roberts v. Louisiana*[31] that mandatory death penalties violated the Eighth Amendment. Those decisions raised serious questions about the constitutionality of the anti-hijacking statute, at least as it would apply in some cases. Although the Department of Justice never conceded a problem, it also apparently never pursued a death sentence under the 1974 statute before Congress repealed it upon passing new death-penalty procedures in 1994.[32]

Various other bills aimed at providing a general sentencing procedure for federal capital crimes also appeared but failed between 1972 and 1988. The Senate passed such legislation only a few months after *Furman*, but it did not survive in the House,[33] which, instead, passed the more narrowly applicable anti-hijacking statute. Bills were introduced in the following Congress, but action was postponed to await the Supreme Court rulings in the 1976 cases.[34] After 1976, death-penalty bills were regularly introduced, but no legislation ultimately passed.[35] Professor Rory Little has noted that this period of "political deadlock seems unsurprising in

---

[27] *See* DEATH PENALTY INFO. CTR., FEDERAL EXECUTIONS 1927-2003, *available at* http://www.deathpenaltyinfo.org/federal-executions-1927-2003 (last updated Oct. 21, 2011).

[28] *See id.*

[29] *See* Pub. L. 93-366 (93d Cong. 2d Sess.), 88 Stat. 409, 411-13, *originally codified at* 49 U.S.C. App. § 1472(I), 1473(c) (1983 ed.), *repealed by* Pub. L. 103-322, sec. 60003(b), 108 Stat. 1970 (1994).

[30] 428 U.S. 280 (1976).

[31] 428 U.S. 325 (1976).

[32] *See* Little, *supra* note 1, at 373-76 & n. 149.

[33] *See* S. REP. No. 99-282, at 2-3 (1986); 120 CONG. REC. 6757 (daily ed. March 13, 1974).

[34] *See id.* at 3.

[35] *See id.*

a federalist system governed by congressional delegations from states that fundamentally disagree about the death penalty."[36] A major part of the underlying explanation was that the Supreme Court regularly issued opinions during this period that "adjusted the requirements for imposing the death penalty" and that "serious concerns" continued to be raised about racial and economic inequality in the use of the penalty.[37] Not until 1987, when the Court decided *McCleskey v. Kemp*,[38] did the broad constitutional challenge to post-*Furman* capital sentencing, based on allegations of arbitrariness and racial discrimination, finally fail.

§ 24.03   MODERN FEDERAL DEATH PENALTY PROCEDURES

[A]   The 1988 Drug Kingpin Act

One year after *McCleskey*, Congress passed the first post-*Furman* sentencing procedure under which death sentences have been imposed.[39] The law, known as the Drug Kingpin Act ["DKA"], provided capital sentencing procedures only for those who intentionally kill or cause an intentional killing in connection with a complicated, narcotics-related offense known as a "Continuing Criminal Enterprise."[40] Because of the narrow application of the DKA, the government has obtained very few death penalties under this provision. The first was imposed on David Ronald Chandler in 1991, but President Clinton ultimately commuted his sentence to life imprisonment on January 20, 2001.[41]

Three more defendants, all members of a gang in Richmond, Virginia, were sentenced to death under the provision in 1993 for their involvement in a series of drug-related murders.[42] However, their executions scheduled for May, 2006, were stayed based on a claim that the chemicals used to carry out federal executions pose an unacceptable risk of causing undue pain, violating the Eighth Amendment.[43]

Although the DKA provisions have not produced many death sentences, they were important because they "provided a template for future death penalty legislation."[44] The provisions mandate a bifurcated sentencing hearing after a

---

[36] Little, *supra* note 1, at 378.

[37] *Id.*

[38] 481 U.S. 279 (1987).

[39] *See* Continuing Criminal Enterprise, Pub. L. No. 100-690, § 7001a, 102 Stat. 4181, 4387 (codified at 21 U.S.C. § 848(e)-(r) (1988)).

[40] *See* 21 U.S.C. § 848(c) (1988).

[41] *See* Commutations, Remissions, and Reprieves Granted By President Clinton, *available at* http://www.justice.gov/pardon/clinton_comm.htm (last visited Dec. 22, 2011).

[42] *See* Death Penalty Info. Ctr., Federal Death Row Prisoners, *available at* http://www.deathpenaltyinfo.org/federal-death-row-prisoners#list (last updated Oct. 21, 2011).

[43] *See* Tom Campbell, *Execution dates for members of Richmond gang put on hold*, Richmond Times Dispatch B-02 (March 9, 2006).

[44] Little, *supra* note 1, at 381.

finding of conviction.[45] They also provide for narrowing of the death-eligible group by requiring the jury to unanimously identify at least one aggravating circumstance before further considering a death sentence.[46] In addition, they require the jury to consider the presence of mitigating factors and allow any juror to consider such factors even if not found by other jurors.[47] Regardless of the balance of aggravating against mitigating factors, the statute also does not direct that the jury must impose a death sentence.[48]

[B] The 1994 Federal Death Penalty Act

In September, 1994, Congress approved and President Bill Clinton signed a new Federal Death Penalty Act,[49] ["FDPA"] which provided death sentencing procedures for a sweeping array of previously existing and new capital crimes. One provision made the new procedures applicable, "if death results," to fifteen federal statutes that previously contained death-penalty provisions that were probably unconstitutional under *Furman*.[50] Other sections made the new death-penalty procedures applicable to seventeen existing federal statutes that had not previously carried a death penalty. Still other sections created ten new capital crimes.

In a few cases, the FDPA purported to make the death penalty applicable to non-homicide crimes. One provision created capital crimes for certain major drug dealers and for certain other drug kingpins who unsuccessfully attempt to kill.[51] Another provision authorized the death penalty for non-homicidal espionage where the information "directly concerned" nuclear weapons, military spacecraft or satellites, or certain other national security information.[52] Another provision authorized the death penalty for non-homicidal treason.[53]

The constitutionality of the death penalty for these non-homicidal offenses is uncertain. The Supreme Court has not approved capital punishment in the absence of a human death since 1977, when it proscribed the death penalty for the crimes of

---

[45] *See* 21 U.S.C. § 848(i)(1) (1988).

[46] *See* 21 U.S.C. § 848(k) (1988).

[47] *See* 21 U.S.C. § 848(m) (1988).

[48] *See* 21 U.S.C. § 848(k) (1988).

Some special features also appear in the DKA death penalty provisions that go beyond those required by Supreme Court precedent and that do not generally appear in state capital-sentencing procedures. For example, the DKA requires that the judge instruct the jury not to consider "the race, color, religious beliefs, national origin, or sex of the defendant or victim" and, further, that the judge direct the jury not to recommend death unless it has determined that it would recommend death regardless of those factors. 21 U.S.C. § 848(o)(1).

[49] Pub. L. No. 103-322, 108 Stat. 1796, 1959, *reprinted in* 1994 U.S.C.C.A.N. 1801.

[50] The offenses included transportation of explosives, kidnapping, hostage-taking, murder, train wrecking, and car-jacking, among others. *See* 108 Stat. 1968-70 (1994).

[51] *See* 108 Stat. 1960, *codified at* 18 U.S.C. §§ 3591(b)(1) & (2) (1994).

[52] 108 Stat. 1969 (1994).

[53] *See* 108 Stat. 1960 (1994).

rape and robbery where no death results.[54] The constitutionality of the provisions applicable to non-homicidal drug crimes are particularly debatable since there is no modern history of imposing the death penalty for such crimes.[55]

The number of federal crimes to which the death penalty now attaches is substantial. After 1994, Congress made the FDPA procedures applicable to additional crimes.[56] The list of federal capital offenses has been summarized as follows:[57]

Homicide related Crimes:

Murder related to the smuggling of aliens. (18 U.S.C. § 1342)

Destruction of aircraft, motor vehicles, or related facilities causing death. (18 U.S.C. § 32-34)

Murder committed during a drug-related drive-by shooting. (18 U.S.C. § 36)

Murder committed at an airport serving international civil aviation. (18 U.S.C. § 37)

Retaliatory murder of a member of the immediate family of law enforcement officials. (18 U.S.C. § 115(b)(3) [by cross-reference to 18 U.S.C. § 1111])

Civil rights offenses resulting in death. (18 U.S.C. § 241, 242, 245, 247)

Murder of a member of Congress, an important executive official, or a Supreme Court Justice. (18 U.S.C. § 351 [by cross-reference to 18 U.S.C. § 1111])

Death resulting from offenses involving transportation of explosives, destruction of government property, or destruction of property related to foreign or interstate commerce. (18 U.S.C. § 844(d),(f),(I))

Murder committed by the use of a firearm during a crime of violence or a drug trafficking crime. (18 U.S.C. § 930)

Murder committed in a Federal Government facility. (18 U.S.C. § 924(I))

Genocide. (18 U.S.C. § 1091)

---

[54] *See* Coker v. Georgia, 433 U.S. 584, 598 (1977) (plurality opinion) (rape); Hooks v. Georgia, 433 U.S. 917 (1977) (per curiam) (robbery).

[55] Some scholars have questioned whether the death penalty remains constitutional even for treason. *See, e.g.,* James G. Wilson, *Chaining the Leviathan: The Unconstitutionality of Executing Those Convicted of Treason,* 45 U. PITT. L. REV. 99 (1983). In *Kennedy v. Louisiana,* 128 S.Ct. 2641 (2008), in which the Court outlawed the death penalty for child rape, the majority declined to address the constitutionality of the death penalty for "crimes defining and punishing treason, espionage, terrorism, and drug kingpin activity, which are offenses against the State." *Id.* at 2659.

[56] The Antiterrorism and Effective Death Penalty Act of 1996 added four new capital offenses. *See* Pub. L. No. 104-132, 110 Stat. 1214, 1286, 1292, 1296, 1330 (1996).

[57] *See Capital Punishment, 2009 — Statistical Tables, supra* note 2, at 7, tbl. 3.

First-degree murder. (18 U.S.C. § 1111)

Murder of a Federal judge or law enforcement oficial. (18 U.S.C. § 1114)

Murder of a foreign official. (18 U.S.C. § 1116)

Murder by a Federal prisoner. (18 U.S.C. § 1118)

Murder of a U.S. national in a foreign country. (18 U.S.C. § 1119)

Murder by an escaped Federal prisoner already sentenced to life imprisonment. (18 U.S.C. § 1120)

Murder of a State or local law enforcement oficial or other person aiding in a Federal investigation; murder of a State correctional officer. (18 U.S.C. § 1121)

Murder during a kidnapping. (18 U.S.C. § 1201)

Murder during a hostage-taking. (18 U.S.C. § 1203)

Murder of a court officer or juror. (18 U.S.C. § 1503)

Murder with the intent of preventing testimony by a witness, victim, or informant. (18 U.S.C. § 1512)

Retaliatory murder of a witness, victim or informant. (18 U.S.C. § 1513)

Mailing of injurious articles with intent to kill or resulting in death. (18 U.S.C. § 1716)

Assassination or kidnapping resulting in the death of the President or Vice President. (18 U.S.C. § 1751 [by cross-reference to 18 U.S.C. § 1111])

Murder for hire. (18 U.S.C. § 1958)

Murder involved in a racketeering offense. (18 U.S.C. § 1959)

Willful wrecking of a train resulting in death. (18 U.S.C. § 1992)

Bank-robbery-related murder or kidnapping. (18 U.S.C. § 2113)

Murder related to a carjacking. (18 U.S.C. § 2119)

Murder related to rape or child molestation. (18 U.S.C. § 2245)

Murder related to sexual exploitation of children. (18 U.S.C. § 2251)

Murder committed during an offense against maritime navigation. (18 U.S.C. § 2280)

Murder committed during an offense against a maritime fixed platform. (18 U.S.C. § 2281)

Terrorist murder of a U.S. national in another country. (18 U.S.C. § 2332)

Murder by the use of a weapon of mass destruction. (18 U.S.C. § 2332a)

Murder involving torture. (18 U.S.C. § 2340)

Murder related to a continuing criminal enterprise or related murder of a Federal, State, or local law enforcement officer. (21 U.S.C. § 848(e))

Death resulting from aircraft hijacking. (49 U.S.C. § 1472-1473)

Non-Homicide Related Crimes

Espionage. (18 U.S.C. § 794)

Treason. (18 U.S.C. § 2381)

Trafficking in large quantities of drugs. (18 U.S.C. § 3591(b))

Attempting, authorizing or advising the killing of any officer, juror, or witness in cases involving a Continuing Criminal Enterprise, regardless of whether such killing actually occurs. (18 U.S.C. § 3591(b)(2))

The procedures specified by the FDPA are similar to those specified in the DKA.[58] The FDPA requires a separate sentencing hearing after conviction for a capital offense.[59] The defendant is entitled to a jury at sentencing, and, unless the defendant pled guilty or elected a judge as fact-finder at the guilt phase or benefitted from a reversal of a previous death sentence, the jury at the sentencing hearing can be the same as at the guilt phase.[60] For the defendant to be death eligible, the jury must find beyond a reasonable doubt and unanimously that the defendant directly caused a death (except when a non-homicide statute applies) and had a mental state of at least gross recklessness.[61] For the defendant to continue to be death eligible, the jury must also find beyond a reasonable doubt and unanimously that at least one statutory aggravating factor is present.[62] The FDPA sets forth 26 possible aggravating factors, although some of those apply only for drug offenses, some only for espionage and treason, and some only for homicide.

At the selection stage of deliberations, the jury may consider both statutory and non-statutory mitigating factors.[63] However, the prosecution must have given the defendant advance notice of any statutory or non-statutory aggravating factors to

---

[58] The procedures are not identical, however, and courts in DKA cases have confronted questions about the relation between the two laws. The FDPA purports to apply to all federal crimes that carry a death sentence. *See* 18 U.S.C. § 3591(a) (Supp. II 1998). However, it has not been thought clear that Congress intended to impliedly repeal the 1988 procedures applicable to DKA homicides. *See* Little, *supra* note 1, at 392. The DKA provided defendants with certain benefits, such as investigation resources and expert services, not provided by FDPA, and it appears that courts "in post-1994 DKA cases have responsibly attempted to 'meld' the two statutes, opting for the measures most protective of the capital defendant when confronted with meaningful differences." *Id.* For a detailed comparison of the procedures mandated by each of the laws, *see id.* at 392-406.

[59] *See* 18 U.S.C. § 3593(b) (Supp. II 1996).

[60] *See id.*

[61] *See* 18 U.S.C. § 3591(a)(2)(A), (D) (1994).

[62] *See* 18 U.S.C. § 3593(c), (d) (1994).

[63] *See* 18 U.S.C. § 3592(a), (b), (c), (d) (1994); 21 U.S.C. § 848(n) (1994). There is disagreement among lower federal courts about whether 18 U.S.C. § 3592(a) allows federal defendants to present and have the sentencer consider a broader range of mitigating evidence than they are entitled to present under the Eighth Amendment. This question recently was discussed in United States v. Gabrion, 648 F.3d 307 (6th Cir. 2011).

be proven and may not offer aggravating evidence irrelevant to those factors.[64] Jurors need not be unanimous in finding mitigating factors and, indeed, even a single juror may conclude that a mitigating factor is present.[65] Jurors must be instructed to determine whether the aggravating factors "sufficiently outweigh" the mitigating factors so as to "justify" a death sentence.[66] The latter requirement means that jurors are not required to return a death verdict even if there are no mitigating factors or even if aggravating factors are deemed to outweigh mitigating factors. In addition, the judge must give an anti-discrimination instruction, and the jurors, if rendering a death verdict, must individually certify that they would have recommended death regardless of the prohibited considerations.[67] The decision of the jury either unanimously in favor of death or not is binding on the trial judge.[68]

In addition to rules regarding appeals, the FDPA also provides rules regarding the implementation of death sentences. Certain persons who have been sentenced to death are protected from execution. For example, a woman is not subject to execution while pregnant, nor is any person who "lacks the mental capacity to understand the death penalty and why it was imposed."[69] The method of execution for federal capital crimes depends on the location of the trial. The 1988 DKA law did not provide for an execution method. However, the 1994 FDPA provided that the method of execution should proceed according to the law of the state where the sentence is imposed.[70]

[C] Facial Constitutionality of Federal Death-Penalty Statutes

There has been little controversy among the federal appellate courts over the facial constitutionality of the federal death-penalty statutes. In *Jones v. United States*,[71] the Supreme Court first upheld a death sentence imposed under the FDPA against a multi-faceted constitutional attack.[72] Three federal prisoners have also been executed under that statute.[73]

After *Ring v. Arizona*,[74] defendants have raised several new facial challenges to the FDPA. *Ring* held that a jury must determine beyond a reasonable doubt the existence of any aggravating circumstances rendering a defendant death eligible. Based on the view expressed in *Ring* that such aggravating circumstances are the equivalent of "elements" of a crime, defendants have argued, for example, that the

---

[64] *See* 18 U.S.C. § 3593(b).

[65] *See* 18 U.S.C. § 3593(a) (Supp. II 1996).

[66] 18 U.S.C. § 3593(e) (1994).

[67] *See* 18 U.S.C. § 3593(f) (1994).

[68] *See* 18 U.S.C. § 3594 (1994).

[69] *See* 18 U.S.C. § 3596(b), (c) (1994).

[70] *See* 18 U.S.C. § 3596(a) (1994).

[71] 527 U.S. 373 (1999).

[72] *See id.* at 375-76.

[73] *See* DEATH PENALTY INFO. CTR., FEDERAL EXECUTIONS 1927-2003, *supra*, note 27.

[74] 536 U.S. 584 (2002).

FDPA is facially unconstitutional because it does not require a grand jury to find aggravating circumstances in the indictment process and because it provides a standard for admission of evidence at the sentencing hearing that is more relaxed than the standards applicable at the guilt-or-innocence trial.[75] The federal appellate courts that have considered these claims have rejected them as grounds to strike down FDPA on its face, concluding that the problems either had been appropriately cured, such as by a superceding indictment that included the aggravating circumstances, or that the FDPA standards complied with the Constitution.[76]

The full implications of *Ring* ultimately will have to await further clarification from the Supreme Court. Litigation based on *Ring* challenging death sentences imposed under the FDPA will continue just as such litigation challenging death sentences imposed under state statutes will also continue. To date, however, the lower federal appellate courts have not struck down the DKA or the FDPA as facially unconstitutional under *Ring*.

§ 24.04   ADMINISTRATION OF THE FEDERAL DEATH PENALTY

Equitable administration of the federal death penalty faces complications, just as in state jurisdictions, due to the potential for unconscious racial bias by decision-makers and the disparate levels of acceptance of capital punishment in different regions. To try to address these problems, the Department of Justice has instituted procedures to exercise centralized influence over prosecutorial decision-making in federal capital cases. Despite these efforts, fairness questions have continued to arise.

[A]   Centralized Review by the Department of Justice

Before the promulgation of the DKA in 1988, the Department of Justice had created policies that required U.S. Attorneys in the 94 federal judicial districts to seek approval from the Attorney General to pursue a death sentence. A decision not to seek the death penalty in an otherwise appropriate case was left to the discretion of the U.S. Attorney. A decision to charge a defendant with a crime punishable by death (a capital crime) also did not require submission of the case for approval if the U.S. Attorney did not plan to seek capital punishment. Between

---

[75] Critics have argued that, because the FDPA allows the government to introduce testimonial hearsay evidence to support the existence of the aggravating circumstances used to establish death eligibility, the statute violates a defendant's Sixth Amendment right of confrontation, applicable at all stages of his "criminal prosecution" and, thus, is facially unconstitutional. *See, e.g.*, Michael D. Pepson & John N. Sharifi, *Two Wrongs Don't Make a Right: Federal Death Eligibility Determinations and Judicial Trifucations*, 43 Akron L. Rev. 1, 4 (2009).

[76] *See, e.g.*, United States v. Sampson, 486 F.3d 13 (1st Cir. 2007); United States v. LeCroy, 441 F.3d 914 (11th Cir. 2006); United States v. Allen, 406 F.3d 940, 949 (8th Cir. 2005); United States v. Barnette, 390 F.3d 775, 788-90 (4th Cir. 2004); United States v. Robinson, 367 F.3d 278, 290 (5th Cir. 2004); United States v. Fell, 360 F.3d 135 (2d. Cir. 2004).

1988 and the end of 1994, the Attorney General approved 47 of the 52 requests to pursue a death sentence.[77]

In early 1995, after the appointment of Janet Reno as Attorney General, the Department adopted a new policy that requires U.S. Attorneys to submit for approval all cases in which the defendant was charged with a capital offense, even if the U.S. Attorney did not intend to seek the death penalty. This policy is known as the death penalty "protocol"[78] and was instituted because of Attorney General Reno's concern that only twenty percent of capital defendants were white.[79] A committee of senior Department lawyers initially considers each submission and makes a recommendation to the Attorney General. Neither the committee members nor the Attorney General are informed of the race or ethnicity of the defendant. Between January, 1995, and July, 2000, United States Attorneys submitted 682 cases, and the Attorney General authorized pursuit of a capital sentence in 159 of them.[80] Attorney General Reno overruled a recommendation of a U.S. Attorney against pursuing the death penalty in only 26 cases.[81]

Shortly after President George Bush appointed John Ashcroft as Attorney General, changes in the administration of the policy followed. These changes reflected the desire of Attorney General Ashcroft to promote geographical uniformity in the use of the federal death penalty.[82] First, the Department amended the protocols in June, 2001, to require a submission whenever a defendant was charged with a capital offense or even simply conduct that could have been charged as a capital offense.[83] This change prevented United States Attorneys from avoiding review in a potentially capital case by charging a lesser offense. A second change eliminated a prior admonition that a federal capital charge should be pursued only when the "Federal interest in the prosecution is more substantial than the interests of the State or local authorities."[84] This amendment implied that U.S. Attorneys could pursue the death penalty even if the state did not have a death penalty or if the state prosecutor had decided against pursuing it. The third change was in the level of deference given to recommendations of U.S. Attorneys against pursuit of the death penalty. The Attorney General began directing U.S. Attorneys to pursue the death penalty in a much larger percentage of cases involving such recommendations than during the era of Attorney General Reno.[85]

---

[77] *See* Department of Justice, *The Federal Death Penalty System: A Statistical Survey* (1988-2000) 1-2 (September 12, 2000).

[78] *Id.* at 2.

[79] *See* John Gleeson, *Supervising Federal Capital Punishment: Why the Attorney General Should Defer When U.S. Attorneys Recommend Against the Death Penalty*, 89 VA. L. REV. 1697, 1699 (2003).

[80] *See id.*

[81] *See id.* at 1697.

[82] *See id.* at 1698-99.

[83] *See* U.S. DEP'T OF JUSTICE, UNITED STATES ATTORNEYS' MANUAL 9-10.020, 9-10.040 (2011), *available at* http://www.justice.gov/usao/eousa/foia_reading_room/usam/.

[84] *See* Little, *supra* note 1, at 413 (quoting U.S. DEP'T OF JUSTICE, UNITED STATES ATTORNEYS' MANUAL 9-10.040 (1999).

[85] *See, e.g.*, Gleeson, *supra* note 79, at 1697. Federal Judge Frederic Block recently noted:

Since the reinstatement of the federal death penalty through September, 2010, the Attorneys General had approved 466 defendants for capital prosecutions.[86] Of these cases, 25 were awaiting or on trial. One hundred twenty-two resulted in non-capital sentences due to a plea bargain, and 65 other requests for the death penalty were withdrawn before or at trial. Twenty-three other cases were dismissed after notice by a Federal District Judge. Nineteen defendants either were acquitted or had charges dismissed based on innocence or were convicted of only non-capital offenses. Two death sentences were vacated and pursuit of the death penalty abandoned. One hundred thirty-eight defendants were sentenced to less than death after the jury or the judge rejected the capital sanction. Three awaited retrial or resentencing after a reversal on appeal. One received clemency. Three died while incarcerated. Sixty were sentenced to death and were in the appeals or post-conviction stages. Three were executed.[87]

[B] Questions about Racial Disparities

Despite the efforts of the Department of Justice to achieve racial neutrality in the administration of the federal death penalty, the existence of disparate outcomes has continued to raise questions about the appearance of unconscious racial bias. Of the 466 approved federal capital prosecutions between 1988 and September, 2010, 344, or 74 percent, were against minority defendants.[88] Taking account of all defendants, "122 have been white, 85 Hispanic, 18 Asian/Indian/Pacific Islander/Native American, 3 Arab and 238 African American."[89] Further, among the federal inmates currently sentenced to death, 59 percent are minorities.[90] Although the gap has narrowed somewhat in the last decade, the proportion of federally death-sentenced defendants who are non-white is higher than the comparable figure for state death row prisoners, which is currently 56 percent.[91]

Federal death penalty prosecutions reappeared in 1988, and since 1990 the attorneys general have authorized 416 prosecutions nationwide: 180 during the 1990s, an average of 18 per year; and 236 from 200 to the present, a jump to almost 40 per year. Frederic Block, *A Slow Death*, THE NEW YORK TIMES, A25 (March 18, 2007).

[86] *See* DEATH PENALTY INFO. CTR., FEDERAL DEATH PENALTY, *available at* http://www.deathpenaltyinfo. org/federal-death-penalty?scid=29&did=147#statutes (last visited Dec. 22, 2011).

The financial cost of the federal death penalty is great. A recent report found that "The median cost [for trial defense counsel alone] of a case in which the Attorney General authorized seeking the death penalty was nearly eight times greater than the cost of a case that was eligible for capital prosecution but in which the death penalty was not authorized." The study found that the median cost for defense representation in a federal death case that went to trial was $465,602. For authorized death cases that settled by a guilty plea, the median cost was $200,933. The median cost for defense representation in a death-eligible case in which the death penalty was not sought or authorized was $44,809. *See* Jon B. Gould & Lisa Greenman, *Report to the Committee on Defender Services, Judicial Conference of the United States: Update on the Cost and Quality of Defense Representation in Federal Death Penalty Cases*, App. C (Sept. 2010), *available at* http://www.uscourts.gov/uscourts/FederalCourts/ AppointmentOfCounsel/FDPC2010.pdf.

[87] *See* DEATH PENALTY INFO. CTR., FEDERAL DEATH PENALTY, *supra* note 86.

[88] *See id.*

[89] *Id.*

[90] *See id.*

[91] *See* DEATH PENALTY INFO. CTR., FEDERAL DEATH PENALTY, *available at* http://www.deathpenalyinfo.

Critics contend that these figures create at least an appearance of unconscious racial bias,[92] even if they do not establish the intentional discrimination required to make out a constitutional violation under *McCleskey v. Kemp.*[93] However, defenders of the system, including former Attorney General Ashcroft, have contended "that the disproportionate numbers of black and Hispanic defendants who face capital charges are due not to bias but rather to the over-representation of those groups in the pool of federal defendants who are accused of death-eligible crimes."[94]

[C]   Continuing Geographical Issues

In recent years, Attorneys General have tried to promote geographical uniformity in the use of the federal death penalty. Changes introduced by Attorney General Ashcroft resulted in reduced deference given to the recommendations of U.S. Attorneys against seeking the death penalty in particular cases. Many more such recommendations have been rejected than during the administration of Attorney General Reno, particularly during the tenures of Attorney General Ashcroft and his successor, Attorney General Alberto Gonzalez. This outcome has occurred as a result of efforts to try to produce more death sentences in federal jurisdictions, such as New York, in which the federal death penalty was previously not often pursued.[95]

The effort to achieve uniformity has been criticized, and it has been of questionable success. Many of the criticisms focus on the increased number of overrides of recommendations by U.S. Attorneys against pursuing a death sentence. The local U.S. Attorney in a jurisdiction, rather than a Department committee in Washington, is plausibly thought better able to evaluate the strengths and weaknesses of a case, especially when tried by specific lawyers and in front of a particular trial judge.[96] Also, the local U.S. Attorney is likely to have better knowledge of the relevant jury pool, and jurors are likely to react less favorably to a death-penalty request in some federal districts than in others. Indeed, as of 2010,

---

org/article.php?scid=29&did=193http://www.deathpenaltyinfo.org/FactSheet.pdf (last updated Sept. 20, 2010).

[92] *See, e.g.*, G. Ben Cohen & Robert. J. Smith, *The Racial Geography of the Federal Death Penalty*, 85 Wash. L. Rev. 425, 428 (2010) (characterizing as "alarming" that "[b]lack inmates constitute twenty-eight of the fifty-seven (49%) inmates on federal death row," although "blacks constitute less than 13% of the population"); Little, *supra* note 1, at 478 (describing the public statistics available in 2000 as "disappointing" and noting that critics have not been impressed with the efforts to achieve racial neutrality).

[93] 481 U.S. 279 (1987).

[94] Gleeson, *supra* note 79, at 1699-1700. One recent study suggests that part of the explanation may rest on the use in federal court of wider, district-level jury pools rather than county-level jury pools covering the county of the crime. The effect in certain federal districts, such as the Western District of Missouri, encompassing Kansas City, or the Eastern District of Missouri, encompassing St. Louis, is to dilute minority representation in the jury pool. The authors of the study suggest that this practice may also help explain some of the pronounced geographical disparities in the use of the federal death penalty. They note that federal death sentences tend to come disproportionately from a few federal districts, such as the Western and Eastern Districts of Missouri. *See* Cohen & Smith, *supra* note 92, at 428-36.

[95] *See* Block, *supra* note 85, at A25.

[96] *See* Gleeson, *supra* note 79, at 1720.

only seven of the 94 federal districts were responsible for 40% of the federal death row population, while two-thirds of the districts had not sentenced anyone to death in the modern era.[97] Likewise, forcing prosecutors to pursue death sentences that they actually do not believe are appropriate may not inspire ardent advocacy on behalf of the government.[98] If these assumptions are correct, the rate at which death sentences are secured in cases in which the U.S. Attorney recommends against seeking a death sentence would not be as high as in cases in which the local U.S. Attorney supports the effort. On this score, one federal judge has asserted: "The federal death penalty is already so difficult to obtain — sixteen of the last seventeen federal juries asked to sentence someone to death have refused to do so — that it scarcely makes sense to seek it if the prosecutor handling the case believes the evidence will not bear the weight of a capital case."[99]

A second criticism of the uniformity goal focuses particularly on efforts to secure death sentences in states that do not authorize the death penalty. Six offenders are currently on federal death row for crimes committed in states without capital punishment.[100] Efforts to obtain death sentences in such jurisdictions have, in some cases, engendered widespread opposition and public outcry.[101] Some legal scholars have also concluded that such death sentences violate the Eighth Amendment.[102] The argument has been made that the Bill of Rights was largely motivated as an effort to preserve state sovereignty from federal encroachment.[103] On this view, the Eighth Amendment prohibition on "cruel and unusual punishments" could be understood as a limitation on the federal power to punish in ways prohibited by a particular state.[104] However, this argument has not yet been adopted by a federal court to prohibit or reverse a death sentence, and the Department of Justice has continued to seek death sentences in non-death penalty jurisdictions.

---

[97] *See* Cohen & Smith, *supra* note 92, at 429-30.

[98] *See* Gleeson, *supra* note 79, at 1715.

[99] *Id.* at 1719. *See also* Block, *supra* note 85, at A25 (noting that in 17 cases authorized by the Attorney General in New York, only one has resulted in a death sentence and concluding that "New Yorkers have sent a clear signal to the attorney general: He should be more circumspect and realistic in authorizing death penalty prosecutions. . . . ").

[100] The death sentences arose in the following states: Iowa(2), Massachusetts, Michigan, North Dakota, and Vermont. *See* DEATH PENALTY INFO. CTR., FEDERAL DEATH PENALTY, *available at* http://www.deathpenalyinfo.org/article.php?scid=29&did=147 (last visited Dec. 22, 2011).

[101] *See, e.g.*, Matthew Hay Brown, *Prospect of Executions Angers Island; Two Puerto Ricans May Be Put to Death for Murder, Spurring a Torrent of Protest*, ORLANDO SENTINEL A17 (April 10, 2005).

[102] *See, e.g.*, Michael J. Zydney Mannheimer, *When the Federal Death Penalty is "Cruel and Unusual*," 74 U. CINN. L. REV. 819, 822 (2006). *Cf.* Ricardo Alfonso, *The Imposition of the Death Penalty in Puerto Rico: A Human Rights Crisis in the Path Towards Self-Determination*, 76 REV. JUR. U. P.R. 1077, 1078-80 (2007) (contending that the application of the federal death penalty in Puerto Rico violates the Puerto Rico Federal Relations Act by extending a federal law that should be understood as not "locally applicable" on the island, given that the Constitution of Puerto Rico, adopted in 1952, declares that "The Death Penalty Shall Not Exist.").

[103] *See, e.g., id.* at 849-66.

[104] *See id.* at 873-85.

Chapter 25

MILITARY DEATH PENALTY

§ 25.01 INTRODUCTION

The military court system stands independent from the civilian courts. The two systems differ not only in procedure and structure but, more fundamentally, in their underlying purpose. Civilian courts, primarily established under Article III of the U.S. Constitution, are designed to decide cases and controversies. Military Courts (or courts-martial) are Article I courts. These courts are an extension of the Executive power (provided by Congress) to aid the President in the supervision and smooth operation of the military. It has been said that courts martial are not courts "but are, in fact, simply instrumentalities of the executive power provided by Congress for the President as Commander-in-Chief to aid him in properly commanding the army and enforcing discipline therein."[1]

Historically, courts martial do not afford defendants the same due process protections as civilian courts are required to offer. Scholars and participants in the military justice system have criticized the military justice system as too focused on command control and discipline while under-emphasizing the fair administration of justice.[2] Others within the military have resisted efforts to impose reforms or to incorporate civil procedural protections into the military system arguing that it could pose a direct threat on the ability of the military to run a strong and effective defense system.[3]

In the first half of the 20th century, high ranking military commanders brought capital charges against soldiers and exercised tight control over military trials. The Articles of War governed military executions until 1950[4] and did not provide many fundamental rights to criminal defendants, including the right to the assistance of legal counsel or the right to judicial review of cases in federal or state courts. Under the Articles of War, a defendant in a military court had no right to seek clemency

---

[1] 1 WILLIAM WINTHROP, MILITARY LAW 54 (1886); *see also* JOHN M. LINDLEY, "A SOLDIER IS ALSO A CITIZEN": THE CONTROVERSY OVER MILITARY JUSTICE IN THE ARMY, 1917–1920, at 27, 67 (1990).

[2] *See* Colonel Samuel T. Ansell, *Military Justice*, 5 CORNELL L.Q. 1, 5 (1919) (arguing that the military justice system is "un-American" with too little independence from the military command system); *see also* Kenneth J. Hodson, *Military Justice: Abolish or Change?* 22 KAN. L REV. 31 (1973) (recommending seven major changes including random selection of court martial panels, independent defense counsel, additional resources and removal of commanders from court martial functions except prosecution and clemency).

[3] *See generally* LINDLEY, *supra* note 1.

[4] Michael I. Spak, *Its Time to Put the Military's Death Penalty to Sleep*, 49 CLEV. ST. L. REV. 41, 55–56 (2001). The Articles of War was originally enacted in 1776 and was revised four times before being replaced by the Uniform Code of Military Justice (UCMJ) in 1950.

until World War One. Only high-ranking officers in the war department had the power to stop executions.[5]

Professor Morgan, the man who eventually led the congressional overhaul of the military justice system in 1950, explained:

> To maintain discipline, military command dominated and controlled the [capital] proceedings from its initiation to the final execution of the sentence. While the trial [had] the semblance of a judicial proceeding . . . in its essence it's a mere administrative investigation; for the final determination of whether the trial [had] legally and properly been conducted [lay] not with a judicial body or officer, but with the military."[6]

Under the original system, the military and its commanders oversaw numerous executions. The military executed thirty-five soldiers during World War One and 141 more by the end of World War Two.[7]

The number of military executions decreased as commander control over the military capital system waned. In 1950, Congress passed the Uniform Code of Military Justice (UCMJ) to govern military criminal courts.[8] The UCMJ mimicked federal and state criminal procedures, established judicial review, and eliminated commander control of death cases.[9] With the UCMJ in place, the number of military executions decreased. The military executed ten men from 1950 to 1961. Since 1961, not one service member has been executed.[10]

The current military capital system has little in common with the scheme that existed in the first half of the 20th century. The newest death penalty laws were put into place by executive order in 1984. Since then, military juries have sentenced only sixteen soldiers to death. Twelve of those soldiers have exhausted their direct appeals. Ten of the twelve appeals were reversed by the military appellate courts.

§ 25.02   HISTORICAL BACKGROUND

In 1789, Congress established the nation's first military justice system by enacting the American Articles of War.[11] These Articles of War were modeled after the 1765 British Articles of War and specified the military offenses eligible for

---

[5] *See generally Ansell,* note 2, *supra; and* Major Joshua M. Toman, *Time to Kill: Euthanizing the Requirement for Presidential Approval of Military Death Sentences to Restore Finality of Legal Review,* 195 MIL. L. REV. 1, 34 (2008).

[6] Edmund Morgan, *The Existing Court-Martial System and the Ansell Army Articles,* 29 YALE L.J. 53, 67 (1919).

[7] *See* Toman, *supra* note 5, at 33.

[8] Pub. L. No. 81-504, 64 Stat. 107 (codified as amended at 10 U.S.C. §§ 801–940 (2006)).

[9] *See* Spak, *supra* note 4, at 56.

[10] In 1961 President Eisenhower approved the death sentence of John Bennett and the military hanged him for raping and attempting to kill an 11-year old girl. *See* Associated Press, *Military Sets Date for First Execution Since 1961,* MSNBC (Nov. 20, 2008), http://www.msnbc.com/id/27828874/ns/us_news-miltary/; *Executions in the Military,* DEATH PENALTY INFORMATION CENTER, http://www.deathpenaltyinfo.org/executions-military (last visited Feb. 2, 2012).

[11] Loving v. United States, 517 U.S. 748 (1996).

capital punishment.[12] These capital crimes were adjudicated under civil, rather than military, court jurisdiction.[13]

Over the next century and a half, Congress revised the Articles of War and expanded the military court jurisdiction.[14] In 1863, Congress amended the military court jurisdiction to include trials of capital crimes and the power to sentence a serviceman to death during time of war.[15] In 1920, Congress enacted a new Articles of War, which provided a structure for capital and non-capital military trials, including a provision providing counsel for the defendant, criteria for selecting a court-martial panel member, and requiring an investigation of any charges before submission to trial.[16]

§ 25.03   THE 1950 UNIFORM CODE OF MILITARY JUSTICE

In 1950 Congress enacted the Uniform Code of Military Justice (UCMJ). The primary purposes of the UCMJ were to "(1)[i]ntegrate the military system of the three services; (2) modernize the system to promote public confidence and protect rights of servicemembers without impeding the function of the military; and (3) improve the arrangement and draftsmanship of the articles."[17]

The UCMJ marks the beginning of America's modern military justice system. It provides service members with basic Constitutional Rights including the right to counsel and the right to remain silent. The UCMJ also created a Court of Military Appeal (today's Court of Appeals for the Armed Forces or CAAF) to review cases tried in a military justice court. In response to earlier concerns about the military system, the UCMJ criminalized improper command influence or the "improper use, or perception of use of superior authority to interfere with the court-martial process."[18] Congress revised the UCMJ in 1968 establishing the position of military judge.[19]

The UCMJ formalized general (trial) courts-martial and automatic review while subjecting servicemembers to charges ranging from the uniquely military to the

---

[12] American Articles of War of 1776 and British Articles of War of 1765, *reprinted in* William Winthrop, Military Law and Precedents, 964 (Gov't Printing Office, 2d ed. 1920) (1896).

[13] *Id.*

[14] *See* Articles of War of 1916, ch 418, § 3, arts. 92–93, 39 Stat. 619 (1916) (granting military courts jurisdiction over peacetime common law felonies committed by a servicemember excluding rape and murder charges which were referred to civilian courts). *See also* Christopher W. Benan, *Don't Tug on Superman's Cape: Defense of Convening Authority Selection and Appointment of Court Martial Panel Members*, 176 Mil. L. Rec. 190, 215–20 (2003) (discussing congressional revisions to the Articles of War, noting the most substantial change coming in 1916 and 1920).

[15] *See* Coleman v. Tenn., 97 U.S. 509, 514 (1879).

[16] Benan, *supra* note 15, at 219–20.

[17] Walter T. Cox III, The Army, *The Courts and the Constitution: The Evolution of Military Justice*, 118 Mil. L. Rev. 1, 13 (1987) (citing an Aug. 18, 1948, letter outlining the purposes of the Committee on a Uniform Code of Military Justice).

[18] *See* Spak, *supra* note 4, at 56.

[19] Colonel Dwight H. Sullivan, *Playing the Numbers: Court-Martial Panel Size and the Military Death Penalty*, 158 Mil. L. Rev. 1, 15 (1998).

civilian. The UCMJ also extended military courts' jurisdiction to include the crimes of rape and murder.[20] The Code provided that rape and two of the four types of murder were punishable as capital crimes.[21]

Death-eligible offenses include mutiny and attempted mutiny;[22] failure to suppress or report mutiny or sedition;[23] and misbehavior before the enemy (including running away, casting aside arms or ammunition, and cowardly conduct).[24] Willful disobedience of a superior officer "in time of war" is also punishable by death;[25] as is compelling or attempting to compel a commander to surrender[26]; improper use of countersign[27]; forcing a safeguard[28]; aiding the enemy[29]; improper hazarding of a vessel[30]; and being asleep or drunk while being a look-out in time of war.[31] The only offense for which the death penalty was mandated in the 1950 UCMJ was spying.[32]

A particular procedural device existed for certain military capital offenses. The 1950 UCMJ provided "[n]o person shall be convicted of an offense for which the death penalty is made mandatory by law, except by the concurrence of all the members of the court-martial . . . "[33] A unanimous vote is also required to impose death where discretionary.[34] Officers sentenced to death have their cases reviewed by the Court of Military Appeals,[35] and, ultimately, the President of the United States before the death penalty may be carried out.[36]

§ 25.04   RESPONSE TO *FURMAN v. GEORGIA*

In 1972, the U.S. Supreme Court handed down the landmark decision of *Furman v. Georgia* finding the civilian death penalty unconstitutional as applied under existing state statutes.[37] Specifically, the Court held that the unlimited and unguided discretion employed by juries in capital trials violated the Cruel and

---

[20] *See* UCMJ art. 1, 10 U.S.C. § 801 (West 2000).

[21] Hodson, note 2, at 35, *supra*.

[22] UCMJ art. 94(b).

[23] *Id.*

[24] *Id.* art. 99.

[25] *Id.* art. 90(2).

[26] *Id.* art. 100.

[27] *Id.* art. 101.

[28] *Id.* art. 102.

[29] *Id.* art. 104.

[30] *Id.* art. 110.

[31] *Id.* art. 113.

[32] *Id.* art. 106.

[33] *Id.* art. 52(a)(1).

[34] *Id.* art. 52(b)(1).

[35] *Id.* arts. 66(b), 67(b)(1).

[36] *Id.* art. 71(a).

[37] Furman v. Georgia, 408 U.S. 238 (1972).

Unusual clause of the Eighth Amendment. While *Furman* struck down existing death penalty statutes in every state system, the majority opinions did not discuss whether or not it applied to military courts.[38]

While state legislatures responded quickly to *Furman*, passing new death penalty statutes within the year, neither the President nor the Congress initiated any reform of the existing military system. Military courts continued to hand down death sentences under the old protocols set up by the UCMJ in 1950.[39]

Just four years after *Furman*, the Supreme Court reviewed several of the new state statutes and held the new capital systems in Georgia, Florida, and Texas were constitutionally permissible.[40] However, military courts-martial continued to apply the 1950 UCMJ. Between 1972 and 1983, military courts sentenced seven service members to death.[41] In 1981, the Navy-Marine Corps Court of Military Review held that the military law governing capital punishment and procedures did not require any change in the military statute in response to *Furman*.[42] They noted that the military procedures had to be reviewed and evaluated in the context of the military system as a whole whose primary purpose is to "establish and maintain the armed forces" and "a disciplined, ever-ready and effective military community."[43]

In 1983, in *United States v. Matthews*, the Court of Military Appeals finally responded to the new death penalty jurisprudence of the Supreme Court. The court reversed Army Private First Class Wyatt Matthews' death sentence, invalidated the existing military death penalty system, and reversed the death sentences of all seven death row inmates.[44] The Court found that because the military statute failed to require a court-martial panel to "[s]pecifically identify aggravating factors" as required under *Furman* and *Gregg*, it was unconstitutional.[45] The court suggested that the President or Congress establish constitutionally valid procedures for the military death penalty system.[46]

---

[38] Justices Powell and Blackmun, dissenting in *Furman*, discussed the application of the case to military courts. 408 U.S. at 417–18 (Powell, J., dissenting) (noting that the majority's "departure from established precedent" invalidates "numerous provisions of the . . . Uniform Code of Military Justice"). In a separate dissent, Justice Blackmun remarked: "Also in jeopardy, perhaps, are the death penalty provisions in various Articles of the Uniform Code of Military Justice." 408 U.S. at 412 (Blackmun, J., dissenting).

[39] Colonel Dwight H. Sullivan, *Killing Time: Two Decades of Military Capital Litigation*, 189 MIL. L. REV. 1, 4 (2006); *see also* United States v. Gay, 16 M.J. 586, 596 (C.M.A. 1983) (noting "absolute discretion is permitted the sentencing authority").

[40] Gregg v. Georgia, 428 U.S. 153 (1976); Proffit v. Florida, 428 U.S. 242 (1976); Jurek v. Tex., 428 U.S. 262 (1976).

[41] *See* Sullivan, note 39, at 5 & n.16, *supra*.

[42] United States v. Rojas, 15 M.J. 902, 928–29 (N.M.C.M.R. 1981).

[43] *Id.* at 929 (discussing how the military system is an outgrowth of the constitutional requirement that Congress and the President establish and maintain "a disciplined, ever-ready and effective military").

[44] Sullivan, *Killing Time*, note 39, at 7, *supra*.

[45] United States v. Matthews, 16 M.J. 354 (C.M.A. 1983).

[46] *Id.* at 382.

President Reagan responded quickly. In January, 1984, President Reagan signed an Executive Order setting forth new procedures to be used in a military death penalty trial.[47] The new rules require a unanimous finding that the accused is guilty of a capital offense, a unanimous finding that at least one of the eleven enumerated aggravating factors exist, and a unanimous finding that any mitigating evidence is "substantially outweighed" by the aggravating factor(s).[48] With these procedures, the military death penalty law, at least facially, came very close to resembling the civilian death penalty law in many state statutes.

In 1996, the Supreme Court reviewed the new military system in *Loving v United States*.[49] The Court upheld the new military death penalty as constitutional and validated the President's constitutional power to enact R.C.M. 1004. The following year, the UCMJ was amended to replace the sentence of life (with eligibility for parole after ten years) with a sentence of life without the possibility of parole.[50]

§ 25.05   CAPITAL PUNISHMENT PROCEDURES UNDER THE MODERN UNIFORM CODE OF MILITARY JUSTICE

The UCMJ authorizes the death penalty as a possible punishment for first degree pre-meditated murder and first degree felony murder committed by military personnel regardless of where the offense is committed.[51] Death penalty eligibility under the UCMJ may stem from offenses both related and unrelated to military operation and function. It is broader than most civilian statutes in that, under certain circumstances, it authorizes the death penalty for rape and other non-homicide crimes.[52]

In the military system, death penalty procedures include several distinct stages and two decision makers. The first decision maker is the "convening authority." The convening authority decides whether or not to bring a case as a capital case and has exclusive authority to allow a plea bargain that includes the waiver of the death

---

[47] Exec. Order No. 12,460, 49 Fed. Reg. 3169 (Jan. 26, 1984) (codified as Rule for Courts-Martial 1004 *in* Dep't of Def., Manual for Courts-Martial Pt. II (2008) [hereinafter MCM]).

[48] *See* MCM, note 47, R.C.M. 1004, *supra*.

[49] Loving v. United States, 517 U.S. 748 (1996).

[50] *The U.S Military Death Penalty: Overview*, Death Penalty Information Center, http://www.deathpenaltyinfo.org/us-military-death-penalty#overview (last visited Feb. 2, 2012).

[51] UCMJ art. 118, 10 U.S.C. § 918 (2006), provides "any person subject to this chapter who, without justification or excuse, unlawfully kills a human being, when he (1) has a premeditated design to kill; (2) intends to kill or inflict great bodily harm; (3) is engaged in an act which is inherently dangerous to another and evinces a wanton disregard of human life; or (4) is engaged in the perpetration or attempted perpetration of burglary, sodomy, rape, robbery or aggravated arson; is guilty of murder, and shall suffer such punishment as a court-martial may direct, except if found guilty under clause (1) or (4) he shall suffer death or imprisonment for life as a court martial shall direct."

[52] *Id.* art. 120. Congress amended Article 120 in 2006 and it still authorizes the death penalty for rape. National Defense Authorization Act for Fiscal Year 2006, Pub. L. 109-163, § 552(b), 119 Stat. 3136, 3263. Some non-homicide offenses are eligible for death in times of war only. *See* UCMJ arts. 85, 90, 101, 106, 113. Others are available at any time. *See* UCMJ arts. 94, 99, 100, 102, 104, 106(a), 110.

penalty. The second decision maker is the court martial panel members. These military personnel sit as jurors during a capital trial and first decide whether a defendant is guilty of a capital offense and then, if necessary, determine whether or not to impose a sentence of death or life imprisonment.

The military death penalty process begins with an investigation of the crime.[53] This investigation is conducted in an article 32 proceeding. This proceeding is similar to a civilian grand jury except that defense counsel is permitted to participate, call witnesses, and cross-examine prosecution witnesses. The investigating officer, usually a judge advocate, provides a written report to the convening authority with a recommendation as to whether the case should be tried as a capital case. The convening authority has sole, complete, and unreviewable discretion on the final decision on whether to seek a sentence of death.

The convening authority is the highest ranking member in command, often a general staff officer in charge of a large force or fleet.[54] Although the convening authority may not have any legal training or background, he does, by virtue of rank or assignment, have command authority over most persons involved in the proceeding including the defendant, the trial counsel, witnesses, and members of the panel. The convening authority holds significant power — playing both the role of a traditional civilian prosecutor as well as a judicial officer.[55] He decides whether to seek a death sentence initially but he does not personally try the case.

If the convening authority decides to refer the case as a capital one, the case goes to a capital court-martial for prosecution.[56] Once a case is referred for trial, an accused may choose to be tried by either an all-officer panel or a one-third enlisted soldier panel; but in a capital trial a defendant may not elect to be tried by only one judge.

The convening authority selects and appoints the members of the court-martial jury panel subject to the defense and prosecution challenges to potential panel-members.[57] The CAAF held that under UCMJ article 25, a "military defendant

---

[53] Jonathan Turley, *Tribunals and Tribulations: The Antithetical Elements of Military Governance in a Madisonian Democracy*, 70 Geo. Wash. L. Rev. 649, 668–71 (2002); UCMJ art. 32.

[54] Turley, note 53, at 668, *supra*; Major Stephen A. Lamb, *The Court Martial Panel Selection Process: A Critical Analysis*, 137 Mil. L. Rev. 103, 125 (1992) ("Although the President or service secretary can designate any officer, general court martial convening authorities usually are general or flag officers, but almost always are of the rank of colonel or higher (captain or higher in the Navy or Coast Guard) and in command of a spate brigade, wing, station or larger unit.").

[55] Colonel Dwight H. Sullivan, *A Matter of Life and Death: Examining the Military Death Penalty's Fairness*, Fed. Law., June 1998, at 38, 40.

[56] Turley, *supra* note 53, at 679 n.175; *see also* Lieutenant Colonel Theodore Essex and Major Leslea Tate Pickle, *A Reply to the Report of the Commission on the 50th Anniversary of the Uniform Code of Military Justice (May 2001): "The Cox Commission,"* 5 2 A.F.L. Rev. 233, 266 (2002), *and* Meredith Robinson, *Comment: Volunteers for the Death Penalty? The Application of Solorio v. United States to Military Capital Litigation*, 6 Geo. Mason L. Rev. 1049, 1061 n.115 (citing Brief in Support of Petition for Extraordinary Relief in the Nature of a Writ of Mandamus at 1–6, Levell v. Oullette, 36 M.J. 26 (C.M.A. 1992) (No. 92-93/MC)).

[57] *See* Hon. Walter T Cox III et al., Nat'l Inst. of Military Justice, Report of the Commission on the 50th Anniversary of the Uniform Code of Military Justice (2001) [hereinafter Cox Commission] (on file with author); MCM, *supra* note 47, R.C.M. 601, R.C.M. 504(a).

does have a right to have members of a panel who are fair and impartial." The convening authority alone selects those who, in his opinion, are best qualified to serve based on age, education, training, experience, length of service, and judicial temperament.[58] Some argue that a convening authority has a good perspective on the suitability of those he selects to be members of the panel since these are generally individuals with whom he interacts on a daily basis. Critics raise concerns that military structure could impact the deliberations and voting on the panel.[59] The convening authority is a superior officer to all members involved in the court-martial including the judge, trial counsel, each member of the panel and the defendant.

When the convening authority selects the members of the panel, both the defense and the prosecution hold unlimited challenges for cause.[60] A panel-member's removal for cause requires an expression that he or she has formulated an opinion of the defendant's guilt or a showing that the member's participation would lead to "substantial doubt as to legality, fairness, and impartiality" of the proceeding.[61] Unlike capital trials in U.S. District Courts, where each side is given 20 peremptory challenges, the prosecution and defense in courts-martial have only one peremptory challenge to those selected by the convening authority.[62]

A panel should have twelve members but in a capital case may have no fewer than five members.[63] If a member is removed with a challenge, he is not required to be replaced unless the panel contains less than five members. At that point a convening authority selects replacement members to reach the minimum of five.

Once a panel is selected, the case proceeds to trial. There are four fundamental requirements in order for a death penalty to be imposed. First, panel members must unanimously find the accused guilty beyond a reasonable doubt of a death-eligible offense. Second, panel members must unanimously find beyond a reasonable doubt that at least one aggravating factor exists. Third, panel members must unanimously conclude that an aggravating factor substantially outweighs any mitigating factors. Finally, panel members must unanimously vote for a sentence of death.[64] Members may decline to impose a sentence of death for any reason even when all of the eligibility factors are present. A single vote for life results in a life sentence.[65]

---

[58] MCM, *supra* note 47, R.C.M. 502(a).

[59] Sullivan, *Playing the Numbers, supra* note 19, at 28.

[60] *Id.* at 15; *see also* MCM, *supra* note 47, R.C.M. 912(f).

[61] MCM, *supra* note 47, R.C.M. 912(f)(1)(N).

[62] *Id.* R.C.M. 912(g)(1).

[63] *Id.* R.C.M. 501(a)(1)(A) (establishing "[i]n a case in which the accused may be sentenced to death, the number of members shall be not less than 12, unless 12 members are not reasonably available because of physical conditions or military exigencies in which case the convening authority shall specify a lesser number of members not less than five. . . . "); UCMJ art. 25(a), 10 U.S.C. § 825 (2006).

[64] MCM, note 47, *supra*, R.C.M. 1004(a)(2), R.C.M. 1004(b)(7), R.C.M. 1004(b)(4)(c), R.C.M. 1006(d)(4)(A).

[65] Mary M. Foreman, *Military Capital Litigation: Meeting the Heightened Standards of United States v. Curtis*, 174 Mil. L. Rev. 1 (2002) (contrasting the strategy of capital defense counsel who present all theories in penalty phase even if they failed in the guilt phase in hopes of convincing one member of the panel from non-capital counsel who may abandon theories to preserve credibility).

The UCMJ sets out even more detailed procedures the panel must follow before it may vote on a sentence of death. After the guilt stage, a jury panel must first consider whether life imprisonment is an appropriate sentence. Only once there is a unanimous vote for life imprisonment may a panel consider and vote on a sentence of death. The court described the voting requirements as a "valuable right" extended to all those accused in capital cases.[66] This procedure promotes a policy that any one member of a panel can prevent the death penalty from being imposed."[67]

§ 25.06　APPEAL OF A MILITARY CAPITAL CASE

The military death penalty appellate process includes three levels of automatic appeals. When a death sentence is imposed, the record is initially reviewed by the convening authority, who has the power to reduce sentences and to set aside guilty findings.[68] The convening authority can reduce the sentence, but cannot increase it.[69] If the convening authority approves a death sentence, the condemned service-member will be moved to military death row and the case automatically moves to the intermediate Court of Criminal Appeals for that particular branch of the armed-forces.[70] Courts of Criminal Appeals[71] consider the factual sufficiency of all the evidence and the appropriateness of the sentence.[72] While the Judge Advocates General have discretion forming rules for the Courts of Criminal Appeals,[73] the Courts must sit in panels of at least three appellate military judges.[74] A military judge assigned to a Court of Criminal Appeals must be certified by the Judge Advocate General to perform the duties of a military judge and serve in that function as his primary duty.[75]

If the intermediate court affirms, then the Court of Appeals for the Armed Forces ("CAAF") must review the case.[76] Unlike the intermediate courts of appeal,

---

[66] Id.

[67] Id. at 3.

[68] Id.; United States v. Turner, 25 M.J. 324 (C.M.A. 1987).

[69] UCMJ art. 62(b)(3), 10 U.S.C. § 862(b)(3) (2006).

[70] UCMJ art. 66(b). Four intermediate courts of appeal exist: the courts of appeals for the army, navy-marine, air force, and coast guard. Article 69 also grants the Judge Advocate General discretionary authority to refer other cases to the Court of Criminal Appeals. UCMJ art. 69.

[71] The name of the intermediate-level court has varied over the decades. The 1950 UCMJ referred to these bodies as "boards of review." Ch. 169, 64 Stat. 128. The Military Justice Act of 1968 substituted in the name Courts of Military Review. Pub. L. No. 90-632, § 2(27), 82 Stat. 1335, 1341 (1968). Subsequent amendments replaced Courts of Military Review with Court of Criminal Appeals. National Defense Authorization Act for Fiscal Year 1995, Pub. L. No. 103-337, § 924, 108 Stat. 2663, 2831 (1994); National Defense Authorization Act for Fiscal Year 1996, Pub. L. No. 104-106, § 1153, 110 Stat. 186, 468. While readers should be familiar with the change in nomenclature for reviewing case-law secondary authority, the current statutory formulation is used throughout this chapter.

[72] UCMJ art. 66(c).

[73] Id. art. 66(f).

[74] Id. art. 66(a).

[75] Id. art. 23(c); United States v. Beckerman, 27 M.J. 334, 224 (C.M.A. 1989).

[76] UCMJ art. 67(a)(1). Up until 1994, the CAAF was called the Court of Military Appeals. See supra

the CAAF does not hold fact-finding powers and only examines matters of law.[77] The CAAF is a five-member, Article I court that sits atop the military justice system. Its judges are civilians appointed by the President with the advice and consent of the Senate to serve 15-year terms.[78] If the Court of Appeals for the Armed Forces affirms the sentence, the case is eligible for Supreme Court review.[79] The Supreme Court's certiorari jurisdiction over military justice cases was enacted in 1983.[80] If the Supreme Court affirms the sentence or denies certiorari in a military capital case, the death sentence is then reviewed by the executive branch.[81]

Unlike civilian capital systems, the President must "approve" all military death sentences after direct appeals are exhausted and after a "final judgment" on the legality of the death sentence.[82] There are no guidelines, criteria, or timetables to inform the President to follow in deciding whether or not to approve a sentence of death.[83] After presidential approval, a defendant may file for habeas corpus review in the federal courts.[84]

§ 25.07   CAPITAL OFFENSES UNDER THE UNIFORM CODE OF MILITARY JUSTICE

The military makes more than a dozen crimes death eligible in the Uniform Code of Military Justice. Twelve of these offenses are uniquely military offenses and have no similar provisions in civilian death penalty law.[85] These include desertion, espionage, or disobeying a superior. Some of these military offenses carry the death penalty only in the time of war and others do not impose that requirement. The last two death eligible offenses (with civilian analogue) are murder (premeditated murder or felony murder) and rape. Both of these apply to offenses committed by any U.S. military personnel anywhere in the world and regardless of whether they occur during peacetime or wartime.

Since *Matthews* in 1983, every service member sentenced to death by a military jury has been convicted of premeditated murder or premeditated murder and felony murder.[86] Imposing the death sentence requires a unanimous jury finding that at least one aggravating circumstances occurred in the commission of the

---

note 71. Cases before the switch occurred use the "CMA" citation.

[77] *Id.* art. 67(a).

[78] *Id.* art. 67(a)(1).

[79] *Id.*

[80] Military Justice Act of 1983, Pub. L. No. 98-209, § 10, 97 Stat. 1393, 1406 (codified as amended at 28 U.S.C. § 1259 (2000)).

[81] UCMJ art. 71(a).

[82] *Id.* arts. 71(a), 71(c)(1).

[83] *See* Sullivan, *Killing Time*, note 39, at 28, *supra*; Toman, note 5, at 62, *supra*.

[84] *Id.*

[85] *See* UCMJ arts. 86–134.

[86] *See* Toman, *supra* note 5, at 13 (2008). In fact, this has been the case since 1972. *See* Sullivan, *supra Killing Time*, note 39, at 4–5 & n.16.

crime.[87] The Rules for Courts-martial inventory 11 aggravating circumstances.[88] Less than half that list, however, may apply to charges of murder or rape due to limiting phrases in the possible circumstances. Only two aggravating circumstances apply to any death-eligible offense: knowingly creating a grave risk of substantial damage to the national security of, or mission, system, or function of, the United States;[89] and committing the offense with intent to avoid hazardous duty.[90] Except for the two unlimited circumstances, murder is subject to four aggravating circumstances, and rape may be aggravated by proving one of two circumstances.[91]

Defendants have the opportunity to "present matters in extenuation and mitigation regardless whether the defense offered evidence before findings."[92] Matters in extenuation include reasons for the crime which do not amount to a legal defense.[93] Mitigating evidence may include "particular acts of good conduct or bravery and evidence of the reputation or record of the accused in the service for efficiency, fidelity, subordination, temperance, courage, or any other trait that is desirable in a servicemember."[94] In capital cases particularly, "[t]he accused shall be given broad latitude to present evidence in extenuation and mitigation."[95] Additionally, defendants have a right to either sworn allocution, subject to cross-examination, or unsworn allocution not subject to cross.[96]

§ 25.08   THE COX COMMISSION AND EXAMINATION OF THE MILITARY SYSTEM

In 2000, Congress created the Cox Commission to study the UCMJ.[97] In its report, the Cox Commission recommended Congress implement four principal changes to the UCMJ.[98] First, the Commission suggested modifying the role of the convening authority, in both selecting members of the panel and in making pre-trial legal decisions. Second, it recommended providing the military judge with more autonomy and responsibilities. Third, it suggested additional safeguards in capital punishment trials, including a 12 member court martial panel, an anti-discrimination instruction and closer examination in to the quality of defense counsel. Finally, the commission recommended abolishing the UCMJ rape and sodomy provision.

---

[87] UCMJ art. 52; MCM, *supra* note 47, R.C.M. 1004(b).

[88] MCM, *supra* note 47, R.C.M. 1004(c).

[89] *Id.* R.C.M. 1004(c)(2).

[90] *Id.* R.C.M. 1004(c)(5).

[91] *See id.* R.C.M. 1004(c)(4) (murder), R.C.M. 1004(c)(7) (murder), R.C.M. 1004(c)(8) (murder), R.C.M. 1004(c)(6) (murder or rape), R.C.M. 1004(c)(9) (rape).

[92] *Id.* R.C.M. 1001(c)(1).

[93] *Id.* R.C.M. 1001(c)(1)(A).

[94] *Id.* R.C.M. 1001(c)(1)(B).

[95] *Id.* R.C.M. 1004(a)(3).

[96] *Id.* R.C.M. 1001(c)(2).

[97] *See* Cox Commission, *supra* note 57.

[98] *Id.* at 5–6.

The Commission was particularly critical of the role of the convening authority observing that it presented the possibility for corruption in the proceedings.[99] Its report reflected long standing criticisms of the role of the convening authority in selecting the members of the panel and argued that a fair and impartial panel is the most fundamental protection afforded a serviceman.

Ultimately, Congress decided not to implement any of the commission recommendations and kept the UCMJ in its current form.[100] Supporters of the UCMJ argue that the UCMJ represents the best of all worlds because it creates a "fair, efficient and practical system" while allowing commanders to maintain "the needs of the military institution."[101]

§ 25.09   MILITARY APPELLATE REVIEW OF DEATH SENTENCES

Despite the strong criticisms and concerns raised about the fundamental fairness of the UCMJ, a review of capital cases in the military shows that the military appears to be very judicious in its applications of the death penalty. Only one-third of the capital cases tried in a court-martial results in a guilty verdict and a sentence of death.[102] The rate of reversal on appeal, however, dwarfs this percentage. Since 1984 sixteen men have been sentenced to death in capital courts-martial.[103] The military appellate courts reversed the death sentences for ten men.[104] Four men have appeals pending.[105] Only two men who have exhausted their direct appeals remain on death row.

Reversals in military court are based on a number of factors. Todd Dock, Joseph Thomas, Jose Simoy, and Jessie Quintanilla were all found guilty of capital crimes and sentenced to death. The appellate courts reversed their death sentences based on a finding that the trial judge had not properly applied the law. In Todd Dock's case, the court found that the trial court had, contrary to UCMJ 45(b), allowed Dock to plead guilty to an offense that was the predicate for a sentence of death.

---

[99] *Id.* at 7.

[100] Benan, *supra* note 14, at 195–96.

[101] *Id.* at 196.

[102] At the end of 2006, only 15 out of the 47 known capital courts-martial returned death sentences. Catherine M. Grosso et al., *The Impact of Civilian Aggravating Factors on the Military death Penalty*, 43 U. MICH. J.L. REFORM 569, 569–70. Since then, two men have been acquitted and Timothy Hennis has been sentenced to death, making the current ratio 16 out of 50.

[103] Those men are: Ronald Gray, Dwight Loving, Todd Dock, Melvin Turner, James Murphy, Ronnie Curtis, Joseph Thomas, Curtis Gibb, Jose Simoy, Kenneth Parker, Wade Walker, William Kreutzer, Jesse Quintanilla, Andrew Witt, Hassan Akbar, and Timothy Hennis.

[104] The ten men whose death sentences have been reversed are: Todd Dock, Melvin Turner, James Murphy, Ronnie Curtis, Joseph Thomas, Curtis Gibb, Jose Simoy, Wade Walker, William Kreutzer, and Jesse Quintanilla. As of Spring, 2011, there has never been a death sentence reinstated after an appellate court reversed a sentence of death or ordered a new trial. *See* Sullivan, *Killing Time*, note 39, at 37–39, *supra*.

[105] The four men on death row pursuing appeals are: Kenneth Parker, Hasan Akbar, Andrew Witt, and Timothy Hennis. *See The U.S Military Death Penalty*, DEATH PENALTY INFORMATION CENTER, http://www.deathpenaltyinfo.org/us-military-death-penalty (last visited Feb. 2, 2012).

In the trial of both Joseph Thomas and Jose Simoy, the trial judges failed to instruct the jury panel on proper voting procedures in accordance with Rule for Courts-Martial 1006. The CAAF court found that the jury panel was not instructed to vote on the lightest proposed sentence first; the jury panel failed to unanimously agree that life imprisonment would be an appropriate sentence before it considered and voted on a sentence of death.[106]

Jesse Quintanilla's sentence of death was reversed when the court found that the military judge improperly excused two potential members of the panel "for cause" during *voir dire*.[107] Both jurors expressed concerns about being able to impose the death penalty based on their religious background and beliefs. Both, however, stated they would be able to vote for death.[108] Concluding that the religious beliefs of both panel members would inhibit their abilities to consider the entire range of punishment, the trial judge granted the two challenges for cause.[109] The CAAF reversed based on the Supreme Court case of *Wainwright v. Witt*[110] that prevents challenges for cause based on a panel member's view of capital punishment unless it "prevents or substantially impairs" the juror's performance.[111]

§ 25.10   "DEATH IS DIFFERENT" IN MILITARY COURTS

Like its civilian counterpart, military death penalty jurisprudence adheres to the notion that, due to the severity and irrevocable nature of the punishment, "death is different."[112] As a result, an accused in a death penalty case receives extra protection in the military court system. Military appellate review must work to insure that the results in capital cases are fair and reliable.[113] *Thomas, Simoy*, and *Murphy* demonstrate how the "death is different" principle leads to a heightened standard of review which fosters death sentence reversals. Defendants William Kreutzer, Wade Walker, Ronnie Curtis, and James Murphy were all convicted of premeditated murder and sentenced to death. In all four cases the appellate courts overturned the death sentences because defense counsel did not adequately develop the mitigation case or because defense counsel's performance was deficient, incomplete, and ineffective. Even though the court cited *Strickland*,[114] it imposed a more narrow and exacting standard for counsel in capital cases. The court concluded that in death penalty cases, an accused deserves a "skilled, trained, and

---

[106] United States v. Thomas, 46 M.J. 311 (C.A.A.F. 1997); United States v. Simoy, 50 M.J. 1 (C.A.A.F. 1998). When Simoy's trial occurred, the CAAF had yet to make its decision in Thomas.

[107] United States v. Quintanilla, 63 M.J. 29 (C.A.A.F. 2006).

[108] *Id.*

[109] *Id.* at 35.

[110] Wainwright v. Witt, 469 U.S. 412, 424 (1985).

[111] *Quintanilla*, 63 M.J. At 36 (quoting *Wainwright*, 469 U.S. at 424).

[112] Loving v. United States, 62 M.J. 235, 236 (C.A.A.F. 2005).

[113] *Id.*

[114] Strickland v. Washington 466 U.S. 668 (1984). In *Strickland*, the Court created a two-pronged test that a defendant must satisfy to prevail on a claim of ineffective assistance of counsel. First, a defendant must show that counsel's performance was *deficient*. Deficient means the attorney was not functioning effectively as counsel. Second, a defendant must establish *prejudice*; a defendant must show that counsel's failures were so serious that the sentence of death was not reliable. *See also* Section 16.03[D].

experienced attorney."[115] The CAAF disregarded defense counsel's proffered trial strategies and concluded that the sentence case "was not fully developed because the trial defense counsel lacked the necessary training and skills to know how to defend a death-penalty case."[116]

§ 25.11 ROADBLOCKS TO MILITARY EXECUTIONS AFTER A DEATH SENTENCE IS AFFIRMED ON APPEAL

In 1989, a court-martial convicted Army Private First Class Dwight Loving of murder, felony murder, attempted murder, and robbery and sentenced him to death.[117] Loving exhausted his direct appeals in 1996 when the Supreme Court affirmed his sentence.[118] At this juncture, UCMJ article 71(a) requires the President to review the case, and if appropriate, approve the sentence.

Even though Loving completed his direct appeals in 1996, the CAAF continued to exercise continuing jurisdiction to hear collateral habeas petitions. In light of its "pivotal role" in the military justice system, the CAAF concluded that it retained jurisdiction until the case was "approved" and "final" under military law.[119] The President cannot, under UCMJ article 71, consider and approve the sentence before a "final judgment as to the legality of the proceedings" exists.[120] Pursuant to UCMJ article 76, a death sentence does not become absolute and final until the President signs and "approves" the sentence.[121] Taken together, these rules provide that the terminal point of the military proceedings does not occur at the completion of direct review. Rather, CAAF jurisdiction to hear collateral attacks continues until the President approves the sentence.[122] In Loving's case, the CAAF heard at least six collateral appeals after direct review ended in 1996.[123]

The Army did not deliver Loving's case to the President until January 23, 2006.[124] Part of this delay can be attributed to the UCMJ. The UCMJ requires the Judge Advocate General of the Army to transmit the entire case, along with a sentence recommendation, to the Secretary of the Army. The Secretary may, at his discretion, make a written recommendation to the President. Then, the Army forwards the entire case to the Secretary of Defense to do the same. Only then does the case go to the President.[125]

---

[115] *Id.* at 331–32.

[116] Unites States v. Curtis, 48 M.J. 331, *3 (C.A.A.F. 1997).

[117] *See* Loving v. United States, 517 U.S. 748, 751 (1996).

[118] *Id.* at 774.

[119] *Loving*, 62 M.J. at 239–46.

[120] *Id.*

[121] *Id.* at 243–45.

[122] *Id.* at 244.

[123] *See* Toman, *supra* note 5, 58–62.

[124] *Id.*

[125] *Id.*

When the Army delivered Loving's case to the President in 2006, an evidentiary hearing on Loving's ineffective assistance of counsel claim was still pending in the CAAF.[126] During this time, the President took no action on whether to approve Loving's death sentence.[127]

In 2009, the CAAF completed the evidentiary hearing and denied his claim of ineffective assistance of counsel.[128] The Supreme Court denied certiorari in 2010.[129] The President has yet to make a decision on Loving's death sentence and Loving has yet to file more additional collateral habeas appeals. As a result, Loving's execution remains pending.

Only one other capital case completed direct appeal and went to the President for final approval. In 1988 a court-martial found Army Specialist Ronald Gray guilty of rape and premeditated murder of two women and the rape of a third woman and sentenced him to death.[130] Gray completed direct review in 2001 when the Supreme Court denied certiorari.[131] He made no subsequent court filings but the military did not deliver his case to the President until September 2005.[132]

President Bush "approved" the military's request to execute Gray in July 2008.[133] The military scheduled for Gray to die by lethal injection on December 10, 2008.[134] On November 26, 2008, the United States District Court for the District of Kansas, where the military death row barracks are located, stayed the execution to allow Gray to file a habeas petition.[135] Gray's habeas petition remains pending and the execution remains stayed.

The scope of review on habeas review remains uncertain. The congressional statutes governing federal habeas review, including the USA Patriot Act and the Antiterrorism and Effective Death Penalty Act of 1996, omit any reference to the military habeas petitions.[136] No federal district court has ruled on a military habeas petition in the modern era and no death row inmate had filed a habeas petition since 1961. The District Court that stayed Gray's execution acknowledged the petition raised new issues as yet unresolved.[137]

---

[126] Loving v. United States, 64 M.J. 132, 141–43 (C.A.A.F. 2006).

[127] Toman, note 5, 61 n.368, *supra*. This would suggest that Loving's defense counsel intentionally delayed the execution by filing numerous collateral appeals. *See* Sullivan, *Killing Time*, note 39, at 29 n.112, *supra*.

[128] Loving v. United States, 68 M.J. 1 (C.A.A.F. 2009).

[129] Loving v. United States, *cert. denied*, 131 S. Ct. 67 (2010).

[130] *See* United States v. Gray, 54 M.J. 231 (C.A.A.F. 2000).

[131] United States v. Gray, *cert. denied*, 532 U.S. 919 (2001).

[132] *See* Toman, *supra* note 5, 62; Sullivan, *Killing Time*, *supra* note 39, at 29 n.112.

[133] *See The U.S. Military Death Penalty*, DEATH PENALTY INFORMATION CENTER, http://www.deathpenaltyinfo.org/us-military-death-penalty (last visited Feb. 2, 2012).

[134] Mike Mount, *First military execution since 1961 scheduled next month*, CNN (Nov. 11, 2008), http://www.cnn.com/2008/CRIME/11/20/military.execution/index.html?iref=mpstoryview.

[135] Order granting stay of execution, Gray v. Gray, No. 08-3289-RDR (D. Kan. Nov. 26, 2008).

[136] Sullivan, *Killing Time*, *supra* note 39, at 28.

[137] *See* Associated Press, *Judge Won't Lift Stay of Execution for Soldier Convicted of Murder, Rapes*, FOX NEWS (Dec. 5, 2008), http://www.foxnews.com/story/0,2933,462788,00.html.

§ 25.12   CONCLUSION

The military maintains the punishment of death for specific offenses. In recent years, there are only a small number of cases in which a death penalty trial has occurred. Of those, there are a handful of death sentences imposed and few of those survive a direct appeal. In his review of two decades of military capital litigation, Col Dwight H. Sullivan sums up the military death penalty by quoting Professor Gary D. Solis: "The death penalty in the Armed Forces: Yes, but No."[138]

---

[138] Sullivan, Killing Time, *supra.* Note 39 at 50 (quoting Professor Gary D. Solis Marines and Military Law in Vietnam. Trial by Fire 8 (1989).

Chapter 26

THE DEATH PENALTY IN A GLOBAL CONTEXT

§ 26.01 OVERVIEW

The United States is not the only country with the death penalty. In fact, the division among states in the U.S., some with and some without the death penalty, is similarly reflected in divisions internationally. On the international level, however, there is a more noticeable trend to abolish the death penalty. As of December 2011, 140 countries do not have the death penalty or have not imposed it in over 10 years.[1] According to Amnesty International's statistics, 96 countries have abolished the death penalty for all crimes; 9 have abolished the death penalty for ordinary crimes, retaining it for crimes such as military crimes or treason; and 35 have not executed anyone in more than ten years in circumstances thought to reflect a policy or practice against using the death penalty.[2] Fifty-eight countries, including the United States, actively maintain capital punishment.[3] Most notably, as a block, the 47 countries that are members of the Council of Europe have eliminated or no longer use the death penalty. In Africa, 38 of the 54 countries no longer use capital punishment. In the Americas, most of Central and South America have abolished the death penalty, as have Canada and Mexico. Most of the countries that retain the death penalty, other than the United States, are in the Middle East, Asia, and some parts of Africa.[4]

Most of the executions in the world occur in China.[5] In 2010, the 6 countries that executed the most individuals were: China (more than 1,000); Iran (at least 252); North Korea (at least 60); Yemen (at least 53); United States (46); and Saudi Arabia (at least 27).[6] Excluding China, Amnesty International reported that there were 527 executions in 23 countries in 2010.[7]

In countries that retain the death penalty, there is some variation on which crimes are death-eligible and in methods of execution. In general, murder is a death-eligible crime as it is in the United States. In other countries, death-eligible

---

[1] *See* Amnesty International statistics at Death Penalty Information Center (DPIC) http://www.deathpenaltyinfo.org/abolitionist-and-retentionist-countries (last visited Jan. 21, 2012).

[2] *Id.*

[3] *Id.*

[4] *Id.*

[5] *But see* Roger Hood, *Abolition of the Death Penalty: China in World Perspective*, 1 City Univ. of Hong Kong L. Rev. 1-21 (2009) (discussing changes in Chinese law and attitudes about the death penalty).

[6] *See* Amnesty International statistics at DPIC, *supra* note 1, at http://deathpenaltyinfo.org/death-penalty-international-perspective#interexec (last visited Jan. 21, 2012).

[7] *Id.*

crimes also include non-homicide crimes, *inter alia*, of robbery,[8] drug-trafficking,[9] rape of an adult,[10] adultery,[11] same-sex consensual sexual relations,[12] and economic offenses.[13] In contrast, in the United States, it is more unusual to find non-homicide crimes that are death-eligible.[14] Methods of execution worldwide include, *inter alia*, lethal injection,[15] hanging,[16] firing squad,[17] beheading,[18] and stoning.[19] For example, in 2009, a woman in Somalia was stoned to death for adultery and two men in Iran were stoned to death for adultery and murder.[20] Another aspect of stoning is that it is typically a public execution, rather than done out of the public eye as is the case with most executions.

---

[8] *See* China, Democratic Republic of the Congo, Cuba, Equatorial Guinea, Indonesia, Iran, Jordan, Lebanon, Malaysia, Nigeria, Saudi Arabia, Sudan, Uganda, and Vietnam. This list is from the Northwestern University School of Law, Center for International Human Rights (Northwestern) database at http://www.deathpenaltyworldwide.org (last visited Feb. 4, 2012), but includes only those countries considered retentionist by Amnesty International. For the Amnesty International information, *see* DPIC, *supra* note 1.

[9] *See* Bahrain, Bangladesh, China, Cuba, Democratic Republic of the Congo, Egypt, India, Indonesia, Iran, Iraq, Jordan, Kuwait, Libya, Malaysia, Oman, Pakistan, Qatar, Saudi Arabia, Singapore, South Sudan, Sudan, Syria, Taiwan, Thailand, United Arab Emirates, United States, Vietnam, Yemen. This list is from the Northwestern website, *supra* note 8, but includes only those countries considered retentionist by Amnesty International.

[10] *See* China, Iran, and Saudi Arabia. This list is from the Northwestern website, *supra* note 8, but includes only those countries considered retentionist by Amnesty International.

[11] *See* Iran and Saudi Arabia. This list is from the Northwestern website, *supra* note 8, but includes only those countries considered retentionist by Amnesty International.

[12] *See* Iran, Nigeria, Saudi Arabia, and Yemen. This list is from the Northwestern website, *supra* note 8, but includes only those countries considered retentionist by Amnesty International. A bill was also introduced in Uganda that would have made "aggravated homosexuality" a death penalty offense. *See* the Anti Homosexuality Bill, Uganda, 2009, *available at* http://www.truthwinsout.org/blog/2010/02/6848/. However, in February 2012, the bill was reintroduced without the death penalty provision. *See Uganda Revives Anti-Gay Bill but Drops Death Penalty, available at* http://www.bbc.co.uk/news/world-africa-16928608 (February 7, 2012).

[13] *See* China (death-eligible economic crimes include, *inter alia*, producing or selling fake medicine or tainted food, causing serious injury; certain economic fraud to the extreme detriment of the state; forgery, fraudulent issue, or improper sale of tax items or papers). Northwestern website, *supra* note 8.

[14] *See* discussion of non-homicide crimes, Section 8.05, *supra*.

[15] China, Guatemala, Taiwan, Thailand, United States, and Vietnam. Northwestern website, *supra* note 8.

[16] *Id.* Most of the retentionist countries have hanging as a method.

[17] *Id.* Similar to hanging, shooting is a method authorized in most retentionist countries.

[18] *Id.* Iran, Saudi Arabia, and Yemen.

[19] Indonesia, Iran, Nigeria, Pakistan, Saudi Arabia, Sudan, United Arab Emirates, and Yemen. *Id.*, but includes only those countries considered retentionist by Amnesty International.

[20] *See Somali Woman Stoned for Adultery*, BBC NEWS, *available at* http://news.bbc.co.uk/2/hi/8366197.stm (Nov. 18, 2009); *Men Stoned to Death for Adultery, Murder in Iran*, CNN WORLD, *available at* http://articles.cnn.com/2009-01-13/world/iran.stoning_1_stoned-amnesty-international-sentences?_s= PM:WORLD (Jan. 13, 2009). In January 2012, Iran was poised to change a stoning sentence to hanging in the face of international protest. *Iranian Woman to Face Death by Stoning or Hanging*, CBS NEWS, *available at* http://www.huffingtonpost.com/2011/12/25/iran-stoning-woman-adultery_n_1169429.html (December 25, 2011).

Despite the continuation of the death penalty, with the variations on death-eligible crimes and methods of execution, the trend internationally is to abolish capital punishment. Within the last 10 years alone, from 2002-2012, 19 countries have ceased using the death penalty.[21] According to Professors Hood and Hoyle, the rate of change in abolishing the death penalty has increased dramatically. In an 11-year period, from 1989-1999, 40 countries moved to abolition, compared with only 26 countries in the 23-year period from 1966-1989.[22] What are some of the developments in this trend? To answer that question, the next two sections will explore international treaties and national judicial decisions or executive actions. A third section will focus on two issues that occur with some frequency in other countries, mandatory death sentences and the death row phenomenon. A final section will examine the extradition practices of those countries without the death penalty and the consequences for countries, such as the United States, which retain the death penalty.

§ 26.02 INTERNATIONAL TREATIES

Similar to the U.S. Supreme Court's interpretation of the 8th Amendment as prohibiting arbitrary imposition of a death sentence under the cruel and unusual punishment clause, all major human rights treaties protect individuals against arbitrary deprivation of life, and prohibit torture, and cruel, inhuman or degrading punishment and treatment. For example, the International Covenant on Civil and Political Rights (ICCPR), with 167 countries as parties to the treaty, including the United States, provides:

> Every human being has the inherent right to life. This right shall be protected by law. No one shall be arbitrarily deprived of his life.[23]

The Universal Declaration of Human Rights,[24] the American Convention on Human Rights,[25] the European Convention on Human Rights,[26] and the African Charter on Human and Peoples' Rights[27] also enshrine the principle of a right not to be deprived of life arbitrarily.

The ICCPR further restricts the use of the death penalty in several ways. It provides that only the "most serious crimes" may be subject to the death penalty. The treaty states:

---

[21] Death Penalty Information Center, "Abolitionist and Retentionist Countries," *available at* http://www.deathpenaltyinfo.org/abolitionist-and-retentionist-countries#1976 (last visited Jan. 21, 2012).

[22] Roger Hood and Carolyn Hoyle, *Abolishing the Death Penalty Worldwide: The Impact of A "New Dynamic"*, 38 CRIME & JUST. 1, 6 (2009).

[23] International Covenant on Civil and Political Rights (ICCPR), 999 U.N.T.S. 171, 6 I.L.M. 368, *entered into force* Mar. 23, 1976, at art. 6 (1).

[24] Universal Declaration of Human Rights, G.A. Res. 217A (III), UN GAOR, 3d Sess., Supp. No. 13, UN Doc. A/810 (1948) 71.

[25] American Convention on Human Rights, Nov. 22, 1969, 1144 U.N.T.S. 123.

[26] Council of Europe, European Convention for the Protection of Human Rights and Fundamental Freedoms, 4 November 1950, E.T.S. 5 *entered into force*, Sept. 3, 1953.

[27] African Charter on Human and Peoples' Rights, 21 I.L.M. 58, June 27, 1981.

> In countries which have not abolished the death penalty, sentence of death
> may be imposed only for the most serious crimes in accordance with the law
> in force at the time of the commission of the crime and not contrary to the
> provisions of the present Covenant . . .

The treaty further prohibits the death penalty for those who are under 18 years old
when they committed the crimes and for pregnant women.[28] The ICCPR is also
interpreted as encouraging abolition of the death penalty[29] and precluding a state
without the death penalty from reinstating it.[30]

The international community has gone further than prohibiting arbitrary death
sentences. In more recent years, countries have established optional protocols to
three of the well-established human rights treaties that explicitly abolish the death
penalty. The Second Optional Protocol to the ICCPR states the basic principle that
"all measures of abolition of the death penalty should be considered as progress in
the enjoyment of the right to life."[31] The Protocol then states that "each State Party
shall take all necessary measures to abolish the death penalty within its jurisdiction."[32] There presently are 73 countries that are parties to the Protocol.[33] There is
a similar protocol to the American Convention.[34] The European Convention has two:
Protocol 6 abolishes the death penalty in peacetime[35] and Protocol 13 abolishes the
death penalty even in wartime.[36]

International bodies have also called for a moratorium on the death penalty. The
General Assembly of the United Nations,[37] the U.N. Sub-Commission on the
Promotion and the Protection of Human Rights,[38] and the African Commission on

---

[28] ICCPR, *supra* note 23, at art. 6.

[29] ICCPR, *supra* note 23. Art 6 states: Nothing in this article shall be invoked to delay or to prevent
the abolition of capital punishment by any State Party to the present Covenant. *See also* Hood & Hoyle,
supra note 22, at 32.

[30] Hood & Hoyle, *supra* note 22, at 20.

[31] Second Optional Protocol to the International Covenant on Civil and Political Rights, Aiming at
Abolition of the Death Penalty, 29 I.L.M. 1464, *entered into force* July 11, 1991.

[32] *Id.* at 1467.

[33] *See* list of signatories as of Feb. 10, 2012 at http://treaties.un.org/Pages/ViewDetails.aspx?src=
TREATY&mtdsg_no=IV-12&chapter=4&lang=en.

[34] Protocol to the American Convention on Human Rights to Abolish the Death Penalty, 29 I.L.M.
1447, *entered into force* upon deposit of instruments of ratification or accession (13 countries are parties
to the treaty) (last visited Feb. 4, 2012).

[35] Protocol No. 6 to the Convention for the Protection of Human Rights and Fundamental Freedoms
Concerning the Abolition of the Death Penalty, Eur. T.S. 114, *entered into force,* Mar. 1, 1985 (46
countries are parties to the treaty) (last visited Feb. 4, 2012).

[36] Protocol No. 13 to the Convention for the Protection of Human Rights and Fundamental
Freedoms, Concerning the Abolition of the Death Penalty in All Circumstances, Eur. T.S. 187, *entered
into force* July 1, 2003 (43 countries are parties to the treaty) (last visited Feb. 4, 2012).

[37] UN General Assembly, *Moratorium on the use of the death penalty: resolution/adopted by the
General Assembly*, Feb. 26, 2008, A/RES/62/149, *available at* http://www.unhcr.org/refworld/docid/
47c814e32.html (last visited Feb. 5, 2012).

[38] UN Sub-Commission on the Promotion and Protection of Human Rights, *Resolution 2004/25 on
the Imposition of the Death Penalty on Civilians by Military Tribunals or by Tribunals Whose
Composition Includes One or More Members of the Armed Forces,* Aug. 12, 2004, E/CN.4/Sub.2/RES/

Human and Peoples' Rights have each issued resolutions urging a moratorium.[39]

Moreover, international bodies charged with interpreting the treaties have restricted the use of the death penalty through their decisions. For example, the Human Rights Committee, which is responsible for cases involving the ICCPR, has interpreted the limitation to the "most serious crimes" to preclude the death penalty for drug offenses, robbery, and embezzlement.[40] A similar interpretation has been offered by the U.N. Special Rapporteur on Extrajudicial, Summary, or Arbitrary Executions.[41]

In line with the trend on the international level, none of the international criminal courts has the death penalty. These courts include the International Criminal Court, the International Criminal Tribunal for the former Yugoslavia, the International Criminal Tribunal for Rwanda, the Special Court for Sierra Leone, the Extraordinary Chambers in the Courts of Cambodia, and the Special Tribunal for Lebanon. The absence of the death penalty is noteworthy in part because the international criminal tribunals are adjudicating some of the worst crimes that occur on a large scale: war crimes, crimes against humanity, and genocide. Further evidencing the global trend towards abolition on a national level, even Rwanda, the site of a horrific genocide, has abolished the death penalty.

The trend towards abolition and the increased use of international instruments reflect an emphasis on the death penalty as a human rights issue. According to Professors Hood and Hoyle, the death penalty has changed from being a national criminal justice issue to an international human rights issue.[42] A human rights approach, through both legal and political frameworks, and through bodies such as the Council of Europe and the European Union, is having a strong impact on countries to move towards abolishing the death penalty.[43] This pressure is reflected, for instance, in the refusal of abolitionist countries to extradite to retentionist countries unless there are assurances that the death penalty will not be imposed.[44] In the increasingly global world of crime, including terrorism, extraditions are extremely important for political and security issues. Further discussion of extradition follows in Section 26.05, *infra*.

2004/25, *available at* http://www.unhcr.org/refworld/docid/41640b564.html.

[39] African Commission on Human and People's Rights, *Resolution Calling on State Parties to Observe the Moratorium on the Death Penalty*, 10-24 November 2008, ACHPR/Res. 136 (XXXXIIII) 08, *available at* http://www.achpr.org/english/resolutions/resolution136_en.htm.

[40] Rick Lines, *A "Most Serious Crime"? — The Death Penalty for Drug Offences and International Human Rights Law*, 21 Amicus J. 21, 22 (2010).

[41] *See* UN Human Rights Council, *UN Human Rights Council: Report of the Special Rapporteur on Extrajudicial, Summary or Arbitrary Executions*, Jan. 29, 2007, A/HRC/4/20, *available at* http://www.unhcr.org/refworld/docid/461e40f82.html.

[42] Hood & Hoyle, *supra* note 22, at 17.

[43] *Id.* at 23-27.

[44] *Id.* at 25; *see also* discussion, *supra*, Section 23.05.

§ 26.03 NATIONAL JUDICIAL AND GOVERNMENTAL DECISIONS

Part of the overall international trend towards abolition is evidenced by decisions of courts that have directly found the death penalty unconstitutional. One of the leading constitutional decisions invalidating the death penalty is from the Constitutional Court of South Africa. In *State v. Makwanyane*,[45] the Court found that capital punishment "annihilates human dignity . . . ," has "elements of arbitrariness," and is "irremediable." As a result, it constitutes "cruel, inhuman and degrading punishment."[46] Other national courts, in addition to South Africa, that have interpreted their constitutions as prohibiting the death penalty include the courts of Hungary, Lithuania, Albania, Nepal, and the Ukraine.[47] In each case, the court grounded its decision on the constitutional right to life or the right to be free from inhumane punishment.[48]

One of the issues that arises with constitutional interpretation is whether the national constitution provides for an absolute right to life or a qualified right to life. The South African Constitution contains an absolute, unqualified right to life. The South African Constitution states: "Everyone has the right to life."[49] A "qualified" right to life provision is one in which the constitution protects against the "arbitrary" deprivation of life or the taking of life "without due process of law," but does not provide for a right to life in absolute terms. The U. S. Constitution follows this model of a qualified right to life with the language stating: "nor shall any State deprive any person of life, liberty, or property, without due process of law . . . "[50] The U.S. Supreme Court and a number of other national courts[51] with qualified right to life constitutional provisions have held that the qualification supports a finding that the death penalty is not *per se* unconstitutional. On the other hand, decisions from the Ukraine,[52] Hungary, and Albania courts found the death penalty unconstitutional despite having a qualified right to life in their constitutions.[53]

Further evidence of a trend towards abolition is a call for legislative action, such as occurred in a decision by the Supreme Court of Uganda. The Ugandan Court, similar to the U.S. Supreme Court, must interpret the Constitution, not legislate. Recognizing that limitation, the Ugandan Supreme Court, while upholding the

---

[45] 1995 (3) SA (CC) (S. Afr.).

[46] *Id.* at para. 95 (Chaskelson, J.).

[47] Hood & Hoyle, *supra* note 22, at 11.

[48] Paolo G. Carozza, *"My Friend Is a Stranger": The Death Penalty and the Global Ius Commune of Human Rights*, 81 Tex. L. Rev. 1031, 1046-1077 (2003).

[49] S. Afr. Const., 1996, Ch. 2, section 11.

[50] U.S. Const. amend. XIV, section 1.

[51] Carozza, *supra* note 48, at 1046-1055; 1061-1062 (describing the court decisions in India; Tanzania; and Nigeria). More recently, the Supreme Court of Uganda took a similar position under their constitution. *See Attorney General v. Susan Kigula & 417 Others*, Constitutional Appeal No. 3 of 2006, 2009 UGSC 6, at 33-34.

[52] "Every person has the inalienable right to life. No one shall be arbitrarily deprived of life." *See* Opinion of the Venice Commission on the Constitutional Aspects of the Death Penalty in Ukraine, *available at* http://www.venice.coe.int/docs/1998/CDL-INF(1998)001rev-e.asp.

[53] Carozza, *supra* note 48, at 1063-69.

constitutionality of the death penalty under a qualified right to life provision, explicitly called upon the Ugandan legislature to reconsider whether to continue the retention of the death penalty.[54]

Another similarity to the United States can occur with executive clemency. As discussed *supra* in Chapter 18, recent years have seen governors in the United States grant blanket commutations to death row inmates due to concerns about the administration of the death penalty. Similarly, although on a larger scale, in August 2009 in Kenya, the President commuted the death sentences of over 4,000 individuals and asked for a re-evaluation of the use of the death penalty.[55]

What is the reasoning behind the general trend towards abolishing the death penalty? The reasoning of the Constitutional Court of South Africa is probably the most comprehensive. The Court referred to arbitrariness in imposition of the death penalty; the fact that mistakes cannot be remedied; society's value of human dignity; and that retribution can be served by a long prison sentence.[56] In a strong statement of the state's role in exemplifying respect for human dignity, Justice Langa wrote:

> . . . For good or for worse, the State is a role model for our society. A culture of respect for human life and dignity, based on the values reflected in the Constitution, has to be engendered, and the State must take the lead. In acting out this role, the State not only preaches respect for the law and that the killing must stop, but it demonstrates in the best way possible, by example, society's own regard for human life and dignity by refusing to destroy that of the criminal. Those who are inclined to kill need to be told why it is wrong. The reason surely must be the principle that the value of human life is inestimable, and it is a value which the State must uphold by example as well.[57]

§ 26.04   RECURRING ISSUES: MANDATORY DEATH SENTENCES AND DEATH ROW PHENOMENON

[A]   Mandatory Death Sentences

One issue that arises with some frequency in other countries is the legality of mandatory death sentences. Similar to the situation in the United States in which the U.S. Supreme Court held mandatory death sentences unconstitutional, national and international bodies around the world are taking the same position. For example, the Supreme Court of Uganda struck down mandatory death sentences in 2009 under the national constitution.[58] Similarly, the High Court of Malawi struck

---

[54] *Kigula, supra* note 51, at 63.

[55] Kenya State House, http://www.statehousekenya.go.ke/. *Kenya Empties its Death-Row Cells*, BBC NEWS, *available at* http://news.bbc.co.uk/2/hi/8181864.stm (Aug. 3, 2009).

[56] *Makwanyane, supra* note 45.

[57] *Makwanyane, supra* note 45, at para. 222 (Langa, J., concurring).

[58] *Kigula, supra* note 51.

down mandatory death sentences under its national constitution in 2007.[59] The Human Rights Committee, charged with interpreting the ICCPR, has repeatedly found mandatory death sentences in violation of the treaty. This has occurred, for example, in cases involving Zambia,[60] Sri Lanka,[61] Trinidad and Tobago,[62] The Philippines,[63] and St. Vincent and the Grenadines.[64] The Committee has said that it is necessary to be able to take into account "the defendant's personal circumstances or the circumstances of the particular offence."[65] Similarly, the Inter-American Court of Human Rights has found mandatory death sentences in violation of the American Convention on Human Rights in cases involving Barbados[66] and Trinidad and Tobago.[67] The Privy Council, formerly the appeals court for Commonwealth countries in the Caribbean, also found mandatory death sentences violative of national constitutions in Belize[68] and St. Lucia.[69] Similar to the reasoning of the U.S. Supreme Court, the flaw in mandatory sentences was considered to be the inability to consider mitigation and the individual circumstances of the defendant.

[B] Death Row Phenomenon

The death row phenomenon, an issue yet to be considered by the U.S. Supreme Court, is a second issue that arises around the world in national and international courts. Courts in Uganda[70] and the Privy Council with regard to Jamaica[71] have set limits on the constitutionality of years on death row. The Privy Council, in cases from Caribbean nations, found that more than five years on death row constitutes a constitutional violation.[72] The Ugandan Court set the limit at three years. In its

---

[59] Kafantayeni v. Attorney General, Constitutional Case No. 12 of 2005, 2007 MWHC 1 (Malawi) (holding that a mandatory death sentence for murder amounts to inhumane treatment or punishment in its application).

[60] Mwamba v. Zambia, Hum. Rts. Comm., Communications No. 1520/2006, dec. of 10 March 2010 at para. 6.3.

[61] Weerawansa v. Sri Lanka, Hum. Rts. Comm., Communications No. 1406/2005, dec. of 17 March 2009 at paras. 2.1 and 7.4.

[62] Kennedy v. Trinidad and Tobago, Hum. Rts. Comm., Communications No. 1077/2002, dec. of 26 March 2002.

[63] Carpo v. The Philippines, Hum. Rts. Comm., Communication No. 1077/2002, dec. of 28 March 2003.

[64] Thompson v. St. Vincent and the Grenadines, Hum. Rts. Comm., Communications No. 806/1998, dec. of Dec. 5, 2000.

[65] *Mwamba, supra* note 60, at para. 6.3.

[66] Case of Boyce et al. v. Barbados, Series C N. 169, Inter-American Court of Human Rights (IACrtHR), Judgment, 20 November 2007.

[67] Case of Hilaire, Constantine and Benjamin *et al.* v. Trinidad and Tobago, Series C N. 94, Inter-American Court of Human Rights (IACrtHR), Judgement, 21 June 2002.

[68] Reyes v. The Queen, UKPC 11 (Privy Council 2002) (Belize).

[69] The Queen v. Hughes, 2 App. Cas. 259 (Privy Council 2002) (St. Lucia).

[70] More than 3 years is inordinate delay. *Kigula, supra* note 51.

[71] Pratt et al. v. Attorney General for Jamaica *et al.*, 4 All E.R. 769 (Privy Council 1993) (Jamaica).

[72] *Pratt et al., supra* note 71 (finding that it would be inhumane or degrading punishment to hang two defendants after more than fourteen years and holding that cases which take more than five years to proceed to execution will be commuted to life imprisonment in the future); *see also* Attorney General et

decision, the Supreme Court of Uganda considered the time that is necessary for appeal and a clemency petition balanced against the difficult prison conditions in which the inmate is confined. The Court carefully noted how important the judicial and clemency processes are, including quoting from the U.S. Supreme Court in *Herrera v. Collins*[73] on the role of clemency, but concluded that 3 years was sufficient to complete these processes.[74]

§ 26.05   EXTRADITION

Another consequence of the increased number of countries without the death penalty is a refusal to extradite to countries with the death penalty without assurances that it will not be sought. For example, if a defendant commits a crime in the United States and then flees to another country, the state or federal government will want to extradite the defendant from the foreign country to stand trial here. Foreign courts and international tribunals are increasingly refusing to extradite to the United States or other countries if the defendant could face the death penalty or be subject to the death row phenomenon.[75] The courts are finding that extradition under these circumstances would violate either their own national constitutions or international treaty obligations.

One of the most cited cases that addressed an extradition issue is *Soering v. United Kingdom.*[76] Soering was accused of murder in the United States, but was arrested in England. He raised the death row phenomenon as a reason to preclude his extradition. The European Court of Human Rights[77] held that England would violate the European Convention for the Protection of Human Rights and Funda-

---

al. v. Joseph & Boyce, CCJ Appeal No CV 2 of 2005 (2006) (Barbados) (affirming *Pratt* in principle, but declining to set a specific time limit and expressing the opinion that where the condemned person initiates international human rights processes exceeding eighteen months, that time should be disregarded for the purposes of *Pratt*).

[73] 506 U.S. 390, 411-12 (1993); *see also* discussion on *Herrera, supra,* Section 18.05.

[74] *Kigula, supra* note 51, at 52-55.

[75] John Quigley, *The Rule of Non-Inquiry and Human Rights*, 45 Cath. U.L. Rev. 1213, 1227-29 (1996) (describing the inquiry and requisite assurances of no death penalty or of mistreatment by countries in Europe and Latin American. *Cf.* Daniel J. Sharfstein, *European Courts, American Rights: Extradition and Prison Conditions*, 67 Brook. L. Rev. 719, 729-731 (2002) (commenting on changes in extradition policies in Israel and some Latin American countries in response to pressure from the United States); Elizabeth Burleson, *Juvenile Execution, Terrorist Extradition, And Supreme Court Discretion To Consider International Death Penalty Jurisprudence*, 68 Alb. L. Rev. 909 (2005); Kent Roach, *Wrongful Convictions and Criminal Procedure*, 42 Brandeis L.J. 349 (2003-04); David A. Sadoff, *International Law and the Mortal Precipice: A Legal Policy Critique of the Death Row Phenomenon*, 17 Tul. J. Int'l & Comp. L. 77, 111 (2008) (referring to increasing trend not to extradite without assurances of no death penalty). *See* Section 19.02, *supra*, on the death row phenomenon.

[76] Jens Soering, a German national, killed his girlfriend's parents in Virginia and fled to England, where he was detained for check fraud. Soering v. United Kingdom, 11 Eur. Ct. H.R. 439, 443 (1989). During his detention he admitted to the killings. *Id.* The U.S. subsequently requested Soering's extradition under the terms of the Extradition Treaty of 1972 between the United States and the United Kingdom. *Id.* at 444.

[77] The European Convention for the Protection of Human Rights and Fundamental Freedoms, and its subsequent Protocols, established the European Court of Human Rights to hear complaints of violations under the European Convention, *available at* http://www.echr.coe.int/NR/rdonlyres/DF074FE4-96C2-4384-BFF6-404AAF5BC585/0/Brochure_en_bref_EN.pdf (last visited Jan. 28, 2012).

mental Freedoms if they extradited Soering to the United States to stand trial under these circumstances. The European Court focused on the confluence of four factors: 1) a delay of 6-8 years on death row, 2) restrictive living conditions, 3) the young age of the defendant at the time of the crime (18 years old) along with some mental disturbance, and 4) the possibility of trying the defendant in Germany.[78] On the basis of their findings, the European Court found that, under these conditions, extradition to the United States to face the death row phenomenon would violate the prohibition that no one be "subjected to torture or to inhuman or degrading treatment or punishment."[79] A decision from the European Court of Human Rights affects a significant number of countries in Europe. Thus, *Soering* potentially has a serious impact on the ability of the United States to extradite defendants to stand trial in capital cases.

A number of countries currently refuse to extradite individuals to the United States without assurances that the death penalty will not be imposed.[80] For instance, in *United States v. Burns*,[81] the Canadian Supreme Court unanimously held that two Canadians could not be extradited to the United States on murder charges without assurances that they would not face the death penalty, unless there were "exceptional circumstances." The extradition otherwise would violate the Canadian Charter of Rights and Freedoms. Thus, the general rule in Canada after *Burns* is not to extradite without assurances that the death penalty will not be imposed.[82] The South African Constitutional Court similarly found that an individual had been illegally turned over to the United States to face trial with the possibility of the death penalty.[83] Other countries that have required assurances

---

[78] *Soering*, 11 Eur. Ct. H.R. at ¶¶ 107, 108, 110.

[79] Soering was ultimately extradited with assurances that the death penalty would not be imposed. Sharfstein, *supra* note 75, at 743.

[80] *See* Sharfstein, *supra* note 75 at 744-47 (describing prison conditions in capital and noncapital cases as potential bar to extradition); Alan W. Clarke et. al., *Does the Rest of the World Matter? Sovereignty, International Human Rights Law and the American Death Penalty*, 30 Queen's L.J. 260 (2004) (commenting on European governments' increasing refusal to extradite to the U.S. without assurances of no death penalty); Elizabeth Burleson, *Juvenile Execution, Terrorist Extradition, And Supreme Court Discretion To Consider International Death Penalty Jurisprudence*, 68 Alb. L. Rev. 909, 910 (2005) (noting that, even though the death penalty itself is not yet considered to be a violation of customary international law, it still has a significant impact on extradition; further noting that a "growing body of case law provides a warning to States that still use the death penalty that their extradition treaties may not be upheld without assurances that capital punishment will not be imposed"); Roger Hood & Carolyn Hoyle, *Abolishing the Death Penalty Worldwide: The Impact of A "New Dynamic"*, 38 Crime & Just. 1, 25 (2009) (discussing the pressure by non-death penalty countries on countries with the death penalty by refusing extradition).

[81] United States v. Burns, 2001 S.C.R. 283 (Can.), *also available at* 40 I.L.M. 1034. In *Burns*, the Canadian Court also stated that the death row phenomenon was a factor that weighed in the balance against extradition without assurances.

[82] For discussion of the *Burns* case, *see*, Alan Clarke, *Justice in a Changed World: Terrorism, Extradition, and the Death Penalty*, 29 Wm. Mitchell L. Rev. 783, 799-803 (2003); Burleson, *supra* note 75 at 913-14; Melissa A. Waters, *Mediating Norms and Identity: The Role of Transnational Judicial Dialogue in Creating and Enforcing International Law*, 93 Geo. L.J. 487, 523 (2005); Kent Roach, *supra* note 75, at 367; and Andrea Cortland, *United States v. Burns: Canada's Extraterritorial Extension of Canadian Law and Creation of A Canadian "Safe Haven" in Capital Extradition Cases*, 40 U. Miami Inter-Am. L. Rev. 139, 144 (2008).

[83] Case of Kahlfan Mohammed, Constitutional Court of South Africa 2001(7) BCLR 685 (CC) (finding

that the death penalty would not be imposed include The Netherlands,[84] France,[85] Germany,[86] Spain,[87] and Mexico.[88] The Italian Constitutional Court took an even

---

violation of South African Constitution to deport or extradite Mohammed to the United States without assurances of no death penalty); also described in United States v. Bin Laden, 126 F. Supp. 2d 295, 363-64 (S.D.N.Y. 2001) (describing court decision on behalf of Mohamed, a co-defendant of Bin Laden's; Mohamed was one of four men convicted for the 1998 bombings of two American embassies in Tanzania and Kenya.). It is also interesting to note that the U.S. federal court permitted use of the decision from South African Constitutional Court as mitigating evidence to show that equally culpable co-defendants would not face the death penalty because of assurances given to Germany and likely to be given to the United Kingdom. *See also* Clarke, *supra* note 82, at 803-05; John Paul Truskett, *The Death Penalty, International Law, and Human Rights*, 11 Tulsa J. Comp. & Int'l L. 557, 574 (2004); Chimène I. Keitner, *Framing Constitutional Rights*, 40 Sw. L. Rev. 617, 618-20 (2011).

[84] Short v. Kingdom of the Netherlands, 29 I.L.M. 1375 (1990) (finding the extradition of Short (an American serviceman) to the United States, where he would face the death penalty, would violate the European Convention on Human Rights which prevailed over a NATO agreement). *See also* Ved P. Nanda, *Bases for Refusing International Extradition Requests — Capital Punishment and Torture*, 23 Fordham Int'l L.J. 1369, 1391-92 (2000) (describing the *Short* opinion). Ultimately an assurance of no death penalty was given and Short was extradited. Sharfstein, *supra* note 75, at 743-44. *See also Dutch Court Forbids Extradition of Dutch Man to US*, Xinhua News Agency via Comtex, *available at* Westlaw NewsRoom (Oct. 13, 2005) (District Court in the Hague ruled that an unnamed defendant could not be extradited for "telecom fraud with the intention of facilitating telephone conversations between members of Al Qaeda" because the U.S. had not given sufficient assurances that he would not face additional charges and that his fundamental human rights would be respected); *Netherlands: Court Authorizes Extradition of Terror Suspect*, Associated Press, *available at* http://www.loc.gov/lawweb/servlet/lloc_news?disp3_l205402021_text (June 2, 2010) (Court of Rotterdam ruled that a terror suspect from Somalia could be extradited to the U.S. after receiving assurances from the U.S. that he would not face the death penalty); *In the News, Baghdad*, CNN.com, at 6, *available at* http://articles.cnn.com/2007-01-29/world/monday_1_cnn-ministers-orange-bowl/6?_s=PM:WORLD (Jan. 29, 2007) (Wesam Al Delaema, a Dutch citizen of Iraqi descent was extradited to the U.S. on terrorism-related charges after the U.S. agreed to certain conditions, including not seeking the death penalty).

[85] *See, e.g.*, Nanda, *supra* note 84, at 1392-93 (describing the case of Ira Einhorn, who was extradited to the United States in 1999 with assurances of no death penalty); *Cases of U.S. Extradition Deals*, A.P. Online, (Dec. 1, 2001) (stating that France agreed to extradite James Charles Kopp, wanted by the U.S. in the 1998 killing of a New York doctor who performed abortions, because the U.S. promised that Kopp would not face the death penalty).

[86] *See* Christopher Newton, *U.S. May Bend on Trials, Concessions are Likely*, San Antonio Express-News, Dec. 2, 2001) (reporting that, in 1998, the U.S. Justice Department gained custody of Mamdouh Mahmud Salim, Osama bin Ladin's suspected finance chief, by promising Germany he would not be executed); Associated Press, *Germany to Keep Terrorism Evidence*, Wall St. J. Europe (June 10, 2002), at A3 (explaining that Germany refused to hand over evidence against Zacarias Moussaoui, an alleged member of the Al Qaeda terrorist network, because "European Union law states it is illegal to extradite suspects to a country where they face the death penalty, or to provide evidence that could incriminate someone on death row"); *Germany OKs Extradition of Yemenis*, CNN.com, *available at* http://articles.cnn.com/2003-07-21/world/germany.extradition_1_mohammed-al-hasan-al-moayad-extradition-mohammed-mohsen-yahya-zayed?_s=PM:WORLD (July 21, 2003) (German court approved extradition of two Yemeni men on charges relating to providing weapons and financial support to al Qaeda after U.S. gave assurance it would not seek the death penalty).

[87] *See* Daniel J. Sharfstein, *Human Rights Beyond the War on Terrorism: Extradition Defenses Based on Prison Conditions in the United States*, 42 Santa Clara L. Rev. 1137 (2002) (noting that Spain was likely to refuse extradition of 9/11 suspects on the basis of the death row conditions); *U.S. Mulls Conceding to European Sensibilities in Seizure of Terror Suspects*, Guelph Mercury (Dec. 2, 2001) (stating that Spain refused to extradite eight suspected terrorists to the United States because extraditing prisoners, without assurance that the death penalty will not be imposed, violates the European Convention on Human Rights) *Spain Extradites Notorious Terrorist Arms Dealer to U.S. for Trial*, FoxNews.com, *available at* http://www.foxnews.com/story/0,2933,366327,00.html (June 13, 2008)

stronger position on extradition to a country with the death penalty. In *Venezia v. Ministero di Grazia e Giustizia*,[89] the Court found that extradition to a country with the death penalty would violate the Italian Constitution, even if there were assurances that the death penalty would not be imposed. The Court blocked the extradition of Venezia to the United States despite the assurance of the United States that the death penalty would not be "imposed or inflicted" on Venezia.[90] The Court found the discretion of the Italian officials to decide what constituted adequate assurances was inconsistent with the absolute protection of life in the Italian Constitution.[91]

Another forum in which extradition issues can arise is the Human Rights Committee, which is charged with hearing complaints about compliance with the ICCPR. In the early 1990s, the Human Rights Committee found no violation of the ICCPR when Canada extradited three individuals to the United States, even though the individuals could face the death penalty.[92] In one of the three cases, however, the

---

(stating that Spain had agreed to extradite Al-Kassar on the condition that the U.S. agree not to seek the death penalty or life imprisonment without parole).

[88] *See* Hugh McDiarmid, Jr., *Longo Missed Chance by Agreeing to Return, Mexican Extradition Out If Execution Seen*, DETROIT FREE PRESS (Jan. 17, 2002) at 6B (quoting a press secretary from the Mexican Embassy in Washington, D.C., Miguel Monterrubio, as stating that Mexico does not extradite if the country seeking extradition will seek the death penalty because it would violate Mexico's Constitution); Bob Baker, *Mexico Butts Into U.S. Justice; Criminals are Finding a Haven to the South*, L.A. TIMES (Feb. 11, 2003), § 2 at 13 ("Since Oct. 2, 2001, Mexico has repeatedly refused to return suspects to the U.S. for prosecution. There are reportedly more than 60 alleged killers from Los Angeles County alone that officials believe have fled to Mexico to escape punishment; as of last year [2002], the Justice Department had about 800 open extradition cases for fugitives in Mexico."); *Mexico extradites record number of fugitives to U.S.*, ASSOCIATED PRESS, *available at* 2006 WLNR 18624398 (Oct. 25, 2006) (noting an increase in the number of extraditions from Mexico to the U.S., but also noting Mexico's continued policy of refusing extradition where the suspect faces the death penalty); *Ex-Leader of Drug Cartel Pleads Guilty*, LOS ANGELES TIMES, *available at* 2012 WLNR 208715 (Jan. 5, 2012), (noting that drug kingpin Benjamin Arellano Felix, extradited from Mexico to the U.S. could not receive the death penalty based on the extradition agreement). *See also* Clarke, *supra* note 82, at 807. *See also* Devin McNulty, *The Changing Face Of Extraditions Between Mexico And The United States*, 31 CHAMPION 32 (2007) (detailing the current situation between Mexico and the United States regarding extradition of capital defendants). *See also* Kathryn F. King, *The Death Penalty, Extradition, and the War Against Terrorism: U.S. Responses to European Opinion about Capital Punishment*, 9 BUFF. HUM. RTS. L. REV. 161 (2003) (noting several cases dealing with extraditions and assurances with the United States as a party).

[89] 79 Rivista di Diritto Internazionale 815 (1996) (in Italian); described and discussed in Andrea Bianchi, *U.S.–Italy Extradition Treaty — Challenge Regarding Constitutionality — Protection of Fundamental Human Rights, Including Right to Life — Prohibition of Death Penalty in Requested Party's Constitution — Inadmissibility of Assurances That Death Penalty Shall Be Imposed or Enforced*, 91 AM J. INT'L L. 727, 729 (1997).

[90] Bianchi, *supra* note 89, at 729 (explaining that the Italian Constitutional Court found the "discretionary appraisal" by the Italian authorities of the sufficiency of the assurances from the receiving state was inconsistent with the absolute prohibition of the death penalty in the Italian Constitution; noting that a treaty that provided that the receiving state had to substitute the Italian penalty for the crime might allow for extradition to a country with an authorized death penalty). *See also* discussion of Venezia in Ved P. Nanda, *supra* note 84; Mark E. DeWitt, *Extradition Enigma: Italy and Human Rights vs. America and the Death Penalty*, 47 CATH. U. L. REV. 535 (1998).

[91] Bianchi, *supra* note 89, at 728; William A. Schabas, *International Law and Abolition of the Death Penalty*, 55 WASH. & LEE L. REV. 797 (1998) (describing international agreements and norms that prohibit or limit the use of the death penalty).

[92] Kindler v. Canada, U.N. Hum. Rts. Comm., Communications No. 470/1991, dec. of July 30, 1993,

Human Rights Committee found that Canada did violate the ICCPR by extraditing Charles Ng to California where he would face possible execution by lethal gas, a method the Committee found constituted "cruel and inhuman treatment."[93] In 2003, the Human Rights Committee changed its position on extradition where a defendant faces a possible death penalty. The Committee found that, if a country has abolished the death penalty, that country violates the ICCPR if they extradite an individual to a country with the death penalty without assurances that the death penalty will not be imposed.[94]

---

reprinted in 14 HUM. RTS. L.J. 307 (1993); Ng v. Canada, U.N. HUM. RTS. COMM., Communications No. 469/1991, dec. of Nov. 5, 1993, reprinted in 15 HUM. RTS. L.J. 149 (1994); Cox v. Canada, U.N. Hum. Rts. Comm., Communications No. 539/1993, dec. of Oct. 31, 1994, reprinted in 15 HUM. RTS. L.J. 410 (1994). *But see* dissenting opinions in each case. *E.g.*, the position is taken that "a State party that has abolished the death penalty is . . . under the legal obligation, according to article 6 of the Covenant, not to reintroduce it. This obligation must refer both to a direct reintroduction within the State's jurisdiction, and to an *indirect* one, as it is the case when the State acts — through extradition, expulsion or compulsory return — in such a way that an individual within its territory and subject to its jurisdiction may be exposed to capital punishment in another State." (Kindler, 15 HUM. RTS. J. at 318 (Pocar, F., dissenting) (emphasis added). *Compare* with more recent *Judge* case cited *infra* note 94 and accompanying text.

[93] Ng v. Canada, 15 HUM. RTS. L.J. 149 (1994). *See* discussion of *Ng* and other extradition cases in Quigley, *supra* note 75.

[94] Judge v. Canada, Hum. Rts. Comm., Communications No. 829/1998, dec. of Aug. 5, 2003. The Committee found that Canada violated Judge's right to life under article 6 of the ICCPR when, as a country that has abolished the death penalty, it deported him to the United States where he was already sentenced to death. The Committee viewed the actions of Canada as providing "the crucial link in the causal chain that would make possible the execution of [Judge]." *Id.* at ¶ 10.6. The dissenting opinions from *Kindler*, *see* note 92, *supra*, were attached as appendices by one of the concurring members.

Chapter 27

EVOLVING ATTITUDES ON CAPITAL PUNISHMENT: THE MOVE AWAY FROM THE DEATH PENALTY

§ 27.01   BACKGROUND

When the Supreme Court struck down existing death penalty statutes in 1972[1] states responded quickly. Within one year, more than thirty states adopted new capital punishment schemes and began to impose sentences of death. By 2000, the number of states with the death penalty reached a high of thirty-eight states. By 2012, the number of states had decreased to thirty-three states with death penalty statutes.[2]

Modern support for capital punishment peaked during the 1990s.[3] In 1999, there were ninety-eight executions in the United States, the highest number since the Supreme Court reinstated the death penalty in 1976.[4] Public support of the death penalty reached an all-time high of eighty percent during 1994[5] and for most of the 1990s, the number of death sentences handed down annually totaled between 280 and 300.[6]

During the 1990's, the Supreme Court jurisprudence did little to narrow or limit the application of the death penalty. The Court rejected a systemic challenge to the death penalty based on statistical evidence that the death penalty was applied in a

---

[1]   Furman v Georgia 408 U.S. 238 (1972) Furman struck down existing death penalty statutes in the U.S. *See* Chapter 6, *supra*.

[2]   THE DEATH PENALTY INFORMATION CENTER, *State by State Death Penalty Information, available at* http://www.deathpenaltyinfo.org/article.php?amp;did=121&scied=11 (last visited Feb. 5, 2012). The thirty-four states with the death penalty are: Alabama; Arizona; Arkansas; California; Colorado; Delaware; Florida; Georgia; Idaho; Indiana; Kansas; Kentucky; Louisiana; Maryland; Mississippi; Missouri; Montana; Nebraska; Nevada; New Hampshire; North Carolina; Ohio; Oklahoma; Oregon; Pennsylvania; South Carolina; South Dakota; Tennessee; Texas; Utah; Virginia; Washington; Wyoming. The U.S. government and U.S. military also have death penalty statutes. The seventeen states (year abolished in parentheses) without the death penalty are: Massachusetts, Michigan (1846); Wisconsin (1853); Maine (1887); Minnesota (1911); Hawaii (1948); Alaska (1957); Vermont (1964); Iowa (1965); West Virginia (1965); North Dakota (1973); Rhode Island (1984); New Jersey (2007); New York (Pragmatically, 2007); New Mexico (2009); Illinois (2011); Connecticut (2012). The District of Columbia also does not have the death penalty.

[3]   Mike Simmons, *The Tide Shifts Against the Death Penalty*, TIME MAGAZINE (Feb. 3, 2009), *available at* http://www.time.com/time/nation/article/0,8599,1876397,00.html.

[4]   *Gregg v. Georgia* 428 U.S. 153 (1976).

[5]   Simmons, *supra* note 3.

[6]   *Id.*

racially discriminatory manner.[7] Although there were cases where defense counsel failed to investigate, prepare or present evidence for the penalty trial, the Court either declined to review these cases or to reverse a death verdict on the basis of ineffective assistance of counsel.[8]

By the year 2000 capital punishment began to lose momentum.[9] States conducted fewer executions each year.[10] In 2000, there were eighty-five executions nationally, fifty-two during 2009, forty-six during 2010 and forty-three in 2011.[11] Although thirty-four states had death penalty statutes, only thirteen states carried out executions during 2011, and only eight states carried out more than one execution.[12] The practice of carrying out executions is limited almost entirely to the South, where thirty-four of the last forty-five executions took place.[13]

Each year since 2000, juries returned fewer death sentences in favor of the punishment of life without parole.[14] In 2000, there were 234 new sentences of death imposed, 112 during 2009, and 114 during 2010. In 2011 there were 78 sentences of death marking the first time since the reinstatement of the death penalty in 1976 that the number fell below 100.[15] Active death penalty states such as Virginia,

---

[7] McClesky v. Kemp, 481 U.S. 279 (1987). For a discussion of race and the death penalty *see* Chapter 20, *supra*.

[8] For a discussion of ineffective assistance of counsel, *see* Chapter 16. Strickland v. Washington, 466 U.S. 668 (1984) Burger v. Kemp 483 U.S. 776 (1987).

[9] Simmons, *infra* note 43.

[10] *See* DEATH PENALTY INFORMATION CENTER, *Executions by Years, available at* http://www. deathpenaltyinfo.org/executions-year, *and* DEATH PENALTY INFORMATION CENTER, *Number of Executions by State and Region Since 1976* (last updated Mar. 10, 2011), *available at* http://www.deathpenaltyinfo.org/ number-executions-state-and-region-1976.

[11] THE DEATH PENALTY INFORMATION CENTER, *Number of Executions by State and Region Since 1976, available at* http://www.deathpenaltyinfo.org/number-executions-state-and-region-1976 (last accessed Feb. 6, 2012).

[12] *Id. States Conducting Executions* (and number of executions): Texas (13), Virginia (1), Oklahoma (2), Florida (2), Missouri (1), Alabama (6), Georgia (4), Ohio (5), South Carolina (1), Arizona (4), Delaware (1), Mississippi (2), and Idaho (1).

[13] THE DEATH PENALTY INFORMATION CENTER, *Number of Executions by State and Region Since 1976, supra*.

[14] THE DEATH PENALTY INFORMATION CENTER, *Death Penalty Sentences Have Dropped Considerably in the Current Decade, available at http://www.deathpenaltyinfo.org/death-penalty-sentences-have-dropped-considerably-current-decade*. Compared to the 1990s, there has been a marked decline in death sentences in the U.S. since 2000. Every region of the country and every state that averaged one or more death sentences per year has seen a decline in the annual number of death sentences. *See also* Editorial, *Still Cruel, Less Usual*, THE NEW YORK TIMES (Dec. 30, 2010), *available at* http://www.nytimes.com/2010/ 12/31/opinion/31fri3.html.

[15] *See* THE DEATH PENALTY INFORMATION CENTER, *Death Penalty Sentences Have Dropped Considerably in the Current Decade, available at* http://www.deathpenaltyinfo.org/death-penalty-sentences-have-dropped-considerably-current-decade (last accessed Feb. 6, 2012). Compared to the 1990s, there has been a marked decline in death sentences in the U.S. since 2000. Every region of the country and every state that averaged one or more death sentences per year have seen a decline in the annual number of death sentences. *See also* Editorial, *Still Cruel, Less Usual* THE NEW YORK TIMES (Dec. 30, 2010), *available at* http://www.nytimes.com/2010/12/31/opinion/31fri3.html (last accessed Feb. 6, 2012). While juries imposed 114 death sentences during 2010 and 112 death sentences during 2009, these rates were still only about half of what they were during the 1990s.

Georgia, Missouri, and Indiana had no new death sentences in 2010.[16] The total number of persons on death row also decreased, from 3,652 in 2000, to 3,297 in 2009, 3,261 in 2010, and to 3,251 in 2011.[17]

Since 2000, there has been a growing movement around the country away from capital punishment. It began as a movement to impose a moratorium on executions.[18] Community and religious groups, professional organizations, and local governments all began to pass moratorium resolutions.[19] While none of these measures have the force of law, they reflected the growing public opinion questioning capital punishment. Legislatures formed commissions to examine the capital punishment system in the state.[20] The moratorium movement in several states evolved into efforts to abolish the death penalty in favor of a sentence of life without parole. Five of the sixteen states without the death penalty in 2012 abolished the practice between 2004 and 2012.[21] During the 2011 legislative term alone, legislation was introduced in fourteen states to abolish the death penalty.[22] Nine states

---

[16] The Death Penalty Information Center, *The Death Penalty in 2010: Year End Report* (Dec. 2010), *available at* http://www.deathpenaltyinfo.org/documents/2010YearEnd-Final.pdf (last accessed Feb. 6, 2012).

[17] THE DEATH PENALTY INFORMATION CENTER, *The Death Penalty in 2011: Year End Report* (Dec. 2011), *available at* http://www.deathpenaltyinfo.org/documents/2011__Year__End.pdf (last accessed Feb. 6, 2012).

[18] For an in-depth discussion providing a historical perspective of the moratorium movement see Jeffrey L. Kirchmeier, *Another Place Beyond Here: The Death Penalty Moratorium Movement in the United States*, 73 U. COLO L. REV. 101 (2002). Kirchmeier lists five major "events" that have created this current moratorium movement including: 1) Sister Helen Prejean writing Dead Man Walking which was then made into a movie, 2) Justice Harry Blackmun rejecting the death penalty in Callins v Collins in 1994, 3) the American Bar Association passing a resolution in favor of a moratorium on executions in 1997, 4) the use of DNA evidence in capital cases to exonerate individuals on death row, and 5) specific moratorium activity including the action of Republican Governor George Ryan in Illinois.

[19] In 1997, the American Bar Association (ABA) called for a moratorium and began to actively raise concerns about the adequacy of representation, the limits imposed on habeas corpus review, and the effect of racial bias on the decision of who is sentenced to death. From 2001-2003 each of the 38 states with death penalty statutes introduced some form of moratorium, abolition or reform legislation. Only two measures passed; the Nebraska legislature passed a moratorium bill and the new Hampshire legislature passed a bill calling for abolition. Both measures were vetoed by the governor of the state.

[20] The Maryland Commission on Capital Punishment, the legislative commission to examine the death penalty in Maryland, released its final report on December 12, 2008 detailing the reasons for its recommendation to abolish the death penalty. *Available at* http://www.goccp.maryland.gov/capital-punishment/index.php, Kansas Judicial Council Death Penalty Advisory Committee on Certain Issues Related to the Death Penalty, November 2004, Tennessee Legislative Study Committee Recommendations (2009). A 16-month analysis of the state's capital punishment process by the committee with recommendations for achieving a more fair and accurate system.

[21] *Id.* The Death Penalty Information Center, *Part II: History of the Death Penalty*, *available at* http://www.deathpenaltyinfo.org/part-ii-history-death-penalty (last visited Feb. 6, 2012). New Jersey, by legislation in 2007; New York, by state court order finding capital punishment to be unconstitutional in June, 2004; New Mexico, by legislation in March 2009; Illinois, by legislation in March 2011, Connecticut by legislation in April 2012.

[22] DEATH PENALTY INFORMATION CENTER, *2011 Proposed or Passed Legislation*, *available at* http://www.deathpenaltyinfo.org/2011-Legislation (last visited Feb. 5, 2012). The twelve states are: California; Connecticut; Florida; Illinois; Indiana; Kansas; Kentucky; Maryland; Missouri; Montana; Nebraska Ohio; Pennsylvania; Texas; and, Washington. Mississippi and Nevada had bills introduced that would

introduced similar legislation in the first month of 2012.[23]

Supreme Court decisions since 2000 also contributed to a move away from capital punishment. In 2002 the Court forbid the execution of defendants who are mentally retarded and in 2005 excluded from eligibility for death those who were juveniles at the time of their offense. In 2000, for the first time in almost 70 years, the Court reversed a capital sentence, finding that the lawyer was ineffective.[24] In 2007 the Court placed executions on hold throughout the country to examine whether lethal injection violated the Eighth Amendment prohibition against cruel and unusual punishment.[25]

Many long-time supporters of the death penalty began to question its effectiveness. As the conversation turned to the *process* of imposing the death penalty rather than the *morality* of killing convicted murderers, new voices are speaking out in opposition to the death penalty.[26] Judges in lower courts began to write opinions and dissents expressing their concern for the often daunting barriers facing death row prisoners to appeal their convictions or voicing their concern for the death penalty process.[27] Former wardens who presided over state executions started

---

have imposed a moratorium on the death penalty. Only Illinois successfully passed and received their governor's ratified of their bill. *Id.*

[23] The Death Penalty Information Center, *2012 Proposed or Passes Legislation, available at* http://www.deathpenaltyinfo.org/recent-legislative-activity#2012_Legislation (last visited Feb. 5, 2012). The nine states are CT, FL, GA, KS, MD, NE, PA, OH, WA.

[24] In 1932 the Court reversed the sentences of death of the so-called Scottsboro Boys in Powell v. Alabama 287 U.S. 45 (1932). Beginning in 2000 the Court reversed sentences of death on the grounds of ineffective assistance of counsel in Williams v. Taylor, 529 U.S. 362 (2000), Wiggins v. Smith, 539 U.S. 510 (2003), and Rompilla v. Beard, 545 U.S. 374 (2005).

[25] *See* Baze v. Rees, 553 U.S. 35 (2008); *and* Mike Simmons, *The Tide Shifts Against the Death Penalty*, TIME MAGAZINE (Feb. 3, 2009), *available at* http://www.time.com/time/nation/article/ 0,8599,1876397,00.html. The Court ruled 7-2 that lethal injection did not violate the Eight Amendment's prohibition against cruel and unusual punishment.

[26] *See* Donald A. McCartin, *Second Thoughts of a 'Hanging Judge,'* THE LOS ANGELES TIMES (Mar. 25, 2011), *available at* http://www.latimes.com/news/opinion/commentary/la-oe-mccartin-death-penalty-20110325,0,4609310,print.story (quoting Judge McCartin) ("It's a waste of time and taxpayers' money," Judge McCartin stated. "It cost 10 times more to kill these guys than to keep them alive in prison. It's absurd. And imagine the poor victims' families having to go through this again and again" David Kravets, *Top Judge Calls Death Penalty "Dysfunctional" Legislature Blamed for Inadequate Funding*, SAN JOSE MERCURY NEWS, May 1, 2006 at B4 (quoting Ronald M George former Chief Justice of the California Supreme Court) Jim Petro, former Attorney General of Ohio, now opposed the death penalty and states "We are probably safer, better and smarter to not have a death penalty." Petro's recent book, FALSE JUSTICE: EIGHT MYTHS THAT CONVICT THE INNOCENT (2010), describes the risks of mistakes in how police and prosecutors handle capital cases.

[27] *See* John Schwartz, *Judges' Dissents for Death Row Inmates Are Rising*, THE NEW YORK TIMES (Aug. 13, 2009), *available at* http://www.nytimes.com/2009/08/14/us/14dissent.html ("There is an increasing frustration among federal judges throughout the system . . . Judges are likely to have less and less patience for being hogtied by legalistic mumbo-jumbo . . . which prevents them from reaching fair results"). *See* Editorial, *Capital Punishment*, THE NEW YORK TIMES (Mar. 10, 2011), *available at* http://topics.nytimes.com/top/reference/timestopics/subjects/c/capital_punishment/index.html;   *and* Debra Cassens Weiss *'Fervent, Lonely Dissents' on the Rise in Death Penalty Cases*, ABA LAW JOURNAL (Aug. 14, 2009), *available at* http://www.abajournal.com/news/article/fervent_lonely_dissents_on_the_ rise_in_death_penalty_cases/.

voicing their opposition to the death penalty.[28] Newspapers in active death penalty states like Texas and Alabama published editorials questioning the use of capital punishment.[29]

Recent polls show that public support for the death penalty is softening and, in some cases, declining. Although the death penalty's current national approval rating of sixty-one percent suggests that the majority of Americans favor capital punishment, the statistic decreases when people are asked when they would support an alternative of life without the possibility of parole.[30] Polling in California found a life imprisonment had overtaken the death penalty as the preferred punishment between 2000 and 2011.[31]

For years, opposition to the death penalty was based primarily on moral concerns about state killing. The public now considers a broad range of factors including the high financial costs associated with capital punishment,[32] the risk of innocent people being executed,[33] and most recently, the nature of the drugs used in an execution.[34] The pendulum appears to be swinging in the other direction as fewer legislators and judges are willing to "tinker with the machinery of death."[35]

---

[28] Frank Thompson, a former state penitentiary warden in Oregon and who supervised the only two executions carried out in the state since capital punishment was reinstated in 1984, described the death penalty as a "failed public policy,", Jeanne Woodford, former warden at San Quentin in California is now the executive director of Death Penalty Focus and speaking out in CA in support of the initiative to abolish the death penalty. Donald A. Cabana, warden at Parchment State Prison in Mississippi wrote Death at Midnight: The Confession of an Executioner voicing his concerns about the death penalty.

[29] See Editorial, *A Decade of Progress on Death Penalty Justice*, THE DALLAS MORNING NEWS (Dec. 24, 2009), *available at* http://www.dallasnews.com/opinion/editorials/20091224-Editorial-A-decade-of-progress-4435.ece ("[C]ourts, prosecutors, politicians, and the public are recognizing the programs in our imperfect system of justice. This newspaper feels more strongly than ever that those false are sufficiently widespread that the justice system cannot be trusted to impose irreversible sentences of death"); *and* Birmingham News, Editorial, OUR VIEW: Alabama lawmakers should pass legislation to put a three-year halt to imposing death sentences or carrying out executions. April 25, 2011. *Available at* http://www.deathpenaltyinfo.org/editorials-birmingham-news-calls-moratorium-alabamas-death-penalty.

[30] See GALLUP POLL, *Death Penalty Gallup Poll* (Oct. 2011), *available at* http://www.gallup.com/poll/1606/death-penalty.aspx?version=print. While sixty-one percent of Americans are in favor of the death penalty for a person convicted of murder, thirty-five percent are against it, and four percent do not have an opinion.

[31] Safe California, *Historic Turn Away From the Death Penalty in California*, September 29, 2011, *available at* http://www.safecalifornia.org/downloads/5.4.B_9.29.11pressrelease.pdf (last visited Feb. 5, 2011). Statewide support for life imprisonment without the possibility of parole and the death penalty were forty-two and forty-one percent, respectively. These were a significant shift from ten years earlier, when the death penalty garnered forty-four percent and life imprisonment without parole only thirty-seven percent support.

[32] See Section 27.05, *infra*.

[33] See Chapter 17, *supra*.

[34] See Chapter 5, *supra*.

[35] See Callins v. Collins, 510 U.S. 1141 (1994) (Blackmun, J., dissenting); *and* Mike Simmons, *The Tide Shifts Against the Death Penalty*, TIME MAGAZINE (Feb. 3, 2009), *available at* http://www.time.com/time/nation/article/0,8599,1876397,00.html.

§ 27.02   STATE ABOLITION OF THE DEATH PENALTY

The past decade has seen an increase in the number of states considering an end to their capital punishment systems. Both legislative efforts and judicial challenges have resulted in a small but growing number of states rejecting death sentences as a means of punishment.

[A]   New York

New York's death penalty was struck down in 2004 when the state supreme court held the statute unconstitutional.[36] The New York legislature has been unsuccessful in passing new legislation resulting in a *de facto* repeal in the state. New York had not executed anyone under their new death penalty statute; their last execution was in 1963, when Eddie Mays was electrocuted in Sing Sing Prison.[37]

In 1972, when the *Furman* decision declared unconstitutional various death penalty statutes, New York attempted to enact a new death penalty law that would comply with the Supreme Court's holdings. Beginning in 1975, legislation to restore capital punishment was passed by the legislature each year over a period of twenty years but vetoed each year by Governors Carey (1975-82) and Cuomo (1983-94). Together they vetoed eighteen consecutive death penalty bills.[38] Although Cuomo was characterized as "[a]lmost alone as the last holdout against capital punishment,"[39] the Governor stated that "stopping the death penalty [was] his overriding priority" and that he would veto any death penalty law that was enacted"[40]

In 1995, newly elected Republican Governor George Pataki fulfilled his campaign promise and signed legislation reinstating the death penalty in New York, establishing lethal injection as the method of execution.[41] The next year,

---

[36]   People v. LaVelle, 817 NE 2d 341 (2004).

[37]   THE DEATH PENALTY INFORMATION CENTER, *State by State Database: New York, available at* http://www.deathpenaltyinfo.org/state_by_state (last visited Feb. 6, 2012); *and* The DEATH PENALTY INFORMATION CENTER, *Executions in the U.S. 1608-2002: The Epsy File, available at* http://www. deathpenaltyinfo.org/executions-us-1608-2002-espy-file. New York had 1,130 recorded executions since 1608, Virginia had 1,385 and Texas had 1,221. Since 1976, Virginia executed 108 individuals, Texas executed 466, and New York had no executions.

[38]   *See* Editorial, *Governor Paterson Padlocks New York's Death Chamber,* THE NEW YORK OBSERVER (Jul. 29, 2008), *available at* http://www.observer.com/2008/politics/governor-paterson-padlocks-new-york-s-death-chamber. Governors Carey and Cuomo vetoed the legislation on the grounds that they were "morally opposed to state-sponsored executions."

[39]   Michael Kramer, *The Political Interest: Cuomo, the Last Holdout,* TIME MAGAZINE (Apr. 2, 1990), *available at* http://www.time.com/time/magazine/article/0,9171,969742,00.html.

[40]   *Id.* (quoting Cuomo). Cuomo argued the death penalty did not deter and had been wrongly applied, pointing to one study showing that in New York alone, eight innocent people had been executed since 1905. Cuomo stated the death penalty "demeans and debases us".

[41]   *See* Joseph Lentol, Helene Weinstein, Jeffrion Aubry, *The Death Penalty In New York,* NEW YORK STATE ASSEMBLY STANDING COMMITTEES ON CODE, JUDICIARY AND CORRECTION (Apr. 3, 2005), *available at* http://assembly.state.ny.us/comm/Codes/20050403/deathpenalty.pdf. The law authorized the death penalty for thirteen categories of intentional murder, including felony murders.

Pataki removed Bronx District Attorney Robert Johnson from a case of a murdered police officer after Johnson declined to seek the death penalty in the case.[42] Despite these efforts, during Pataki's twelve years as New York's Governor, not one execution was carried out.[43]

In 2004, New York's State Court of Appeals ruled in a four to three decision that the state's death penalty statute was unconstitutional, effectively nullifying Pataki's legislation.[44] Pataki promised to pass a new statute, but by January, 2005, the political climate in New York had turned against the death penalty. Supporters of the death penalty passed a bill in the Republican-controlled State Senate only to have it voted down in the Democratically-controlled assembly.[45]

After lengthy public hearings where 146 witnesses testified, the State Committee on Codes, Judiciary and Correction wrote a scathing report and declined to pass a "quick fix" of the defective death penalty statute. This ended the state's ten year experiment with the death penalty.[46] The reported noted that "[i]n the past ten years, the state and local governments have spent over $170 million administering the law. Yet, not a single person has been executed."[47]

The death penalty presented a political issue in the Manhattan District Attorney election in 2005. Incumbent Robert Morgenthau's campaign criticized his opponent Leslie Crocker Snyder who stated in one case, she would have been willing to give

---

[42] *See* Richard Perez-Pena, *Split Court Backs Pataki's Decision in Capital Case,* The New York Times (Dec. 5, 1997), *available at* http://www.nytimes.com/1997/12/05/nyregion/split-court-backs-pataki-s-decision-in-a-capital-case.html?ref=kevingillespie. The Governor removed Johnson in March, 1996, after he refused to seek the death penalty against Angel Diaz, a former convict accused of shooting Officer Gillespie. Chief Judge Judith S. Kaye wrote for the majority, stating, "[c]learly, the legislature did not allow one or all 62 District Attorneys to functionally veto the statute by adopting a 'blanket policy,' thereby in effect refusing to exercise discretion."

[43] The Death Penalty Information Center, *State by State Database: New York, available at* http://www.deathpenaltyinfo.org/state_by_state (last visited Mar. 15, 2011).

[44] *See* People v. LaVelle, 817 N.E.2d 341 (2004). The statute provided that if a jury deadlocked on penalty, the trial judge would be required to impose a sentence that would make the defendant eligible for parole in 20 to 25 years. The court held this provision unconstitutional as it could coerce jurors to vote for the death penalty, given that the only alternative was the eventual release of a person charged with murder) *See* William Glaberson, *4-3 Ruling Effectively Halts Death Penalty in New York,* The New York Times (Jun. 25, 2004), *available at* http://www.nytimes.com/2004/06/25/nyregion/4-3-ruling-effectively-halts-death-penalty-in-new-york.html; *and* Pro-Death Penalty Resource Community, *On This Day: New York Overturns Death Penalty Law* (Jun. 24, 2008), *available at* http://off2dr.com/smf/index.php?topic=4183.0.

[45] *See* Thomas P. Morahan, *Senate Passes Death Penalty Legislation,* New York State Senator Website Blog (Mar. 9, 2005); *and* Michael Cooper, *Metro Briefing|New York: Albany: Senate Votes to Restore Execution,* The New York Times (Mar. 10, 2005), *available at* http://query.nytimes.com/gst/fullpage.html?res=9901E6DE173CF933A25750C0A9639C8B63. Michael Cooper, *Metro Briefing| New York: Albany: Senate Votes to Restore Execution,* The New York Times (Mar. 10, 2005), *available at* http://query.nytimes.com/gst/fullpage.html?res=9901E6DE173CF933A25750C0A9639C8B63.

[46] *See* Lentol, *supra* note 41. New Yorkers For Alternatives to the Death Penalty, *New York's Death Penalty: Did You Know? available at* http://www.nyadop.org/content/nys-death-penalty-did-you-know.

[47] *See* Lentol, *supra* note 41. "Only seven persons have been sentenced to death. Of these, the first four sentences to reach the Court of Appeals were struck down. One sentence was converted to a sentence of life imprisonment without the possibility of parole after the *LaValle* decision. Two sentences are awaiting review.

a lethal injection to the defendant herself."[48] Morgenthau won the election and declined to seek the death penalty during his tenure.[49]

In 2008, the State Senate again passed legislation to impose the death penalty for the murder of law enforcement officers; but it was never acted on in the assembly.[50] Governor David Paterson, a Democrat, issued an executive order to remove execution equipment in the state's prison penitentiary.[51]

[B] New Jersey

In 2007, New Jersey became the first state to legislatively repeal the death penalty. This served as an important catalyst for other states.[52] In New Jersey, the argument by death penalty opponents was simple; it was ineffective and expensive. Keeping inmates on death row cost the state $72,602 per year for each prisoner,[53] while inmates kept in the general population cost $40,121 per year each to house. The corrections department estimated that a repeal of the death penalty could save New Jersey as much as $1.3 million per inmate over the inmates lifetime — and that figure did not include the millions spent by the state and public defender attorneys on inmates' appeals in the case.[54]

In twenty-four years with the death penalty, New Jersey had failed to execute any defendants. After a state appeals court ruled in 2004 that New Jersey's

---

[48] *See* Leslie Eaton, *The Ad Campaign; A Morgenthau Attack, for Liberal Voters* (Aug. 31, 2005), *available   at*   http://query.nytimes.com/gst/fullpage.html?res= 9503E4D71631F932A0575BC0A9639C8B63. Synder had said that she would request the death penalty if it were available for particularly heinous crimes and given corroborating evidence like DNA. Editorial, *When to End an Era*, THE NEW YORK TIMES (Aug. 30, 2005), *available at* http://www.nytimes.com/2005/ 08/30/opinion/30tue2.html?_r=1. "While the newspaper acknowledged that Snyder was a lawyer of unquestioned ability and broad experience, 'there [were] some aspects of Ms. Snyder's record that gave us pause," including her support of the death penalty.' "

[49] Michael Powell, Benjamin Weiser, and William K. Rashbaum, *Morgenthau Heads for Door, Legacy Assured*, THE NEW YORK TIMES (Feb. 27, 2009), *available at* http://www.nytimes.com/2009/02/28/nyregion/ 28legacy.html. "[a] liberal Democratic lion, he never once sought the death penalty; and yet the city's most confrontational mayors, Edward I. Koch and Rudolph W. Giuliani, hesitated to slash at him."

[50] Martin J. Golden, *Senate Passes Bill to Establish Death Penalty for Cop Killers*, WEBSITE OF NEW YORK STATE SENATOR MARTIN J. GOLDEN (May 30, 2008), *available at* http://www.nysenate.gov/news/senate- passes-bill-establish-death-penalty-cop-killers. The legislation (S.6414) would have established the death penalty for the intentional murder of a police officer, peace officer or an employee of the Department of Correctional Services. The bill mandated the sentence of life without parole if the jury is deadlocked.

[51] Brendan Scott, *Gov Pulls Switch on Death Cell*, THE NEW YORK POST (Jul. 24, 2008), *available at* http://www.nypost.com/seven/07242008/news/regionalnews/gov_pulls_switch_on_death_cell_121295.htm.

[52] *See* Jeremy W. Peters, *New Jersey Nears Repeal of Death Penalty*, THE NEW YORK TIMES (Dec. 11, 2007), *available at* http://www.nytimes.com/2007/12/11/nyregion/11death.html. During 2007 the legisla- tures in Nebraska, Montana, Maryland, and New Mexico debated bills to repeal those states' death penalties; however, each measure failed, often by slim margins. In 2000, the New Hampshire state legislature voted to repeal capital punishment; but, the bill was vetoed by then Democratic Gov. Jeanne Shaheen. Death penalty opponents had succeeded only through court rulings, or through moratoriums imposed by a governor, as in Illinois and Maryland.

[53] *See generally* NEW JERSEY DEATH PENALTY COMMISSION REPORT. (January 2007), *retrievable at* http://www.njleg.state.nj.us/committees/dpsc_final.pdf (Law Accessed January 31, 2012).

[54] *Id.*

procedures for administering the death penalty were unconstitutional,[55] the Department of Corrections never finalized a new procedural manual.[56] The state senate imposed a moratorium on executions while a commission studied the death penalty. This marked the first time a moratorium was enacted legislatively, rather than by executive order as in Illinois and Oregon.[57] On December 17, 2007, Governor Jon Corzine signed the abolition bill into law. He commuted the sentences of the eight men on New Jersey's death row to life in prison with no possibility of parole.[58]

[C]　New Mexico

Following New Jersey and New York, New Mexico abolished the death penalty on March 18, 2009 making it the fifteenth state without the death penalty.[59] A year before abolition, a statewide poll of New Mexico showed that 64 percent of New Mexicans supported replacing the death penalty with life without parole.[60]

Public concerns of the added costs of the death penalty dominated the legislative debate. A 2009 study conducted by the New Mexico State Public Defender Department estimated that the state could save several million dollars per year on Public Defender costs alone if the death penalty was replaced with an alternative sentence.[61] New Mexico Supreme Court Justice Richard Bossom estimated that the cost of death penalty cases in New Mexico was six times higher than other murder cases. Other researchers concluded that the death penalty cost Mexico between $3 to $4 million per year. The result of this expense was only one execution in New Mexico since 1960.[62]

---

[55] *Id.*

[56] *See* Bobbye Alley, *New Jersey Death Penalty Moratorium*, eHow.com (Jul. 23, 2010), *available at* http://www.ehow.com/facts_6768394_new-jersey-death-penalty-moratorium.html. *See* Laura Mansnerus, *Panel Seeks End to Death Penalty for New Jersey*, The New York Times (Jan. 3, 2007), *available at* http://www.nytimes.com/2007/01/03/nyregion/03death.html.

[57] Nancy Solomon, *New Jersey's Death Penalty Moratorium*, NPR (Jan. 15, 2006), *available at* http://www.npr.org/templates/story/story.php?storyId=5158551. P.L. 1983, c.245, *available at* http://www.njleg.state.nj.us/2004/Bills/PL05/321_.PDF; Celeste Fitzgerald, *Codey Signs Bill Suspending Executions in New Jersey*, New Jerseyans For Alternatives to the Death Penalty (Jan. 12, 2006), *available at* http://www.njadp.org/forms/codeymor.html; William Yardley, *Oregon Governor Says He Will Block Executions*, The New York Times (November 22, 2011), *available at* http://www.nytimes.com/2011/11/23/us/oregon-executions-to-be-blocked-by-gov-kitzhaber.html.

[58] Jeremy W. Peters, *New Jersey Nears Repeal of Death Penalty*, The New York Times (Dec. 11, 2007), *available at* http://www.nytimes.com/2007/12/11/nyregion/11death.html. Governor Corzine declared an end to what he called "state-endorsed killing," and said that New Jersey could serve as a model for other states."

[59] The Death Penalty Information Center, *State by State Database: New Mexico:* http://www.deathpenaltyinfo.org/state_by_state.

[60] The Death Penalty Information Center, *Death Penalty Abolished in New Mexico — Governor Says Repeal Will Make the State Safer* (Mar. 19, 2009), *available at* http://www.deathpenaltyinfo.org/death-penalty-abolished-new-mexico-governor-says-repeal-will-make-state-safe.

[61] Fact Sheet, *Cost*, New Mexico Coalition to Repeal the Death Penalty, *available at* http://nmrepeal.org/issues/cost.

[62] After reenacting its death penalty statute in 1979, New Mexico did not execute anyone until 2001. At the time of the repeal, New Mexico had two people on death row.

Concerns about executing innocent persons also permeated the New Mexico legislative debate.[63] Senator Cisco McSorley, an Albuquerque Democrat, emphasized that "[a]s beautiful as our justice system is . . . it is still a justice system of human beings, and human beings make mistakes."[64] The U.S. Conference of Catholic Bishops and Lieutenant Governor Diane Denish were among those urging the governor to sign the bill.[65] Governor Bill Richardson, a death penalty supporter, ultimately decided to sign the abolition bill.[66] In a public statement, Richardson cited the 130 inmates around the country exonerated and freed from death row since 1973, adding, "[t]he sad truth is the wrong person can still be convicted in this day and age, and in cases where that conviction carries with it the ultimate sanction, we must have ultimate confidence, I would say certitude, that the system is without flaw or prejudice. Unfortunately, this is demonstrably not the case."[67]

[D] Illinois

After a decade of studies, debates and a moratorium, Illinois Governor Pat Quinn signed Senate Bill 3539 on March 9, 2011, making Illinois the sixteenth state without the death penalty.[68] Illinois' disturbingly high rate of exonerations and the skyrocketing costs of financing the capital system were important in the final decision to repeal capital punishment.

A shift in public attitudes may be traced to 1998 when the Center on Wrongful Convictions at Northwestern University hosted twenty-nine exonerated death row inmates. The conference included a public recitation of the stories from the men and women who were sentenced to death and almost executed for crimes they did not commit. This put a human face to the death penalty's errors. The exoneration of

---

[63] Fact Sheet, *Innocence*, NEW MEXICO COALITION TO REPEAL THE DEATH PENALTY, *available at* http://nmrepeal.org/Issues/Innocence. In 1974, New Mexico sentenced to death four innocent men, Thomas Gladis, Ronald Keine, Clarence Smith, and Richard Greer, based on false witness testimony and police misconduct. They were released two years later when the actual killer confessed.

[64] Editorial, *New Mexico Abolishes Death Penalty*, CBS NEWS (Mar. 18, 2009), *available at* http://www.cbsnews.com/stories/2009/03/18/national/main484296.shtml.

[65] *Id.* The overwhelming majority of responses indicated that the death penalty should be repealed. New Mexico Sheriffs' and Police Association opposed repeal, saying capital punishment deterred violence against police officers, jailers and prison guards. District attorneys also opposed the legislation, arguing that the death penalty was a useful prosecutorial tool.

[66] Editorial, *New Mexico Governor Repeals Death Penalty in State*, CNN (Mar. 18, 2009), *available at* http://articles.cnn.com/2009-03-18/justice/new.mexico.death.penalty_1_penalty-trial-death-row-death-penalty-information-center?_s=PM:CRIME (quoting Richardson). "Throughout my adult life, I have been a firm believer in the death penalty as a just punishment — in very rare instances, and only for the most heinous crimes. I still believe that."

[67] THE DEATH PENALTY INFORMATION CENTER, *Death Penalty Abolished in New Mexico — Governor Says Repeal Will Make the State Safer* (Mar. 19, 2009), *available at* http://www.deathpenaltyinfo.org/death-penalty-abolished-new-mexico-governor-says-repeal-will-make-state-safe.

[68] *See* ILLINOIS GENERAL ASSEMBLY, *Full Text of SB 3539*, *available at* http://www.ilga.gov/legislation/96/SB/PDF/09600SB3539lv.pdf. SB 3539 repeals SB 3539 repealed the death penalty (720 Ill. Comp. Stat. 5/9-1) and provided that the funds remaining in the Capital Litigation Trust Fund be used for murder victims' families services and law enforcement.

Anthony Porter and the media coverage that followed fueled the debate.[69] Porter had been within hours of execution when a judge issued a stay to explore Porter's low IQ. During that brief reprieve, Northwestern journalism students established Porters innocence. Porter was exonerated and released.

One year after the Wrongful Conviction conference, the Chicago Tribune also did a five-part series illuminating the deep persistent problems in the state's system of capital punishment.[70]

Prompted by the release of thirteen men from death row over a period of little more than ten years, Governor Ryan established a Blue Ribbon Commission on Capital Punishment. The Commission was charged with examining the death penalty system and to determine "what reforms, if any, would ensure that the Illinois capital punishment system is fair, just and accurate."[71] The Governor declared a moratorium on executions in Illinois so that the Commission could work without the specter of an upcoming execution.[72] The Commission filed its report on April 15, 2002. A narrow majority of the Commission favored abolishing the death penalty in Illinois. Others felt that the death penalty still served a useful purpose in the state punishment scheme. Despite this divergence of views on what they characterized as the "ultimate question," the Commission reached a "strong consensus" that reforms of the system were necessary to ensure a "fair, just, and accurate death penalty scheme." The Commission report then made 85 recommendations; some to be implemented by the legislature, others by the Illinois Supreme Court or the Governor.

None of the Commission's recommendations were enacted by the legislature. Still concerned about the possibility of error and frustrated by the inaction of the legislature, Governor Ryan granted executive clemency to 167 death row inmates reducing most of their sentences of death to life without parole.[73] Ryan also took the unusual step of granting a pardon and releasing four men from death row who

---

[69] Center on Wrongful Convictions, *Anthony Porter*, *accessible at* http://www.law.northwestern.edu/ cwc/exonerations/ilPorterSummary.html (last visited Feb. 6, 2012); Steve Mills, *What Killed Illinois' Death Penalty*, CHICAGO TRIBUNE (Mar. 10, 2011), *available at* http://articles.chicagotribune.com/2011-03-10/news/ct-met-illinois-death-penalty-history20110309_1_death-penalty-death-row-death-sentences.

[70] Ken Armstrong and Steve Mills, *The Failure of the Death Penalty In Illinois*, THE CHICAGO TRIBUNE (Nov. 14-19, 1999), Part One of Five *available at* http://articles.chicagotribune.com/1999-11-14/news/chi-991114deathillinois1_1_capital-punishment-death-row-criminal-justice-system.

[71] REPORT OF THE GOVERNOR'S COMMISSION ON CAPITAL PUNISHMENT (Apr. 15, 2002), (preamble); *available at* http://www.chicagojustice.org/foi/illinois-govenor-george-ryans-commission-on-capital-punishment/ Report_of_the_Commission_on_Capital_Punishment_Com.pdf.

[72] William Fisher, *Illinois Ends the Death Penalty, The Public Record* (Mar. 10, 2011), *available at* http://pubrecord.org/nation/9039/illinois-ends-death-penalty/print/. Ryan cited the exoneration of Porter as one of the reasons for the moratorium, stating, "[a]nd so I turned to my wife, and I said, how the hell does that happen? How does an innocent man sit on death row for 15 years and get no relief . . . And that piqued my interest, Anthony Porter."

[73] *Governor's Blanket Pardon Spares Lives of 167 Condemned Inmates*, AP (Jan. 11, 2003), *available at* http://www.foxnews.com/story/0,2933,75170,00.html. The clemency included 157 inmates who were on death row and sentenced to death and 10 inmates who were awaiting a new sentencing hearing. Four of the 157 inmates had their sentences reduced to forty years.

Ryan said he was convinced were innocent.[74]

The following year the Illinois legislature did enact a number of procedural reforms but failed to pass much needed reforms of the forensic labs.[75] The Illinois General Assembly created the Capital Punishment Reform Study Committee[76] to study the effects of the reforms. The Committee issued its sixth and final report on October 28, 2010 and concluded that Illinois capital punishment system was misused, capricious, and very costly.[77]

On January 11, 2011, legislation to abolish the death penalty in Illinois passed both houses of the legislature.[78] Governor Pat Quinn, previously a death penalty supporter,[79] spent nearly two months deciding whether or not to sign the bill. Ultimately Quinn concluded that the death penalty system was inherently flawed and the only way to ensure justice was to abolish it.[80]

[E] Connecticut

In Connecticut, it took two legislative bills to finally replace the death penalty with a sentence of life without parole. In 2011, the Senate and the House of Representatives passed legislation that Governor Rell vetoed in the face of a highly publicized death penalty trial with particularly horrific facts. In the spring, 2012,

---

[74] Jodi Wilgoren, *4 Death Row Inmates Pardoned*, NEW YORK TIMES (Jan 11, 2003), *available at* http://www.nytimes.com/2003/01/11/us/4-death-row-inmates-are-pardoned.html?pagewanted=all&src= pm. Pardons were given to Madison Hobley, Stanley Howard, Leroy Orange, and Aaron Patterson who all said that they had confessed to Cmdr. Jon Burge when they were tortured. Burge was fired from the police department in 1993. No other inmate since 1973 in any state had been pardoned directly off death row.

[75] *Id.*

[76] *See* 20 ILCS 3928, *Capital Punishment Reform Study Committee Enabling Statute* (Nov. 19, 2003), *available at* http://www.icjia.state.il.us/public/pdf/dpsrc/CPRSC%20Enabling%20Statute%20_ 20%20ILCS%203929_.pdf.

[77] *See* ILLINOIS CAPITAL PUNISHMENT REFORM STUDY COMMITTEE, *Sixth and Final Report* (Oct. 28, 2010), *available at* http://www.icjia.state.il.us/public/pdf/dpsrc/CPRSC%20-%20Sixth%20and%20Final% 20Report.pdf. *See also* Thomas P. Sullivan, *Leave The Death Penalty in Dustbin*, CHICAGO TRIBUNE (Mar. 23, 2011), *available at* http://articles.chicagotribune.com/2011-03-23/news/ct-oped-0323-penalty-20110323_1_death-eligible-death-penalty-death-sentences.

[78] Staff, *Illinois Abolishes the Death Penalty*, NPR (Mar. 9, 2011), *available at* http://www.npr.org/ 2011/03/09/134394946/illinois-abolishes-death-penalty?ft=1&f=1001. James Warren, *With Some Surprising Support, a Historic Week in Illinois*, THE NEW YORK TIMES (Jan. 14, 2011), *available at* http://www.nytimes.com/2011/01/14/us/14cncwarren.html.

[79] Doug Finke, *Poll Takes Deeper Look at Death Penalty*, JOURNAL STAR (Jul. 18, 2010), *available at* http://www.pjstar.com/news/x999357427/Finke-Poll-takes-deeper-look-at-death-penalty. Quinn's campaign spokeswoman stated, "[Quinn] believes the death penalty underscores our shared belief as a society that some crimes deserve the most severe punishment, when meted out fairly and justly."

[80] Editorial, *Quinn Explains Decision to Abolish Death Penalty*, AUSTIN WEEKLY NEWS (Mar. 9, 2011), *available at* http://www.austinweeklynews.com/print.asp?ArticleID-3190&SectionID= 1&SubSectionID=1. Quinn stated, "[f]or me, this was a difficult decision, quite literally the choice between life and death. This was not a decision to be made lightly, or a decision that I came to without deep personal reflection." Quinn consulted with retired Anglican Archbishop Desmond Tutu of South Africa and Sister Helen Prejean, among others. William Fisher, *Illinois Ends Death Penalty*, THE PUBLIC RECORD (Mar. 10, 2011), *available at* http://pubrecord.org/nation/9039/illinois-ends-death-penalty/.

the legislature again passed a bill. This time, newly elected Governor Dannel Malloy, signed the legislation.[81]

§ 27.03   OTHER STATE LEGISLATIVE ACTION

In the wake of death penalty repeals in New York, New Jersey, New Mexico, Illinois and Connecticut, concern and caution about the use and continued viability of capital punishment "have moved from the fringes to the center of public discourse in universities, in the media, and perhaps most significantly in the federal and state legislatures."[82]

[A]   California

In California there have been a series of events culminating in a death penalty abolition initiative on the ballot for November 2012.[83] The Taxpayers for Justice Coalition gathered the necessary signatures to qualify the measure for the ballot.[84] California currently has over 700 people on death row, almost 20% of the national death row population.[85] Because of the large number of inmates who would be affected, abolition of the death penalty in California would have a significant impact on legislative action in other states.

In 2004, the California State Senate created the California Commission of the Fair Administration of Justice.[86] The Commission worked for four years examining causes of wrongful conviction and reviewing the implementation of the death penalty in California. This was the first comprehensive study of the death penalty by any official body since its implementation in 1977. On June 30, 2008, after three public hearings and hundreds of pages of submitted materials and statements on various aspects of the death penalty, the Commission issued its report and

---

[81] *See* THE DEATH PENALTY INFORMATION CENTER, *Current Legislative Activity, available at* http://www. deathpenaltyinfo.org/recent-legislative-activity. *See* Susan Haigh, *Conn. Lawmakers Take Up Death Penalty Repeal Bill*, NORWICH BULLETIN (Mar. 7, 2011), *available at* http://www.norwichbulletin.com/news/x1643898622/Connecticut-lawmakers-take-up-death-penalty-repeal-bill#axzz1KrU57i8c. *See also* http://www.nypost.com/p/news/local/connecticut_governor_signs_bill_q9S2PE2xF9LUoemqpjF9TJ.

[82] Carol S. Steiker & Jordan M. Steiker, *Should Abolitionists Support Legislative "Reform" of the Death Penalty?* 63 OHIO ST. L.J. 417 (2002). Connecticut also abolished the death penalty by legislative enactment in April, 2012.

[83] Since the death penalty was established in California by initiative, under California law it may only be repealed by initiative. Cal. Const. art. II, sec. 10(c) provides, "The Legislature may amend or repeal referendum statutes. It may amend or repeal an initiative statute by another statute that becomes effective only when approved by the electorate unless the initiative statute permits amendment or repeal without their approval."

[84] Supporters had to collect signatures from almost 510,000 registered California voters in order to have the initiative included on the ballot. The total signatures were close to 800,000.

[85] California currently houses 719 individuals on its death row, or 22.3% of the 3,220 Death Row inmates throughout the United States. Death Penalty Information Center, *Death Row Inmates By State and Size of Death Row By Year* (July 1, 2011), *available at* http://www.deathpenaltyinfo.org/death-row-inmates-state-and-size-death-row-year.

[86] The California Commission on the Fair Administration of Justice web site is found at http://www.ccfaj.org/.

recommendations.[87] The Commission agreed with the testimony of California Chief Judge Ron George who stated the death penalty system in California is "dysfunctional"[88] The report concludes:

> The system is plagued with excessive delay in the appointments of counsel for direct appeals and habeas corpus petitions, and a severe backlog in the review of appeals and habeas petitions before the California Supreme Court. Ineffective assistance of counsel and other claims of constitutional violations are succeeding in federal courts at a very high rate. Thus far courts have rendered final judgment in 54 habeas corpus challenges to California death penalty judgments. Relief in the form of a new guilt trial or a new penalty hearing was granted in 38 of the cases, or 70%. . . . The failures in the administration of California's death penalty law create cynicism and disrespect for the rule of law, increase the duration and costs of confining death row inmates, weaken any possible deterrent benefits of capital punishment, increase emotional trauma experienced by murder victims' families and delay the meritorious capital appeals.[89]

Litigation in both state and federal courts caused executions to come to a halt in 2006 with a de facto moratorium.[90] Death row inmates filed challenges in federal court to the implementation of the lethal injection procedure. In 2006, Judge Jeremy Fogel granted hearings on this issue and stayed all executions in California pending the outcome of the hearing.[91] After five days of hearings and thousands of pages of stipulated testimony, Judge Fogel found California's procedure to be unconstitutional — but added that it could be fixed.[92]

The Governor and state officials responded to Judge Fogel's order by setting out a new three-drug lethal injection procedure.[93] Death row inmates filed a challenge in state court arguing that the procedure was enacted in violation of the state's Administrative Procedures Act.[94] The Marin County District Court agreed, creat-

---

[87] The CCFAJ final death penalty report can be found at http://www.ccfaj.org/rr-dp-official.html.

[88] CCFAJ report p. 114 death penalty referencing Testimony of California Chief Justice Ronald M. George January 10, 2008.

[89] CCFAJ report at 114-115.

[90] The last execution in California was in 2006 with the lethal injection of Clarence Allen. Death Penalty Information Center, *Clarence Allen*, *available at* http://www.deathpenaltyinfo.org/clarence-allen.

[91] *Morales v. Tilton* No. C-06-0219-JF (N.D. Ca. Sept. 27, 2006) *see* Ellen Kreitzberg and David Richter, *But Can it Be Fixed? A Look at Constitutional Challenges to Lethal Injection Executions.* 47 SANTA CLARA L. REV. 445 (2007) *see* Ch. 5.05.

[92] *Morales v. Hickman* (Feb. 14, 2006), *available at* http://www.deathpenaltyinfo.org/Calif.leth.inj. Order.pdf.

[93] Then Governor Schwarzenegger and the California State Attorney General had their initial efforts to enact new procedures struck down by the Marin Court once earlier before losing an appeal to the California Courts of Appeals in 2009. The decision discussed here struck down the procedure enacted following the litigation in 2009. For full discussion, *see* Maura Dolan and Carol J. Williams, *Schwarzenegger Changes Strategy In Execution Debate*, LOS ANGELES TIMES (Feb. 24, 2009), *available at* http://articles.latimes.com/2009/feb/24/local/me-california-executions24.

[94] *See also* Ch. 5.04, Paul Elias, *supra. Marin Judge Rejects Lethal Injection Procedure*, ASSOCIATED PRESS (Dec. 17, 2011), *available at* http://www.mercurynews.com/breaking-news/ci_19562494.

ing another obstacle to overcome before executions in California can resume.[95]

In December 2011 California's new Supreme Court Chief Justice, Tani Cantil-Sakauye spoke candidly of California's death penalty system, describing it as requiring "structural change, and we don't have the money to create the kind of change that is needed"[96]

[B]   Other State Action

Several other states have come very close to abolishing their death penalty by legislative action. In Montana, repeal was passed by the Senate but defeated in the House Judiciary Committee.[97]

During the 2011 legislative term, proposals to abolish the death penalty were also introduced in the legislatures of Florida, Illinois, Indiana, Kansas, Kentucky, Maryland, Missouri, Ohio, Pennsylvania, Texas, and Washington. Proposals to establish a moratorium were introduced in Mississippi, Missouri, and Texas. A proposal urging district attorneys to not seek the death penalty and instead reinvest resources into solving cold cases was discussed in Georgia.

Governor Kitzhaber of Oregon recently announced that he would not allow any executions during his term in office which runs until January, 2015.[98] The governor also called for Oregon's legislators to take up legislation ending the death penalty in 2013.[99] Oregon still has thirty-seven individuals still on death row.[100] Oregon has held only two executions in the 27 years since voters authorized the death penalty,

---

[95] Carol J. Williams, *Judge Rejects California Execution Plan*, Los Angeles Times (Dec. 16, 2011), *available at* http://latimesblogs.latimes.com/lanow/2011/12/judge-tosses-california-execution-protocols.html.

[96] Maura Dolan, *California Chief Justice Urges Reevaluating Death Penalty*, Los Angeles Times (Dec. 24, 2011), *available at* http://articles.latimes.com/2011/dec/24/local/la-me-1222-chief-justice-20111221, The Justice stated, "It's no longer effective in a sense that it is the kind of program that needs to be re-examined because of the fiscal arrangements facing the state." While Justice Cantil-Sakauye's statements do not indicate an absolute opposition to capital punishment, her pragmatic recognition of the current system's cost failings and the state's economic inability to address those failings have been seized upon by supporters of the state's initiative abolition efforts. *See* fn. 109, *infra*. *See* LaDoris Cordell, *Take It From Two Judges: California's Death Penalty Is Broken*, SAFE California (Jan. 11, 2012), *available at* http://www.safecalifornia.org/news/blog/take-it-from-two-judges-california-death-penalty-is-broken.

[97] The Senate Judiciary Committee passed the bill followed by passage in the Senate on February 15; the bill was defeated in the House Judiciary Committee on March 18, 2011. *See* Allison Maier, *Emotional Crowd Testifies on SB 185*, Helenair.com (Mar. 16, 2011), *available at* http://helenair.com/news/article_b28c371a-4f8e-11e0-9aa9-001cc4c03286.html?print=1. *See* Associated Press, *Plan to Repeal Death Penalty in Montana in Key House Committee After Clearing Senate* (Mar. 15, 2011), *available at* http://www.therepublic.com/view/story/1f6d1e539354665aac950376637ca15/MT-XGR-Death-Penalty/. Randy Steidl, who spent twelve years on death row after being wrongly convicted in a 1986 double murder testified at the hearings.

[98] Kim Murphy, *Oregon Governor Declares Moratorium On Death Penalty*, Los Angeles Times (November 22, 2011), *accessible at* http://latimesblogs.latimes.com/nationnow/2011/11/oregon-governor-kitzhaber-executions-death-penalty.html.

[99] Patrick Sheenahan, *Oregon Legislator: Debating Capital Punishment: We Can Be Tough On Crime Without the Death Penalty*, Oregonians For Alternative to the Death Penalty (Dec. 2, 2011), *available at* http://www.oadp.org/?q=node/152. There were no bills introduced that would abolish Oregon's death penalty in the first two months of 2012. *See* Death Penalty Information Center, *2012 —*

both approved by Governor Kitzhaber during his previous administration. In both cases the inmates had waived their appeals.

§ 27.04   COST AND THE DEATH PENALTY DEBATE

Where concerns of executing innocent persons previously fueled the death penalty debate, the economic crisis has shifted the discussion in a new direction:[101] With so many states facing budget deficits, state legislatures began to discuss capital punishment in terms of its financial costs.[102] With death sentences and executions already on the decline, financial considerations as a basis for legislative arguments to abolish the death penalty began to emerge.[103]

There is no single figure for the cost of the death penalty. Each state's assessment of cost is dependent on that state's laws, pay scales, and the extent to which it uses the death penalty.[104] Each year new studies emerge from groups who oppose the death penalty, from legislative commissions that study the death penalty, and most recently by a senior judge for the U.S. Court of Appeals.[105] Every study concludes that the death penalty is far more expensive than an alternative system where the maximum sentence is life in prison without the possibility of parole.[106]

Proposed or Passed Legislation, *available at* http://www.deathpenaltyinfo.org/recent-legislative-activity#2012_Legislation.

[100] William Yardley, *Oregon Governor Says He Will Block Executions*, THE NEW YORK TIMES (Nov. 22, 2011), *available at* http://www.nytimes.com/2011/11/23/us/oregon-executions-to-be-blocked-by-gov-kitzhaber.html.

[101] Barbara Goldberg, *Tight Budgets May Spell Death of Death Penalty in Some States*, REUTERS.COM (Mar. 15, 2011), *available at* http://www.reuters.com/assets/print?aid=USTRE72E4SY20110315 (quoting Richard Dieter). "Innocence is the biggest issue, but what's getting these bills heard is the cost of the death penalty."

[102] Maya Srikrishnan, *Could Abolishing the Death Penalty Help States Save Money?* ABC NEWS (Dec. 7, 2010), *available at* http://abcnews.go.com/Politics/abolishing-death-penalty-states-cut-costs/story?id=12324697. In an interview with ABC News, Richard Dieter stated, "[t]he public feels the budget and the economic recession directly . . . When it affects your paycheck, you say, well what other things can be cut? I support the death penalty, but if we're spending $10 million a year and getting one execution a year, you may be able to let it go."

[103] *See* Richard Dieter, *Smart on Crime: Reconsidering the Death Penalty in a Time of Economic Crises*, THE DEATH PENALTY INFORMATION CENTER (Oct. 2009), *available at* http://www.deathpenaltyinfo.org/documents/CostsRptFinal.pdf.

[104] *See* Dieter, *Smart on Crime*. There are many ways to approach the question of how much the death penalty costs; to calculate the cost of each individual step in a death penalty case, to measure the extra cost to the state of arriving at one death sentence or one execution, or to assess the total extra costs to the state for maintaining the death penalty system instead of a system in which life in prison was the maximum sentence, on a yearly or multi-year basis.

[105] *See* MARYLAND COMMISSION ON CAPITAL PUNISHMENT, *Final Report to the General Assembly*, (Dec. 12, 2008), *available at* http://www.goccp.maryland.gov/capital-punishment/documents/death-penalty-commission-final-report.pdf, California Commission on the Fair Administration of Justice, *Report and Recommendations on the Administration of the Death Penalty in California* 82 (June 30, 2008) *available at* http://www.ddfaj.org, Arthur L. Alarcón & Paula M. Mitchell, *Executing the Will of the Voters? A Roadmap to Mend or End the California Legislature's Multi-Billion-Dollar Death Penalty Debacle*, 44 LOY. L.A. L. REV. S41, S109 (2011).

[106] Arthur L. Alarcón & Paula M. Mitchell, *Executing the Will of the Voters? A Roadmap to Mend*

Pennsylvania's state Senate initiated a study of its capital punishment system in 2012.[107] Citing an estimated average of $2 million spent per case, the Senate directed the study, among other issues, to determine the cost of the death penalty in Pennsylvania.[108]

The Maryland General Assembly created the Maryland Commission on Capital Punishment in 2008 to study all aspects of capital punishment and to make recommendations regarding its future use. The Commission concluded that the costs associated with cases in which a death sentence was sought were substantially higher than the costs associated with cases in a sentence of life without the possibility of parole. The Commission recommended that the state abolish the death penalty.[109]

A Kansas legislative audit in 2003 concluded that capital cases were seventy percent more expensive than comparable non-death penalty cases providing the basis for a significant legislative debate for abolition in both 2009 and 2010.[110] The Board of Indigents' Defense Services testified that since re-enactment of the death penalty there have been twenty-six death penalty trials in Kansas and twelve death sentences at a cost of $19.9 million just for the defense services.[111] Despite spending millions of dollars in the pursuit of the death penalty, Kansas has not carried out even one execution since 1965.[112] The abolition vote in the Kansas Senate was a tie.[113]

The financial debate was central to the Colorado effort to abolish the death penalty in 2009. The legislature came within one vote of abolishing the death penalty with a bill that directed the savings be used for unsolved homicides.[114]

The debate in California around the abolition initiative is framed, in large part, on the financial cost of the death penalty. A report by Justice Arthur Alarcon and

---

or *End the California Legislature's Multi-Billion-Dollar Death Penalty Debacle*, 44 Loyola Of L. A. L. Rev. S41, S109 (2011).

[107] Tom Shortell, *With Executions Backlogged, Pennsylvania Senate Calls For Review of Death Penalty*, The Express-Times (Jan. 2, 2012), *available at* http://blog.lehighvalleylive.com/breaking-news_impact/print.html?entry=/2012/01/with_backlog_of_executions_pen.html.

[108] Charlee Song, *Bipartisan Task Force Will Study Death Penalty*, Public Radio (Feb. 9 2012), *available at* http://www.essentialpublicradio.org/story/2011-12-23/bipartisan-taskforce-will-study-death-penalty-9705.

[109] Maryland Commission on Capital Punishment, *Final Report to the General Assembly*, (Dec. 12, 2008), *available at* http://www.goccp.maryland.gov/capital-punishment/documents/death-penalty-commission-final-report.pdf.

[110] *See* Senator Carolyn McGinn, *Death Penalty Too Costly, Not Deterrent*, The Wichita Eagle (Mar. 1, 2009), *available at* http://www.deathpenaltyinfo.org/new-voices-republican-senator-says-kansas-death-penalty-too-costly.

[111] *See* Erin Brown, *Kansas Could Abolish Death Penalty to Cut Costs*, Kansan.com (Jan. 27, 2010), *available at* http://www.kansan.com/news/2010/jan/27/kansas-could-abolish-death-penalty-cut-costs/.

[112] *Id.*

[113] WIBW.com, *Kansas House Introduces Bill to Abolish the Death Penalty* (Feb. 11, 2011), *available at* http://www.wibw.com/politics/headlines/Kansas_House_Introduces_Bill_to_Abolish_the_Death_Penalty_115986009.html.

[114] *Id.*

Paula Mitchell examines the costs of administering California's death penalty.[115] The numbers in the Alarcon and Mitchell study were staggering; California's system of capital punishment had cost more than $4 billion since 1978. This price was $184 million per year more than sentences of life without the possibility of parole.[116] The SAFE California campaign argues that the money spent in pursuit of the death penalty has not made the citizens of California any safer. In fact, the campaign argues, a shocking 46% of all murder and 56% of all reported rapes are unsolved in California every year.[117] The campaign suggests that the money saved by replacing the death penalty with life in prison without parole could be used to bolster law enforcement and solve these open cases.[118]

§ 27.05 CONCLUSION

With the use of the death penalty declining and becoming more isolated in only a few Southern states, and the costs to finance capital punishment increasing, the public is increasingly pushing legislators to implement moratoriums to study the continued viability of the death penalty.[119] The same states that are spending millions of dollars on the death penalty are facing severe cutbacks in other justice areas, "where courts are open less, trials are delayed, and police are being furloughed."[120] While economic difficulties continue, the costs of implementing capital punishment has forced some states into a crisis of administering the death penalty itself.[121] This economic pressure will likely continue to impact the death penalty debate. Justice Alarcon expressed the decision this way:

"Unless California taxpayers want to tolerate the continued waste of billions of tax dollars on the state's now defunct death penalty system, they

---

[115] Judge Arthur L. Alarcon and Paula M. Mitchell, *Executing the Will of the Voters?: A Roadmap to Mend or End the California Legislature's Multi-Billion Dollar Death Penalty Debacle.* 44 Loy. L.A. L. Rev. S41, 42 (2011) Alarcon is a Senior Judge for the U.S. Court of Appeals for the Ninth Circuit and has participated in every aspect of a death penalty case including as a Deputy District Attorney, legal advisor to Governor Edmund "Pat" Brown, and as a judge on superior court and the court of appeals. Mitchell is an adjunct professor of Law at Loyola Law school and was a law clerk to Judge Alarcon.

[116] *Id.*

[117] *See* www.safecalifornia.org.

[118] The initiative provides that $30 million each year for three years should be allocated to local law enforcement agencies. www.safecalifornia.org.

[119] Richard C. Dieter, *A Crises of Confidence: Americans' Doubts About the Death Penalty*, THE DEATH PENALTY INFORMATION CENTER (Jun. 2007), *available at* http://www.deathpenaltyinfo.org/CoC.pdf. A 2007 poll conducted by the Death Penalty Information Center found that fifty-eight percent of respondents believed that it was time for a moratorium on the death penalty while the process undergoes a careful review.

[120] Richard Dieter, *Smart on Crime: Reconsidering the Death Penalty in a Time of Economic Crises*, THE DEATH PENALTY INFORMATION CENTER (Oct. 2009), *available at* http://www.deathpenaltyinfo.org/documents/CostsRptFinal.pdf. For example, in 2009, New Hampshire, civil and criminal trials were halted for one month to save money. In one county, 77 criminal trials were delayed for up to six months.

[121] *Id.* In Georgia pursuing the death penalty in the Brian Nichols case in 2009 cost the state over $2 million in defense costs. There was no question of Nichol's guilt; and the case could have been resolved with a plea. The case resulted in a crisis in indigent funding across the state. The head of the death penalty unit of the public defender's office resigned because his office could no longer fairly represent its clients.

must either demand meaningful reforms to ensure that the system is administered in a fair and effective manner or, if they do not want to be taxed to fund the needed reforms, they must recognize that the only alternative is to abolish the death penalty and replace it with a sentence of life imprisonment without the possibility of parole.[122]

---

[122] Alarcon, and Mitchell, *supra* note 116.

Chapter 28

FUTURE ISSUES IN CAPITAL PUNISHMENT LAW

§ 28.01 OVERVIEW

The past 40 years have seen dramatic changes in death penalty laws in the United States. In 1972 the death penalty was struck down, only to be reinstated again in 1976. In the years that followed, the Supreme Court reviewed numerous death penalty statutes and ruled on a wide variety of issues, including systemic challenges to the death penalty,[1] specific claims of constitutional violations based on ineffective assistance of counsel,[2] jury instructions,[3] eligibility of crimes or classes of persons for the death penalty,[4] and the application of international laws and treaties to capital cases.[5] The Supreme Court has held that it is unconstitutional to execute a person who was a juvenile at the time of his offense[6] or who is mentally retarded,[7] and that a defendant is entitled to have a jury determine whether a statutory aggravating circumstance is present to make a case eligible for a sentence of death.[8] The next decades will no doubt bring more changes to death penalty law and practice.

Although most changes in the past came from decisions on constitutional issues from the United States Supreme Court, it is likely that legislative and executive-branch actions will play a greater role in shaping capital punishment law in the future. The Innocence Commission established in North Carolina[9] is one example of a legislative response to a problem in the system, the inadequacies of the judicial process to determine innocence post-conviction. On an executive level, there have been significant grants of clemency by governors in recent years.[10] Yet another nonjudicial development is the increased number of legislative or executive decisions to either study or impose a moratorium on the death penalty, often due to

---

[1] *E.g., see* challenges to the death penalty as arbitrary in *Furman* or *per se* as in *Gregg*, discussed in Chapter 4 *supra*; and challenges on the basis of the racial impact of the death penalty in *McCleskey* as discussed in Chapter 20, *supra*.

[2] *See* Chapter 16, *supra*.

[3] *See, e.g.,* Section 13.05, *supra*, discussing juror confusion about life without parole instructions.

[4] *See* Chapter 8, *supra*.

[5] *See* Chapter 23, *supra*.

[6] Roper v. Simmons, 543 U.S. 551 (2005). *See* Section 8.04, *supra*.

[7] Atkins v. Virginia, 539 U.S. 304 (2002). *See* Section 8.03, *supra*.

[8] Ring v. Arizona, 536 U.S. 584 (2002). *See* Sections 9.02[A] and 10.02, *supra*.

[9] *See* Chapter 17, *supra*.

[10] *See* Chapter 18, *supra*.

errors in the system or the exorbitant cost of imposing death sentences.[11]

While it is impossible to predict what may develop on judicial, legislative, or executive levels with regard to the death penalty, this chapter will address some of the issues that continue to arise or may develop. These issues include televising or recording executions, the use of the death penalty in military commissions, and the status of "fast-tracking" death penalty cases under Anti-Terrorism and Effective Death Penalty Act (AEDPA).

§ 28.02   PUBLICIZING EXECUTIONS

The question of whether or not an execution should be televised or otherwise publicized has been raised numerous times over the years.[12] The media has sued under the First and Fourteenth Amendment for access to the execution chambers.[13] Although no court has ordered that the press has a right to tape, record or broadcast an execution, that has not silenced the debate. Opposition to televising executions has come from both death penalty supporters and opponents.[14]

There are three main arguments raised to support televised executions: 1) access is mandated under the First and Fourteenth Amendment, 2) televising executions will increase any deterrent impact of the death penalty, and 3) to educate the public.[15] Opponents to televising executions raise four principle arguments: 1) media access is no greater than that of the general public; 2) restrictions on access are reasonable in light of safety and security concerns of the institution; 3) executions may be "shocking", upsetting or, at a minimum, tasteless entertainment that trivializes the process; and 4) it would turn a defendant into a victim by only showing the last step in a long legal process.[16]

---

[11] *See* Chapter 27, *supra.*

[12] For a discussion of this issue *see* John D. Bessler, *Televised Executions and the Constitution: Recognizing a First Amendment Right of Access to State Executions*, 45 FED. COMM. L.J. 355 (August 1993).

[13] Garrett v. Estelle 556 F.2d 1274 (5th Cir. 1977) (upholding statute that denied the press the opportunity to record an execution); Entertainment Network, Inc, v. Lappin, 134 F. Supp. 2d 1002 (2001) (finding statute prohibiting recording or broadcasting of an execution is constitutional and serves legitimate penological interests); Lawson v. Dixon 336 N.C. 312 (1994) (finding no right under First and Fourteenth Amendments of the U.S. Constitution or under the North Carolina state constitution to audiotape or videotape defendant Lawson's scheduled execution); KQED, Inc. v. Vasquez, 1995 WL 489485 (N.D. Cal., 1991) (Amended Judgment) (finding for defendants to exclude cameras from execution); Halquist v. Department of Corrections, 113 Wash. 2d 818, 783 P.2d 1065 (1989) (holding that the First Amendment does not provide the press any constitutional right of access to information not available to the public).

[14] Steve Keeva, *Watching a Killer Die: California TV Station Sues To Televise Execution*, 76 A.B.A.J. 24 (Oct. 1990) (concerns expressed by ACLU and former Attorney General Edwin Meese); Anthony Lewis, *Their Brutal Mirth*, TIMES, May, 20, 1991 at A15 (arguing that television will trivialize executions and reduce them to the level of entertainment).

[15] Philip J. Wiese, *Popcorn and Primetime v. Protocol: An Examination of the Televised Execution Issue*, 23 OHIO N.U. L. REV. 257, 270-271 (1996).

[16] Jeff I. Richards and Bruce Easter, *Retrospective Forum: The Robert Alton Harris Execution: Televising Executions: The High Tech Alternative to Public Hangings*, 40 UCLA. L. REV. 381 (1992).

In addition to challenges by the press, a religious group raised a First Amendment claim as a member of the "public." This claim, too, was rejected by the court. In *Rice v. Kempker*,[17] the New Life Evangelistic Center argued that their First Amendment right was violated when they were denied permission to videotape an execution. The Eighth Circuit Court of Appeals found no First Amendment violation, upholding the state's media policy that barred cameras or videotaping. In the court's view, there was no constitutional right to videotape even a public proceeding, such as a criminal trial. Consequently, there was no such right regarding an execution.[18] The court further stated that it did not matter if New Life was considered to be the "public" rather than the "press."[19]

Since the issue of publicizing executions has not yet been addressed by the United States Supreme Court and raises policy issues related to deterrence, it is likely this debate will continue to surface.

§ 28.03   TERRORISM, CIVILIAN TRIALS, AND MILITARY COMMISSIONS

The terrorist acts of September 11, 2001, and other subsequent events in the United States and around the world have challenged the United States in many ways, including how to try those who have allegedly committed the terroristic acts. Both U.S. courts and military commissions have been invoked as venues. Although there are many issues associated with these trials, especially procedural protections in the military commissions,[20] some issues arise specifically because of the intersection of international terrorism and American use of the death penalty.

One issue is the need to extradite individuals from other countries to the United States to stand trial. If the prosecution in the United States is seeking the death penalty, the country with custody of the individual may refuse to extradite. One death penalty scholar described America as placing itself in the position as the "world's executioner" at a time when much of the world has rejected the death penalty.[21] The potential political and international implications are significant.[22]

---

[17] 374 F.3d 675 (8th Cir. 2004).

[18] *Id.* at 678-679.

[19] *Id.* at 680.

[20] *See, e.g.*, Peter Jan Honigsberg, *Essay Inside Guantánamo*, 10 Nev. L.J. 82, 105 (2009) (discussing impact on attorney-client privilege from review of attorney's notes of interview with client by a government "privilege team" to secure classified information); Mark Denbeaux, et. al., *No-Hearing Hearings: An Analysis of the Proceedings of the Combatant Status Review Tribunals at Guantánamo*, 41 Seton Hall L. Rev. 1231, 1233-1235; 1259-1264 (2011) (criticizing use of hearsay by Combatant Status Review Tribunals and inability of detainees to confront all of the evidence against them). For attorney-client privilege issues arising in the *Al-Nashiri case*, discussed in the text *infra, see, e.g., United States v. Al-Nashiri*, Defense Motion to Bar JTF-GTMO from Interfering with the Defendant's Right to Receive Confidential Legal Mail and Access to the Courts (AE027, filed Dec. 19, 2011); Defense Motion to Bar the Department of Defense From Monitoring Defense Counsel's Computers and Electronic Communications (AE016, filed Nov. 28, 2011) 1, *available at* http://www.mc.mil/CASES/MilitaryCommissions.aspx (Abd al-Rahim Hussein Muhammed Abdu Al-Nashiri (2)).

[21] David Bruck, *Capital Punishment in the Age of Terrorism*, 41 Cath. Law 187 (Winter 2001).

[22] *See* Section 26.05, *supra*, discussing extradition issues.

The use of capital punishment in terrorism cases may create a potential conflict in any strategy to combat terrorism. Many countries have announced that individuals will not be extradited to the United States without adequate assurances that he or she will not face the death penalty.[23] In addition, in some cases, countries have refused to provide any information or intelligence that would assist the U.S. in the prosecution of that terrorist.[24] There is, thus, a tension between increasing the use of the death penalty in reaction to terrorism and decreasing the use of the death penalty in order to obtain cooperation from other countries.

Military commissions, or *military tribunals* as they are also called, are a second controversial issue. Following the September 11, 2001, attacks and the U.S. incursion into Afghanistan, many individuals were captured and taken to the Guantánamo Bay Naval Base in Cuba. President Bush issued a military order establishing military commissions to try those individuals at Guantánamo.[25] This announcement was controversial both in the U.S. and abroad.[26] The Order did not provide defendants the same rights and protections as civilian courts,[27] and yet the Commissions were given the authority to impose sentences of death.[28] The only review afforded defendants who were convicted under these tribunals was a final review by the President or the Secretary of the Defense, if the President so

---

[23] *Id.*

[24] *See* Section 19.02, *supra. See also* Daniel J. Sharfstein, *Human Rights Beyond the War on Terrorism: Extradition Defenses Based on Prison Conditions in the United States,* 42 Santa Clara L. Rev. 1137 (2002) (noting that Spain was likely to refuse extradition of 9/11 suspects on the basis of the death row conditions); *See U.S. Mulls Conceding to European Sensibilities in Seizure of Terror Suspects,* Guelph Mercury, *abstract available at* http://pqasb.pqarchiver.com/guelphmercury/access/ 446538261.html?FMT=ABS&FMTS=ABS:FT&type=current&date=Dec+2%2C+2001&author= &pub=Daily+Mercury&edition=&startpage=B.08&desc=U.S.+mulls+conceding+to+European+ sensibilities+in+seizure+of+terror+suspects (Ontario, Canada), Dec. 2, 2001, at B08 (stating that Spain refused to extradite eight suspected terrorists to the United States because extraditing prisoners, without assurance that the death penalty will not be imposed, violates the European Convention on Human Rights); Stephen J. Hedges, *German Law Keeps Evidence from U.S. in Moussaoui Case,* 2002 WLNR 12661901 (Oct. 26, 2002) (noting German law prohibiting assistance in obtaining death penalty). Eventually, evidence was turned over to the United States after assurances that the evidence would not be used to directly or indirectly seek the death penalty. *See Germany, France to Aid Moussaoui's Prosecution,* L.A. Times, 2002 WLNR 12421526 (Nov. 28, 2002).

[25] Military Order of Nov. 13, 2001: Detention, Treatment, and Trial of Certain Non-Citizens in the War Against Terrorism, 66 Fed. Reg. 57, 833-36 (Nov. 13, 2001), *available at* http://www.mc.mil/Portals/ 0/MilitaryOrderNov2001.pdf.

[26] *See, e.g.,* Toni Locy, *Fates Unsure at U.S. Base in Cuba,* USA Today, *available at* http://www. usatoday.com/news/world/2003-09-21-gitmo-usat_x.htm (Sept. 22, 2003), at 9A (noting tribunals are controversial due to fewer rights accorded to defendants than in civilian courts); Rahshmee Z. Ahmed, *UK Wants to Discuss Trial of British Al-Qaeda Men,* The Times of India, *available at* http://timesofindia. indiatimes.com/world/UK-wants-to-discuss-trial-of-British-al-Qaeda-men/articleshow/61774.cms (July 5, 2003) (describing concern of U.K. regarding trial in military tribunals).

[27] "Given the danger to the safety of the United States and the nature of international terrorism, . . . it is not practicable to apply in military commissions under this order the principles of law and the rules of evidence generally recognized in the trial of criminal cases in the United States district courts." Military Order of Nov. 13, § 1(f). *See also* Peter M. Shane, *The Obama Administration and the Prospects for a Democratic Presidency in a Post-9/11 World,* 56 N.Y.L. Sch. L. Rev. 27 (2011/2012).

[28] *Id.* at § 4(a).

designated.[29] The Order did not authorize access to a civilian court.[30]

The U.S. Supreme Court found in favor of detainees in two cases in 2004 that challenged aspects of the commissions. In *Rasul v. Bush*,[31] the Court held that the detainees had access to U.S. courts for habeas petitions on the legality of their detentions. In *Hamdan v. Rumsfeld*,[32] the Court invalidated the tribunals on the basis that they were improperly constituted without an express congressional act and that, without a showing of "impracticability," the failure of the procedures to provide the same protections as the Uniform Code of Military Justice (UCMJ) was in violation of the UCMJ and Common Article 3 of the Geneva Conventions that requires a "regularly constituted court" that is "established and organized in accordance with the laws and procedures already in force in a country."[33]

In response to *Rasul* and *Hamdan*, Congress passed the Military Commission Act of 2006.[34] Although there were a few more procedural protections than before, the Act also provided that the federal courts did not have jurisdiction to hear habeas corpus petitions from the detainees.[35] In *Boumediene v. Bush*,[36] the U.S. Supreme Court held that the constitutional right to habeas (in contrast to the statutory right to habeas) had not been suspended by the congressional act and, therefore, the detainees at Guantánamo still maintained a right to habeas petitions in federal courts on the legality of their status. The Court found that the constitutional provisions applied, even though Guantánamo is the territory of another sovereign country, because the base is "under the complete and total control"[37] of the United States.[38]

After President Obama took office, the Act was amended and re-enacted as the Military Commission Act of 2009.[39] Although most of the 2006 Act remained in place, there were several changes that were made, including a prohibition of admitting statements that were obtained through cruel, inhuman and degrading treatment.[40]

---

[29] *Id.* at § 4(c)(8).

[30] *Id.*

[31] 542 U.S. 466 (2004).

[32] 548 U.S. 557 (2006).

[33] *Id.* at 632.

[34] The Military Commission Act of 2006, Pub.L. No. 109-366, 120 Stat. 2600 (West 2006), codified at 28. U.S.C. § 2241(e)(1).

[35] *Id.* at § 7, amending 28 U.S.C. § 2241. Another controversial provision included relaxed rules on the admission of hearsay. § 3 at § 949(a)(2)(E).

[36] 553 U.S. 723 (2008).

[37] *Id.* at 771.

[38] The Court, thus, did not decide whether detainees in other locations, such as in Afghanistan, would have the same constitutional right to habeas.

[39] The Military Commission Act of 2009, Pub. L. No. 111-84, 123 Stat. 2190, (codified as amended at 10 U.S.C. § 948 (a)).

[40] According to Professor Shane, five changes were made, which "(1) prohibit the admission of statements obtained through cruel, inhuman, and degrading treatment; (2) give detainees greater latitude in their choice of counsel; (3) afford protection for those defendants who refuse to testify; (4) place the burden of justification for using hearsay on the party trying to use it; and (5) confirm that

In the fall of 2011, charges in a military commission with the possibility of the death penalty were filed in *United States v. Al-Nashiri.*[41] Al-Nashiri is charged, *inter alia*, with murder and attempted murder in violation of the law of war, terrorism, and attacking a vessel.[42] These charges arise out of the attack on the USS Cole in 2000 and on other ships.[43] Pretrial motions were scheduled for April 2012, but, as of February 2012, no trial date had yet been set.

The procedures in a death penalty case in the military commissions are similar in many respects to civilian death penalty trials. One difference is that there is no lay jury; 12 military commissioners sit in judgment and sentence.[44] The death-eligible crimes fall into three categories: 1) those always resulting in death — murder crimes; 2) those crimes for which death is only authorized if a victim dies — e.g., taking hostages, hijacking, torture, and terrorism; and 3) a non-homicide crime — spying.[45] Similarities in procedure to civilian trials include the requirement of finding at least one aggravating circumstance beyond a reasonable doubt, the admission of mitigating evidence, and a requirement that a decision of death be unanimous. The provision on mitigating evidence appears to be broad, although it will remain to be seen if it is interpreted as broadly as the U.S. Supreme Court has interpreted mitigation in civilian cases. The military commission provision states: "The accused shall be given broad latitude to present evidence in extenuation and mitigation."[46] Death is only a permissible punishment if all 12 commissioners agree that ". . . any extenuating or mitigating circumstances are substantially out-weighed by any aggravating circumstances."[47]

The aggravating circumstances are:[48]

"(1) That the offense was committed in such a way or under circumstances that the life of one or more persons other than the victim was unlawfully and substantially endangered;

(2) That the offense resulted in the death of more than one person;

---

military judges are empowered to determine their own jurisdiction." *See* Shane, *supra* note 27, at 34–35.

[41] *See* Referred Charges, 9/28/11 (Charge Sheet), *available at* http://www.mc.mil/Portals/0/pdfs/Al%20Nashiri%20II%20%28Sworn%20Charges%20II%29.pdf.

[42] The complete list of charges also includes perfidy, conspiracy, intentionally causing serious bodily injury, attacking civilians, and attacking civilian objects. *Id.*

[43] The other incidents were an attempted attack on the USS The Sullivans in 2000 and an attack on the MV Limburg in 2002.

[44] *See* Rules for Military Commission (R.M.C.) 501(a)(2), Manual for Military Commissions (M.M.C.) (2010), *available at* http://www.mc.mil/Portals/0/2010_Manual_for_Military_Commissions.pdf.

[45] Military Commissions Act of 2009, 10 U.S.C.A. § 950(t) (West 2012). Death eligible crimes include Murder of protected persons and Murder in violation of the law of war. If death results to a victim, the death-eligible crimes include: Attacking civilians; Taking hostages; Employing poison or similar weapons; Using protected persons as a shield; Torture; Cruel or inhuman treatment; Intentionally causing serious bodily injury; Mutilating or maiming; Using treachery or perfidy; Hijacking or hazarding a vessel or aircraft; Conspiracy; and Terrorism. Regardless of a resulting death, the crime of Spying is death eligible.

[46] R.M.C., *supra* note 44, at 1004(b)(3).

[47] *Id.* at 1004(b)(4)(C).

[48] *Id.* at 1004(c).

(3) That the offense was committed for the purpose of receiving money or a thing of value;

(4) That the accused procured another by means of compulsion, torture, mutilation, or cruel, inhuman, or degrading treatment to commit the offense;

(5) That the crime was preceded by the intentional infliction of substantial physical harm or prolonged, substantial mental or physical pain and suffering to the victim or to another person. . . .[49]

(6) That the accused has been found guilty in the same case of another capital crime;

(7) That the victim was under the age of 15;

(8) That the victim was a protected person or that the offense was committed in such a way or under circumstances that the life of one or more protected persons other than the victim was unlawfully and substantially endangered, except that this factor shall not apply to a violation of Offenses 1 (Murder of Protected Persons) and 9 (Using Protected Persons as a Shield);

(9) That the offense was committed —

   (A) through the employment of a substance or a weapon that releases a substance and that such substance causes death or serious damage to health in the ordinary course of events through its asphyxiation, poisonous, or bacteriological properties, except that this factor shall not apply to a violation of Offense 8 (Employing Poison or Similar Weapon); or

   (B) through the employment of a weapon that causes unnecessary suffering in violation of the law of war;

(10) That the offense was committed through the use of treachery or perfidy, except that this factor shall not apply to a violation of Offense 17 (Treachery or Perfidy);

(11) That the offense was committed with the intent to intimidate or terrorize the civilian population, except that this factor shall not apply to a violation of Offense 24 (Terrorism);

(12) That the offense was committed while the accused intentionally targeted a protected place . . . "

The aggravating circumstances are similar in concept to civilian death penalty statutes in creating aggravating circumstances based on circumstances of the offense or the status of the victim. They differ, however in specifically identifying circumstances that relate to terroristic acts, such as use of a weapon in violation of

---

[49] This provision further provides: "For purposes of this subsection, "substantial physical harm" means fractures or dislocated bones, deep cuts, torn members of the body, serious damage to internal organs, or other serious bodily injuries. The term "substantial physical harm" does not mean minor injuries, such as a black eye or bloody nose. The term "substantial mental or physical pain or suffering" is accorded its common meaning and includes torture."

the law of war, the use of treachery or perfidy,[50] and commission with an intent to terrorize a civilian population.

§ 28.04 "FAST-TRACKING" DEATH PENALTY CASES

The Antiterrorism and Effective Death Penalty Act (AEDPA) allows a state to apply for and be allowed to "opt-in" to a "fast-track" status for handling capital cases in federal courts.[51]

To meet the opt-in requirements, a state must establish a system for appointing and compensating attorneys for indigent petitioners in state habeas proceedings. In addition, the state must set up standards for the competency of the attorneys appointed. Under AEDPA, the federal courts were given the power to determine whether or not a state qualified for the "opt-in" provisions. Only one state has possibly qualified and no cases have been decided under the opt-in procedures.[52]

Once a state is designated as an "opt-in" state, AEDPA imposes shorter filing deadlines for capital cases in that state in federal courts and strict guidelines on federal judges for deciding appeals.[53]

In 2006, as part of the re-authorization of the "Patriot Act," the Attorney General of the United States was given the power to determine whether a state is eligible for a "fast-track" determination of cases in federal court.[54] In 2007, significant controversy erupted when it became public that the Justice Department was finalizing regulations to implement the power given to the Attorney General under the Patriot Act.[55] After an extended public comment period, final regulations for

---

[50] Treachery and perfidy are defined as: "Any person subject to this chapter who, after inviting the confidence or belief of one or more persons that they were entitled to, or obliged to accord, protection under the law of war, intentionally makes use of that confidence or belief in killing, injuring, or capturing such person or persons shall be punished, if death results to one or more of the victims, by death or such other punishment as a military commission under this chapter may direct, and, if death does not result to any of the victims, by such punishment, other than death, as a military commission under this chapter may direct." 10 U.S.C.A § 950(t) (17).

[51] See Section 15.01 supra. Antiterrorism and Effective Death Penalty Act of 1996 (AEDPA), Pub. L. No. 104-132, 110 Stat. 1214 (1996). For the opt-in provisions, see 28 U.S.C.A. § 2263 et seq.

[52] See Spears v. Stewart, 283 F.3d 992 (9th Cir. 2002), cert. denied, 537 U.S. 977 (2002) (finding that Arizona has a capital punishment system that facially complies with the opt-in criteria, but not applying the standards in the case because Arizona failed to timely appoint counsel to represent petitioner in state habeas proceedings).

[53] Under the opt-in system, there is a 180-day statute of limitations for a capital habeas case, in contrast to the 1-year limitation for noncapital cases. The federal district court must decide the case within 180 days of the date of the filing of the habeas application, with the possibility of only one 30-day extension for specified reasons. The federal court of appeals must decide the case within 120 days of the filing of the reply brief, with a second 120-day period if there is a rehearing en banc. The capital amendments also create specific rules for claims that were not raised in state court. Such a claim is only allowed if the failure to raise it was the result of unconstitutional state action, a new federal right recognized by the Supreme Court as retroactive, or the non-discovery of a factual predicate despite due diligence. 28 U.S.C.A. § 2263 et seq.

[54] See USA PATRIOT Improvement and Re-authorization Act of 2005, Pub. L. No. 109-177, 120 Stat. 192 (2006) (codified at 28 U.S.C. § 2265(1)).

[55] Richard B. Schmitt, Gonzales Could Get Say in State's Execution, L.A. Times, available at

certifying whether a state has opted-in to the "fast-tracking" provisions were approved and published in December 2008, but the regulations were enjoined before enactment by a federal district court in California and ultimately removed by the new Attorney General in December 2010.[56]

§ 28.05   THE CONTINUING CONTROVERSY

Capital punishment will continue to be a controversial topic. For now, the death penalty remains part of our legal system in 33 states and in federal prosecutions. Constitutional issues challenging many different aspects of the imposition of the death penalty continue to wind their way through the court system to review in the United States Supreme Court. Interpretations of the Eighth Amendment to the Constitution have dominated the jurisprudence of capital punishment law, and will still contribute to the substance and procedures of the legal systems for imposing the death penalty. It is also likely, however, that state legislatures and Congress will play a larger role in defining the parameters of capital punishment law in the next few years. Studies on the fairness of the system, the moratorium movement, and concerns about terrorism will all shape capital punishment law in the future.

---

http://articles.latimes.com/2007/aug/14/nation/na-penalty14 (August 14, 2007); Dan Eggen, *Gonzales to Get Power in Death Penalty Cases*, WASHINGTON POST, *available at* http://www.washingtonpost.com/wp-dyn/content/article/2007/08/14/AR2007081401707.html?nav=emailpage (August 15, 2007).

[56] *See* 28 C.F.R. §§ 26.20-26.23 (July 1, 2009), 2008 WL 5169264 (Final Regulations published December 2008); Habeas Corpus Resource Center v. U.S. Dept. of Justice, 2009 WL 185423 (N.D. Cal. 2009) (enjoining DOJ from putting regulations into effect); 75 Fed. Reg. 71353, 2010 WL 4719252 (removing Dec. 2008 regulations). *See also* Casey C. Kannenber, *Wading Through the Morass of Modern Federal Habeas Review of State Capital Prisoners' Claims*, 28 QUINNIPIAC L. REV. 107 (2009) (discussing "opt-in factors" identified in Spears v. Stewart and applying the factors to explain why no states, except Arizona, have satisfied the certification requirements).

TABLE OF CASES

[References are to pages]

[References are to pages]

[References are to pages]

[References are to pages]

[References are to pages]

[References are to pages]

[References are to pages]

TABLE OF CASES

[References are to pages]

TABLE OF STATUTES

[References are to pages]

[References are to pages]

WYOMING

Wyoming Statutes

Sec.	Page
6-2-102(h)(xi)	151

FEDERAL STATUTES, RULES, AND REGULATIONS

United States Constitution

Amend.	Page
amend.:1	4; 45
amend.:1:to:10	24; 39; 43; 409; 425
amend.:4	215; 237
amend.:5	24; 28; 75, 76; 156–158; 215; 217; 224–227; 250
amend.:6	24; 77, 78; 81–83; 86; 88; 135; 141; 149; 156–158; 182; 184; 215; 217; 218; 223; 237; 247; 249; 255; 257; 262; 270; 273; 275; 371; 374; 376; 378; 421
amend.:8	3; 5; 7; 15; 23–25; 27–36; 39; 43, 44; 46–49; 51, 52; 54; 64; 75; 129; 131; 139; 142; 143; 147, 148; 159–161; 173; 175, 176; 184; 192; 200, 201; 205, 206; 209–214; 237; 244; 245; 247; 279; 319; 348; 350–354; 365; 371; 374–377; 384; 389, 390; 395, 396; 398; 408–410; 412; 414, 415; 419; 425; 431; 445
amend.:13	343
amend.:14	24; 27, 28; 39; 47; 64; 82; 86; 88; 148; 157; 202; 317; 319; 343; 345; 350, 351; 354; 391; 397
amend.:14:1	24; 28; 142; 448
art.:1:27	23
art.:6:2	25; 392, 393; 404; 406
art.:6:11(a)	215
art.:I:9:2	235
art.:II:2	390
art.:II:2:1	311
art.:II:2:2	390
art.:II:10(c)	469
art.:III:	427
art.:V:	311
art.:VI:	390
art.:VI:2	25; 390

United States Code

Title:Sec.	Page
10:801	430
10:801 to 940	428

United States Code—Cont.

Title:Sec.	Page
10:825	434
10:841	83
10:862(b)(3)	435
10:918	432
18:32-34	417
18:36	417
18:37	417
18:115(b)(3)	417
18:241	417
18:242	417
18:245	417
18:247	417
18:351	417
18:794	419
18:844(I)	417
18:844(d)	417
18:844(f)	417
18:924(I)	417
18:930	417
18:1091	417
18:1111	417, 418
18:1114	418
18:1116	418
18:1118	418
18:1119	418
18:1120	418
18:1121	418
18:1201	418
18:1203	418
18:1342	417
18:1503	418
18:1512	418
18:1513	418
18:1716	418
18:1751	418
18:1958	418
18:1959	418
18:1992	418
18:2113	418
18:2119	418
18:2245	418
18:2251	418
18:2280	418
18:2281	418
18:2332	418
18:2332a	418

[References are to pages]

INDEX

[References are to page numbers.]

[References are to page numbers.]

[References are to page numbers.]

[References are to page numbers.]

[References are to page numbers.]

[References are to page numbers.]

[References are to page numbers.]